THE BEST PLACES TO KISS™

IN NORTHERN CALIFORNIA

A Romantic Travel Guide

COMPLETELY REVISED **5th** EDITION AND UPDATED

by
Linnea Lundgren

BEGINNING PRESS

Other Books in the

BEST PLACES TO KISS™

Series:

The Best Places to Kiss in Southern California, 4th Edition $13.95

The Best Places to Kiss in the Northwest, 7th Edition $16.95

The Best Places to Kiss in Hawaii, 3rd Edition $14.95

Any of these books can be ordered directly from the publisher.

Please send a check or money order for the total amount of the books, plus $5 for shipping and handling per book ordered, to:

**Beginning Press
13075 Gateway Drive, Suite 160
Seattle, WA 98168**

All prices are listed in U.S. funds.
For information about ordering from Canada or
to place a credit card order, call (206) 444-1616.
Visit our web site to order on-line:
www.bestplacestokiss.com

Art Direction and Production: Studio Pacific, Deb McCarroll
Cover Design: Studio Pacific, Deb McCarroll
Managing Editor: Laura Peterson
Editors: Sigrid Asmus and Kris Fulsaas
Printing: Publishers Press
Contributors: Paula Begoun, Elizabeth Janda, and Laura Peterson

Copyright 1990, 1992, 1994, 1997, 1999 by Paula Begoun
First Edition: June 1990
Second Edition: June 1992
Third Edition: June 1994
Fourth Edition: January 1997
Fifth Edition: October 1999
1 2 3 4 5 6 7 8 9 10

BEST PLACES TO KISS™

is a registered trademark of Beginning Press
ISBN 1-877988-27-8

This book is distributed to the U.S. book trade by:
Publisher's Group West
1700 Fourth Street
Berkeley, CA 94710
(800) 788-3123

This book is distributed to the Canadian book trade by:
Raincoast Books
8680 Cambie Street
Vancouver, B.C. V6P 6M9
(800) 663-5714

"As usual with most lovers

in the city, they were

troubled by the lack

of that essential need

of love—a meeting place."

Thomas Wolfe

Publisher's Note

Travel books have many different criteria for the places they include. We would like the reader to know that this book is not an advertising vehicle. As is true for all *The Best Places to Kiss* books, the businesses included were not charged fees, nor did they pay us for their review. This book is a sincere, unbiased effort to highlight those special parts of the region that are filled with romance and splendor. Sometimes those places were created by people, such as restaurants, inns, lodges, hotels, and bed and breakfasts. Sometimes those places are untouched by people and simply created by God for us to enjoy. Wherever you go, be gentle with each other and with the earth.

"What of soul was left,

I wonder, when the

kissing had to stop?"

Robert Browning

Contents

The Fine Art of Kissing 1

Why It's Still Best to Kiss in Northern California 1

You Call This Research? 1

Rating Romance 2

Kiss Ratings 3

Cost Ratings 3

Wedding Bells 4

North Coast 5

Wine Country 69

San Francisco 149

Marin County 197

East Bay 213

South of San Francisco 229

Lake Tahoe and Environs 241

Gold Country 265

Yosemite National Park and Environs 311

South Coast 325

Index 397

The Fine Art of Kissing

Why It's Still Best to Kiss in Northern California

It is no secret that northern California is a splendid part of the world. For those of us who kiss and tell for a living, it is simply our favorite place to visit again and again. Every region is brimming with romantic potential. From the brilliant lights of San Francisco, it is only a short drive to mountains, forests, vineyards, rugged shorelines, and sandy beaches. Regardless of the season or the area, misty mornings, sultry afternoons, and cool evenings are standard. The seasons themselves are all exhilarating and temperate: mild winters, lush autumns, vivid springs, and perfect summers. In short, there probably is not a more diverse, yet compact place in the world in which to pucker up.

From the North Coast and South Coast to Wine Country, the Bay Area, Lake Tahoe, and the mesmerizing terrain of Yosemite National Park—all will ignite your imagination and your passions. If you've ever longed for a special place to share time together, you'll find it in northern California. Charming wineries, elite bed and breakfasts, fanciful hot-air balloon rides, alluring restaurants, scenic hikes, lofty woods, city streets filled with extravagant shopping, expansive parks, not to mention the ocean and the bridges and the valleys and the entertainment and ... in short, northern California is an adult carnival. From the Sierras to the shore, the vitality and romance here are contagious, and when you're accompanied by the right someone, the only challenge will be finding the lovable niche that serves your hearts best.

You Call This Research?

This book was undertaken primarily as a journalistic effort and is the product of ongoing interviews, travel, thorough investigation, and critical observation. Although it would have been nice, even preferable, kissing was not the major research method used to select the locations listed in this book. If smooching had been the determining factor, several inescapable problems would have developed. First, we would still be researching, and this book would be just a good idea, some breathless moments, random notes, and nothing more. Second, depending on the mood of the moment, many kisses might have occurred in places that do not meet the requirements of this travel guide. Therefore, for both practical and physical reasons, more objective criteria had to be established.

You may be wondering how, if we did not kiss at every location during our research, we could be certain that a particular place was good for such an activity? The answer is that we employed our reporters' instincts to evaluate the heartfelt, magnetic pull of each place we visited. If, upon examining a place, we felt a longing to share what we had discovered with our special someone, we considered this to be as reliable as a kissing analysis. In the final evaluation, we can guarantee that when you visit any of the places listed, you will be assured of some degree of privacy, a beautiful setting, heart-stirring ambience, and romantic accommodations. What you do when you get there is up to you and your partner.

Rating Romance

The three major factors that determine whether or not we include a place are:

- **Privacy**
- **Location/view/setting**
- **Ambience**

Of these determining factors, "privacy" and "location" are fairly self-explanatory, but "ambience" can probably use some clarification. Wonderful, loving environments are not just four-poster beds covered with down comforters and fluffy pillows, or tables decorated with white tablecloths and nicely folded linen napkins. Instead, there must be other engaging features that encourage intimacy and allow for uninterrupted affectionate discourse. For the most part, ambience was rated according to degree of comfort and number of gracious appointments, as opposed to image and frills.

If a place has all three factors going for it, inclusion is automatic. But if one or two of the criteria are weak or nonexistent, the other feature(s) have to be superior before the location will be included. For example, if a breathtakingly beautiful panoramic vista is in a spot that's inundated with tourists and children on field trips, the place is not included. If a fabulous bed and breakfast is set in a less-than-desirable location, it is included if, and only if, its interior is so wonderfully inviting and cozy that the outside world no longer matters. Extras like complimentary champagne, handmade truffles, or extraordinary service earn brownie points and frequently determine the difference between three-and-a-half- and four-lip ratings.

Kiss Ratings

The lip rating preceding each entry is our way of indicating just how romantic we think a place is and how contented we were during our visit. The following is a brief explanation of the lip ratings awarded each location.

No lips	=	Reputed to be a romantic destination, but we strongly disagree
💋	=	Romantic possibilities with potential drawbacks
💋💋	=	Can provide a satisfying experience
💋💋💋	=	Very desirable
💋💋💋💋	=	Simply sublime
Unrated	=	Not open at the time this edition went to print, but looks promising

Romantic Note: If you're planning to celebrate a special occasion, such as an anniversary or birthday, we highly recommend telling the proprietors about it when making your reservation. Many bed and breakfasts and hotels offer "special-occasion packages," which may include a complimentary bottle of wine, breakfast in bed, fresh flowers, and special touches during turndown service, such as dimmed lights and your beloved's favorite CD playing in the background to set the right romantic mood. Restaurants are also sometimes willing to accommodate special occasions by offering free desserts or helping to coordinate a surprise proposal.

Cost Ratings

We have included additional ratings to help you determine whether your lips can afford to kiss in a particular restaurant, hotel, or bed and breakfast. (Almost all of the outdoor places are free; some charge a small fee.) The price for overnight accommodations is always based on double occupancy; otherwise there wouldn't be anyone to kiss. Unless otherwise indicated, eating establishment prices are based on a full dinner for two (which includes an appetizer, entrée, and dessert for each person), excluding the cost of liquor. Because prices and business hours change, it is always advisable to call each place you plan to visit, so your lips will not end up disappointed.

Lodgings

Inexpensive	Less than $100
Moderate	$100 to $130
Expensive	$130 to $175
Very Expensive	$175 to $250
Unbelievably Expensive	More than $250

Restaurants

Inexpensive	Less than $30
Moderate	$30 to $50
Expensive	$50 to $80
Very Expensive	$80 to $110
Unbelievably Expensive	More than $110

Wedding Bells

One of the most auspicious times to kiss is the moment after you've exchanged wedding vows. The setting for that magical moment can vary, from your own cozy living room to a lush garden perched at the ocean's edge to a grand ballroom at an elegant downtown hotel. As an added service to those of you in the midst of prenuptial arrangements, we have indicated which properties have impressive wedding facilities. For more specific information about the facilities and services offered, please call the establishments directly. They should be able to provide you with menus, prices, and all the details needed to make your wedding day as spectacular as you have ever imagined.

Romantic Note: If wedding bells aren't in your near future and you are going to an establishment that specializes in weddings and private parties, call ahead to ensure that a function isn't scheduled during your stay. Unless you hope that seeing a wedding will magically inspire your partner to "pop the question," you might feel like uninvited guests.

North Coast

If you've never witnessed the North Coast's incredibly dramatic and arresting scenery, be prepared for the visual experience of a lifetime. Unlike the developed coastline south of San Francisco, this rugged, breathtaking shoreline remains relatively pristine and unblemished. Much of the surrounding region consists of sprawling pastoral farmland, poised in serene contrast to the dynamic Northern California surf. In some areas, turbulent, foaming whitecaps thunder against the coast's tall, rocky cliffs; in other areas, waves lap gently at beaches or at sand dunes overgrown with grass and wildflowers. Not surprisingly, the coast offers many superlative places to stay, eat, and hike, though not in such abundance that the region's natural beauty has been obstructed in any way. We can't think of a better setting for romance—kissing here seems inevitable.

Romantic Note: Many of the Hotel/Bed and Breakfast Kissing options in this chapter are situated on Highway 1. In some cases, traffic noise is a drawback, but a location on Highway 1 can also mean a remarkable oceanfront setting. Throughout this chapter, we describe an establishment's relation to the highway (when applicable) and specifically note if road noise is a romantic distraction.

Outdoor Kissing

❤❤❤❤ **HIGHWAY 1** The Northern California Coast Highway 1 is an exhilarating roller-coaster ride of a lifetime. A compact two-lane roadway writhes along terrain that would otherwise seem impassable. Hugging the ocean from atop towering cliffs, each turn capriciously switches back on itself, following the edge so closely that you may feel like you're hang-gliding instead of driving. At other times, feeling the ocean mist on your face and hearing the surf's constant roar, you can almost imagine you're sailing on the high seas.

Be sure to allow enough time to travel this highway at a leisurely, touring pace. With myriad coiled turns and a minimum of passing lanes, maneuvering and speeding are impossible. Scads of scenic turnoffs will demand your attention, so go slowly and stop at any intriguing point to take in the visual glory. Each corner and each turn has views so astonishing that a warning seems in order: Driving and kissing don't mix! Before you indulge, pull over and park the car; you can return to negotiating the narrow turns later. *Highway 1 breaks off from Highway 101 just north of the Golden Gate Bridge in Marin County and continues northward to the town of Leggett, about 80 miles south of Eureka.*

Romantic Suggestion: If you are in a hurry to get to points north, do yourselves and the rest of the traffic on Highway 1 a favor: Take Highway 101.

Stinson Beach

Although technically part of Marin County, this area is the gateway to the North Coast. Until recently, the only way to stay in Stinson Beach (without moving there) was to spend the night with local friends or rent a vacation home. Several bed and breakfasts have since opened, but this seaside town, located within the **GOLDEN GATE NATIONAL RECREATION AREA**, is happily far from overdeveloped. **STINSON BEACH STATE PARK**, three miles of sandy white beach, is crowd-crazed in the summer, but you can still take off your shoes, close your eyes, and bask in the sun and sand. Although San Francisco is barely an hour away and the Golden Gate Bridge is in clear sight, you'll feel light-years away from the city.

Hotel/Bed and Breakfast Kissing

❦❦❦ **CASA DEL MAR, Stinson Beach** Succulent tropical foliage, Balinese statues, and flowering cacti fill the beautifully landscaped grounds of this towering Italian-style villa. Pass through the gate and up a terraced stone pathway to these bright and cheerful accommodations. Casa del Mar ("house of the sea") is what you'd expect to see along the sun-kissed Mediterranean, not the fog-entrenched northern California coast. Yet, the warmth of this place is certain to brighten up any day in these parts.

Vivacious local art adorns the six colorfully decorated guest rooms. Each features a queen-size bed, down comforter and heated mattress, brightly patterned linens, and a private patio. Ocean views (beyond rooftops) from terra-cotta-tiled patios make the Shell Room and the Heron Room especially attractive, while the smaller, more affordable Hummingbird Room has a serene view of neighboring Mount Tamalpais (and, unfortunately, views of the home below). The Passionflower Room features a balcony with mountain view.

The spacious, top-floor Penthouse Suite has exquisite views of both mountain and ocean from cement patios on each side of the building. Compared to the other rooms, the suite's decor is somewhat sparse and, besides the queen-size bed, there's the odd placement of two single beds in the room, including one in the closet. The bathroom, however, with its two-person soaking tub and skylight views, can't be beat. Coziness prevails in the Garden Room. Even though it's located on the ground level, this room has a decent ocean view from its quaint garden patio, and such romantic perks as a private entrance, a wood-burning fireplace fronting the bed, a large soaking tub, and a small kitchenette. Best of all, breakfast is delivered to your door. For everyone else, a delightfully creative, full breakfast is served in the sunny dining room. Apple-ricotta pancakes flavored with cinnamon, Granny's French toast, cranberry-orange-pecan scones, and quiches accented with herbs from the garden will prepare you for the walk to the nearby beach. **37 Belvedere Avenue; (415) 868-2124, (800) 552-2124; www.stinsonbeach.com; expensive to very expensive; minimum-stay requirement on weekends.**

Olema

Hotel/Bed and Breakfast Kissing

❤❤❤ **POINT REYES SEASHORE LODGE, Olema** Although this provincial yet polished cedar lodge is set just off Highway 1 in the small town of Olema, the sound of nearby traffic all but disappears once you step inside. Each of the property's 18 rooms and three suites surveys views of a vast grassy yard bordered by the lively Olema Creek, and backed by the pristine **POINT REYES NATIONAL SEASHORE** (see Outdoor Kissing in Inverness and Point Reyes Station). Here guests can lounge under shade trees in Cape Cod–style lawn furniture and watch red-tailed hawks soar over the rolling hills. Outdoor lovers will appreciate the lodge's easy access to recreational areas. Hiking, bird-watching, biking, horseback riding, and other nature-oriented activities are a hop, skip, and jump away. If rainy conditions prohibit such excursions, the lodge offers a well-stocked library filled with local-interest books, and a downstairs game room complete with an antique billiards table, puzzles, and board games.

If you can afford to indulge, three spacious two-story suites have wood-burning fireplaces, whirlpool tubs, separate sleeping lofts with sensuous feather beds, and the added luxury of breakfast delivered to your doorstep. If a splurge is out of the question, you won't be disappointed with the lodge's less expensive rooms, many of which feature tiled wood-burning fireplaces, whirlpool tubs with peekaboo views of the mountains, and private patios or balconies. All rooms are enhanced by natural wood accents, plush down comforters, and elegant lodge-style furnishings. Simple and pleasant, these rooms distinguish themselves from typical hotel rooms by their step-down living rooms and bedrooms or, in some cases, step-up bathrooms.

Unless you've booked a suite (where breakfast is served to your room), you can wake up to a deluxe continental breakfast. Your morning meal is served in the sunny dining room that opens to the courtyard and is warmed by an immense stone hearth crowned with dried flowers. **10021 Coastal Highway 1; (415) 663-9000, (800) 404-5634 in California only; www. pointreyesseashore.com; moderate to very expensive; recommended wedding site.**

❧❧ **ROUNDSTONE FARM, Olema** We were immediately drawn to Roundstone Farm's semirural landscape, where flocks of red-winged blackbirds nest by a tranquil pond, and Connemara and Arabian horses graze in surrounding golden pastures. Named after a district of western Ireland, this ten-acre ranch offers a hushed refuge for those seeking to escape the city. Guests can savor views of the pastoral scenery through a wall of windows in the inn's homey communal living room, or, if the weather's nice, from the adjacent outdoor deck. Better yet, such scenes can be enjoyed from the privacy of your room.

Built to serve as a bed and breakfast, the inn was designed with seclusion in mind; the five guest rooms are situated on different levels of the guest wing, and all are equipped with private standard baths. Although the outdated linens and eclectic decor are a little worn and could use some sprucing up, Roundstone Farm still deserves its reputation as a romantic destination. You can't argue with views of the sun setting in the distance over Tomales Bay, or with the warmth of a crackling fire in the hearth (found in four of the five guest rooms). A full breakfast, including fresh baked goods, is served family-style in the airy dining room or on the garden patio, depending on the weather. **9940 Sir Francis Drake Boulevard; (415) 663-1020, (800) 881-9874; www.roundstonefarm.com; moderate to expensive; minimum-stay requirement on weekends.**

Restaurant Kissing

❧❧❦ **OLEMA INN RESTAURANT, Olema** A juxtaposition of country comfort and contemporary style is exactly what you'll find at the charming Olema Inn Restaurant. Surrounded by a wraparound porch and white picket fence and backed by a large yard and orchard, this yellow Victorian-style farmhouse has turned this roadside restaurant into quite an attraction. Inside, there's little in the decor that reflects the Victorian exterior; instead you'll discover modern touches with white-on-white hues, recessed skylights, high ceilings, and soft jazz music. Lamp-like candles, colorful china, and fresh flower arrangements top the linen-covered tables, and attractive sconces and dried floral wreaths accent the walls. Black-and-white coastal photographs hint at modernism, as do the stylish muslin draperies covering the tall, paned windows and French doors. Two-person tables strategically line the windows, and most are spaced well enough apart for quiet conversation. Warmer months bring diners outside to the pretty garden patio overlooking the orchard.

The unchanging continental menu delivers straightforward and consistently good meals. Try the crispy tarragon roasted chicken breast, fettuccine with scallops and prawns in a creamy pesto sauce, or the pan-roasted trout topped with mandarin orange relish and toasted pine nuts. Portions border on large, so be prepared. **10000 Sir Francis Drake Boulevard, at the Olema Inn; (415) 663-9559; moderate to expensive; lunch and dinner daily, brunch Sunday.**

Romantic Note: Overnight accommodations are also available at OLEMA INN (moderate). Upstairs are six small guest rooms, each with a simple interior and antique touches. Although the inn's past is colorful, travelers with romance (not history) on their minds should stay at one of the nearby places that has received our kiss of approval (see Hotel/Bed and Breakfast Kissing).

Inverness and Point Reyes Station

Bordering the **POINT REYES NATIONAL SEASHORE** (see Outdoor Kissing) and Marin County, Inverness and Point Reyes are the entry points into this gorgeous coastal area. Scattered along the shore of Tomales Bay, these two quaint villages harbor numerous waterside and hillside romantic retreats. Even though this region is sparsely populated and particularly quiet in the winter months, it is well traveled in the spring and summer. Nevertheless, if you can ignore the crowds or travel off-season, a stay at one of the special bed and breakfasts in this area can be utterly romantic and memorable.

Hotel/Bed and Breakfast Kissing

❤❤❤ **BLACKTHORNE INN, Inverness** Like a child's tree house, only better, the Blackthorne Inn is a four-story fantasy home nestled high in the woods. The multidimensional redwood castle spares no expense when it comes to unique touches, including twin turrets, peaked gables, stained glass windows, and a firefighters' pole that descends to the driveway below (just in case you don't want to use the stairs). The main floor is surrounded by an expansive redwood deck, while up another flight of stairs you'll discover a hot tub nestled among the trees. Inside the common room, an immense stone hearth cranks out the heat and the vaulted, open-beam ceiling captures all the warmth, not to mention the filtered sunlight from the numerous windows. This home is pieced together with plenty of history—

such as the railroad door and the beams salvaged from a San Francisco pier—so be sure to ask if something interesting captures your curiosity.

Skylights, mix-and-match antiques, and knotty wood walls are some of the features found in each of the five guest rooms. None of the rooms have TVs or phones, and the stairway climb to some of the rooms will develop your leg muscles in no time flat. Two rather dull rooms that share a detached bath are situated on the ground floor, while a narrow spiral staircase leads up to the more private ones. The Lupine Room is divinely cozy, with a sloped ceiling and its own entrance. The larger Overlook Room has the disadvantage of a hallway bathroom, but the advantage of two terraces—a small outdoor terrace looking out onto the forest as well as a strangely situated, Juliet-style balcony overlooking the living room. Head into the treetops for one of northern California's most unique rooms, appropriately named the Eagle's Nest. This dazzling aerie occupies the top of the octagonal tower with windows on all sides and a steep ladder leading to a private sundeck (or stargazing deck). The only drawback to the Eagle's Nest is that the bathroom lies across a 40-foot-high outdoor walkway—a potentially chilly jaunt on a rainy night. The jetted hot tub, which, by the way, fronts the Eagle's Nest's bathroom facilities, is available to all guests until 10 P.M., when it is designated for the private use of Eagle's Nest occupants.

A full breakfast buffet is served every morning and can be enjoyed on the deck, weather permitting, or in the sunny breakfast room at your own table for two. There's plenty of wildlife wandering and flying around the inn, so keep your eyes open and you might see a furry or feathered creature. **266 Vallejo Avenue; (415) 663-8621; www.blackthorneinn.com; expensive to very expensive; minimum-stay requirement on weekends.**

❧❧❧ **COTTAGES ON THE BEACH, Inverness** At first glance, these two beachfront cottages seem an unlikely setting for a romantic encounter. Situated just footsteps from a busy road, the cabins' weathered exteriors and neglected grounds are hard to ignore. But much to our surprise, our first impressions were forgotten after one peek at the cabins' lovely, upscale interiors. Richly colored Oriental carpets cover gleaming hardwood floors, and French doors open onto private decks overlooking tranquil Tomales Bay. Contemporary, stylish artwork graces beige sponge-painted walls, and dried flowers, baskets, and antiques accent the cabins' cozy, cheery living areas. A ladder in one cottage leads to a snug sleeping loft, and cushy down comforters drape the beds in both units. Breakfast fixings are provided ahead of time in the fully equipped modern kitchens, where copper teakettles sparkle against fresh white tiles. **12788 Sir Francis Drake Boulevard; (415) 663-9696; www.ptreyescountryinn.com; expensive to very expensive; minimum-stay requirement on weekends.**

❦❧ **DANCING COYOTE BEACH GUEST COTTAGES, Inverness** Nestled on the shore of Tomales Bay, this getaway is a wonderful retreat when you're in need of quiet time together. Dancing Coyote's four adjoining beachfront cottages are sheltered from the busy road by a stand of sturdy pine and cypress trees that climb a small hillside. A lovingly landscaped garden enfolds a small outdoor deck furnished with wooden lounge chairs where guests can enjoy close-up views of pelicans swooping down to the water's edge.

Decorated in pastel shades of peach and green, Acacia, Birch, and Beach are three weather-worn, two-story cottages with all the right romantic touches: wood-burning fireplaces, cozy loft bedrooms, two private decks, abundant skylights, and floor-to-ceiling windows (the closer the cottage is to the water, the better the view). Touch-ups are needed here and there, but for the most part this shouldn't interfere with your enjoyment of the surroundings. A less expensive, slightly more rustic studio cottage, called Skye, is outfitted with rough-hewn wood beams and walls, a small sleeping loft (big enough for just a bed) with a glimpse of the bay, and a funky but surprisingly invigorating outdoor shower. Breakfast provisions are provided for guests to eat at their leisure in the privacy of their own small kitchen. Each cottage has access to private beachfront a few feet from its front door. However, keep in mind that your sense of privacy is minimized when all four cottages are occupied and neighboring guests are trekking past to reach the beach. If this is a romantic distraction, take advantage of the fact that all the windows have Venetian blinds. **12794 Sir Francis Drake Boulevard; (415) 669-7200; moderate to expensive; no credit cards; minimum-stay requirement on weekends.**

❦❦❦ **GRAY'S RETREAT, Point Reyes Station** Framed by flower gardens and a sprawling horse pasture, Gray's Retreat is an idyllic country getaway, just right for two. Sunshine streams through expansive multipaned windows in the living room and adjacent spacious kitchen, highlighting the golden color scheme and terra-cotta-tiled floors. Landscape art, eclectic furnishings, floral fabrics, and a wood-burning fireplace blend to create a stylish, cheerful ambience. Cozy up in the four-poster bed covered with inviting, rich linens or dazzle your beloved with your culinary talents in the fully equipped gourmet kitchen (provisions are your responsibility). Although Gray's Retreat is in town, views of Point Reyes' surrounding countryside are plentiful, and French doors in the bedroom and the dining area open onto a private wooden deck that overlooks a lovely pasture. **(415) 663-1166; very expensive; minimum-stay requirement on weekends.**

Romantic Alternative: If Gray's Retreat is booked, consider the property's other option, JASMINE COTTAGE (very expensive), surrounded by herb, flower, and vegetable gardens. The self-contained wood cottage is charmingly cozy, with lace curtains, a wood-burning Franklin stove, and a full kitchen stocked with tasty breakfast items (including eggs from the resident chickens). Oriental rugs are strewn over a rock floor, and a floral-cushioned window seat affords views of the garden. Another romantic perk is the hot tub situated just outside, secluded behind a latticed-wood fence, and available to guests of both Gray's Retreat and the Jasmine Cottage. Also outside on the garden patio is a fireplace to warm you up on cool nights, and a double hammock and several lounge chairs offering plenty of sit-and-kiss spots. Though it feels like the country, don't forget that the innkeeper's home is just on the other side of the garden.

❧❧❦ **HOTEL INVERNESS, Inverness** Want to paint fun and colorful memories into your romantic picture? Then a stay at this historical and beautifully renovated inn is a must-do and a must-see. The creative owners of Hotel Inverness have boldly gone where few innkeepers have dared to go ... and, thanks to a background in interior decorating, have succeeded.

Walls of solid bold color define each of the three sunny, south-facing rooms: Sunflower yellow dominates Room One, bright red covers the walls in Room Three (aka the Chile Sauce Room), and a peaceful blue permeates lovely Room Five. Basically, color choice determines preference of rooms since all are similar in size (small) and appointments. However, Room Five has the advantage of a balcony with bay and mountain views, while Room Three delights with a beautiful bent-willow canopied bed. Each room has colorful, slightly whimsical artwork, bent-willow furnishings, and light 'n' bright bathrooms with unusual green rubber floors, oversize showers, pedestal sinks, and, for a flush of originality, sculptural toilets designed by a Swedish artist.

Two new north-facing rooms, larger than the others, tend to be more tailored and softer than their bold, across-the-hall cousins. Identical in size, these two rooms offer sitting areas, mahogany antique headboards backing queen-size beds, and subtle color schemes of chocolate, taupe, cream, and black. Room Two tends to be a bit darker and cozier, while Room Four has a private balcony. Breakfast is delivered to all the rooms, but if it's a sunny morning, you can ask to have yours served on the common deck area overlooking the residential neighborhood. **25 Park Avenue; (415)**

669-7393; www.hotelinverness.com; moderate to expensive; minimum-stay requirement on weekends.

Romantic Alternative: The nearby TEN INVERNESS WAY (10 Inverness Way; 415-669-1648; www.teninvernessway.com; expensive to very expensive; minimum-stay requirement on weekends) is a traditional bed and breakfast with five rooms done in pleasant country motifs. All have queen-size beds and private baths. First choice on our kissing list is Room One, a sun-filled corner retreat with a beautiful, long window seat and sloping ceilings. More complete accommodations await downstairs in the ground-floor Garden Suite, which has a full kitchen, dining area, and private patio. Best of all, breakfast is delivered to your door if you stay in this suite. Other guests dine in the toasty living room and feast on such savories as pecan Belgian waffles or blue cheese–portobello mushroom quiche. Morning entertainment is provided by two lively Siamese cats.

💋💋💋 **MANKA'S INVERNESS LODGE, Inverness** Since Manka's Inverness Lodge runs one of the sexiest restaurants in all of northern California (see Restaurant Kissing), it's no surprise that its overnight accommodations are equally seductive. Eleven units are available in and around this turn-of-the-century hunting lodge set on a densely forested hillside. The rooms incorporate romance into the hunting lodge theme with huge unpeeled-log beds, rough-hewn wood walls, cozy fireplaces, and bold hunting prints and plaids. Unfortunately, only hunting types will be impressed by the stuffed fish, fur rugs, and big game trophies.

The four rooms located directly above the restaurant are subject to too much crowd noise during dinnertime, but are entirely intimate after-hours or on nights when the restaurant is closed. Two cabins on the property make distinctive retreats for embracing, particularly the Fishing Cabin, with its Adirondack-style furnishings, two-person antique tub, al fresco shower, and redwood hot tub on the private deck.

Breakfast is not included with your stay, but the restaurant is open for guests every morning from 8:30 A.M. until 10 A.M., and prices range from $6 to $12 per dish. A morning meal of, say, eggs scrambled with shiitake mushrooms and local goat cheese, accompanied by homemade wild boar sausage and cream biscuits, should more than prepare you for the day. (Don't worry; lighter options are also offered.) If you're impressed with what the kitchen produces in the morning, plan ahead by making reservations for dinner, when Manka's chefs really shine. **Argyle Avenue and Callendar Way; (415) 669-1034, (800) 585-6343; www.mankas.com; moderate to unbelievably expensive.**

Romantic Alternative: Manka's also operates the CHICKEN RANCH (unbelievably expensive), a rustic cabin set at the edge of Tomales Bay. This one-bedroom home, built in the 1850s as a hunting cabin, is one of the oldest buildings in West Marin. Although the cabin's interior shows some wear and tear, features like its waterside location and wraparound deck with trailing vines add an incredible amount of charm.

❀❀❀ MARSH COTTAGE BED AND BREAKFAST, Point Reyes Station

As you might deduce from the name, this small, weathered wood cottage sits on the shore of a marsh on Tomales Bay. Although the cabin is situated just off a fairly busy road, a fence deflects most of the traffic noise. Cattails, wildflowers, and long, honey-colored grass grow around the cabin, framing a nature lover's paradise. Country prints and fabrics, a wood-burning fireplace, and French doors that open onto a sundeck overlooking the marsh enhance the cabin's natural setting. A two-person hammock swinging outside provides the perfect spot to bird-watch or witness the sun setting over the rolling hills across the bay.

A more-than-generous breakfast of fresh orange juice, home-baked bread or muffins, seasonal fruits, milk and granola, as well as a basket of eggs, cheeses, tea, and coffee awaits guests in the semimodern, fully equipped kitchen. Your only complaint here will be that you can't stay longer. **(415) 669-7168; www.marshcottage.com; expensive; no credit cards.**

❀❀❀❀ THE NEON ROSE, Point Reyes Station

Thankfully, the only neon to be found at this private country retreat is one red rose, set above the bedroom's arched door frame. Situated in a supremely serene neighborhood, the geometrically inspired Neon Rose caters to lovers who really want to escape the city—neon lights included. Pass through a flourishing flower garden into the self-contained one-bedroom cottage that commands sweeping views of the **POINT REYES NATIONAL SEASHORE** (see Outdoor Kissing) and the bay beyond. The simply decorated and uncluttered interior features hardwood floors, white walls with hints of color, skylights, and modern appointments. Experiencing the sun's daily cycle was important to the owner, so an abundance of windows allow natural light to shine through. No curtains cover the living room windows, but with undisturbed meadows before you, lack of privacy isn't a problem. The conveniences of home, such as a full kitchen, stereo system, and telephone, are here, plus cozy touches like a living area warmed by a woodstove, a small bedroom with a queen-size bed and plush down comforter, and a jetted tub in the bathroom. A generous continental breakfast, concentrating on organic foods, is supplied for you to prepare at your own pace. Neon Rose provides peace, quiet, and a healthy dose of relaxation. What more could a city-weary couple ask for? **Overlook Road; (415) 663-9143,**

(800) 358-8346; www.neonrose.com; expensive to very expensive; no credit cards.

❀❀❀❀ **SANDY COVE INN, Inverness** Sandy Cove Inn is aptly named, due to its location just off a stretch of sandy shore along peaceful Tomales Bay. This weathered gray Cape Cod–style home is enveloped by four acres of country landscape and abundant herb and flower gardens, while tall trees completely conceal it from the road. Two resident sheep, two horses, and one barn cat call the quaint nearby barn home, adding to the pastoral charm of this property.

The innkeepers do everything to ensure a peaceful, romantic stay for guests, and their attention to detail is beyond compare. Guests are greeted with chocolates, sparkling wine in the mini-refrigerator, and a selection of fruits, cheeses, and crackers. Even a tin of breath mints is included for kissing purposes. Thoughtful touches continue with straw hats and back-packs for daily jaunts, heart-shaped chocolates placed pillowside at evening turn-down service, and newspaper delivery each morning. At the time requested, an abundant breakfast is brought to your room and served by one of the innkeepers, who presents the feast on white linen and fine china and embellishes the table with garden-fresh flowers or herbs. By the warmth of the fire, you and your honey can enjoy such sweet delights as freshly squeezed tangerine juice; berries with ginger and cream; banana-pecan pancakes and chicken-apple sausage; or creamy scrambled eggs with roasted potatoes, Canadian bacon, and golden thyme. Suffice it to say, these breakfasts are some of the best we've had anywhere.

Breakfast may be the only time you'll see the innkeepers, since privacy is highly prized here. Each of the three guest rooms has its own private entrance, queen-size bed, fireplace, private tiled bath, telephone, CD player, coffeemaker with fresh-ground coffee and cream in the fridge, plush robes and slippers, and a "lap secretary" for writing love notes in bed. French-country pine and wicker furnishings, hardwood floors embellished by colorful rugs, and charming antiques lend a rough-hewn elegance to every room, while subtle motifs (equestrian, nautical, and ornithological) make each room unique. Vaulted ceilings in the second-story North Room and South Room supply an open, airy feel, while the ground-level West Room has a large private deck, spacious bathroom, and lovely window seat fronting the gas fireplace. What you won't find in any room is a TV or VCR, and we guarantee you won't need one at Sandy Cove. Romance reigns supreme here. **Sir Francis Drake Boulevard; (415) 669-2683, (800) 759-2683; www.sandycove.com; moderate to very expensive.**

Romantic Suggestion: Within walking distance from Sandy Cove, BLUE WATERS KAYAKING (at the Golden Hinde Inn and Marina; 415-669-2600; www.bwkayak.com; rental prices start at $25) has guided moonlight kayak tours every Saturday ($49 per person). It's a perfect way for the two of you to see what the night brings to Tomales Bay (besides kissing, of course!).

SEA STAR COTTAGE, Inverness A 75-foot-long wooden walkway stretches over the tidal waters and leads to the door of this petite, weathered cottage. Comfortable, albeit timeworn, furnishings and a corner woodstove give warmth to the living room, which faces placid Tomales Bay. The adjacent bedroom features a four-poster queen-size bed with a down comforter, and the small bathroom is adorned with blue and white tiles. The overall effect is somewhat sparse and mismatched, but don't despair; the absolute *best* place to kiss here is in the sunroom that spans the front of the building, where a large hot tub is bubbling away. From this vantage point, watch a variety of seabirds fly or float by. In the morning, a breakfast of fresh juice, fruit salad, quiche, and home-baked scones is left in the kitchen and can be enjoyed in the simple breakfast room. Just be careful about having breakfast in the buff. The Inverness Yacht Club, located right next door, has a long dock that can infringe on your sense of privacy. **Sir Francis Drake Boulevard; reservations through Holly Tree Inn and Cottages, (415) 663-1554; www.hollytreeinn.com; very expensive; minimum-stay requirement on weekends.**

Romantic Warning: We must also warn you that time and the elements have taken their toll on the cottage. But with its on-the-water location, Sea Star Cottage still gets bookings despite the lofty price tag. The location certainly *is* special, but at these rates, finer appointments are expected.

VISION COTTAGE, Point Reyes Station Camouflaged by old-growth Bishop pines and cypresses at the top of a hushed, tree-laden hillside, this self-contained cottage specializes in quiet seclusion. Although the shores of Tomales Bay are nowhere in sight, neither is the highway, which adds to your sense of solitude and supreme privacy. A large black stove heats the cottage's rustic interior, which is outfitted with knotty pine walls, floor-to-ceiling windows, and a mismatched assortment of country knickknacks and antiques. Handmade quilts and down comforters cover antique pine beds in two separate, sparsely appointed bedrooms. Although a far cry from polished, all of the amenities required for a romantic getaway are here for the taking: a welcome plate of fresh fruit and chewy chocolate chip cookies, a full kitchen stocked with continental breakfast provisions, and two decks that survey views of the surrounding forest. Best of all, you can soak uninterrupted for hours in an oversize outdoor Jacuzzi tub beneath a canopy of stars twinkling in the night sky. **Sir Francis Drake Boulevard; reservations through Holly Tree Inn and Cottages, (415) 663-1554; www.hollytreeinn.com; very expensive; minimum-stay requirement on weekends.**

Restaurant Kissing

❧❧❧❧ MANKA'S INVERNESS LODGE RESTAURANT, Inverness
Dinner at Manka's is a once-in-a-lifetime romantic dining experience, though if you're lucky it will turn out to be more than once. Although this turn-of-the-century hunting lodge is set alongside a steep residential street, the dense greenery surrounding the inn makes you feel like you're nestled deep within the forest. A fire blazes in the first of three seductively lit dining rooms, while candles flicker on white linen–cloaked tables. The fire also serves as the kitchen's grill, filling the room with delicious aromas. Dark wood paneling in one dining room adds to the warm and cozy lodge surroundings, and the largest room has a massive flower arrangement at its center. Tables are nicely spaced for intimate conversation, but if you're searching for some mood-making music, the tranquil melodies from a grand piano should fill the bill.

Manka's kitchen prides itself on using regional ingredients and locally caught fish, so much so that the menu each night is determined by what the farmers and fishing boats bring in that day. Grilled game is the house specialty, but what it will be—venison, quail, or rabbit—remains a nightly surprise. Fish and vegetarian entrées also span the lineup, but one thing is for sure: Nothing will bore the taste buds. Appetizers such as clam and mussel soup with fennel and cilantro purée or grilled polenta with local wild mushrooms start things off on a scrumptious note. The house-cured grilled pork chops, served with mashed potatoes, Italian black cabbage, and pear-kumquat chutney, or the fireplace-grilled wild sturgeon served with smoky sweet pepper broth will continue to please. But you won't want to forgo dessert. Strawberries with amaretto cream and Belgian chocolate, or creamy cheesecake with warm caramel sauce and toasted pecans are two heavenly creations worth splurging on. **Argyle Avenue and Callendar Way, at Manka's Inverness Lodge; (415) 669-1034, (800) 585-6343; expensive; reservations recommended; call for seasonal hours.**

Romantic Note: Reservations are highly recommended. Monday is designated "Casual Night," with a sampler menu featuring smaller portions and lower prices (in the moderate range), an absolute steal in our opinion.

💐❀ **TOMALES BAY FOODS, Point Reyes Station** Crashing waves, windswept grasslands, and long, lonely beaches in the **POINT REYES NATIONAL SEASHORE** (see Outdoor Kissing) create the perfect backdrop for a lovely picnic for two. Luckily, all those delicious fixings needed for such an al fresco occasion are ready and waiting at Tomales Bay Foods, a delightful store specializing in gourmet foods to go. The interior, a converted barn redone with sophisticated touches, is enchanting enough to make you want to stay and sip a cappuccino at one of the small tables. But, for kissing purposes, stock up on the to-go goods, starting in the wine and cheese department with its ample selection of local cheeses, handmade crackers, and artisan breads, as well as California wines at their peak. The picnic food selection at the takeout counter is like reading from a fine restaurant's menu: rockfish with broccoli and remoulade sauce, cured salmon salad with celery root, smoked trout, roasted eggplant sandwiches, chicken liver pâté, and smoked chicken with potato salad. All are deliciously fresh and packed in sturdy containers for carrying to your favorite spot. With a place like Tomales Bay Foods supplying the delicacies, you and your sweetie might find yourselves going on more picnics than planned. **80 Fourth Street; (415) 663-9335; www.cowgirlcreamery.com/tomales.htm; inexpensive to moderate; call for seasonal hours.**

Outdoor Kissing

💐💐💐💐 **POINT REYES NATIONAL SEASHORE** The force of the frothy sea crashing into the rocky shore is one spectacle that definitely edges on the dramatic. Such a production plays continuously at the Point Reyes National Seashore and, luckily, there are plenty of spots for enjoying the show. Jutting out into the Pacific, this land mass is noted for acre after exquisite acre of untamed terrain, filled with rustling grasses, chiseled rock, cascading waterfalls, calm sandy beaches, precarious primitive coastline, and turbulent breakers crashing against haystack rocks. These sights are best seen by getting out of your car, donning those hiking boots, and hitting the multitude of trails that weave throughout this prime hiking kingdom. There are too many spectacular treks in this area to list each one. Luckily, the pucker potential is great everywhere in the Point Reyes National Seashore, but some of our favorite areas to explore are **ALAMERE FALLS, TOMALES POINT,** the **POINT REYES LIGHTHOUSE** (see the Whale

Watching review below), and **WILDCAT BEACH**. Each spot is dramatically different from the others, but their natural glory is worth discovering for yourselves. Helpful park rangers at the Bear Valley Visitor Center in Olema can give you specific hiking information. Some trails lead to vista points where the ocean reveals itself nestled between interwoven hills. Stop for a while, savor the scenery, and share a kiss in the fresh sea air. **Bear Valley Visitor Center; (415) 663-1092; free admission.** *The visitor center is located a quarter mile west of Highway 1 on Bear Valley Road in Olema.*

Romantic Suggestions: Point Reyes National Seashore may be the big draw in these parts, but don't miss out on the many smaller parks around the area. One such romantic destination is **HEART'S DESIRE BEACH**, in Tomales Bay State Park, right on Tomales Bay. Do the views from this tranquil, sparkling bay live up to the beach's name? Go and see for yourselves.

Rent a pair of horses at **FIVE BROOKS STABLES** (8001 Highway 1; 415-663-1570; www.fivebrooks.com; reservations required), three and a half miles south of Olema. This is a fabulous horse ranch with hourly rentals or half-day trips around Point Reyes National Seashore and the beach. Rental prices start at $30 per hour per rider.

Some people consider oysters to be a powerful aphrodisiac. We won't argue either way, but if you like these mouthwatering mollusks, stop at **JOHNSON'S OYSTER COMPANY** (17171 Sir Francis Drake Boulevard, just off the Sir Francis Drake Highway in Point Reyes National Seashore; 415-669-1149; inexpensive), or the **TOMALES BAY OYSTER COMPANY** (15479 Highway 1, Marshall; 415-663-1242; inexpensive; no credit cards). There is nothing fancy about either of these establishments (in fact, they look rather dumpy), but you can purchase extremely fresh oysters just plucked from the bay.

❤❤❤❤ **WHALE WATCHING** If you have always longed to witness firsthand the passage of whales on their yearly migration, then the northern California coast is a great place to fulfill your cetaceous fantasy. December to March is the best time to witness this odyssey, particularly when the weather conditions are clear and sunny. Be sure to go early in the morning, about the time the sun is warming the cool morning air. As you stand at the edge of a towering cliff near the **POINT REYES LIGHTHOUSE**, you will have a tremendous view of the coastline. Find a comfortable position, snuggle close together, and be patient.

Take in the open, endless ocean, lined with staggered cliffs dotted with green and gold chaparral for as far as the eye can see. Allow your vision to slowly scan the calm, azure waters. Suddenly, in the distance, breaking the stillness of a silent, sun-drenched morning, a spout of water explodes from the surface. A giant black profile arches boldly against the blue sea, followed by an abrupt tail slap—and then all is calm once more. It's hard to explain the romance of that moment, but romantic it is. Perhaps it's the excitement of observing such an immense creature gliding effortlessly through the water with playful agility and ease. Or perhaps it's the chance to celebrate a part of nature's mysterious aquatic underworld together. *Numerous viewpoints line the Coast Trail in the Point Reyes National Seashore, but Point Reyes Lighthouse, at the end of the Sir Francis Drake Highway, is a particularly outstanding vantage point from which to see the whales.*

Marshall

Hotel/Bed and Breakfast Kissing

❧❧❧ **POET'S LOFT, Marshall** Even if you aren't a poet, a weekend here just might inspire you to pen a few love poems. Though Poet's Loft is set just off the highway, the otherwise spectacular setting speaks volumes. Perched on stilts, this trilevel, multiangled wood home juts out over the placid waters of Tomales Bay. Skylights and floor-to-ceiling glass windows infuse the home's interior with daylight and showcase views of the bay. Throw rugs accent the hardwood floors, and contemporary pastel furnishings fill the living room, kitchen, and two bedrooms. One of the coziest spots in the house is the upstairs sleeping loft, accessible via a ladder. A wood-burning fireplace will keep you toasty warm, as will the spacious outdoor hot tub, which also offers a sweeping panorama of the bay and Point Reyes Peninsula. If this doesn't fuel your poetic inclinations, nothing will. **19695 Highway 1; (415) 721-3601; expensive to very expensive; no credit cards; minimum-stay requirement on weekends and holidays.**

Romantic Warning: This is a vacation rental, not a bed and breakfast. Guests must provide their own food and linens. However, if you are from out of town, linens and towels can be provided for an extra charge.

Bodega

Hotel/Bed and Breakfast Kissing

❧❧ **SONOMA COAST VILLA, Bodega** You can't miss this prodigious property, nestled among 60 acres of rolling hills scattered with oak trees, grazing cattle, and roaming horses. Sonoma Coast Villa's red-tiled roof, terra-cotta and stucco exterior, and terraced grounds and courtyard might remind you of a mansion tucked into the Italian countryside.

If you arrive before check-in (or if the weather is uncooperative), there's a wonderful circular staircase in the lobby that leads to the tower library brimming with dog-eared novels, homey knickknacks, and panoramic windows showcasing lovely views of the surrounding countryside. In the courtyard, a shaded walkway lined with cacti, succulents, and blossoming rosemary bushes proceeds past a scintillating outdoor swimming pool shaded by elegant cypress trees. Surrounding the pool are the inn's six original guest rooms, while six newer rooms await around back.

In contrast to the warm exterior and elegantly landscaped grounds, the rooms' interiors have mismatched furnishings, draperies, and decorations that seriously detract from the clean and simple Mediterranean look. Private entrances, wood-burning fireplaces, slate floors, stucco walls, and private baths are common features in all rooms, while some are embellished by skylights, recessed ceilings with dimming lights, Jacuzzi tubs, and private patios. To spice up the villa's romantic potential, we recommend visiting the new spa for a massage, sharing a late-night dip in the indoor communal Jacuzzi tub, or going for a moonlit walk through the lavish property. A hot, country-style breakfast is included with your stay; it's served each morning at two-person tables in an open and airy dining room adorned with dried flower arrangements and large windows looking onto the courtyard. Dinners, which aren't included in the price, are available only on Friday and Saturday nights (expensive; in-house guests receive reservation priority). **16702 Coast Highway 1; (707) 876-9818, (888) 404-2255; www.scvilla.com; expensive to very expensive; minimum-stay requirement on weekends.**

Bodega Bay

Perched above the rocky coast, Bodega Bay and an array of other small towns dot this shoreline, boasting spectacular views, wonderfully romantic accommodations, and several marvelous beaches accessible from Highway 1. Keep watch for the "COASTAL ACCESS" signs, which will direct you to secluded, windswept beaches—enticing to beachcombers and romantics alike.

Hotel/Bed and Breakfast Kissing

❦❦ **BAY HILL MANSION, Bodega Bay** This hillside bed and breakfast can be seen long before you approach it, thanks to the words "Bed and Breakfast" oddly painted across the front. While Bay Hills Mansion is certainly large, we aren't sure why the word "mansion" is included in the inn's name, since you won't find gilt-edged refinement nor a substantial estate here. What you will find are five comfortable guest rooms in a contemporary Victorian-style home. Soft pastels, dainty florals, queen-size beds with down comforters, and touches both modern and antique decorate every room; none have TVs. We recommend only the three rooms with private or detached private baths (the other two rooms share one hallway bath). Located in the home's turrets, the Whale Watch and Jenner's Reach Rooms feature an octagonal shape and expansive windows. The slightly larger Honeymooner's Hideaway, unromantically located off of the common area, holds some of the prettiest antiques in the house and is the perfect place to lie in bed and look out onto the bay. Views can also be soaked up from the communal hot tub that overlooks the driveway and the bay beyond.

In the evening, Sonoma County wines, seafood appetizers, and glorious sunsets draw guests to the main-floor parlor, with its immense woodstove, homey furnishings, and expansive bay windows. In the late morning, a full gourmet breakfast is served family-style in the dining room or on the deck if the weather is warm. **3919 Bay Hill Road; (707) 875-3577, (800) 526-5927; www.bayhillmansion.com; expensive to very expensive; minimum-stay requirement on holidays.**

❤❤❤ **BODEGA BAY AND BEYOND VACATION RENTALS, Bodega Bay** It's hard to believe that the owners of these spectacular custom-built homes don't live here year-round, but their absence is your romantic gain. These dream houses and cozy cottages can become a reality with just one phone call to Bodega Bay and Beyond. The rental properties are scattered in and around Bodega Harbour, a community of stylish, contemporary homes with water views, and many hug an 18-hole golf course. No matter which place you select, you'll feel right at home.

Currently, 57 attractive homes and cottages are on the list, all nicely furnished and equipped with everything you could ever need and more: full kitchens, TV/VCRs, wood-burning fireplaces, firewood, and even barbecue grills. Listen to the distant blare of the foghorn from the deck of the Sea Cottage, a rustic little number that overlooks the 15th green and onward to the beach and bay. More water views, ample sunlight, stylish decor, and extra touches like double-headed showers and plush linens are some of the enticing features of Cedar Cove. Harbour Nest, which has a definite "cabin feel," is popular with couples because of its large hot tub on the outside deck and cozy knotty pine interior. On the contemporary side is the Bay House, replete with nautical accents, an outdoor Jacuzzi tub off the second bedroom, and an expansive deck overlooking the inner bay. Fisherman's Cottage may not have ocean views, but the creekside location is a plus, and the sea is only seconds away. Inside this light and bright two-bedroom cottage, you'll find a woodstove, CD player, three decks to sit on, and Edward Hopper prints to set a nautical mood. **575 Highway 1; (707) 875-3942, (800) 888-3565; www.sonomacoast.com; moderate to unbelievably expensive; minimum-stay requirement.**

Romantic Note: A two-night minimum is required, but we recommend staying longer and taking advantage of the generous midweek specials (four nights for the price of three).

❤❤❤ **BODEGA BAY LODGE, Bodega Bay** At first glance, Bodega Bay Lodge looks like little more than a run-of-the-mill highway motor lodge, but a closer examination reveals its wondrous water views, charming restaurant, and contemporary interior. Even the lobby is surprisingly upscale and comfortable, outfitted with floor-to-ceiling bookshelves, overstuffed sofas snuggled next to a large fieldstone fireplace, and two fabulous fish tanks featuring creatures you'd find in both local and tropical waters. Such a setting becomes more welcoming near dinnertime when you can partake of the complimentary wine reception.

Perched atop an oceanfront bluff, the lodge's 84 spacious guest rooms and suites survey gorgeous views of Bodega Bay and the windswept grasslands of the adjacent **DORAN BEACH REGIONAL PARK** and nearby bird sanctuary. Only the occasional sound of the harbor horn interrupts the remote peace of this sprawling property. Distinctive touches like shell lamps and seascape sculptures add individuality to the hotel-style rooms, which are done up in shades of green, accented by avian or nautical motifs, and comfortably furnished with classical appointments. Best of all, every room features a private deck overlooking the water, and most have the romantic luxury of wood-burning fireplaces. TVs, coffeemakers, plush white towels and robes, and the convenience of a refrigerator and wet bar are appreciated amenities. If your budget allows, spring for one of the five new Executive Whirlpool Suites, in particular the ground-level Trumpeter Swan Suite, which resides adjacent to the restaurant. Besides having nature right outside your private patio, this corner suite dazzles lovebirds with its king-size bed, CD player, and an ultradeluxe bathroom complete with two-person whirlpool tub and a glass-enclosed shower brightened by a skylight.

A walk to the beach takes only five minutes, but if you want to stay on the property, there's plenty to do here, too. Seashore vegetation borders trails that meander to an exercise room, sauna, heated outdoor pool, and glass-enclosed whirlpool with an open-top gazebo and ocean views. If all that exercise and water doesn't help you unwind, try the spa's offerings, including massages, body treatments, and facials. **103 Coast Highway 1; (707) 875-3525, (800) 368-2468; www.woodsidehotels.com; expensive to unbelievably expensive; minimum-stay requirement on weekends.**

Romantic Suggestion: After a day spent enjoying the lodge's spectacular surroundings, we recommend a candlelight dinner at the property's very own DUCK CLUB RESTAURANT (expensive; reservations required; breakfast and dinner daily). An immense river-rock fireplace warms this bay-view dining room, which is decorated with duck sculptures and paintings. Large (a little too large) circular tables are draped in white linens. Trained in Italy, the chef is well known for his seasonal California cuisine emphasizing local goods from Sonoma County. At breakfast time, be sure to bring binoculars and watch the bird life in the wetlands below.

Jenner

If it weren't for its spectacular vistas, the sleepy little town of Jenner would be little more than a big curve in the road where the Russian River meets the sea. Calm river waters, a sandy shoreline, and, of course, the sparkling Pacific Ocean give Jenner a special identity all its own. There aren't many kissable overnight options, but you should at least consider stopping for lunch to get your fill of this incredible scenery.

Restaurant Kissing

❤ **RIVER'S END, Jenner** Views of swirling white water and turbulent eddies that explode over and around the rock outcroppings of the Pacific Ocean can change at twilight into a placid, almost surreal, composition. As sunset nears, a single path of sunlight glosses the surface of the water, illuminating it and the horizon, with the hills veiled in darkness. Evening announces its finale with a crescendo of colors that fade slowly to black. From the deck, dining room, or solarium lounge of the River's End restaurant, perched at the edge of the Russian River estuary, this daily, sparkling performance is yours to behold. Thank goodness for nature's show, since the restaurant's cabin-like decor (including a dusty stuffed seal above the bar) doesn't wow the senses. The menu showcases everything under the sun and sea, from coconut fried shrimp, to medallions of venison, to East Indian chicken or beef curry. Our meal was just average, but with the glistening ocean outside, we found it easier to forgive the kitchen's shortcomings. **11048 Highway 1; (707) 865-2484; moderate; call for seasonal hours.**

Romantic Warning: River's End also offers four cabin accommodations, which we don't recommend for kissing purposes.

Outdoor Kissing

❤❤❤ **GOAT ROCK STATE PARK, Jenner** This dramatic location would have been awarded our premium four-lip rating except that, like many other state parks, it is so packed with people during the summer and on weekends that privacy is hard to find. Still, this place is so alluring that you shouldn't let the crowds deter you. Here the milky green and blue waters of the Pacific crash into the surf and meet the mouth of the Russian River estuary. Water laps on both sides of this small strip of beach, and massive rocks protrude from the sea where colonies of sea lions and seals often bask in the sun. **Free admission.** *From Highway 1, watch for signs to Goat Rock State Park.*

Romantic Suggestion: There might be fewer people at **SHELL BEACH**, just south of Goat Rock State Park. A well-used trail leads down to this little section of sand, which is best visited at low tide when there are diverse tide pools to explore.

Cazadero

Hotel/Bed and Breakfast Kissing

❤❤❤❤ **TIMBERHILL RANCH, Cazadero** If you're hoping to escape the pressures of the daily grind, look no further than the Timberhill Ranch. Nothing about this pastoral ranch is remotely reminiscent of the real world (except maybe the price tag). Poised on a ridge above the Sonoma coast, this property encompasses 80 serene wooded acres of nature's finest greenery.

Secluded among trees, the ranch's 15 handsome cedar log cabins are rustic yet elegant, with knotty pine walls, colorful handmade quilts, tiled wood-burning fireplaces, and a variety of location choices ranging from pondside to tucked-in-the-woods toasty. Amenities like oversize tiled bathrooms, CD players, mini-bars, and fridges stocked with refreshments add to your comfort. What you won't find are those trappings of civilization: phones and TVs.

Hike to your hearts' content through seemingly endless acres of rambling woodland. Beyond the ranch itself are 6,000 acres of protected wilderness, where dozens of footpaths wind through redwood forests, past shimmering ponds and fields of wildflowers in adjacent **SALT POINT STATE PARK** and **KRUSE RHODODENDRON RESERVE**. The kitchen will even pack you a to-go knapsack filled with treats for your trip. You can also make use of the property's premier tennis courts or simply enjoy the scenery from the soothing comfort of a 40-foot heated pool and nearby steaming Jacuzzi tub.

Although the room rates seem quite steep, keep in mind that they include an ample continental breakfast brought to your cottage every morning and a six-course evening meal served in the inn's handsome dining room.

Dinners here are remarkable and served at intimate tables set with silver and crystal. On any given day the menu may include a noteworthy chilled artichoke appetizer with tarragon and Maine crab; a robust old-fashioned split-pea soup; perfectly seared Chilean sea bass; wonderful grilled swordfish with a black bean and roasted corn relish; homemade mango sorbet as a palate refresher; and, for dessert, strawberry buttercream cake. Consider a walk around the grounds between courses, especially if you can catch the sunset. **35755 Hauser Bridge Road; (707) 847-3258; www.timber hillranch.com; unbelievably expensive (price includes breakfast and dinner); minimum-stay requirement on weekends; closed January; recommended wedding site.**

Fort Ross

Hotel/Bed and Breakfast Kissing

❤❤ **FORT ROSS LODGE, Fort Ross** Encircled by rolling meadows dotted with wildflowers and dried golden brush, this very casual destination offers some affordable, affectionate options for an overnight stay. Because of its great prices and child-friendly policy, Fort Ross Lodge caters mostly to families (especially during summer vacation). However, if you're on a budget and you don't mind the slight motor-lodge feel, you're in luck.

Fort Ross Lodge is divided into two sections: "The Lodge" rooms are located below the road near the sea, and "The Hill" rooms are situated in the hills. Food isn't provided, but a well-stocked deli/store across the street should provide most essentials. The 16 Lodge rooms comprise four buildings and are all decorated differently, ranging from colorful, simple florals to Southwest prints. Furnishings cover all decorating bases, from modern oak tables to early '80s-style dressers and side tables. Each room is equipped with a small refrigerator, microwave, coffeemaker, and TV. On the private, enclosed deck there's a barbecue for your use, along with charcoal.

The best Lodge rooms (the King and Queen Room Nos. 14 through 16) overlook the unobstructed beauty of the Pacific Ocean, and come romantically equipped with fireplaces, hot tubs on private patios, and champagne in the refrigerator. (All other rooms without hot tubs receive a bottle of wine for two.) For rooms lacking in bubbling fun, a glass-enclosed hot tub with ocean view is available for all guests on the property, as is a Finnish sauna. Another favorite feature for all guests is a mowed path leading to the edge of 150-foot coastal cliffs where you can watch the waves crash on the shore or catch a stupendous sunset.

Six more units are set in "The Hill," a rambling ranch home high above the road on 35 acres of forested hillside. (Guests here will need to drive down to use the Lodge's communal hot tub and sauna.) These rooms are billed as the more romantic (and more expensive) suites because they are designated "couples only." Four have in-room spa tubs and saunas. Due to the location, a walk to the shore isn't an immediate option, but a tree-framed view of the sea is visible from most units. These rooms are decorated in a more contemporary style and feel like studio apartments where you can host your own private party for two. No. 20, the large Honeymoon Suite, comes with a two-person Jacuzzi tub and sauna, a large covered porch, mini library, pedestal bed tucked in between the windows, and a flagstone fireplace. Although it's smaller, we also liked the ground-floor Room No. 24 with its black and burgundy decor, Jacuzzi tub with forest view, and porch showcasing panoramic views. **20705 Highway 1; (707) 847-3333; www.fortrosslodge.com; very inexpensive to very expensive; minimum-stay requirement on weekends for some rooms.**

Romantic Note: When making reservations, you should know that Lodge Room Nos. 9 through 12 have no view at all. Also, be sure to ask about midweek discounts and specials.

Sea Ranch

Hotel/Bed and Breakfast Kissing

❤❤❤ **SEA RANCH ESCAPE, Sea Ranch** Views of the thundering surf crashing onto Sea Ranch's rugged, rocky shoreline can be best appreciated from the seclusion of your very own luxury rental home. Sea Ranch Escape's vacation properties are some of the prettiest we've seen, scattered along more than ten miles of exquisite coastline. Ranging from cozy cottages tucked among trees to enormous oceanfront homes equipped with every imaginable luxury and amenity, there's sure to be something to match your budget and personality. Many homes are newly built and stylishly outfitted, while others represent that quintessential simple beach cabin. No matter which you choose, all come stocked with the basic necessities (a full kitchen and cooking utensils, towels, linens, blankets, firewood, etc.). Many have spectacular ocean views, decks, fireplaces or wood-burning stoves, and even Jacuzzi tubs. Homes are categorized as oceanfront, hillside, cluster, oceanside meadow, and forest, so pick where you want to hibernate from the world, and head out!

As for romantic suggestions, here are two: Cuddling couples often gravitate to the Wild Fern, a upscale hillside home with panoramic views, a hot tub, a woodstove, and wooden pillars accenting the open kitchen. Jungle lovers head to the hills to find the Treehouse, a one-bedroom wonder that's hidden in the forest. This multidimensional home features a rustic wood interior, large windows, a loft bedroom, and a hot tub on its deck. **60 Sea Walk Drive; (707) 785-2426, (888) SEA-RANCH; www.888searanch. com; moderate to unbelievably expensive.**

❤❤❤ **SEA RANCH LODGE, Sea Ranch** The boundless drama of the Pacific Ocean harbors plenty of romantic possibilities, so the closer your accommodations are to this magnificent shoreline, the better. They don't get much closer than Sea Ranch Lodge, nestled on a bluff directly above the grassy dunes and ocean. Architecturally interesting and angular in shape, the Lodge offers gorgeous pristine views from most guest rooms. In fact, the 20 guest rooms are simply but elegantly attired, so that nothing competes with the world outside the picture windows. Stylish taupe colors, natural fibers, woven chairs, dried vine wreaths, and knotty pine walls free from unnecessary adornments help bring nature indoors. (None of the rooms contain a TV, and with these vistas, you won't miss it.) Wonderful window seats and wood-burning fireplaces turn Room Nos. 1 and 7 into popular picks, while No. 11, a corner room, boasts the most wide-reaching views. If a soaking tub is more important than a sweeping vista, Room No. 20 has a dandy of a hot tub in its private backyard, plus a wood-burning stove indoors. There's no view at all, but the compromise is worth it.

Breakfast is not included with your stay, but you won't have to walk far for food. The **SEA RANCH RESTAURANT** (see Restaurant Kissing) serves up outstanding ocean vistas with breakfast, lunch, and dinner. An intimate connection with nature and each other is what makes this small lodge so special. However, plans are in the works to add a whopping 70 additional rooms, all with ocean views! While this may be better for business, we worry that romantic ambience may suffer. Stay tuned. **60 Sea Walk Drive; (707) 785-2371, (800) 732-7262; www.searanchlodge.com; expensive to unbelievably expensive; minimum-stay requirement on weekends; recommended wedding site.**

Romantic Suggestion: A barn might not be your first idea of a wedding venue, but wait until you see how the owners have raised a barn to new heights here. Located on a seaside bluff, this weathered old barn has been transformed into a study of true rustic elegance. For weddings (summers only), fabrics are draped from the rafters, and hay-covered floors add just the right country touch to that special day.

Restaurant Kissing

❤❤ **SEA RANCH RESTAURANT, Sea Ranch** Like the Sea Ranch Lodge's decor, the namesake restaurant's interior does little to compete with the magnificent beauty outside. From the restaurant's towering wall of windows, look out onto windswept grasslands that reach down to the fringes of the turbulent ocean. Although fresh flowers and crisp white linens adorn every table, the restaurant retains an exceedingly casual, lodge-style ambience. Breakfast, lunch, and dinner are served daily, but dinner is by far the most romantic meal, especially if your reservation time corresponds with the sunset.

We especially enjoyed the light portobello-stuffed ravioli garnished with goat cheese as well as the coriander-crusted salmon marinated in a fennel-onion slaw, pink peppercorns, and rice wine vinegar. Most heavenly of all was the Chocolate Landslide—rich milk chocolate and pecans topped with fresh raspberries and whipped cream. After you've eaten, head to the fireside room, where you can relish the warmth of a fire flickering in the stone fireplace, or take in more delicious ocean views in the adjacent solarium. **60 Sea Walk Drive, at Sea Ranch Lodge; (707) 785-2371, (800) 732-7262; searanchlodge.com; moderate to very expensive; breakfast, lunch, and dinner daily, brunch Sunday.**

Gualala

One surefire way to spot tourists in this region is to hear how they pronounce Gualala. Don't worry; locals won't hassle you if you say it wrong, but the correct pronunciation is *"wah-LA-la."* Gualala is a Native American word that means "water coming down place." Luckily, the phrase does not mean you should expect rain (it is sunny here an average of 300 days a year); instead it refers to the place where the Gualala River meets the sea. Gualala offers a number of romantic overnight options and several excellent restaurants, which is surprising, considering the size of this small, friendly coastal village.

Hotel/Bed and Breakfast Kissing

❦❦❦ **BREAKERS INN, Gualala** As you pull into Breakers Inn's parking lot, you may feel apprehensive about our recommendation. The nondescript exterior gives no indication of the impressive suites that await. In fact, from the outside this could be any seaside motel or apartment complex. Inside, it is a completely different story. Each of the 27 rooms is decorated according to a city, state, or country theme, from San Francisco (a stunning room with elegant cream-colored furnishings, a king-size carved sleigh bed, and beveled glass windows) to Virginia (a Colonial-style room featuring wingback chairs and a mahogany four-poster bed). Themes aren't limited to American styles: Japan has a two-person jetted corner tub made of rare Japanese cypress, Denmark has a Danish sauna, and Provence has rattan furnishings and an intricate iron bed. Basically, Breakers Inn offers something for everyone … you just need to choose in which part of the world you'd like to spend the night.

Other romantic advantages include the fact that every room has a spectacular view; some feature large patios facing the Gualala River estuary, the sandy beach, and the pounding surf. Radiant-heated floors warm every room, and all oceanfront luxury rooms have wood-burning fireplaces, whirlpool tubs for two, and king-size beds. Other room categories vary in romantic amenities, so be sure to specify your hearts' desire. A continental breakfast of fresh fruit and store-bought pastries and muffins is served in the main lobby but, luckily, trays are provided to take back to your room, where the view combined with privacy makes for the best breakfast spot in town. **39300 South Highway 1; (707) 884-3200, (800) 273-2537; www. breakersinn.com; expensive to very expensive; minimum-stay requirement on holiday weekends.**

❦❦ **NORTH COAST COUNTRY INN, Gualala** Set at the edge of busy Highway 1, this cluster of terraced, weathered redwood cottages—housing six suites in all—scales a forested hillside and provides many essentials for a romantic escape. The four original suites all have private decks, and two offer peekaboo ocean views (across the busy highway). High peaked ceilings and open beams give the eclectic rooms a feeling of sparse spaciousness despite their country collectibles, old logging tools, and botanical art. Cloth throw rugs warm the wood floors, and patchwork quilts dress up the antique four-poster beds. All four original rooms also feature fireplaces, skylights, and fully equipped kitchenettes. While each makes for a pleasant retreat, romantics may want to venture farther up the hillside steps to the new Forrest House, where two deluxe suites await. Both the Southwind and Evergreen are identical in layout and comfortably outfitted with one-person Jacuzzi tubs in the bathroom, high king-size beds, lovely appointments, and sitting areas overlooking floor-to-ceiling windows. Unfortunately, neither has an ocean view. Southwind takes on a French country theme with yellow and white walls accented by blue carpeting, while Evergreen tends toward the natural look, with its knotty pine walls and ceiling. A delicious breakfast buffet is served in the cheerful and sunny common room, where you'll find round tables for two, a gas fireplace, and a cupboard displaying a colorful plate collection.

One of the property's best features awaits at the end of a charming lighted pathway trimmed with flowers and greenery. Here, sequestered among the pines, is an enclosed hot tub and outdoor shower. Lock the wooden gate and let the bubbles take the two of you away. If you continue on to the hillside's crest, you'll discover a meadow punctuated by a gazebo, comfortable lounge chairs, and a small fountain. While road noise is audible from this natural retreat, the seclusion is so seductive you'll forget civilization and let the forest sounds and distant ocean roar engulf you. **34591 South Highway 1; (707) 884-4537, (800) 959-4537; expensive to very expensive; minimum-stay requirement on weekends and holidays.**

❧❧ **SEACLIFF, Gualala** Seacliff's four modern cedar structures sit on an oceanfront bluff overlooking the mouth of the Gualala River. They look like an ordinary apartment complex from the parking lot, but once you step inside and get a load of the extraordinary view, you'll see why this is a fabulous place to kiss the day away.

The eight rooms on the first floor may appeal to your budget, but the eight second-floor rooms will appeal to your hearts, thanks to their vaulted ceilings, large windows, and superior views from corner decks. Since the decor in all units can only be described as hotel standard (boring bathrooms, modest furniture, and drab color schemes), we recommend spending the additional $25 per night to perch on the second floor. Regardless of the floor you choose, each room has a gas fireplace, king-size bed, private patio with provided binoculars, and a two-person whirlpool tub where you can watch seagulls swoop overhead as you revel in the perfectly unobstructed ocean views. Even if the room decor doesn't tug at your heartstrings, the cost of these rooms and their romantic amenities make them worthy of a toast with the complimentary sparkling wine or cider. **39140 South Highway 1; (707) 884-1213, (800) 400-5053; www.seacliffmotel.com; moderate to expensive; minimum-stay requirement on holiday weekends.**

❧❧ **ST. ORRES INN, Gualala** Finding words that succinctly express the architectural intrigue of this inn is a challenge. Across the highway from a cloistered sandy cove, this structure appears suddenly out of nowhere, a fascinating hand-carved, wood-and-glass Russian-style chalet. Stained glass windows in two intricately crafted towers twinkle in the daylight; inside, prismatic light bathes the interior in a velvety amber glow. Varied guest accommodations range from eight simple, drab rooms in the main house with shared baths (not recommended) to 12 small cottages scattered about the grounds. Each cottage has its own spirit and tone, with rustic furnishings, a small kitchen, and varying color schemes. Some feature unobstructed ocean views, while others have skylights, sundecks, fireplaces, and sunken tubs. Having said all this, we must mention that although rustic simplicity has its charm, the interiors of the cottages could use some sprucing up.

(The Blue Iris Cottage is the only one that has been recently updated with a new bathroom, Jacuzzi tub, and sauna.) While staying here, a dinner at **ST. ORRES RESTAURANT** (see Restaurant Kissing) is a romantic must. As for the first meal of the day, a full breakfast, including homemade granola and freshly baked bread, is delivered to your door in a large basket. **36601 South Highway 1; (707) 884-3303; www.saintorres.com; inexpensive to very expensive; minimum-stay requirement on weekends.**

Romantic Note: Make your reservations early. In summer the cottages are booked up to eight weeks in advance.

❦❦❦❦ **WHALE WATCH INN, Gualala** Whale watching has never been more luxurious than at this well-known inn. From the comfort of your own private balcony (or, in some cases, a whirlpool tub), you and your sweetheart can witness the fantastic migration of earth's largest animals. Yet whale-watching season isn't the only time to visit. Couples wanting to spend quality time together in private surroundings migrate here year-round.

Eighteen rooms and suites, each endowed with its own unique style, are housed in five wooden buildings spread throughout the cliffside property. Sounds of the careening surf are as clear as a bell from almost every room, and if you get the urge to see the ocean for yourselves, it's just 134 steps to the beach below (although it feels more like 234 coming back up).

Which room to choose? Our favorites are the eight suites in the Pacific Edge Building and the two rooms in the Quest House. Although the decor varies dramatically, from contemporary to classic, each room offers stunning views and a wood-burning fireplace; some even have private decks and whirlpool tubs for two. In particular, the private Pacifica Suite won our hearts over, thanks to its picture-perfect window seat, whirlpool tub for two with mirrored backdrop, and location away from other rooms. Ocean Sunrise and Crystal Sea, both located in the Quest House and identical in layout, have that "cabin-in-the-woods" feeling due to their wooded surroundings. (For the best ocean views, book the second-floor Crystal Sea.) Rooms in the Sea Bounty and Cygnet House Buildings deserve some romantic consideration, but are not nearly as stylish or well put together as some of the others. In keeping with the romantic theme, none of the rooms have TVs or phones.

At the hour you request, a delicious gourmet breakfast is served in your room. Along with the food, you can savor ocean views and hopefully spot a whale pod from your perfect vantage point. **35100 Highway 1; (707) 884-3667, (800) 942-5342; www.whale-watch.com; expensive to unbelievably expensive; minimum-stay requirement on weekends and holidays.**

Restaurant Kissing

❧❧❧ **THE OLD MILANO HOTEL RESTAURANT, Gualala** As you veer off the highway and start down the gravel driveway toward the ocean, you will readily appreciate the enveloping seclusion of this modest turn-of-the-century building. Besides its wondrous location (a stone's throw from the edge of an ocean bluff), this restaurant's most irresistible attribute is its enthusiasm for antique country finery. Every corner of the Victorian dining area reveals a memento from the past. The cozy tables are draped in rose linens and topped with oil lanterns, and a roaring fire crackles in the river-rock fireplace.

The continental menu brings to the table dishes that will satisfy for the most part, although we've heard that the kitchen can be inconsistent. Grilled black prawns served with roasted red pepper aioli, lemon-feta chicken, and filet of salmon garnished with a citrus–red onion relish make up the relatively small menu. After dinner, take a stroll through the gardens and along the bluff to admire the celestial scenery. **38300 Highway 1; (707) 884-3256; www.oldmilanohotel.com; expensive; no credit cards; call for seasonal hours.**

Romantic Note: Old-fashioned authenticity continues in the 13 guest rooms and cottages at **THE OLD MILANO HOTEL** (inexpensive to very expensive). The six rooms above the restaurant share two baths, but if you don't mind sharing the facilities, Room Nos. 1, 4, and 6 have great views. The master suite, directly off the dining room, offers a private bath and a sitting area with incredible ocean views. For the train lover, a cozy caboose-turned-guest-room is quite a special accommodation, although the view is nil. Two new large cottages, complete with fireplaces and spa tubs, might be potential kissing places if their Victorian decor weren't so sparse and the overwhelming smell of cleaning materials didn't drive us out so soon. Perhaps the most romantic features of the Old Milano are the cliffside hot tub (available for private soaks), the beautifully cared-for gardens, and the outdoor sitting area with chairs facing the rugged coast.

❧❧❧ **ST. ORRES RESTAURANT, Gualala** St. Orres' Russian-inspired architecture is anything but ordinary, and the restaurant exemplifies the inn's flair for the unusual (see Hotel/Bed and Breakfast Kissing). A three-story-high wooden tower, adorned with stained glass windows and stenciled woodwork, houses a dramatic dining room ideal for romancing the night away. Trailing plants hang from the walls, and the atmosphere is formal yet entirely comfortable. Catch the light of the setting sun by sitting at one of the candlelit two-person tables clustered at the base of the tower. The only letdown is that this clustering of tables can be tight in spots. One couple we saw moved together to one side of the table so they could talk privately.

Dinner here is a prix-fixe, three-course delight (including soup, salad, and entrée), with unusual dishes like wild boar stuffed with dates and walnuts to more subdued offerings like breast of pheasant presented on wild mushroom risotto cakes. Another enticing entrée is the grilled Sonoma County quail marinated in tequila and served with yam and green onion pancakes, pheasant wontons, and a blood orange–jalapeño pepper glaze. If you can't tell already, the specialty here is wild game of the North Coast, and vegetarian options are limited. Desserts are equally engaging. The house-made Jack Daniels ice cream with roasted pecans and maple syrup proves to be a delightfully mellow and creamy surprise. **36601 South Highway 1, at St. Orres Inn; (707) 884-3303; www.saintorres.com; expensive to very expensive; credit cards accepted for lodging guests only; call for seasonal hours.**

❀❀❀ **TOP OF THE CLIFF, Gualala** You may be wondering why we're sending you to this little redwood shopping center along Highway 1, but take a closer look. Spanning the second floor you'll find Top of the Cliff, a lovely, open restaurant that's trying hard to please, and doing a mighty fine job of it. The small restaurant with adjoining bar holds only 13 tables, but each one has an ocean view ranging in quality from good to excellent. Glass oil candles, long-stem flowers on each table, and low lighting create a casual yet intimate atmosphere. Service is friendly and professional, and on certain weekends, local talent plays pleasing, often passionate, tunes on an acoustic guitar. Once you're snuggled inside, there's no indication that Highway 1 and a parking lot are right outside. However, we only wish the silent yet visually distracting TV in the bar could be turned off.

Plenty of seafood dishes, steak, and pasta specialties are served in extremely generous portions, and each meal includes warm bread, hot soup, and fresh salad. Halibut baked with crab and brie, a house specialty, is richly satisfying. The hot pot of seafood—shellfish and fresh fish in a mussel broth topped with a puff pastry—is a must-try. Full of delectable clams, the light and creamy New England clam chowder proves a favorite on this coastline too. Don't skip dessert or else you'll miss such treats as a luscious tiramisu surrounded by warm, frothy cream. **39140 South Highway 1; (707) 884-1539; expensive; call for seasonal hours.**

Outdoor Kissing

❀❀❀ **KAYAKING, Gualala** Whether braving ocean waves and currents or just meandering up the Gualala River, lovers of the great outdoors will thoroughly enjoy a kayak excursion in this area. A paddle upriver is perfect for spotting ospreys, great blue herons, and brown pelicans; if you're lucky you may see river otters playing in the water. There is room in each kayak to bring along a picnic lunch (see the Romantic Suggestion), and if you have a waterproof container for your camera (a plastic bag will do), the photo opportunities are innumerable. Canoes and double kayaks are also available for couples who wish to paddle in synchronicity. **Adventure Rents: Cantamare Center; (707) 884-4386, (888) 881-4386; www. adventurerents.com; rental prices start at $20 per kayak.**

Romantic Warning: Kayaking on a gentle river is fine for beginners, but sea kayaking is for the more experienced only.

Romantic Suggestion: Those interested in exploring Gualala's spectacularly private beaches might want to pack a lunch and make a day of it. **THE FOOD COMPANY** (Highway 1 and Robinson Reach; 707-884-1800; inexpensive; breakfast, lunch, and dinner daily), located right off Highway 1 in Gualala, is an excellent place to purchase a carry-out gourmet lunch. Whether it's polenta tart, tamale pies, green bean and artichoke salad, barbecued pork ribs, or a tempting slice of chocolate cake with raspberry filling, you're sure to find something appetizing (so appetizing, in fact, that it might be consumed before you reach the beach). Call on the day you plan to picnic, and the friendly staff can put together something delicious for you. Or better yet, stop by and see the mouthwatering goodies displayed in glass cases. The price for two is typically around $20, not including wine. While we're on the subject, there's a good selection of splits as well as full-sized bottles from local wineries.

Point Arena

Hotel/Bed and Breakfast Kissing

❦❦ **COAST GUARD HOUSE HISTORIC INN, Point Arena** Formerly a lifesaving station, the Coast Guard House Historic Inn proudly overlooks the pier and Arena Cove. The six various-sized guest rooms in this venerable, weather-beaten Cape Cod–style home and separate cottage are comfortable and simply decorated, with an emphasis on Arts-and-Crafts furnishings and accents. In the main house, couples who like to be close can snuggle up in the ultra-cozy Flag Room. Although its near-the-living-room location isn't the best, this nautical-inspired hideaway will wow guests with its cozy sitting nook for two and queen-size bed tucked into a windowed alcove. From either vantage point, ocean views are prominent. Seclusion seekers should opt for The Boathouse, a separate cottage with gold sponge-painted walls, high ceilings, tiled floors, a potbellied stove, a jetted two-person tub in the living room, and all the privacy you could hope for. The other four rooms in the main house offer pleasant accommodations, but lack the romantic character of the Flag Room and The Boathouse. Breakfast time brings to the dining table in the main home such dishes as spinach soufflé, potato pie with Gruyère cheese, and berry pancakes. **695 Arena Cove; (707) 882-2442, (800) 524-9320; www.coast guardhouse.com; moderate to expensive.**

❀❀ **WHARF MASTER'S INN, Point Arena** This quiet, tree-covered hillside is where the wharf master once surveyed the comings and goings of fishing vessels in Arena Cove Harbor below. Now the site of the sprawling Wharf Master's Inn, the hillside hosts a handful of wooden, two-story buildings that overlook the still-bustling harbor. While the weather outside isn't always pleasant, the property's 23 spacious guest rooms make perfect retreats from the elements. Done up with pastel color schemes and pleasant floral accents, every room has a sumptuous four-poster queen-size bed and a private deck with either ocean or courtyard views. All but two rooms feature fireplaces and large, beautifully tiled Jacuzzi tubs. Unrivaled water and sunset views make the original wharf master's refurbished 1870s Victorian home irresistibly romantic and undeniably the best (albeit most expensive) spot to kiss on the property. Its location, separate from the rest of the inn, is also perfect for privacy seekers.

Breakfast is not included with your accommodations so be sure to pick up provisions the night before. Some restaurants in nearby Point Arena have the reputation of opening whenever the owners feel like it, especially during the off-season. **785 Port Road; (707) 882-3171, (800) 932-4031; www.wharfmasters.com; inexpensive to unbelievably expensive; minimum-stay requirement on holidays.**

Restaurant Kissing

❀❅ **PANGAEA, Point Arena** From near and far, locals and visitors alike travel to the tiny town of Point Arena for the outstanding food at Pangaea. And, with seasonal specialties like duck tacos on homemade corn tortillas, seared rare ahi in a sesame oil and soy sauce, and chicken roasted in *herbes de Provence*, your taste buds will quickly understand why so many make the journey. (Just keep your eyes open, since the nondescript exterior is difficult to spot from the street.) Operated by a group of artists, culinary and otherwise, the restaurant possesses an artistic bent with dramatic and generous food presentations, not to mention bold flavors. The decor also reflects an artistic touch, most notably the butter-yellow walls set off by vivid, colorful paintings. Track lighting, black chairs, and simple wooden tables bring out a modern flair, rather than a cozy romantic feel. However, there's no doubt you'll fall in love with what's on your plate, and such a prelude is often enough to make the rest of the evening turn out right. **250 Main Street; (707) 882-3001; moderate to expensive; no credit cards; dinner Wednesday–Sunday.**

Manchester

Hotel/Bed and Breakfast Kissing

❦❦❦❦ **VICTORIAN GARDENS, Manchester** Not at all visible from the road, Victorian Gardens is a striking gray and white Victorian farmhouse set among 92 acres of meadows and forest. From the moment you arrive, quiet serenity envelops you as the gracious hosts welcome you like a personal friend into their beautifully appointed residence. Although the exterior is thoroughly Victorian, the interior is not outfitted in accompanying fashion. Instead of taking the traditional route of matching interior with exterior, the innkeepers here have created a refreshing blend of old and new, with a bent toward all things Italian. Polished hardwood floors, hand-loomed Italian rugs, hand-stenciled wallpapers, and exquisite artwork from the innkeepers' world travels fill the main floor, and the same stylish elegance continues in the four guest rooms upstairs.

Sloped ceilings, hardwood floors, and exquisite artwork prevail in all the guest rooms, and each is reasonably spaced apart from the next. The spacious Master Bedroom is the premier suite. Distant ocean views can be enjoyed from its comfortable sitting area, the claw-foot tub fronts an elegant etched-glass window, and a fluffy down quilt warms the queen-size bed. (Note the color of this bedframe. It's painted with the *very* same paint used to cover that famous bridge by the bay.) The Northwest Bedroom, another favorite, has an enormous tiled bath, queen-size bed with sumptuous linens and a down comforter, and ocean and pastoral views from the large soaking tub for two. The other two bedrooms, Golden and Poppy, share a detached bath; however the innkeepers will not rent out both rooms at the same time. Of these two, Golden is our choice for romance, with its wrought-iron queen-size bed and wicker chairs set beside a bay window showcasing awesome sunsets. None of the rooms come with TV or fireplace, but with such warmth and beauty surrounding you, they certainly won't be missed.

A lavish, multicourse breakfast, featuring eggs from resident hens, is served in the elegant dining room beside a crackling fire or in the adjacent sunny sitting room. Early evening brings wine and hors d'oeuvres, which you can enjoy on the wraparound porch if weather permits. There's little need to leave the property to find things to fill your day. The formal library offers a bounty of books and a letter-writing desk (stationery included), while the parlor houses the only TV and VCR, along with a collection of classical movies, perfect for rainy-day entertainment. Others may want to breathe deep in the meditation garden or flex those leg muscles along various trails on the property. However, you may not be totally alone on your trek. The resident donkeys have been known to accompany couples hoofin' it to the hills. **14409 South Highway 1; (707) 882-3606; moderate to very expensive.**

Romantic Suggestion: Once you get comfortable here (it won't take long), you need not even step out for dinner. We highly recommend the five-course gourmet Italian meal lovingly prepared by the resident chef/ innkeeper. Designed to resemble a dinner party, the meal brings back the lost art of dining, when meals weren't rushed, but instead savored throughout the evening accompanied by fine wine and conversation. Your innovative Italian host prepares historically authentic classics such as succulent roasted pork loin; thin slices of ham rolled around diced potatoes, carrots, and green beans with homemade mayonnaise; and hand-rolled pasta stuffed with savory wild mushrooms. Desserts are equally mouthwatering. To keep things interesting, a new, hand-printed menu is presented daily, and many of the ingredients are plucked straight from the garden. Each course is served family-style in the fireside dining room, but if you'd rather dine together (and you call early enough), you can reserve a table à deux. As you would expect from the attention to detail here, fine Italian china, linens, crystal, and silver accompany the meal, as do wonderful wines and after-dinner drinks.

The only requirement for dinner is that you make reservations ahead of time. The price is $125 per couple (not including tax and gratuity, but it does include wine and additional beverages, making it an excellent value). Dinner is also open to nonguests on the same basis (reservations required; based on availability—no drop-ins). Dinners start at 7:30 P.M. and last as long as your hearts (and taste buds) desire.

Elk

Hotel/Bed and Breakfast Kissing

❤❤❤ **ELK COVE INN, Elk** Views from this bed and breakfast are stunning, and sunsets will leave you speechless (which makes kissing that much easier). Set above a driftwood-scattered beach and facing ancient rocks that jut out of the sea, Elk Cove Inn offers six rooms in the Victorian main house, four neighboring cabins, and, best of all, four new luxury suites adjacent to the home.

Decorated in authentic Craftsman style, the new suites are *the* places to pucker up, as far as our lips are concerned. All are similar in design and amenities; what differs is the upstairs or downstairs location. Hunter green motifs blend naturally with the redwood vaulted ceilings and the wooden blinds, while private decks offer unobstructed ocean views. Luscious linens and plenty of pillows cover the king-size beds (one room downstairs has a queen-size bed), and the roomy bathrooms come equipped with jetted tubs, glass-enclosed showers, and heated floors to keep your tootsies happy. In the morning before breakfast, whip up a latte with your own espresso machine and sit-and-sip on the comfortable Craftsman-style chairs beside the fireplace.

While the luxury suites can't be beat for romance, those wanting a style more in keeping with the Victorian main home have a few options, too. Wood paneling, arched ceilings, down comforters, and floral linens create a homey feeling in the three rooms on the second story. Each one has a private standard bath. Standing out as the romantic favorite, Seascape delights the eye with dormer windows facing windblown cypresses and the shimmering sea. The remaining three rooms on the main floor overlook the inn's grounds and gardens. Of these, book the Lumber Baron's Suite for kissing purposes. This beautiful French-inspired room has a private entrance, a king-size bed, and a click-on gas fireplace. Unfortunately, the bathroom is average, and there's no view. Luckily, guests in this room can head to the communal rooftop deck if they need a bird's-eye view of the ocean.

Higher on the kissing scale, but not quite as high as the new suites, are the four small guest cabins perched at the edge of a bluff for even closer sea views. (The structures aren't actually individual cabins—they are more like duplexes—but they do offer a high degree of privacy and extremely cozy interiors.) Two have bay windows, high beamed ceilings, skylights, and wood stoves, while all offer fluffy feather beds and down comforters. We'll take the Greenwood Cottage for its "window-to-the-sea" shower alone.

Besides some kiss-worthy accommodations, warm hospitality and freshly baked goodies are another important part of your stay. There's a four-legged tour guide who regularly escorts guests to and from the beach. (We recommend taking the tour ... you'll need it before conquering breakfast.) A lavish buffet, featuring no fewer than 20 items, is presented in the casual, oceanfront dining room come morning. The delicious array of homemade scones, fruit parfaits, gourmet egg dishes, and five varieties of juices will leave you satisfied until dinner, or at least late afternoon. If you're hungry by midday, try the homemade cookies, wine, and fruit in your complimentary gift basket. If all this eating isn't enough, the inn features candlelight dinners served in the dining room every Tuesday and Wednesday night (moderate to expensive; open to the public; reservations recommended). Sit at the white-laced tables, listen to 1940s jazz, and enjoy such rich specialties as salmon cakes, ravioli in cream sauce, or spicy Thai shrimp. Now *this* is living. **6300 South Highway 1; (707) 877-3321, (800) 275-2967; www.elkcoveinn.com; moderate to very expensive; minimum-stay requirement on weekends and holidays.**

❦ **GREENWOOD PIER INN, Elk** Lush flower and herb gardens border walking paths that zigzag through the Greenwood Pier Inn's eclectic and arty landscaped grounds, leading you past an assortment of fantasy-style cottages set on an oceanside bluff. Several cottages are inhabited by gift and garden stores, while another houses the **GREENWOOD PIER CAFE** (see Restaurant Kissing) which makes good use of the fresh vegetables, herbs, and edible flowers grown here year-round.

To our delight, the four cottages perched closest to the cliff's edge are reserved exclusively for overnight guests who wish to indulge in staggering views of the untamed ocean below. These quirky cottages resemble something straight out of a fairy-tale book, and people who are tall, large, or claustrophobic should note that interior space is limited. Mismatched country fabrics, antiques, and knickknacks blend with funky, artistic touches to create an eccentric, although slightly worn-out, look in each of the cottages. All feature knotty pine paneling and either fireplaces or wood-burning stoves; some have private decks, stained glass windows, and canopied beds. Ceramic sinks and deep blue tiles add pizzazz to the otherwise nondescript bathrooms. Private decks jut daringly out over the precipice from North Sea Castle, South Sea Castle, and the Cliffhouse, and spiral staircases lead to indoor soaking tubs on the second story of all three (the best features as far as we're concerned). The smaller, less expensive rooms in two other buildings have decent views, but they are decorated in a shabby fashion, are noticeably more run-down, and are not at all desirable for a romantic encounter. (Sometimes you really do get what you pay for.)

In the morning, a continental breakfast is delivered to your room for you to enjoy at your leisure. Although breakfast in bed is an affectionate option, enjoying your morning meal in the garden perched at the edge of the Pacific may be reason enough to get out of bed. Freshly baked breads and muffins taste so much better outside overlooking enormous ocean-carved rocks and the brilliant frothy-blue sea below. **5928 South Highway 1; (707) 877-9997, (800) 807-3423; www.greenwoodpierinn.com; moderate to very expensive; minimum-stay requirement on weekends.**

❀❀ **GRIFFIN HOUSE AT GREENWOOD COVE, Elk** Clustered behind a friendly Irish pub, where you might think you'd find a parking lot, are eight tiny 1920s cottages. Don't expect anything too fancy here. Each small unit is modestly decorated with country prints and the interiors could use some updating, but wood-burning Franklin stoves and incredible ocean views from three of the cottages offer romantic potential. These ocean-view cottages, set at the bluff's edge, are the only ones we recommend. Both Greenwood and Donohue feature queen-size brass beds and private decks overlooking the endless Pacific. Matson has a private deck with the same great view, plus a window-side claw-foot tub, but only a double bed. If you need to spread out to be truly comfortable, these units are probably too snug for you, but the views are spectacular, the pub is a convenient and fun place for a nightcap, and the prices are relatively reasonable. A hearty full breakfast is delivered to your door in the morning. **5910 South Highway 1; (707) 877-3422; www.griffinn.com; moderate to expensive; minimum-stay requirement on weekends.**

❀❀❀ **THE HARBOR HOUSE INN, Elk** This 1916 redwood inn is balanced atop an oceanfront bluff with astonishing views of haystack boulders and sea-worn rock arches that rise above the ocean's ever-changing surface. Since our last visit, new owners have transformed the six guest rooms and four cottages into some of the nicest in town. Although rooms differ in style, most offer classic-contemporary touches, Berber carpeting, crisp linens, and fireplaces. Small, standard baths prove to be the only blemish. Even without a fireplace, the tiny Lookout Room remains a kissing favorite, due in part to its private location, wonderful balcony, and outstanding views. More stately and larger is the Harbor Room, a light, bright room with a regal king-size bed that made our hearts go pitter-patter. Seclusion is ensured in the self-contained, casually rustic Seaview and Oceansong Cottages, which have semiprivate decks, king-size beds, fireplaces, and full ocean views.

Although room rates are some of the steepest in town, a full gourmet breakfast and four-course dinner are included with your stay. Guests can savor their meals in the contemporary dining room warmed by a wood-burning fireplace and enhanced by enormous windows. Prix fixe dinners change nightly but may start with such delicacies as smoked duck dumplings surrounded by a mango-sesame sauce, traditional crab cakes followed by grilled filet mignon on a potato-mushroom cake, or seared rare ahi tuna served with a zing of horseradish cream. (Nonguests are invited to partake in dinner; however reservations are extremely limited.) Breakfast, an equally extraordinary affair, includes delicious hot baked entrées, fresh fruit, pastries, coffee, tea, and juice. After breakfast or dinner, we recommend taking a romantic walk hand in hand along the property's cliffside vegetable gardens, or savoring the sea from one of the numerous lookout benches. **5600 South Highway 1; (707) 877-3203, (800) 720-7474; www.the harborhouseinn.com; very expensive to unbelievably expensive (breakfast and dinner included); minimum-stay requirement on weekends; closed the first two weeks of December.**

Restaurant Kissing

◆ **GREENWOOD PIER CAFE, Elk** Lunch spots are difficult to come by in this region, particularly in the off-season. Thank goodness for the Greenwood Pier Cafe, where you can fill your growling stomachs with hearty, healthy meals accented with herbs and vegetables from the property's lavish gardens. You're in for a treat with piping-hot vegetable soup, tasty pastas, grilled fish dishes, and salads made from the freshest ingredients, plus scrumptious homemade desserts. Sunlight floods into the casual, airy dining room through surrounding windows that overlook the beautifully landscaped grounds. Luckily, you'll have something nice to look at while you wait and wait and wait for your food. The staff can be exceedingly laid-back and leisurely (bordering on rude). Don't be in a rush to go anywhere if you dine here. **5928 South Highway 1; (707) 877-9997, (800) 807-3423; www.greenwoodpierinn.com; moderate to expensive; call for seasonal hours.**

Albion

Hotel/Bed and Breakfast Kissing

◆◆◆◆ **ALBION RIVER INN, Albion** Spontaneity is sometimes the most memorable aspect of a romantic vacation, but at other times it pays to plan ahead. If you're thinking of taking a trip up the North Coast, we suggest you book reservations at the Albion River Inn immediately (or at least two months in advance). Everybody wants to stay here, and if you're lucky enough to get a room, you'll see why.

Fortunately, the inn's popularity in no way diminishes its romantic virtues. Set on a precipice towering above Albion Cove and the Pacific, this New England–style inn offers 20 stunning ocean-view units. All boast wood-burning fireplaces, elegant country touches, floral linens, down comforters, cozy robes, and complimentary wine and coffee. All but two rooms have private decks with superlative views. Six of the luxury rooms feature Jacuzzi tubs with ocean vistas, while several others have two-person soaking tubs. Be sure to stroll the inn's private headland pathway that leads to expansive vistas of water and sky. If, after a long day of touring, you're looking for a secluded, first-class spot to watch the sky turn fiery red as the ocean thunders against the shore below, this is the place to be.

In the morning, enjoy a generous complimentary breakfast of fresh breads, homemade granola, eggs cooked to order, breakfast potatoes au gratin, fresh fruit, and juices, served in the inn's waterfront restaurant (see Restaurant Kissing). Dinner here is another romantic must. The food is as delicious as the view is mesmerizing. **3790 North Highway 1; (707) 937-1919, (800) 479-7944; www.albionriverinn.com; very expensive to unbelievably expensive; minimum-stay requirement on weekends and holidays; recommended wedding site.**

Restaurant Kissing

❀❀❀ **ALBION RIVER INN RESTAURANT, Albion** ALBION RIVER INN (see Hotel/Bed and Breakfast Kissing) shares its glorious clifftop setting with this highly acclaimed restaurant. Expansive ocean views help make this stylish dining room a worthwhile romantic venture. Although the number of tables limits intimacy and the dining room is filled to capacity most days, the amorous mood is undeniable and engaging from the moment you enter. The interior is awash in soft lighting and flanked by floor-to-ceiling windows affording wonderful views of the scenery.

The menu focuses primarily on fresh seafood dishes, each one deftly executed by the skilled chef. Don't miss the pan-roasted halibut topped with a flame grape and roasted pistachio salsa. In addition to seafood, you'll also find delicious, creative dishes like the oven-roasted quail wrapped in bacon and marinated with a tantalizing mixture of balsamic vinegar, soy, and rosemary. Everything is thoroughly satisfying, yet the chef's light touch should leave you with enough room for dessert. Even if you don't think you can eat another bite, you'll be sweetly tempted by caramelized coconut bananas in warm rum-caramel sauce served with French vanilla ice cream, or tangy rhubarb-and-wildberry cobbler topped with homemade lemon-poppyseed ice cream. **3790 North Highway 1; (707) 937-1919, (800) 479-7944; www.albionriverinn.com; expensive; dinner daily.**

❀❀❀ **THE LEDFORD HOUSE RESTAURANT, Albion** You would never guess it from just driving by, but this large Craftsman is one of the loveliest places to dine along the entire North Coast. Situated alone on a bluff with spectacular ocean views, The Ledford House Restaurant is a peaceful place to linger over dinner and romance the night away. Soft jazz filters in from the mellow bar area, single long-stemmed flowers adorn every table, and candlelight casts flickering shadows on whitewashed walls, infusing the dining room with warmth. When the area is shrouded in fog (which occurs more often than some would like to admit), Ledford House becomes even more cozy and inviting.

A straightforward, yet diversified menu delivers bistro-style treats like cassoulet and braised rabbit as well as traditional entrées, most notably grilled swordfish; a Dijon-herb encrusted rack of lamb; and a hearty risotto filled with roasted vegetable ragout, shiitake mushrooms, and Asiago cheese. The amorous atmosphere and gracious wait staff make The Ledford House Restaurant a wonderful place to spend a memorable evening on the coast. **3000 North Highway 1; (707) 937-0282; www.ledfordhouse.com; expensive; dinner Wednesday–Sunday; closed mid-February–mid-March.**

Little River

Hotel/Bed and Breakfast Kissing

❤️❤️❤️ **GLENDEVEN INN, Little River** Glendeven Inn promises country living at its best. Its ten guest rooms are situated in two buildings poised on verdant meadowland brushed by fresh ocean breezes. Of special interest are the four airy Stevenscroft annex rooms, decorated in a refined country fashion with wood-burning fireplaces, vaulted ceilings, large tiled baths, and French doors opening to sunny private decks and water glimpses. If these rooms don't help set a romantic mood, nothing will. Rooms in the historic New England Federalist-style manor are equally engaging, although road noise from Highway 1 is slightly audible. These spacious, handsome rooms feature lovely bay or garden views, affectionate details, and decor similar to that in the Stevenscroft building.

In the morning, snuggle in front of your fireplace as you consume your hand-delivered breakfast of warm homemade muffins, a piping-hot egg entrée, fruit, and freshly squeezed orange. Then take a refreshing hike to the beach; it is an easy 20-minute walk down to Van Damme Beach. On a rainy day, explore the on-site art gallery, featuring a stunning array of local artwork. **8221 North Highway 1; (707) 937-0083, (800) 822-4536; www.glendeven.com; moderate to very expensive; minimum-stay requirement on weekends and holidays.**

❀❀❀ **HERITAGE HOUSE, Little River** Boasting one of the North Coast's most spectacular panoramas, this renovated farmstead holds a series of small cottages, duplex units, and fourplex units terraced above the mighty Pacific on 37 acres of spellbinding waterfront. Decor, views, and amenities vary from room to room, but most of the 66 accommodations here offer fireplaces, and some on the luxury end feature jetted tubs in the bathrooms. We were partial to the higher-priced cottages with better views of the pristine coast and more luxurious appointments, including ocean-view decks, fireplaces, and oversize Jacuzzi tubs. Views from the Sunset, Seacliff, or Vista Cottages are pure inspiration. The roar of the ocean engulfs you in the Next Year's Cottage, so throw open the windows and welcome the Pacific's music inside. Better yet, sink into the big whirlpool tub while you soak in the sounds. All the cottages and rooms are free of phones and TVs to ensure a distraction-free getaway. As for the fourplex units, try to reserve an upper level unit for better views and less noise.

If you've got your heart set on one of the property's exclusive, ocean-view cottages, book your reservations as soon as possible; some of these cottages require reservations *a full year* in advance. Since we last visited, the complimentary breakfast and complimentary dinner for two at the restaurant (see Restaurant Kissing) have been discontinued. At the prices you're paying for the luxury-end units, that's disappointing. **5200 North Highway 1; (707) 937-5885, (800) 235-5885; www.heritagehouseinn.com; moderate to unbelievably expensive; minimum-stay requirement on weekends and holidays; closed January–mid-February; closed Thanksgiving–mid-December.**

❀❀ **INN AT SCHOOLHOUSE CREEK, Little River** Don't let the "Inn" in the name fool you. This place is mostly about cottages, some of which are ideally suited for couples who enjoy snuggling up in their own comfy quarters. Six blue-and-white well-kept cottages sit above Highway 1, along with half a dozen other rooms housed in adjoining units that, while pleasant, don't fit our romantic qualifications. The turn-of-the-century cottages differ from one another in size and layout, but the underlying theme is clean, comfortable country decor, accented by wood-burning stoves (a few have gas stoves), kitchenettes, hardwood floors warmed by throw rugs, redwood wall paneling, and old-fashioned paned windows. Some cottages feature decks and most offer ocean peek-a-views. Featherbeds and lovely linens dress up the sparse rooms, and gas heaters take over when the fire fades. A favorite retreat for kissing couples is the solitary Cypress Cottage. This one-bedroom wonder, standing alone in a lovely little meadow, delivers more privacy than any other cottage. However, the bathroom is small, and the accompanying fluorescent lighting doesn't help fuel the flames of romance.

A communal hot tub resides above the cottages in an open meadow and, if you look farther, you'll discover a double hammock hidden in the trees. Spend a carefree day down at the beach exploring tide pools, or journey through the woods to nearby Schoolhouse Creek for some peace and solitude. Each morning a delicious buffet breakfast (heavy on the carbos and fruits for all those hikers) is served in the historic main home. Trays are available to load up and take back to your cottage, too. Come evening, sample local wines and hors d'oeuvres while warming up by the home's brick fireplace. **7051 North Highway 1; (707) 937-5525, (800) 731-5525; www.binnb.com; moderate to expensive; minimum-stay requirement on weekends and holidays.**

Romantic Warning: From some cabins, road noise can be heard from Highway 1; however, come nighttime, traffic dies down.

❀❀❀ **LITTLE RIVER INN, Little River** Although all 65 rooms at the Little River Inn face the ocean, the inexpensive to expensive rooms don't measure up to our romantic criteria—the interiors of these rooms are too minimalist and hotel-like to be considered for a special interlude. However, rooms in the very expensive to unbelievably expensive categories are an entirely different story. The higher the price, the greater the distance from the busy parking lot and highway, and the better the amenities and decor.

The most luxurious accommodations are set across from the main property, on the ocean side of the highway. Four suites comprise a contemporary rambler known as the Van Damme House, and a separate cottage next door is called Coombs Cottage. Both the cottage and the spacious suites feature a wood-burning fireplace, country-chic furnishings, open-beam ceilings, a two-person Jacuzzi tub in the bathroom, and magnificent ocean views from the hot tub on each deck. (Yes, each room has two tubs for your bubbling delight.) All are similar in design, but the unbelievably expensive Coombs Cottage offers more space and sublime privacy, while the Van Damme South and Margaret Bullard Rooms within the rambler boast inside Jacuzzi tubs placed window side so you can enjoy spectacular views as you soak.

Breakfast is not included in your stay, but a short walk takes you to the inn's restaurant (inexpensive to moderate), where you can savor egg dishes, hot-from-the-griddle specialties, and an olallieberry cobbler. The restaurant is also open for dinner and weekend brunch, plus you can request to have your meal delivered right to your room. **7751 North Highway 1;**

(707) 937-5942, (888) INN-LOVE; www.littleriverinn.com; inexpensive to unbelievably expensive; minimum-stay requirement on weekends and holidays.

♨♨♨ **STEVENSWOOD LODGE, Little River** Look for the magnificent metal sculptures along Highway 1 and you'll know you've arrived at this art-oriented, luxury inn. Set far back from the road on lush landscaped grounds, this quiet inn offers ten contemporary rooms in an upscale lodge setting. Although this is a lodge first and foremost, it is also an art gallery with modern artwork, photographs, and sculptures adorning the rooms, hallways, lobby, and gardens.

Rooms come in two sizes, demi-suite and grand suite, and those on the second floor have vaulted ceilings that make the already spacious interiors even larger. Wood-burning fireplaces, private bathrooms, and queen-size beds are standards in each individually decorated suite; neutral colors and natural woods add warmth. Depending on which way your room faces, you'll enjoy either forest vistas or ocean glimpses across the meadow. For bubbling pleasures, venture to one of the two spas near the garden; romantics may want to reserve the one with the locked gate to ensure private soaking.

Complimentary breakfasts are not included in your stay, but that doesn't mean you should pass up such delicious morning offerings as huckleberry crêpes, French omelets, and wild rice and toasted pecan waffles. Breakfast and dinner are served at **STEVENSWOOD LODGE RESTAURANT** (see Restaurant Kissing), an intimate, firelit room bordering the backyard gardens. For a *real* treat, have dinner (or breakfast) delivered course-by-course to your room. To ensure the utmost in private dining, the waiter calls to let you know the next course is on its way. This way you can really get some kissing in between courses. **8211 North Highway 1; (707) 937-2810, (800) 421-2810; www.stevenswood.com; expensive to very expensive.**

Restaurant Kissing

♨♨♦ **HERITAGE HOUSE RESTAURANT, Little River** What makes this place worthy of a kiss or two is that nearly every linen-cloaked table in the three dining rooms has a glimpse of the sparkling Pacific below. In one room, a painted dome ceiling softly illuminated by chandeliers endows the restaurant with a feeling of spaciousness. Tall candles and white linens in the remaining two dining rooms contribute to an elegant, yet simple ambience. The menu changes daily and may include savory starters such as grilled polenta with wild mushroom ragout or local cod cakes, and such entrées as grilled salmon with spinach, *pommes noisette*, and lemon-tarragon vinaigrette. Luscious desserts, most notably the chocolate-rum pot de crème and the peach crumble, top off the evening ever so sweetly. **5200 North Highway 1, at Heritage House; (707) 937-5885, (800) 235-5885; www.heritagehouseinn.com; expensive; reservations required; breakfast and dinner daily, brunch Saturday–Sunday.**

Romantic Note: If you plan to dine during the peak summer season, make your dinner reservations pronto!

❦❦❦ **STEVENSWOOD LODGE RESTAURANT, Little River** Surround yourselves with contemporary artwork in a lovely, intimate dining room where a crackling fireplace keeps the mood warm and a handful of beautifully attired tables provide a sense of elegance. Tucked away in the forest, **STEVENSWOOD LODGE** (see Hotel/Bed and Breakfast Kissing) and its namesake restaurant promote the pleasures of art and food all under one roof. Subtle colors and surroundings serve to highlight the artwork on the walls, and small halogen lamps hanging above each table set an intimate mood.

Masterpieces of the culinary kind are brought forth from the kitchen. Begin by sampling cured gravlax napoleon with wild rice pancakes; red beets combined with chèvre, baby spinach, and cilantro vinaigrette; or the oh-so-creamy roasted butternut squash bisque. Choosing just one entrée per person is difficult with such selections as pine-nut-crusted salmon fillet, tarragon roasted chicken with brown-butter spinach spaetzle, and the mosaic of seared scallops with sweet pea risotto. Each dish is better than the previous one, so pace yourselves and be prepared for the sweet grand finale for two: a heart-shaped "lovers" baked apple pie with maple crème anglaise and "red hot" ice cream. This hot tart is certain to spice things up for kissing later on. **8211 North Highway 1, at Sevenswood Lodge; (707) 937-2810, (800) 421-2810; www.stevenswood.com; expensive; breakfast daily, dinner Friday–Tuesday.**

Mendocino

The streets of this quaint Cape Cod–style seaside town are lined with old-fashioned storefronts housing art galleries and specialty shops. Its many bed and breakfasts are frequently booked on weekends, often months in advance. Of course, Mendocino's main attraction is its view of the magnificent bay and surrounding rugged bluffs. Unfortunately, the very elements that make Mendocino so alluring also make it very crowded, especially in the late spring and summer. Still, there is the off-season, when the people and the sun are less prevalent and fog shrouds the area in a veil of misty white. That's when you can best appreciate this area's abundance of cozy restaurants and bed and breakfasts, not to mention off-season discounts.

Hotel/Bed and Breakfast Kissing

❤️❤️❤️ **AGATE COVE INN, Mendocino** Twenty-four hours a day, the sounds, sights, and smells of the sea are alive at this charming oceanfront accommodation. Agate Cove Inn, ensconced on a bluff across the street from the ocean, truly lets you experience the Pacific in all its glory. Set in an 1860s historic farmhouse, the small, antique-filled lobby and glass-enclosed dining room revel in ringside views of the rugged shoreline. Here, you can witness spectacular sunsets by the fireside hearth or, if you're lucky, catch a glimpse of migrating whales while savoring a scrumptious hot breakfast that has been prepared on a 100-year-old wood-burning stove. Trays are available to take the fixings back to your room, but after you see this view, you might stick around.

Stone walkways ramble through gardens surrounding the property's collection of cozy country-style cottages and duplex cottages. The ten guest rooms differ in size and decor, and a few offer mesmerizing views of the ocean. All boast an underlying French or English country theme, thoughtfully appointed features, TVs and CD players, and large four-poster or sleigh queen- or king-size beds covered with down comforters and luscious floral motif spreads. Last but not least, private patios grace each accommodation, although views vary in quality. Gas-burning fireplaces warm all but one room, and some upper-end rooms feature cedar-lined closets, bringing the forest fragrance indoors. The best bets for romance are the Emerald Room and the Obsidian Room, located in the duplex cottage. Both these rooms offer extra-large tubs for two, private decks, double-headed showers, king-size beds, fireplaces, and spectacular white-water panoramas. Obsidian is the cream of the crop; it has a better view plus a telescope for whale watching or evening stargazing. **11201 North Lansing Street; (707) 937-0551, (800) 527-3111; www.agatecove.com; moderate to expensive; minimum-stay requirement on weekends.**

Romantic Warning: When making reservations, steer clear of the small cottages at the very back of the property; they have limited ocean views and are literally yards from an adjacent highway.

❤️❤️❤️ **C. O. PACKARD HOUSE, Mendocino** We usually don't have a difficult time deciding which room is our favorite in the smaller bed and breakfasts, but we did at the C. O. Packard House. Each of the three rooms in this landmark 1878 Carpenter Gothic–style Victorian are delightfully romantic. However, before we go further in describing them, we must first point out to lace lovers and antique admirers that, despite the Victorian facade, there is nothing remotely Victorian about this place inside. Instead, contemporary elegance prevails, along with an outstanding collection of ancient Greek art, Persian prints, and masks from New Guinea and beyond.

Now, back to the rooms, starting with common denominators in each. Romantic must-haves are all here: bedside gas fireplaces, two-person jetted tubs, robes and slippers, glass-enclosed showers, TVs hidden within antique French amoires, and beautiful big beds covered by lush linens and pillows. Creamy neutral hues, large-paned windows, and sparkling marbled baths add brightness to each room. Peer over the rooftops to the sea in the Pacific View Room. This is the largest room, complete with a king-size Parisian sleigh bed and an arched entrance leading to the magnificent bathing area. Speaking of baths, the loo is even lovelier in the Garden Court Room, where you actually enter through the bathroom. While such an entrance is indeed odd, the light-filled bathroom is a stunner, particularly the jetted tub framed by a large window opening to garden views. Privacy prevails in the Chapman Point Room. Just be careful not to knock yourselves out on the hallway's sloping ceilings, which add dimension to these tucked-away quarters. The pine and iron sleigh bed stands out as the most cozy bed of all with a feathered comforter and plenty of pillows to prop yourselves up for viewing the sea beyond. A fourth bedroom downstairs was under construction when we visited and the owners wouldn't let us look. We're sure it will be nice, but the off-the-living room location isn't prime privacy territory. There are also two cottages on the property, but even the brochure notes that these accommodations aren't as elegant as the other rooms.

A two-course breakfast, highlighting rich dishes such as pear puff pastries, Dutch babies with berries, and espresso flan, is served at the dining room table. In the evening, admire the museum-quality artworks while sampling wine and hors d'oeuvres in the living room. When dinnertime arrives, stroll hand in hand to any one of Mendocino's restaurants; all are within walking distance of C. O. Packard House. **45170 Little Lake Street; (707) 937-2677, (888) 453-2677; www.packardhouse.com; expensive; minimum-stay requirement on weekends.**

❤❤❤❤ **COAST RETREATS, Mendocino** Having traveled the world over looking for romantic retreats of their own, the owners of this impressive rental company finally found their slice of heaven in Mendocino. Fortunately, they're eager to share. Some of Mendocino's most dramatic ocean views are visible from the decks, porches, and front yards of Coast Retreat's six sensational, ultraprivate rental properties.

Built as close to the ocean as possible, four of these rental homes are perched atop steep bluffs that jut out over the incoming tide. French doors open onto a spacious water-view deck at the Jameson House, showcasing seagulls and osprey sailing at eye level. A large hot tub, a walk-in shower for two, a beautiful jade-colored tile kitchen, and even a telescope are other romantic features here. Just down the road, the artistically decorated Bungalow shares the same breathtaking oceanfront stage, plus a hot tub and a deck that wraps around three sides of the house. Copper countertops in the kitchen, mosaic tiles in the bathrooms, and other hand-worked details give the one-bedroom home added personality. No matter which property you decide on, you're in for a treat, with amenities and views designed to cater to your romantic sensibilities. **(707) 937-1121, (800) 859-6260; www.coastretreats.com; expensive to very expensive; minimum-stay requirement.**

❦❦❦❦ **CYPRESS COVE, Mendocino** Believe us when we say it is worth the effort to plan your special getaway around the availability of the two suites at Cypress Cove. Your heart won't be disappointed. Perched on a rocky bluff, this two-story beach house has wraparound floor-to-ceiling windows showcasing spectacular views of Mendocino and the bay. Both suites are simply decorated in a contemporary, Scandinavian style, highlighting natural wood accents and colorful bedspreads and decorations. Amenities include private decks, indoor whirlpool tubs for two, separate showers, wood-burning fireplaces, complete entertainment systems, and sublime comfort. In both suites, the bed faces seaward, and ambience is easily adjusted by dimming lights.

Pacifica, the second-floor suite, is accented with teal colors, large bouquets of fresh flowers, and terra-cotta-tiled floors. The ground-level Cove Suite comes in a more subdued style, with shades of gray, black, and sea green. One particularly noteworthy aspect of the Cove Suite is its corner window seat with magnificent views—this has to be one of the absolute *best places to kiss* in all of California.

In addition to all this, one of the best features of Cypress Cove is that you can hear the ocean as well as view it. This is something most of us do not have the pleasure of hearing at home, and there is something very special about being lulled to sleep by such a pure and powerful sound. **Chapman Drive; (707) 937-1456, (800) 942-6300; www.cypress cove.com; very expensive; minimum-stay requirement on weekends and holidays.**

Romantic Note: Coffee, tea, brandy, and chocolates are provided; breakfast is not. Luckily, you're not far from Mendocino's many restaurants and bakeries, and each suite is equipped with a kitchen so you can prepare your own meals. In keeping with the seclusion theme, there is no daily maid service either.

❦❦❦❦ **THE HAYLOFT, Mendocino** If you love hunkering down in the forest with your honey, this is the ideal hideaway for two—just don't let the name fool you into thinking it is some type of barn. About five miles from the sea and surrounded by cypress and fir trees, this perfectly maintained one-bedroom cottage is a delight, and since it is owned by the same innkeepers who operate **CYPRESS COVE** (see review above), you can expect the best. Occupying the second story only (a garage is below), the cottage features a feast of romantic features. Watch for shooting stars as you heat up in the hidden hot tub on the back deck, or stargaze through skylights while cuddling beneath the down comforter on the queen-size bed. On the homemaking side, a fully equipped kitchen will have you cooking in style; the wood-burning fireplace, embellished by Portuguese tile, will keep things toasty; and, in the armoire, a TV, VCR, and CD player with a CD and video selection should keep you entertained when you're not kissing. Soft white and beige tones, natural woods, and pine furnishings create a warm contemporary feel, and everything is spic 'n' span. Off the bedroom, French doors open onto a small balcony, which overlooks the driveway and the owner's home nearby. A basket of fruits and bakery goods—good for two days' worth of breakfasts—comes with the cottage, and such appliances as a coffeemaker and juice squeezer make mornings much easier. A five-minute drive takes you into town, but we bet you won't want to roll out of the Hayloft to make the trip. **Reservations through Cypress Cove, (707) 937-1456, (800) 942-6300; www.mendocino preferred.com; expensive; minimum-stay requirement on weekends.**

❦❦ **THE HEADLANDS INN, Mendocino** Charm, comfort, and a cheerful atmosphere distinguish this pretty 1868 Victorian located in the heart of Mendocino, just a few blocks from the ocean. Several of the inn's five distinctive rooms (and one cottage) offer full views or glimpses of the surf. Warmed by a fireplace or parlor stove, each guest room is adorned with thick carpeting and antique furnishings, while handmade quilts and overstuffed reading pillows cover sumptuous feather beds. Views of the Pacific's churning water are outstanding from the large bay window in the spacious and handsome Bessie Strauss Room. Arched ceilings and a cozy window seat facing the ocean add character to the light and bright John Barry Room, situated at the top of the house. Designed for privacy, the self-contained Casper Cottage is hidden behind the main house (read: no view), with a four-poster queen-size bed, wood-burning fireplace, and large sunken soaking tub that's looking worn out.

In the morning you can lounge in bed as you await an exceptional gourmet breakfast brought directly to your room. Be prepared for such delicacies as artichoke egg casserole or orange French toast, and fresh pastries and fruits on your personalized tray. **Howard and Albion Streets; (707) 937-4431, (800) 354-4431; www.headlandsinn.com; expensive to very expensive; minimum-stay requirement on weekends and holidays.**

❧❧ **THE JOSHUA GRINDLE INN, Mendocino** The Joshua Grindle Inn is a traditional and rather large bed and breakfast offering some romantic room choices. Set on the edge of town, this 1879 Victorian farmhouse has ten rooms decorated with period and country antiques, new but standard bathrooms, and wood-burning fireplaces in some of the rooms. All rooms are devoid of TVs and phones, but loaded with treats, including chocolate chip cookies and a split of wine. Our favorites for romance are the two rooms in the Saltbox Cottage, the spacious Master Suite in the main house (the only one with a whirlpool tub), and the Watertower II, a sunny, small room uniquely located, as the name implies, in a historic watertower. A bountiful breakfast is served in the country-style dining room, or in-room if you request this service the night before. We recommend the latter. **44800 Little Lake Road; (707) 937-4143, (800) GRINDLE; www.joshgrin.com; moderate to very expensive; minimum-stay requirement on weekends.**

❧❧ **MENDOCINO SEASIDE COTTAGE, Mendocino** Kitties, and duckies, and frogs, oh my! Kitties, and duckies, and frogs! You'll feel like you're in a cutesy version of *Wild Kingdom* at this vacation retreat situated beside the **MENDOCINO HEADLANDS STATE PARK** (see Outdoor Kissing). Four rooms in the main home—all sporting cute 'n' cuddly, somewhat overbearing, animal themes—will have your eyes occupied for a long time to come. The ornately decorated rooms *do* compete with the outstanding views of the grasslands and the sea. But if such decor appeals to your fancy, you'll love what the rooms have to offer in the way of romantic perks. All feature gas fireplaces, small kitchens, and private entrances and patios, and three have two-person Jacuzzi tubs fronting million-dollar views.

Hopping to the top of our kissing list is the second-story Frog Pond Suite, thanks to its lovely bay window sitting area, three-way fireplace, step-up whirlpool tub (complete with rubber frogs), and a "ribbiting" two-person steam, shower, and foot-massaging spa. Views from this very private room rank as some of the best in town, too. Need we mention amphibian art, figurines, stuffed animals, and motifs are everywhere? Downstairs, the

Kit-Kat Room and Just Ducki both have Jacuzzi tubs, although the Kit-Kat is the cat's meow when it comes to views. There's even a telescope near the tub for whale watching while bubbling. The least expensive room, Vista View, may not have the intense animal theme or a luxurious tub, but the name certainly defines this ground-floor room. The property also holds the Tropical Paradise Cottage, but the overlapping animal prints, faded animal photographs, stacks of old *National Geographics*, fuzzy white carpeting, and white satin bed surrounded by mirrors was too tacky for our animalistic tastes. All the rooms in the main house come with queen-size beds piled high with pillows and ruffled bedskirts, matching puffy draperies, and details at every turn including towels wrapped in ribbons and theme-appropriate books. All except the cottage are light, bright, and certainly cheerful. Breakfast is not included with your stay, although coffeemakers and coffee are provided in each room. And town is only a hop, skip, and waddle away. **Lansing Street; (707) 485-0239, (800) 94-HEART; www.mcn. org/b/seacottage; very expensive to unbelievably expensive.**

❦❦❦❦ **REED MANOR, Mendocino** If opulent luxury is what you're looking for in a bed and breakfast, check into the stately Reed Manor. Located on a grassy knoll adjacent to a historic cemetery, this large, relatively new home has architecture reminiscent of a New England–style manor. Upon entering, you'll pass by museum-quality glass display cases where halogen lights illuminate the innkeepers' antique collections, including hundreds of miniature model cars and dozens of collector's dolls and ceramic wildlife figurines. Not only is such a display extraordinary, but it also serves as one of the many reminders of the care and attention to detail invested in this home.

Each of the five palatial guest rooms features a gas log fireplace, two-person whirlpool tub, sumptuous and classic decor, a high beamed ceiling, mini-fridge, coffeemaker, teapot, stereo, and a TV with bedside VCR access. Collections of ceramics, plates, and artwork are beautifully displayed, once again, in illuminated glass cabinets in each room. If that's not enough to look at, high-powered telescopes are provided on some of the Pacific-facing decks for viewing the village below and the ocean beyond. Privacy is a priority here, as demonstrated by the secluded patios, right down to the telephones with personalized answering machines. A complimentary split of wine awaiting in your room encourages you to make a toast to it all (and to each other).

In the second-floor Napoleon Room, a double-sided fireplace warms both the bathroom, with its Jacuzzi tub and dual-headed shower, and the silvery French provincial bedroom, with its romantic four-poster bed.

Josephine's Garden Room opens to a delightful private patio and garden, while Morning Glory lets you savor A.M. sunshine and town views from a private balcony. Imperial Garden, the smallest, least expensive room (still in the expensive category), is elegant and cozy. Lastly, there's the Majestic and English Rose, a two-bedroom suite that's better suited for couples traveling together.

A continental breakfast of baked goods, fruit, and locally made apple juice is carefully placed in a basket and delivered to your room in the evening, so you can enjoy it at your leisure the following morning. **10751 Palette Drive; (707) 937-5446; www.reedmanor.com; expensive to unbelievably expensive; minimum-stay requirement on weekends.**

❦❦❧ SEA ROCK BED AND BREAKFAST INN, Mendocino

The inspired innkeepers here are continually improving and upgrading their oceanfront inn, so expect things to keep getting better ... and more romantic. In fact, the kissing potential has already increased with the addition of four deluxe suites housed in a new, two-story building. Of these, we highly recommend hiking up the many steps to the two top rooms, Nos. 11 and 12. Once up in the treetops, ocean views reign supreme and the privacy is delightful. Both spacious quarters are decorated with dark, solid-color carpeting offset by creamy white walls, beautiful floral linens, and a blend of contemporary art. Vaulted knotty pine ceilings and wood-burning fireplaces add to the romantic ambience, but the pièces de résistance are the two-person soaking tubs that overlook the ocean. Room Nos. 7 and 8 below are similar in decor, but each offers two large bedrooms and a tempting whirlpool tub in the bathroom.

The inn's other accommodations consist of six gray cottages and four rooms in the two-story Stratton House. While the style and decor vary drastically in every cottage and room, from old-fashioned to country, all offer down comforters, mini-patios, cable TVs, and VCRs; many boast Franklin fireplaces and feather beds as well. The Stratton House rooms have the best views on the property (particularly from the second story), although the interiors, while pleasant, can't compete with those in the newer building. However, the innkeepers are keeping the renovation momentum going and will soon be upgrading these rooms as well. As for the cottages, No. 1 remains *numero uno* for romance due to its unobstructed ocean view from the deck.

An expanded continental breakfast is presented beside the reception area, and you can dine at tables set along windows that view the ocean beyond Lansing Street. If you prefer, take a tray back to your room or to one of the benches scattered around the grounds. One bench, set at the edge of a bluff across the street from the inn, is especially picturesque. **11101 Lansing Street; (707) 937-0926, (800) 906-0926; www.sea rock.com; moderate to unbelievably expensive; minimum-stay requirement on weekends and holidays.**

Romantic Warning: Although Sea Rock Bed and Breakfast Inn has plenty of charm, sounds from the highway behind the property may interrupt the peace and quiet you are seeking.

❀❀❀❀ **STANFORD INN BY THE SEA, Mendocino** A perfect marriage of luxury and rustic elegance, this expansive redwood lodge takes advantage of its beautiful setting. All 33 rooms and suites feature private decks where you can observe the sun setting on the distant horizon. Enjoy views of the nearby Pacific, as well as the inn's sloping lawn, gardens, and llamas grazing in corralled pastures. If the evening is chilly, as it usually is in this region, cuddle by the fire in your knotty pine–paneled room and slide a mood-setting CD into your stereo. Even the smallest rooms have fireplaces, private balconies, stereos, TV/VCRs, and sleigh or four-poster beds covered with richly colored, plush linens. If you want to surround yourselves with plenty of space, we recommend the large suites at the end of the property.

In the morning, visit the alluring greenhouse-enclosed pool, spa, and sauna. The warmth of this bright and humid solarium and its abundance of tropical plants, orchids, and ceiling fans might make you think you're actually in a warmer region of the world. After you've heated yourselves thoroughly, enjoy a complimentary, cooked-to-order vegetarian breakfast— heavy on interesting egg dishes, but also featuring delicious blue-corn waffles and organic, shade-grown coffee—presented in the sunny dining room. Come dinnertime, you won't have to wander far to enjoy the fruits (and vegetables) of Stanford Inn's meticulous organic gardens. The beautiful, window-filled restaurant called **THE RAVENS** (inexpensive to moderate; breakfast daily, dinner Thursday–Monday) showcases some of northern California's best gourmet vegetarian cuisine. **Coast Highway and Comptche-Ukiah Road; (707) 937-5615, (800) 331-8884; www.stan fordinn.com; very expensive to unbelievably expensive; minimum-stay requirement on weekends.**

Romantic Suggestion: Down where the river meets the sea, the inn's recreational outfit CATCH A CANOE AND BICYCLES, TOO (707-937-0273) offers state-of-the-art mountain bikes for guests' complimentary use. If pedaling isn't a passion, rent a canoe, kayak, or outrigger and paddle away to a private picnicking spot to smooch.

❀❀❀ **WHITEGATE INN, Mendocino** In some towns, Victorian-style bed and breakfasts are so abundant they start to look like carbon copies of each other, but that's not the case in Mendocino. The Whitegate Inn, a milky white Victorian with black trim, stands out as one of the few traditionally Victorian places to stay in town, with its elegant crystal chandeliers, antique furnishings, claw-foot tubs, and floral and textured wall coverings. It also stands out as an excellent example of why some people fall in love with the bed-and-breakfast experience. A warm greeting (including a personalized hello by Violet, the welcoming kitty), friendly hospitality, and lavish breakfasts and snacks are just a few things you can expect from the very gracious hosts.

An expansive redwood deck, charming gazebo, and garden benches provide prime kissing spots, where you can smell the flowers, gaze at the clear blue sea, and then venture to the parlor for afternoon wine and cheese. Six comfortably elegant guest rooms await in the main house, each with ocean or village views, cozy down comforters, unremarkable bathrooms, and gas or wood-burning fireplaces. A separate cottage with its own private garden deck, king-size bed, corner woodstove, and claw-foot tub, is set behind the house, and guests staying here can opt to have breakfast delivered. With advance notice, a table for two can be arranged in the parlor for anyone else who wants some morning privacy. Otherwise, the multicourse gourmet breakfast, which might showcase apple-caramel French toast or an artichoke frittata, is served family-style in the formal dining room. Sitting family-style may not be very intimate, but you might overhear some good ideas on how to spend your day (just in case you've already done everything we've suggested). **499 Howard Street; (707) 937-4892, (800) 531-7282; www.whitegateinn.com; moderate to very expensive; minimum-stay requirement.**

Restaurant Kissing

❤❤ **955 UKIAH STREET RESTAURANT, Mendocino** When it comes to dinner recommendations in Mendocino, 955 Ukiah is on the tip of every local's tongue. A long boardwalk embellished with greenery leads to the entrance of this popular restaurant, set overlooking a stand of trees draped with tiny white lights. A 20-foot vaulted ceiling in the split-level dining room absorbs some (but not all) of the sounds coming from the busy open kitchen. Local artwork and trailing plants accentuate partially wood-paneled walls. Adequately spaced tables covered with white linens, fresh flowers, and votive candles create a comfortable atmosphere in which to enjoy delicately flavored California cuisine. Giant ravioli filled with five cheeses, slow-roasted duck, and Pacific red snapper accented with pesto and wrapped in phyllo dough are just some of the menu items, in addition to nightly seafood specials. Grandpa's favorite bread pudding with huckleberry compote is a must for dessert. If you're too full to eat it right there, be sure to have your server pack it to go. **955 Ukiah Street; (707) 937-1955; www.955 restaurant.com; moderate to expensive; dinner Wednesday–Sunday.**

❦❦❦ CAFE BEAUJOLAIS, Mendocino

Some say Cafe Beaujolais is the most romantic restaurant in Mendocino; others argue that the tables are too close together for comfort. In the end, everyone agrees that the candles at every table, pleasing country motifs, and wood-burning stove do create a pretty cozy atmosphere. Even if you're closer to other diners than you prefer, the incredible cuisine and gracious service make up for the compact seating. A casual, glassed-in porch overlooking the gardens holds additional tables; this is a lovely spot to dine on a pleasant day, but the room can get too hot when the sun beats down.

Despite the French name, Cafe Beaujolais specializes in creative European-style cuisine with Mexican and Asian influences. Portions are generous, so be careful not to fill up on the hearty breads made daily at the on-site bakery. Freshness and quality are the kitchen's top priorities, and the chefs' dedication is apparent in dishes like pan-roasted sturgeon fillet with truffle emulsion sauce or roasted free-range chicken served with saffron-chanterelle sauce and mashed yellow potatoes. The desserts, such as the homemade brioche bread pudding with maple-whiskey sauce and the bittersweet chocolate mousse terrine with vanilla and hazelnut crème anglaise, are just as interesting and just as delicious. **961 Ukiah Street; (707) 937-5614; www.cafebeaujolais.com; expensive; reservations recommended; dinner daily.**

❦❦❦ MACCALLUM HOUSE RESTAURANT, Mendocino

Walking into the MacCallum House Restaurant is like taking a pleasant step back in time. While the ground level of this turn-of-the-century mansion has been converted into a restaurant, many of the home's original features were kept in place. A substantial cobblestone fireplace warms the first of two dining rooms, classical books yellowed by age embellish the built-in shelves, and oil paintings and delicate plates adorn the redwood paneled walls. In both dining rooms, tables are adequately spaced apart and set with all the essential elements necessary for fine dining. Some choice seating spots include in front of the fireplace or next to the multipaned windows overlooking the porch and garden.

Such an authentic ambience is complemented by a seasonal menu of fresh regional fish, meats, and produce. Start by dipping warm slices of bread into a trio of locally made olive oils and, if that's not filling enough, try the light potato gnocchi in a walnut-arugula pesto topped with a slice of melted Cambozola cheese. If you bring a hearty appetite with you to dinner, consider the pan-seared duck breast served atop a bed of wilted spinach, roasted golden beets, and glazed yams. Everything on the changing menu satisfies the palate, so enjoy. Couples who can't decide on dessert can easily share the restaurant's signature ice-cream creation: a taco-shaped praline cookie filled with six scoops of homemade ice-creams, ranging from ginger-mango sorbet to a flavorful chocolate mint (made from garden-fresh mint ... what a difference!). **45020 Albion Street; (707) 937-5763; www. maccallumhouse.com; moderate to expensive; dinner daily.**

Romantic Alternative: For a more casual dinner or just for drinks, consider the **GREY WHALE BAR AND CAFE**, at the same address (moderate; dinner daily). The charming window-framed sunporch at the front of the restaurant overlooks greenery and the nearby street scene. If it's a chilly evening, share some goodies while seated on the couch next to the fireplace.

Romantic Note: Under separate management from the restaurant, **THE MACCALLUM HOUSE INN** (707-937-0289, 800-609-0492; www. maccallumhouse.com; inexpensive to very expensive; minimum-stay requirement on weekends) is one of the most unusual bed and breakfasts we've seen. The rooms, suites, and cottages range in style from overly rustic and dark to somewhat romantic. For kissing purposes, the best units are Nos. 1 and 2 in the main house (both are large, bright, and equipped with clawfoot tubs à deux) and No. 18, an upper unit in the restored Barn. You'll have a heyday here, thanks to its brass queen-size bed fronting a massive stone fireplace and the double whirlpool tub in the bathroom. This room tends toward the small side, but the semi-private patio in front, overlooking the property, town, and sea, helps compensate for the tight quarters.

❧❧ MENDOCINO HOTEL VICTORIAN DINING ROOM, Mendocino

Transport yourselves back in time as you cuddle next to the fire in the Mendocino Hotel's elegant lobby among its tapestried settees and Persian carpets. After your pre-dinner warm-up, gravitate to the authentic Victorian dining room where flickering candles cast a soothing glow on dark wood accents, deep red wall coverings, and faceted glass partitions. Such soft lighting and dark, cozy quarters are perfect for casting amorous glances at one another, but a little difficult for menu reading. If you do manage to decipher the menu, you'll discover an ordinary lineup of meat, seafood, and pasta dishes, including baked scallops, prime rib au jus, herb-crusted ahi, and pasta du jour. Take note of the prix fixe menu; it's quite a bargain, with a glass of wine, appetizer, entrée, and dessert all for one price. **45080 Main Street; (707) 937-0511, (800) 548-0513; www.mendocinohotel. com; expensive; dinner daily.**

Romantic Note: If you visit the hotel earlier in the day, a pleasant option for breakfast or lunch is in the hotel's GARDEN CAFE AND BAR (inexpensive to moderate; breakfast and lunch daily, brunch Sunday)—a gloriously lush greenhouse setting that's especially inviting when the sun streams in. Don't miss the bountiful spinach salad or a local favorite, French onion soup topped with bubbly Swiss cheese. Just be sure to end lunch with a slice of olallieberry deep-dish pie. Topped with homemade ice cream, this treat will win your taste buds over faster than you can say olallieberry.

Romantic Suggestion: Although most rooms at this historic hostel-style hotel share bathrooms and are not the least bit conducive to romance, we do recommend the higher-priced Garden Suites, which range from very expensive to unbelievably expensive. Situated in self-contained buildings behind the original hotel and surrounded by beautiful rose gardens and sweet-scented walking paths, many of these suites have parlors, fireplaces, balconies, private baths, and soaking tubs. None, however, have decent ocean views and, for these prices, that can be a letdown. Some suites in the original building do offer excellent sea views, but the well-worn, tired decor and communal patios will likely distract from matters of the heart.

☙☙ **THE MOOSSE CAFÉ, Mendocino** Sparking up a little noontime romance is easy at this cozy, home-turned-casual café. On a chilly, foggy day, cuddle up at a fireside table where there's enough warmth to defrost you and enough privacy to carry on an intimate conversation. Large windows look out to the garden and street, and plenty of modern artwork dresses up the plain walls. Daily specials excite the palate, starting with a hot 'n' spicy Cajun meatloaf sandwich followed by applewood-smoked salmon served on a toasted bagel. Or sink your spoon into one of the many hearty soups that change with the seasons. Gourmet coffees and scandalously rich desserts, such as the irresistible Blackout Cake—two layers of pure chocolate delight—will win the hearts of chocoholics. The dinner menu offers similarly imaginative dishes, and nighttime brings an even cozier atmosphere with sparkling window lights setting the perfect glow for a romantic evening. **390 Kasten Street; (707) 937-4323; www.theblueheron.com; inexpensive to moderate; lunch and dinner daily.**

Romantic Note: Operating directly above the restaurant, THE BLUE HERON INN (707-937-4323; www.theblueheron.com; inexpensive) offers three rooms, two of which share a bath. All are sparsely decorated, but feature down comforters covering queen-size beds. However, the restaurant noise, bathroom situation, and no view (in the two town-facing rooms) doesn't exactly rank them high on the kissing scale. The inexpensive price (which includes a continental breakfast) is really the most convincing reason to stay here.

Romantic Alternative: If the sun is shining, grab some goodies from THE MENDOCINO BAKERY (Lansing at Ukiah; 707-937-0836; inexpensive; open daily) and find a picnic place far away from this popular (and crowded) spot. A variety of to-go items, including several types of frittatas, focaccia pizzas, and bakery goods, should please any picnic goer.

Outdoor Kissing

❀❀❀ **MENDOCINO COAST BOTANICAL GARDENS** Fronted by a rustic garden shop and a country café, the garden's entrance gives little indication of the 47 beautiful acres of botanical wonders found inside. Natural gardens unfold with ever-expanding layers of brilliance, each one surprising and evocative. Follow walkways festooned with rhododendrons as you stroll hand in hand past formally landscaped colorful annuals, hillsides laced with hydrangeas, and meadows mellow with heather. No matter what time of year you visit, something will be in bloom. Wander to the farthest reaches of the garden to find a stunning seascape with welcoming benches perched high above the crashing surf. In the winter you may even see a whale pass by, its water spout punctuating the vast horizon. **18220 North Highway 1; (707) 964-4352; www.gardenbythesea.org; $6 entrance fee per adult; call for seasonal hours.** *The garden is located on the west side of Highway 1, approximately eight miles north of Mendocino, in the town of Fort Bragg.*

Romantic Suggestion: If you've worked up an appetite after exploring the nearly three miles of paths in this heavenly garden, consider eating a meal at GARDEN'S GRILL (18218 North Highway 1; 707-964-7474; inexpensive to moderate; lunch Monday–Saturday, dinner Thursday–Saturday, brunch Sunday). Located just off the highway near the parking lot at the garden's entrance, the café is a very casual affair. Although the inside decor is done in a charming country style, we highly recommend sitting on the large outdoor deck if the sun cooperates. Here, overlooking the gardens, you can truly appreciate the beauty of the surroundings. The kitchen serves up California grill and vegetarian cuisine, from pasta specials to juicy burgers and tasty soups. We enjoyed a grilled portobello sandwich the size of a sunflower and topped it off with slice of pecan pie dabbed with a dollop of whipped cream.

❤❤❤❤ **MENDOCINO HEADLANDS STATE PARK** Perhaps more than any other attraction, the Mendocino Headlands State Park is the primary draw of this region. The protected, flawless curve of land is an easily accessible place to see, hear, and feel nature in all its magnitude and glory. On calm sunny days, the glistening ocean reveals hidden grottos, sea arches, and tide pools, as foamy white surf encircles the rock-etched boundary of Mendocino. If you happen to be here December through March, you may see whales migrating along the coast. Even on days when the thick ocean fog enfolds the area in a gray cloak, this is still a prime place to explore and daydream. Bundle up and snuggle close—the cool mist tingling against your cheeks is delightfully chilly. **(707) 937-5804; free admission.** *The coastal headlands and the park surround Mendocino on all sides.*

Romantic Option: MACKERRICHER STATE PARK (three miles north of Fort Bragg off Highway 1; 707-937-5804; free admission) is a wondrous assortment of nature's most engaging features: waterfalls at the end of forested trails, grass-covered headlands overlooking the Pacific, white sandy beaches, rolling dunes, and haystack rocks where harbor seals spend the day sunning themselves. Actually, the most outstanding feature of this state park is its distance from Mendocino; the extra few miles make it less popular, giving it a definite kissing advantage.

Garberville

Hotel/Bed and Breakfast Kissing

❤❤ **BENBOW INN, Garberville** Mile after mile of ancient towering redwoods draw tourists north on Highway 101 but, surprisingly, few overnight accommodations in this region offer haven to the romantically inclined. This National Historic Landmark, set just off the highway and surrounded by stands of oak and redwood, makes a perfect stopover on your way through the redwoods. Built in 1926, the Tudor-style hotel hosted dignitaries such as Eleanor Roosevelt and Herbert Hoover in its glory days. Today, the Benbow is a little worn around the edges but still elegant, filled with a blend of old-world antiques and accents. Complimentary hors d'oeuvres are served every afternoon in the spacious, rustic lobby, where Oriental carpets cloak hardwood floors, rocking chairs beckon near the hearth, and a life-size teddy bear lounges around in life-like positions.

Although the hotel's 55 small rooms have all been renovated, they retain a historic feeling, replete with antiques and old-fashioned wallpaper, red velvet lounge chairs, Oriental carpets, paisley linens, and nicely tiled but otherwise standard baths. We especially like the Terrace Rooms, with private patios that overlook the landscaped grounds and nearby burbling river. Three guest rooms feature wood-burning fireplaces, and one has a Jacuzzi tub for your soaking pleasure. A basket of mystery novels is provided in each guest room for added amusement, and bikes are available for those who want to explore the outlying grounds. There is even a film projector in the lobby showing favorite black-and-white flicks starring Charlie Chaplin and Clara Bow. **445 Lake Benbow Drive; (707) 923-2124, (800) 355-3301; www.benbowinn.com; moderate to unbelievably expensive; minimum-stay requirement on weekends; closed January–mid-April.**

Romantic Suggestion: For lack of nearby alternatives, the BENBOW INN RESTAURANT (moderate to expensive) is a convenient and reasonably romantic option for breakfast, lunch, dinner, or Sunday brunch. Chandeliers and candle lanterns cast dim light across the Tudor-style dining room, where an abundance of two-person tables are arranged next to large windows with views of the trees. Whet your palate with appetizers such as an artichoke tart with sweet onions or grilled portobello mushrooms; the kitchen's pasta and seafood specialties are also excellent.

Ferndale

Several hours north of San Francisco via Highway 101 (much longer if you drive up the coast), the Victorian village of Ferndale hugs the hills of the Eel River Valley. Beautifully preserved Victorian homes line the residential streets, and dozens of boutiques, antique stores, and art galleries lure visitors from the busy highway to this out-of-the-way town, now a State Historic Landmark. Even if Ferndale weren't so affable, it would still be worth visiting for the famous GINGERBREAD MANSION INN alone (see Hotel/Bed and Breakfast Kissing).

Hotel/Bed and Breakfast Kissing

❤❤❤❤ **GINGERBREAD MANSION INN, Ferndale** With its elaborate trim and turrets, manicured shrubs, and towering palm tree, the peach and yellow Gingerbread Mansion Inn graces the pages and covers of innumerable guidebooks. It's not surprising that this three-story Victorian mansion is one of northern California's most photographed homes—the Gingerbread is as pretty as a picture. Built in 1899 as a private residence, the expansive mansion now operates as an 11-room bed and breakfast. It is evident from top to bottom that the owner of this marvelous home has attended to every detail with painstaking care.

Each elegant room has been lovingly and individually decorated with period wallpaper, beautiful antiques, romantic fireplaces, and luscious linens and fabrics. Two claw-foot tubs placed toe-to-toe or side-by-side in several of the spacious, sunlit bathrooms add a frolicking touch. Deciding among the different but equally gorgeous rooms can be difficult, but if a splurge is in your plans, the extraordinary Empire Suite should be your first choice. Situated at the top of the house, this dramatic suite is actually a converted attic with peaked 12-foot ceilings, alcoves, and gables. Rich gold and black Regency Revival wallpaper has been artistically applied to the angular walls. White classical ionic columns frame an enormous king-size bed draped with luxurious, sexy black-and-gold Egyptian cotton linens. A claw-foot tub and an oversize glass-enclosed shower (with five massage jets and three shower heads) face a gas fireplace at one end of the suite. At the other end, a cozy love seat fronts a second fireplace, and a sumptuous reading chair (big enough for two) is tucked into a corner alcove under a softly lit lamp. You'll feel on top of the world in this spectacular room. If the Empire Suite has already been conquered, second choices for romantic escapes include the second-floor Fountain Suite (home to the side-by-side tubs and two fireplaces), the Rose Suite embellished by a magnificent four-poster bed, and the main-floor Garden Suite with French doors opening onto the well-tended gardens. Wherever you rest your head, you'll be delighted with both the evening turndown service (complete with house-made chocolates) and the coffee/tea service set outside your door before breakfast.

Downstairs in the regal dining room, a lavish spread of fruits, freshly baked cakes and pastries, breakfast meats, and a baked egg dish will keep your stomach satisfied until afternoon teatime. That's when an appetizing array of hors d'oeuvres, tea sandwiches, and petit fours is served on silver platters and hand-painted china in the formal sitting room that is brimming with turn-of-the-century antiques. Truly, the Gingerbread Mansion is a destination for couples who appreciate the romantic qualities of a magnificent Victorian setting, not to mention decadent delights for the heart and palate. **400 Berding Street; (707) 786-4000, (800) 952-4136; www. gingerbread-mansion.com; expensive to very expensive.**

Restaurant Kissing

❦❦ **CURLEY'S GRILL, Ferndale** Romantic restaurants are few and far between in this area, but Curley's excels even without competition. Casual but classy, this one-room restaurant features a handful of nicely spaced tables topped with whimsical salt and pepper shakers. Track lighting illuminates vivid local artwork as well as more salt and pepper shakers that line the windowsills. For the most privacy (and the best kissing), request one of the tables tucked into a window alcove. The menu curls to the casual side, with an abundance of entrée-sized salads, grilled sandwiches, and seafood, but everything is superbly prepared and so well flavored that you won't be needing those charming little table adornments. If nothing else, be sure to try the restaurant's signature item: grilled polenta topped with mushrooms, sage, and sautéed tomatoes. At the end of the meal, desserts are showcased on a tray brought to your table; save room, because all are irresistible! **460 Main Street; (707) 786-9696; moderate; breakfast Saturday–Sunday, lunch and dinner daily.**

Eureka

Eureka, the northernmost town included in this book, is located about five and a half hours from San Francisco via Highway 101 or about three hours from Mendocino if you are traveling up the coast on Highway 1.

Located 75 miles south of the Oregon border, the modern-day logging town of Eureka is considerably more than a hop, skip, and a jump from the coastal village of Mendocino. In fact, it is hard to recommend a trip here just for the sights. Yes, the redwoods on the way are amazing, and yes, the town has a lot of Victorian buildings to admire and antique shops to browse through. Still, we are hesitant to recommend that you make the three-hour drive up here from Mendocino. However, if you happen to be in this neck of the redwoods, you'll be glad to know we found a wonderful place to kiss.

Hotel/Bed and Breakfast Kissing

❧❧❧❧ **HOTEL CARTER, Eureka** You'll shout "Eureka!" once you arrive at the Hotel Carter, a northern California destination in and of itself. Comfort, style, and gracious service are immediately evident as you enter the warm, sun-filled lobby. Soft beige couches and chairs are placed around a crackling fireplace, and afternoon wine and hors d'oeuvres are set out for all to enjoy. Twenty-three rooms, all with taupe walls, dimming lights, Southwest-style couches or chairs, weathered pine furnishings, plantation-style shutters, and entertainment centers hidden in antique pine armoires, are spread out over three floors in the hotel. The most luxurious rooms are on the third floor; they feature marble wood-burning fireplaces, jetted tubs for two, and double-headed showers, and some have massive pine four-poster beds.

While the hotel's rooms are truly exceptional, the ultimate romantic retreat awaits across the street in the new Carter Cottage. This restored Victorian is vibrantly decorated with French country–chic flair and endowed with beautiful appointments and lots of windows. In addition to the full gourmet kitchen, you'll also find fireplaces at every turn, dimming lights, and the bedroom of your dreams. A black metal four-poster bed enclosed by white curtains fronts a gas fireplace while French doors lead into the large bathroom. Soothe sore muscles in the two-person whirlpool tub (with head pillows for extra comfort) or have some good, clean fun in the double-headed shower. As an extra bonus, there's an enclosed back-yard deck adorned with a fountain for your private pleasure. There's no need to leave this love nest for dinner if you so choose. Upon prior arrange-ment, a multicourse dinner (expensive to very expensive) can be prepared and served in the cottage.

While not as extravagant or private, the adjacent Bell Cottage holds three guest bedrooms, each with double whirlpool tubs and two with fire-places. These rooms have a modern edge, with dimming halogen lamps, black leather furniture, parquet wood floors, and boldly printed fabrics in shades of gray, taupe, and black.

In addition to all this, the best restaurant in town is located on the hotel's main level (see Restaurant Kissing), and you should definitely re-serve a table for dinner. Before bedtime, sweeten up in the lobby where warm homemade cookies and soothing herbal tea make for perfect evening snacks. A delicious gourmet breakfast, also included with your stay, is served in the restaurant each morning. If you wish to explore Eureka and its sur-roundings, don't hesitate to ask the gracious innkeepers, whose enthusiasm for their hometown is infectious. **301 L Street; (707) 444-8062, (800) 404-1390; www.carterhouse.com; expensive to very expensive.**

Romantic Alternative: Kitty-corner to the Hotel Carter, and under the same ownership, is the **CARTER HOUSE** (expensive to unbelievably expen-sive). This is where the Carter family's hotel business started nearly two decades ago, with the construction of an impressive dark brown Victorian with towering brick chimneys. There are five guest rooms here, each with polished hardwood floors, antique headboards and furnishings, plantation-style wooden blinds, and varying fabrics. Although pleasant, these rooms aren't as stunning as those in the Hotel Carter or the two cottages. However, plans are in the works to update the Carter House quarters, so stay tuned.

Restaurant Kissing

❤❤❤ **RESTAURANT 301 AT THE HOTEL CARTER, Eureka** Restaurant 301 at the Hotel Carter brings a whole new level of dining to Eureka, not only in terms of food but with its exquisitely sophisticated dining room. Stylish tapestries hang from the high ceiling, modern artwork dresses the warm beige walls, and candles and little lanterns flicker at every white linen–covered table. Pale pine furnishings lend European flair, and tall win-dows look out to the street and the harbor in the distance.

The regionally influenced à la carte menu changes weekly, but consistently features local seafood, meat, and produce; there are also several prix fixe menus, which we highly recommend. Many ingredients are picked fresh from the hotel's own organic garden, including the aptly named salad of garden-gathered greens. After your starting course and possibly a glass of wine (the wine list is award winning), consider anything on the menu and you'll be satisfied. Pan-roasted pork chops with pear chutney, potato gnocchi with chanterelles and oven-dried tomatoes, and pan-seared salmon bathed in a fresh lemon verbena tomato sauce are some of the choice entrées from both types of menus. The kitchen focuses on keeping flavors clear and full, and the presentation is lovely. Top off your meal with an unforgettable dessert—perhaps the bread pudding drenched in warm caramel sauce—then call it a night (an exceptional night, we might add). **301 L Street, at Hotel Carter; (707) 444-8062, (800) 404-1390; www.carter house.com; expensive to very expensive; dinner daily.**

Romantic Suggestion: You won't have to whisper those sweet nothings if you book the one and only table hidden in the hotel's cozy wine shop. The two of you will be surrounded by hundreds of vintages. Rest assured, wine bottles don't talk.

"To be thy lips

is a sweet thing and small."

e. e. cummings

Wine Country

Wine Country is approximately an hour and a half north-east of San Francisco. From the city take Highway 101 north (over the Golden Gate Bridge) to Highway 37 east. Highway 37 connects with the Sonoma Highway (Highway 12), which accesses the Sonoma Valley. If you continue on Highway 37, it connects with the St. Helena Highway (Highway 29), which heads north through the Napa Valley.

Hills in this countryside are given over to vineyards and the succulent grapes they produce. Once you visit this region, you will understand the vivacious, impetuous temperament that is the hallmark of California's Wine Country: its robust regard for living life to the fullest. The boroughs and hamlets of the area are well stocked with an enormous selection of bed and breakfasts, restaurants, spas, wine-tasting rooms, hot-air balloon companies, and the most remarkable picnic turf around. The most difficult part of traveling here is deciding where to concentrate your time and what time of year to visit. Each season brings on a new, completely different array of colors and sights. In spring, dormant grapevines awaken to mustard-colored fields. By summer, the vines are draped in lush green foliage, and the warm temperatures bring visitors in a constant flow. Fall heralds the celebration of the annual harvest (called the "crush" by folks in these parts), and the grape leaves start to turn golden. Winter, the quietest season, is when the vines become dormant again and the splaying branches are trimmed back to a craggy stalk. Winter can be a good time to visit because traffic is light and getting reservations is easy, but be forewarned that the weather can be iffy, and many establishments close or have limited hours (particularly during the month of January). Still, at any time of year, Wine Country offers memories to last a lifetime.

Romantic Note: The number of wineries scattered throughout these picturesque hills and valleys is staggering. Even if you were merely to sip your way in and out of tasting rooms for a week, you would make only a nominal, intoxicating dent in the possibilities that exist here. Because this book is about sentiment and not necessarily about choosing a vintage wine, we've selected a handful of wineries, some lesser known and off the beaten path, and others well known and more highly trafficked but still noteworthy. These are the places we found to be the most appealing for tasting and embracing. Winery reviews are listed under Wine Kissing for each town.

Romantic Suggestion: The wineries are scattered throughout the two valleys (not exactly within walking distance of one another), so you will probably be driving. A single taste of wine is barely a gulp, but sips add up quickly. Please, know your limits and do not drink and drive. One option that is not only safe but also a lot of fun is to have a chauffeur drive you around in a limousine for an afternoon. Many limousine companies operate throughout the Wine Country. In the Napa Valley, a reputable company that offers two-person tours is **ANTIQUE TOURS LIMOUSINE SERVICE** (707-226-9227; www.antiquetourslimousines.com). If you rent a limousine for six hours or more, a gourmet picnic lunch can be included for $10 per person. Prices range from $70 to $90 an hour with a three-hour minimum. In Sonoma County, consider using **BAUER'S TRANSPORTATION** (415-522-1212, 800-LIMO-OUT) or **STYLE 'N COMFORT LIMOUSINE** (707-578-3001, 800-487-5466; www.snclimos.com). The latter offers, among other cars, a very unique 1966 Austin Princess that's perfect for two. For both these companies, prices range from $50 to $150 per hour. Minimum rental times usually apply, too.

Napa Valley

The heavily trafficked St. Helena Highway (Highway 29) cuts through most of the towns in the Napa Valley, detracting from the quiet splendor of the area. Nevertheless, the abundance of gorgeous wineries, charming bed and breakfasts and inns, and world-acclaimed restaurants found in the beautiful surrounding countryside of the Napa Valley make this area one of northern California's most sensational places to pucker up. Helpful information packets about the Napa Valley can be obtained from the **NAPA VALLEY CONFERENCE AND VISITORS BUREAU** (1310 Napa Town Center, Napa, CA 94559; 707-226-7459; www.napavalley.com).

Romantic Alternative: If battling traffic on busy St. Helena Highway doesn't fit into your romantic plans, consider touring along the **SILVERADO TRAIL**, a serene stretch of highway that follows the east side of the Napa Valley, starting in the town of Napa and going north to Calistoga. At some points, Highway 29 and the Silverado Trail are separated by only one or two miles, but in spirit and atmosphere they are eons apart. Highway 29 is just that, a highway, encumbered with cars, billboards, tourists, gas stations, and other "civilized" necessities. In contrast, the Silverado Trail is a meandering drive through nature at its most charming. You'll discover contiguous, undulating hillsides endowed with a profusion of vineyards, forests, and olive groves. As you map your course through Napa Valley's Wine Country, it would be a grievous mistake not to allow enough time to cruise along the Silverado Trail more than once. The wineries tucked away in the network of back roads are less commercial and more personal than those that line the main road. Plus, when you do require provisions or restaurants, the towns of Napa, Yountville, Oakville, Rutherford, St. Helena, and Calistoga are only a short drive away.

Romantic Suggestion: If you notice tummy rumblings during your tour of the valley, stop by **OAKVILLE GROCERY** (Highway 29; 707-944-8802, 800-973-6324; www.oakvillegrocery.com; moderate; open daily), one of Napa Valley's most popular picnic supply places. (If you're touring along the Silverado Trail, you'll need to cross over to the St. Helena Highway along Oakville Crossroad to get here. It won't take more than ten minutes.) When it comes to gourmet California-style picnic lunches, the very popular and tightly packed country-style store has everything you'll need. The collection of pâtés, cheeses, olives, cured meats, salads, and breads all are luscious to look at, delectable to eat, and, unfortunately, much more expensive than your little grocery deli back home.

Napa

It would be nice if the Napa Valley's namesake town was more peaceful and country-like, but the truth is that Napa is where most of the locals come to shop and do business. Consequently, shopping plazas, fast-food stops, and gas stations abound. Thankfully, affectionate establishments also exist here—you just have to know where to look.

Hotel/Bed and Breakfast Kissing

❤❤❤ **BLUE VIOLET MANSION, Napa** A pretty white gazebo rests on the manicured front lawn of this colorful Queen Anne Victorian. Inside the home, fantasy-inspired touches from around the world will intrigue romantic spirits who come to stay. The embossed leather wainscoting, Oriental carpets, and modern sculptures and art in the main foyer make it clear that this is not your run-of-the-mill bed and breakfast. Of the 14 guest rooms spread out on three floors, 11 feature single or double whirlpool tubs, all but two have fireplaces, and five have king-size beds. Those on the first two floors contain an eclectic mix of antiques and are decorated in Victorian style. The third floor, affectionately called the Camelot Floor, holds four of the home's most romantic accommodations. Rooms up here are decorated in a King Arthur theme, with exquisite antiques, stained glass windows, and hand-painted murals. Romantic perks include CD players, gas fireplaces, and private baths with two-person whirlpool tubs. Once you are in one of these spectacular rooms, pour your complimentary bottle of wine into two silver goblets and make a toast to romance.

A full, two-course breakfast might include fresh fruit and cinnamon rolls for starters, plus an egg dish, vanilla French toast, or crêpes filled with artichoke hearts and sun-dried tomatoes as a tempting main course. Before your morning meal, take a cup of coffee and snuggle up beneath the gazebo. When temperatures start rising, cool off in the outdoor pool and spa surrounded by a lush green lawn. **443 Brown Street; (707) 253-2583, (800) 959-2583; www.bluevioletmansion.com; expensive to unbelievably expensive; minimum-stay requirement on weekends and holidays; recommended wedding site.**

Romantic Suggestion: If playing lord and lady of the manor appeals to your *Masterpiece Theatre* sensibilities, the innkeepers will happily play along. A five-course candlelit dinner can be served in your room or in the formal dining room known as **VIOLETTE'S AT THE MANSION** (very expensive; reservations required). Ask the innkeepers for complete details.

❧❧❧ **CEDAR GABLES INN, Napa** If Shakespeare were alive today and touring the Napa Valley, you can bet he would be staying at the Cedar Gables Inn. Every inch of this dark-brown-shingled mansion, trimmed in white and sheltered by immense cedar trees, exudes Renaissance England. Stepping through the large front doors, guests are engulfed by the sheer grandeur of the rich burgundy carpeting, dark redwood walls, tall leaded windows, and Gothic-style antiques. Most guest rooms are on the second and third floors, up a wide carpeted stairway embellished with bold wooden banisters. While enormous, the home has several cozy "conversation corners" tucked away here and there. Don't miss the opportunity to kiss in the mezzanine level's quaint seating area; the only one watching will be the armored knight standing guard.

Each of the six rooms offers exquisite antiques, lush carpeting, and opulent fabrics in rich, warm tones. All rooms have queen-size beds and private baths (four include two-person jetted tubs), and four rooms feature gas fireplaces. The handsome Churchill Chamber, done in delicious shades of black, gray, and cream and complemented by intricately designed antiques, has a whirlpool tub that will seduce you in seconds. This two-person jetted tub is surrounded by a dark wood canopy ... as if it were a bed. Also boasting a luscious bubbling bath is Count Bonzi's Room, the largest room in the house. To enjoy this pool-size jetted tub, bring a bottle of wine and sip 'n' soak beneath the dimmed lights of the chandelier. The Count Bonzi Room also boasts the largest walnut headboard we've seen (eight feet tall, to be exact) crowning its inviting bed. On the other end of the home resides the most private accommodation, Lady Margaret's Room. Tucked away from the others and equipped with its own "secret entrance," this spacious room is the perfect place to snuggle up and not be bothered. No matter which room you claim as your own, extra special touches like the evening wine-and-cheese reception, nightly turndown service, and having your bed made while you're enjoying breakfast add to the home's regal atmosphere.

Breakfast is served in a bright, black-and-white–tiled sunroom with two-person tables clothed in crisp white linens. A variety of homemade baked goods, fresh fruit, and a hot entrée of French toast soufflé or chile-sausage-cheese-egg bake are just some of the delectable treats you may encounter. **486 Coombs Street; (707) 224-7969, (800) 309-7969; www.cedargablesinn.com; expensive to very expensive; minimum-stay requirement on weekends seasonally.**

❦❦❦ **CHURCHILL MANOR, Napa** Tall, perfectly manicured hedges effectively enclose this stately mansion in welcome privacy. Its pretty fountain, immaculate lawn, and towering white columns offer a lasting first impression, one that may take your thoughts back to plantation mansions of the deep South. You know your stay will be a grand one once you enter the historic home and glimpse the two elegant parlors on the main floor; both feature high ceilings, intricately carved columns, velvet-draped windows, original fireplaces, stunning antiques, and ornate chandeliers. Victorian opulence—fluctuating between masculine and feminine motifs—continues in the nine upstairs guest rooms, which feature antique bedroom sets and private baths. Many have fireplaces as well. Our two favorites are the Edward Churchill Room (No. 5), the home's largest room, and the third-floor Mary Wilder Room (No. 8). The former, located on the second floor, features a stunning walnut king-size bed from France, a gold-leaf tiled fireplace, pleasing floral motifs, and a giant cast-iron bathtub highlighted by a crystal chandelier. There's also a two-person shower if the tub isn't enough. Grape motif wallpaper and deep hunter-green carpeting define the handsome Mary Wilder Room, with its king-size bed, gas fireplace, and sunny corner-room location. Although the green tiled bathroom has a lovely claw-foot tub, the bonus is the walk-in shower room. (Yes, it is so large we call it a room!) Other accommodations throughout the house vary in style, from violet motifs to golf themes. Most will do for romance, although some are rather snug. The only accommodation we can't wholeheartedly recommend is No. 1, a ground-level room that's too close to the common areas for peace and quiet.

Step into the marble-floored sunroom for a full breakfast of baked apples or poached pears, muffins or croissants, and your choice of a cooked-to-order omelet or orange French toast. On warmer days, this morning feast can be enjoyed on the huge veranda that wraps around the entire front of the house. Freshly baked cookies in the afternoon, wine and cheese in the evening, and the availability of croquet gear make your stay at this beautiful and majestic inn exceedingly comfortable. **485 Brown Street; (707) 253-7733; www.virtualcities.com; inexpensive to very expensive; minimum-stay requirement on weekends; recommended wedding site.**

Romantic Warning: The opportunity to enjoy this mansion during summer weekends is limited, thanks to its popularity as a wedding venue. On most Friday and Saturday nights, the entire mansion is booked by wedding parties. Call ahead and ask about any openings; you may just be lucky.

THE HENNESSEY HOUSE, Napa Standing tall among the ordinary buildings on Main Street, this multicolored Queen Anne Victorian houses a pleasant and well-maintained bed and breakfast. A manicured lawn and colorful flower beds frame the main residence where six guest rooms reside, all decorated with a combination of beautiful English and Belgian antiques, and most with four-poster or canopy beds. Room features include high ceilings, fireplaces (in some), cozy feather beds with down pillows, marbled bathrooms, stained glass windows, and claw-foot tubs (in most). The adjacent Carriage House holds the most romantically appointed accommodations on the property. All four of these suites offer more privacy and considerably more space, along with whirlpool tubs for two, fireplaces, double vanities, lovingly restored antiques, and separate entrances. Sport and hunting themes also give these rooms a more masculine mood: The second-floor Bridle Suite has an equestrian theme, while the first-floor Fox's Den is decorated with an English hunt in mind. Vaulted ceilings and skylights lend an airy feel to the two upstairs suites, while the two downstairs suites feature huge doors that open onto private patios.

With light classical music as the auditory backdrop, a full gourmet breakfast is served in the dining room beneath a beautiful hand-painted, stamped-tin ceiling. Creatively prepared entrées await each morning, along with homemade granola, fruit plates, yogurt, and freshly baked goodies. Caramel French toast, spicy baked eggs with chiles, and blueberry-stuffed French toast all go perfectly with a cup of the inn's house-blended coffee. In the evening, sample wine and hors d'oeuvres on the shaded back patio while listening to the bubbling fountain and the birds. There's also a dry sauna near the patio, available to guests 24 hours a day. **1727 Main Street; (707) 226-3774; www.hennesseyhouse.com; moderate to very expensive; minimum-stay requirement on weekends.**

LA BELLE EPOQUE, Napa Situated in a quiet residential neighborhood, this colorful Queen Anne–style home speaks volumes about the love and attention that goes into maintaining its beautiful condition both inside and out. A consistent and opulent Victorian theme runs through six of the seven guest rooms, which are located on the first and second floors of the home. Some of these rooms have 20-foot ceilings, hardwood floors covered with Oriental rugs, beautiful Victorian antiques, ornately patterned wallpapers, floral linens, and sitting areas with authentic stained glass windows. All six of these Victorian-style rooms have standard private baths (one with a jetted tub), and two feature wood-burning fireplaces. The seventh room is located in the daylight basement, near the common area and small wine-tasting room. This suite has a more contemporary tone, with floral linens, dark green carpeting, a small sitting area, an elevated king-size bed, and a spacious bathroom with a shower big enough for two. Even though this suite is close to the common area where vintage wines and hors d'oeuvres are served nightly, it is by far the most spacious and private room this inn offers. Plus, after wine and cheese hour ends at 7 P.M., you'll have the entire common area to yourselves.

Every morning guests gather at one magnificently decorated table in the regal dining room. What comes your way can only be called gourmet: apples baked in pastry with crème fraîche, roasted beef tenderloin in a merlot sauce, Grand Marnier French toast, and Southern spoon bread with fresh Napa corn. Finish breakfast off with a sweet kiss, and you'll be set for the day. **1386 Calistoga Avenue; (707) 257-2161, (800) 238-8070; www.labelleepoque.com; expensive to very expensive; minimum-stay requirement on weekends and holidays.**

❧❧❧ **LA RESIDENCE, Napa** Casual refinement and great kissing potential abound at La Residence. Two impressive buildings, a cedar-shingled manor (called the French Barn) and a stately Victorian mansion (appropriately named the Mansion), hold 19 beautifully appointed guest rooms. Not too far away, a small cottage holds one additional getaway. The rooms in the French Barn feature French and English pine antiques, soft and pleasing color schemes, and rich designer linens and bedspreads with matching window treatments and slipcovers. Fireplaces and balconies (or patios) are highlights in these rooms. Rooms in the Victorian mansion live up to the elegant exterior of the building with polished, dark wood furnishings, chandeliers, white shutters, and ten-foot-high ceilings. Standard but beautiful private bathrooms contain all the usual comforts. Our favorite Mansion room is No. 31, a ground-level hideaway with its own entrance. Inside, an enormous four-poster bed is tucked into a bay window, and the fireplace, CD player, and deep soaking tub further enhance the room's romantic appeal. A new arrival to the property, and the most private accommodation of all, is found in the small cottage next to the vineyards. From its semi-private patio, French doors open into a spacious two-room suite that's a divine place to spend the night.

Brick paths meander throughout the property, inviting you to admire the well-tended grounds punctuated with rose trellises, grape arbors, an ancient oak tree, and two towering fountains. A casual wine and cheese hour is held nightly on the back patio (or in the second-floor salon, depending on the weather). You might consider a dip in the pool on hot afternoons, but a much more affectionate option would be a moonlit soak in the Jacuzzi tub behind the mansion, where you can stargaze and luxuriate any time of year. In the morning, a three-course breakfast is served to individual tables in the French-country dining room or, if the sun shines, on the backyard terrace. **4066 St. Helena Highway (Highway 29); (707) 253-0337; www.laresidence.com; expensive to unbelievably expensive; minimum-stay requirement on weekends.**

Romantic Note: Considering the inn's proximity to the highway, road noise is hardly noticeable inside the guest rooms (especially in rooms facing away from the highway). Obviously, traffic can be heard from any of the outside patios, but a wall of tall trees fronting the property conceals the road from your view.

❤❤❤❤ **OAK KNOLL INN, Napa** If you're headed to the Napa Valley specifically for romance, this is the place to kiss and kiss and kiss some more. Oak Knoll Inn is one of those incredibly special places that epitomizes all that is wonderful about bed and breakfasts. From the country road, turn into the tree-lined property and you'll quickly realize that you have stumbled upon a one-of-a-kind retreat. There is nothing else for miles around but the fertile vineyards, lush meadows, and abundant bird life. Enter through the cozy living room (where Nolan Oaks, the living room cat, regularly presides) and take in the charming decorations, books, and a wood-burning fireplace; then continue through the French doors into the courtyard area. Here, two wings of suites overlook a long swimming pool, steaming spa, and spectacular scenery. Suffice it to say, you'll have plenty of room here to fall in love.

Each of the four spacious suites has a remarkable 17-foot-tall vaulted ceiling, double-stone walls (for soundproofing), and a wood-burning fireplace with a comfortable sofa in front for snuggling. Light-filled marble bathrooms are the norm, as are plush king-size beds smothered in soft pillows and fine linens. Fresh flower bouquets are everywhere, and French doors open onto the inner courtyard. A complimentary bottle of wine, as well as an assortment of bottled waters and sodas, await your enjoyment. Bird-watching guides and binoculars let you take a closer look at what is flying around outside. All rooms are equally wonderful; however, the two end units both feature a dramatic 12-foot cathedral window facing neighboring vineyards.

The evening wine-and-cheese hour with gourmet goodies and freshly made appetizers should not be missed. Almost every night, a local winemaker comes to pour his or her wines and personally answer questions. It's a perfect way to educate your palate by sampling what many small, out-of-the-way wineries produce. There's also a bounty of delicious breads, cheeses, vegetables, and dips, beautifully presented by the gracious innkeepers.

Not surprisingly, breakfast is also a gourmet's delight. Different entrées are served each morning. We sat at the fireside dining room table and savored an apple crisp topped with lavender ice cream, followed by puffed toast adorned with fresh berries and accompanied by sausage. Other treats include chocolate tacos full of tropical fruits, and an Anaheim chile quiche spiced up with fresh salsa. On warmer mornings, the outside deck serves as the dining room, and hot-air balloons occasionally float overhead. Such serenity isn't found just anywhere. **2200 East Oak Knoll Avenue; (707) 255-2200; www.virtualcities.com; unbelievably expensive; minimum-stay requirement on weekends.**

Romantic Suggestion: Personal service is another one of Oak Knoll Inn's specialties, and the innkeepers are eager to make your visit to Napa Valley memorable. If you've never been to the area before (or even if you come here regularly but want to see some different wineries and restaurants), put your schedule in their capable hands. You won't be disappointed with the detailed itinerary they put together for you.

❦❧ **OLD WORLD INN, Napa** If the path to your heart is through your stomach, you'll be smitten by the Old World Inn. Afternoon tea, including cookies and a bountiful assortment of homemade treats, will win over your sweet tooth; the early evening wine-and-hors d'oeuvres feast might prompt you to postpone dinner; and (as if you haven't been spoiled enough) a chocoholic's dream dessert buffet is set out before bedtime. After sampling these delectable creations, even the latest risers will be eager to get up for breakfast the following morning. A generous buffet-style breakfast is served in the dining room where intimate tables for two await.

As for the decor, the writing is on the wall ... literally. Written thoughts abound throughout the living room, dining room, and stairwell. Most appropriately, "WELCOME HOME, ROMANCE SPOKEN HERE" is stenciled on the wall leading to the guest rooms. The nine cheerful rooms and one cottage are uniquely decorated, but hand-stenciled accents, comfortable furnishings, and a complimentary bottle of wine are common to all. Private bathrooms are standard and have that old-fashioned flair thanks to pedestal sinks, pull-chain toilets, and claw-foot tubs. Only two rooms feature private spas, but all guests can enjoy the large hot tub on the outdoor patio.

While parts of the home could use some touching up, and the shaggy rust-colored carpet in the hall definitely needs an update, the owners are trying hard to please and improve. The recently redone Garden Room shines with its large skylights, many windows, designer fabrics, and private entrance. Stockholm has a private sunroom with a spa tub for two but, unfortunately, this room is situated near the dining room (not the most private location). Birch is extremely pretty, with a white eyelet bedspread and small stand-up balcony, while the smallest room of all, Carl Larsson's, boasts the biggest bathroom. Behind the house near the parking lot is the newest romantic retreat, a private cottage complete with two bedrooms, a fireplace, and a tucked-into-an-alcove jetted tub. You'll be sure to read the writing on the walls here; it spells romance. **1301 Jefferson Street; (707) 257-0112, (800) 966-6624; www.oldworldinn.com; moderate to very expensive; minimum-stay requirement on weekends.**

Romantic Warning: The Old World Inn's location on a busy downtown street is hardly tranquil, especially if your room faces Jefferson Street. Traffic thins out after dark, but road noise becomes apparent again in the early-morning hours.

Restaurant Kissing

❤❤ **AUGUSTINO'S, Napa** A commonplace strip mall is not where you'd expect to find a charming dining spot, but tucked far enough away from it all to be considered a "find," Augustino's is about as cozy as mall restaurants come. Knotty pine walls, painted wood floors, candles at every table, country motifs, and a two-sided stone fireplace aglow in the room's center create an enchanting atmosphere. In warmer months be sure to dine outdoors on the creekside patio, the restaurant's showpiece. Tulip-style garden lamps and white holiday lights draped from the towering bay laurels create a festive, warm glow. The lush, natural setting will certainly inspire a kiss or two.

The menu at Augustino's consists of mostly Italian creations, some with California twists, such as the enormous portobello, feta, and spinach salad; pesto-crusted salmon; garlic linguine chicken salad; and beef lasagne. When we visited, desserts were limited to tiramisu and cheesecake. **3253 Browns Valley Road; (707) 224-0695; moderate; lunch Monday–Friday, dinner daily.**

❤❤ **BISTRO DON GIOVANNI, Napa** Bistro Don Giovanni is one of the many Napa Valley restaurants that have earned a reputation for fine food and fine wine. Thankfully, the owners of this Italian eatery have also made efforts to create a stylish dining environment. The warm and inviting interior sports pale yellow walls, terra-cotta–tiled floors, antique copper cookware, and a large gas fireplace in the corner. Regretfully, the tables are too packed in for our romantic sensibilities, the booths need higher backs to create some privacy, and the noise level can get out of hand on busy nights. An outside patio, complete with a wood-burning fireplace, is another seating option, although noise from the nearby highway can be distracting. Even if kissing between courses isn't a viable option, you can at least savor the *fritto misto*, a popular seafood and vegetable appetizer for two, along with well-flavored homemade pastas, flat-bread pizzas topped with all sorts of gourmet goodies, and grilled or wood-oven–roasted meats and fish. Such a meal is certain to set the stage for romance later on. **4110 St. Helena Highway (Highway 29); (707) 224-3300; moderate to expensive; lunch and dinner daily.**

LA BOUCANE, Napa In a valley where nouvelle cuisine and hot new French bistros regularly make the headlines, it's nice to find a charming, unpretentious, and classical French restaurant. Nestled in a cozy Victorian home along a residential street, La Boucane has been a Napa mainstay for more than two decades. What is its formula for success? Straightforward and sinfully rich French fare, with a menu that's easy to understand and food that's simply delicious.

Straightforward also describes the decor in the dining room, where each table is cloaked with white linens, surrounded by simple wooden chairs, and topped off with a single red rose and candles. Soft classical music and a stunning orchid centerpiece provide pleasures for the ears and eyes. There's not much here to distract you from each other except, of course, the food. We started by savoring a creamy lobster bisque so decadent it should be called a dessert, followed by rack of lamb that proved simple and satisfying. Couples may want to indulge in the crisp-roasted duckling à l'orange, a dish that's made for two. A taste of homemade crème brûlée, sealed by a golden caramelized crust, left us feeling simply *magnifique*. **1778 Second Street; (707) 253-1177; expensive; dinner Monday–Saturday; closed January.**

Wine Kissing

DOMAINE CARNEROS, Napa Carneros is the wine-growing region spanning the base of the Napa and Sonoma Valleys. Many visitors use the Carneros Highway to get to and from Napa or Sonoma without realizing there are worthwhile places to visit along the way. Domaine Carneros, an impressive winery that specializes in sparkling wines, is one such place— that is, if you want an elegant and somewhat formal tasting experience.

Perfectly trimmed hedges and stately stone fountains frame the stairway leading to the chateau. Marble floors, brass-edged tables, and crystal chandeliers adorn the tasting salon, which functions more like a café. Hors d'oeuvres and crackers accompany your sparkling glass of champagne. In the warmer months you can sit outside on a terrace and enjoy your bubbly along with an exquisite vineyard view. **1240 Duhig Road; (707) 257-0101; www.domaine.com; open 10:30 a.m.–6 p.m. daily.**

Romantic Warning: Tour buses make stops at this popular winery, so be prepared for crowds.

❦❦❦ **THE HESS COLLECTION WINERY, Napa** A fine wine should be lingered over, and so should this exceptional winery and contemporary art gallery. Located on a quiet side road far removed from the rush of Highway 29, The Hess Collection Winery seduces you into slowing your pace with its self-guided tour. A 12-minute audiovisual presentation demonstrates the Hess philosophy of grape growing and winemaking, while three floors showcase Donald Hess' contemporary art collection, including many provocative and intriguing pieces. As you walk through the gallery, windows interspersed with works of art allow you to view the winemaking operation. Sadly, picnic tables are not provided here, but a leisurely walk in the garden courtyard may be just the tranquil escape you are seeking.

Don't even think of leaving without tasting one of the award-winning vintages in the sparse tasting room. You will soon find out why all of Napa is buzzing about The Hess Collection wines. **4411 Redwood Road; (707) 255-1144; www.hesscollection.com; open 10 a.m.–4 p.m. daily.**

❦❦ **JARVIS, Napa** Jarvis is a stunning example of what a person with a vision, a passion for wine, and an unlimited expense account can create. Come here to see how the other half, or, perhaps more appropriately, the other one percent, lives. The imposing entrance to the wine caves looks like something out of a James Bond movie. Massive arched doors open to the caves, and modern bronze sconces line the walls. This is where the tour begins. Toward the center of the tunnels, waterfalls plummet into a flowing stream, both for looks and practical reasons—the running water helps maintain the cave's natural humidity. The tour continues into a grand room called the Crystal Chamber, used for social gatherings. Immense, dazzling outcroppings of amethysts and crystals at each end of the room are quite a sight to see. Finally, after stopping for a glimpse of the fiber-optic chandelier in the ladies room (yes, men get to peek for just a moment), you'll be taken to a formal tasting room with a long marble table and elegant royal-blue chairs trimmed in gold. Here, gourmet cheese and crackers accompany tastings of two or three different wines. **2970 Monticello Road; (707) 255-5280, (800) 255-5280; tours and tasting by appointment only.**

Romantic Warning: All in all, Jarvis is a one-of-a-kind experience, but we must admit that the serious and somewhat pretentious tone became tiresome by the end of the almost hour-long tour. If you are aware of this one drawback in advance and still want to see what Jarvis is all about, you will surely appreciate the unique quality of this winery tour.

❤❤ MONTICELLO VINEYARDS, Napa

In this bustling valley, Big Ranch Road is a road less traveled, and taking it to the peaceful country setting of Monticello Vineyards can make all the difference. Framed by acres of vineyards on either side, a long driveway leads to a stately mansion—modeled after Monticello, Thomas Jefferson's home—and its adjacent informal tasting room. After touring and sipping, check out the picnic area, which is concealed by white lattice. A garden full of roses blooms beside the picnic tables, and several old walnut trees provide shade on sunny days. If you plan ahead and bring your own lunch, all you'll need is a bottle of wine, available for sale in the tasting room. Isn't life in Wine Country wonderful? **4242 Big Ranch Road; (707) 253-2802, (800) 743-6668; open 10 a.m.– 4:30 p.m. daily; recommended wedding site.**

❤❤❤ NAPA VALLEY WINE TRAIN, Napa

Although it is the most touristy excursion in the Napa Valley, the Napa Valley Wine Train can be a lot of fun. Your journey begins at the train depot in downtown Napa. You'll leave the station's tapestry sofas, tasting area, and small art gallery to board a line of 1915 Pullman cars. Each car has been carefully and beautifully restored with glowing mahogany paneling, polished brass, stenciled ceilings, etched glass partitions, and gold and burgundy velvet draperies. Depending on which tour you choose, you will be directed either to the dining car or the lounge car first. Tables line each side of the dining car, so everyone has a window seat. Polished silver, fine bone china, and perfectly pressed white linens enhance the elegant setting, and silver candle lanterns and single red roses are the crowning romantic touches.

Dinner begins with an appetizer and seasonal salad; then select one of three or four entrées such as roasted lamb, broiled sturgeon, pasta du jour, or veal loin. (Vegetarians may need to special order.) Dessert and coffee follow. Some tours include a glass of champagne while others offer paired wine tastings with the meal. A lunch or brunch excursion is the best way to view the scenery. The view of the vineyards *is* one of the best parts of the tour (although the train's route parallels Highway 29, so if you have driven through the valley, you have probably seen these sights). If you prefer to ride the dinner train, which departs at 6:30 P.M. and returns around 9:30 P.M., we recommend doing so in the warmer months, when the days are longer. Another option, either day or night, is to just come along for the ride and pick up something in the deli car (expensive; lunch daily). Another car is devoted exclusively to wine tasting (extra charge). Trips last a minimum of three hours, so be prepared to sit, sip, and eat. **1275 McKinstry Street; (707) 253-2111, (800) 427-4124; www.winetrain.com; unbelievably expensive (includes train fare, tax, and gratuity); reservations required; restaurant: lunch and dinner daily, brunch Saturday–Sunday; closed the first week of January.**

Romantic Bonus: Due to the popularity of the wine train tours, stops along the route have been added. Passengers can now disembark at various wineries to stretch their legs and whet their palates on the latest vintages.

❦ **RMS DISTILLERY, Napa** If you're tired of "pouring" over the innumerable merlots, chardonnays, and fine cabernet sauvignons in the area, take a trip to the RMS Distillery for something different: the making and aging of fine brandy. Be sure to take the half-hour tour that begins in the visitors center, starting with a demonstration depicting the unique process of creating brandy. You'll then be led outside to a rustic stone building called the Still House, where the distillation tanks are kept. Sunlight dances off these beautiful copper tanks as they concentrate wine into brandy. The tour finishes in the dimly lit barrel house, filled with the aroma of aging brandy. Gregorian chants, piped through hidden speakers, help set the perfect mood. Sadly, brandy tastings are not available, but you can purchase a bottle for a delightful nightcap on another romantic occasion. **1250 Cuttings Wharf Road; (707) 253-9055; tours only, no tasting; call for seasonal hours.**

❦❦❦ **WILLIAM HILL WINERY, Napa** Not every winery in the Napa Valley has great views to accompany its wine-tasting facility. To its romantic credit, William Hill takes advantage of a remarkable setting while providing an attractive tasting room. Placed on top of a grassy embankment, this small winery overlooks verdant hills peppered with symmetrical rows of grapevines and sprawling shade trees, while mountains rise majestically in the distance. Inside, faux antique painted walls and a terra-cotta floor create a lovely atmosphere for tasting. Massive windows look down on hundreds of wooden barrels filled with aging wine. Black wrought-iron picnic tables are set outside near the gravel parking lot, overlooking the inspiring panorama. If you're lucky, you might snatch up the only table set away from the others on a soft lawn; it's a spectacular place to catch a sunset. **1761**

Atlas Peak Road; (707) 224-4477; www.williamhillwinery.com; tours and tasting by appointment only.

Romantic Suggestion: If you want to bring a basket full of lunchtime treats to this or any other Napa Valley winery, consider stopping at GENOVA DELICATESSEN (1550 Trancas; 707-253-8686; inexpensive; open daily) for made-to-order picnic goodies.

Yountville

Yountville is one of the few Napa Valley towns that allow the two of you to veer off the crowded St. Helena Highway and into a slice of small-town tranquillity. In fact, Yountville's distinctive, quiet charm makes it one of our top picks for places to kiss. There are boutiques and galleries to peruse, not to mention several very romantic locales and some world-class restaurants.

Hotel/Bed and Breakfast Kissing

❧❧ **CROSS ROADS INN, Yountville** If your day of kissing in Wine Country has left you walking on air, ascend to the Cross Roads Inn—a multilevel, contemporary wood house set high above the rolling, vineyard-laden valley. The view from its spacious, firelit living room and redwood deck is enchanting. Enjoy magnificent sunsets from the guest rooms' double whirlpool tubs and private decks. (Views don't get much better than this!) The only other property in Wine Country that even begins to compete with this vantage point is the exclusive AUBERGE DU SOLEIL (see Hotel/Bed and Breakfast Kissing in Rutherford). However, the view is the only romantic element these two properties have in common—their styles and atmospheres are totally different.

While Auberge du Soleil caters to an upscale crowd, Cross Roads Inn offers four homey guest rooms with a comfortable, albeit lived-in, feeling. Rooms are named after Beatrix Potter characters, and each features a music box depicting its namesake. The upper-floor Puddleduck Room, with a pink bedspread and mirrored closet doors, has a two-person Jacuzzi tub framed between two corner windows that overlook the valley to the west and a wild ravine to the north. Another good choice on the upper floor is the Peter Rabbit Room. Although its location is poor (off the front entrance), this room is done in a country motif with a beautiful pencil-post bed, plenty of windows, and a double Jacuzzi tub with outstanding views. The two downstairs rooms offer more seclusion but, unfortunately, their views are disrupted by balconies and railings.

Features like whirlpool tubs for two, king-size beds, semiprivate decks, full breakfasts delivered to your room, afternoon tea, and evening brandy and chocolates help make up for some of the out-of-date decor; however, prices in the very expensive range may lead you to expect more. On the other hand, the innkeepers are adding more amenities, most recently a heated pool and spa overlooking the valley. Above all, it is the view that makes Cross Roads Inn stand apart. If vineyard vistas are of premier importance (and you aren't traveling on a limited budget), then this hillside inn is worth your romantic consideration. Hiking trails zigzag above the inn to **ATLAS PEAK**, where views get even better, stretching as far as San Francisco on clear days. **6380 Silverado Trail; (707) 944-0646; www. crossroadsnv.com; unbelievably expensive; minimum-stay requirement on weekends and holidays.**

❀❀❀❀ **MAISON FLEURIE, Yountville** Creeping ivy covers the brick and stone exterior of Maison Fleurie, a luxurious getaway that combines an in-town location with country-like ambience. Housed in a charming 1873 hotel, the Main Building holds several guest rooms, along with the dining room, lobby, and kitchen area. More rooms are found next door in two small brick buildings named the Old Bakery and the Carriage House. Charming French-country details like delightful hand-painted murals, elegantly rustic antiques, warm color schemes, and floral linens appoint each of the 13 rooms. Four of the most spacious rooms are found in the Old Bakery. Each boasts a king-size bed, a one-person whirlpool tub in the bathroom, and a gas fireplace. Guests in these rooms can enjoy their bottle of complimentary wine on their small patio or deck surveying the outdoor pool, spa, and nearby restaurants. The two Carriage House rooms feature private entrances, and one has a gas-log fireplace. Seven more rooms, some extremely tiny, are located on the upper floor of the Main Building and have easy access to the expansive sundeck overlooking acres of nearby vineyards. The Main Building's most romantic room, a deluxe queen room, features the inn's only double Jacuzzi tub. However, its next-to-the-lobby location and accompanying noise are detracting factors. Whichever room you select, afternoon wine and hors d'oeuvres as well as evening turndown service are part of the impeccable package.

Breakfast is another notable element at Maison Fleurie. Venture to the teddy-bear–filled lobby of the Main Building, where a full breakfast is served buffet style. Down some steps, you'll find a crackling fire warming the terra-cotta–tiled floors in the provincial dining room; here, tables for two allow for a semiprivate morning affair. A stay at Maison Fleurie is like visiting the French countryside, only without the language barrier. **6529**

Yount Street; (707) 944-2056, (800) 788-0369; www.foursisters.com/maison.html; moderate to very expensive.

❀❀ **OLEANDER HOUSE, Yountville** What you see is what you get at this French-country bed and breakfast, but what you hear is less pleasant. The sound of cars whizzing by on the adjacent highway is more than irksome; it's distracting. What a disappointment for an otherwise peaceful, romantic find. If you can put the outside traffic aside (it's at its worse during midday), inside you'll discover a lovely blend of old-fashioned decor with modern architecture and amenities distinguishing all five guest rooms. You can kiss by the fireplace in each accommodation except the main-floor Garden Room; however, this room has a private brick patio to compensate. Bright standard bathrooms, winter and summer quilts, and mix-and-match furnishings are common to all guest rooms, while vaulted ceilings and private balconies lend a sense of spaciousness in the four upstairs units.

After a cup of morning coffee, guests can tiptoe to the backyard for a wake-up soak in the hot tub or venture to the front garden to smell the roses. Every so often, a loud *whoosh* pierces the tranquillity of the morning as a brightly colored hot-air balloon floats overhead. Later, guests can meet in the sunny dining room for such dessert-like breakfast specialties as a pleasing pear tartlet or oatmeal brûlée topped with sweet berries. **7433 St. Helena Highway (Highway 29); (707) 944-8315, (800) 788-0357; www.oleander.com; expensive to very expensive; minimum-stay requirement on weekends.**

❀❀ **PETIT LOGIS, Yountville** *Petit logis* is French for "small, temporary lodgings," a term that surely fits this unique inn situated in the middle of town. A long shingle-style building, fronted by a vine-covered trellis and a small lawn, is home to five side-by-side rooms. For those seeking freedom from ornate, over-styled decor, the French-country minimalist feel here should soothe your senses. All rooms are similar in size, and each has simple furnishings, rough-textured walls painted pale yellow, and a hand-painted mural depicting a garden scene (the only art on the otherwise bare walls). Romantic highlights in each room include a queen-size bed fronting a gas fireplace, and a cavernous bathroom where a six-foot-long Jacuzzi tub and separate tiled shower await. The beds are all from the Pottery Barn, and styles vary from a pine sleigh bed (Room No. 3) to a whitewashed wood bed (Room No. 2). TVs are hidden away in wall cabinets—a nice touch—and small, semiprivate patios offer a trio of vistas: a nearby restaurant, the town's buildings and roads, and the mountains beyond. Our favorite rooms are Room No. 3, with its pine bed and matching furniture, and Room No.

1, which, although closest to the road, best captures the sun's rays and boasts a four-poster bed nestled in the corner.

As the definition states, Petit Logis is a lodging, not a bed and breakfast. However, a delicious, complimentary breakfast has been arranged for you by the innkeepers at two participating local restaurants. Simply walk over to the restaurant of your choice and order whatever suits your fancy. **6527 Yount Street; (707) 944-2332, (877) 944-2332; www.petitlogis. com; expensive; minimum-stay requirement on weekends and holidays.**

❦❦❦ **VILLAGIO INN AND SPA, Yountville** The clean and classic Mediterranean look of earthy stucco finishes, tiled roofs, and bubbling fountains sets this inn apart from the rest in town. Only a few months old when we visited, Villagio is the younger sibling of the **VINTAGE INN** (see review below), and affords the same standards, luxury, and features. Being brandnew, a few things still need ironing out (such as remembering to do turndown service and developing the landscaping) in order for Villagio to run as smoothly as its predecessor. Nevertheless, the inn is a delightful retreat, complete with a full spa, a workout room, two pools, and a lovely, sunfilled lobby where afternoon and morning treats are presented.

Like the those at the Vintage Inn, guest rooms at Villagio are clustered in small buildings spanning the property; a long fountain runs through the middle of the grounds, creating a soft, comforting sound that helps you forget about nearby traffic noise … somewhat. Unfortunately, such a clustered building design often doesn't allow the best views, and, depending on your room location, you might see more of your neighbor than you wish. Luckily, room interiors are wonderfully warm and appealing, with dimming lights, soothing earth tones, luxurious linens and towels, and plantation-style shutters. Some suites boast two-person whirlpool tubs in their slate and marble bathrooms, and a bottle of complimentary wine awaits in the mini-bar. All guest rooms have a patio or deck as well as a fireplace. Like other inns in town, Villagio parallels noisy Highway 29. Because the inn lacks mature vegetation to absorb the noise, earplugs may be necessary if you don't want to wake to the sounds of traffic.

A continental breakfast buffet, complete with champagne, a half dozen pastry choices, and plenty of fruit, should get those taste buds prepared for wine tasting. If you have no zip after a day spent sipping, be sure to take advantage of the soothing spa services on the property. **6481 Washington Street; (707) 944-8877, (800) 351-1133 in California; expensive to unbelievably expensive; minimum-stay requirement on weekends.**

❦❦❦ **VINTAGE INN, Yountville** Soft classical music breezes through the Vintage Inn's serene lobby, with its plum-colored chairs, brick hearth, and high, peaked, open-beam ceiling. Outside, beauty awaits at every turn: Fountains, reflecting pools, and flowers embellish the apartment-like complex of brick and clapboard buildings. Within these buildings reside 80 inviting guest rooms. Wood-burning fireplaces, warm neutral tones, plantation-style shutters, small and shallow jetted bathtubs (that are due for an updating), and private patios all help make for a suitably romantic stay. A complimentary bottle of wine is included with your stay, and hotel-like amenities such as TVs, refrigerators, and coffeemakers are found in every room. Room service and a concierge are also available. We prefer the spacious mini-suites and the upstairs rooms with vaulted ceilings, particularly the ones in the inner courtyard, which are less likely to be bothered by road noise from Highway 29. These Inner Court rooms are more expensive, but a good night's sleep is worth the extra money—especially if you're willing to spring for the inn's very expensive to unbelievably expensive room rates in the first place.

A continental champagne breakfast is served fireside in the lobby every morning. If a bubbly mimosa with breakfast doesn't wake you up, then a dip in the inn's outdoor heated pool should rejuvenate you for a day of wining and dining. **6541 Washington Street; (707) 944-1112, (800) 351-1133 in California; www.vintageinn.com; very expensive to unbelievably expensive; minimum-stay requirement on weekends and holidays.**

❧❧ **YOUNTVILLE INN, Yountville** Set on the quieter edge of town (although not far enough away from the noisy freeway), the new Yountville Inn offers a few romantic choices in its assortment of 51 roomy accommodations spread throughout seven buildings. The elegant New England–style inn, embellished by a stylish river-rock facade and white-trimmed windows and balconies, is nestled against historic Hopper Creek. It's here, near the water's edge, that you'll find the most romantic rooms on the property. Patios off these superior rooms are a stone's throw from the unassuming creek. Besides the waterfront advantage, these rooms will also tempt you with vaulted ceilings and more peace and quiet than you'll find in other locations. Creekside or not, all rooms are brightened by a French-country flair and warmed by fieldstone fireplaces. Adjacent to the lodge-like lobby, where a continental breakfast buffet is served, you'll find a heated pool and spa for your enjoyment. **6462 Washington Street; (707) 944-5600, (800) 972-2293; www.yountvilleinn.com; expensive to unbelievably expensive; minimum-stay requirement on weekends.**

Restaurant Kissing

❧❧ **BISTRO JEANTY, Yountville** With its warm, inviting interior and such French comfort staples as cassoulet and *entrecote frites* (steak with fries),

Bistro Jeanty has won over the hearts and palates of most Napa Valley residents. Authentic French-country antiques and classic bistro touches like a blackboard menu, vintage French posters, and butcher paper–topped tables add plenty of authentic charm. We suggest you bypass the front dining room; it tends to be quite noisy due to the waiting crowd, communal eating table, and casual bar. The back room, next to the fireplace, affords a little more peace and quiet, but not much when the place gets busy.

Even if you can't get close and cuddly here, your taste buds will certainly fall in love with the French bistro–style fare. Must-try items are the signature tomato and puff-pastry soup, the robust and hearty coq au vin (a chicken and red wine stew), and, for the finishing touch, a gigantic crêpe smothered in orange butter. Ooh la la. **6510 Washington Street; (707) 944-0103; reservations recommended; lunch and dinner daily.**

DOMAINE CHANDON, Yountville Domaine Chandon is certainly one of the most beautiful properties for dining in Northern California. Secluded on the grounds of a country winery, this immense three-terraced dining room spares no expense in its quest for luxury. Inlaid stone walls, arched-wood-beam ceilings and doorways, and views of well-tended lawns and gardens combine to create a sensuous, elegant dining climate. If it weren't for the dining room's overwhelming popularity, large size, and poor acoustics (it can get noisy in here), we would have awarded this restaurant four lips without a second thought. Despite these shortcomings, it is still a stunning place to dine, and the sparkling wines just add more splendor to the experience.

The ultraluxe menu brings forth an assortment of delicacies, starting with the appetizers. If you crave caviar, are tempted by tartare, or favor foie gras, you'll find quite a generous selection with the starters. We began our meal with smoked salmon tartare accompanied by a fennel salad. Entrées bring fresh fish and local meats and poultry to the forefront. The roasted Chilean sea bass was by far one of the best presentations we've tasted of this popular fish. Unfortunately, our rack of lamb proved much too fatty to be easily consumed. Be sure to finish with Domaine Chandon's decadent signature dessert: a hot "gooey" chocolate cake topped with a scoop of vanilla ice cream. Sounds wonderful, doesn't it? If you can get a reservation before prime dining hours, you're likely to find the experience rapturous. **One California Drive; (707) 944-2280, (800) 736-2892; www.dchandon. com; very expensive to unbelievably expensive; reservations required with credit-card guarantee; call for seasonal hours; dress code: no T-shirts, jeans, or shorts.**

Romantic Suggestion: Even if you do not plan to dine here, visit **DOMAINE CHANDON WINERY** (call for seasonal hours). Although it is located just off Highway 29, a hillside completely conceals the road from view, and the entry to the grounds passes vineyards and a flower-rimmed pond. Tours do not include tasting, but you can purchase champagne by the glass or by the bottle in the Salon, a comfortable outdoor area that looks out to vineyards and oak-covered hills. In addition, cabaret performances and evening concerts are periodically offered at the winery. Call for information on special events.

❀❀❀❀ **FRENCH LAUNDRY, Yountville** Look closely when searching for this restaurant—the French Laundry could easily be mistaken for a private country home. Housed in a lovingly renovated two-story brick building, this restaurant is one of the finest in Napa Valley, if not the entire state. Several dining rooms comprise the interior, including one upstairs, and the elegantly adorned tables provide plenty of elbow room. Subdued colors and a simple French-country decor give prominence to the artwork that arrives on your plate. First and foremost, the French Laundry is a food lover's paradise. Romance comes second—although a close second, we might add.

A superlative chef's-choice menu changes daily and ranks as the most popular choice, although an additional prix fixe menu lets you choose from several selections for each course. The menu may include such exotic and superbly executed dishes as chilled cauliflower panna cotta topped with sevruga caviar; a Maine lobster pancake surrounded by a delicate carrot-ginger butter; a New Zealand venison chop with red wine–braised cabbage; or herb-roasted monkfish served with a ragout of wine-braised oxtail, glazed pearl onions, and pan-roasted salsify (oyster plant). For dessert, you may be offered a luscious chocolate soufflé or the chef's signature "coffee and doughnuts," a cappuccino semifreddo topped with frothed milk and served in a coffee cup alongside two hot-from-the-fryer sugar doughnuts. Service is faultless, although if you're trying to have an intimate conversation, the constant replacement of silverware may be cause for many a pause. **6640 Washington Street; (707) 944-2380; unbelievably expensive; reservations required; lunch Friday–Sunday, dinner daily; closed the first two weeks of January.**

Romantic Note: Due to French Laundry's popularity, reservations are almost impossible to obtain, usually requiring booking 60 days in advance for limited seatings. Most innkeepers in the area are well aware of this fact and try to make advance reservations for you when you book a stay at their inn. (They deserve a kiss for this!) While spontaneous romance is always a big plus in our book, planning ahead is a must in this case. If you're food lovers, you don't want to miss the opportunity to dine here.

❧ **MUSTARDS GRILL, Yountville** Mustards' popularity precludes it from being considered either intimate or romantic, so why would we send you here? Despite crowds and a boisterous atmosphere, the extensive wine list and inventive menu will appeal to those looking for a fun, relaxed lunch spot. If you don't mind an audience, you might even be able to sneak in a kiss across the table. Dinner can be more difficult to experience, especially without reservations. Hearty bistro-style entrées complete with heapings of comfort-food accompaniments (such as mashed potatoes or onion rings) are the specialty here. Try the famous pork chops or any of the grilled items, and you won't be disappointed. **7399 St. Helena Highway (Highway 29); (707) 944-2424, (800) 901-8098; moderate to expensive; reservations recommended; lunch and dinner daily.**

Outdoor Kissing

❧❧❧❧ **ABOVE THE WEST HOT-AIR BALLOONING, Yountville** Nobody will argue that a hot-air balloon ride is the best way to get enthralling views of Wine Country. The arise-with-the-birds launch time may seem like a drawback at first, but once you witness the glow of sunrise over the colorful valley, you'll be thrilled to be awake, alive, and floating along above acres of Wine Country.

A hot-air balloon adventure could feel a little too close for comfort if the two of you are squashed into a balloon basket with many other people. Above the West takes a special approach to ballooning, recognizing that crowds can be a deterrent to those who only have eyes for each other. By limiting the number of passengers allowed on every flight (the maximum is six), this company caters to those who are looking for a more intimate experience. Private flights (including weddings aloft) can be arranged for a price. After touring the sky above Napa Valley, return to earth for a post-flight champagne breakfast featuring a variety of cooked-to-order treats. **6525 Washington Street; (707) 944-8638, (800) 627-2759; www.nva loft.com; prices start at $195 per person; reservations required.** *Call for directions to the meeting site.*

Romantic Note: Read Above the West's brochure carefully when you make reservations so you are aware that balloons can be launched only when the weather allows. Also note that hats are recommended for particularly tall people (the burner above your heads puts out a lot of heat) and jackets are advisable.

❧❧❧❧ **NAPA VALLEY BALLOONS, INC., Yountville** Your excursion commences at sunrise, when the air is still and cool (yes, that means somewhere between 5 A.M. and 9 A.M.). As you step into the balloon's gondola, your eyes will gape at the towering, billowing bag of fabric overhead, and your heart will race with wild expectation. Once your craft is aloft, the wind guides it above countryside blanketed with acres of grapes. Up here, the world seems more serene than you ever imagined possible. You will be startled by the sunrise from this vantage point; daylight awakens the hills with new vigor and warmth. After your flight, a gourmet champagne brunch awaits at a nearby hotel. This isn't everyone's way to start an early morning, but for those who can handle the noise and heat (from the overhead flame thrower that fills the balloon with hot air), it is a stimulating way to spend an early morning together. **(707) 944-0228, (800) 253-2224; www.napavalleyballoons.com; prices start at $175 per person; reservations required.** *Call for directions to the meeting site.*

❀❀❀ **NAPA VALLEY MODEL A RENTALS, Yountville** How about splurging on your romantic getaway with some old-fashioned fun? Cruise down country roads in either a convertible 1929 Model A Roadster or a 1929 Mercedes SSK while the warm California breeze blows through your hair. No one will know it's a rental car, which is all the better for your classy image. In addition to the two cars mentioned, there's also a 1930 Model A Phaeton. All are convertibles, all are automatic, and all are guaranteed to turn heads about town. Period costumes are available if you want to complete the picture, and picnic lunches can be included. Just be sure to include a good old-fashioned kiss, and you're set to toot about town. **6795 Washington Street; (707) 944-1106; rentals start at $40 per hour; reservations recommended.** *Going northbound from Napa, take Highway 29 until you reach Madison Street in Yountville. Take a right onto Madison Street and continue for one block. The rental location is at the corner of Madison and Washington Streets.*

Wine Kissing

❀❀❀❀ **S. ANDERSON VINEYARD, Yountville** As you tour Wine Country, you might hear terms like "mossy," "chewy," or, our personal favorite, "barnyard," used to describe the taste and smell of a fine wine. At S. Anderson Vineyard, these terms are accompanied by a healthy dose of humor. This is not to say that the people at S. Anderson don't take themselves seriously. On the contrary, this endearing family-owned and -operated winery would not be where it is today if they did not take their business extremely seriously. The hour-long tour, complete with generous tastes of the winery's famous champagnes and wines, is as insightful as it is entertaining. The twice-daily tours begin in the main house, where the winemaking facility resides, then proceeds through the vineyards and into the dramatic champagne caves. These ancient-looking caves, boasting 18-foot-high ceilings, exposed volcanic rock walls, uneven cobbled floors, and more than 400,000 bottles of some of the finest champagnes in the area, are by far the biggest of any tour in the valley. Incredible! The darkness is punctuated with bare lightbulbs strung on a single black wire and softened by the glow of candles flickering against the barren walls.

You might enter these magical caves under the impression that champagne is only for special occasions. After sipping S. Anderson's latest vintage, however, you may be convinced that a fine champagne makes any occasion special. After the tour, purchase your own bottle of bubbly, sit at one of the picnic tables surrounded by the scent of fragrant roses, and toast your special time here. **1473 Yountville Crossroad; (707) 944-8642, (800) 428-2259; www.4bubbly.com; open 10 a.m.–5 p.m. daily.**

Oakville

Wine Kissing

❤❤ **MUMM NAPA VALLEY, Oakville** If you have grown weary of chatting with fellow wine enthusiasts and listening to discussions of different blending and crushing techniques, you may find a place like Mumm Napa Valley refreshing. In other words, come here if you are looking for a hands-off experience. Mumm's tasting room is run like a restaurant, where you can sit at your own table and enjoy a variety of sparkling wines (for a price) while looking out at the vineyards and mountains. The patio area, set beside lush rows of grapes, makes for a lovely summer setting. What we like most about Mumm is that no one interrupts you after the champagne is poured. **8445 Silverado Trail; (707) 942-3434, (800) 686-6272; call for seasonal hours.**

Rutherford

Hotel/Bed and Breakfast Kissing

❤❤❤❤ **AUBERGE DU SOLEIL, Rutherford** If the words "splurge" and "pamper" come to mind when planning your romantic getaway, Auberge du Soleil may be the place for you. In this case, we hope that the phrase "unlimited expense account" is also part of your vocabulary. This upscale resort hotel has some of the most well-known, heart-stirring, and certainly first-class accommodations in the area. In fact, the 50 rooms here are all outrageously spacious and beautiful.

Perched on a forested hillside, Auberge du Soleil overlooks the thriving Napa Valley. Forty-eight suites are spread throughout 11 Mediterranean-style buildings. Many rooms have Jacuzzi tubs (or oversize tubs) where candles and fragrant bath salts await; all have wood-burning fireplaces and private terraces with stupendous views. These are stunning retreats, with blond wood furnishings and sun-kissed interiors. Further enlivening each room are bright yellow pillows and a fuchsia-colored bedspread on the California king-size bed (the colors sound odd, but they work here). Modern artwork above the bed, the bathtub, and throughout the living room are individually highlighted by halogen lights. Even though the architecture is southern French, the brilliant colors and rustic touches like terra-cotta–tiled floors and warm taupe walls combine to create a festive Mexican ambience. Two additional guest rooms, located in the main building, are slightly smaller and lack fireplaces.

Every convenience you can imagine is merely a phone call away. In-room massage treatments are available, there is 24-hour room service, and your suite is equipped with a stereo, TV/VCR, and gourmet wet bar. Stroll around the grounds and you'll find a full-service spa, a swimming pool and sundeck, and a quiet path leading through an olive grove and sculpture garden. If the rest of Wine Country wasn't so inviting, you might want to spend your entire romantic escape here. **180 Rutherford Hill Road; (707) 963-1211, (800) 348-5406; www.aubergedusoleil.com; unbelievably expensive; minimum-stay requirement on weekends; recommended wedding site.**

Romantic Suggestion: Even if you do not stay overnight, you should spend some time enjoying the view from Auberge du Soleil's decks in the restaurant and lounge (see Restaurant Kissing). Have lunch or an early dinner while daylight still covers the valley.

Restaurant Kissing

❤❤❤❤ **AUBERGE DU SOLEIL RESTAURANT AND LOUNGE, Rutherford** Perched atop a ridge high above the Napa Valley, Auberge du Soleil has a commanding perspective on the entire countryside. Ensconced in hills blanketed with flourishing olive groves, the restaurant and its neighboring buildings are so well integrated with the landscape that they seem to be organically linked. Walls of taupe-colored stucco, light pine-paneled ceilings, wooden tables, and a Spanish-style hearth all add to this elegantly natural effect. The dining room and lounge are designed to supply premium viewing pleasure from every nook and corner. Tables in the lounge are positioned near a fireplace large enough to generate ample warmth.

However, the absolute best place to kiss at Auberge du Soleil Restaurant and Lounge is on the expansive outdoor deck. A properly timed evening visit allows you to bask in the warm hues of day yielding to night.

The view is a hard act to follow, but the kitchen does a satisfactory job of keeping up. Although the restaurant's name is French, the menu offers an international variety of dishes with a focus on fresh regional ingredients. The Seven Sparkling Sins, a decadent appetizer for two, offers caviar and other delicacies for those who want to be a little naughty. For more subdued starters, try the cumin-chervil crab cakes or tempura ahi-salmon sashimi. Main courses are nicely divided between fish/shellfish, meat, and poultry dishes. Surprisingly, there's also a three-course vegetarian tasting dinner. The portobello-and-prosciutto-roasted chicken was good, but didn't wow our taste buds. Better bets are the grilled California striped bass and the roasted-garlic lamb medallions served with truffle risotto and a triple-mint essence. Whether you indulge in a dining adventure here or simply toast each other in the bar, the potential for romance is more than likely—it's guaranteed. **180 Rutherford Hill Road, at Auberge du Soleil; (707) 967-3111, (800) 348-5406; www.aubergedusoleil.com; very expensive to unbelievably expensive; breakfast, lunch, and dinner daily; recommended wedding site.**

Romantic Suggestion: Rising above Auberge du Soleil is RUTHERFORD HILL WINERY (200 Rutherford Hill Road; 707-963-7194; www.rutherfordhill.com; open 10 A.M.–5 P.M. daily). It's located just off the Silverado Trail and up Rutherford Hill Road. This small winery is a heart-tugging spot to bring a picnic for a leisurely lunch and private wine tasting. Spread your blanket in the shade of a leafy tree to capture a splendid view of the valley. Or save your appetite and, as the cool of evening approaches, saunter down to Auberge du Soleil and toast the beginning of an amorous night.

❤❤❤ **LA TOQUE, Rutherford** This recent arrival to the Napa Valley restaurant scene is making a splash among food aficionados, and its intimate dining room is making waves when it comes to romance. The large, one-room dining area borrows a bit from the surrounding Rancho Caymus Inn, which has a classic hacienda look. Inside, the restaurant's decor is simple Southwest. Fourteen large, linen-covered tables are well placed around the room's perimeter, and a soaring floral arrangement holds court in the center. High-pitched ceilings and a stone fireplace are the only other embellishments besides the wall sconces. If only the lights were dimmed more, the austere room could be cozier.

Flexibility in dining times isn't a strong point here. With only 12 tables, seating times are understandably limited to twice an evening. (The first seating occurs between 5:30 P.M. and 6:30 P.M.; the second takes place between 8 P.M. and 9 P.M. Expect dinner to last two and a half to three hours.) A set menu featuring five courses changes nightly, but always delivers uncomplicated, yet well-balanced French dishes with local flair. Duck breast with peppered Bosc pear in red wine, spaetzle with spinach and grilled portobello mushroom, and striped bass bathed in a bourride sauce and aioli are just a sample of the delectable delights. While the dinner prices are high, the generous portions won't disappoint, so prepare for this dinner by eating a light lunch. **1140 Rutherford Road, at the Rancho Caymus Inn; (707) 963-9770; www.latoque.com; unbelievably expensive; reservations recommended; dinner Wednesday–Sunday.**

St. Helena

This picturesque town embodies everything there is to love about Wine Country. The town's center is lined with boutiques, cafés, restaurants, and a couple of art galleries, while the town's country outskirts are laden with wineries and cozy bed and breakfasts. Of all the towns in Wine Country, St. Helena has the most abundant selection of places to explore, eat, stay, and (last, but never least) kiss. Unfortunately, popularity comes with a price. The highway runs through town and traffic is often bumper-to-bumper during peak hours. Don't expect to rush through this town.

Hotel/Bed and Breakfast Kissing

❧❧ **CHESTELSON HOUSE, St. Helena** Just two short blocks from St. Helena's town center, this blue-and-white Queen Anne cottage has an old-fashioned bed-and-breakfast charm. Firelight warms the parlor and adjacent dining area, where wine and cheese are presented every evening. Three of the four guest rooms are located on the main floor and have floral linens or patchwork quilts, brass or antique beds, and beautifully restored wooden furniture. Each room has a TV/VCR along with a romantic movie to help set the mood. Our favorite main-floor room is Escape, where you can do exactly that on a private deck sheltered by an ancient elm tree. To experience the inn's most kissable retreat, head downstairs to the secluded Shadow Suite, a bright and airy room accented by a soothing color scheme of pale green, gold, and cream. Ceiling-high bay windows frame the queen-size bed's brass and iron headboard. Inside the sizable tiled bathroom awaits a two-person Jacuzzi tub (candles and bath salts included), set beside a greenhouse-style window.

In the morning, awake to a full breakfast of fresh fruit salads; hot-from-the-oven croissants, scones, or London sausage rolls; and a baked egg dish such as a spinach ricotta omelet or asparagus cheese frittata. You can enjoy your morning meal at the large table in the main parlor or, better yet, park yourselves underneath a parasol on the large front deck. **1417 Kearney Street; (707) 963-2238; www.chestelson.com; moderate to very expensive; minimum-stay requirement on weekends.**

❤❤ **HARVEST INN, St. Helena** Flowering gardens and manicured lawns edge the brick walkways that meander through the Harvest Inn's lovely grounds and lead to clusters of English Tudor–style buildings. Brick chimneys, spiral turrets, iron lanterns, and stucco walls accented by wood beams enhance the Old English atmosphere, while tall trees completely conceal the inn from Highway 29. The 54 recently renovated rooms come in a choice of seven categories, ranging from Cozy Queen Rooms to two-story Executive Suites. Some of the names are certain to appeal to romantics with a funny bone: Earl of Ecstasy, Count of Fantasy, Duchess of Delight, and, let's not forget those star-crossed lovers, Romeo and Juliet. Interiors vary, but Old English decor dominates with hardwood floors, heavy draperies, wood beam ceilings, and enormous brick fireplaces. Furnishings tended to be a mix and match of antiques, and despite the renovations, some pieces look like they've been here since time began.

As in most cases, romantic amenities, views, and choice location improve as prices increase. Luckily, most rooms have a "U-build-it" woodburning fireplace that helps enhance the mood (assuming you know how to start a fire), and many feature patios or balconies. Rooms with patios/balconies adjacent to the 14 acres of vineyards behind the inn are noteworthy romantic possibilities, as are the Executive Suites that boast two-person jetted tubs in their upstairs loft bedrooms. If you don't get a room with a view, don't despair. Vineyard vistas can be enjoyed in the coffee shop, where a continental breakfast buffet is presented every morning. Framed by stained glass windows and warmed by a large brick fireplace, the coffee shop makes for a nice morning retreat. Or simply head to the outdoor deck for an al fresco breakfast. The property's two outdoor swimming pools, Jacuzzi tubs, and complimentary mountain bikes are also available for guests. **One Main Street; (707) 963-9463, (800) 950-8466; www.harvestinn.com; very expensive to unbelievably expensive; minimum-stay requirement on weekends and holidays.**

❤❤ **INK HOUSE, St. Helena** Authenticity is the hallmark of this three-story, yellow Victorian built in 1884. (Some say its real claim to fame is the fact that Elvis Presley filmed *Wild in the Country* here in 1959, but if you are not partial to the King, do not panic—there is no Elvis paraphernalia in sight.) Wrought-iron gates and landscaped gardens surround the home, lending privacy to the wraparound veranda, although the neighboring highway is still visible and audible. Inside, the noise seems to disappear, due in part to the ornate decor that takes over your senses. The main floor offers two cozy parlors brimming with antiques. The seven guest rooms on the main and upstairs floors are all individually decorated with soft colors; lace half-canopies and curtains; queen-size antique wood, brass, or wrought-iron beds; eclectic antiques; and Oriental carpets. All but two rooms feature private baths and none have TVs or telephones. Some touch-ups and structural improvements could be had here and there, but if you're a lover of Victorian decor, this won't matter.

For the best views (and the best kissing), climb upstairs to the observatory at the top of the house. Furnished with comfortably worn wicker chairs and area rugs covering hardwood floors, the room is encircled by windows that allow panoramic views of the vineyards below. In the morning, a delicious array of freshly baked breads and muffins, a hot entrée, and plenty of coffee and tea are served in the dining room at one large table, or by the fireplace in one of the parlors. **1575 St. Helena Highway (Highway 29); (707) 963-3890; www.napavalley.com/inkhouse; moderate to very expensive; minimum-stay requirement on weekends and holidays.**

❤❤❤ **THE INN AT SOUTHBRIDGE, St. Helena** Although it is the younger sibling of the celebrated **MEADOWOOD** property (see review below), The Inn at Southbridge has carved out its own sense of style. Set near the heart of St. Helena on Highway 29, this Mediterranean-style inn has inherited the same high quality and service as its older counterpart (which is saying a lot). All 21 spacious guest rooms boast California-French decor with modern walnut furnishings, wrought-iron lamps, down comforters, wood-burning fireplaces, and butter-yellow walls and sage green accents. Upper-level rooms have vaulted ceilings, and some bathrooms are illuminated by skylights. The overall look is clean-lined and modern, a refreshing change of pace for this region.

If your hearts are set on a quiet country setting, the Highway 29 location is a drawback. (If your budget allows, you should consider Meadowood instead.) However, guests' privacy and comfort are a top priority, and you will not be disappointed. Guest rooms are soundproofed, and continuous landscaping efforts around the property block out some of the traffic noise. Also, the inn is within easy walking distance of downtown St. Helena, numerous wineries, and many restaurants.

As an added bonus, the inn's guests have complimentary use of the beautiful **HEALTH SPA NAPA VALLEY** (1030 Main Street; 707-967-8800;

www.napavalleyspa.com) adjacent to the inn. This new facility features an outdoor lap pool and Jacuzzi tub, a spacious workout room, steam rooms, and some very soothing spa treatments. Enjoy a massage on a private patio bordering the peaceful aromatherapy gardens, or treat yourselves to a healthy grape-seed mud wrap, the spa's signature treatment. There's even a couple's room, where both of you can delight in a massage together. This is truly one of the nicest spas we've seen in the Napa Valley. **1020 Main Street (Highway 29); (707) 967-9400, (800) 520-6800; very expensive to unbelievably expensive; minimum-stay requirement seasonally.**

❀❀❀❀ **MEADOWOOD, St. Helena** Although the address states St. Helena, Meadowood is discreetly tucked into the forested foothills of the Napa Valley, nowhere near a highway or any potential noise (except perhaps the occasional *thwack* of a tennis racquet). This grand dame of the Wine Country is reminiscent of an elegant Cape Cod resort, with its tiers of gables, gray clapboard siding, and sparkling white trim and balustrades. Meadowood believes in the three Rs: refinement, relaxation, and rejuvenation. Manicured croquet lawns, two miles of hiking trails, a nine-hole golf course, seven tennis courts, two swimming pools, a state-of-the-art fitness center, and a full-service health spa are all available for guests.

Eighty-five guest rooms are scattered among the resort's 250 wooded acres. Styles vary from studios to cozy cottages all the way up to multiroom suites. Locations vary too: Some rooms overlook the croquet lawns, numerous cottages are set around the property, and several Hillside Terrace rooms provide the ultimate in privacy. We stayed in one of the Oakview Terrace cottages (conveniently located above the pool and spa area), and found it absolutely wonderful. Most rooms offer private entrances, stone hearths, and wood-burning fireplaces, while private balconies, dimming lights, cathedral ceilings with skylights, and subtle, softly hued interiors create a sense of serenity. Down comforters, gourmet honor bars, and air-conditioning ensure comfort. Even the tile floors in the bathrooms are heated, so as not to startle your toes.

This is one of the most expensive places to stay in the Napa Valley, but a place as grand as Meadowood validates the old cliche, "You get what you pay for." If you are celebrating a special occasion or just want to splurge, Meadowood justifies the expense. **900 Meadowood Lane; (707) 963-3646, (800) 458-8080; www.meadowood.com; unbelievably expensive; minimum-stay requirement on weekends and holidays; recommended wedding site.**

Romantic Suggestion: A visit to Meadowood would not be complete without a dinner at **THE RESTAURANT AT MEADOWOOD** (see Restaurant Kissing).

❦❦❦ **VINEYARD COUNTRY INN, St. Helena** If only this beautiful French-country inn resided a little farther away from the highway, it would be prime kissing territory. Other than its poor location, no detail has been overlooked. All 21 guest rooms are gracious two-room suites, situated in a complex of one- and two-story stucco and tiled buildings. The simply decorated bedrooms have full baths, four-poster or sleigh beds, and sumptuous down comforters; the sitting areas are equally attractive and comfortable, with wet bars, large brick fireplaces, and light mauve and soft-white color schemes. Some rooms even offer private patios and balconies that overlook neighboring vineyards. A generous continental breakfast is served at two-person tables in the sun-filled communal dining room each morning. From this vantage point, you can take in views of the vineyards on one side and a brick courtyard with an outdoor pool and Jacuzzi tub on the other. **201 Main Street (Highway 29); (707) 963-1000; expensive to very expensive; minimum-stay requirement on weekends.**

❦❦ **WINE COUNTRY INN, St. Helena** Situated on a beautifully landscaped knoll overlooking tranquil acres of tree-hemmed vineyards, this large inn has all the makings for a romantic country getaway. The 24 guest rooms, spread throughout three different buildings, are individually decorated with old-fashioned country accents of calico and floral wallpapers, handmade patchwork quilts, homespun local art, and white wainscoting in the recently renovated bathrooms. Most of the rooms feature wood-burning fireplaces and small balconies or decks that view the pastoral surroundings. Three rooms have outdoor hot tubs set out on private decks, and one sports a whirlpool tub in its bathroom. Need we say that we recommend these four rooms for the best in romantic accommodations?

The outdoor swimming pool, bordered by colorful flowers and greenery, affords the best views of the vineyards and stunning evening sunsets. We can't think of a better spot in which to enjoy a newly purchased vintage as you dabble your toes in the cool sparkling water. Mornings feature an extensive buffet breakfast of hot scones and croissants, a hot egg dish, and fresh fruit served in the main house's parlor. **1152 Lodi Lane; (707) 963-7077; www.winecountryinn.com; expensive to unbelievably expensive; minimum-stay requirement on weekends for select rooms.**

❦❦ **ZINFANDEL INN, St. Helena** Set on a relatively quiet street between Highway 29 and the Silverado Trail, this stone-and-wood English Tudor–style home is enhanced by a spouting fountain on the manicured front lawn. Guests can enjoy the forested surroundings that enclose two acres of gardens, an aviary, two gazebos, a small swimming pool, a hot tub, and a fish pond and waterfall.

The three guest rooms exude homespun European ambience. The ground-floor Chardonnay Room features a large stone fireplace, a wood-beamed ceiling, a large jetted tub, and bay windows overlooking the garden. Oak furnishings, a tiled Jacuzzi tub, fireplace, private deck, and stained glass window enhance the upstairs Zinfandel Suite. The third room, Petite Sirah, is indeed petite and not necessarily the best option due to its detached bath. Snuggly down comforters, a complimentary chocolates-and-champagne basket upon arrival, and a lavish full breakfast (served family-style every morning) add to the personal touches here. While not as upscale as many Wine Country properties, the Zinfandel Inn gives travelers a taste of what an old-fashioned bed and breakfast can offer. **800 Zinfandel Lane; (707) 963-3512; www.zinfandelinn.com; expensive to unbelievably expensive; minimum-stay requirement on weekends and holidays.**

Restaurant Kissing

❦❦❦ **GREYSTONE RESTAURANT, St. Helena** Discussions about the CIA occur frequently in the Napa Valley, but it is not because of an abundance of covert activities. Most likely when someone mentions the CIA, it's a reference to the Culinary Institute of America and its fantastic restaurant, Greystone. Located at the northern reaches of the Napa Valley, this stunning restaurant has become a destination in and of itself.

Formerly the Christian Brothers Greystone Winery, this monumental Gothic stone structure first opened its doors in 1889. After being extensively remodeled, Greystone is now serving a dual function as a continuing education center for chefs from around the world and, luckily for us, a first-rate restaurant for visitors from around the world. The atmosphere is entirely festive and usually noisy, with voices resonating off the thick stone walls and high ceiling, but we found the whole experience so memorable that a three-kiss rating is in order. Copper hanging lamps illuminate colorful chairs and beautifully adorned wooden tables, and an open "show" kitchen allows you to watch the chefs in action. Two acres of organic gardens on the premises provide the freshest produce available, and local products are used in abundance (including area wines).

The Mediterranean-influenced menu is designed so guests can enjoy a variety of dishes, and the reasonable prices allow samplings of many flavors. Call them tapas, hors d'oeuvres, or meze, but most of all call them delicious: The list of small tastings is amazing, ranging from Spanish potato tortillas to dolmas to pork kebabs sprinkled with North African spices. If you're in the mood for sharing an entrée, the restaurant's signature paella for two fits the bill. When we paid Greystone a wintertime visit, comfort food topped the list of main courses. Try rotisserie chicken stuffed with sun-dried tomatoes and served with braised lentils and broccoli, Portuguese white bean stew with shellfish, or roasted rack of lamb marinated in pomegranates and red wine. As the seasons change, so does the menu, so you might have to try this place at least four times. Dessert provides the perfect finale. Lavender flan with brandied orange slices, and a pear and date tart with walnut ice cream are two tantalizing selections. It is not always easy to get a reservation at Greystone, but your effort will reap great culinary rewards (not to mention a kiss for choosing such a tasty place). **2555 Main Street (Highway 29); (707) 967-1010; www.ciachef. edu; moderate to expensive; reservations recommended; call for seasonal hours.**

Romantic Note: Mostly during the off-season, Greystone offers some special dinners featuring noted winemakers, chefs, and other food personalities. While these culinary festivities aren't necessarily romantic, they are interesting and informative, and the food and wine are divine.

🌸🌸 **PAIRS PARKSIDE CAFE, St. Helena** Although its earthy atmosphere is more like that of a casual café or espresso bar than a fancy dining establishment, Pairs Parkside Cafe is a lovely place for a light bite or evening dessert and drinks. Votive candles at each simply adorned table illuminate the burnished yellow walls, wrought-iron and wicker chairs, and hardwood floors. New Age music whispers soothingly in the background.

The menu offers a taste of California-Asian cuisine at affordable prices, and service is low-key and friendly. Try the lemon basil–roasted salmon on sweet corn polenta with tomato-caper compote, or the grilled peppered sirloin steak with a blue cheese and caramelized onion tart. The inventive dessert choices include a triple chocolate truffle brownie sundae topped with espresso ice cream, and a coconut milk custard enlivened by an exotic jasmine-tea caramel and strawberries. Unlike so many other St. Helena restaurants, Pairs Parkside Cafe is not about seeing or being seen, and the peacefulness is a welcome change of pace. **1420 Main Street (Highway 29); (707) 963-7566; www.pairscafe.com; moderate; lunch and dinner Thursday–Monday.**

🌸🌸🌸 **PINOT BLANC, St. Helena** Pinot Blanc is one restaurant that's turning heads in the Napa Valley dining scene. An interior painted in brilliant shades of yellow and pale green is home to sensational, upscale French decor and richly upholstered chairs and booths. This highwayside restaurant has undergone several makeovers since it first opened several years ago, and we hope this choice of decor will stay. Although the restaurant is rather large, the eating area is divided into several rooms, and tables in each section are spaced well apart. While all the dining areas are quite romantic, one little room off the main entrance caught our eye. It has only four linen-topped tables set against bright red walls and picture windows. During summer, the outdoor patio, sheltered by trees and hidden from the highway, is a perfectly divine place to park yourselves for a leisurely lunch.

Hit and miss best defines the French-influenced cuisine. Our Provençal appetizer plate, featuring four Mediterranean-inspired dips served with French bread, offered some great and not-so-great tastes. The grilled chicken entrée, presented with a herb potato purée, proved tasty although we wondered if the chicken was actually grilled; it lacked the accompanying texture and smoky flavor. What proved excellent was the bountiful bowl of risotto with wild mushrooms. Despite the inconsistency of our meal, Pinot Blanc remains a beautiful restaurant worth kissing in. **641 Main Street (Highway 29); (707) 963-6191; moderate to expensive; lunch and dinner daily.**

❧❧❧❧ **THE RESTAURANT AT MEADOWOOD, St. Helena** The Restaurant at Meadowood exudes a rejuvenating serenity and quiet elegance rarely found anywhere. Simultaneously spacious and intimate, the dining room has high peaked ceilings, plush upholstered chairs, and exquisite table settings. Ceiling-high windows look out to a perfectly manicured golf course bordered by dense forest. Classical music and a formal but unpretentious staff add to the refinement. Most romantically appealing of all, however, is the exquisite lighting. As the sunlight fades, candles and dimmed lights take over, contributing just the right light for kissing. The extensive wine selection, including 250 vintages from the Napa Valley alone, will please any palate, as will the menu. A variety of French- and Asian-influenced dishes featuring local ingredients are offered either à la carte or on the chef's tasting menu.

Just to give you an idea of what your taste buds can expect, our meal started with a marinated calamari Napoleon punctuated by a lively blend of lime, mint, and fresh coriander. The restaurant's signature local baby-greens salad, uniquely encased by a crispy apple ring, proved as interesting to look at as it was to eat. As for main courses, choose from light seafood preparations such as ahi tuna pepper steak and pancetta-wrapped monkfish to more succulent selections like the unique filet of Limousin beef (a meat similar to tender lamb) and the pan-roasted loin of venison. For dessert we indulged in lemon cream brûlée and a slice of double chocolate cake served warm. Our relaxed, two-hour dinner was worth every minute, the impeccable food worth every calorie, and the wonderful experience worth every penny. **900 Meadowood Lane, at Meadowood; (707) 963-3646, (800) 458-8080; www.meadowood.com; very expensive to unbelievably expensive; reservations recommended; dinner daily, brunch Sunday; recommended wedding site.**

❀❀❀ SHOWLEY'S AT MIRAMONTE, St. Helena

The Yountville–Rutherford–St. Helena area of Wine Country has its share of award-winning restaurants. The gourmet-savvy crowds that flock to this part of the world keep a handful of talented chefs very busy. It is a feat to continually execute smashing meals that please the finicky palates of these visiting connoisseurs. Though not as in-vogue as some of the other restaurants in the area, Showley's does a superior job of keeping up with the demand while providing a low-key, pleasant atmosphere. Inside this large, unadorned white stucco building is a simple, subdued dining room featuring local artwork, French-country touches, and a creative locally inspired menu.

Those who have seen the sensuous (and food-filled) movie *Like Water for Chocolate* should start by indulging in the *Chile en Nogada*, a classic dish from the movie. Other dishes worthy of movie-star status include the pan-seared Columbia River sturgeon with wasabi butter and the grilled tenderloin of pork coated with whole-grain mustard. Portions are generous, and service is congenial and professional. **1327 Railroad Avenue; (707) 963-1200; moderate to expensive; lunch and dinner Tuesday–Sunday.**

❀❀❀❀ TERRA RESTAURANT, St. Helena

Antiques and icons of the past do not automatically promote thoughts or deeds conducive to kissing. But skillfully blend the artifacts of yesteryear with appropriate contemporary flourishes, and you have all the romantic atmosphere you need. Terra Restaurant effortlessly achieves this heartwarming balance.

The century-old stone building has a noble yet unpretentious aura. As you enter, it appears as if you're setting foot in a miniature French castle. The wood beams that loom overhead, the terra-cotta–tiled floor, and the stone walls are complemented by large contemporary paintings and floor-to-ceiling wine racks spanning the back walls. This is a setting fit for award-winning cuisine. The menu lists an exotic assortment of fresh fish and game, accompanied by intriguing sauces and side dishes. The grilled salmon fillet with Thai red curry sauce and the sake-marinated sea bass with shrimp dumplings are both exquisite. You will not be disappointed by the desserts either—the lemon crème brûlée will have you puckering up in no time. **1345 Railroad Avenue; (707) 963-8931; expensive to very expensive; reservations recommended; dinner Wednesday–Monday; closed part of January.**

Romantic Suggestion: For a quieter evening, request a table in the dining room to your left as you enter. The other room receives too much traffic due to the location of the host's desk.

❀❀❀ **TRA VIGNE, St. Helena** In an epicurean region like Wine Country, fine wine goes hand in hand with fine food. Many restaurants in the Napa Valley have achieved success with this concept, while providing ultrastylish dining rooms to further enhance the overall experience. Unfortunately, stylish interiors and romance don't always go together. Some of the most popular places in the valley have incredible food, great wine lists, and chic interiors, but they lack warmth and intimacy. Tra Vigne is a perfect example. Reservations are nearly impossible to get on weekend nights, and even if you can get a table, the noise in the dining room discourages closeness. Still, if you want to dine in a restaurant that everyone has been talking about for years, an evening at Tra Vigne may be in order.

Trailing ivy covers the handsome brick exterior of Tra Vigne, and wrought-iron gates open to a brick courtyard. Inside, 25-foot-tall ceilings, a stunning oak bar, and towering wrought-iron–embellished French windows create a very impressive, almost castle-like setting. The tables are individually spotlighted from above, and every detail, including the food, is attended to with sophistication and panache. Fried skate wing on lemon-infused whipped potatoes, smoked and braised beef short ribs, and a wild mushroom flat-bread pizza are all tantalizing and beautifully presented. A must for chocolate lovers is the truffle cake, a dessert so breathlessly rich you might need extra oxygen just to finish it. **1050 Charter Oak Avenue; (707) 963-4444; expensive; reservations recommended; lunch and dinner daily.**

Romantic Alternative: Although it is not nearly as grand as the interior dining room, a quieter and more casual dining option is Tra Vigne's small outside eatery known as **CANTINETTA DELICATESSEN** (707-963-8888; moderate; lunch and early dinner daily). Wrought-iron tables and chairs are set beneath trees in the small brick courtyard, and a great selection of Italian breads, cheeses, and meats is available. Takeout is also an option if you are planning a picnic.

Outdoor Kissing

❀❀❀ **BALE GRIST MILL STATE HISTORIC PARK, St. Helena** You won't see any grape arbors at this cool, forested park located a short drive and a world away from the area's sun-soaked vineyards. Stroll along restful paths that meander past a gurgling stream hemmed with wildflowers in early spring. One easy trail leads to a restored wooden grist mill with a 36-foot waterwheel; tour the mill together on weekends to experience life in simpler times. Or follow the path through meadow and forest to a kissing spot that nature has saved just for you. **(707) 963-2236, (707) 942-4575; $3 day-use fee per car.** *On the west side of Highway 29, five miles north of downtown St. Helena.*

Wine Kissing

❀❀❀ **BURGESS CELLARS, St. Helena** There are many reasons why you should visit one winery rather than another. If you are a consummate oenophile, you may be lured by the exceptional quality of the grapes at a particular vineyard or by the sterling reputation of an established estate. But it is also a treat when you become acquainted with the offerings of a small up-and-coming winery and can take pride in your discovery. Burgess Cellars, in the hills of Napa Valley, is one of these wineries. In addition to its winemaking craft, Burgess is famous for striking views of the Napa countryside. Your emotions and your taste buds will soar to new heights here. **1108 Deer Park Road; (707) 963-4766; www.burgesscellars.com; open by appointment only.**

❀❀❀ **FLORA SPRINGS WINERY, St. Helena** You'll find this attractive winery far from the hustle of Highway 29, surrounded by spectacular views of rolling vineyards. Several picnic tables are set in a charming brick courtyard, surrounded by copious flowers and dotted by sturdy shade trees. Beyond a stone fountain lies the cozy tasting room, with dark wood accents and friendly, unpretentious service. Sip to your hearts' content, with tastes of Flora Springs' complex merlot, a beautifully blended Sangiovese, or Soliloquy and Trilogy, both blends of several different varieties of fruit. **1978 West Zinfandel Lane; (707) 963-5711; www.florasprings.com; tours and tasting by appointment only.**

Romantic Note: Since tastings are done by (limited) appointments at the winery, a more convenient but less romantic tasting option is to stop by Flora Springs' tasting room (677 St. Helena Highway; 707-967-8033) that's open daily to the public.

❀❀❀ **JOSEPH PHELPS VINEYARD, St. Helena** Wind up and away from the busy Silverado Trail to this large and unpretentious winery with natural wood accents, Asian-style landscaping, and beautiful views. Set on a verdant, secluded hillside, Joseph Phelps is one of the only wineries along the Silverado Trail that escapes traffic noise completely. Wine tastings are served exclusively as part of a tour, but to join in you need only make a reservation. An adjacent outdoor terrace presides over a stunning view of a sparkling lake enclosed by vineyards and rolling hills; it's an inspiring spot for a picnic after taking the tour. **200 Taplin Road; (707) 963-2745, (800) 707-5789; www.jpvwines.com; tours and tasting by appointment only.**

❦❦ **MERRYVALE VINEYARDS, St. Helena** There is nothing particularly outstanding about Merryvale Vineyards in terms of its location or picnic facilities. But the entertaining and extremely educational two-hour seminar ($10 per person) with extensive tasting is well worth the time. Guests learn how to understand and appreciate the taste of a wine's many different components, such as its tannin and sugar content, how it was aged, and what it was stored in. If you are not in the mood for a two-hour-long seminar, visit the attractive tasting bar, which features a nice array of Merryvale wines. On your way out, you may want to check out the charming gift shop filled with delightful souvenirs of the valley. **1000 Main Street (Highway 29); (707) 963-7777, (800) 326-6069; www.merryvale.com; call for seasonal hours, wine seminar Friday–Sunday mornings.**

❦❦❦ **ST. CLEMENT VINEYARD, St. Helena** Neatly cropped vineyards climb toward this picturesque Victorian house perched at the crest of the hillside. The home's original living quarters are filled with antiques and serve as a quaint tasting room. Once you've filled your glasses, wander outside to the porch swing or to the picnic tables arranged around the patio and terraced grounds, and drink in lovely views of the surrounding countryside along with your wine. **2867 St. Helena Highway (Highway 29); (707) 967-3033, (800) 331-8266; www.stclement.com; open 10 a.m.– 5 p.m. daily.**

Romantic Suggestion: In the busy summer months it is a good idea to call ahead to reserve a picnic table. At less busy times, you only need to let your hosts know you are on the premises, then head outside to enjoy the expansive hillside grounds.

Calistoga

There is no other place in the United States quite like Calistoga, California. The entire town is dedicated to the rejuvenation of the body and spirit through an ingenious variety of treatments. We have added a special "Miscellaneous Kissing" section here to highlight spas that offer services just for couples. In addition to spending a day at a spa, devote some time to exploring Calistoga, which has a laid-back atmosphere (even at the height of tourist season) and a fun mix of places to stay, eat, and shop. For additional information about Calistoga, contact the **CALISTOGA CHAMBER OF COMMERCE** (1458 Lincoln Avenue, No. 9, Calistoga, CA 94515; 707-942-6333; www.napavalley.com/calistoga).

Hotel/Bed and Breakfast Kissing

❀❀❀❀ **CHRISTOPHER'S INN, Calistoga** Although Christopher's Inn is located near a jam-packed intersection of Highway 29, you'd never know it. The architect-innkeeper reduced the traffic's impact with numerous soundproofing efforts when he turned these three buildings into an English-country inn. Once you settle into your delightful accommodations for a quiet evening, you will be comforted to find that the street sounds are hardly noticeable.

Gracing most of the 22 beautiful guest rooms are intriguing antiques, high ceilings, private entrances, and gas or wood-burning fireplaces. All rooms have matching Laura Ashley prints that drape the beds and cover the large windows. Receiving rave kissing reviews are the inn's nine newest rooms, all with fireplaces, and seven of which sport fabulous jetted tubs. Those on the ground-floor feature enclosed garden patios as well. Sublime kissing is certain to happen in any of these new accommodations, but romantic favorites include Room 16, known as simply "The Room." Gracing this beautiful blue-and-white retreat is a glass-enclosed jetted tub (with head pillows) that fronts the fireplace, as well as a carved four-poster bed. Another fantastic jetted delight is found in Room 11, where a two-person sunken tub is encircled by glass. Room 12, done in light apricot tones, is another romantic favorite, thanks to its enclosed patio, jetted tub, and snug daybed. If the steep price tag of these new beauties is beyond your budget, opt for the simply outfitted Secret Garden Room. Off on its own, this pocket-size room has a wonderful enclosed patio overflowing with camellias and star jasmine.

Mornings are leisurely at Christopher's, with an expanded continental breakfast delivered to your door in a basket. **1010 Foothill Boulevard (Highway 29); (707) 942-5755; www.chrisinn.com; expensive to very expensive; minimum-stay requirement on weekends.**

❀❀❀❀ **COTTAGE GROVE INN, Calistoga** Whatever decor turns you on to romance—Victorian, a touch of nautical, the fly-fishing motif, or a fantasy of flowers—you'll find it here. Located in an old elm grove at the edge of town, these 16 cottages offer decors of all kinds. Thankfully, the themes aren't overstated or contrived here but, rather, charm the eye with tasteful touches. We stayed in the Fly Fishing Cottage (No. 9), and absolutely loved it—and we don't even fish! Antique fishing rods adorn the walls, tackle baskets are transformed into bedside lamps, a fishing net graces the wood-burning fireplace mantle, and mosquito netting delicately hangs over the king-size bed. The large bathroom holds a separate shower and a two-person Jacuzzi tub that's so deep you might mistake it for a fishing hole. Slip in a mood-setting CD (available for complimentary use from the front desk), open the peekaboo windows to the fireplace, light a candle, and bubble away. Who could ask for more?

All the cottages have impressive features like hardwood floors, Jacuzzi tubs, wet bars, dimming lights and skylights in both bedroom and bath, and soft robes for the two of you. Shaded porches are perfect places to lounge the day away. While decorated differently, each cottage comes with the same accoutrements *d'amour,* although beds range from king- to queen-size. The cottages' roadside location isn't ideal but, luckily, all windows and porches face inward to the quiet courtyard, so traffic noise is minimized. But honestly, these cottages could be in the middle of Manhattan and we wouldn't mind. They have enough charm and personality to make them absolutely lovable anywhere.

A wine-and-cheese reception, featuring several choices of reds and whites, is served in the common area each evening. Come morning, birds chirping at the property's numerous feeders let you know it's also feeding time for the two of you. An expanded continental breakfast buffet is served in the fireside dining room or, if the weather's good, on the outdoor patio. Better yet, take a tray back to your cottage and enjoy the day's first meal on the front porch. Later, work off that buttery croissant by riding through town on the inn's two complimentary 1950s coaster bikes. **1711 Lincoln Avenue; (707) 942-8400, (800) 799-2284; www.cottagegrove.com; very expensive; minimum-stay requirement on weekends and holidays.**

❀❀ **THE ELMS, Calistoga** If you want to wander around downtown Calistoga, this sparkling-white French Victorian bed and breakfast offers a good central location, right next to a quiet residential park and a block away from the main shopping street. Upon arrival, tired guests are welcomed into the snug parlor, with its glowing fireplace and elegant French Victorian antiques. A steep, curved staircase ascends to the second and third floors, where four of the seven guest rooms are located. All of these rooms are a bit on the small side, but you will be extra comfy at night snuggled on top of a fluffy feather bed and under a billowy down comforter. Authentic Victorian decor fills every room, and some have special romantic touches such as canopy beds with white eyelet covers and floral linens, private balconies, window seats, and high ceilings made of pounded tin. All but two rooms have fireplaces.

The three other rooms available at The Elms are located in the separate Carriage House near the main building. Of those in the Carriage House, the Honeymoon Cottage is the largest guest room, and features a private entrance and patio, kitchenette, and wonderful two-person Jacuzzi tub framed by black and white tiles. Even more enticing is the king-size bed overlooking the Napa River right outside your door. Two other rooms, also in the same structure, cater to romantics looking for some "snuggle up and kiss" accommodations. Although small, these two pack a romantic punch with private entrances, one-person Jacuzzi tubs, and lovable beds.

A full breakfast is served downstairs in the main house each morning. Later in the day, a generous assortment of wines and cheeses are offered beside the fire or outside on the patio. **1300 Cedar Street; (707) 942-9476, (800) 235-4316; www.theelms.com; moderate to very expensive; minimum-stay requirement on weekends.**

❦❦❦❦ **FOOTHILL HOUSE, Calistoga** Certain bed and breakfasts have a way of immediately making you feel right at home—and Foothill House is one such place. Perhaps it's the innkeeper's warm welcome, maybe it's the smell of freshly baked cookies in the air, or it could be the way the world seems to slow down the moment you reach the tucked-away-from-the-road property. Whatever the reason, special places like this are worth revisiting time and time again.

The modest exterior of Foothill House gives no indication of the coziness and comfort found in each guest room. There are three rooms in the main house, and each one overflows with everything your sentimental hearts could desire. All have beautiful beds, Laura Ashley prints, and a fireplace or stove complete with chopped wood. The Redwood Room features a two-person whirlpool tub and a private little brick patio. From the king-size bed in the Foothill Lupine Room, look up and see glowing stars (not real ones, but charming nonetheless). The spacious Evergreen Room offers plenty of romantic sitting spots, from a cozy reading nook to a private patio. From the main house, whisk up the steep driveway in the golf cart to a separate cottage that's the property's pièce de résistance. The Quail's Roost cottage wows all those who enter, with its double-sided fireplace and glass-enclosed whirlpool tub for two that overlooks a waterfall cascading from the hillside. Within this 1,000-square-foot space there's also a lovely little kitchen, a delightful reading alcove, and a beautiful four-poster bed. Outside, lounge around on the cushioned chairs on your own sheltered backyard patio.

After a full day of sweeping your way through the wineries and health spas of Calistoga, you'll return to find gourmet appetizers and wine awaiting each afternoon. Later, when you return from dinner, the bed is neatly turned down, and a ceramic canister filled with Foothill House's signature chewy chocolate chip cookies awaits on your pillow next to a mini-size book about love.

In the morning, freshly squeezed orange juice, hot coffee, warm baked goods, a delicious fruit preparation, and an equally engaging egg dish can be delivered to your door in a beautifully prepared breakfast basket or served in the congenial sunroom. As you linger over the last morsel of the French toast soufflé or the Southwest casserole served with corn bread, you will be revitalized for an encore performance of the day before. The super-hospitable innkeeper will gladly help you plan your day if you so desire. **3037 Foothill Boulevard (Highway 128); (707) 942-6933, (800) 942-6933; www.foothillhouse.com; expensive to unbelievably expensive.**

🌑🌑🌒 **LA CHAUMIÈRE, Calistoga** If you aren't looking closely, you might pass by this charming English Cotswold–style home, hidden behind lush foliage and framed by a majestic, vine-covered cedar. With its white-stucco exterior, curved forms, and thatched roof, the home is simply charming. In fact, the entire scene makes you feel as if you're in the countryside rather than in a neighborhood only a block from downtown Calistoga.

Upon arrival, guests are greeted with wine and hors d'oeuvres in the dining area, which is filled with the owner's collection of elephant-themed art and eclectic antiques. Of the three rooms at the inn, the two located in the main home have private baths and more antiques. The handsome and dark Downstairs Room features an exquisite Louis XV bed, a private porch, and a loo you won't soon forget. The black and lavender bathroom features fixtures and tiles from the 1930s, the time when the home was remodeled. The sun-filled Upstairs Room is actually a small suite with two rooms, one of which houses the owner's collection of porcelain clowns.

Even if you aren't newlyweds, you'll want to book the Honeymoon Cottage set behind the house. Built in the early 1900s, the cottage still retains many original rustic touches such as rough-hewn redwood walls and support beams, and a wood-burning fireplace with a petrified-wood hearth. Country-style furnishings, nature-scene paintings, and hardwood floors covered by Southwest-style rugs create a cozy, cabin-like atmosphere. There is a small, sunny kitchen for guests to use, and the private bath (shower only) displays local flair with its walls covered with wooden wine crates.

One of the most interesting features of La Chaumière resides next to the cottage, and is open to all guests. A towering redwood is surrounded by a large deck romantically embellished with a hot tub and hammock. A staircase leads up to a second deck (called The Treehouse) set in the tree's boughs, where, in warmer months, soothing massage treatments can be scheduled for a fee.

Begin breakfast with a fruit course and then move on to such hearty dishes as Italian sausage frittata, homemade lemon pancakes, or Grand Marnier French toast with chicken-apple sausage. This morning repast can be savored at the dining room table with other guests, or outside on the brick patio where the bubbling fountain provides background music and hummingbirds offer fly-by entertainment. **1301 Cedar Street; (707) 942-5139, (800) 474-6800; www.lachaumiere.com; expensive to very expensive; minimum-stay requirement on weekends and holidays.**

❧❧❧ **THE PINK MANSION, Calistoga** Despite the name of this turn-of-the-century Victorian, pink isn't its overall color theme. Sure, the outside is a shade of light pink, but inside the owners are making great efforts to diversify the rooms with additions of neoclassical Bradbury & Bradbury wallpapers done in colors other than you-know-what.

The main parlor, the first room to receive the wallpaper makeover, is decorated with Asian art pieces and an interesting collection of antique angels and cherubs. A curved window seat in the turret remains a favorite kissing spot in this room. Located on the main and second floors, the six guest rooms are each outfitted differently, but all have private baths and TV/VCRs. Views range from garden vistas to stunning panoramas of the mountains. When we visited, the Angel and Oriental Rooms were being remodeled and are certain to be the stars for the romantic set. Besides each offering 800 square feet of space, these two rooms have 12-foot-high vaulted ceilings, king-size beds, wood-burning fireplaces, and Jacuzzi tubs à deux.

To entice you out of your warm bed, a bountiful breakfast of fresh scones, baked apples or poached pears, and Norweigan pancakes or baked French toast is served in the homey dining room. After breakfast, you'll likely want to sneak away to the inviting indoor lap pool, attractively set in an airy sunroom equipped with a fireplace to keep things toasty. A pair of lovebirds, some finches, and a curious parrot keep you company as you swim. Warmer water awaits outside in a hot tub tucked among the backyard greenery. **1415 Foothill Boulevard (Highway 128); (707) 942-0558, (800) 238-7465; www.pinkmansion.com; moderate to unbelievably expensive; minimum-stay requirement on weekends and holidays.**

❧❧❧ **SCOTT COURTYARD, Calistoga** A thoroughly wonderful experience awaits you at Scott Courtyard, located in a residential neighborhood just two blocks from downtown Calistoga. The six private suites are located in four pastel yellow cottages clustered around a pool and garden courtyard. Each room is decorated differently, but they all have a combination of art deco style and tropical flair accentuated by modern furnishings and eclectic antiques and artwork. Hardwood floors and black-and-white striped awnings make these accommodations slightly reminiscent of 1940s Hollywood bungalows.

Those looking for relaxation can lounge by the pool on sunny days. Wine and cheese are offered every afternoon, and full breakfasts are served at individual bistro tables in the main house's dining room. There seems to be something for everyone here, although conservative tastes may be taken aback by the wild style and bold colors. On the other hand, if you are looking for a fun and different bed and breakfast, this is it. In a business where traditional Victorian, country, or contemporary decor rules, Scott Courtyard's unconventional style is a breath of fresh air. **1443 Second Street; (707) 942-0948, (800) 942-1515; www.scottcourtyard.com; moderate to expensive; minimum-stay requirement on weekends.**

❤️❤️❤️ **SILVER ROSE INN & SPA, Calistoga** Perched on an oak-studded knoll a discreet distance from the busy Calistoga spa scene, the Silver Rose Inn & Spa sits on 20 acres of attractive landscaping that blends in nicely with the nearby foothills and trees. There are two handsome buildings, Inn the Vineyard and Inn on the Knoll, each hosting an array of guest rooms. In between these two buildings are two tennis courts, a putting green, and an outdoor pool shaped like a bottle of wine. Behind the Inn on the Knoll is another outdoor pool with an impressive rock garden and a flowing waterfall.

Inn on the Knoll has nine simple but nicely decorated fantasy-theme rooms. The Safari Room features wall-to-wall jungle prints and a net canopy over the bed, while the Western Room offers a terra-cotta floor, a corner Jacuzzi tub, a vaulted ceiling, and a smattering of cowboy paraphernalia. Inn the Vineyard houses an additional 11 rooms that continue the theme concept, although they are marred by a rather contrived, prefabricated ambience. Though the embellishments can be a bit much, the rooms are exceedingly comfortable, roomy, and immaculate. Three suites have two-person Jacuzzi tubs, while six feature gas fireplaces and pleasant views of the nearby vineyards. A rather sparse continental breakfast of fresh fruits, breads, and muffins is served in the inn's spacious common area near a colossal stone fireplace each morning.

The Silver Rose Inn & Spa has a small but charming in-house spa that offers a wide range of services. The half-hour massage, mud water treatment, and herbal body wrap are capable of relaxing even the tensest travelers. **351 Rosedale Road; (707) 942-9581, (800) 995-9381; www. silverrose.com; expensive to unbelievably expensive; minimum-stay requirement on weekends.**

Restaurant Kissing

❦❦❦ **ALL SEASONS CAFÉ AND WINE SHOP, Calistoga** With its delightful menu and classic interior, this old-style storefront café is an enchanting place to enjoy a romantic dinner for two. Colorful art pieces, white linen–topped tables, large windows, a black-and-white checkerboard floor, and an old-fashioned bar lend depth to this cozy restaurant, reminiscent of a '40s café. Tables are packed in tightly around the edges; try the tables in the restaurant's center for more elbow room. Entrées are exceptionally light and fresh, and portions are more than generous. We shared the delicious house-smoked-salmon salad and the Chilean sea bass covered by a mild mango-chipotle-mint salsa. A rich espresso pot de crème ended our meal on an up note. **1400 Lincoln Avenue; (707) 942-9111; moderate to expensive; lunch Thursday–Tuesday; dinner daily.**

❦❦ **BRANNAN'S GRILL, Calistoga** This architecturally stunning restaurant seems a bit too stylish to be set along Calistoga's "down-home" main street, but its modern touches are a refreshing change of pace. Embellished by metal and wood rafters, a beautiful mahogany wood bar, and stylish lighting, the vast interior may also seem too spacious for seduction; luckily, there are the booths. Yes, booths, the saving romantic grace for large restaurants like this. Hide yourselves away in a high-backed booth near the bar, or look out onto the restaurant from one of the upper-level booths. (If you can't get one of these special spots, the tables are reasonably spaced apart.) Our favorite spot is that quintessential corner booth by the fireplace; just be sure to avoid those booths that front the open kitchen.

The varied menu, featuring small and large plates, doesn't quite complement the eye-popping architecture. Our entrée of short ribs atop pumpkin risotto proved to be a hit-and-miss dish (the risotto excellent, the ribs dry). Hopefully the diverse menu, concentrating on American cuisine with regional flavors, will even out as the restaurant's kitchen gains momentum. In the meantime, snuggle in your booth and enjoy the sights, each other, and a dessert. Our gooey banana spoon bread sent us soaring! **1374 Lincoln Avenue; (707) 942-2233; moderate to expensive; lunch and dinner daily.**

❦❦ **CALISTOGA INN RESTAURANT & BREWERY, Calistoga** The Calistoga Inn Restaurant is like two different restaurants, depending on the time of year when you visit. In summer, lunch and dinner are served on the garden patio; in cooler months, the antique-filled main floor of the inn serves as the dining room. The same menu applies both seasons, and microbrews from the small Napa Valley Brewing Company (located on the premises) are always available. You'll find hearty salads, traditional sandwiches, and plenty of grill plates, including Jamaican jerk chicken, Missouri-style spare ribs, and a tri-top sirloin cured in the brewery's Calistoga red ale. Service is friendly but not always prompt, and tables are packed in like wine bottles on a rack. **1250 Lincoln Avenue, at the Calistoga Inn; (707) 942-4101; www.napabeer.com; moderate; lunch and dinner daily.**

Romantic Warning: The low rates for the 18 rooms at the CALISTOGA INN (inexpensive) are unheard of in Wine Country, but we cannot recommend staying here. Noise from the main-floor kitchen, dining room, and bar is a problem. Also, all the rooms here have shared baths.

🍃🍃 WAPPO BAR & BISTRO, Calistoga

Try coming here on a warm summer day, since Wappo's courtyard patio is the most romantic in town. Tucked between two buildings, the brick-lined patio receives the cool covering of the trees and a vine-covered trellis. As an added bonus, this al fresco spot is sufficiently sheltered from distractions so you can whisper sweet nothings without competing with the roar of traffic. If the day is gray, the interior will do for a quiet dinner. The building's historic nature shines through with a wood-beamed ceiling, large multipaned windows, and mirrors framed by old barn wood. Some interesting accents, such as henna-painted lampshades, help round out the rustic look. For better or worse, the banquette seats—set against the wainscoting without back cushions—will have you sitting up straight to eat.

Dimension in presentation, flavor, and variety mark the international menu that draws on influences from India, Southeast Asia, and Mexico. Our culinary journey started in Vietnam with delicate spring rolls dipped in a spicy and hot *nam pla* sauce. From here we ventured to the Middle East by filling our forks with flavorful Lebanese lemon chicken. Next, it was on to India as the Chilean sea bass with garam masala, mint chutney, and basmati rice graced our table. We ended in a traditional American fashion with coconut cream pie, piled high with cool whipped cream. No matter whether you eat inside or out, these flavors will sit well with your taste buds. **1226 Washington Street; (707) 942-4712; www.napa valley.com/restrnts/wappo; moderate to expensive; lunch and dinner Wednesday–Monday.**

Wine Kissing

🍃🍃 CLOS PEGASE, Calistoga

Clos Pegase is a dramatic, terra-cotta–colored winery named after Pegasus, the winged horse of Greek mythology. As the story goes, Pegasus brought forth wine and art into the world when his hooves unleashed the sacred Spring of the Muses. The water irrigated the vines and inspired the poets who drank of them. We can't guarantee that you will be moved to verse, but you can enjoy the fine wine here and debate whether the neoclassical Greek architecture and bold, abstract sculptures enhance the surroundings. **1060 Dunaweal Lane; (707) 942-4981, (800) 366-8583; www.clospagase.com; open 10:30 a.m.–5 p.m. daily.**

❤❤❤ **SCHRAMSBERG VINEYARDS, Calistoga** It is no exaggeration to say that there are dozens of wonderful wineries in the Napa Valley. One of the more distinctive and beautiful is Schramsberg. Set in the Napa Valley highlands, this 1862 estate is full of historical and enological interest. The stone buildings of the winery are located far enough away from the traffic of the main road to provide quiet refuge. Because only private tours are allowed, your introduction to the world of champagne will be sparklingly intimate. After you roam through the labyrinth of underground cellars that were tunneled into the rocky ground years ago, be certain to stop at the wine shop. By this point, you will have learned almost all the secrets of *methode champenoise*, so purchase your own bit of effervescent history to share. **1400 Schramsberg Road; (707) 942-2414; www.schramsberg. com; tours and tasting by appointment only.**

Miscellaneous Kissing

❤❤❤ **LAVENDER HILL SPA, Calistoga** Because Lavender Hill Spa specializes in treatments for couples, intimacy and privacy are at the top of its list, and the calming atmosphere adds to a highly romantic experience. With a variety of treatments to choose from, you'll be able to find the right combination for rejuvenation and renewed peace of mind. We highly recommend the volcanic-mud bath, which is actually a wonderful mixture of soft ash, sea kelp, and essential oils, followed by a warm blanket wrap and light foot massage. These treatments take place in the bathhouse, which is fully insulated for noise protection and warmth. Side-by-side mineral bathtubs and two tables for the after-bath blanket wrap and foot massage are perfectly suited for couples. We also urge you to try the hour-long massage, which was everything we had hoped and then some. The professional staff works wonders on tense muscles, and the overall result is simply amazing. An hour or a day at Lavender Hill Spa is something you and your bodies will remember forever. **1015 Foothill Boulevard (Highway 29); (707) 942-4495, (800) 528-4772; www.lavenderhillspa.com; prices vary, depending on the service.**

❀❧ **LINCOLN AVENUE SPA, Calistoga** Besides offering spa services that range from a tranquillizing massage to an invigorating rubdown (both will knead away any anxieties you may have brought with you), the staff members here are also skilled at foot reflexology and acupressure "face-lifts." You can custom-design services that fit your personal preferences, such as body mud treatments, herbal facials, and more. As for couples' massage, the spa's claim to fame is the side-by-side herbal blanket wraps done on a specially designed table for two. While you may be too relaxed to notice, we found the spa to be a bit worn out, and the tall rock walls said "medieval castle" rather than "cozy spa." **1339 Lincoln Avenue; (707) 942-5296; www.lincolnavenuespa.com; prices vary, depending on the service.**

Sonoma Valley

Unlike the towns of the Napa Valley, which are bisected by the St. Helena Highway, Sonoma Valley towns are set off the highway and, consequently, feel more rural and are often less accessible. If you're in a hurry, this might be an inconvenience. If you're touring at a slower pace, however, you'll realize that the lack of nearby traffic creates a climate that is much more conducive to romance. More information about the Sonoma Valley is available from the **SONOMA VALLEY VISITORS BUREAU** (453 First Street East, Sonoma, CA 95476; 707-996-1090; www.sonomavalley.com).

Sonoma

Despite its tourist appeal and bustling popularity, the town of Sonoma is a prime place for a romantic rendezvous. The village itself wraps around a park-like square shaded by sprawling oak trees and sculpted shrubbery. This central area is peppered with park benches, flowering walkways, a fountain, and a duck pond. Beyond the square's perimeter, branching out in every direction, is an array of shops, restaurants, and wineries that have retained much of their original charm.

Romantic Warning: As is the case in most Wine Country towns, summer crowds in Sonoma can be overpowering all week long and unbearable on the weekends. Off-season is the best time to find a degree of solitude as well as cooler, more comfortable weather conditions.

Hotel/Bed and Breakfast Kissing

❀❀ **EL DORADO HOTEL, Sonoma** What the El Dorado Hotel lacks in warmth and personality, it makes up for with privacy, comfort, and convenience. For some travelers, these factors are enough to inspire romantic inclinations. Located at the edge of Sonoma's town square, this hotel has 26 modestly proportioned rooms with four-poster iron beds, pale peach bedspreads, terra-cotta–tiled or hardwood floors, TVs displayed on the dressers, and bare walls (except for mirrors uniquely framed by branches). The rooms lack decoration and have a minimalist feel, which isn't cold—but then again, it isn't warm and intimate, either. French doors in most rooms open to small patios that overlook either the hotel's inner courtyard and its heated pool or the nearby town square. Continental breakfast for two and a split of wine are also included with your stay, and most of the typical hotel amenities are provided for your comfort. **405 First Street West; (707) 996-3030, (800) 289-3031; www.hoteleldorado.com; moderate to very expensive; minimum-stay requirement on weekends and holidays seasonally.**

Romantic Warning: Rooms facing the street and town square provide great views, but can be extremely noisy. (The vocal rooster in the town square doesn't help much either.) If you are a light sleeper, we highly recommend a courtyard-view room and/or bringing a pair of heavy-duty earplugs.

Romantic Note: Located in the El Dorado Hotel, PIATTI RESTAURANT (707-996-2351; moderate to expensive; lunch and dinner daily) is a chain restaurant known for its bustling atmosphere and fresh, well-prepared Italian cuisine. This location is no different from the others except that it is incredibly convenient if you are a guest at the hotel.

❤❤❤❦ MACARTHUR PLACE, Sonoma

Sonoma's newest addition to the hospitality scene is a perfect example of how the old blends in well with the new. This magnificent, lush property holds two stunning buildings: a circa-1860 Victorian manor house (reputed to be one of the oldest homes in Sonoma) and its adjacent barn. Both have been magnificently restored in recent years to their present glory. Add to this several new buildings that complement the two original structures, as well as mature gardens, a small swimming pool, and a quiet, in-town setting, and you have a place more than worthy of a romantic getaway.

Thirty-five guest accommodations comprise the historic Manor House, six nearby cottages, and one single-suite cottage. Each room displays an individual charm that's certain to inspire a smooch or two. Upscale country decor, soothing solid color schemes, magnificent beds with designer floral duvets, and plenty of windows are common to all. Furnishings range from antique pine to whitewashed woods, and signature bathroom features include taupe and white ceramic-tiled floors and walk-in showers.

Guest rooms in the cottages (four rooms to a two-story cottage in most cases) are similar in size and layout, and afford guests more privacy in their comings and goings. The classic Manor House's selling points are many: unique room layouts, private patios in some rooms, enormous windows, and a sense of history not found in the more modern structures.

Although all rooms at MacArthur Place are romantically appealing, we must admit to falling in love with the Burris Suite, a spacious room done in a soft dusty rose color, located on the second floor of the Manor House. Two French doors lead to a balcony overlooking the gardens, classical botanical art adorns the walls, and an elegant four-poster bed resides beside a comfortable sitting area. You can also survey the garden from the windowside claw-foot tub in the bathroom. Another romantic favorite on the property is the Garden Suite, which, unlike the other six cottages, is the only free-standing accommodation. It's perfect for couples seeking the utmost in privacy. Natural light floods the large, one-story suite, highlighting the king-size bed, sleigh daybed, and spacious bath with jetted tub for two.

Although there are no guest rooms in the barn, a continental breakfast is served in this building's Tack Room each morning. Tractor-size doors open to this charming space filled with western art, antique farm equipment, wood floors, and towering ceilings. Enjoy your morning meal by the fireplace or on the barn's terrace overlooking the gardens. Later in the day, lounge by the pool that serves as the property's centerpiece, stroll along the grounds to smell the flowers, or rent a bicycle (rental prices start at $7 per person) and journey through nearby neighborhoods. When you come back, re-invigorate with a massage at **THE SPA** (707-933-3193; rates vary, depending on the service), located adjacent to the pool. After all that exercise and a soothing massage, you'll have no problem kissing the night away at this fabulous place. **29 East MacArthur Street; (707) 938-2929, (800) 722-1866; www.macarthurplace.com; expensive to unbelievably expensive; minimum-stay requirement on weekends and holidays; recommended wedding site.**

Romantic Note: At press time, MacArthur Place was adding 30 additional rooms, plus converting the Tack Room into a full-time restaurant called **SADDLES** (moderate to expensive; breakfast, lunch, and dinner daily). Open both to guests and the public, the restaurant will serve up California-western cuisine.

❤❤ **RAMEKINS, Sonoma** Kissin' and cookin', two elements essential to romance, blend together quite beautifully at this unique bed and breakfast. The large, unadorned, Mediterranean-style building resides just a few blocks from Sonoma's town square. Inside, you'll find a culinary school downstairs and six delightful and luxurious guest rooms upstairs. Not surprisingly, food decor is a theme throughout, ranging from colorful modern prints of eggplants and tomatoes to whimsical banisters sculpted and painted to resemble asparagus. An underlying English-country theme brings in lovely antiques and old-fashioned cooking utensils and gadgets.

Whipping up some romance on your own is easy in one of the spacious, sunny guest rooms. Elegant English-country decor, highlighted by beautiful wood or four-poster beds, pine chests, textured yellow walls, and rich floral duvets, is complemented by modern bathrooms featuring tiled walk-in showers and oversize ceramic sink bowls. Large windows, antique cooking utensils, and, once again, whimsical food art add a distinctive touch. Some rooms also feature balconies, and most come with either king- or queen-size beds. One room has two twin beds and is not recommended for kissing purposes.

A continental breakfast, including pastries made by Ramekin's official pastry chef, is served at a quiet upstairs dining table. Downstairs, there's a flurry of activity as apron-clad culinary students head from kitchen to kitchen with notebooks in hand. **450 West Spain Street; (707) 933-0452; www.ramekins.com; moderate to unbelievably expensive; minimum-stay requirement on weekends and holidays.**

Romantic Suggestion: Couples who relish kissing and cooking together are the clientele best suited for Ramekins. This may be a bed and breakfast, and a lovely one at that, but the orientation is different from most. If cooking together sounds like the right romantic recipe, a variety of classes are geared to cooks of all levels. Topics range from kitchen survival to soups and stocks to pastry preparation. Contact Ramekins for a class catalog and more details.

☙☙❧ **SONOMA MISSION INN & SPA, Sonoma** The usual spa scenario—rigorously scheduled activities, limited quantities of diet food, and militant aerobics instructors—does not constitute a romantic getaway. Nor is it what the Sonoma Mission Inn & Spa promotes. Although a variety of workout classes and spa-style treatments are offered and a state-of-the-art fitness facility is available, guests choose for themselves the type of spa experience they desire—the only limitation is the price tag.

Because this is a place with loads of activities, you probably won't spend a lot of time in your room—which is to your advantage, since many of the guest accommodations are just average. Remember: The *real* reason to come here is to use the full-service spa or for dinner at **THE GRILLE** (see Restaurant Kissing). Many of the 198 rooms, spread throughout the large property in separate buildings, are merely hotel-like with pastel pink and beige interiors—not exactly what you expect from the grand, rose-colored, Mission-style exterior of the original building and its elegantly appointed lobby. When choosing a room, request one of the Historic Inn rooms, appropriately found in the original building. These rooms may be on the small side, but they do have more character with floral bedspreads, half-canopies, and wood shutters; some rooms also feature wood-burning marble fireplaces. Larger suites, available throughout the property, are quite lovely but also very expensive. (Be sure to ask for midweek and off-season rates; they won't be volunteered unless you inquire.) At the time of our visit, 30 new suites were in the beginning phases of construction; only time will tell if these suites will be kiss-worthy accommodations. If you really want to splurge on spa treatments, and a full-service property suits your needs, Sonoma Mission Inn & Spa may be just right for you. **18140 Sonoma Highway (Highway 12); (707) 938-9000, (800) 862-4945; www. sonomamissioninn.com; very expensive to unbelievably expensive; minimum-stay requirement on weekends.**

Romantic Note: To give you an idea of what to expect, massage prices start at $89 per person, and "The Revitalizer," a one-hour-and-45-minute package including an herbal body scrub, lymphatic massage, and hot linen body wrap, costs $179 per person. (You will probably end up spending more on à la carte spa treatments than on your standard guest room, which is already expensive.) However, the spa staff is expertly trained and these pampering treatments will definitely put you in the mood for romance.

☙☙ **THISTLE DEW INN, Sonoma** Just a block away from Sonoma's busy town center, this restful retreat is comprised of two turn-of-the-century homes. The common area and dining room in the main house are appointed with Arts and Crafts–style antique furniture mixed with contemporary effects, and warmed by a wood-burning fireplace. The six guest rooms, divided between the two homes, are filled with more Arts and Crafts antiques, handmade Amish patchwork quilts, queen-size beds, bright sponge-painted walls, and private bathrooms. The home farthest from the road is where real romance (or, at least, the rooms with the most romantic perks) can be found. All four rooms here boast private entrances, one has a gas fireplace as its romantic highlight, and two feature gas fireplaces coupled with whirlpool tubs, wonderful for warm, bubbling ambience.

Mornings at the inn are a treat, and might feature banana-buckwheat pancakes, fruit-filled oven-baked Dutch babies, mushroom and Brie omelets, or cinnamon-raisin French toast. After breakfast, cactus lovers may want to inspect the inn's greenhouse, where the innkeeper has collected hundreds of different species of this prickly plant. Later, borrow two of the inn's complimentary bikes for a day of exploring Sonoma and its environs. Evenings at Thistle Dew Inn are set aside for hors d'oeuvres and pleasant conversation near the warmth of the stone fireplace. **171 West Spain Street; (707) 938-2909, (800) 382-7895; www.thistledew.com; moderate to very expensive.**

❦❦ **TROJAN HORSE INN, Sonoma** Weary wine tasters immediately feel welcomed upon entering this turn-of-the-century Victorian farmhouse. The spacious, sun-filled parlor holds a pleasant mixture of contemporary and antique country furnishings, and the glowing hearth creates a warm atmosphere as you visit with the hospitable innkeepers over evening refreshments. Even though this home borders Highway 12, the clean, comfortable, and colorful surroundings create an environment where the outside world doesn't matter.

The six standard guest rooms, all with private baths and contemporary and antique furnishings, vary in decor and mood. Three standouts include the airy and feminine Bridal Veil Room, with a white Battenburg lace canopy over the bed and a woodstove in the corner; the sensual and inviting Victorian Room, dressed in light and dark shades of burgundy; and the Grape Arbor Room, adorned in a soft silver-lavender hue and romantically equipped with a queen-size bed fronting a gas fireplace and a two-person jetted tub in the bathroom.

In the morning, a full gourmet country breakfast ensures a hearty start to a full day of wine tasting. Savory and sweet dishes rotate daily and may include spinach and mushroom quiche, banana-walnut pound cake, or orange zest French toast. Snacks are served later in the evening and, if the sun cooperates, can be enjoyed on the garden patio below the home. Last, but not least, there's also an outdoor Jacuzzi tub sheltered by an ancient bay tree in the backyard. **19455 Sonoma Highway (Highway 12); (707) 996-2430, (800) 899-1925; www.trojanhorseinn.com; moderate to expensive; minimum-stay requirement on weekends.**

❦❦ **VICTORIAN GARDEN INN, Sonoma** Petite but extraordinary grounds envelop the Victorian Garden Inn, set in a peaceful Sonoma neighborhood only blocks from the town square. Fountains and white iron benches dot the glorious garden, and a trellised brick walkway leads to the front door. If the garden doesn't provide enough cooling shade on summer afternoons, a swim in the pool behind the house should do the trick, or you can simply retreat to your air-conditioned room. Much attention has been lavished on the garden, which, as the name indicates, is the centerpiece here. We only wish more attention could be paid to the house, which is a lovely Victorian farmhouse in need of a few touch-ups and a fresh coat of paint.

Four comfortable guest rooms are available on the property; however, we only recommend the three detached units, since the room in the main house does not have its own bath. Top o' the Tower, housed in an old water tower, is the least expensive of the detached units. Although this room is quite small and equipped with only a shower, it is ultraprivate, and the high ceilings and pastel blue decor help to create the illusion of more space. The pretty Garden Room features a gas fireplace, a cut-lace duvet, wicker furnishings, and a claw-foot tub. We also like the handsome, cabin-like Woodcutter's Cottage, with its high, open-beam ceiling, hunter-green interior, claw-foot tub, and wood-burning fireplace.

A California-style continental breakfast, featuring plenty of locally grown fruit, granola, fresh cherry juice, and pastries, is set out in the main dining room every morning. Guests are welcome to take breakfast back to their room or partake on the patio next to the garden. **316 East Napa Street; (707) 996-5339, (800) 543-5339; www.victoriangardeninn.com; expensive to very expensive; minimum-stay requirement on weekends.**

Restaurant Kissing

❀❀ **DELLA SANTINA'S, Sonoma** A little slice of Italy is tucked behind a stone facade, not far from Sonoma's main square. Opera music fills the tiny front dining room where 11 tables are packed in, each adorned with crisp white linens and a yellow rose. Whitewashed walls featuring framed antique doilies lend a nostalgic touch, while above the gas fireplace, beautiful portraits of the owner's children give the restaurant a homespun feel. Such familiarity with family and friends isn't new here; the owner greets locals with a kiss on the cheek. For those who'd rather kiss each other, try requesting one of the four tables in the second dining area hidden within a covered interior courtyard. Summertime dining on the large outdoor patio out back is another ideal choice, although tables are tight here, too.

Straightforward and traditional Italian dishes grace the menu, ranging from pesto tortellini to spit-roasted chicken garnished with fresh herbs. Prices are reasonable, and they become even more so if you order the Della Santina Cena, a special dinner for two featuring salad, pasta, and your choice of a rotisserie entrée. Desserts dazzle, especially the rum-soaked panna cotta that packs a punch or two. **133 East Napa Street; (707) 935-0576; moderate to expensive; lunch and dinner daily.**

❀❀❀ **THE GENERAL'S DAUGHTER, Sonoma** Set in the heart of Sonoma Valley, this massive yellow Victorian building houses a show-stopping restaurant known as The General's Daughter. Inside, the illusion of coziness is captured by large plants and half walls that help conceal and separate the dining rooms. Soothing shades of yellow, cream, or peach brighten up each dining space, while life-size paintings of farm scenes and farm animals add a whimsical touch. After sunset, twinkling chandeliers provide a soothing, soft glow. In the warmer months, you can enjoy your meal on the outdoor patio, which unfortunately faces the parking lot, or at a more private table on the restaurant's wraparound porch.

Starters and entrées include such exceptional dishes as grilled pork chops accompanied by a tomato–ancho chile mole; fresh pasta topped with butternut squash, baby spinach, and Gorgonzola cheese; and a mixed grill of Chilean sea bass and tiger prawns accented by a red pepper and pickled ginger salsa. For dessert, anything goes. We went with the cheese blintzes in blueberry sauce, which proved mighty fine. **400 West Spain Street; (707) 938-4004; www.thegeneralsdaughter.com; moderate to expensive; lunch and dinner daily, brunch Sunday.**

❤❤❤ **THE GRILLE, Sonoma** The SONOMA MISSION INN & SPA (see Hotel/Bed and Breakfast Kissing) is one the most impressive structures in the valley. The warm pink exterior of this Mission-style beauty is enhanced by perfectly maintained grounds. Expensive cars typically line the circular drive fronting the inn, an indication of this property's clientele.

As you enter through the casually elegant lobby, take note of the Lobby Bar, where you can sit fireside and enjoy after-dinner drinks. The Grille is slightly more formal than the lobby, but its sophistication is without pretense. Recessed lighting, pale peach walls, candles and fresh flowers at every table, and crisp white table linens create an environment that is both refined and serene.

A distinct French influence is evident in the menu, although locally grown products are the main attraction and, in true spa tradition, several light options are available (calories and fat grams are listed). Unlike typical spas, however, even the lightest dishes are flavorful and extremely good. The grilled Petaluma chicken breasts with forest mushrooms and braised greens is excellent, as is the roasted sea bass wrapped in eggplant. If you aren't too put off by the scale provided in the bathroom (reminding you that this is a spa), consider one of The Grille's brilliantly presented desserts. **18140 Sonoma Highway (Highway 12), at Sonoma Mission Inn & Spa; (707) 938-9000, (800) 862-4945; www.sonomamissioninn.com; expensive to very expensive; dinner daily, brunch Sunday.**

Wine Kissing

❤❤❤❤ **BUENA VISTA WINERY, Sonoma** Gather your picnic goodies in Sonoma Plaza before heading off to this historical winery. We suggest filling up your basket with award-winning sourdough bread, local deli meats and mustards, and scrumptious pesto jack from the **SONOMA CHEESE FACTORY** (2 Spain Street, in Sonoma Plaza; 707-996-1931; www.sonoma jack.com; inexpensive; open daily). Once you have provisions, a smooth chardonnay and a peaceful picnic spot are all you'll need, and both can be found at Buena Vista. Rugged stone walls covered with tangles of ivy lend an ancient feel to this winery. Established in 1857, it is one of California's oldest. A bevy of picnic tables is set by a woodsy creek and on a hillside terrace, all shaded by sweet-scented eucalyptus trees. The air-conditioned tasting room offers a small selection of fine gifts to commemorate your time together, and a mezzanine gallery showcases local art. **18000 Old Winery Road; (707) 938-1266, (800) 926-1266; www.buenavista winery.com; open 10:30 a.m.–5 p.m. daily; recommended wedding site.**

❧❧❧ **GLORIA FERRER CHAMPAGNE CAVES, Sonoma** As the name suggests, the focus here is on champagne, that effervescent drink that almost always goes hand in hand with special occasions. Regardless of the occasion, any afternoon here is sure to be special. Gloria Ferrer's stunning Spanish-style villa is set a half mile from the highway at the base of gently rolling hills. After taking a tour of the caves and learning how fine champagne is created, stay and taste some. You can purchase a full glass of sparkling wine in the spacious tasting room, where plenty of two-person marble-topped tables sit beside a crackling fire. Or you can sit, sip, and smooch outside on the vast veranda that faces acre upon acre of grapes. **23555 Carneros Highway (Highway 121); (707) 996-7256, (800) 799-7256; www.gloriaferrer.com; wines sold by the glass; open 10:30 a.m.–5:30 p.m. daily.**

Romantic Note: Tour times vary from day to day. Your best bet is to call the day you plan to visit to find out about times.

❧❧ **VIANSA WINERY, Sonoma** Viansa, a winery run by the established Sebastiani winery family, offers not only fine wine but an extensive Italian marketplace where you can purchase gourmet picnic necessities and plenty of edible mementos of your time spent in Wine Country. Fresh herbs and vegetables complement pâtés, salads, and other tasty Italian treats, all made right on the premises. Try one of the freshly baked focaccia sandwiches and a luscious dessert, followed by a smooth cappuccino (if you've already tasted enough wine). You can enjoy this small feast inside the casual, brightly lit Italian marketplace, but the attractive grounds outside beckon. Numerous picnic tables are set beneath a grape trellis, overlooking young grapevines and a 90-acre waterfowl preserve. **25200 Arnold Drive; (707) 935-4700, (800) 995-4740; www.viansa.com; open 10 a.m.–5 p.m. daily.**

Romantic Note: The picnic area is reserved for people who purchase their picnic items from Viansa.

Glen Ellen

Glen Ellen, a quiet rural community located just off Highway 12, is so small that there isn't much to say about it except that the relaxed country atmosphere is a welcome change of pace from city life or even life in one of the larger Wine Country towns. Luckily, there are some wonderful restaurants and bed and breakfasts here where you can stop, stay, and savor the quietness.

Hotel/Bed and Breakfast Kissing

❤️❤️ **BELTANE RANCH, Glen Ellen** A working farm, vineyard, and down-home bed and breakfast are effectively combined at this Wine Country destination, making it a truly countrified place to stay. A dusty driveway off the main road winds up to the yellow wood-frame farmhouse set in the midst of gentle hills and green pastures. It is primarily the setting of this 1,600-acre ranch that makes it ideal for long, lazy afternoons and quiet, loving evenings.

Of the five guest rooms in the century-old, modestly renovated main home, the three upstairs are the most desirable. Guests in these rooms can sit on the wraparound deck and eat a hearty breakfast while surveying the front yard's lush garden. (Breakfast can also be enjoyed in the country-style kitchen or in the garden.) Although none of the rooms in the main home are sophisticated or endearing, they do offer unmistakable coziness and country-style comfort. The new Garden Cottage is more appealing (and more romantic) than the other rooms, thanks to its private, separate location, tucked-away garden, colorful decor, and, best of all, a two-way silent-butler pantry where breakfast is left for you in the morning. **11775 Sonoma Highway; (707) 996-6501; moderate to very expensive; no credit cards; minimum-stay requirement on holiday weekends.**

❤️❤️❤️❤️ **GAIGE HOUSE INN, Glen Ellen** Stunning, simply stunning, is the only way to describe the rooms inside this impressive Italianate Victorian. Capturing the beauty and simplicity of Balinese and Southeast Asian decor and skillfully blending it with a varied collection of antiques and modern artwork, the innkeepers have transformed the Gaige House into a luxurious boutique inn that is one of the finest in the Sonoma Valley.

Guests are greeted by the concierge and escorted to their room. After settling in, visit the fireplace-warmed parlor, where afternoon wine and cheese are served along with plenty of interesting conversation. If you miss these appetizers (and with these romantic rooms, you just might), drop by the small kitchenette for a freshly baked cookie or two. The 13 guest rooms are located throughout the main house, the attached Garden Annex, and the separate Pool House. All are spacious retreats with private entrances. The corner Gaige Suite is the grandest of the rooms in the main house, with its own expansive deck, a king-size carved mahogany bed with a crocheted canopy, and an immense blue-tiled bathroom with a whirlpool tub large enough for four, but much more romantic with just two. Built on a teak base, the bed takes center stage in Room No. 10, although the pillow-plush window seat, steamy double shower, and bubbling Jacuzzi tub might overshadow its glory a bit. While all the rooms are exceptional, our favorite is the Creekside Suite, located in the Pool House. Sophisticated Asian-inspired touches, beautiful orchids, cement floors covered by natural-fiber rugs, dimming lights, a gas fireplace, and a wall of windows looking onto your own creekside patio are offerings too wonderful for romantics to pass up. The carved glass sink in the bathroom is a work of art, and the two-person Jacuzzi tub works wonders on sore muscles. Need we mention there's a two-person shower, too? This is one room you will never want to leave.

After a day spent tasting wine, refresh yourselves with a dip in the inn's pool or nearby Jacuzzi tub. Continue living the lush life by sinking into the garden furniture on the communal creekside patio and stealing a kiss or two. After a morning walk along country roads, return to enjoy a two-course breakfast served in the elegant sunroom. The creative chef whips up such delights as Creole eggs in a spicy tomato sauce, chocolate-chip pancakes with banana compote, or apple-Gruyère-ham crêpes. With meals like this and such splendid surroundings, one night here is definitely not enough. **13540 Arnold Drive; (707) 935-0237, (800) 935-0237; www. gaige.com; expensive to unbelievably expensive; minimum-stay requirement on weekends.**

Romantic Note: At the time of our visit, two additional rooms were being constructed on the property, one in the Pool House and the other in the main house. We have no doubt that these new rooms will be as sumptuous and inviting as the other accommodations at the Gaige House.

❀❀ **GLENELLY INN, Glen Ellen** This 1916 inn is a legacy of Glen Ellen's heyday, when San Franciscans considered this woodsy town an invigorating getaway and ventured here via train. Today, when you come by car, you'll find the inn's setting to be just as enchanting; it is nestled at the base of a steep hill and shaded by the gnarled branches of century-old oak and olive trees. A soothing Jacuzzi tub and a brick courtyard are found in the lower rose garden, and a double hammock swings lazily in the breeze on the more naturally landscaped upper terrace.

Although the architectural design is from an era when standard rooms were smaller, the country decor, Norwegian down quilts, and claw-foot tubs in most of the eight rooms add to the intimacy. Wood-burning stoves in two of the rooms further enhance the coziness. All rooms open onto either a large common veranda or a patio where chairs are ready and waiting for you to sit all day if you so desire.

A full breakfast, served fireside in the spacious upstairs common room, always includes freshly squeezed juice, baked goods still warm from the oven, and a seasonal fruit dish. A tasty, filling main dish, such as a salsa Jack soufflé or hash-brown decadence, varies from day to day. If the weather permits, enjoy breakfast on the oak-shaded patio out back. **5131 Warm Springs Road; (707) 996-6720; www.glenelly.com; moderate to expensive; minimum-stay requirement on weekends.**

Restaurant Kissing

❤❤❤ **GLEN ELLEN INN RESTAURANT, Glen Ellen** During the high season, you'll need to make a reservation early to enjoy an evening at this charming little gem, owned and operated by an equally charming couple (he is the chef and she is the server). Everyone in town and from out-of-town seems to visit tiny Glen Ellen for the delicious food served here. Luckily, romance seekers will be pleased by the seating choices. The main dining room, done in a soothing shade of butter yellow and accented by big baskets, modern art, and dried floral arrangements, is a wonderful place to dine (especially by the windows), and the open kitchen isn't too noisy. However, more serene surroundings are found on the sunporch; its interior is embellished with abundant greenery and white holiday lights, creating the ideal romantic glow come sundown. If the weather cooperates, dine al fresco on the backyard patio near a lovely koi pond, where a waterfall washes away any sounds that nearby traffic might bring.

From the kitchen comes one mouthwatering dish after another. Seasonal entrées change, but you'll be treated to such specialties as grilled mango-papaya-ginger Chilean sea bass or roasted chicken stuffed with Gruyère cheese, pine nuts, and spinach. The field, stream, and sky risottos offer a new taste each day, and there's always a special or two worth trying. As satisfied as you'll be by dinner's end, the desserts are all too tempting to pass up. The gooey banana bread pudding with a warm 'n' creamy chocolate center is unforgettable. **13670 Arnold Drive; (707) 996-6409; www.glenelleninn.com; moderate to expensive; reservations recommended; dinner Thursday–Tuesday.**

❦❦❦ **IL MULINO, Glen Ellen** From mill to distillery to charming Italian restaurant, the 150-year-old building housing Il Mulino has had a long, interesting history. Fortunately, much of its historical ambience has been retained, and contributes to the restaurant's romantic flair. Topped with a red tin roof and bordered by an enormous waterwheel, the pale yellow building is located in **JACK LONDON VILLAGE**, a classy yet quaint shopping area nestled among the forested hills of Glen Ellen. Inside the dining room, Tuscan yellow walls complement the old wooden beams and rafters that support the ancient building. Choose a seat beside the wood-burning fireplace on a nippy night or, when the sun shines, savor the outside scenery near the windows that encompass half the restaurant. For more views of nature, there's always the lovely outside terrace overlooking a tranquil brook.

Northern Italian dishes fill the menu, including homemade gnocchi, roasted chicken and prosciutto ravioli, and lightly fried calamari served with a spicy marinara sauce. House specialties take advantage of the oak-burning grill; especially noteworthy are the grilled veal chops with fennel, cracked peppercorns, and crispy potatoes. Seafood lovers shouldn't pass up the zesty orange-fennel cioppino filled with all sorts of savories from the sea.

If, after enjoying a meal here, you find that things start looking a little crooked, don't blame it on the wine, the robust Italian fare, or being madly in love. The ancient building actually slopes a bit, adding to its authentic character. **14301 Arnold Drive, in Jack London Village; (707) 938-1890; www.ilmulino.net; moderate to expensive; call for seasonal hours.**

Outdoor Kissing

❦❦ **JACK LONDON STATE HISTORIC PARK, Glen Ellen** Besides being a fascinating historical site, Jack London State Historic Park offers some of the most pastoral picnic sites around, with lovely wooded paths suitable for an old-fashioned stroll after lunch. Sit at one of the picnic tables set among the trees, or bring a blanket and spread it out on the rolling lawn that overlooks the small cottage where London penned many of his famous adventure stories. A forested trail leads to the granite ruins of Wolf House, the castle that London was building for himself and his beloved wife, Charmian. Tragically, Wolf House mysteriously burned down before they could move in, and London died shortly thereafter. Nearby is another grand stone structure, the House of Happy Walls, which Charmian built as a memorial to the love of her life. It holds memorabilia from their life and exotic travels together. **2400 London Ranch Road; (707) 938-5216; www.**

parks.sonoma.net/jlpark.html; $6 day-use fee per car. *From Glen Ellen's center, head west uphill on London Ranch Road to the park.*

Romantic Warning: In the summer, when tourism is at its peak and the kids are out of school, Jack London's "Beauty Ranch," as he called it, can feel more like a zoo than a park.

Romantic Suggestion: On your way to Jack London State Historic Park, stop at the **BENZIGER FAMILY WINERY** (1883 London Ranch Road; 707-935-4046, 888-490-2739; www.benziger.com; open 10 A.M.–5 P.M. daily) for wine tasting and a self-guided tour. Here you can get a brief lesson about winemaking and wander through lush, well-maintained grounds. Watch out for heavy equipment, though; this working ranch gets hectic around harvest time.

Kenwood

Kenwood is a modest village located north of Glen Ellen on Highway 12. Don't let the small-town look fool you into simply driving through; there are several places worth visiting.

Hotel/Bed and Breakfast Kissing

❤❤❤ **THE KENWOOD INN & SPA, Kenwood** If an Italian count and countess were to greet you at the door of The Kenwood Inn, you probably wouldn't be surprised. This Tuscan-style villa was built in the later half of this century, but it looks ancient, as if transplanted to Kenwood right from a Mediterranean hillside. Ivy embraces the walls, a rose garden abounds with blooms, and tall hedges and a cement wall conceal the courtyard and its swimming pool, hot tub, and central fountain.

Twelve opulent guest rooms are dispersed throughout several buildings. The decor varies slightly, but dark, rich brocade fabrics, faux marble walls, feather beds, and wood-burning fireplaces are found in every room. Some rooms have small ivy-framed stone balconies that face the lovely garden, pool, and, unfortunately, nearby Highway 12. The Italian theme continues in the breakfast room, with its trompe l'oeil murals and tapestry-covered high-backed chairs. Here, an Italian-accented three-course gourmet breakfast is served at intimate two-person tables. **10400 Sonoma Highway (Highway 12); (707) 833-1293, (800) 353-6966; www.kenwoodinn.com; unbelievably expensive; minimum-stay requirement on weekends.**

Romantic Suggestion: The Kenwood Inn also operates a full-service spa adjacent to the reception lobby. If you care to be pampered, schedule an in-room "Togetherness Massage" or venture to the spa's private rooftop patio for a couple's massage al fresco.

Restaurant Kissing

❧❧ **KENWOOD RESTAURANT AND BAR, Kenwood** Kenwood Restaurant's elegant dining room is accented by white linens, cane chairs, a peaked ceiling with exposed beams, and whitewashed walls enlivened by contemporary Impressionist paintings. Floor-to-ceiling windows reveal intoxicating views of the pastoral fields and vineyards. Unfortunately, after the dining room fills up with devoted patrons, it loses some intimacy due to the increased noise level. Because of this, you might want to opt for an early lunch or late dinner.

The international and creative menu features tantalizing choices such as poached salmon, grape leaves stuffed with wild rice and lamb, Bodega Bay bouillabaisse, and pork chops served with sweet-and-sour red cabbage. Smaller dishes, such as the warm goat-cheese salad or crab cakes, appeal to those with lighter appetites. Large or small, all dishes are designed to go well with a glass of local wine. **9900 Sonoma Highway (Highway 12); (707) 833-6326; moderate to expensive; lunch and dinner Wednesday–Sunday.**

Wine Kissing

❧❧❧ **CHATEAU ST. JEAN, Kenwood** Getting stuck in a huge tour group is never romantic, which is why we love Chateau St. Jean. This elegant winery estate allows you take a self-guided tour at your own pace. During harvest time you can witness the winemaking process, but regardless of when you visit, be sure to climb up to the observation tower. From this perspective, you have a wonderful view of the expansive vineyards, rolling green hills, and beautifully manicured property. Purchase a bottle of Chateau St. Jean's highly acclaimed wine, choose a prime picnic spot on the lush green lawn, and then kiss everyone in your intimate, two-person tour group. **8555 Sonoma Highway (Highway 12); (707) 833-4134, (800) 543-7572; www.chateaustjean.com; open 10 a.m.–4:30 p.m. daily.**

Santa Rosa

If you're in a provincial mind-set, Santa Rosa can be a disappointment. Kiss the grape arbors, sleepy hills, and sweet, fresh air goodbye, because this is the city. Not only is Santa Rosa a detour from the country, it is also California's largest city north of San Francisco. Despite this, Santa Rosa provides a handful of very distinctive romantic locales, several of which are located on the city's outskirts.

Hotel/Bed and Breakfast Kissing

❤❤❤ **THE GABLES, Santa Rosa** Three and a half acres of picturesque farmland surround this gabled Victorian Gothic Revival home, so we were tempted to call it a country getaway; unfortunately, traffic zooming along on the nearby highway convinced us otherwise. However, once you step inside this lovely inn, you will be won over by the beauty of the main parlor and the aroma of afternoon tea.

The Gables offers seven remarkable rooms to choose from, plus a cozy cottage next door. The Parlor Suite, located on the main floor, is the largest and most elegant possibility. Decorated in hunter green and burgundy, it is equipped with a king-size bed, down comforter, and Italian marble fireplace. The other refined yet unpretentious guest rooms are reached via a curving mahogany staircase. The house features 15 gables that crown keyhole-shaped windows, which are incorporated into each room's decor. Floral wallpapers, richly colored linens, attractive antiques, and private bathrooms accompany every room, and three also have wood-burning fireplaces to warm your toes on cold nights.

The most enticing (and most private) accommodation is the self-sufficient cottage adjacent to the main house. Knotty pine walls, a Franklin stove, and attractive handcrafted wood furniture are enduring touches. You'll also find a loft bedroom with a feather bed and down comforter, a double whirlpool tub, and a full kitchen for your comfort and convenience. After a day of wine tasting, return to the cottage, snuggle up in your plush bathrobes, and watch a classic romantic movie (provided in-room) for some kissing inspiration.

To lure you out of your snug bed in the morning, a gourmet country breakfast is served in the formal dining room. Your meal includes fresh fruit, home-baked breads with homemade jam, and an ever-changing hot entrée, such as French toast with caramelized bananas. **4257 Petaluma Hill Road; (707) 585-7777, (800) GABLES-N; www.thegablesinn.com; moderate to very expensive; minimum-stay requirement on weekends and holidays.**

❤❤❤ **VINTNERS INN, Santa Rosa** The drive to Vintners Inn, surrounded by well-groomed rows of grapevines, feels as though you are passing through a magic portal into southern France. A fountain splashes in the central plaza, and brick pathways lead to the Mediterranean-style, sand-colored buildings with red tile roofs. (It seems more like a vintner's private estate than a hotel, even though the freeway is in sight.) The 44 spacious, uncluttered guest rooms are appointed with contemporary and antique reproduction pine furnishings. French doors open to brick patios or iron grillwork balconies that overlook 50 acres of surrounding vineyards or the inner courtyard's fountain. Upper-story rooms have high, peaked ceilings, and all feature oversize oval tubs in the standard bathrooms. Sip a mellow cabernet by the wood-burning fireplace if you are in a fireplace suite, or head to the common-area library, where overstuffed chairs provide comfy fireside snuggling. A huge Jacuzzi spa is also available for guests' use, but it is placed so close to the road that traffic noise can be distracting.

A deluxe continental breakfast is served at tables for two in the reception building. You can enjoy home-baked breads, cereals, yogurt, and fruit in the bright sunroom overlooking the lawns, or pile the goodies on your Belgian waffle while seated by the wood-burning hearth. As for dinner, you won't have to venture far to find excellent food. The highly acclaimed JOHN ASH & CO. (see Restaurant Kissing) is on the property. **4350 Barnes Road; (707) 575-7350, (800) 421-2584; www.vintnersinn.com; expensive to very expensive; minimum-stay requirement on weekends seasonally.**

Restaurant Kissing

❤❤❤ **JOHN ASH & CO., Santa Rosa** A view of the vineyards doesn't get much better (or closer) than at this restaurant next to **VINTNERS INN** (see Hotel/Bed and Breakfast Kissing). Clusters of candlelit, linen-covered tables overlook the panoramic country scene through floor-to-ceiling windows; tables on the outdoor brick patio offer the same magnificent view. In the evening, an inviting fire casts a warm glow in the restaurant, which is truly an ideal showcase for Sonoma Valley foods and wines. The menu changes seasonally, but it is always as contemporary and fresh as the decor, with choices such as grilled tenderloin of pork served with a delicious sweet-potato purée, rack of lamb over root vegetables and surrounded by a sun-dried cherry and cabernet reduction, or pan-seared, pepper-coated ahi tuna. For dessert, we highly recommend sharing the sampler plate, featuring numerous treats du jour. Before you plan your evening, be forewarned that this restaurant is always busy (make reservations early!) and decibel levels rise accordingly. Service is prompt, friendly, and professional. **4330 Barnes Road, at Vintners Inn; (707) 527-7687, (800) 421-2584; www. johnashco.com; expensive to very expensive; reservations recommended; lunch Tuesday–Saturday, dinner daily, brunch Sunday.**

❤❤ **JOSEF'S RESTAURANT AND BAR, Santa Rosa** This 1907 hotel's granite exterior may give it a somber face, but the parlor and dining room inside are warmly inviting. Upon entering, diners are greeted by an ebony grand piano that is enlivened by live jazz music Friday and Saturday nights. The dining room's mauve, green, and sand color scheme is restful, and tables are elegantly adorned with white linen, fine china, and silver. Relax with an aperitif on the love seat in front of the wood-burning fireplace as you review the French continental menu. Once seated, savor prawns in Chef Josef's garlic-herb sauce; sautéed chicken topped with lemon, capers, and artichokes; or a classic rack of lamb roasted in a mustard–red wine sauce. **308 Wilson Street, at Hotel La Rose; (707) 579-3200, (800) 527-6738; www.hotellarose.com; moderate to expensive; lunch Tuesday–Friday, dinner Monday–Saturday.**

Romantic Warning: Rooms at HOTEL LA ROSE (expensive to unbelievably expensive) don't begin to compare with the restaurant for kissing ambience. They are not recommended.

❤❤❤ LISA HEMENWAY'S BISTRO, Santa Rosa

Who would have thought a romantic and elegant restaurant specializing in creative world cuisine could be found in a small shopping mall? We did, once we experienced a meal at Lisa Hemenway's. From just about any one of the cozy tables, take in views of colorful flower beds and lovely landscaping through bistro-style windows. Faux wall painting and plush, dark carpeting create an intimate setting, while white linen tablecloths, gold upholstered chairs, and soft lighting complete the picture. The menu is intriguing. Asian rice rolls with rice noodles, crisp vegetables, and sweet chile dip make a perfect starter. Try the sensational signature main dish of chicken, lemon grass, and peanut hash rolled in Napa cabbage and served with jasmine black rice and chile-mint sauce. Another noteworthy choice is the wild mushroom ravioli with fresh chive mascarpone sauce. The service is as excellent as everything else. **710 Village Court Mall; (707) 526-5111; moderate to expensive; lunch and dinner Monday–Saturday.**

❤❤ WILLOWSIDE CAFE, Santa Rosa

It would be easy to pass by this red roadhouse if you were not aware of the delicacies that await inside. Only a modest sign marks this café, and yet plenty of people have managed to discover this much-talked-about little treasure—finding it is half the fun. Polished copper tabletops, hardwood floors, and an assortment of ornately framed mirrors and soft-toned lights create a cosmopolitan, stylish atmosphere that is unexpected in this rural setting. Low lighting and candles at each table add a subtle romantic touch.

Although the small menu changes weekly, beautifully presented California-French cuisine is a constant. A buckwheat crêpe wrapped around duxelles started our meal off right. Appointed with a generous assortment of mussels and oyster mushrooms, the grouper proved fresh, but the broth was too delicate for our tastes. Escolar, served over wasabi-infused red rice, gets points for creativity, as does the tasty portobello mushrooms with asparagus and mustard beurre blanc. Dessert—a coffee caramel custard—proved so divine, we almost ordered another. **3535 Guerneville Road; (707) 523-4814; expensive; dinner Wednesday–Sunday.**

Wine Kissing

❤❤❤❤ **MATANZAS CREEK WINERY, Santa Rosa** What's different about Matanzas Creek Winery? How about the 2 million lavender stems that blanket the front hills of the sprawling property? Often compared with the lavender hills found in Provence, the sight (and scent) is simply breathtaking. If you happen to visit in June or July (which is lavender harvest time), the aroma that wafts through the air is almost as intoxicating as the aging wines. The main building/winemaking facility is set back behind the lavender fields and hidden by tall trees and shrubs. Daily tastings of the winery's latest triumphs are offered, but better yet, purchase a bottle and stroll through the lavender fields arm in arm, or set up a picnic lunch at one of the two tables located at the back of the property in a serene wooded area.

If you want to take more than memories back home with you, visit the main building. Here you'll find a whole range of Matanzas Creek products for sale, including bath oils, bath salts, potpourri, sachets, and soaps, all infused with this fragrant purple herb. **6097 Bennett Valley Road; (707) 528-6464, (800) 590-6464; www.matanzascreek.com; open 10 a.m.–4:30 p.m. daily.**

Occidental

This charming town may be a bit off the beaten path, but then again, that's where many romantic destinations like to hide. From **THE INN AT OCCIDENTAL** (see Hotel/Bed and Breakfast Kissing), savor views of the town and surrounding redwoods while enjoying one of the nicest accommodations in Wine Country.

Hotel/Bed and Breakfast Kissing

❤❤❤❤ **THE INN AT OCCIDENTAL, Occidental** Notorious for his exuberance and enthusiasm, the innkeeper here has used his energy, attention to details, and artistic flair to create a work of art. Set high on a redwood-covered hillside overlooking the small historical town of Occidental, this beautifully restored gabled Victorian home brims with country charm.

Oriental carpets cover the hardwood floors, and country collectibles and antiques fill common areas where guests can lounge in overstuffed sofas and enjoy the warmth of a crackling fire in the brick hearth. Outside, the flower-laden veranda, furnished with comfortably cushioned white wicker furniture, is a perfect place to sip wine and enjoy each other's company.

There is nothing the conscientious innkeeper has overlooked; even the smallest of the inn's eight guest rooms is convincingly elegant. Each room has an unusual but attractive color scheme reflecting the warm hues of the nature photographs and artwork adorning the walls. Antique collections vary from room to room, complementing the contemporary mood with a historical flavor. Fluffy down comforters cover sumptuous feather beds, and rich chocolates await guests at their bedside tables. Any room is a delight to stay in, but a few have extra-special touches. In the Cut Glass Room, sliding French doors open onto a private patio, garden, and full-size hot tub. A corner fireplace glows in the airy and whimsical Quilt Room, which features high ceilings, a Jacuzzi spa built for two, and some cutting-edge art in the form of a five-foot-tall pair of scissors. A mahogany four-poster canopy queen-size bed, set in front of a brick fireplace, distinguishes the Tiffany Room, while The Marbles Suite delights with an antique marble collection, not to mention a king-size bed, fireplace, and spa tub for two.

Awaken in the morning to the enticing aromas of freshly baked pastries, orange-thyme pancakes, homemade granola, and other gourmet delights served family-style in the wine cellar. When the weather is warm, you can enjoy this repast outside on the attached patio. With such beautiful accommodations and lovely setting, you and your beloved might just forget about touring the wine country and decide to stay put. **3657 Church Street; (707) 874-1047, (800) 522-6324; www.innatoccidental.com; expensive to unbelievably expensive; minimum-stay requirement on weekends.**

Romantic Note: The Inn at Occidental was expanding at the time of our visit. Construction was underway on a new building adjacent to the main house, where eight fabulous new rooms will sport private entrances, spa tubs, fireplaces, and private decks; hot tubs will grace two of the rooms. Without a doubt, this inn is on its way to kissing perfection.

Healdsburg

You might assume that if you've seen one small town in Wine Country, you've seen them all. Guess again. Amazingly enough, each town in this area has a character and disposition of its own, which makes traveling here an ongoing adventure. Healdsburg is one of our favorite towns in the

Sonoma Valley, for several reasons: Its charming town plaza and park green are lined with interesting boutiques and restaurants, and the gorgeous surrounding countryside harbors numerous bed and breakfasts and wineries secluded on quiet, winding roads—perfect spots for kissing. For additional information, contact the **HEALDSBURG CHAMBER OF COMMERCE** (217 Healdsburg Avenue, Healdsburg, CA, 95448; 707-433-6935, 800-648-9922 in California; www.healdsburg.org).

Hotel/Bed and Breakfast Kissing

❦❦❦❦ **BELLE DE JOUR INN, Healdsburg** The four cottages and separate Carriage House Suite at Belle de Jour Inn are equally irresistible and private, but just different enough to make it hard to choose one. The four cottages stand out against the property's gentle green hills, tall eucalyptus and olive trees, and bright flowers. Although they are connected, each one is a private hideaway offering modern furnishings mixed with plenty of country charm. Romantic bonuses include hardwood floors, sumptuous linens and robes, and private entrances. With the exception of the Morning Hill Room with its two-person shower/steam unit, all have whirlpool tubs. Of the cottages, our favorite is the Terrace Room, which features a high vaulted ceiling, private patio, wood-burning stove, and whirlpool tub with a stunning view of the surrounding vineyards and lush greenery. Running a close second is the Caretaker's Suite, a large, yet cozy room with a king-size canopy bed.

The pièce de résistance, however, is the inn's newest suite, encompassing the second story of the Carriage House. Its interior is decorated in creamy whites and highlighted by redwood salvaged from an old barn. Enhancing such a wonderful space are luscious crimson- and gold-toned linens, a four-poster king-size bed, a fireplace, a two-person whirlpool tub framed with green tile, and a large glass shower. Because of its out-of-the-way location, privacy is guaranteed and the sunrise views are exceptional.

Breakfast at Belle de Jour is a cornucopia of ever-changing daily delights such as fresh fruit and yogurt, Parmesan baked eggs, cranberry scones, and fresh muffins. The innkeeper will also whip up your favorite coffee drink, be it a full-strength espresso or double latte. This morning feast is enjoyed in the breakfast room of the main house. **16276 Healdsburg Avenue; (707) 431-9777; www.belledejourinn.com; expensive to unbelievably expensive; minimum-stay requirement on weekends and holidays.**

Romantic Suggestion: See the wineries in grand style from the back of the innkeeper's 1925 Star Touring Car. Personally chauffeured tours are available April through October for guests, and reservations are needed.

Prices start at $45 an hour (three-hour minimum). You're certain to turn heads kissing in the backseat of this beauty.

CALDERWOOD INN, Healdsburg Nestled in a quiet residential neighborhood and secluded behind old-growth cypress and spruce trees, this Queen Anne Victorian inn is the perfect place for relaxed refinement. Sip a refreshing glass of lemonade with your honey as you unwind on the front-porch swing, or enjoy the cool shade by the koi pond. Savor the splendor of the parlor, which is filled with period furnishings, towering flower arrangements, and thoughtful decorations. Wine and cheese are served here every afternoon, complemented by the sounds of a player piano that's wired to stereo speakers. The resulting melodies are delightful.

Custom-designed Bradbury & Bradbury silk-screened wall and ceiling papers enhance the Victorian mood throughout the home, including the six guest rooms. Cozy alcoves and sloping ceilings, attractive linens and plush robes, and period antiques highlight each guest accommodation; most offer claw-foot tubs in their private baths (one room has a detached bathroom), and one room features a Jacuzzi tub. Small decorating details throughout make the common rooms and hallways equally attractive.

An opulent full breakfast is served in the formal dining room each morning. The tasty special of the day may include eggs Benedict or croissants stuffed with mascarpone cheese; accompaniments include home-baked breads, seasonal fruits, and breakfast meats. Such a meal certainly puts the finishing touch on any romantic interlude. **25 West Grant Street; (707) 431-1110, (800) 600-5444; www.calderwoodinn.com; expensive to very expensive; minimum-stay requirement seasonally.**

CAMELLIA INN, Healdsburg The Camellia Inn combines Victorian elegance with modern amenities to put travelers in a peaceful state of mind. The two parlors of this 1869 Italianate Victorian home are trimmed with intricate, leaf-motif plasterwork and adorned with Oriental carpets, floral-patterned sofas, eclectic antiques, tapestried chairs, and marble fireplaces. These parlors are lovely, if visually busy, places in which to enjoy afternoon wine and hors d'oeuvres.

The inn's nine individually decorated guest rooms will appeal to almost any bed-and-breakfast connoisseur. All rooms have private baths (one is down the hall but still private), and four feature Jacuzzi tubs. Beautiful antiques and family heirlooms mixed with some modern furnishings are found in most, as well as pretty linens, comfy sitting areas, and gas-log fireplaces. Our favorite rooms are Royalty, with its Scottish canopy bed, and Tiffany, which sports Bradbury & Bradbury wall coverings, a four-poster queen-size bed, and a large Jacuzzi tub for two.

A full buffet breakfast, served at one large table in the dining room, includes a hearty main dish such as quiche or huevos Mexicanos, cinnamon rolls or rhubarb torte, and plenty of fresh fruit. Before you sneak off to your room, take a dip in the swimming pool in the backyard. Afternoon refreshments are served outside near the pool in the summer months. **211 North Street; (707) 433-8182, (800) 727-8182; www.camelliainn.com; inexpensive to expensive; minimum-stay requirement on weekends.**

Romantic Note: The inn offers some nice romance packages ranging from simple seductions to elaborate productions. Chocolate lovers who are in town on Wednesday should not miss the "Chocolate Inn-dulgence" package. You'll be treated to chocolates in-room, a pairing of chocolate and an evening refreshment, and chocolate treats at breakfast. Who could resist a chocolate and strawberry crêpe? Not us.

❧❧❦ **GRAPE LEAF INN, Healdsburg** It's hard to miss this refurbished Queen Anne Victorian set in an otherwise ordinary neighborhood. Why? Because it is painted lavender with bright purple trim. A winsome and welcome combination of eccentricity and solace, the inn offers seven suites done in seven personalized styles. Viewing the building from the outside, it's hard to imagine that there is room for more than one suite, much less seven, but the accommodations are more than ample. Highlights include sloped ceilings with skylights in the four upstairs rooms, multicolored leaded-glass windows throughout, separate sitting areas, hardwood floors, and double whirlpool tubs in five of the rooms. When we visited, new owners were outfitting each room with new designer wallpapers, luscious linens, matching bed skirts, window treatments, and accents. By the looks of the finished rooms, the overall results will be very romantically pleasing.

Being in the heart of wine country, the innkeepers incorporate local wines and produce into their breakfast treats. The results: pears poached in zinfandel or apricots cooked in a late-harvest wine. Corn and cheddar pancakes, as well as other homemade goodies, fresh fruit, and juices are served in the two living rooms or on the patio when weather permits. Early-evening wine tastings, plenty of chocolate treats, and overall Victorian elegance make the Grape Leaf Inn an ideal resting and romancing spot. **539 Johnson Street; (707) 433-8140, (877) 547-4654; www.grapeleaf inn.com; moderate to very expensive; minimum-stay requirement on weekends.**

❧❧ **HAYDON STREET INN, Healdsburg** Harbored on a quiet residential street, this gabled Queen Anne Victorian home and its two-story cottage provide a convenient setting for exploring Healdsburg by day and relaxing in elegant comfort by night. Located behind the home, the cottage houses the two most desirable accommodations: the Victorian Room, which has cathedral ceilings, Ralph Lauren linens, a queen-size wicker bed, restored antiques, and a two-person whirlpool tub; and the Pine Room, which features whitewashed walls, a Battenburg lace canopy over the queen-size bed, and a skylight above its whirlpool tub. The six antique-filled guest rooms in the main house are smaller, less private, and more ordinary than romantic. One standout, however, is the Turret Room, with its bed tucked under the eaves and a claw-foot tub placed beside a fireplace.

Breakfast, served in the main dining room, is a full country affair with home-baked breads and muffins, fresh fruit and juice, and a hot entrée such as quiche or oat-nut pancakes. **321 Haydon Street; (707) 433-5228, (800) 528-3703; www.haydon.com; inexpensive to expensive; minimum-stay requirement on weekends seasonally.**

❀❀❀ **HEALDSBURG INN ON THE PLAZA, Healdsburg** You may wonder whether you are in the right place when you first arrive here. The entrance to the Healdsburg Inn on the Plaza is located in an art gallery and gift shop on the ground floor. (On your way through, be sure to admire the work of the talented local artists featured here; you may even find a memento to take home.) A staircase leads to the bed-and-breakfast area on the second floor, where ten guest rooms adjoin a mezzanine. Every room has a private bath, some feature gas fireplaces and bay windows, and three rooms share a lovely outdoor balcony. Detailing original to the turn-of-the-century building, such as crown moldings, wainscoting, and pressed-wood walls, is found throughout. The very lovely Garden Suite, also known as the Honeymoon Suite, is the most romantically attired room, featuring a whirlpool tub for two, corner gas fireplace, and king-size iron and brass bed. All rooms are affectionately decorated with American antiques, down comforters and quilts, firm canopy beds adorned with handmade rag dolls or teddy bears, and cozy sitting areas trimmed in pastel colors and textured country fabrics. The art theme also continues upstairs; the hallways and guest rooms double as mini-galleries for local artwork.

One of the most outstanding features of this inn is the rooftop garden and solarium set above the plaza—a charming setting for a savory buffet breakfast and/or an afternoon wine-and-popcorn reception. A champagne brunch is served for guests on Saturdays and Sundays and, if you happen to get hungry midday, there's always freshly baked treats in the cookie jar. **110 Matheson Street; (707) 433-6991, (800) 431-8663; www.healds burginn.com; expensive to very expensive; minimum-stay requirement on weekends and holidays seasonally.**

❤❤❤❤ **THE HONOR MANSION, Healdsburg** Once in a while we visit a place that is so close to perfect, it quickly reminds us why we do what we do. The Honor Mansion is one of those special places. Beauty and grace emanate from the very foundation of this white Italianate Victorian home, set next to a 100-year-old magnolia tree in a reasonably quiet residential neighborhood.

Your first glimpse of elegance is found in the guest parlor, with its period antiques, deep burgundy wallpaper, and crackling fire in the hearth. Five rooms, two suites, and a private cottage are available at this small luxury inn, and each accommodation offers thoughtful touches and varied decor. Amenities in all rooms include feather beds with richly colored down comforters, private bathrooms (many with claw-foot tubs), and exquisite antiques. Everything is here for your comfort and pleasure, too: CD players and CDs, fluffy robes and soft slippers, lap desks for writing love letters, and even garment steamers so you'll look freshly pressed for that romantic night out. Turndown service with chocolates adds to the elegance.

Which room to choose? The ground-floor Rose Room dazzles with a private porch and a claw-foot tub surrounded by floor-to-ceiling windows. If you're seeking romance on a budget, we recommend the cozy Angel Room, with a cherub mural in the corner above the bed and a handmade patchwork quilt on the cozy bed. Certainly the most private option is the self-contained Squire's Cottage situated near the koi pond. Snuggle up on big pillows next to the gas fireplace or relax on your own garden patio. There's also a TV/VCR and video library, a king-size canopy bed fronting the fireplace, and a claw-foot tub for two framed by stained glass windows. Jewel-toned linens, a vaulted ceiling with clerestory windows, and a sparkling whitewashed interior make this our top romantic pick.

Two new luxury suites shaded by a beautiful tulip tree were being constructed when we visited, and closely compete with the cottage for the most kissing appeal. Amorous offerings in these two-bedroom suites include cozy sitting areas, corner fireplaces, two-person showers, and outdoor jetted tubs tucked into enclosed gardens. Romantic offerings just keep getting better here.

Early-evening refreshments are served in the dining room of the main house. If the weather cooperates, take your drink to the outdoor deck, which is furnished with green wrought-iron tables and chairs, and hemmed by colorful gardens and a pond full of "kissing koi" (they'll actually kiss your finger). In the back of the home, an outdoor swimming pool promises recreation and relaxation for tired wine enthusiasts.

An easy-to-use espresso maker is available for guests who need their latte early in the morning. At a later hour, breakfast is presented in the grand dining room. We enjoyed a lavish breakfast of cranberry-apricot scones, poached pear smothered in a fruit compote and topped by whipped cream, and Mexican crêpes filled with scrambled eggs, zesty salsa, and fresh avocado. If you can't figure out what to do the rest of the day (besides lounge around), the inn's concierge can direct you to wineries and also make reservations for dinner. How's that for fine living? **14891 Grove Street; (707) 433-4277, (800) 554-4667; www.honormansion.com; expensive to unbelievably expensive; minimum-stay requirement on weekends and holidays.**

❧❦ **MADRONA MANOR, Healdsburg** A royal crest adorns the white arch that welcomes you to this landmark inn and restaurant (see Restaurant Kissing). Beautifully landscaped gardens and surrounding woods completely hide the stately 1881 mansion from any sign of the nearby city and highway. The setting is truly one of the most majestic and peaceful in Healdsburg. That is why it saddens our hearts to find that the guest rooms don't begin to live up to the splendor outside. Distributed throughout the three-story Victorian mansion, the adjacent Carriage House, the Garden Cottage, and the Meadow Wood Complex, nearly all of Madrona Manor's 21 rooms and suites are designer disappointments. We can only truly recommend the mansion's second-floor rooms, which are outfitted in a lavish Victorian style with exquisite period antiques, tall ceilings and windows, spacious bathrooms, ornate window treatments, large fireplaces, and queen- or king-size beds backed by massive wood headboards.

Every other guest room we saw on the property is a confusing mix of outdated and mismatched furnishings and cheap artwork; many have bland bathrooms as well. The only exception is Suite 400, where the star attraction is a magnificent two-person Jacuzzi tub. (The entire bath is done in Mediterranean marble, and shutters open for a fireplace view from the tub.) Even the Meadowood Complex, romantically situated away from the other buildings, has a disappointing motel feel. It's all too bad, since, with a little love and a talented interior designer, this place could be spectacular.

A buffet breakfast of baked scones, fresh fruit, cereals, and coffee and tea is served to guests in the main house's beautiful dining room. We recommend lingering over breakfast, since the home's common areas will please the senses more than the guest rooms. **1001 Westside Road; (707) 433-4231, (800) 258-4003; www.madronamanor.com; very expensive to unbelievably expensive.**

Romantic Note: At press time, new owners had taken over Madrona Manor and plan to redecorate the rooms. We hope for the best.

Restaurant Kissing

💋 **MADRONA MANOR RESTAURANT, Healdsburg** Be sure to arrive ten or 15 minutes before your dinner reservation so you can wander through the handsomely landscaped grounds of this estate. If it's raining, so much the better: Sit by the fire on an overstuffed sofa in the cozy parlor. The manor's dining room is characterized by high ceilings, lace curtains, and rose-colored wallpaper. Intimate tables covered in white linens are scattered throughout the house's original living and dining rooms. Dinner options include either ordering à la carte or choosing the prix fixe menu. With dishes ranging from satisfactory to good, the prix fixe dinner includes several entrée choices, such as rack of lamb in a Dijon-pistachio crust and pan-seared Atlantic salmon with zinfandel sauce. You also get four choices for dessert and, luckily, most will please any sweet tooth. **1001 Westside Road, at Madrona Manor; (707) 433-4231, (800) 258-4003; www.madronamanor.com; very expensive; dinner daily.**

Romantic Note: MADRONA MANOR (see Hotel/Bed and Breakfast Kissing) had just come under new ownership at press time. We look forward to more romantic changes, both in the restaurant and the accommodations.

💋💋💋 **RAVENOUS, Healdsburg** Looking for a romantic evening out? Then make dinner reservations to rendezvous with your sweetheart at Ravenous, a popular hideaway adjacent to the Raven Theater in downtown Healdsburg. Only eight tables fill this small space that beautifully incorporates a modern flair with Mediterranean warmth. The combination of tortoiseshell-framed mirrors and bistro-style wood chairs and banquettes accented by animal-print fabrics may sound far-out and funky, but it works in a subtle fashion here. Artistic touches flourish throughout the dining room, from the wall sconces that resemble small wheat sheaves to the antique French posters on the yellow walls. Ideal kissing spots are the two small corner tables.

Light and lively California cuisine is the name of the game here. Don't miss such treats as a portobello mushroom sandwich topped with tapenade and roasted red peppers, potato fennel soup, beef short ribs in a red wine–brandy sauce, and a grilled pork tenderloin quesadilla topped with an avocado-melon salsa. One thing is guaranteed about eating the plentiful portions here: You certainly won't be ravenous when you leave. **117 North Street; (707) 431-1770; moderate to expensive; no credit cards; lunch and dinner Wednesday–Sunday.**

Russian River Area

More than 50 wineries grace the Russian River area, which stretches from the Pacific Coast inland to Healdsburg, then north through Geyserville. Many are family-run operations far off the beaten path that are a pleasure to discover together.

Hotel/Bed and Breakfast Kissing

❀❀❀ **APPLEWOOD INN, Russian River Area** Built in 1922, this Mission-style pink stucco inn once served as a private family estate. Today its European allure and historic elegance enchant guests in search of amorous accommodations. Footpaths wind through the lovingly landscaped property, past a stone courtyard with a burbling lion's-head fountain and a large outdoor swimming pool set among sparse stands of trees.

Eight of the inn's 16 guest rooms are located in the spacious original building. Appropriately, these rooms exude historic authenticity, with English-style antiques, dark wood accents, and brightly colored fabrics. Several rooms in this building have private balconies, and most offer lovely views of the landscaped grounds. However, we can't wholeheartedly recommend these rooms after seeing the seven rooms in the Piccola Casa, which are much more stylish, light, and contemporary. Here, vibrant pastel walls make a colorful backdrop for eye-catching artwork, and thick down comforters drape sensuous queen-size sleigh beds. All of these rooms have gas fireplaces, as well as Jacuzzi tubs or double-headed showers in their spacious, modern bathrooms inlaid with gorgeous tile work. As an added pleasure, each ground-level room comes complete with a private patio and fountain. When we visited, three deluxe suites were being built next to Piccola Casa. With their jetted tubs, fireplaces, and private decks, these could be the property's most romantic accommodations yet.

In the morning, a vast array of hot breakfast entrées like sautéed apples, Brie omelets, and eggs Florentine are served along with pastries and fresh fruit in the airy new dining room designed in the style of a French barn. Dinner (expensive to very expensive; reservations recommended) is also served here Tuesday through Saturday evenings. After a day spent playing at the shore or touring the Sonoma Valley, treat yourselves to such California-Provençal–inspired dishes as black sea bass with quinoa and chive crust, pan-roasted chicken served alongside roasted potatoes and a bing-cherry mustard reduction, or herbed buttermilk crêpes with grilled endive, onions, and spinach. **13555 Highway 116; (707) 869-9093, (800) 555-8509; www.applewoodinn.com; moderate to unbelievably expensive; minimum-stay requirement.**

Outdoor Kissing

❤❤❤❤ **RUSSIAN RIVER WINE ROAD, Russian River Area** The handful of wineries along this backwoods road are set apart from the rest of the Sonoma Valley by their isolation and beauty. Coiling through the hillsides and ravines, your path crisscrosses the tributaries and creeks of the Russian River. Along the way, the vineyards, redwoods, and forests take turns revealing their distinctive virtues and profiles. Whenever you see a winery sign along here, consider stopping and resting for a bit under the shade of a tree or in the coolness of a cellar tasting room. **Highway 128 to Chalk Hill Road.** *From Healdsburg, follow Healdsburg Avenue north until it becomes Alexander Valley Road. Follow this road to Highway 128 and turn south. Highway 128 branches off to the east; to the west is Chalk Hill Road.*

Wine Kissing

❤❤❤❤ **RUSSIAN RIVER AREA WINERIES TOUR, Russion River Area** Most of the wineries in the Russian River area offer quiet, romantic picnic spots where you can savor a bottle of wine with the repast you've packed in your basket. For maps and information on this area, contact the **RUSSIAN RIVER REGION VISITORS BUREAU** (Post Office Box 255, Guerneville, CA, 95446; 707-869-9212, 800-253-8800; www.russian river.org) or call the **RUSSIAN RIVER WINE ROAD INFORMATION LINE** (800-723-6336). Most maps of this area suggest beginning your tour at Healdsburg and making a westward loop through the Russian River area. The following wineries are recommended for kissing purposes, and are listed in the order in which you will encounter them along the way if you follow this route.

No trip to this area would be complete without a stop at the **FERRARI-CARANO WINERY** (8761 Dry Creek Road, Healdsburg; 707-433-6700, 800-831-0381; www.ferraricarano.com; open 10 A.M.–5 P.M. daily). Formal flower gardens with perfectly trimmed shrubs line the path to this Italianate mansion where a lovely gift shop and tasting room await. Unfortunately, because this is one of the most upscale (and popular) wineries in Sonoma Valley, there is no picnic area. However, you can stop and smell the roses while strolling along the brick walkways that pass through the gardens.

Set deep in the country, **A. RAFANELLI WINERY** (4685 West Dry Creek Road, Healdsburg; 707-433-1385; tours and tasting by appointment only) is a refreshing departure from many of this area's chic and somewhat pretentious wineries. Although there is no picnic area, you'll enjoy sipping wine in the wood-barn tasting room or wandering around the grounds, which are hemmed by lovely grape arbors.

DRY CREEK VINEYARD (3770 Lambert Bridge Road, Healdsburg; 707-433-1000, 800-864-9463; www.drycreekvineyard.com; open 10:30 A.M.– 4:30 P.M. daily) is situated on a flatland surrounded by vineyards and sloping hills, deep within the countryside. You'll have to make a small detour off West Dry Creek Road (where most of the other wineries we recommend are located) to get here, but it is worth it. Stained glass windows flank ivy-covered stone barns that serve as tasting rooms. When you've selected your wine, head outdoors to the picnic tables, set beneath shade trees on a manicured lawn framed by flower gardens.

At the **LAMBERT BRIDGE WINERY** (4085 West Dry Creek Road, Healdsburg; 707-431-9600, 800-975-0555; www.lambertbridge.com; open 10:30 A.M.–4:30 P.M. daily), a roaring fire in the massive stone fireplace warms the large barn-like building. Rows of barrels line one wall, and the tasting bar is hosted by a casual, unpretentious staff. A gazebo and several picnic tables are set next to the parking lot, but if you look away from the cars you'll see only vineyards.

Follow a winding farm road and a long gravel drive to **EVERETT RIDGE VINEYARDS & WINERY** (435 West Dry Creek Road, Healdsburg; 707-433-1637; www.everettridge.com; open 11 A.M.–4:30 P.M. daily). Two picnic tables sit next to an old red barn overlook rolling vineyards with mountains on the horizon. Roaming chickens and weatherworn antique farm equipment accent the rural setting.

HOP KILN WINERY (6050 Westside Road, Healdsburg; 707-433-6491; open 10 A.M.–5 P.M. daily) is one of the most romantic picnic spots in the area. Its sun-soaked picnic tables border a pond that is surrounded by vineyards and home to many a waterfowl. More tables are found in the cozy, shaded garden. Wine tasting takes place in the impressive stone historic landmark that was once a hop kiln and now doubles as a small gallery for local art.

ROCHIOLI VINEYARD AND WINERY (6192 Westside Road, Healdsburg; 707-433-2305; open 10 A.M.–5 P.M. daily) is another winery with an intoxicating picnic setting. Spend a lazy afternoon lingering at a table on a shaded patio with ambrosial views of rolling vineyards backdropped by mountains.

KORBEL CHAMPAGNE CELLARS (13250 River Road, Guerneville; 707-887-2294, 800-793-7983; www.korbel.com; call for seasonal hours) is situated farther west than most of these wineries, but is a superb stop for romance if you're heading to the coast. The tasting room is one of the grandest in the area—a spacious, elegant chamber, complete with a crystal chandelier, in a castle-like stone building. Before tasting, take a tour of the winery or the stunning gardens. Colorful flowers and towering shade trees enhance the picnic area but, unfortunately, noise from the busy street isn't conducive to vintage kissing.

Geyserville

Hotel/Bed and Breakfast Kissing

❦❦ **HOPE-BOSWORTH HOUSE, Geyserville** This attractive Queen Anne Victorian has four guest rooms, all with queen-size beds, views of the neighborhood, and private baths (one is private but situated across the hall). The Oak Room, with its Jacuzzi tub for two and charming country atmosphere, deserves special mention. We also like the Sun Porch Room, accented by wicker furnishings and hardwood floors. The Hope-Bosworth House is the kissing cousin of the **HOPE-MERRILL HOUSE** (see review below).

A full country breakfast of fresh breads, a hot egg entrée, and fruit is served in the antique-filled dining room on the main floor each morning. **21238 Geyserville Avenue; (707) 857-3356, (800) 825-4233; www. hope-inns.com; moderate to expensive; minimum-stay requirement on weekends and holidays.**

❦❦❦ **HOPE-MERRILL HOUSE, Geyserville** Staying in one of the eight rooms at this elaborately restored turn-of-the-century Victorian is like stepping back in time. The Eastlake Stick–style home showcases Victorian intricacies alongside modern amenities. Stunning silk-screened Bradbury & Bradbury wall coverings and ceiling papers add the proper flourish to the Sterling Room, while the romance of a whirlpool tub for two enhances both the beautiful Peacock Room and the Carpenter's Gothic Room. The Vineyard View Room has a cozy fireplace and a beautifully restored antique armoire, not to mention a shower suited for twosomes.

Before you indulge in the full, country-style breakfast of fresh fruit, pastries, a hot egg dish, and breakfast meats, take a dip in the refreshing outdoor swimming pool. It's set behind the home, near a latticed gazebo and a vineyard. **21253 Geyserville Avenue; (707) 857-3356, (800) 825-4233; www.hope-inns.com; moderate to very expensive; minimum-stay requirement on weekends and holidays.**

Romantic Suggestion: For $32, the inn will prepare a gourmet picnic lunch for two. This includes appetizers, entrées, salads, desserts, fruit, and a bottle of the innkeeper's wine, all packed in a keepsake basket. Make reservations ahead of time to enjoy this delicious experience.

Restaurant Kissing

❧❧❧❧ CHATEAU SOUVERAIN CAFÉ AT THE WINERY, Geyserville

No matter which Wine Country town you spend the night in, make sure you head north to Geyserville to dine at Chateau Souverain at least once during your visit. A stately stone and wrought-iron archway sets the mood as you approach the elegant chateau, set atop a vineyard-laden knoll. Sweep up the regal stone steps to the main dining room, where picture windows on three sides frame a view that is as intoxicating as the fine wines offered here. A massive fireplace, magnificent bent-brass chandeliers hanging from a cathedral ceiling, and soft, neutral tones enhance the French chateau feel. In the warmer months, tables are set on the grand terrace overlooking the vineyards of the Alexander Valley.

The country-French cuisine is equally wonderful, with appetizers like Redwood Hill goat cheese and leek tart with pine nuts, chives, and baby greens. Entrées include such mouthwatering dishes as roasted Sonoma chicken served over creamy polenta, and risotto with prawns enhanced by an orange-scented fennel broth. If you go for lunch, don't miss the generous and refreshing Dungeness crab salad served with avocado and heart of palm. We saved room for the almond cannoli with lime mascarpone filling and mango sauce, and highly recommend that you do the same. **Independence Lane (Highway 101); (707) 433-8197, (888) 80-WINES; www. chateausouverain.com; expensive; reservations recommended; lunch daily, dinner Friday–Sunday.**

"Every kiss provokes another."

Marcel Proust

San Francisco

Shrouded by fog and harbored between the Pacific Ocean and San Francisco Bay, the city of San Francisco pulsates with electric intensity. Colorful Victorian-style homes crowd together in lively hillside neighborhoods, while the arcing cables of the landmark Golden Gate Bridge gracefully ascend above clouds hovering over the bay. On sunny days the various parks and beaches come alive with picnickers, bicyclists, and walkers. Cafés and bakeries permeate the city's many ethnic neighborhoods, filling the air with the aroma of roasted garlic or freshly baked bread.

In such a diverse city, there is something for everyone, especially those with romance on their minds. Options are endless when it comes to luxury hotels and opulent bed and breakfasts, and world-renowned chefs dazzle diners in restaurants that range from quaint neighborhood cafés to glittery downtown showstoppers. Wildlife and greenery abound in **GOLDEN GATE PARK** (see Outdoor Kissing), where you can seek refuge from city life in nature's splendor. Depending on your mood, a visit to San Francisco may include spending an evening at the theater, symphony, or opera; taking a morning walk through the architecturally renowned **PALACE OF FINE ARTS** (see Outdoor Kissing); riding up those famous hills on a cable car; or exploring the bustling international district or some of San Francisco's trendy areas like Fillmore and Union Streets. No matter how you choose to spend your time, San Francisco's sights and sounds are sure to inspire fun, romance, and plenty of kissing.

Romantic Warning: Parking in San Francisco can be a nightmare, especially in crowded areas like Union Square or Chinatown. (We won't even mention how challenging it is to *drive* through town.) Don't let the frustration of searching for a space spoil your adventure before it begins. If you are downtown or nearby, do yourselves a favor and catch a cab, a bus, or a cable car, or simply walk (but go on foot only if you're wearing good walking shoes and are prepared to climb some hills). San Francisco is one city where a car may hinder your romantic excursions.

Hotel/Bed and Breakfast Kissing

❤❤❤❤ **THE ARCHBISHOP'S MANSION, San Francisco** Just a few houses down from San Francisco's "Painted Ladies" (those famous pastel-colored Victorian homes with a city backdrop) resides an equally engaging property that is sure to inspire romance: The Archbishop's Mansion. From the outside, you'll enjoy its regal facade—but cross the threshold and you'll discover what truly makes this place so spectacular.

Built in 1904 for the archbishop of San Francisco, the mansion retains much of its old-world elegance. The formal parlor, where complimentary wine and cheese are presented each evening, is a study in opulence and home to two of the inn's most interesting features: an impressive triple-vaulted, hand-painted ceiling and, for the film lover, a chandelier featured on the set of *Gone with the Wind*. Opera music fills the massive foyer, where a stained glass dome crowns the formidable three-story staircase. Noel Coward's grand piano in the hallway and furniture pieces that once belonged to Mary Todd Lincoln are a few of the more notable appointments in this mini-museum of sorts.

Each of the 15 lavish guest rooms is superbly designed for intimacy, although a few stand out as particularly kiss-worthy. Keep toasty-warm as you soak in the Carmen Suite's claw-foot tub, which sits in the middle of the large bathroom facing an elaborately carved fireplace. If love has your head spinning, you'll fit right into Der Rosenkavalier Suite. This curvaceous room, once the archbishop's library, is light and bright, with an accompanying spacious bathroom and Jacuzzi tub for two. Yet nothing compares to the grand Don Giovanni Suite. With its seven-headed shower, separate sitting room with fireplace, and mahogany four-poster French bed, you won't want to leave this fantasy room. In fact, we're told many people don't, preferring to have dinner delivered via a local gourmet caterer for an intimate candlelit meal in-room.

All guest rooms feature choice antiques, comfortable sitting areas, embroidered linens, and partial or full canopies gracing queen-size feather beds (except for the Gypsy Baron Room, which has the only king-size bed in the mansion). Several rooms offer city views, many have fireplaces, and two boast Jacuzzi tubs, while others have soaking tubs for two. Each room has been christened with the title of a well-known opera, and come singing season, this inn is a popular place to stay.

At the morning hour of your choice, a simple continental breakfast is brought to your door along with the newspaper. If you care to take a morning walk, **ALAMO SQUARE** (see Outdoor Kissing) is right across the street. However, you may just want to stay put since the surroundings and service at The Archbishop's Mansion allow you to partake in an amorous and aristocratic adventure all in one place. **1000 Fulton Street, at Steiner; (415) 563-7872, (800) 543-5820; www.sftrips.com; expensive to unbelievably expensive; minimum-stay requirement on weekends; recommended wedding site.**

Romantic Note: While The Archbishop's Mansion resides in a lovely neighborhood, the streets a few blocks away aren't so impressive. This shouldn't interfere with your stay, but you may want to consider a cab for nighttime excursions.

❦❦❦ THE BED AND BREAKFAST INN, San Francisco The fun part about this delightful bed and breakfast is finding it. Leave behind the urban pace of Union Street and turn into a mews (a British term for "alley") called Charlton Court, where you will discover this charming hideaway. Formerly a neighborhood carriage house, the picturesque place was one of the first bed and breakfasts in San Francisco, and proves the staying power and appeal of a hidden location in a hectic city.

Of the 11 guest accommodations, four share baths while the rest have private facilities. All are surprisingly comfortable and quaint, appointed with eclectic antiques and thick down comforters. A few rooms, including the Giverney Room, even open onto their own private gardens. (Even though it is a "shared bath" room, the Giverney Room's private garden and inexpensive price compensate for the bathroom inconvenience.) Tucked away on the top floor is the popular Celebration Suite, a snug, narrow room romantically equipped with a queen-size brass bed, a comfortable sitting area, and a delightful soaking tub à deux. A spiral staircase in the spacious Mayfair Penthouse winds upstairs to a bedroom with a sloped ceiling and a large, two-person Jacuzzi tub. Another favorite is the wonderfully luxurious and self-contained Garden Suite, located across the alley from the main building. This suite features a solarium, a whirlpool tub that looks onto a private garden patio, two bedrooms (including a loft bedroom), and a fully equipped modern kitchen.

A continental breakfast is served in the main building's small, country-style dining room for all guests except those staying in the Garden Suite. (Couples in this suite won't have to venture far from bed to find their refrigerator stocked with breakfast goodies.) Guests also have the option of having their morning repast delivered directly to their room, a choice too tempting for the romantically inclined to resist. After breakfast, explore the multitude of cosmopolitan shops and dining establishments on Union Street, just steps away from the inn's front door. **4 Charlton Court, at Union Street between Laguna and Buchanan; (415) 921-9784; www. 1stb-bsf.com; inexpensive to expensive.**

❦❦❦ CAMPTON PLACE HOTEL, San Francisco Imagine a valet service that unpacks your baggage, brings fresh bouquets to your room, and provides shoe shines. There is only one word for the Campton Place Hotel: aristocratic; and there is only one word for you during your stay: pampered.

From the marble lobby with its Asian accents to the rooftop garden to the extravagant dining room (see Restaurant Kissing), the Campton Place Hotel has spared no expense. The hotel's management is continuing to spend with a planned renovation that looks very promising. Gone will be the warm but outdated tones of golds and browns, standard baths, and nondescript furnishings. When we visited, the mock-up room exuded sleek and contemporary touches, with blond wood accents, shoji-screen doors that open to large marble bathrooms, and window seats for admiring the city below. The 110 rooms are spread out over 17 floors in order to ensure privacy, and from the ninth floor up, there are only four rooms per floor. No matter which level you choose for your love nest, you'll be delighted by the new stylish rooms, the award-winning restaurant downstairs (room service is available too), and the hotel's convenient location near Union Square and the Financial District. **340 Stockton Street, between Sutter and Post; (415) 781-5555, (800) 235-4300; www.camptonplace.com; very expensive to unbelievably expensive.**

❤❤ **CLIFT HOTEL, San Francisco** Situated in the theater district not far from Union Square, this regal hotel has stood the test of time as one of San Francisco's most notable grand dame hotels. The lobby makes an attempt at being elegant, with wood paneling, high ceilings, ornate murals, and lovely chandeliers; however, some outdated and frumpy furnishings detract from the splendor. These are minor points, really, since you won't be living in the lobby and can check into one of the lovely rooms upstairs.

Each of the 326 guest rooms is slightly different in layout and theme, but common denominators include alluring spaciousness, dark wood furnishings, comfortable linens and down comforters, lavish swagged valances, and large windows that let in plenty of California sunshine. Most rooms feature blue or rose color schemes, with a few mismatched touches here and there. French doors separate the bedroom from the sitting area in both the Petite and Executive Suites. If your pocketbook can handle it, we recommend one of the 12 Grand Suites. The one we visited boasted an incredible view, a large dressing room and marble bathroom, and an overall roominess that may well be unmatched in the city. Surprisingly, none of the rooms have Jacuzzi tubs or fireplaces, and breakfast is not included in the price of your stay.

If you choose to stay in one of the Grand Suites, consider splurging on the hotel's Romance Package. This includes a dozen long-stemmed red roses, a bottle of champagne, chocolate-dipped strawberries, and a pair of monogrammed pajamas (although this begs the question: What will the other person wear?). In the morning, enjoy a full breakfast for two served in-room.

Perhaps the most romantic aspect of the Clift Hotel awaits downstairs, past the lobby, in the exquisite and intimate restaurant called the RED-WOOD ROOM (see Restaurant Kissing). It's the kind of dining room you won't see anywhere except in California, home of the giant redwoods. **495 Geary Street, at Taylor; (415) 775-4700, (800) 65-CLIFT; www.clifthotel. com; very expensive to unbelievably expensive; recommended wedding site.**

❀❀ **EDWARD II BED AND BREAKFAST, San Francisco** The endless procession of cars on Lombard Street is enough to make you want to pass this one up. Don't. If you're willing to contend with intense traffic noise, this is one of San Francisco's best kissing bargains. While prices are comparable to the plethora of nearby economy motels, the Edward II is in a class of its own in every other sense. Stained glass windows add color to the bright and cheerful lobby, where country knickknacks and cozy clusters of tables and chairs fill this inviting space. An adjacent London-inspired pub, ornamented with beautiful green tile work, enhances the property's authentic English disposition.

Although ten of the inn's 32 guest rooms share baths and are reminiscent of European hostel accommodations, the remaining rooms at the Edward II have many of the essentials for a romantic encounter. If you can afford it, book one of the three suites in the main building, all of which feature spectacular beds, plenty of room, and whirlpool bathtubs. (There are also four suites across the street in a pink house sandwiched between a motel and a Thai restaurant. While pleasant and private, they reminded us too much of apartments.) If suite prices are too steep, bargain hunters looking for love will find the Queen Bedrooms with private bath just the right catch. Our favorites are the light-filled corner Queen Rooms; however, you'll need earplugs at night to drown out traffic noise. Decor throughout is a mix of styles, including hunter-green carpeting, floral wallpaper, wicker furniture, and wooden shutters. There's no elevator here, and the walk up to the second and third floors can be tiring with heavy luggage. A continental breakfast is served each morning in the window-filled dining room. **3155 Scott Street, at Lombard; (415) 922-3000, (800) 473-2846; www. citysearch.com/sfo/edwardiiinn; inexpensive to very expensive; minimum-stay requirement on weekends.**

Romantic Warning: Designated parking spaces are limited, and metered street parking is difficult to find. For better or worse, the inn is not located near the downtown core, so your best bet is to use public transportation.

❀❀❀❀ **EL DRISCO HOTEL, San Francisco** Perched at the peak of the regal Pacific Heights neighborhood, this lovely boutique hotel is the find of our San Francisco trip. Who wouldn't fall in love with the oh-so-quiet residential location, the intimate yet relaxed atmosphere, and the exquisitely appointed rooms and suites? Here's a part of San Francisco where lovers can stroll hand in hand through peaceful neighborhoods while enjoying breathtaking city vistas, exploring nearby parks and shopping streets, and admiring the plethora of mansions along the way. Afterward, they return to El Drisco's lovely sitting room for refreshments: Coffee and tea are served here all day, and a delightful evening wine-and-cheese reception takes place here each evening.

The major selling point of the four-story El Drisco is the view. Depending on which room you choose, you'll look out onto the Golden Gate Bridge, East Bay, or everything in between. If, by some strange chance, the view doesn't entice you, the rooms will definitely do the trick. All 43 guest accommodations were designed by the same interior decorator who outfitted the sublime **RITZ-CARLTON** (see review below), so expect only the best in design and comfort. Creamy yellows, beiges, and whites brighten the nicely sized rooms, which come equipped with classical European furnishings, CD stereos, plush robes, and two-poster beds covered with the softest of linens. Bright private bathrooms grace every room, except for six rooms that have detached bathrooms across a semiprivate hallway. (Guests are compensated for the inconvenience by outstanding views or discounted rates.)

In the morning, venture down to the elegant dining room, find a table for two, and enjoy a complimentary continental breakfast. Later, pay a visit to the nearby health club with indoor swimming pool, or head into town via the complimentary drop-off limousine service (available mornings only). Better yet, just stay put. The privacy and serenity that prevail here are addicting, and with El Drisco's regal location, you will feel like you're on top of the world. **2901 Pacific Avenue, at Broderick; (415) 346-2880, (800) 634-7277; www.eldriscohotel.com; very expensive to unbelievably expensive.**

Romantic Warning: We hate to taint this wonderful review with bad news, but here it is: Parking around El Drisco is next to impossible. Even if you're lucky enough to find a spot, you'll have to move the car every three hours (8 A.M.–6 P.M. weekdays). That might take some fun out of hiding away in your room all day.

❦❦❦ **FAIRMONT HOTEL, San Francisco** You might recognize the legendary Fairmont Hotel even if you've never been there—it's one of the most photographed hotels in the country. Built in 1907, this classically designed building is also one of San Francisco's oldest and most popular hotels. From the deep red carpet to the red velvet couches and settees, the hotel's spectacular lobby is cloaked in this rich color, setting the stage for romance. Grandiose crystal chandeliers hang from towering ceilings, and marble columns continue the theme of extravagance and elegance.

Of the hotel's 600 guest accommodations, the newer Tower Rooms are the most inviting, with large picture windows that showcase stunning views of the distant bay. For those who like to soak in the historic ambience, rooms in the main building are your best bet ... plus they have larger bathrooms. (However, be forewarned about room views, some of which aren't good at all. As always, the more expensive the room, the better the view.) When we visited, a $100 million renovation was underway in which all the rooms were being remodeled with yellow, cream, and blue tones; lavish window treatments; and marble bathrooms. Plans are also in the works to redecorate the lobby. The overall goal is to bring back the opulence and grandeur of the hotel's glory days. While the breathtaking lobby certainly doesn't need any more glorification, many rooms in the main building could do with some edification. We look forward to the results.

Even if you don't stay at the Fairmont, be sure to visit **MASON'S** (see Restaurant Kissing) for American grill cuisine in a formal setting. **950 Mason Street, at California; (415) 772-5000, (800) 527-4727; www.fairmont.com; expensive to unbelievably expensive; recommended wedding site.**

Romantic Note: We aren't usually awed by hotel banquet/conference rooms, but those at the Fairmont are an exception. If you're planning a special event, be sure to check out the opulent Gold Room or the intimate Pavilion Room with its rooftop garden.

❤❤❤ **THE HOTEL MAJESTIC, San Francisco** Pacific Heights, known for posh and upscale residences, is also home to one of San Francisco's classic hotels. The former home of a turn-of-the-century railroad magnate, the gleaming white Majestic lets you sample San Francisco in grand style. A mirrored marble entrance leads into a plush lobby area brimming with antique tapestries, etched glass, and French Empire furnishings. You may want to stop here and sip a cocktail at the genuine 19th-century French mahogany bar and admire the exquisite (and rare) butterfly collection adorning the walls. But don't flutter here too long—the real romance is waiting upstairs.

The centerpiece of many of the 57 elegantly historic rooms is a canopy bed dressed in plump feather pillows with fine linens and a plush down comforter. Lace curtains, subtle color schemes, large and light marble bathrooms (many with claw-foot tubs), and beautiful antiques create an upscale, turn-of-the-century ambience, while gas fireplaces in some rooms add an instant glow. Small crystal chandeliers embellish every room, and bay windows allow in ample sunlight, especially in the corner rooms, which feature a semicircular wall of tall windows. Only two points detract from the elegance of this five-story, architecturally stunning hotel. First, busy Gough Street is below and the windows aren't soundproofed. (Of course, that tends to be the case no matter where you stay in San Francisco.) To avoid undue traffic noise, we recommend the rooms that face somewhat less-trafficked Sutter Street. Second, touch-ups throughout the hotel are needed to correct flickering lights, exposed extension cords, and sloppy paint jobs in some rooms.

For a very convenient romantic repast, dine at **CAFE MAJESTIC** (see Restaurant Kissing), located downstairs adjacent to the lobby. **1500 Sutter Street, at Gough; (415) 441-1100, (800) 869-8966; moderate to unbelievably expensive.**

Romantic Suggestion: Take a stroll through **LAFAYETTE PARK**, at the corner of Octavia and Sacramento, a few blocks north of the hotel. Panoramic views of San Francisco await, along with well-tended gardens and hilly lawns.

❤❤❤❤ HOTEL MONACO, San Francisco

The Côte d'Azur is closer than you think. In fact, if you happen to be in San Francisco's theater district, it's just around the corner. As you step over the threshold of this French-inspired luxury hotel, you'll feel as if you have traveled halfway around the world. In the front lobby a life-size portrait of a woman draped in stars and moonlight is visible at the top of a sweeping marble staircase. Just beyond, an ornate chandelier hangs from a cathedral ceiling, and floor-to-ceiling mirrors reflect a mural depicting hot-air balloons amid the clouds. Armchairs close to the raging fireplace invite guests to sit down and unwind. In a second even cozier common room, flamboyant fabrics and flourishes provide an air of chic opulence. Modern artwork graces the terra-cotta walls, and a second fireplace casts a warm glow over the richly decorated parlor. Wine and cheese are served every afternoon in this handsome room.

You know you're in for something different when you check in at the front desk, which has been playfully patterned after a classically styled steamer trunk. As strange as it sounds, the designers here have done more than pull off the unusual—they've created a showpiece. The 201 extravagant and luxurious guest rooms are works of art, boasting brilliantly colored and intriguingly patterned fabrics and linens. In some rooms, red-striped canopies hover above fluffy yellow down comforters. Eastern wildlife paintings contrast with green and yellow pin-striped wallpaper. Antique trunks hint of exotic travels, while modern comfort is ensured by jetted two-person Jacuzzi tubs in 20 suites, and shower heads with massage options in the rest of the rooms. A full-service fitness center and spa are available to guests, complimentary shoe shines and newspapers are provided, and Nintendos are featured in every room—although we can think of better games to play in these surroundings. **501 Geary Street, at Taylor; (415) 292-0100, (800) 214-4220; www.hotelmonaco.com; expensive to unbelievably expensive; recommended wedding site.**

Romantic Note: Hotel Monaco's adjacent restaurants, THE PETITE and GRAND CAFES (415-292-0101; moderate to expensive), are open daily for breakfast, lunch, and dinner, as well as Sunday brunch. Toulouse-Lautrec artwork, brass sculptures, and spherical chandeliers create an intriguing environment, but echoing cathedral ceilings and an open kitchen are distracting, to say the least—especially when the restaurants are full. We recommend filling up on tasty French-California cuisine here and relying on the hotel itself to inspire your romantic inclinations.

❤❤❣ **HOTEL TRITON, San Francisco** If, after Alice went through the looking glass, she had needed a hotel room, she might have stayed at the Hotel Triton. The interior is a combination of surrealistic and unconventional detailing, offering some of the more intriguing visual stimulation in town. Chairs shaped like puzzle pieces adorn the lobby, in-house phones come bedecked with faux jewels, and you'll see stars when looking at the hallway carpeting. Guest-room walls prove more than colorful with hand-painted white-and-taupe checkers or sponge-painted pink and iridescent gold patterns. Beds are strewn with oversize throw pillows and backed with cloud-shaped, upholstered headboards. All 140 rooms have up-to-date amenities to make your stay exceedingly comfortable, albeit amusingly eccentric.

For a breath of fresh air, both figuratively and literally, request a room on the seventh floor, otherwise known as the EcoFloor, where the ecologically minded meets the superchic. These rooms come equipped with water- and air-filtration systems and all-natural linens, as well as biodegradable soaps and shampoos.

Hotel Triton also has seven designer suites, all of which are stellar attractions. The Jerry Garcia Suite displays a collection of his fabulous silks, the Wyland Suite is decorated with colorful seascapes and boasts an impressive fish tank, and Suzan Briganti's Love Letter Suite is the perfect spot to rendezvous with your favorite pen pal.

Fresh cookies, along with complimentary wine and beer, await in the lobby each evening. Once in a while, a Tarot card reader shows up to read fortunes. **342 Grant Avenue, at Bush; (415) 394-0500, (800) 433-6611; www.hotel-tritonsf.com; expensive to unbelievably expensive.**

❦❦ **HOTEL VINTAGE COURT, San Francisco** Hotel Vintage Court has one of the cozier hotel lobbies in downtown San Francisco. Circular couches surround a marble hearth where a crackling fire inspires guests to kick off their shoes, listen to classical music, and enjoy the evening wine reception. Once you've selected your vintage of choice, head upstairs to the guest rooms, named after some of California's best-known wineries. Though names differ, the rooms share the same fresh, countrified decor, with floral draperies accenting large windows and matching linens draping queen-size beds. The only drawbacks: Views are nonexistent in some rooms (ours looked into a rundown apartment building), and the basic rooms border on tiny with equally small and rather bland bathrooms. If you're willing to pay just a bit more for extra space, book one of the suites with an oversize Jacuzzi tub. In spite of the pervasive hotel-style ambience and lack of scenic views, rooms of this caliber rarely go hand in hand with such reasonable rates. **650 Bush Street, between Powell and Stockton; (415) 392-4666, (800) 654-1100; www.vintagecourt.com; moderate to very expensive; minimum-stay requirement on weekends.**

Romantic Suggestion: Guests get preferred reservations at MASA'S (see Restaurant Kissing), the Vintage Court's world-famous restaurant. Dining here is a romantic must whether you're an overnight guest or not.

❦❦❦❦ **THE HUNTINGTON HOTEL, San Francisco** Our highest recommendation when it comes to kissing in San Francisco goes to the elegant Huntington Hotel, perched on the upper tier of Nob Hill. Originally built as a luxury apartment building, The Huntington has 140 commodious, wonderfully quiet rooms brimming with individuality and romantic flair. Because it's an independently owned hotel with no corporate-set definitions on decor, the owners have invited noted designers to transform guest rooms into works of art. Styles range from contemporary Asian to English classical, all with luxurious touches at every turn: marble foyers and bathrooms, large windows that let in the crisp San Francisco air, ultra-comfortable beds, and enough space to rank these rooms as some of the largest in town. Large mirrors, artwork fit for a museum, mini-bars or kitchenettes, and TVs hidden within armoires are other heartwarming features. Guests are offered complimentary tea or sherry service upon arrival to their room—a perfect way to unwind in privacy. Many rooms enjoy views of pleasantly manicured Huntington Park, across the street, where the sight of locals doing tai chi at dawn inspires guests to slow their pace and enjoy their surroundings. For dazzling delights, book a city-facing room to see San Francisco in all its illuminated glory.

Although The Huntington's room rates may be high, you get what you pay for here. You'll want for nothing at this hotel, and the gracious staff ensures that your stay will be private and thoroughly comfortable. **1075 California Street, at Taylor; (415) 474-5400, (800) 652-1539 in California, (800) 227-4683; www.slh.com/huntingt; expensive to unbelievably expensive.**

Romantic Suggestion: Off the lobby of The Huntington Hotel resides THE BIG 4 restaurant (415-771-1140; expensive to very expensive; breakfast and dinner daily, lunch Monday–Friday). Mahogany walls, dark green leather banquettes and chairs, and historical photos give it a traditional "men's club" look, yet the subdued lighting and elegantly appointed tables can charm those seeking sophistication and romance. The best spot for cuddling up to your sweetie is next to the crackling fire in the cozy lounge. In this alluring location, listen to the soft piano music and enjoy a nightcap before retiring to your choice accommodations.

☙ **THE INN AT UNION SQUARE, San Francisco** You won't have to carry those shopping bags far if you stay at this small, European-style inn, located a half block west of Union Square. Add to this convenience a friendly staff and some unique policies (no tipping, no smoking), and The Inn at Union Square may just suit your needs. All 30 rooms are appointed with sitting areas, standard baths, matching bedspreads and draperies, and brass lion-head door knockers. As for a view, don't expect any (you may even be looking at a brick wall). Some rooms are a bit on the small side and in need of a decorator, but not the choice Penthouse Suite. This top-floor retreat has its own sauna, deep Asian soaking tub, fireplace, and wet bar. Yet improvements in the standard rooms were underway at the time of our visit. Rooms were being renovated with updated bedspreads and draperies, new rugs, and marble accents in the bathrooms.

Painted with murals of bookshelves and lovely garden scenes, the main lobby is too small and too close to noisy Post Street to be relaxing. Thankfully, each of the six floors has its own fireplace in a lounge where evening wine and hors d'oeuvres can be enjoyed (or taken back to the privacy of your room). In the morning, a complimentary continental breakfast is served in each floor's lounge. **440 Post Street, between Mason and Powell; (415) 397-3510, (800) 288-4346; www.unionsquare.com; expensive to unbelievably expensive; minimum-stay requirement on weekends.**

☙☙ **JACKSON COURT, San Francisco** A small brick courtyard hemmed with potted plants fronts the entrance of this turn-of-the-century brownstone mansion, located in the Pacific Heights neighborhood. Despite its grand size, the warmth of a home prevails inside this charming bed and breakfast, thanks to its reasonably quiet residential location, gracious but unobtrusive staff, wood-paneled library stocked with local newspapers and magazines, and an inviting front parlor where a complimentary afternoon tea is served in front of the impressive fireplace.

Upon arrival, guests are ushered to their room and welcomed with a bottle of nonalcoholic California wine. The ten eclectic guest rooms each have their own charms and differ dramatically from one another. Set off the parlor, the sunlit Garden Court (originally the home's dining room) has dark wood walls accented by a showy marble fireplace. Other romantic features of this room include a king-size bed, large windows, and a private outdoor garden patio—a perfect place for puckering up. Next door, the sunny Executive Room wows romantics with its queen-size bed, fireplace, Italian marble accents, and seductive spaciousness. Upstairs in the popular Library Room, a large sitting area is warmed by a wood-burning fireplace. One of the sunniest rooms in the house, the Corner Room, is appointed with white and beige fabrics and features two comfortable window seats. Luscious linens and comfy antique beds compensate for the rather bland bathrooms and discordant style of some of the rooms, including mismatched carpets and wallpaper. Last, the walls are thin, so if you're a light or late sleeper, try the quieter rooms on the third floor. (Just pack lightly because there's no elevator.)

One of the more generous continental breakfasts in town is served each morning in the second-floor dining room. If you want privacy, however, trays are available to take the juices, coffee, fruits, and pastries back to your quarters. **2198 Jackson Street, at Buchanan; (415) 929-7670, (800) SF-TRIPS; www.sftrips.com; expensive to very expensive; minimum-stay requirement on weekends.**

Romantic Note: Because this property is operated as a time-share, reservations are accepted no sooner than two months in advance to allow owners the opportunity to choose the rooms they want well ahead of time. Except for this rule, Jackson Court has the look and feel of a typical professionally run bed and breakfast—you'll never notice the difference.

Romantic Warning: Parking is a problem here. While street parking is available, you'll have to move your car every two hours (between 8 A.M. and 6 P.M. Monday–Saturday), and that can certainly interrupt kissing. A parking lot a few blocks away sometimes has space, but at a price.

💋💋💋 **MANDARIN ORIENTAL, San Francisco** We debated including this exclusive business-oriented hotel in our kissing book, but not for long. The Mandarin Oriental has by far the most stunning vistas of any hotel in the city. How could it not, when guest rooms start on the 38th floor? With such unparalleled scenery awaiting upstairs, you'll quickly forget the

Financial District locale and the suit-and-tie crowd down in the lobby. You can also overlook the outrageous room costs if you visit on Friday and/or Saturday night when rates drop like a stock gone sour.

Unobstructed city and bay views from huge windows are standard in all 158 rooms and suites, so just decide which part of California you'd like to gaze upon with the in-room binoculars. (Some rooms even have peekaboo ocean views when the weather cooperates.) Soothing sage, crimson, gold, and cream colors; plenty of square footage; and luxurious marble baths delight the senses, while extra touches such as Thai silk slippers presented at turndown, silk-covered headboards, and terry-cloth robes clearly demonstrate why the Mandarin Oriental is a first-class hotel. If you want to soak in more than just the view, book one of the Mandarin Rooms, where the bathtub fronts a floor-to-ceiling window. Better yet, in the Taipan or Oriental Suites go outside and enjoy the views from your private terrace. If the height of these suites doesn't make you dizzy, their price tags certainly will.

Descending from cloud nine can be difficult, but back on earth you'll find a state-of-the-art fitness center and the hotel's superb restaurant, **SILKS** (see Restaurant Kissing). After sampling such amenities, scale the heights of tranquillity back to your luxurious love nest and enjoy the bird's-eye view. **222 Sansome Street, between Pine and California; (415) 276-9888, (800) 622-0404; www.mandarin-oriental.com; unbelievably expensive.**

❦ **NOB HILL INN, San Francisco** Classical music in the cozy lobby of this 1907 Edwardian mansion takes your mind off the busy thoroughfare just outside, although traffic noise poses more of a distraction in the upstairs guest rooms. The cheap linens and lack of amenities in some of the 21 guest rooms don't even merit one kiss, but according to management, many of these rooms are filled by time-share owners. So why do we consider this a find? Approximately half of the inn's guest rooms have attractive linens and enticing gas fireplaces; some even have sexy marble bathrooms with glass-enclosed showers or claw-foot tubs. Bed choices range from canopy to brass to four-poster, and some street-facing rooms feature the bed tucked into the curved bay window. And while they may be tempting to the pocketbook, stay away from the inexpensive rooms (no view whatsoever).

Included with your stay is a generous continental breakfast, served in-room or downstairs at individual tables in a cozy wine cellar adjacent to the lobby. A bargain like this is bound to inspire a kiss or two—as long as you're careful to reserve one of the nicer rooms. **1000 Pine Street, at Taylor; (415) 673-6080, (888) 982-2632; inexpensive to very expensive.**

❦❦❦ **NOB HILL LAMBOURNE, San Francisco** After a day exploring the city and walking up those hills, you'll be happy to return home to this boutique hotel that concentrates on keeping you healthy, both mentally and physically. Quiet, serene, and uncomplicated in its decor, the Nob Hill Lambourne offers soothing relief from the world outside. With only 20 rooms and suites, guests are ensured privacy and attentive service. Neutral colors and contemporary French-style furnishings please the eye, while kitchenettes, TV/VCRs, and high-tech stereos satisfy the other senses. Although standard looking, bathrooms come equipped with features designed to promote relaxation and romance: temperature-controlled deep tubs, waffle-weave robes, a homeopathic remedy bar, and built-in stereo speakers. The hotel's six suites offer even more perks. Besides spaciousness, each suite features a separate parlor, in-room exercise equipment, and a hard-to-find feature in San Francisco: a tiny (no view) veranda off the bedroom that's perfect for two.

No matter which room you choose, mind and body benefits remain standard, including an on-site spa treatment room, a wine-and-cheese reception every evening, a complimentary low-fat continental breakfast, and evening turndown service. But, no, you won't find chocolates on your pillow here. Instead, the health-conscious hotel provides Performance Packs®, capsules of antioxidants designed "for men and women who demand top performance." **725 Pine Street, between Powell and Stockton; (415) 433-2287, (800) 274-8466; www.sftrips.com; expensive to very expensive.**

❧❧ **PARK HYATT, San Francisco** Granted, San Francisco's Financial District tugs more at the purse strings than at the heart strings, but this shouldn't discourage you from staying at the Park Hyatt, one of the truly romantic choices in this part of town. The intimate lobby and even cozier library are as inviting as a residential living room, with rich textures, marble and wood accents, and an abundance of windows. A delightful tea is served here every afternoon, as well as pre-dinner cocktails and complimentary morning coffee.

With 360 rooms, the Park Hyatt may seem rather large for an intimate getaway, but once you enter your cozy enclave, size won't matter. Decorated in warm earth tones, the guest rooms vary in layout, and the best views, via floor-to-ceiling windows, are found on the top floors. Italian-style furnishings, modern art pieces, and granite-lined bathrooms with separate showers and bathtubs make these some of the classiest rooms in town.

Guests are encouraged to take advantage of the hotel's fitness center and complimentary Mercedez-Benz drop-off service. One aspect that sets the Park Hyatt apart from other downtown hotels is its magnificent art collection. If that's not enough entertainment, the hotel is located across the street from The Embarcadero, an outdoor galleria of upscale shops, restaurants, and movie theaters. **333 Battery Street, at Embarcadero Center; (415) 392-1234, (800) 323-7275; www.parkhyattsf.com; very expensive to unbelievably expensive.**

Romantic Note: A weekend visit here rates high on the romance scale. The business crowd is gone, and room prices drop several percentage points.

❧❧❧ PETITE AUBERGE, San Francisco

A collection of stuffed teddy bears and the aroma of freshly baked cookies greet you in the lobby of this winsome downtown hotel. It doesn't matter which of the 26 guest rooms you choose; even the eight smallest rooms are endowed with the gracious charm of a French-country inn. Creamy lace window treatments, thick comforters, and muted color schemes ensure comfort and calm during your stay, and the staff's attention to detail guarantees satisfaction. Sixteen rooms feature fireplaces, and the deluxe Petite Suite is the only room with its own private entrance, Jacuzzi tub, and patio (just don't expect a petite price). The largest rooms face Bush Street and, consequently, are more subject to street noise. Thankfully, fairly effective soundproofing efforts have been made throughout the inn, but the smaller rooms at the back of the hotel are still the quietest.

As the smell of baked goods suggests, the kitchen takes great care in preparing a full breakfast, served buffet-style in the lower-level French-country dining room each morning. (Late-afternoon wine and hors d'oeuvres are also presented here.) Terra-cotta–tiled floors, an expansive mural depicting a country marketplace, and a glowing gas fireplace in the neighboring parlor add to the charming setting. You will never be left hungry at Petite Auberge, but if you'd like to venture out for dinner, the downtown location presents countless dining options. **863 Bush Street, between Mason and Taylor; (415) 928-6000, (800) 365-3004; www.foursisters.com/petite.html; moderate to very expensive.**

❧❧❧❧ THE PRESCOTT HOTEL, San Francisco

While The Prescott is much too large to be considered charming or intimate, that doesn't keep the management from trying to make things feel that way. A fire glows in an immense stone hearth in the hotel's elegant "living room," where beautiful flower arrangements, antique writing desks, comfortable chairs, and a collection of early California arts and crafts welcome visitors to sit and stay awhile.

Although The Prescott has 164 guest accommodations, the hotel feels much more intimate due to the fact that rooms are nicely spread out between two connected buildings. For a splurge, book one of the 46 rooms or 23 suites on the Executive Club Level. Here you'll find the "hotel within a hotel" concept in full swing, with a private concierge, complimentary continental breakfast and evening cocktail reception, and free morning limousine service within the general area. Moreover, stationary bicycles and rowing machines can even be delivered to your room upon request. And if that's not enough, complimentary head and neck massages are available from 5 P.M. to 7 P.M. in the Executive Club's lounge. If all these amenities can't prep you for romance, nothing will. Ralph Lauren bedspreads; deep color schemes of hunter green, eggplant, and taupe; cherrywood tables and chairs; elegant armoires; large mirrors; and brass accents are attractive features in the Executive Club's guest rooms. Bathrooms, while standard, come beautifully appointed with black-and-taupe striped shower curtains, marble accents, and gold and pewter fixtures. Executive Club Suites are slightly more expensive, but have more space and the added luxury of whirlpool tubs.

The remaining 83 regular rooms and nine deluxe suites also maintain the highest degree of style and comfort, and come equipped with every imaginable modern convenience. These accommodations feature color TV/VCRs, stocked bars and refrigerators, hair dryers, and terry-cloth robes.

Roosting at the top of The Prescott is what may be the most extraordinary suite in the city: the Mendocino Penthouse (one of three luxury suites residing on the seventh floor). You'll be instantly enchanted by the rich Edwardian furnishings and hardwood floors in the parlor and bedroom, the grand piano in the formal dining room, the two wood-burning fireplaces, and the rooftop deck with a Jacuzzi tub and garden. Staying here is the height of romantic pampering, which makes its unbelievably expensive price tag a little easier to swallow. **545 Post Street, between Taylor and Mason; (415) 563-0303, (800) 283-7322; www.prescotthotel.com; very expensive to unbelievably expensive; recommended wedding site.**

Romantic Note: POSTRIO (see Restaurant Kissing), located just off the hotel's lobby, is a stunning, chic eatery with sensational cuisine. Hotel guests get priority seating at this popular Wolfgang Puck restaurant—a plus when things get busy.

❤❤❤❤ **THE RITZ-CARLTON, San Francisco** Simply put, The Ritz is the crème de la crème of San Francisco's hotels. If you're in the mood to be waited on, catered to, and simply spoiled, book a night at this fabulous neoclassic hotel on Nob Hill. From the expansive rose garden to the Persian carpets and Bohemian crystal chandeliers, everything is first class. You'll marvel at the exquisite 18th- and 19th-century furnishings, fabrics, and antiques decorating the polished-marble lobby. Just off the foyer is **THE LOBBY LOUNGE**, a regal room with cream-colored walls, ornate chandeliers, floor-to-ceiling windows, and life-size portraits of aristocratic women. Here guests can savor afternoon tea accompanied by the soothing melodies of a classical harp. Come evening, a sushi chef appears with an accompanying sushi cart and rolls out made-to-order delicacies for you to enjoy.

All 336 rooms and suites are sights to behold, featuring antique-style furnishings, elegant window treatments, richly upholstered furniture, Italian marble bathrooms with double sinks, and plush terry-cloth bathrobes. Views aren't the best in town, but you'll never miss them with rooms like these. The 42 spacious suites are the most grand, with separate dining, living, and sleeping rooms, and private balconies, some of which offer glimpses of the city. In the 52 Ritz-Carlton Club rooms that comprise the eighth and ninth floors, guests are provided with a dedicated concierge and continuous culinary treats: a complimentary continental breakfast, mid-morning snacks, an afternoon tea, cocktails and hors d'oeuvres, and late-evening cordials and chocolates.

Overindulging can be a concern here, but don't worry. The Ritz is one of only a few luxury downtown hotels to feature an in-house fitness center complete with a fully equipped workout room, heated indoor pool, whirlpool, and spa. Massage therapy is also offered in case you climb one too many of San Francisco's infamous hills.

Everything you need is at your fingertips when you stay at The Ritz, including one of the city's most elegant restaurants, the opulent **DINING ROOM** (see Restaurant Kissing). On warm days, **THE TERRACE** (415-773-6198; expensive to very expensive; breakfast, lunch, and dinner daily, brunch Sunday) offers courtyard seating at white wrought-iron chairs and tables with peach-colored umbrellas. Enjoy contemporary Mediterranean cuisine accompanied by a pianist and jazz vocalist Friday through Sunday evenings. A haven for dessert aficionados awaits adjacent to the Dining Room in **THE RITZ BAR** (see Restaurant Kissing). **600 Stockton, at California; (415) 296-7465, (800) 241-3333; www.ritzcarlton.com; unbelievably expensive; recommended wedding site.**

❤❤❤❤ **THE SHERMAN HOUSE, San Francisco** When *Architectural Digest* features a bed and breakfast in its illustrious pages, you usually know you're in for an interior decorator's dream. You might also surmise that you would pay for such photogenic surroundings ... and you'd be right. Dubbed by many the "mini-Ritz," The Sherman House will turn your hearts inside out with elegance—and so will the bill, unless you have an unlimited expense account. An "absurdly expensive" price category is more appropriate for many of the rooms in this exquisitely restored 1876 French-Italianate mansion. Still, this is San Francisco's most aristocratically intimate hotel. Renovations inspired by the French Second Empire radiate royal ambience, from the grand music room with its cathedral ceilings and hardwood floors to the sweeping wood staircase that winds through the center of the home.

Pampering starts at check-in with complimentary valet service (essential in the posh Pacific Heights neighborhood), followed by champagne and hors d'oeuvres. After being escorted to your room, you will be left alone to savor the splendor. All 11 guest rooms in the mansion are simply magnificent, so choosing one won't be difficult. Many have full canopy beds with heavy velvet-lined tapestry draperies that can be wrapped around the bed to create a plush hideaway during nightly turndown service. All have lovely sitting areas, some of which feature comfortable window seats with abundant pillows and billows of drapes above. Gas fireplaces, luscious linens and down comforters, gorgeous antique armoires and writing desks, CD players, and black-granite bathrooms with deep, black soaking tubs are more of the seemingly endless luxuries. Views range from garden scenes to sweeping vistas of the bay. One magnificent room (at $700 a night) boasts a rooftop patio with views worth the price.

Stone walking paths lead from the main house, past manicured courtyards with splashing fountains and a gazebo, to the quiet confines of the Carriage House, a favorite for sweethearts. While all three suites in the Carriage House border on divine, we instantly fell in love with the Thomas Church Garden Suite on the lower level, which is enveloped by multilevel gardens. Two walls of French-paned windows allow plenty of daylight into this striking suite, highlighting its latticed walls, rattan furnishings, slate floors, teak-trimmed jetted tub, and free-standing fireplace.

A complimentary full breakfast, served in the main home's solarium, lets you soak in the rays as you sip your coffee. In the evening, wine and hors d'oeuvres are served in the Gallery, and at dinnertime, guests have exclusive use of the intimate dining room where seasonal specialties are prepared by the chef. (We'd give it four kisses, if only it were open to the public.) Dinner can also be served in-room, but here at The Sherman House, both options are equally enticing.

If you're hesitating to stay at The Sherman House because of the steep price, keep in mind that the sumptuous surroundings are unparalleled anywhere else in San Francisco. You might want to save up for a special celebration you'll never forget. **2160 Green Street, at Webster; (415) 563-3600, (800) 424-5777; www.theshermanhouse.com; very expensive to unbelievably expensive; minimum-stay requirement on weekends and holidays.**

❦❦❦ **THE SPENCER HOUSE, San Francisco** The Spencer House has little need for advertising. In fact, there isn't a "SPENCER HOUSE" sign to be seen anywhere near this grand multicolored Queen Anne Victorian. It isn't even listed in the phone book. So how do guests find out about this extraordinary bed and breakfast? The answer is simple: word of mouth from satisfied customers, and repeat business. This fact alone gives you some idea of the kind of intimacy guests experience here.

Although The Spencer House has all the trappings of a noble Victorian home—spacious firelit parlors, hardwood floors, Oriental carpets, and period antiques—its real focus is on comfort. All six guest rooms have feather beds, rich fabrics, and private baths; some feature large bay windows that offer glimpses of nearby Buena Vista Park and the city beyond. Bradbury & Bradbury silk-screened wall and ceiling coverings, crisp linens trimmed with antique lace, gas and electric chandeliers, and a collection of gorgeous antiques contribute to the authentic but fantastically comfortable Victorian ambience. The French Room remains a popular romantic hideaway, thanks to its magnificent king-size bed flanked by a backboard of smiling cherubs. The bathroom may be tiny, but the bed certainly makes up for this shortcoming. What you won't see among all this loveliness are TVs in any of the rooms. For many seeking romance, that's reason enough to stay here.

Aromas from the kitchen will tempt you downstairs to enjoy a delicious full breakfast of eggs Benedict or Belgian waffles topped with warm strawberries. Such culinary delights are served at one long table in the ornate, wood-paneled dining room that's so stunning it looks like it came straight out of a *Masterpiece Theatre* special. No wonder The Spencer House doesn't need to advertise! **1080 Haight Street, at Baker; (415) 626-9205; www.spencerhouse.com; moderate to very expensive; minimum-stay requirement on weekends and holidays.**

❦❦❦ **THE WARWICK REGIS HOTEL, San Francisco** In a city where many hotels strive to be hip and modern, The Warwick stands its ground as a classic-style hotel set in the heart of San Francisco's theater district. Its reputation for romance stems from its enticing, luxurious atmosphere, where old-world charm combines with modern amenities to create an exceedingly comfortable yet elegant ambience. All 84 regal guest rooms are decorated with comfortable French and English antiques, mirrored armoires, lace curtains surrounded by lush draperies, charming bee-motif wallpaper, and black-marble bathrooms adorned with fresh flowers. High ceilings and plenty of windows help brighten the olive and beige rooms. Some exceptionally romantic suites have balconies, canopy beds, and fireplaces.

Coffee and cookies are served downstairs at the **LA SCENE CAFE** (see Restaurant Kissing) every weekday afternoon. Once you've satiated your romantic inclinations, you'll appreciate that The Warwick is just a short stroll from much of what makes San Francisco famous: Union Square, the cable cars, art galleries, exclusive shops, fabulous restaurants, and, of course, the theaters. **490 Geary Street, at Taylor; (415) 928-7900, (800) 827-3447; www.warwickhotels.com; moderate to very expensive; minimum-stay requirement.**

Romantic Note: When making your reservations at The Warwick, ask about the different romantic packages (including theater packages). These include such extras as valet parking, dinner at **LA SCENE CAFE**, red roses on your pillows with turndown service, and charming mementos.

❦❦❦ **WHITE SWAN INN, San Francisco** Magically, the White Swan Inn brings the English countryside to life in the heart of downtown San Francisco. The 26 guest accommodations are masterfully decorated with stately antiques, floral and striped wallpapers, dried-flower wreaths, and lace curtains. Personal touches like turndown service (complete with chocolates left on your pillows), homemade cookies available day and night, and soothing bath salts in every bathroom make a stay in the city exceedingly comfortable. Every room has a gas-log fireplace as well, which helps warm the poorly insulated rooms when temperatures fall. The two spacious Romance Suites, each with a separate dressing area, canopy queen-size bed with a down comforter, and even more flowers and lace, are particularly inviting. For extra space, book the two-room Ashleigh Suite with its canopy bed, two fireplaces, and two bathrooms. A bottle of champagne is left for guests in the suites, although every room comes with complimentary soft drinks in its small refrigerator.

As wonderful as the guest rooms are, you should venture downstairs to the handsome fireside library in the afternoon. High tea and an abundance of appetizers are served here daily. A full breakfast buffet is also presented downstairs in the cozy dining room, where individual tables provide ample privacy. Overall, the White Swan Inn effectively sustains the illusion of being a small European boutique hotel. Unless you look out a window (Bush Street is an extremely busy thoroughfare), you may forget you're within walking distance of Union Square. We were delighted with our accommodations, but the staff's indifferent attitude soured the sweetness a bit. And speaking of sweets, the staff forgot our turndown service, so we missed those chocolates. **845 Bush Street, between Mason and Taylor; (415) 775-1755, (800) 999-9570; www.foursisters.com/white. html; expensive to very expensive.**

Restaurant Kissing

❤❤❤❣ **ACQUERELLO, San Francisco** In a city of ritzy, trend-setting restaurants where showiness is taken to extremes, it's refreshing to find a place that stands apart. Acquerello, a pretty and cozy Italian hideaway, allows elegance to speak for itself. Nothing competes for your attention in the dining room. Round two-person tables are simply adorned with lamp-like candles and elegant china, while butter-colored walls are softly illuminated by wall sconces and graced with watercolors of Italy. Pay attention to the subtle detailing here and you'll notice that Acquerello is housed in an old church. Ornate ironwork, a round stained glass window, and vaulted ceilings that still retain the original hand-painted designs add a sense of history and serenity.

Just as notable as the surroundings is the service, which ranks close to flawless. Special touches include a complimentary aperitif and tableside decanting service for the restaurant's outstanding selection of Italian reds. No need to worry about choosing between such innovative Italian entrées as pumpkin gnocchi tossed with butter and sage, pink-pepper–crusted loin of pork, and almond-amaretti–crusted sea bass: All are superb. We ended our meal with an almond panna cotta adorned with caramel-Frangelico sauce. Simply heavenly. **1722 Sacramento Street, between Van Ness and Polk; (415) 567-5432; www.acquerello.com; expensive to very expensive; dinner Tuesday–Saturday.**

❤❤ **BIX, San Francisco** The elegance and sophistication of the '30s comes to life as you step over the threshold of Bix's back-alley entrance. The dramatic two-story restaurant/jazz club speaks both Art Deco and classic decor with Corinthian columns, ornate cathedral ceilings, and dark wood paneling from top to bottom. Positioned above the long bar is an expansive mural of a lively '30s dance club scene. Upstairs along an open balcony, cozy banquettes and booths offer the best opportunities for quiet conversations. (The downstairs area is too busy and noisy, especially near the bar.) Ellington-era jazz sets the mood for romance, and the professional, tuxedo-clad waitstaff help add that final touch of class.

The menu, which changes daily, sticks with traditional treats such as grilled filet mignon, Dungeness crab cakes, seared ahi tuna, and, a local favorite, chicken hash à la Bix. Stay a while, listen to the sultry sounds of the torch singer, and then indulge in dessert. You'll coo too after experiencing the warm chocolate brioche pudding. **56 Gold Street, an alley between Pacific and Jackson, off Montgomery; (415) 433-6300; www.city search.com/sfo/bix; moderate to expensive; lunch Monday–Friday, dinner daily.**

❀❀ **CAFE JACQUELINE, San Francisco** Forget tea for two! Try a soufflé à deux. Sharing has never been so appealing (or required) than at this tiny hole-in-the-wall restaurant in North Beach where soufflés for two comprise the menu. Although a bit weathered, the interior radiates old-world charm with intimate, closely spaced tables for two, high ceilings, and worn wood floors. A few flower arrangements and mix-and-match artwork near the back are the only attempts to decorate the sparse dining room.

You'll have no difficulty deciding what to order. Besides a two-item salad selection, the menu revolves around build-your-own soufflés. The more goodies you want added—leeks, broccoli, prosciutto, mushrooms, extra Gruyère cheese—the more you pay. Luckily, the prices for even the fullest soufflé won't flatten your wallet. Desserts keep the soufflés coming, offering such classical flavors as chocolate, Grand Marnier, lemon, and seasonal fresh fruit. Such puffery is a perfect prelude to a romantic evening. **1454 Grant Avenue, between Green and Union; (415) 981-5565; inexpensive to moderate; dinner Wednesday–Sunday.**

❀❀❀ **CAFE MAJESTIC, San Francisco** Local reviewers and residents often call Cafe Majestic one of San Francisco's "most romantic" cafés, and we're not surprised. More restaurant than café, the Majestic's tasteful interior is characterized by a lofty ornamented ceiling, Corinthian columns that separate its three dining rooms, and muted apricot and sage green tones. Long-stemmed red roses at every table add to the romantic spirit. In the evenings and during Sunday brunch, a talented pianist tickles the ivories of the baby grand in the corner and encourages special requests. Don't be shy—he's willing (and able) to play just about anything!

Sunday morning is a perfect (and relatively peaceful) time to visit, especially when the sun shines through the restaurant's large windows. Salmon eggs Benedict and French toast drizzled with creamy apple butter start the day off right. The dinner menu is certain to please romance-seeking couples with such dishes as grilled salmon with roasted vegetable ragoût, rack of lamb stuffed with spinach and black chanterelles, grilled Sonoma quail, and pancetta-wrapped veal loin. Service is first-rate, and desserts are divine. **1500 Sutter Street, at Gough, at The Hotel Majestic; (415) 441-1100, (800) 869-8966; moderate to expensive; breakfast and dinner daily, brunch Sunday.**

❀❀❀ **CAFÉ MOZART, San Francisco** For more than two decades, this intimate downtown restaurant has billed itself as "San Francisco's Most Romantic European Restaurant." By the looks of the many twosomes dining here, that claim holds true. Thick red velvet and embroidered white curtains hang in the windows, secluding diners from the busy street. Much of Café Mozart's charm comes from having only a handful of tables, each draped with white linens and set with fine china, silver, crystal, and a single red rose. European antiques, paintings, and delicate chandeliers enrich the interior, and music by the restaurant's namesake is a delightful accompaniment. Service is extremely gracious and considerate of your time, especially if you have plans to attend the opera, theater, or ballet.

When it comes to dinner entrées, Café Mozart sticks to the ordinary rather than the extraordinary. European cuisine featuring such classics as beef Stroganoff, chicken Dijonnaise, and boneless duck roasted in *herbes de Provence* remain typical fare. Dinners may be ordered à la carte or, for an additional $10.50, you can have soup or salad and a pick from the tempting dessert tray. With its traditional cuisine and cozy atmosphere suited for couples, Café Mozart may continue to be San Francisco's most romantic European restaurant for many years to come. **708 Bush Street, between Powell and Mason; (415) 391-8480; www.citysearch.com/sfo/cafe mozart; moderate to expensive; reservations recommended; dinner Tuesday–Sunday.**

❤❤❤ **CAMPTON PLACE RESTAURANT, San Francisco** Campton Place Restaurant is an exceptional culinary landmark where the elite come for very serious dining and very intense romancing. Its elegance and refinement are dazzling, and its quietness proves attractive in a city of hustle and bustle. Extravagant floral arrangements and gilt-framed mirrors surround tables set with crystal and freshly cut flowers, while large potted plants in exquisite vases are precisely positioned around the room. The extremely formal service and regal setting call for Miss Manners–approved etiquette.

The Southern French cuisine is sublime. Foie gras and duck ravioli are merely preludes to the delicious entrées. Tempting dishes like wild striped bass with caramelized fennel, and roasted Colorado rack of lamb are just the tip of the iceberg when it comes to amazing flavors. (Just don't expect portions the size of icebergs.) As for desserts, the vanilla crème brûlée with a touch of cinnamon is a dream come true. If you'd like, you can also visit Campton Place Restaurant for a lovely (albeit expensive) breakfast. The atmosphere is less stuffy in the morning: You could drop your napkin twice and no one in the predominantly business-suit crowd would blink an eye. **340 Stockton Street, between Sutter and Post, at the Campton Place Hotel; (415) 955-5555, (800) 235-4300; www.camptonplace.com; expensive to very expensive; breakfast, lunch, and dinner daily, brunch Sunday.**

Romantic Note: For the same formal style in accommodations, consider splurging on overnight reservations at the deluxe CAMPTON PLACE HOTEL (see Hotel/Bed and Breakfast Kissing).

❦❦❦ **THE CARNELIAN ROOM, San Francisco** Fifty-two floors above it all, The Carnelian Room's distinctive glass-enclosed restaurant and lounge offer mesmerizing views of San Francisco and the East Bay. For a stellar experience, arrive just before sunset as the last light of day casts striking shadows across the city. But, as evening lingers on, be prepared for fog rolling in, which can quickly drown out the view. When it's visible, the dramatic vista provides a heartfelt backdrop to the restaurant's opulent and clubbish interior, resplendent with rich walnut paneling, dim lighting, and 18th- and 19th-century artwork.

Unlike the incredible vistas, restaurant service doesn't stand out as extraordinary, and the contemporary American cuisine didn't excite our senses. Top that off with a wine-by-the-glass selection that is embarrassingly inadequate, and you might be disappointed, considering the amount you are spending here. Budget-wise, your best bet is the three-course, prix fixe dinner, which during our visit included a wonderful sweet pea ravioli in a lovely lemon-mint broth. Aside from that stunner, everything else was simply standard. Perhaps this sky-high establishment has been resting on its laurels (and location) too long. We highly recommend visiting the lounge instead and enjoying a cocktail as the California sun puts on its final show. **555 California Street, at Montgomery, on the 52nd floor of the Bank of America Building; (415) 433-7500, (888) 275-0928; very expensive; dinner and cocktails daily, brunch Sunday.**

Romantic Note: If you've got a special proposal in mind, consider renting the private Tamalpais Room ($75, excluding food and beverage). Here you'll find a cozy table set for two, a cushy love seat, and a green-and-red light outside the room that you control, summoning your own personal waiter only when you require service.

❦❦ **CLEMENTINE, San Francisco** There's a tiny bit of France in the midst of San Francisco's second Chinatown, aka Clement Street. Among dozens of Asian markets and restaurants resides a darling French bistro named Clementine that's winning diners over. Unlike many of the big names downtown, this restaurant caters mainly to the neighborhood crowd, tempting them in with reasonable prices, consistent food quality, and an elegant, inviting atmosphere. A copper bar, large gold-framed mirrors, and photographs of France accent much of the restaurant, while soft beige and green tones along with delicate wall sconces add softness. Banquettes lining the long walls create a cramped seating area with tables too close together; however, if you arrive early enough you'll have plenty of space.

On the rainy night we visited, the French "comfort" food on the seasonally changing menu really hit the spot, most notably the chicken stuffed with rosemary and anchovies served alongside a helping of mashed potatoes. Continue comforting yourselves with such dishes as sage-perfumed veal shank, delectable rack of lamb, or striped sea bass topped with an interesting raisin-and-caper sauce. End dinner with the warm chocolate cake crowned with a coconut sorbet. While the portion is downright dainty, the melting chocolate will win big with your sweet tooths. **126 Clement Street; (415) 387-0408; moderate to expensive; dinner Tuesday–Sunday, brunch Sunday.**

❤❤❤ **THE CLIFF HOUSE, San Francisco** Come evening, busloads of camera-laden tourists flock to The Cliff House to witness stunning ocean views and spectacular sunsets. To avoid being overrun (or run over) by crowds, we recommend dining well before sunset, when there's no wait for a table with a view. Floor-to-ceiling windows in The Cliff House's dining rooms showcase incomparable panoramas of the forceful, frothy sea crashing against the jagged rocks below. You'll be tempted to linger as you watch seals basking on Seal Rock, a spectacle that is vastly superior to any aquarium. The famous San Francisco fog, a common visitor to these parts, often creeps in, putting an end to picturesque views. But look on the bright side: You'll be warm and cozy sitting inside The Cliff House.

Rich red draperies and glowing candlelight create a romantic setting in the Victorian-style dining room, which is appointed with dark wood detailing, tall plants, and photos of celebrities who have wined and dined here. Slightly more casual and crowded, the upstairs dining room shares the same magnificent views and is open for breakfast. The mood, not the continental-style food, is the specialty here, so keep that in mind and you won't be disappointed. **1090 Point Lobos Avenue; (415) 386-3330; www.cliffhouse.com; moderate to expensive; breakfast, lunch, and dinner daily, brunch Sunday; recommended wedding site.**

❤❤❤❤ **THE COMPASS ROSE, San Francisco** Set just off the lobby of the regal St. Francis Hotel, The Compass Rose is a place where you'll hear the pop of champagne corks at noon and the delicate clinking of teacups and saucers later in the day. This room is so splendid that the hotel provides diners with a brochure pointing out all the historical features and artwork that fill this palatial space. Like a museum, the softly lit dining room is filled with treasures from around the world, including hand-painted decorative screens, 19th-century cloisonné vases, and other exquisite Asian, Middle-Eastern, and European artifacts. Overhead, dark wood and black-marble pillars frame the restaurant's ornate cathedral ceiling. Snuggle into one of the plush chairs or love seats and savor the surrounding splendor.

High tea, an impressive affair served from 3 P.M. to 5 P.M. daily, offers a three-tiered tray of delights such as dainty tea sandwiches, freshly baked scones, berries with Grand Marnier cream, and petit fours. Don't pass this place up for lunch either. The dark room offers a respite from the flashy world outside, and the menu features an agreeable variety of rich entrées including sautéed scallops and butternut squash ravioli. **335 Powell Street, between Geary and Post, at the Westin St. Francis Hotel; (415) 774-0167; moderate to expensive; lunch, afternoon tea, and evening appetizers daily.**

❦❦❦❦ THE DINING ROOM AT THE RITZ-CARLTON, San Francisco

Like us, you may be asking yourselves if this dining room could possibly aspire to the stellar reputation of the hotel in which it resides. Well, after a meal here, you will be questioning no more. You and your sweetheart can be assured of service beyond reproach; elegant, intimate surroundings; and some of the best presentations of California cuisine in the Golden State.

Although formal, the decor is far from stuffy. All those touches that make elegant dining elegant are in place—plush chairs, beautifully adorned tabletops, classical oil paintings, flowing fabrics, soft harp music, and glowing candlelight. Blond wood–paneled walls set off the rich red and gold interior. The gracious service and the kitchen's ability to be flexible demonstrate that The Dining Room aims to please.

Choose between a three-, four-, and five-course dinner or simply go with the chef's grand menu. We were surprised by the portions, which for haute cuisine certainly weren't small. A generous dish of daube (beef) ravioli started us rolling, and we continued a steady upward spiral into culinary paradise with the roast Maine lobster on creamy polenta and the tenderloin of beef cooked to perfection. All desserts will certainly please, but for that Midas touch, try the chocolate Ritz *"Palais d'Or"* topped with a tiny leaf of gold foil. **600 Stockton Street, at California, at The Ritz-Carlton; (415) 773-6198; www.ritzcarlton.com; very expensive to unbelievably expensive; reservations required; dinner Monday–Saturday.**

❦❦❦ ÉLAN VITAL, San Francisco

When we called inquiring about Élan Vital's menu, the person answering the phone gave us detailed descriptions of each entrée's preparation and presentation. While that's more information than most people need for a night out, it shows that Élan Vital is a place for serious food lovers. Luckily, its cozy atmosphere also caters to lovers in general. With only ten candlelit tables in this popular Russian Hill restaurant, reservations are a must, especially on weekends. Large, modern artwork adorns the dining room's pale yellow walls, along with some surprisingly sophisticated children's paintings. Nab a window seat if possible, since tables by the semi-open kitchen can be noisy (even though the aromas are wonderful) and those by the wine bar can be a bit cramped. But really, anywhere you sit is just fine; the world around you will quickly disappear as you devour the delectable delights.

The robust Provençal bread salad delivers interesting tidbits for the gourmet, such as quail eggs and caper berries, while the house-rolled potato gnocchi with duck confit and shallot cream was so light it almost had us levitating. Continue pleasing the palate with Dijon roasted rack of lamb or pancetta-wrapped monkfish, each glorified by their own special reduction sauce. One dish is better than the next at Élan Vital, so plan on coming here on an empty stomach and leaving in love with the food and, of course, each other. **1556 Hyde Street; (415) 929-7309; moderate to expensive; reservations recommended; dinner Monday–Saturday.**

❦❦❦ **FLEUR DE LYS, San Francisco** It's not surprising that Fleur de Lys has maintained its long-standing reputation as one of the most romantic restaurants in San Francisco. Completely secluded from the busy street outside, this cozy dining room is the perfect place to spend an enchanted evening together, although on some weeknights the corporate crowd seems all too prevalent. "Plush" best describes the interior. Yards of floral fabric are draped from the ceiling and walls, creating the illusion of dining beneath a big, beautiful tent. In the center of the room, a towering floral arrangement is spotlighted by a Venetian chandelier hanging from the pinnacle of the fabric. Ornamental mirrors surround the dining room, making it appear more spacious than it really is. Service is professional, and the ever-present maître d' tends to all tables, especially those ordering expensive wine.

In spite of its decidedly French disposition, the kitchen also flirts with Mediterranean accents. From truffled vichyssoise to sea bass with a ratatouille crust, every dish is cooked to perfection and artistically presented. Special menu choices worth noting are the seven-course extravaganza, the more moderate three-course prix fixe dinner that changes regularly, and, most surprising of all, a vegetarian prix fixe option. **777 Sutter Street, between Jones and Taylor; (415) 673-7779; expensive to unbelievably expensive; reservations required; dinner Monday–Saturday.**

Romantic Warning: Reservations are de rigueur at Fleur de Lys, and you must also reconfirm them two days prior. This can present a problem, especially when you're concentrating on other things, like kissing.

❦❦❦ **FOURNOU'S OVENS, San Francisco** Breakfast, brunch, lunch, or dinner, you can always expect a gourmet repast at Fournou's Ovens, although the later you go, the more romantic the atmosphere. The Mediterranean/old-world–style restaurant is handsomely decorated with tiled floors, paintings, tapestries, colored pottery, and 18th-century French Provençal antiques. High-backed chairs, candle lanterns, and fresh flowers complement each table. Set within a small alcove in the main dining room, and accented by bottles of wine and hanging copper skillets, are several European-style roasting ovens set off by beautiful blue-and-white Portuguese tiles. As you dine, you can watch the chef bake bread for each evening's meal. You'll also find one of the most extensive wine lists in the world, with more than 10,000 bottles housed in the restaurant's wine cellar.

Fournou's Ovens is really a series of small dining rooms and, depending on your mood, you can select a setting that matches the experience you have in mind. Choose one of the formal dining rooms for a quiet candlelit tête-à-tête. For a casual breakfast or lunch, only the airy tropical-inspired solarium is open; through its conservatory-style windows, you can watch cable cars ascending and descending Nob Hill.

The chefs here prepare contemporary American cuisine that is best described as hearty and flavorful. Rack of lamb is a house specialty, along with roast duck, rack of veal, and fresh seafood dishes. One of the city's best maple crème brûlées is here as well, so save room for dessert. **905 California Street, at Powell, at the Renaissance Stanford Court Hotel; (415) 989-1910; www.renaissancehotel.com/sfosc/restrant; expensive to very expensive; breakfast, lunch, and dinner daily, brunch Saturday–Sunday.**

❦❦❦ **GARDEN COURT, San Francisco** Crystal chandeliers hang from a leaded glass dome ceiling, illuminating the mirrored doors, gold-leaf sconces, marvelous flower arrangements, and marble columns that enhance the Garden Court. Overstuffed sofas and chairs provide relaxed, intimate seating at the back of the room. Tables in the front appear more formal, draped elegantly in white linens and graced with fine china and fresh flowers. Though the ornate splendor of this palatial room surpasses that of any other dining room in San Francisco, so do the prices. To best appreciate the gorgeous surroundings without spending a fortune, you might consider opting for high tea instead of a high-priced continental dinner. **2 New Montgomery Street, between Second and Third, at the Sheraton Palace Hotel; (415) 546-5010; expensive to unbelievably expensive; breakfast and lunch Monday–Saturday, afternoon tea and dinner Wednesday–Saturday, brunch Sunday; recommended wedding site.**

💋💋 **GAYLORD INDIA RESTAURANT, San Francisco** Climb above it all to a place where sitar music stirs the air, spicy foods excite the palate, and views are par excellence. On the third floor of the Chocolate Building in San Francisco's Ghirardelli Square resides one of the few kiss-worthy spots in this tourist mecca: Gaylord's. Hand-carved figurines, antiques, and artifacts from India fill the dining room, which overlooks the harbor and Fisherman's Wharf. Candles glow atop cozy tables draped with cream-colored linens (which are in desperate need of a pressing). Many tables are placed next to large bay window and most are well spaced, although those in the center of the room are a cluttered mess. Overall, we can't say Gaylord's decor is exciting or fresh, and the staff, while professional, is somewhat indifferent. Luckily, terrific views more than make up for such shortcomings.

The traditional East Indian menu brings many tastes to the table, including aromatic curries, freshly baked breads, dal, and vegetable samosas. Herbivores will be pleased by the dozen or so vegetarian entrées and, for couples who like sharing, Gaylord's offers several set dinners to enjoy together. **900 North Point Street, at Ghirardelli Square; (415) 771-8822; www.gaylords.com; expensive; lunch and dinner daily.**

💋💋💋 **GRANDVIEWS RESTAURANT AND LOUNGE, San Francisco** Grand views are exactly what you'll find at this lounge and restaurant, which resides 36 flights above the city in the Grand Hyatt. As you sit high above the rush of traffic and crowds, the magnificent cityscape spans before you, showcasing Fisherman's Wharf and the bay, Telegraph Hill, Nob Hill, and the Financial District. Plush burgundy chairs, elegant low lighting, and marble-topped tables in the lounge create an intimate atmosphere any time of day. (The lounge serves light fare and desserts all day until 10 P.M.) However, we find the lounge most romantic at sunset or after dark Tuesday through Saturday nights, when melodies from the soothing jazz piano accompany the sparkling city lights.

For a full meal of comfort cuisine, head to the adjacent restaurant where tables are positioned along the windows, and candles, white linens, and flowers create a more formal setting. Keep in mind that the view is the primary reason to come here, since the food receives mixed reviews. We enjoyed our pan-roasted sea scallops on lobster risotto, but the roasted chicken with sautéed potatoes, chanterelles, asparagus, and garlic was slightly dry. Desserts are less complicated and reliably more satisfying. **345 Stockton Street, between Post and Sutter, at the Grand Hyatt; (415) 398-1234; moderate; breakfast, lunch, and dinner daily.**

❧❧ **JARDINIÈRE, San Francisco** Champagne, some say, is the elixir of love, so we were not surprised to see this beverage as the decorating theme at Jardinière, a lively restaurant near the Civic Center. Step into this large, upscale establishment through a dramatic entryway and look skyward. Within the large central opening of the two-story room, a dramatic inverted champagne-glass dome twinkles with tiny lights that resemble bubbles, while a balcony railing surrounding the upstairs opening is detailed with lit glass and pewter-colored champagne buckets, appropriately filled with ice. Surely, a toast to the originality of the decor and celebratory ambience is in order here.

Upstairs, away from the crowded entrance and busy bar, is the best place for comfort and coziness. Lush aubergine velvet drapes, exposed brick walls, and rose-colored wall sconces bring a sense of timelessness to the decor, while booths and tables spaced far enough apart create a sense of privacy. Unfortunately, the piped-in music can be a bit deafening, but later in the evening when a jazz duo takes over, the decibel level drops and a sultry mood prevails ... at least upstairs. There is little breathing space downstairs, where the see-and-be-seen crowd congregates and gingerly sips cocktails.

The kitchen showcases French-California cuisine with smashing style. Seared scallops surrounded by mashed potatoes and a black truffle sauce bring comfort food to a whole new (and expensive) level. Any entrée ordered, from loin of venison with juniper sauce to red wine–braised short ribs, will have you coming back for more. Desserts prove just as divine, including a brown-butter walnut cake with crème fraîche, and homemade ice creams and sorbets. Fitting in with the underlying theme, an ample selection of champagnes and sparkling wines are available, as are flights (multiple tastings) of almost every specialty liquor you could want. **300 Grove Street, at Franklin; (415) 861-5555; expensive to very expensive; dinner daily.**

❧❧ **JULIUS' CASTLE, San Francisco** Yes, we know this cliffside restaurant is a tourist trap (and we all know tourist traps hinder kissing), but the spectacular views from this castle are worth mentioning. Nestled on Telegraph Hill below the famous Coit Tower, Julius' Castle's location is a prime spot for watching the city come alive each evening. Bay windows in the series of upstairs dining rooms survey unobstructed views of San Francisco Bay and the Golden Gate Bridge. Crystal chandeliers shed soft light above linencloaked tables in the somewhat timeworn Victorian-style dining room, distinguished by burgundy upholstery and carpeting and dark wood paneling. Although nearly every table has a view, most of them are crowded much too close together for romantic preferences. If you're having trouble over-looking the crowds, turn your attention to the menu, which throws no sur-prises. Straightforward dishes like halibut, grilled beef, rack of lamb, and mustard-marinated pork chops should satisfy the taste buds, while the eyes fill up on the view. **1541 Montgomery Street, north of Union Street; (415) 392-2222; www.juliuscastlerestaurant.com; expensive; dinner daily.**

❤❧ **LA FOLIE, San Francisco** You can't help but like this enticing and fes-tive French restaurant from the moment you set eyes on it. A soft glow illuminates the mullioned windows, and boxes of flowering plants hang from the second story. Inside, puffy clouds adorn the sky blue ceiling, a massive mirror frames the bar, and textured gold-colored walls provide a backdrop for theatrical puppets, many of which are posed within empty painting frames. Snug tables for two are packed a little too close for com-fort in that all-too-common San Francisco fashion. Thankfully, half-curtained windows help conceal the bustling sidewalk and crowds outside.

The fabulous French food is exquisitely presented. If you're in the mood to splurge and sample a bit of everything, consider the "Discovery Menu," which includes four courses, or the "Chef Menu," which can be prepared especially for you upon request. Vegetarians are certain to be pleased by the "Vegetable Lover's" menu, a set feast featuring the garden's seasonal show-pieces. Even if you dine à la carte, you won't be disappointed with items such as wild black bass accompanied by a leek and truffle oil risotto in an oxtail jus, or, for wild game lovers, roasted venison served with a chestnut–celery root flan and caramelized apples. **2316 Polk Street, between Green and Union; (415) 776-5577; www.lafolie.com; very expensive; reservations recommended; dinner Monday–Saturday.**

❤❧ **LA SCENE CAFE, San Francisco** This chic café, located on the main floor of the regal **WARWICK REGIS HOTEL** (see Hotel/Bed and Break-fast Kissing), is a lively spot for an après-theater cocktail or dessert. Soothing apricot-colored walls, white linens, and soft lighting surround you, as you gaze at (and try to identify) chalk sketches of cinema and theater stars of today and yesteryear. La Scene offers California cuisine with a Mediterra-nean flair as well as a three-course prix fixe theater dinner for those in a rush to arrive before the curtain rises. (At our visit the price was $23 per person, quite a bargain for this town.) There are some romantic obstacles, most notably the closely set tables, a prominent and sometimes busy bar in front, and a noisy atmosphere. But, if visited after dinner, especially Thurs-day through Saturday evenings when piano jazz creates an alluring atmo-sphere, La Scene could be just the right setting for a kiss. **490 Geary Street,** at Taylor, at The Warwick Regis Hotel; (415) 292-6430, (800) 827-3447; www.warwickhotels.com/sf/entertain.htm; **moderate to expensive; breakfast and dinner daily.**

❦❦❦ **THE MAGIC FLUTE, San Francisco** A refreshing contrast to the numerous formidable, highbrow dining establishments in San Francisco, the relaxed elegance of The Magic Flute is a romantic's delight. Sunlight streams into the Italianate front dining room, where cozy two-person tables have been arranged with privacy in mind. Warm peach-colored walls and wrought-iron Florentine chandeliers create an inviting climate in which to dine the night away. A second dining room at the back of the restaurant overlooks a garden courtyard hemmed with flowers and greenery, and accented by the sound of water trickling from a stone fountain. On warm evenings, you can dine al fresco in the tranquil courtyard.

A strong Mediterranean influence in the kitchen produces such delights as penne with blue cheese, fresh spinach, and roasted pine nuts, while Californian flair is evident in dishes like the iron skillet–roasted salmon with autumn vegetables and potatoes. Desserts are as tantalizing as you might imagine; don't miss the classic tiramisu for a delightful pick-me-up. **3673 Sacramento Street, between Spruce and Locust; (415) 922-1225; www.citysearch.com/sfo/magicflute; inexpensive to moderate; lunch Monday–Friday, dinner Monday–Saturday.**

❦❦ **THE MANDARIN, San Francisco** Sometimes hidden treasures await in even the most touristy of places. Tucked into a brick building high above Ghirardelli Square is The Mandarin, a landmark restaurant that has been serving Chinese specialties in a sophisticated setting since 1968. Exposed brick walls accented by dark, monochromatic panels set off the sweeping views of San Francisco Bay. Loosely woven bamboo partitions separate a series of interconnecting dining rooms decorated with Asian artwork and exotic flower arrangements; the central dining room holds the restaurant's circular Mongolian fire pit. Tables are set with white linens and equipped with lazy Susans to assist in dining "family style." (Unfortunately, this means The Mandarin caters to groups of people, which reduces its romantic potential by a kiss or two.) Despite such a shortcoming, you can't go wrong with anything on the traditional Chinese menu. House specialties include crisp-skinned smoked tea-leaf duck, seafood mango mango, and pork and eggplant à la Szechuan, a dish guaranteed to heat things up a bit. **900 North Point, at Ghirardelli Square; (415) 673-8812; www.themanda rin.com; moderate to expensive; lunch and dinner daily.**

❧❧❧ **MASA'S, San Francisco** Masa's reputation as one of the best spots in San Francisco to romance the night away is well earned. It doesn't get more formal or more intimate (or more expensive) than in this dimly lit dining room. Deep ruby-red walls and rich red draperies embrace a handful of tables elegantly appointed with crystal, china, and silver. Because there are so few tables here and such a large wait staff, patrons are indulged and catered to—almost to the point of excess.

With glasses of wine that cost more than your average entrée, and entrées that cost more than the price of a good bottle of wine, you should be prepared to splurge. Luckily, you won't be disappointed if you begin with the lobster bisque—more like a consommé in texture—which will bring the tastes of the sea to your palate. From the lamb noisettes to the roasted Maine lobster or grilled swordfish, every dish is close to being a masterpiece. Desserts are equally astonishing, especially the decadent dark chocolate cake served with raspberry ice cream. If you're willing to pay these kinds of prices (the prix fixe dinners start at $75 per person), we can't think of a better place to wine and dine your beloved. For this reason, you'll need to book your reservation several months in advance. **648 Bush Street, between Powell and Stockton, at the Hotel Vintage Court; (415) 989-7154, (800) 258-7694; www.citysearch.com/sfo/masas; unbelievably expensive; reservations required with credit-card guarantee; dinner Tuesday–Saturday.**

Romantic Warning: With such ultraluxe items as foie gras, caviar, and wild mushrooms on the menu, it is little wonder that Masa's requires your credit card number upon making a reservation. Foie gras or not, we still found such a prospect slightly unnerving. You'll be charged $50 per person (and afterward sent a gift certificate for that amount) if you don't show or forget to cancel within 48 hours. Don't kiss the night away by forgetting your reservation!

❧❧ **MASON'S, San Francisco** The lobby of the FAIRMONT HOTEL (see Hotel/Bed and Breakfast Kissing) is refined and luxurious, but its signature restaurant is surprisingly subdued. Attractive brass and blond wood furnishings and the allure of low lights and fresh flowers create an appealing but understated ambience. Tables harbored by the windows have quintessential San Francisco views of the cable cars on California Street. Luckily, many tables here are spaced far enough apart for intimate conversation. Our favorite kissing attractions are the cozy two-person tables and overstuffed sofas surrounding a grand piano in Mason's lounge. The restaurant's congenial staff serves American favorites such as pesto grilled rack of lamb, sautéed filet mignon, and seared Chilean sea bass, all cooked over a wood-fired grill. **950 Mason Street, at California, at the Fairmont Hotel; (415) 772-5233; www.fairmont.com; expensive; dinner daily.**

❦❦ **MCCORMICK & KULETO'S, San Francisco** McCormick & Kuleto's location in touristy Ghirardelli Square has always been a romantic drawback. But the intriguing views of the water and Alcatraz, together with an elegant interior (designed by a famous San Francisco restaurant designer), are worth a closer look. Within 19,500 square feet reside three dining rooms, all of which take full advantage of the view. The main dining room isn't our top pick for romance since it's typically crowded and noisy; however, the crescent-shaped booths on the upper tier might inspire some cuddling. Throughout the restaurant, floor-to-ceiling picture windows accented with stained glass afford amazing views; on a clear evening you can watch the water sparkle as the sun slips beyond the horizon. At the back of the restaurant you'll find the Bay View Room, a quieter environment with hints of British colonial decor, and the clubbish Captain Room, decorated with wood paneling and fabulous seashell-shaped wall sconces. Both these rooms are better suited for quiet conversations.

McCormick & Kuleto's extensive daily menu offers more than 120 items, including 30 different fish and shellfish varieties and more than 275 wine selections. What to order with so many choices? For delectable starters, go traditional with the Dungeness crab cocktail or be more daring by sampling seafood potstickers. Both the grilled white sturgeon with a port-peppercorn butter, and grilled Atlantic salmon adorned with lemon-thyme crème fraîche are delightful entrées, but sometimes the kitchen misses the mark. (Perhaps that's to be expected with such a large menu.) Our oven-baked fish lacked any sort of sauce and was accompanied by dry rice; luckily, the freshly sautéed veggies saved the meal. **900 North Point Street, at Ghirardelli Square; (415) 929-1730; moderate to expensive; lunch Monday–Saturday, dinner daily, brunch Sunday.**

❦❦ **MILLENNIUM, San Francisco** How can lovers resist a restaurant that has a Full Moon Aphrodisiac Night dinner once a month, herbal love potions, and food that is good for your heart, both literally and figuratively? Millennium, located in the Abigail Hotel, has all this, plus the distinction of being one of the only gourmet vegan restaurants in the country. The restaurant's decor says Euro-bistro, with its black-and-white checkered floors, halogen lamps spotlighting each table, and banquette seating in the subterranean level (the best spot to dine in the two-level restaurant). Strategically placed candles provide warm touches, while charming theater-mask wall sconces and matching fabrics add a whimsical twist.

If you're in town, be sure to make reservations for the four-course feast on Full Moon Aphrodisiac Night, served the Sunday closest to the full moon. These dinners come complete with the delicious Love Potion No. 9 (herbs and pomegranate and lime juice), foods to put you in the mood, and, of course, a decadent dessert. But no matter when you visit, the sophisticated food offerings will delight all, vegetarian or not. Because all items on the menu are vegan (no animal products), everything is choles- terol free. And, in our book, what's good for your heart is good for romance. Be sure to try the grilled smoked portobello mushrooms or plantain torte as appetizers, and then move on to such treats as stuffed acorn squash or the delectable Asian-style Napoleon. Desserts will leave you begging for more. Sink your teeth into the luscious and ever-so-silky chocolate-almond mousse cake or pucker up after a bite of the ginger cake topped with tart lemon sorbet. End the evening (at least the dining part) by sharing a sip of Love Potion No. 9. There's no telling what will happen later on, especially if there's a full moon. **246 McAllister Street, at the Abigail Hotel; (415) 487-9800, (800) 243-6510; www.millenniumrestaurant.com; expen- sive; dinner daily.**

Romantic Note: The Full Moon Aphrodisiac Night may include ac- commodations at the **ABIGAIL HOTEL** (415-861-9728; www.sftrips.com; moderate) if you so desire. Unfortunately, the hotel's decor and slightly rundown facilities didn't tug at our heartstrings.

❤❤❤ NEIMAN MARCUS ROTUNDA RESTAURANT, San Francisco

Who would ever guess that you could find a great place to pucker up in a department store? Believe it or not, there is a wonderful kissing spot in Neiman Marcus. On the fourth floor, beneath a spectacular, 26,000-piece stained glass dome, the Rotunda Restaurant provides a respite from the shopping crowds and offers an invitation to afternoon romance. Slip into a cozy booth, or select a table draped in white linen and accented with a single flower near the floor-to-ceiling windows overlooking bustling Union Square. The dining room serves satisfactory lunches, some superb salads, and light meals, but in our opinion, afternoon tea at the Rotunda is the ideal interlude. In a world where late-afternoon romance is too often over- looked because of busy schedules, you'll discover teatime can be a leisurely treat. **150 Stockton Street, at Geary, at Neiman Marcus department store; (415) 362-4777; moderate to expensive; cash, American Express, or Neiman Marcus credit cards only; lunch and high tea daily.**

Romantic Warning: The Rotunda is mostly frequented by female shop- pers, which can give the restaurant something of a "ladies who lunch" atmosphere.

❦❦❦❦ **OVATION AT THE OPERA, San Francisco** After an exhilarating night at the opera, ballet, or symphony, pamper yourselves some more at this bastion of refinement and gourmet cuisine. The main dining area, a handsome and warm room, is accented by a wonderful marble fireplace, mahogany walls, and library-style lamps that cast a soft glow. The second, more intimate dining area continues to impress with Belgian wall tapestries, classical paintings, and towering floral arrangements. Live piano accompanies most dinners, so the entertainment never ends.

Comfortable chairs and banquettes adorned with pillows are positioned around a handful of tables in the main dining room, while tables in the second room are more formal and farther apart. Wherever you end up sitting, you and your darling will enjoy the delights of the ensuing meal—from appetizers to after-dinner drinks. The French-inspired menu sings to the taste buds with such entrées as stuffed chicken breast with spinach and mushrooms, and the oh-so-light Dungeness crab and lobster ravioli. Delicious encores include the tarte Tatin covered with spun sugar, and a rich crème brûlée generous enough for two. We're certain you'll be giving another round of applause after an evening here. **333 Fulton Street, between Gough and Franklin, at The Inn at the Opera; (415) 553-8100, (800) 325-2708; expensive to very expensive; dinner daily.**

Romantic Note: THE INN AT THE OPERA, once a very romantic place to stay, is now operated as a time-share property.

❦❦ **PANE E VINO TRATTORIA, San Francisco** There's much more to Pane e Vino than bread and wine. Its quaint, authentically Italian atmosphere invites devoted hearts to partake in the pleasures of an evening together. Two small dining rooms comprise the restaurant, although the one in back is more romantic with its brick fireplace, clay-tiled floor, soft lighting, and beamed ceiling. A sideboard adorned with fresh flowers and aged cheeses adds rustic charm. Fronted by wine racks and a tempting dessert display case, the open kitchen can prove noisy, although the sounds of Italian chatter and sizzling frying pans add to the atmosphere. Once you settle in, you'll discover that the food is delicious (especially the pastas and the risotto of the day), the wines are wonderful, and the ambience is certainly for lovers. Need we add that desserts, like the white chocolate pistachio gelato, are pure heaven? The restaurant really should be named Pane e Vino e Amore! **3011 Steiner Street, at Union; (415) 346-2111; moderate; lunch Monday–Saturday, dinner daily.**

❦❦❦ **PLUMPJACK CAFE, San Francisco** Despite its name, PlumpJack Cafe is not a café and there is no "plump Jack" to be found. It is more accurately described as an elegantly sophisticated restaurant known for its chic interior and showy clientele. If you like to kiss and be seen, this is the place. Decorated almost exclusively in a grayish-taupe color scheme, the dining room features cylindrical columns; one massive, elegant floral arrangement; and spherical ceiling lamps. A handsome chenille-covered banquette hugs the large windows overlooking fashionable Fillmore Street, and the closely spaced tables are draped with white linens and accented by a small silver bucket of ferns. A curvy iron window treatment, almost medieval in nature, is connected to a transparent screen and displayed in the front window.

PlumpJack offers Mediterranean-influenced California cuisine prepared in grand style. The luscious spinach and garlic soup won our taste buds over, as did the duck confit and lentil strudel. Pastas are well balanced and flavorful, including one special that blended caramelized onions and sundried cherries with smoked chicken. The wine list is also impressive, but just in case your favorite vintage is missing, travel one block to the namesake wine store. Buy there and the café will waive the corkage fee. With the delicious food, excellent wine selection, and innovative decor, PlumpJack is often plumb full; reservations for romance here are a must, even at lunch. **3127 Fillmore Street, between Greenwich and Filbert; (415) 563-4755; expensive; reservations recommended; lunch Monday–Friday, dinner Monday–Saturday.**

❤❤❁ **THE PLUSH ROOM, San Francisco** Remember those late-night black-and-white movies from the 1940s, where hearts were lost, found, broken, and mended, all at a quiet table in the corner of a jazz club? Dramatic music in the background would reach a crescendo just in time for the lovers to join in a torrid embrace. The Plush Room keeps alive this tradition of steamy jazz and soothing contemporary ballads in an appropriately classy, intimate setting. Tables and booths are set beneath a stained glass ceiling, and the large stage seems to spill out into the audience. Whether or not you are a jazz connoisseur, you'll be tempted to share one of the dark mauve booths with your partner. Just don't be surprised to discover that words will be of no practical use all evening long. **940 Sutter Street, between Hyde and Leavenworth, at the York Hotel; (415) 885-2800, (800) 808-9675; www.yorkhotel.com; moderate; cocktails Wednesday–Sunday.**

Romantic Suggestion: Performances are seasonal, so call ahead to find out who is on stage the week you plan to visit.

Romantic Note: Never mind looking for romance at the **YORK HOTEL** (expensive to very expensive); it's just your average city hotel with standard guest rooms and amenities.

❦❦ **POSTRIO, San Francisco** Postrio is an upbeat dinner spot for couples looking for a good time (and good food) rather than quiet togetherness. Everything about Postrio resembles a theatrical production. Diners make their entrance down a sculpted iron staircase to the main dining room. The "set" is an artistic array of colors, textures, and lighting designed to stimulate the senses. Plush, fabric-finished booths alternate throughout the room with striking tables draped in white linen and accented with black chairs. Modern art decorates the walls, while spectacular orb-shaped chandeliers, adorned with curvaceous metal ribbons, draw the eye upward.

Wolfgang Puck, world-renowned chef and owner of Postrio, is without doubt the "director" of this production. His "producers" in the large, open kitchen deserve standing ovations for their dramatic, award-winning interpretations of California-Asian-Mediterranean cuisine. The mesquite-grilled pork and accompanying mustard spaetzle took top honors in our review, although close seconds were the grilled salmon served over wasabi mashed potatoes and the light and lovely sautéed Atlantic sole adorned with a creamy vegetable curry. Meals are served by a lively "supporting cast" that wishes to assist your performance. It's up to you to decide how to play out the evening, but don't forget to end with a grand finale—one of the many scrumptious desserts. (We highly recommend everything.) This may not be the coziest and quietest venue to play out your romance, but you can always kiss post-Postrio. **545 Post Street, between Taylor and Mason, at The Prescott Hotel; (415) 776-7825; www.prescotthotel.com; expensive to very expensive; breakfast, lunch, and dinner daily, brunch Sunday.**

Romantic Alternative: The upstairs bar at Postrio serves gourmet pizzas and lighter fare until midnight. It's the perfect place for a bite to eat and a quick kiss or two after a genuine night at the theater.

❦❦❦❦ **REDWOOD ROOM, San Francisco** One of the most dramatic cocktail lounges in San Francisco, the Redwood Room provides a romantic spot for an intimate tête-à-tête. Cavernous without being cold, this magnificent lounge is a testimony to the beauty of wood and Art Deco design. You'll stand in awe once you realize one 2,000-year-old redwood tree outfitted the entire room. The interior is strikingly handsome, with 22-foot ceilings, plush lounge chairs, and carved redwood paneling adorned with immense reproductions of Gustav Klimt paintings. An elegant bar lines one side of the room while cozy velvet love seats inspire closeness at the many polished wood tables. On selected evenings, the lounge features live piano or jazz music.

A light bistro menu is served all day and offers sophisticated finger foods to complement any cocktail. The imported cheese plate with fresh fruit and housemade crackers is light and satisfying, and you won't go wrong with the exotic wild mushroom strudel with goat cheese, sweet peppers, and chipotle aioli. Lunch and dinner selections include hearty seafood, steak, and pasta dishes. Whether you opt for a full meal or cocktails, your visit to the heart of San Francisco would be incomplete without a visit to the Redwood Room. **495 Geary Street, at Taylor, at the Clift Hotel; (415) 775-4700, (800) 65-CLIFT; www.clifthotel.com; moderate to very expensive; breakfast, lunch, dinner, cocktails, and light fare daily.**

RISTORANTE BACCO, San Francisco We recommend catching the sunset from San Francisco's breathtaking **TWIN PEAKS** (see Outdoor Kissing), and then dining at nearby Ristorante Bacco to top off the evening. This cozy storefront dining room exudes archetypal Italian charm, making it one of the few romantic restaurants in this part of town. Italian art, a Renaissance-inspired wall mural, and triangular wall sconces embellish the butter-colored walls, and single flowers adorn tables simply dressed with white linens. Picture windows lined with flower boxes look out to the residential street beyond. Due to the restaurant's towering ceilings, conversations carry here, especially from the kitchen where Italian is spoken with great vigor.

Like the ambience, the kitchen's menu is classical Italian, featuring a variety of pastas and meat dishes. Try the very light spinach ravioli topped with a sage sauce or the noteworthy braised lamb shank. Desserts, like everything else, are pure Italian. If you want to be perky for passion, try this jolter: full-strength espresso poured over creamy vanilla gelato. **737 Diamond Street, between 24th and Elizabeth; (415) 282-4969; www. citysearch.com/sfo/bacco; moderate to expensive; dinner daily.**

THE RITZ BAR, San Francisco End your evening on a delicious note with a visit to this former cigar bar turned sweet by California's smoking ban. Inside this intimate, wood-paneled room filled with leather couches and chairs, guests can indulge with a prix fixe dessert menu featuring one, two, or three courses. Chocolate bombe, crème brûlée, apple fondant, and a host of other sinfully rich treats can be enjoyed alone or paired with wines and champagnes. The Bar also features the largest single-malt scotch collection in the United States. **600 Stockton Street, at California, at The Ritz-Carlton; (415) 296-7465; www.ritzcarlton.com; inexpensive to moderate; dessert Monday–Saturday.**

❀❀❀❁ **SILKS, San Francisco** To reach Silks, pass through the lovely lobby of the **MANDARIN ORIENTAL** (see Hotel/Bed and Breakfast Kissing) and ascend an elegant, sweeping staircase. A tuxedo-clad waiter greets you at the top and ushers you to a table for two in this exceedingly formal dining room. A splendidly ornate wood table crowned with a lavish tropical bouquet provides a perfect centerpiece, surrounded by tables set far enough apart to allow for a considerable amount of intimacy. Bold, modern art and colorful handblown glass wall sconces and chandeliers add interest to the relatively classic and subdued surroundings. Even more imaginative than the artwork is the food. No expense is spared on presentation or ingredients: Shaved Périgord truffles grace the veal mignon, a dollop of Tobikko caviar adorns the steak-cut ahi, and a seared Thai snapper blazes with chile-spiced turmeric. Eating and kissing at Silks certainly is a sublime experience. **222 Sansome Street, between Pine and California, at the Mandarin Oriental; (415) 986-2020, (800) 622-0404; www.mandarin-oriental.com; moderate to very expensive; breakfast and dinner daily, lunch Monday–Friday.**

❀❀❀❀ **TOMMY TOY'S, San Francisco** If Oscars were awarded for theatrical elegance in a restaurant, Tommy Toy's would win. This elaborate restaurant is patterned after the reading room of the 19th-century Dowager Empress, and she obviously knew how to live. Each dining room is separated by etched glass partitions, filled with exquisite Asian art pieces and rich tapestries and fabrics, and accented with shades of jade and pink. Such ornate surroundings create a regal, museum-like atmosphere.

Dining at Tommy Toy's feels like a formal event (jackets and ties are required for dinner), but it is an event not to be missed if you wish to be treated like royalty for an evening. Hostesses dressed in long kimonos greet you at the door, and tuxedo-clad waiters give you their utmost attention throughout the evening. The service is truly amazing. Don't be surprised if a small troupe of waiters wheels a tray alongside your table and dramatically unveils your meal. Just about everything on the menu earns high marks for both taste and artistic presentation. The signature dinner is very expensive ($55 per person), but its six courses will give you a whole new understanding and appreciation of chinoise (Chinese-French) cuisine. Where else can you order succulent Peking duck with lotus buns for a main course, and then complete your meal with a perfectly fluffy, smooth peach mousse in a strawberry compote for dessert? Other favorites on the menu include pan-fried foie gras with sliced fresh pear and watercress in a sweet pickled-ginger sauce, and the wok-charred beef medallions with garlic, wine, and rosemary, served over four flavors of fried rice. **655 Montgomery Street,**

between Washington and Clay; (415) 397-4888; www.tommytoys.com; very expensive; lunch Monday–Friday, dinner daily.

❀❀❀ **TUBA GARDEN, San Francisco** Begin your morning on a loving note at Tuba Garden, a heartwarming destination best saved for a leisurely sunny day. Sip Bellinis (peach nectar and champagne) as you dine al fresco on the charming patio next to abundant flowers and a burbling fountain, or head inside to the dining room. Given the interesting name of the restaurant, you might expect an abundance of music memorabilia cluttering the interior, or at least a tuba serenade while you eat. You'll find neither. Instead, this restored Victorian home-turned-restaurant is embellished by a lovely garden motif. One of the owners is a classical music lover, but the only "tuba-touches" here are two brass antique tubas, one displayed in the garden and the other hanging in the front window. The instruments lend an eclectic European flair, while wrought-iron tables and fresh flowers at every table create a cheery, inviting atmosphere where you can enjoy your meal in complete harmony.

Noteworthy brunch items include a heavenly quiche Lorraine as well as the Tuba Special: perfectly poached eggs and sautéed spinach served on an English muffin with Hollandaise sauce. For lunch, the salads are consistently fresh and delicious, and the onion soup will make your taste buds sing. The service is well orchestrated, so you won't feel rushed even on a busy weekend morning. **3634 Sacramento Street, between Spruce and Locust; (415) 921-TUBA; inexpensive to moderate; lunch Monday–Friday, brunch Saturday–Sunday.**

❀❀ **VIVANDE RISTORANTE, San Francisco** Located several blocks from San Francisco's opera house, Vivande is often filled with operagoers dressed to the nines. Given the kind of crowds it draws, Vivande is surprisingly jocular. Patrons enter through a door carved to look like a yawning mouth. Murals depicting court jesters adorn the pale yellow walls, which are accented with unusual striped orange and yellow lamps. An open kitchen and bar, framed by collections of Italian ceramics, add to the commotion of the usually packed dining room. However, immense red velvet booths in the back of the restaurant ensure enough privacy for at least one passionate kiss.

The kitchen strives to please with its typically Italian fare, which ranges from homemade penne pasta and egg noodles to risotto served with oven-roasted butternut squash and zucchini. Homemade sorbets and a light but creamy tiramisu should end your evening on a sweet note. **670 Golden Gate Avenue, between Van Ness and Franklin; (415) 673-9245; www.citysearch.com/sfo/vivanderistoran; moderate to expensive; lunch and dinner daily.**

❀❀❀ THE WATERFRONT RESTAURANT AND CAFE, San Francisco

For all the water surrounding San Francisco, waterfront restaurants are few and far between in this city. Luckily, we found one that fits our criteria for romance. Not only does The Waterfront Restaurant and Cafe deliver on-the-bay views, but it also features a stunning interior and food that is certain to start your evening off right. Plan on spending some time here sipping your champagne and watching San Francisco in action. From your perch, you'll survey cars crossing the Bay Bridge, ferries floating by, and couples walking hand in hand along a nearby pier. While this restaurant is located on the "wharf," don't get the impression that it is near ultratouristy Fisherman's Wharf. San Francisco's wharf area stretches quite a ways and, thankfully, this establishment is nowhere near the crowds.

As the name indicates, The Waterfront is actually two restaurants in one. A casual café is located downstairs (complete with outside dining), but we recommend taking the elevator upstairs to the restaurant for a more intimate atmosphere. Asian decor and art dominate the stylish yet simple dining area that's warmed by the colors of chocolate brown, celadon, and burnt yellow. Wraparound windows afford fantastic views, and when the lights of East Bay start to flicker, the warm glow of the restaurant's globe-shaped chandeliers helps set the right mood for loving glances. Request a table in the intimate north dining room if you want privacy. Here, massive antique Asian doors open to a small room with only eight tables. The larger main dining room may have better all-around views, but the decibel level is higher and the seating is tight in spots.

Bold flavors and creativity in preparation come through in whatever you order on the seafood-dominated menu. We started with filo-wrapped asparagus and continued our culinary feast with sautéed snapper in a robust pancetta and shallot sauce. The pumpkinseed-crusted ahi, spiced with a preserved-lemon glace, proved delicious as well. Our sweet and creamy finish, a Tahitian vanilla panna cotta, put us on cloud nine as we watched the evening fog roll over the bay. **Pier 7 at the Embarcadero, at Broadway; (415) 391-2696; expensive to very expensive; reservations recommended; lunch Monday–Friday, dinner daily.**

Romantic Warning: Despite our delicious dinner and attentive server, the wait to be seated bordered on ridiculous. We arrived early (around 5:30 P.M.) and weren't seated until 6 P.M. The crowds hadn't even arrived yet!

❀❀❀ YOYO BISTRO, San Francisco

San Francisco may be famous for its Chinatown, but did you know there is a Japantown as well? One of the most stylish restaurants in this area is YoYo Bistro, tucked into the Radisson Miyako Hotel. Although the downstairs dining area is a bit too casual to wholeheartedly recommend, the upper-level dining room is small, intimate, and well worth a visit. Add to that a modern and sometimes playful decor, and you have a dining atmosphere ripe for romance. High ceilings and wood columns rise up around you, while slate floors blend in with maple chairs and lacquered tables. Handblown glass lights accent the room, and some tables look out to a Japanese garden. The eclectic mix of French bistro, Asian influences, and contemporary fixtures is distinctly cutting edge, but then again so is the food. Sample tantalizing *tsumami*, small dishes of food typically eaten with cocktails. Tamarind-and-black-pepper-glazed chicken wings or ahi tuna tartare served with lotus-root chip should start the mouth watering. Some entrées are decidedly unique. Try the cinnamon-rubbed duck breast with port glaze or the barbecued eel–rice bento box. Of course, there are the more traditional fixings such as tempura prawns or garlic noodle stir-fry with roasted portobello mushrooms. **1611 Post Street, at Laguna, at the Radisson Miyako Hotel; (415) 922-7788; expensive; dinner daily.**

Outdoor Kissing

❤❤❤ **ALAMO SQUARE, San Francisco** San Francisco is famous for its numerous parks, scattered throughout the city in places where you would least expect a grove of trees or lush green grass. Take time to enjoy one of these welcome patches of nature in quiet, tree-dotted Alamo Square. Perched high above the city, this park offers a most remarkable view of San Francisco and the famous pastel homes known as the "Painted Ladies." On a sunny day, it's a lovely spot for a picnic. *Bordered by Fulton, Steiner, Hayes, and Scott Streets.*

❤❤❤ **ANGEL ISLAND, San Francisco** Become castaways for a day on this angelic island in the middle of San Francisco Bay. The ferry ride alone is worthy of a windswept kiss. Once on the island, stop by the **ANGEL ISLAND COMPANY** (415-897-0715; www.angelisland.com; seasonal services), where you can rent mountain bikes ($10 per hour, $25 per day) or sign up for an all-day guided kayak tour of **AYALA COVE** ($100 per person, includes lunch). If you and your sweetie are history buffs, consider taking the hour-long tram tour of the island's historic sites ($10 per person). Did you know that Angel Island has been dubbed the "Ellis Island of the West"? Between 1910 and 1940, the island's immigration station received millions of immigrants from Asia, Russia, and the Pacific Basin to the United States. You'll also discover military garrisons and compounds from the Civil War and every major U.S. war thereafter. If you've got kissing on your mind and not history, ascend primitive trails to private panoramas of the San Francisco skyline or Marin's forested hills. Bring along a picnic lunch to enjoy in a sun-soaked meadow. With its six-mile perimeter trail and rugged climb to a 360-degree view of the Bay Area, Angel Island is sure to yield a secluded kissing spot. **Ferries from San Francisco: Blue and Gold Fleet: (415) 773-1188 for information, (415) 705-5555 for ticket sales; www.blueandgoldfleet.com; $11 per person round-trip. Ferries from Tiburon: Angel Island Ferry: (415) 435-2131; www.angel islandferry.com; $7 per person round-trip.**

❀❀❀ **GOLDEN GATE BRIDGE, San Francisco** Walking over the venerable, symbolically soaring Golden Gate Bridge is an exhilarating, unforgettable journey. This monumental structure offers views that can only be described as astonishing. From this vantage point, you can survey the city's famous hills and skyline unencumbered by buildings or earth. The Pacific Ocean, 260 feet below, is an endless blue apparition framed by the rugged curve of land north to Marin and south to San Francisco. As unbelievable as it sounds, the gusts of wind up here can cause the reinforced, Herculean steel cables to sway to and fro. This is one place where, even without kissing or touching, you can really feel the earth move—and it won't be from an earthquake, either. On a clear, sunny day, put on your walking shoes, don your jackets, and discover this one for yourselves. **Free admission for walkers, $2 toll fee per vehicle.** *Lincoln Boulevard, Park Presidio Boulevard, and Lombard Street all merge in the Presidio and continue onto the Golden Gate Bridge. There is a metered parking area just east of the toll booths, where you gain entrance to the walkway across the bridge.*

❀❀❀❀ **GOLDEN GATE PARK, San Francisco** For those who know this vast acreage of city woodlands and gardens, it is possible to imagine that Golden Gate Park and romance are themselves an adoring couple. There is so much to see in this diverse three-mile-long park that even in a full day you can only scratch the surface. Nevertheless, any of the park's varied attractions can provide a prelude to an enchanting day together. One place to start is the **STRYBING ARBORETUM** (free admission), a horticultural wonderland of plants and trees from all over the world. The gardens comprise 70 acres, and there are plenty of pathways to explore. Another remarkable city escape is the **JAPANESE TEA GARDEN** ($3.50 entrance fee per person), where an exotic display of Japanese landscaping gives a tranquil reprieve from urban life. Besides these attractions, there are miles of secluded walkways to wander through and, of course, the majestic Pacific awaits at the end of the park: a perfect place to catch a sunset. Wherever you find yourselves, this magical San Francisco landmark is the foremost outdoor spot of the city. **(415) 831-2700; civiccenter.sf.ca.us/recpark; free admission; recommended wedding site.** *Bordered by Lincoln Way, Stanyan Street, Fulton Street, and the Pacific Ocean. From the south end of the city, go north on Highway 101. Take the Fell-Laguna Street exit and continue straight onto Fell Street, heading west. Fell Street becomes John F. Kennedy Drive as you enter the park.*

❧❧ **GOLDEN GATE PROMENADE, San Francisco** Golden Gate Promenade winds for three and a half miles around one of the most astounding scenic routes the Bay Area has to offer. If there is a lover's lane to be found anywhere in San Francisco, it would be this projection of land at Fort Point. As you gaze out to the golden rocky hills, the vast lengths of the Golden Gate and Bay Bridges, the glistening blue water, and the formidable cityscape, there is little else to do but move closer and kiss. **Free admission.** *The promenade extends from Aquatic Park at Fisherman's Wharf to Fort Point beneath the Golden Gate Bridge.*

❧❧❧ **PALACE OF FINE ARTS, San Francisco** Nothing in San Francisco compares to the European splendor of the Palace of Fine Arts. Erected in 1915 for the Panama-Pacific International Exposition, it was not built to last. When the structure began to crumble in the late 1960s, San Franciscans who had come to cherish the Palace raised enough money to restore it, making it a permanent city landmark. Reminiscent of European architecture, the mock-Roman rotunda is supported by mammoth Corinthian columns and flanked by majestic colonnades. Walking paths lead beneath the dome and around the adjacent lagoon, where ducks and swans are in abundance. This setting, ethereal any time of day, is especially romantic at night, when the spellbinding architecture is lit up by spotlights, or in early morning when few people are around. **Free admission; recommended wedding site.** *Located between Marina Boulevard and Bay Street, next to The Presidio.*

Romantic Option: A few blocks away, on Marina Boulevard between the Yacht Harbor and Fort Mason (Cervantes and Buchanan Streets), a grassy stretch of land called **MARINE PARK** hugs the bay. On warm weekends, if you don't mind crowds, it's a good place to watch sailboats, fly a kite, or simply sit and enjoy the sunshine.

Romantic Suggestion: Take a cruise on exquisite San Francisco Bay. The **BLUE AND GOLD FLEET** (415-773-1188 for information, 415-705-5555 for ticket sales; www.blueandgoldfleet.com; call for tour options and prices) is docked at Pier 39 and Pier 41. Scenic, yet very touristy excursions depart frequently. You won't be alone, but if you concentrate on the scenery, the crowds will be much less apparent. For more privacy, rent your very own boat for the evening through **DOCKSIDE BOAT AND BED** (see Hotel/Bed and Breakfast Kissing in Oakland).

❧❧❧ **THE PRESIDIO, San Francisco** Back in the 1700s, Spanish settlers were the first to claim this prime piece of real estate; they established the Presidio as their northern military post. Today, the Presidio is still military territory, only now it's home to the U.S. Army's Sixth Division. Fortunately for those who are inclined to kiss in the great outdoors, the Presidio is not just a military installation. This beautiful corner of San Francisco is open to the public and contains hundreds of acres of lush terrain. There's much more to the Presidio than you can see on foot, so start by driving around the grounds on roads lined with redwood and eucalyptus trees. Next, do yourselves a favor: Park the car, clasp hands, and go for a walk. Stroll by some of the historical sites and displays, or take in a tranquil moment at one of the open areas with views of the Golden Gate Bridge and the Pacific Ocean. Or explore the residential area, where old yet immaculate base houses (still occupied) evoke the nostalgic feeling of days long past. **Free admission.** *Located at the very northern tip of the San Francisco peninsula and bordered by the Pacific Ocean, San Francisco Bay, Lyon Street, and West Pacific Avenue.*

❧❧❧ **TELEGRAPH HILL, San Francisco** If you live in or visit San Francisco regularly, there is probably one place that symbolizes for you what this city is all about. For some it's Fisherman's Wharf, for others it's Union Square, and for some eccentrics it may be Alcatraz. For kissing purposes, we nominate Telegraph Hill.

The top of Telegraph Hill is where the famous **COIT TOWER** presides over the city. Built in 1933, this fluted, reinforced-concrete column is noted for its interior murals depicting historic San Francisco scenes. An elevator takes visitors to the top of the tower, and from this vantage point you get a sense of the city's passionate personality and dynamic energy, as well as its orderly, well-contained physique. You will also be exposed to a lot of other sightseers, who may obscure the view and reduce your hope for a romantic moment. But then again, when you actually witness the sights and sounds from this pinnacle, you may find that the crowds around you don't seem to matter. **Free admission.** *From Union Street, head east up Telegraph Hill.*

Romantic Suggestion: When you've finished admiring this magnificent view, make sure you have dinner reservations at nearby **JULIUS'**

CASTLE (see Restaurant Kissing). If you don't, the North Beach area is overflowing with Italian restaurants and cafés that tantalize the senses.

Romantic Warning: If you plan to drive to Coit Tower, be forewarned that the small parking lot accommodates fewer than two dozen vehicles, so you'll probably find yourselves waiting in line to park. We recommend taking the bus or calling a cab. Better yet, get your hearts pumping and walk.

TWIN PEAKS, San Francisco They don't call this the scenic route for nothing. As you follow signs for Scenic Route 49, you'll drive up a steep, winding grade that climbs far above the city, eventually culminating at a peak that feels like the top of the world. From this lofty perspective, San Francisco looks almost minuscule. Truly breathtaking, panoramic views of the Golden Gate Bridge and Marin County reach as far as the Northern Coast. On clear days, the views are awe-inspiring. Though this aerie is by no means a secret, it is still much less frequented than some of San Francisco's other scenic lookouts. We saw several couples smooching without concern, which should inspire you to do the same. **Free admission.** *Follow signs for Scenic Route 49, which will direct you to this hilltop setting.*

"Let him kiss me with the kisses

of his mouth: for thy love is

better than wine."

The Song of Solomon

Marin County

An escape from the city is closer than you might think. A quick drive across the famous Golden Gate Bridge takes you from the crowded urban streets of San Francisco to the picturesque waterfront towns of Sausalito and Tiburon and the forested hills of Mill Valley, Larkspur, and Greenbrae. Whether you've got shopping to do or just want to spend some quality time communing with nature, Marin County offers something for just about everyone.

Romantic Suggestion: One way to get to Marin without getting stuck in traffic is to take the **GOLDEN GATE FERRY** (415-923-2000; www.goldengate.org; one-way fares start at $2.85 per person). The ferry leaves from the San Francisco Ferry Building at the foot of Market Street, and makes its way across the bay every day of the week to Larkspur or Sausalito. For kissing purposes, we recommend traveling during off-peak hours on weekdays. Even when the boat is packed with commuters, the ferry feels like a genuinely San Franciscan way to sightsee in the Bay Area.

Sausalito

Sausalito is often noted for its vast, beautiful view of San Francisco. It's true that this little waterfront town is one of the best vantage points from which to admire the city skyline. Sausalito is also an enjoyable place to escape from the hustle and bustle of San Francisco and browse through stylish boutiques, gift stores, and art galleries.

Hotel/Bed and Breakfast Kissing

❤❤❤ **CASA MADRONA HOTEL, Sausalito** Casa Madrona's Victorian-style property covers a large portion of a residential hillside overlooking sparkling Sausalito Bay. As you climb to your accommodations via a tiered walkway enfolded by greenery, this terraced hotel reveals its many personalities. Guest rooms display the creative work of no fewer than 16 local designers, and each room is more interesting than the last. (Describing all 34 rooms here would require a book in itself.) The Japanese-style decor of the Thousand Cranes Room artistically incorporates ash and lacquer design elements. In the Katmandu Room, purple carpeting and oversize lounge cushions accentuate a bed set beneath a skylight. Brimming with mirrors, secret alcoves, and artifacts from the Far East, this room also offers the luxury of a fireplace and a soaking tub for two. In the Casa Cabana, a festive orange color scheme creates a Southwestern ambience in which potted cacti seem right at home.

At the top of the hill, the property's original Victorian home and surrounding cottages offer incredible harbor views and relatively subdued accommodations filled with old-world antiques. (Just don't bring a heavy suitcase, since two flights of stairs lead to these rooms.) While the Victorian decor up in these parts may appeal to some, we found that these rooms needed more TLC than those below. Most accommodations on the property sport romantic amenities like fireplaces, private decks with brilliant sunlit harbor views, and seductive soaking tubs (only the La Salle Room has a jetted tub). Complimentary continental breakfast is served in Casa Madrona's elegant restaurant, **MIKAYLA** (see Restaurant Kissing), which commands panoramic views of the bay. **801 Bridgeway; (415) 332-0502, (800) 567-9524; www.casamadrona.com; expensive to unbelievably expensive; minimum-stay requirement on weekends and holidays; recommended wedding site.**

❦❦❦ **THE GABLES INN, Sausalito** Take a turn about town and you might miss this hotel tucked into the hillside. Built in 1869, the nine-room historic inn may not be the center of attention in town, but it definitely should be for romance. Subtle beiges, creams, and greens add a soothing, California contemporary touch to each room, while Indonesian furnishings bring about a slightly British-colonial feel. Our top romantic picks are the three suites on the third floor, each with vaulted ceilings, a private balcony, and a king-size bed fronting the fireplace. Of these third-floor suites, the Honeymoon Suite offers the ultimate in bubbles with a view. From the two-person jetted tub, gaze out upon San Francisco's brilliant skyline. Although the two adjacent Skyline Suites lack two-person tubs, vista seekers will relish the first-rate views, and the one-person jetted tub in the bath isn't such a bad deal either. For romance with limited monetary resources, two of the least expensive rooms boast prime privacy territory (read: no shared walls). Views are terrible, but you'll be all alone in Room No. 202 and, downstairs, in Room No. 102. In addition, each of these rooms features a gas fireplace at a height perfect for gazing into the flames from your bed.

The inn's common area turns into a nightly wine-tasting room where guests can sample some of the best vintages from the Napa and Sonoma Valleys. Come morning, return to the same room for a continental breakfast. After that, it's all downhill to Sausalito's sights and shops. **62 Princess Street; (415) 289-1100, (800) 966-1554; www.gablesinnsausalito.com; expensive to unbelievably expensive.**

❦❦❦ **HOTEL SAUSALITO, Sausalito** This boutique hotel bills itself as a French Riviera–style retreat in Sausalito and, by the looks of the bright, beautiful rooms, we'd have to agree. Finding the entrance to this hide-away, however, is a bit tricky; only a small doorway indicates the hotel's presence among the storefronts. (To truly appreciate the hotel's exterior—a 1915 Mission-revival building—view it from across the street in the waterfront park.) Once you've found your way inside, journey up to the second floor to admire the Matisse and van Gogh reproductions displayed against lemon-colored walls. The 16 guest rooms, also located on the second floor, vary in size, price, and color (mainly pretty pastels of apricot, olive green, and raspberry), and each has a private bath with a glass-sided shower. The rooms' furnishings—pine armoires, hand-forged wrought-iron beds, and exquisite mosaic tile work—add to the uniqueness of this chic hotel. Although the hotel is just steps from the water, views aren't a selling point here. The two spacious suites (Nos. 201 and 203) have views of town and the bustling street below. Suite No. 203, while smaller than its counterparts, features a rounded window overlooking a park. Some standard rooms tend toward the small side, but their cheerful decor more than makes up for space difficulties.

Come morning, you'll have to roll out of your comfortable quarters for food. A coupon for a hot drink and pastry is redeemable at the café adjacent to the hotel. If mingling with the café crowd isn't your cup of tea, take your goodies to the hotel's small terraced patio and enjoy your meal in relative privacy. **16 El Portal; (415) 332-0700, (888) 442-0700; www. hotelsausalito.com; moderate to very expensive; minimum-stay requirement on weekends.**

Romantic Warning: Some of the street-facing rooms can be noisy during the day. For better or worse, Sausalito isn't a happening place come nightfall, so things quiet down ... usually.

❤❤❤ THE INN ABOVE TIDE, Sausalito Aptly named, the contemporary

wood-shingled Inn Above Tide sits directly above San Francisco Bay in the picturesque town of Sausalito. Built with views in mind, the inn has 30 modern guest rooms, all with floor-to-ceiling picture windows that survey panoramic water views, with San Francisco's skyline twinkling in the distance. Guests can take advantage of the provided binoculars to catch glimpses of the seabirds and sailboats passing by. Nautical-themed fabrics and contemporary furnishings accentuate the cheery, spacious guest rooms. Potted rosebushes and beautiful hand-carved lounge chairs adorn private waterfront decks attached to most rooms. Oversize pillows decorate queen- or king-size beds in most of the rooms, while swaths of sheer fabric drape a king-size canopy bed in the ultraluxe Vista Suite on the second floor. Twenty-two rooms have fireplaces that are stylishly tucked into rounded brick turrets. All accommodations come with beautifully decorated private bathrooms, many of which feature deep circular soaking tubs.

Sample local vintages on the communal sundeck during afternoon wine hour. In the morning, a generous complimentary breakfast is set out in the front common room or can be delivered to your doorstep (we suggest the latter for serious romancing). **30 El Portal; (415) 332-9535, (800) 893-8433; www.innabovetide.citysearch.com; very expensive to unbelievably expensive; minimum-stay requirement on weekends and holidays.**

Romantic Suggestion: The Inn Above Tide offers "Moonlight Serenade" romance packages, which include extras like chilled champagne, sunset wine service, in-room or deckside massages for both of you, and late checkout so you can sleep in as long as your hearts desire.

Restaurant Kissing

❤❤❤ MIKAYLA, Sausalito Even if you can't stay overnight at the lovely **CASA MADRONA HOTEL** (see Hotel/Bed and Breakfast Kissing), a meal at the property's Mediterranean restaurant is a heart-stirring alternative. Colorful Laurel Burch artwork adorns white and peach stucco walls in the simply adorned dining rooms, complemented by floor-to-ceiling windows that showcase panoramic views of Sausalito Bay and the San Francisco skyline. While nearly every table has a glimpse of the water, tables closest to the windows offer the most exceptional views. Each table is draped with elegant white linens and topped with a lone orchid set afloat in a clear glass bowl. Small and eclectic, the gourmet menu focuses heavily on seafood with international influences, from seared coriander-crusted ahi to grilled butterfish. Classic best defines the desserts, which range from crème brûlée to a flourless espresso cake. After you've sampled the food and the views to your hearts' content, descend to street level and take a stroll through Sausalito. Or, if you are staying at the hotel, head back to your private haven. **801 Bridgeway, at the Casa Madrona Hotel; (415) 331-5888, (800) 567-9524; www.mikayla.com; expensive to very expensive; dinner daily, brunch Sunday; recommended wedding site.**

❤❤ SCOMA'S, Sausalito A dynamite location on the shore of Sausalito's bay makes Scoma's a sure thing for an enticing encounter. Classic seafood dishes like saucy cioppino or steamed clams in white wine and garlic are served in two nautically inspired dining rooms. The tables in these rooms are packed in far too tightly for any degree of intimacy, but if you wait for one in the sunny, glass-enclosed dining area, you can avoid the crowds and your eyes can savor the magnificent view. Service is efficient but hurried (when you see the volume of people going in and out of here, you'll understand why). After dinner, walk along the shore to gaze at San Francisco's city lights and the moon's reflection on the water. **588 Bridgeway; (415) 332-9551; www.citysearch.com/sfo/scomasmarin; expensive; lunch Thursday–Monday, dinner daily.**

❀❀ **THE SPINNAKER, Sausalito** Situated on a rocky point next to the Sausalito Yacht Harbor, The Spinnaker enjoys tremendous views of Sausalito and distant San Francisco. Floor-to-ceiling windows span the entire length of the restaurant, allowing diners to watch sailboats and ships slipping by against the picturesque backdrop of the city skyline. Such views are especially dazzling at dusk on clear evenings. The views nearly make up for the dining room's bland, somewhat dated interior. While the vast array of seafood, pasta dishes, sandwiches, and burgers are usually satisfying, they remain secondary to the splendid waterfront location. **100 Spinnaker Drive; (415) 332-1500; www.thespinnaker.com; expensive; lunch and dinner daily.**

Romantic Alternative: If THE CHART HOUSE (201 Bridgeway; 415-332-0804; www.chart-house.com; expensive; dinner daily) sounds familiar, it's because almost every major city has one. Even so, we've never seen a Chart House with a better view than the one in Sausalito. Huge picture windows frame the bay and the San Francisco skyline, the steak and seafood fare is always good, and the salad bar here is one of the best in the Bay Area.

Outdoor Kissing

❀❀❀ **MARIN HEADLANDS, Sausalito** What is it about the Golden Gate Bridge that evokes passion in all who see it? Find out for yourselves by visiting the Marin Headlands, part of the Golden Gate National Recreation Area. A precipitous road hugs the cliff above this graceful sculpture of a bridge. Several viewpoints are perfect for windblown kisses in front of the Golden Gate, with the San Francisco skyline as a backdrop. It's a magical scene when the fog rolls in, cradling the arching span and city skyscrapers in cottony billows of mist. Intrepid romantics can continue on the winding road to the edge of the Pacific; hike inland to secluded, grassy picnic spots; or comb rocky beaches while exchanging sea-swept caresses. **Northwest of the Golden Gate Bridge, in the Golden Gate National Recreation Area; (415) 331-1540; entrance fee for certain areas.** *From the north: Heading south on Highway 101, take the second Sausalito exit and follow signs to the park. From the south: Heading north on Highway 101, take the Alexander Avenue exit and follow San Francisco signs under the freeway; then follow signs to the Marin Headlands.*

Romantic Note: As a whole, the GOLDEN GATE NATIONAL REC-REATION AREA contains more than 70,000 acres of protected coastline, pristine woodland, regal mountains, rugged hillsides, and meticulously maintained city parks. It is hard to believe that such a massive nature refuge exists so close to San Francisco. Hiking, picnicking, swimming, and any other outdoor activity you can think of is possible in this awesome stretch of land that offers something for the most ardent wilderness lovers to the tamest urban dwellers. Thanks to Mother Nature and the Golden Gate National Park Association, this incredible area is yours to enjoy to the fullest.

❀❀❀ RODEO BEACH AT THE MARIN HEADLANDS, Sausalito This

expanse of white sandy beach is not a secret among locals, but you can be alone during most weekdays before summer vacation releases eager kids from the classroom. Jasper and agate are scattered along the shore, and Bird Island, just a short distance from shore, is often blanketed with fluttering white seabirds. In the distance, rolling hills and jagged cliffs make a distinguished tableau against the bright blue sky. Dozens of hiking trails wind over intriguing terrain to breathtaking panoramas. You won't be at a loss for ways to spend time here; prepare yourselves for the elements (namely, sun and wind) and enjoy long, loving hours together. **Northwest of the Golden Gate Bridge, in the Golden Gate National Recreation Area; (415) 331-1540; free admission.** *From the north: Heading south on Highway 101, take the second Sausalito exit and follow signs to the park. From the south: Heading north from San Francisco on Highway 101, take the Alexander Avenue exit and follow San Francisco signs under the freeway; then follow signs to the Marin Headlands.*

Romantic Possibility: Nearby MUIR BEACH (415-388-2596; free admission) is a much-frequented expanse of white sandy shoreline. While long smooches are probably out of the question, you can still claim your own spot, lie back, listen to the ocean's serene rhythms, and concentrate on each other.

Tiburon

Tiburon has the reputation of being the sunny spot of the Bay Area. Often when other parts of San Francisco and Marin County are veiled in fog, Tiburon is basking in sunshine. Located along the waterfront, the main part of town is brimming with restaurants and shops that can provide plenty of entertainment during your visit here.

Marin County has several outdoor sanctuaries. If you're in Tiburon, stop by the RICHARDSON BAY AUDUBON CENTER AND SANCTUARY

(376 Greenwood Beach Road; 415-388-2524; open Wednesday–Sunday). Housed in a charmingly restored Victorian, the center has a picture-perfect setting by the water. A short, self-guided trail leads up to the crest of a hill for a scenic panorama of Angel Island, San Francisco, Sausalito, and the coastal mountains.

Restaurant Kissing

❧❧❧ **CAPRICE RESTAURANT, Tiburon** Dining at Caprice feels almost like sailing on a boat without all that rocking and rolling. Take advantage of the restaurant's sturdy perch above the swirling waters of Raccoon Strait to enjoy some incredible scenery. Windows in the dining room look out to unobstructed views of Angel Island, San Francisco, and the Golden Gate Bridge. Tables spaced with privacy in mind hug the windows, ensuring that everyone has a share of the remarkable setting.

Dinner here is always an enamored event. Old-fashioned glass lanterns glow atop every table in the softly lit restaurant, and background jazz music sets the right tempo for a tantalizing kiss. The celebrated chef wins patrons over every time with his creative California-influenced European cuisine. Appetizers like pan-fried Dungeness crab cakes spiced with corn relish are just the beginning. Try anything from the varied menu: escargot, grilled coconut prawns, lamb shank pot-au-feu, or roasted Sonoma duck. Can't decide on dessert? Go for the chocolate trio: truffle cake, a mousse tower, and chocolate ice cream all served on one plate. Others may simply appreciate the pistachio crème brûlée, a dessert not seen on just any menu.

Caprice is very popular on weekends, so reservations are a must. If you happen to arrive early (which we recommend), you can enjoy a glass of wine beside the hearth in the entryway or downstairs next to a massive rock fireplace. **2000 Paradise Drive; (415) 435-3400; www.caprice. citysearch.com; expensive to very expensive; reservations recommended; dinner daily; recommended wedding site.**

Romantic Suggestion: After dinner, continue northeast along Paradise Drive to reach **PARADISE BEACH PARK**. This quiet, wooded little corner of the world overlooks the distant hills beyond the bay and the San Rafael Bridge. Depending on the time of day and the season, this place could be yours alone. There is enough strolling and picnicking turf here to make it a significant lovers' point of interest.

❧❦ **GUAYMAS, Tiburon** In every way, Guaymas reflects a south-of-the-border feel and flavor. Named for a Mexican fishing town, this casual waterfront restaurant emphasizes the authenticity of coastal Mexican cuisine instead of the usual Americanized versions. Selections from the immense menu include roasted duck served alongside pumpkinseed sauce, green corn tamales with cactus and plantain, and grilled fresh fish served with chile-tomato butter. Don't miss the house specialty: poblano chiles stuffed with chicken and raisins accompanied by a walnut and pomegranate sauce. Some dishes may sound more exotic than the usual taco and burrito fare, but be adventurous—they are all delicious.

Choose a table in the casual adobe dining room, which is accented with brightly colored paper flags hanging from the ceiling. When the weather cooperates, one of the two waterfront decks can't be beat for sunbathing and sipping margaritas (we prefer the upper level for the best views). The patios are warmed with gas heaters, making them pleasant even when the sun dips below the hills. Blooming bougainvillea climbs over whitewashed log beams, pots of cacti are placed around the decks, and pastel colors set a calming mood. A stunning view of the bay and San Francisco makes outdoor dining even more irresistible. Guaymas may not be fine or intimate dining, but you'll find that sitting back, enjoying the view, and relaxing is very easy to do here. **5 Main Street; (415) 435-6300; www.guaymas. citysearch.com; moderate; lunch and dinner daily, brunch Sunday.**

Romantic Suggestion: The restaurant is a stone's throw from the ferry terminal for the **BLUE AND GOLD FLEET** (415-773-1188 for information, 415-705-5555 for ticket sales; www.blueandgoldfleet.com; call for tour options and prices). If you're staying in San Francisco, taking a ferry to dinner in Tiburon is not only romantic, but also decreases the stress of driving over the bridge.

Mill Valley

Home to a handful of restaurants, art galleries, and boutique stores, the small town of Mill Valley is a charming place to spend an afternoon. Nature enthusiasts will appreciate Mill Valley's rural setting. Red-tailed hawks soar above the rolling hills, and vistas of the mountain peaks and valleys in this region are simply spectacular. **MOUNT TAMALPAIS STATE PARK** and nearby **MUIR WOODS NATIONAL MONUMENT** are ideal for a variety of day hikes (see Outdoor Kissing for reviews of both). We have only one warning about these outdoor spots: Be prepared to contend with crowds on weekends, particularly on clear summer days.

Hotel/Bed and Breakfast Kissing

❀❀❀ **MILL VALLEY INN, Mill Valley** Mill Valley's one and only downtown inn is set near the foot of **MOUNT TAMALPAIS** (see Outdoor Kissing) and surrounded by redwood, eucalyptus, and oak trees. This setting is the only giveaway that you aren't in Europe. Advertised as a European-style pension, the main building fits this description to a tee. From wrought-iron balconies overflowing with flowers to the tiled entryways and natural wood accents to the Tuscan yellow stuccoed exterior, the inn radiates Mediterranean charm.

The 25 guest rooms are located throughout three buildings: the European-style main building, a renovated Victorian, and two cottages tucked in a forest of redwoods. Half of the rooms in the main building face the street and have narrow balconies, while the rest offer wider balconies and overlook a forested area (we recommend these, not only for better views but for less traffic noise). The two private and roomy cottages front a gentle creek and are well suited for those wanting complete privacy. Nearby, a restored Victorian home holds seven rooms, our favorite being Room No. 22 with its roomy veranda facing the creek. No matter where you decide to romance the night away, you'll be completely comfortable. Most rooms have queen- or king-size beds, tiled bathrooms (some with skylights), and French doors leading to the balconies or patios. Fireplaces and Franklin woodstoves are found in many of the rooms as well.

Upscale California decor spiced with rustic touches best describes the inn's interior. Colors are warm and neutral, beds are covered in crisp white linens, and all of the natural wood furnishings have been handcrafted by local artisans, including the "distressed-wood" armoires and the sleigh beds. The look is truly stunning, especially when you discover that many of the rustic touches have been created from leftover materials, such as old window frames turned into bathroom mirrors and coat racks crafted from antique doorknobs.

An extensive continental breakfast is served on the main building's second-floor Sun Terrace. This partially covered deck looks out on tall redwoods and the creek. With its stylish umbrellas and teak tables, the Sun Terrace is a perfect place to enjoy a morning repast. Or you can load up a tray with goodies and take them back to your private patio. Wherever you decide to eat, this delicious breakfast is a great way to start the day. **165 Throckmorton Avenue; (415) 389-6608, (800) 595-2100; www.mill valleyinn.com; expensive to very expensive; minimum-stay requirement on weekends.**

Romantic Warning: Due to the inn's location in downtown Mill Valley, traffic noise can be a problem in rooms facing the street.

❤❤❤ **MOUNTAIN HOME INN, Mill Valley** Views don't get much better than this. Set high above the trees on a ridge of **MOUNT TAMALPAIS** (see Outdoor Kissing), the Mountain Home Inn surveys all the beauty Marin

County has to offer. Hawks soar overhead, and the only sound you'll hear is the wind rustling through the branches of the surrounding trees. Nature-oriented artwork, pine-paneled walls, and wood accents are part of a mountain-lodge motif in the ten guest rooms. All have private decks and boast views of the breathtaking setting (except for Room No. 6, which is tucked into the redwoods). Each room is equipped with different amenities: Some have their own fireplace while others feature either a whirlpool or large soaking tub. Even the smallest guest rooms are worth mentioning since the views are equally terrific. Our favorite kissing accommodation is the secluded Canopy Room, appointed with a king-size four-poster bed made of tree trunks and embellished with a plush down comforter and a lovely canopy. A skylight built into the cathedral ceiling allows ample natural light to filter in, while shutters open from the bathroom's whirlpool tub to views of the tree-laden hillside beyond. Dried-flower wreaths and bouquets enhance the rustic but elegant mood.

A bountiful breakfast here might include entrées like French toast or homemade bagels with smoked salmon, served in the property's elegant (and very popular) dining room. Lunch or dinner at the **MOUNTAIN HOME INN RESTAURANT** (see Restaurant Kissing) is a delicious way to savor the views even if you aren't staying overnight. However, with a perfect perch like this, who would want to descend Mount Tamalpais after dining? We think you'll want to stay. **810 Panoramic Highway; (415) 381-9000; www.mtnhomeinn.com; expensive to unbelievably expensive; recommended wedding site.**

Romantic Warning: In order to enter the Mountain View Room, one of the choice accommodations at this inn, you have to walk through the lower dining room. It's an inconvenient design for such a nice romantic hideaway.

Restaurant Kissing

❤❤❤❤ **EL PASEO, Mill Valley** Don't be fooled by the Spanish name; El Paseo is nothing like the cantina you'd expect. Instead, it's one of the loveliest, most intimate *French* restaurants in Northern California. Potted plants front the entrance to this ivy-laced refuge tucked behind a brick courtyard in the charming town of Mill Valley. Inside, low ceilings with exposed dark wood beams accentuate the dining room's brick walls and rich-colored decor. Bottles of wine are tucked into nooks and crannies around the restaurant, and candles flicker in oversize wineglasses at every table.

Presented on hand-painted china, the authentic French offerings will have your mouth watering in no time. You can't go wrong with pork tenderloin confit accented by an apple marmalade, roasted salmon nested on a bed of leeks, or roasted lamb chops served alongside wild mushrooms in a thyme-scented red wine sauce. It's not surprising El Paseo has won a number of culinary awards, not to mention numerous awards for best romantic atmosphere. It is equally deserving of its four-lip rating for romance in our book. We can't think of a better environment in which to express your love and enjoy fine food. **17 Throckmorton Avenue; (415) 388-0741; expensive; dinner Tuesday–Sunday.**

❤❤❤ **MOUNTAIN HOME INN RESTAURANT, Mill Valley** Situated near the top of **MOUNT TAMALPAIS** (see Outdoor Kissing), this contemporary wood-and-glass restaurant and lodge has some of the best views around on a clear day. Combine these views with simple California-style cuisine and you've created a wonderful dining experience. Dried flowers and crisp linens embellish every table in the elegant dining room on the lower floor, which is warmed by a large tiled fireplace. A second dining room is located just off the bar (which sometimes can get noisy), next to another fireplace. Both these dining areas are perfect when the fog rolls in and those breathtaking views are just a memory. When the weather is clear, however, relish the scenery on the casual outdoor deck. Soups, salads, sandwiches, and seafood are the specialties at lunchtime, and dinner continues in similar California fashion with items such as vegetarian lasagne, grilled salmon in a champagne sauce, and chicken capellini. The walnut-chocolate mousse is an absolute must for dessert. **810 Panoramic Highway, at the Mountain Home Inn; (415) 381-9000; moderate to expensive; reservations recommended; call for seasonal hours; recommended wedding site.**

Romantic Note: The **MOUNTAIN HOME INN** (see Hotel/Bed and Breakfast Kissing) also has ten cozy guest rooms worthy of your romantic consideration.

❤❤ **PIAZZA D'ANGELO, Mill Valley** In spite of its exceedingly casual and noisy atmosphere, Piazza D'Angelo offers some of the best Italian fare this side of San Francisco. Modern in appearance, the restaurant's series of dining rooms are accented with terra-cotta floors, Italian tile, modern artwork, and colorful low-hung lamps. Bottles of wine, Tuscan pottery, and other Italian knickknacks adorn a partition that runs through the center of the busy, and often crowded, restaurant. Favorite romantic sitting spots include the semicircular booths hugging the restaurant's perimeter, as well as the tables for two fronting the large fireplace. In the warmer months, the open-air section of the dining room and the tiled outdoor patio are prime kissing spots.

Besides the chic Italian decor and friendly service, Piazza's moderately priced entrées and hearty portions make this an attractive place to dine. Order any of the pastas, pizzas, and specialty meat dishes, and you might be taking home a doggie bag. Our grilled pork chop topped with caramelized shallots and accompanied by homemade mashed potatoes proved big enough for two to share. Specials of the night are also worth noting. The only disappointment of the evening was the dry tiramisu. For a night out that won't drain your pocketbook but will fill you up with food (and romance), try puckering up at Piazza. **22 Miller Avenue; (415) 388-2000; moderate; lunch and dinner daily.**

Outdoor Kissing

❧❧❧❧ **MOUNT TAMALPAIS STATE PARK, Mill Valley** If you long to be surrounded by nature, you need only cross the Golden Gate Bridge into Marin County and drive along Highway 1 to the crest of Mount Tamalpais. This is without question one of the most absorbing drives in the area. Coiling along the edge of this windswept highland, each turn of the S-shaped road exposes another vantage point from which to scan wondrous views of overlapping hills cascading down to Marin. As you continue your excursion, you can either remain in the car or venture out into the hills with a picnic in hand. The two-mile-long **STEEP RAVINE TRAIL**, which begins at the Pan Toll Station on the Panoramic Highway, is a magnificent deep-forest journey to views of the ocean and bay. Here, in the midst of the earth's simple gifts, a loaf of bread, a jug of wine, and your beloved are all you need. **Panoramic Highway; (415) 388-2070; free admission, $5 parking fee; recommended wedding site.** *From the Golden Gate Bridge, take Highway 101 north to Marin County. Turn off at the Stinson Beach–Highway 1 exit and follow the signs for Mount Tamalpais State Park.*

❧❧❧❧ **MUIR WOODS NATIONAL MONUMENT, Mill Valley** Donated to the federal government in 1908, this well-preserved parcel of redwoods was declared a national monument by President Theodore Roosevelt. Set in the hushed splendor of Redwood Canyon, Muir Woods boasts 560 acres of undisturbed forest and six miles of walking paths. Hawks glide overhead in abundance and sunlight filters through the leafy cathedral canopy. Chipmunks, blue jays, and black-tailed deer are frequently seen in this shady forest. Redwood Creek runs year-round, trickling down from the peaks of Mount Tamalpais to provide sustenance to the trees and animals that live here. Even in the height of summer, you can find secluded spots to admire nature's handiwork and enjoy each other's company in this magical preserve. **Muir Woods Road; (415) 388-2595; www.nps.gov/muwo; $2 entrance fee; recommended wedding site.** *From the Golden Gate Bridge, take Highway 101 north to Marin County. Turn off at the Stinson Beach–Highway 1 exit and follow the signs for Muir Woods National Monument.*

Larkspur

Restaurant Kissing

💋💋💋 **EL QUIJOTE, Larkspur** The structure that houses El Quijote was built more than a hundred years ago. Back then it was the Green Brae Brick Kiln, which supplied bricks for such San Francisco landmarks as Ghirardelli Square, the Cannery, and the St. Francis Hotel. Now, a century later, and after more than a million dollars in renovations, El Quijote retains its historic charm while offering all the contemporary advantages of an alluring Spanish restaurant.

Guests are greeted at the door by the hospitable wait staff and offered a seat at the bar or in the more intimate dining room. Shaped like a large tunnel, the dining room has solid brick walls and a curved brick ceiling. As you'd expect in such a place, it's dark, but low lighting is reflected off the walls from colorful sconces. White linens and blown glass artwork add their own share of brightness to the room. Although the restaurant is rather large, the tables are situated to provide a secluded feeling. A second brick tunnel in back serves as the restaurant's wine cellar.

El Quijote's chefs prepare several different types of paella, including the traditional paella Valenciana, a perfect meat-and-seafood creation for two. Other delicious entrées include chicken breast stuffed with Spanish serrano ham, or sliced pork tenderloins covered in a mild green peppercorn sauce. If you can't decide on an entrée, try sampling several plates of tapas, served both hot and cold. Everything about El Quijote invites you to linger in this place where the past provides the setting for modern-day romance.

If you're in the mood for live entertainment, you may wish to sit at the bar, where you can watch authentic flamenco dancing Friday, Saturday, and Sunday nights. Perhaps this sultry and daring dance will set the mood for you to do your own dancing later on. **125 East Sir Francis Drake Boulevard; (415) 925-9391; expensive; dinner daily.**

💋💋💋 **LARK CREEK INN, Larkspur** As you wind through Larkspur's lovely wooded neighborhoods, be sure to watch for this yellow home-turned-restaurant hidden away on a curvy road. In spite of its somewhat off-the-beaten-path location, the Lark Creek Inn is one of the North Bay's renowned dining spots. Its reputation is well deserved: The home's countrified yet elegant ambience is perfectly conducive to romantic interludes.

The main dining room features hardwood floors, crisp white linens, and a glass ceiling; flowing fabrics covering the glass let diffused light warm the interior. Colorful abstract artwork adds a contemporary touch to the creamy white walls, and a towering flower arrangement draws the eye to the room's center. In the second dining room, the wraparound windows create a distinct sunporch feel, accentuated by plush casual chairs, a green and white color scheme, and plenty of sunshine. When the weather warms up, the restaurant's garden patio, situated near a babbling brook, is a perfect spot for dining on those warm summer days.

Then, of course, there is the unforgettable food. The moment you enter the restaurant, enticing aromas hint at the delights listed on the seasonally changing menu. Brunch specials include dishes like orange soufflé cakes, southern-fried-chicken salad, and nectarine-stuffed brioche French toast. Lunch and dinner are equally creative, with selections such as housemade ravioli, olive-crusted sea bass with sage pasta, and barbecued chipotle-glazed pork medallions certain to spice up your life. Desserts will definitely sweeten your day. Try the melting chocolate cake with hazelnut ice cream or the Lark Creek Inn's famous butterscotch pudding, and savor the divine moment. From appetizers to dessert, the food presentations are as beautiful as the surroundings, making a visit to the Lark Creek Inn an all-around wonderful experience. **234 Magnolia Avenue; (415) 924-7766; expensive to very expensive; reservations recommended; lunch Monday–Friday, dinner daily, brunch Sunday; recommended wedding site.**

Greenbrae

Restaurant Kissing

❤❤ **JOE LOCOCO'S, Greenbrae** Known more for its delicious northern Italian cuisine than its quiet atmosphere, Joe LoCoco's caters to those whose stomachs are the key to their hearts. As you pass the open kitchen near the front entrance, you may be overcome by the irresistible aromas wafting through the dining room. Rest assured: The food is as good as it smells! The focus here is hearty, not heavy, and the kitchen turns out marvelous homemade pastas and fresh seafood dishes. We especially enjoyed the grilled Tuscan bread, served with wild mushrooms and fresh herbs, as well as the angel-hair pasta with rock shrimp in a lemon cream sauce.

Noise from the adjacent open bar and kitchen, combined with the loud shouts of hurried waiters, pose serious romantic distractions for those seeking quiet conversation. Otherwise, the dining room, bathed in the soft glow of candlelight, is unquestionably romantic. Artwork depicting food adorns the peach-colored walls, and exquisite floral arrangements add another gentle touch of color. Large windows at one end of the dining room showcase views of the marina across the street and Mount Tamalpais in the distance. If you're willing to overlook the noise factor, you won't be disappointed. **300 Drakes Landing Road; (415) 925-0808; moderate to expensive; lunch Monday–Friday, dinner daily.**

San Rafael

Hotel/Bed and Breakfast Kissing

❀❀❀❀ **GERSTLE PARK INN, San Rafael** Built in 1895, the Gerstle Park Inn was once a traditional English-style estate; today its timeless charm draws romantics seeking luxury and a quiet location. This wonderful inn is ensconced on one and a half acres in a pleasant residential neighborhood, overlooking the sleepy town of San Rafael. Redwood trees, oaks, and cedars lend ample shade to the expansive gardens and orchards. Deer are frequently seen peacefully grazing on the property in the early evening.

With its small size, romantic amenities, and emphasis on privacy, the Gerstle Park Inn strikes the right balance between intimacy and professionalism. Leaded glass doors open into lovely common rooms, where Asian artwork from the owner's travels is on display and gleaming hardwood floors are accented by handsome Oriental carpets. A fire rages in the large marble hearth in the living room, and every evening wine and cheese are set out for guests to enjoy.

There are three buildings on the property: the main house, the carriage house, and two cottages. Each of the 12 guest rooms is uniquely exquisite, making it very difficult to choose one. All have been lovingly decorated with bright colors, country or classical furnishings, Asian and European accents, and fresh bouquets of flowers. Private baths are common to all. Four rooms feature Jacuzzi tubs, and most have serene views of the gardens or San Rafael's hills.

Harbored on the lower floor of the main house, the Lodge Suite is a favorite for honeymooners and those wanting plenty of time alone. An outdoor stairway winds down to the suite's private entrance and lovely deck appointed with wrought-iron furniture. Inside, bright yellow floral linens and wallpaper have a cheery effect. Tiled steps in the bathroom climb up to an enticing Jacuzzi tub for two surrounded by classical pictures of beach-bathing scenes. In the Gerstle Suite, French doors open onto a private patio and flower gardens. An immense shower–steam bath is an unexpected luxury in its cozy bathroom, where Oriental rugs warm the tiled floor. A private staircase winds upstairs to the elegant Redwood Suite. Green-striped wallpaper, beautiful antiques, a luxurious king-size bed, a Jacuzzi tub, and a private deck overlooking the gardens make this a perfect hideaway. Also very private is the Oak Suite, a second-floor room complete with a king-size bed, a separate parlor, a Jacuzzi tub, and a private deck. The Carriage House holds two beautiful suites, and the two French country–style cottages are perfect for those wanting a fully equipped and romantic place to call home for a while. Trust us: Whichever room you stay in here will be wonderful.

Breakfast includes gourmet specialties like orange French toast, a five-cheese scrambled egg dish, and homemade granola, all served at cozy two-person tables in the snug breakfast room. If you're still hungry after this feast, you'll find cookies and fresh-picked fruit available in the kitchen area. After you've eaten more than your fill (it's impossible not to), stretch your legs in neighboring **GERSTLE PARK**, where trails traverse the tree-covered hills. Or, if you'd rather lie low, sit on the inn's covered veranda and watch the day go by. **34 Grove Street; (415) 721-7611, (800) 726-7611; www.gerstleparkinn.com; expensive to very expensive; minimum-stay requirement on weekends and holidays.**

East Bay

Just across the Bay Bridge from San Francisco, the East Bay stretches from Point Richmond south to the Livermore Valley. In between are Berkeley, home of the well-known University of California at Berkeley campus, and the sprawling metropolis of Oakland. The East Bay may not be a total escape from the City, but if you have only a weekend to spare, it makes for an extremely convenient getaway. You may be surprised to discover several establishments worth your romantic consideration.

Oakland

Can romance be found in Oakland? True, Oakland doesn't have the charisma of San Francisco or the allure of Wine Country, and we have to agree that, by and large, downtown Oakland doesn't hold much fascination for those seeking affectionate encounters. Still, we discovered several semiromantic locales certain to please those with amorous agendas.

Hotel/Bed and Breakfast Kissing

◆◆ **THE CLAREMONT RESORT AND SPA, Oakland** Nestled in the Berkeley Hills and enfolded by acres of deftly cultivated gardens and palm trees, this colossal plantation-style mansion is reminiscent of a European castle. Epic in scale and style, the hotel's exterior can appear overbearing and impersonal if you have something smaller and more intimate in mind. One problem for couples is that large resorts like the Claremont lend themselves to conventions and tour groups. Feeling like part of a software association's annual meeting won't exactly put you in the mood for romance. This famous hotel and tennis club definitely attracts a high percentage of convention-goers and businesspeople, but don't let this fact deter you from seeking romantic possibilities here.

Guests at the Claremont have the opportunity to engage in any of the available activities, and there are plenty. Tennis courts, a large swimming pool plus an additional lap pool, a nearby golf course, saunas, hot tubs, a full-service spa, a state-of-the-art exercise room, a fully equipped weight-training room, and a variety of fitness classes offer invigorating ways to spend the day together. This isn't the place to come, however, if you want to lock yourselves away in a luxurious room for some indoor sports. The 279 rooms have a standard, somewhat dreary hotel feel, and many of the windows are quite small considering the fantastic scenery outside. Some suites have views of Berkeley's hills, the lovely garden grounds, or the distant San Francisco skyline, but the view alone does not justify the cost of these otherwise nondescript rooms. Still, you may want to come to The Claremont Resort and Spa with healthful intentions of being good to yourselves and to each other. Spa Romance packages make it easy (but not exactly affordable) to plan an East Bay getaway. **Ashby and Domingo Avenues; (510) 843-3000, (800) 551-7266; www.claremontresort.com; very expensive to unbelievably expensive.**

Romantic Suggestion: The Claremont's most romantic restaurant, JORDAN'S (moderate to very expensive; reservations recommended; breakfast, lunch, and dinner daily, brunch Sunday), offers some of the most breathtaking views around, especially of the San Francisco skyline during sunset. After regaining your breath, enjoy the standard California cuisine with Pacific Rim influences.

🌸🌸🌸 **DOCKSIDE BOAT AND BED, Oakland** Whether you fancy sailboats or luxury motor yachts, you can kiss like a millionaire (at least for an evening) on your boat of choice in this Oakland port of call. Our 35-foot sailboat would have been a dream come true if the intimate accommodations had been less rustic and confining. More spacious boats cruise into the unbelievably expensive category, but they can be a better way to go if you're willing to share the romance of the evening with another like-minded couple. Complete with several staterooms, modern furnishings (including stereos), and private baths, a large yacht can provide ample space and privacy for two couples. If you'd rather not share, there are boats suited for two. For some sweet dreaming, request *Tiramisu*, a sailing ketch with a wood-burning fireplace to keep you cozy on nippy nights. Whichever boat you choose, a continental breakfast, packed in a picnic basket, is delivered in the morning or stowed on the boat at your arrival.

Most of these boats are strictly kept dockside and can't be taken out for a leisurely sail or cruise. However, if you want to explore the bay's waters, ask about the "snooze and cruise" package when making reservations. This offers you the chance to take a chartered ride around the bay and then stay overnight on the same boat back in port. Romantic extras like limousine service, special floral bouquets, and onboard massages can also be arranged by the Dockside staff. Catered candlelight dinners aboard are also available, although they can be quite expensive; another option is to stroll through the picturesque marina to one of the many (less expensive) restaurants and cafés clustered along the waterfront.

Dockside Boat and Bed also offers similar accommodations at Pier 39 in San Francisco (415-392-5526). Including both sites, there are a dozen or so boats from which to choose, ranging in size from 32 to 68 feet. Most boats have queen-size beds, and some feature lovely teak interior paneling.

Whether you decide to dock near **JACK LONDON SQUARE** in Oakland (see Outdoor Kissing) or near Pier 39 in the City, you're sure to experience fantastic views of the San Francisco skyline. **419 Water Street, at Jack London Square; (510) 444-5858, (800) 436-2574; www.boatandbed. com; moderate to unbelievably expensive; minimum-stay requirement on holiday weekends.**

❦❦ **WATERFRONT PLAZA HOTEL, Oakland** A romance package designed just for kissing is the year-round specialty at this waterfront hotel, harbored along Oakland's charming **JACK LONDON SQUARE** (see Outdoor Kissing). Chilled champagne and fresh strawberries in an edible chocolate bowl are the prelude to an amorous stay in one of the spacious waterfront-view rooms. A continental breakfast is delivered to your door in the morning, saving you the trouble of calling room service or venturing to the hotel's restaurant. Romantics are also given two complimentary nightshirts, which, in this setting, are most likely to go home with you unworn.

Whether or not you splurge for the romance package, the two of you are sure to enjoy the rooms, especially the waterfront accommodations. (Be sure to request a room with a water view—not all of them have one.) Appointed with pine furnishings and brightly colored linens, many of the 144 contemporary guest rooms feature gas fireplaces. Corner suites with wraparound balconies and gorgeous water views are particularly enticing. TV/VCRs, mini-bars, coffeemakers, and access to a public fitness center, sauna, and pool are provided to ensure that all you need to complete the scene is each other.

In spite of the waterfront views and romance package offered here, this hotel draws an almost exclusively business-oriented clientele, particularly on weekdays. You are likely to be the only two people here with something other than business on your minds. **10 Washington Street, at Jack London Square; (510) 836-3800, (800) 729-3638; www.waterfront plaza.com; expensive to unbelievably expensive.**

Restaurant Kissing

❦❦ **IL PESCATORE, Oakland** Marina yachts rock with the waves, and twinkling harbor lights reflect off the water just outside this Italian eatery; luckily, such sights are not lost once you venture inside. Large sloping windows comprising three sides of the restaurant allow for uninterrupted views from most of the well-spaced tables. White linen tablecloths and crystal wine goblets add a dash of elegance, while the nautically inspired woodpaneled interior remains refreshingly unpretentious.

The friendly, down-to-earth wait staff serves up delicious seafood and Italian fare from the mile-long menu. Antipasti specialties, such as grilled eggplant marinated in fresh herbs, provide the perfect start to dinner. Delicious entrées include seafood- and mushroom-filled Italian crêpes; fresh pasta tossed with Dungeness crab, shrimps, and clams; and, one of the restaurant's most popular dishes, veal sautéed with Italian herbs and mushrooms in a sherry sauce. With such dishes coming your way, an evening here is certain to whet your appetite for more waterfront romance as the night continues. **57 Jack London Square; (510) 465-2188; moderate; lunch and dinner daily, brunch Saturday–Sunday.**

SCOTT'S SEAFOOD GRILL AND BAR, Oakland A veritable parade of sailboats, tugs, motor yachts, and even a seal passed by in the estuary outside our window at Scott's. This classy, upscale seafood restaurant can get a bit crowded at times, but don't let that distract you from the fabulous view. Request one of the tables lining the windows; that way you'll be away from the noisy kitchen, but close enough to the lounge area to appreciate the live piano music (every evening) or performing jazz trio (Sunday brunch only). Lanterns and white tablecloths top each table, while gold dome-shaped chandeliers hang from the maroon-colored ceiling.

Fish, fish, and more fish is what you'll find on Scott's menu. Salmon was highlighted the evening we dined, with more than nine different specials ranging from smoked salmon ravioli to baked salmon Florentine. There's also a lot to choose from on the main menu, including charbroiled ahi tuna topped with tropical salsa, grilled whole Pacific sand dabs, and a deep-fried seafood platter featuring prawns, snapper, and scallops. If you're a light eater, simply fill up on appetizers. The Dungeness crab cakes spiced with a mustard sauce are divine. As for the steamed Manila clams, we fell for them hook, line, and sinker. **No. 2 Broadway, at Jack London Square; (510) 444-3456; www.scottseastbay.com; expensive; lunch and dinner daily, brunch Sunday.**

Outdoor Kissing

JACK LONDON SQUARE, Oakland Although most romance-seeking couples prefer the solitude of less-populated destinations, once in a while they may wish to join the crowds and visit a popular local attraction. In a city where amorous options are few and far between, Jack London Square is such a place. This up-and-coming area along Oakland's estuary provides a waterfront home for an abundance of hip restaurants, modern shops, and good old-fashioned museums. At its center stands an immense Barnes & Noble bookstore; at the southeast end is Jack London Village, a series of specialty shops in a turn-of-the-century setting. Festivities and events are scheduled year-round, and every Sunday you'll find a delightful farmers market overflowing with fresh fruits, vegetables, and flowers.

Walk along the sunny boardwalk or tour Franklin D. Roosevelt's restored presidential yacht, otherwise known as the "Floating White House" (510-839-8256; www.usspotomac.org; $3 per person entrance fee; tours Wednesday, Friday, and Sunday). If you would rather not be landlocked, rent a recreational kayak or canoe and paddle off on a self-guided tour of the inner harbor and estuary. Contact **CALIFORNIA CANOE AND KAYAK** (409 Water Street; 510-893-7833; www.calkayak. com; rental prices start at $8 per hour). In addition, you can catch the Alameda/Oakland ferry (510-522-3300; call for prices), which provides daily service to Alameda, Angel Island, Pier 39, and San Francisco. **Event information line: (510) 814-6000.** *From north of Oakland, take the Interstate 880 Alameda–San Jose exit. Follow Interstate 880 to the Broadway-Alameda exit, ease right at the bottom of the ramp, and take the first right on Adeline. Take a left on Third, turn right on Broadway, and follow Broadway until you reach the Square. From south of Oakland, head north on Interstate 880 and take the Broadway exit. Take a left on Broadway and follow it to the Square.*

❧❧❧ **LAKE MERRITT, Oakland** Ask anyone in the East Bay area if downtown Oakland has any amorous potential, and you'll probably hear the same answer: No. If you ask about Lake Merritt, however, people tend to whistle a different tune. Surrounded by 155 acres of park, Lake Merritt is located in, yes, downtown Oakland. Its surprising setting is ideal for picnicking, strolling, canoeing, or myriad other outdoor activities. Autumn is perhaps the best time to discover this city oasis, when the leaves slowly change and frame the lake in vibrant shades of gold and orange.

Start an afternoon here with a picnic near the water, then try a sailing lesson or take a tour on a miniature stern-wheeler. Don't be too disappointed when you find the afternoon has slipped away before you've had a chance to explore many sections of this domain. You'll have to return a few times to see it all, but that leaves you with something to look forward to the next time you happen to be near downtown Oakland. **Free admission.** *From San Francisco, take the Bay Bridge to Interstate 580 east. Take Interstate 580 toward Hayward and exit at Grand Avenue going west. Grand Avenue eventually winds its way into the park.*

Berkeley

People flock from across the country to visit University of California at Berkeley's beautiful campus, set beneath the verdant, rolling Berkeley Hills. This can be a lovely place for a picnic, particularly in the summer, when the student population dwindles significantly. A small array of additional romantic locales are also worth a visit to this university town, especially if you're studying the fine art of love.

Hotel/Bed and Breakfast Kissing

❧❧ **ROSE GARDEN INN, Berkeley** Telegraph Avenue may not be the most romantic street in Berkeley, but then again, surprises often spring up in the most unlikely spots. One such surprise is this Victorian-style inn, comprised of five buildings and hidden from the road by mature trees and lush landscaping. Within the lovely courtyard and throughout the property, English country gardens and literally hundreds of blooming rosebushes infuse the grounds with color and lend a welcome pastoral touch to the urban surroundings.

There is something for everyone at the Rose Garden Inn, which offers 40 guest rooms with a variety of amenities and styles. Dark wood detailing accents the historic Faye Building, built in 1906, and the adjacent Main Building. Guest accommodations in these restored mansions exude turn-of-the-century elegance, with old-fashioned wallpapers, hand-sewn quilts, and period furnishings. Claw-foot tubs, colorful stained glass windows, and working fireplaces are additional enticing period touches. Although it is a hike to the third floor, Room No. 9 in the Faye Building boasts a fabulous patio where you can sit all day and view the distant bay.

Ivy winds around the exterior of the renovated Lott Building (formerly the carriage house), our favorite building on the property. Terra-cotta–tiled floors and hand-painted tiled fireplaces lend a French-country feeling to the four units here, where French doors open to private garden patios. Rose-colored walls give each room a warm blush, highlighted by cathedral ceilings and lovely, plush linens. Rooms in the Garden and Cottage Buildings are more contemporary, with high ceilings, gas fireplaces, hand-painted tile work in several rooms, and modern linens and carpeting.

Since there's such a wide range of amenities and room styles at the inn, be specific when making reservations. Not all of the rooms have private baths, enticing views, balconies, and fireplaces. Don't be shy about asking if these are prerequisites for your romantic interlude.

You won't find fault with the elaborate wine-and-cheese plate set out each afternoon, or the complete breakfast of baked egg dishes, hot-from-the-oven breads, and homemade preserves served in the country-Victorian dining room. If California's famous sunshine is on full blast, take your morning repast out to the covered veranda or head to the gardens, where the scent of roses is sure to sweeten your morning. **2740 Telegraph Avenue; (510) 549-2145, (800) 992-9005; www.rosegardeninn.com; moderate to very expensive.**

Restaurant Kissing

❀❀❀ **CHEZ PANISSE, Berkeley** Many restaurant reviewers say that if you eat out only once in San Francisco, Chez Panisse should be the place (even though it happens to be in Berkeley). Well, far be it from us to argue with the truth. If delicious and ultrafresh California cuisine is your idea of a romantic meal, and you happen to be on the east side of the bridge, the flawless food and comfortable atmosphere here are definitely worth your while.

Chez Panisse offers two dining alternatives with two entirely different menus. The first option is the Arts and Crafts–style upstairs café that offers a casual à la carte menu of soups, salads, a limited selection of entrées, and some fabulous desserts. Our favorite dining spot in this area is a cozy alcove set aglow with lanterns and filled with a handful of tables. The other choice is the more formal and slightly quieter downstairs dining room, which has similar decor but fewer tables, more candlelight accents, and a set three- or five-course dinner menu (depending on the day of the week). Wanting to sample as many tastes as possible, we opted for the upstairs dining room. What culinary wonders awaited us! The Sungold cherry tomato salad with fava bean crostini tasted garden-fresh. (Knowing this restaurant's reputation for freshness, the tomatoes were probably picked that day.) Due to our culinary curiosity, we also tried an item not seen on most menus: *Sopa de Nopales,* or cactus soup. It proved light, slightly sweet, and absolutely delicious. This was followed by entrées of grilled polenta surrounded by a summer bean ragout and baked king salmon, delicately accented by a cherry tomato, cucumber, and chervil vinaigrette. Since we dined during summer, fresh fruit desserts were at the forefront. The nectarine and raspberry crisp topped with vanilla ice cream was the perfect finale to a wonderful meal. **1517 Shattuck Avenue; restaurant: (510) 548-5525, café: (510) 548-5049; www.chezpanisse.com; expensive to very expensive; restaurant: dinner Monday–Saturday, café: lunch and dinner Monday–Saturday; reservations required with credit-card guarantee for restaurant.**

Romantic Warning: Due to Chez Panisse's outstanding reputation, you may have to book your reservation a month in advance if you want to dine in the restaurant. Also, don't be shocked by the request for a credit-card guarantee. Reservations for the café are taken that day; we recommend calling early.

❦❦ **FONTINA CAFFÉ ITALIANO, Berkeley** Fontina Caffé Italiano is an agreeable spot for some informal romancing. The restaurant consists of two dining rooms that share a single fireplace. The brick walls are adorned with everything from modern posters and acrylic landscape paintings to strings of garlic braids and dried peppers. White linens and bottles of olive oil top each of the nicely spaced tables. A small outdoor seating area is also available; unfortunately, its location on busy Shattuck Avenue and its table umbrellas sporting beer logos detract from its romantic appeal. Choose from more than a dozen Italian-style pastas, including pesto tortellini and vegetarian lasagne, or order from the selection of seafood, chicken, and veal dishes. Just don't forget to ask about the daily dessert specials. **1730 Shattuck Avenue; (510) 649-8090; www.fontina.citysearch.com; moderate; lunch and dinner daily.**

❦❦❦ **SKATES ON THE BAY, Berkeley** Simply put, San Francisco has one of the world's most stunning skylines. One way to admire the city's beauty is to travel east across the Bay Bridge to Berkeley. From the dining room at Skates on the Bay, you can observe the golden city's dazzling profile, defined by the expansive blue bay, steep hills, and myriad skyscrapers at water's edge. Windows envelop nearly three-quarters of the dining room, so every table has a glimpse (or more) of the prime views. Chandeliers and track lighting illuminate the crowded dining room, which is filled with circular booths and closely spaced tables. (It's obvious that the view from here is no secret—you're likely to find yourselves competing for reservations and dining in a crowd.) This can make for an exceedingly noisy and cluttered environment, but luckily the food is good and the choices are ample. Garlic-roasted prawns, Dungeness crab grilled over applewood, steak and chicken dishes, as well as a fresh catch du jour menu should please every palate. Just be sure to save room for dessert, so you can linger over the city's lights a bit longer. **100 Seawall Drive; (510) 549-1900; moderate to expensive; lunch and dinner daily, brunch Sunday.**

Romantic Suggestion: After dinner, leave the crowds behind and walk along the water's edge to a nearby pier jutting out into the bay. Follow your instincts to the end of the dock, where the city skyline beckons from across the water. This is one of the best places to kiss we've found yet.

Outdoor Kissing

❤❤❤❤ **BERKELEY MUNICIPAL ROSE GARDEN, Berkeley** Filled with color and fragrance, the Berkeley Municipal Rose Garden is an enchanting realm. From its upper level, you can gaze over an amphitheater of nature's splendor. As you make your way down the stairs, passing one rosebush after another, the sweetly scented air envelops you. This is prime kissing territory, especially in the summer when the flowers are in full bloom. The sedate setting is so expansive that even when others are around, you can usually find an empty park bench to call your own. Spend a few moments (or a few hours) enjoying views of acre after beautiful acre of this earthly paradise. **Free admission; recommended wedding site.** *From San Francisco, take the Bay Bridge east and stay on Interstate 80 going north. Take the University exit east. Go straight to Shattuck Avenue and turn left. At Hearst Avenue, turn right. From here, turn left onto Euclid and follow it to the top of the hill.*

❤❤❤ **TILDEN REGIONAL PARK, Berkeley** Nature's majesty is always close at hand in the Bay Area, and Tilden Regional Park is no exception. One of the most expansive earthy getaways in the area, the park encompasses more than 2,000 acres of forested trails, gardens, and picnic grounds. A hand-in-hand stroll through the park's Botanical Garden is simple romance at its best. Peaceful pathways wind through terraced plantings of native California blooms and trees, while ardent hikers can find their own private paradise along the more rugged trails. Picnic spots abound throughout the park; just drive until you find one that suits your fancy. With so many romantic possibilities, Tilden Regional Park offers a welcome respite from nearby civilization. **(510) 525-2233; www.ebparks.org; free admission.** *From Oakland, take Highway 24 through the Caldecott Tunnel. Exit onto Fish Ranch Road and follow this to Grizzly Peak Boulevard. Look for entrance signs to Tilden Regional Park on the right; several entrances are located along Grizzly Peak Boulevard.*

Point Richmond

Hotel/Bed and Breakfast Kissing

❤❤ **EAST BROTHER LIGHT STATION, Point Richmond** For ringside views of the bay's fabulous scenery, set your course for East Brother Light Station, one of northern California's most uniquely situated bed and breakfasts. Located on the rocky shores of East Brother Island in the strait separating

San Francisco Bay from San Pablo Bay, the 1873 light house is on the National Register of Historic Places. Income from the bed and breakfast is used to preserve the island's buildings and boats. Although the location is off the beaten path, guests certainly don't have to rough it here. The accommodations are tucked away in a creamy white Victorian house connected to the lighthouse, and an additional structure called the Fog Signal Building.

Breathtaking views of the water are definitely the highlight of each guest room; simply gaze out your window to survey the comings and goings of boats crossing over the bay from San Francisco. All four rooms in the Victorian home are sparsely decorated and offer queen-size beds with brass frames and ordinary linens. Unless you don't mind sharing a bathroom with a neighboring couple, request one of the two upstairs rooms with private baths. A fifth accommodation, known as the Water's Quarters, is available in the nearby Fog Signal Building and features a full-size bed and a nautical motif. From the home's common area, ascend a spiral staircase to the light tower, where you can enjoy magnificent views of Mount Tamalpais and the San Francisco skyline. The island offers plenty of restful activities to occupy your time, including fishing and observing the surrounding wildlife. Tours of the island are also provided by the innkeepers.

Overnight accommodations include a ten-minute boat ride from the Point San Pablo Yacht Harbor to and from the island, hors d'oeuvres and champagne upon arrival, a four-course dinner highlighting local wines, and a hot breakfast. (Lunch is served only to guests staying two or more nights.) Day visits to the lighthouse are available Saturdays only ($15 day-use fee per person; reservations required). **117 Park Place, on East Brother Island; (510) 233-2385, (510) 812-1207; www.ebls.org; unbelievably expensive (includes breakfast and dinner).**

Romantic Warning: Due to the island's limited water supply, showers are reserved for guests staying more than one night. In addition, the U.S. Coast Guard's electronic foghorn operates 24 hours a day between October 1 and April 1. Earplugs are provided for guests, but light sleepers may be awakened throughout the night.

Lafayette

Hotel/Bed and Breakfast Kissing

❧❧ **LAFAYETTE PARK HOTEL, Lafayette** From the freeway, the Lafayette Park Hotel looks like an impressive European chalet, but because it is visible from the highway, we were worried. After all, a love nest that borders a highway or a busy road is potentially too noisy for a serene romantic retreat. In this case, however, our skepticism was unfounded. The moment our stay began, the freeway might well have never existed.

In the open and lovely lobby, a profusion of fresh flowers brings soft color to the elegant decor, while skylights illuminate a hand-carved staircase that serves as the room's architectural centerpiece. Soundproofed and spacious, the 140 guest rooms are elegantly appointed with cherrywood furnishings, granite countertops, and wet bars. Our light and bright quarters featured a vaulted ceiling, a wood-burning fireplace, and a king-size bed, along with a cozy sitting area by the window. Exploring the property, we found three charming courtyards to kiss in: one built around an Italian marble fountain, another surrounding a stone wishing well, and the third with a large swimming pool and whirlpool spa. We highly recommend requesting a room with a pool or courtyard view (otherwise you may catch glimpses of the freeway).

Adjacent to the lobby, the **DUCK CLUB RESTAURANT** (moderate to expensive; breakfast, lunch, and dinner daily, brunch Sunday) offers American cuisine in an admirable atmosphere. After dinner, snuggle up near the cobblestone fireplace in the adjacent lounge for a latte or cappuccino, a wonderful way to round out the evening. **3287 Mount Diablo Boulevard; (925) 283-3700, (800) 368-2468; www.woodsidehotels.com; expensive to unbelievably expensive; minimum-stay requirement on holiday weekends.**

Restaurant Kissing

❀❀❀ **POSTINO, Lafayette** Perfectly trimmed hedges and ivy-covered brick mark the entrance to Postino, a charming restaurant set in the town of Lafayette. Its courtyard would be delightful for a leisurely lunch or an intimate evening interlude if it wasn't for the nearby traffic. Thankfully, all distractions dissolve once you step inside, where two dining rooms offer two different experiences. One room has an informal, lively feel, with a glass roof and a big, open kitchen; the other is a beautiful, casually elegant dining area with towering vaulted ceilings, brick walls, and colorful murals. Even though the second room is rather large, it is divided into smaller areas by cozy alcoves, perfect for intimate conversation and loving glances. The restaurant's overall feel is rustic Italian, and the fantastic-tasting food follows suit.

The northern Italian menu changes daily, but offers plenty of palate-pleasing choices. Start off with the Caesar salad, made with whole romaine lettuce leaves so large, you are encouraged to eat them with your hands. For another hands-on experience, there's grilled corn on the cob glistening with red bell pepper butter. As for the entrées, use your silverware to enjoy the specialty pastas, risottos, and other Italian delights that are served in portions worth their price. Some favorites include gnocchi (potato dumplings) in a spicy tomato, smoked bacon, and onion sauce; grilled beef short ribs served alongside soft polenta; and sautéed swordfish adorned with a smoked almond, raisin, and rosemary brown butter. **3565 Mount Diablo Boulevard; (925) 299-8700; expensive; lunch Friday and Sunday, dinner daily.**

Danville

Restaurant Kissing

☙❦ **BRIDGES RESTAURANT, Danville** The noteworthy Asian-inspired California cuisine draws overwhelming crowds to Bridges Restaurant, a fact that doesn't exactly encourage kissing. The closely arranged tables in the chic, ultracontemporary dining room are another romantic hindrance; however, the seating situation is better in the warmer months, when you can choose a table outside on the garden terrace, near a burbling fountain surrounded by trees.

If this restaurant is so packed and noisy, why do we consider Bridges an acceptable place to kiss? Once you taste your meal, you will immediately understand. The seafood is always fresh and beautifully prepared. We recommend the sea scallops and prawns stir-fried with coconut milk, mint, and toasted peanuts. Or try the roasted chicken breast served with caramelized onions and banana-curry coconut fried rice. Bento boxes, traditional Japanese boxed meals, make an occasional appearance on the menu. Each savory bite of your meal here helps you forget about the clamorous surroundings. And don't leave without dessert: The passion fruit ice cream with warm coconut and macadamia nut coffee cake is heavenly. **44 Church Street; (925) 820-7200; expensive; lunch Friday, dinner daily.**

San Ramon

Restaurant Kissing

☙☙❦ **MUDD'S, San Ramon** While the name of this San Ramon restaurant may sound more earthy than romantic, the interior is filled with charm and plenty of amorous possibilities. Tables adorned with candle lanterns are scattered throughout several connecting dining rooms, each with curved wood ceilings and terra-cotta–tiled floors. Request a window seat or a table outside on the patio so you can appreciate the flourishing herb and edible-flower garden that spans the back of the restaurant. A trail winds through the gardens if you care to take a mini-nature walk before or after your meal.

Freshness, creativity, and, of course, flavor are the kitchen's hallmarks. One bite of the sugar-cured pork chop with sweet potato polenta, spinach lasagne with grilled vegetables, or the muscovy duck is enough to convince you to come back again and again. **10 Boardwalk; (925) 837-9387; www.mudds.com; expensive; lunch Monday–Friday, dinner daily, brunch Sunday; recommended wedding site.**

Pleasanton

Hotel/Bed and Breakfast Kissing

❤❤❤ **EVERGREEN, Pleasanton** Have you ever dreamed of living in a woodsy, upscale neighborhood, close enough to the city to be convenient but distant enough to be removed from the city's pressures? Pleasanton is just that kind of community, and Evergreen is the perfect place to taste the good life. This impressive cedar and oak home is tucked into a hillside, with trees and shrubbery enclosing the property. Large windows and high ceilings in the sunny entryway allow the natural splendor outside to complement the interior. Shiny hardwood floors in the living room are warmed by a crackling fire, and plush couches provide a relaxing place to sit and discuss dinner plans.

All four guest rooms exhibit the same comfortable elegance found in the main-floor parlor. Of particular romantic interest is the top-floor Grandview Suite, a spacious, extremely comfortable room with a corner fireplace, a king-size sleigh bed, and a tiled bathroom with a two-person Jacuzzi tub and double-headed shower. From the private deck, you can enjoy serene views of the surrounding treetops. Hideaway, the other romantics' retreat, features a pine four-poster king-size bed, cream and beige accents, and an oval Jacuzzi tub for two. This room also has a deck, but it faces the driveway, so it is not as private as the Grandview Suite's. The two remaining guest rooms are the least expensive, mainly because they have simple bathrooms without Jacuzzi tubs, the beds are queen-size instead of king-size, and they are noticeably smaller. The cozy country interior of the Retreat Room makes for a comfortable getaway, and the Library's rich, dark fabrics make this a choice for those wanting more tailored and traditional surroundings. Even if you choose a room without a tub for two, you can bubble away with your sweetheart in the large communal spa on the large deck. There's also an exercise room on the second floor, complete with TV, and plenty of complimentary goodies in your room's refrigerator.

A generous cooked-to-order breakfast, accompanied by an array of fresh fruits and baked goods, awaits each morning in the main-floor dining area. Stone-topped tables with wrought-iron chairs are set in a sunny breakfast area, or you can take a tray out to the deck or up to your room. Here at Evergreen, you will feel invigorated after a good night's sleep and inspired by the natural beauty around you. **9104 Longview Drive; (925) 426-0901; www.evergreen-inn.com; expensive to very expensive.**

Romantic Suggestion: Not only does Evergreen's location yield much-appreciated seclusion, but it also affords easy access to **AUGUSTIN BERNAL PARK** (8200 Golden Eagle Way; free admission). If you think your legs can handle an uphill walk, it is only about 45 minutes to the top of Pleasanton Ridge from Evergreen, and the view from the top is awe-inspiring. After catching your breath, you'll find this an excellent place to kiss.

Livermore

Hotel/Bed and Breakfast Kissing

☙☙☙❦ **THE PURPLE ORCHID INN, Livermore** Quiet. Peace and quiet. That's exactly what you'll find way out here in the country, where the wind caresses the golden grasses and a dusty road leads to this fabulous inn. Built of hand-hewn logs, The Purple Orchid looks much like a rustic mountain lodge that has been transplanted along acres of olive trees and rolling hills. Inside the large home are eight luxurious accommodations, all with plenty of romantic features to keep every couple kissing. Most noteworthy are the jetted tubs (varying in size) in each guest room, private or semiprivate patios, and plenty of space so the two of you feel alone. Our favorite spot for a few smooches is the main-floor Double Eagle Suite, thanks to a magnificent two-person jetted tub and an enclosed porch where breakfast can be enjoyed in privacy. (The two main-floor suites are the only rooms where breakfast can be served in-room.) The upper-level Uncle Howard's Adventure Retreat runs a close second, with its king-size bed, heart-shaped Jacuzzi tub for two, and semiprivate patio overlooking the countryside. Decor varies from room to room, ranging from a western motif to California contemporary to a charming jungle theme. All are done tastefully without being overbearing.

In addition to the lovely rooms, this inn offers many other romantic treats. A pebble-tiled pool and waterfall out back help cool you off; a full-service day spa meets all your relaxation needs; and the concierge can arrange, among other things, bicycle or horseback rides to Livermore Valley's many wineries (see Outdoor Kissing). Each morning, after the meadowlarks have started to sing, breakfast is served poolside (weather permitting) or in the magnificent dining room. Here cathedral ceilings soar overhead and views of the olive orchards provide a lovely backdrop. Best of all, whatever you want for breakfast is yours for the asking. The creative chef can whip up anything from old-fashioned biscuits and gravy to fancy Grand Marnier French toast. Now that's something unheard of at most bed and breakfasts! But then again, The Purple Orchid is a special place, and one worth the journey out to the countryside. **4549 Cross Road; (925) 606-8855, (800) 353-4549; www.purpleorchid.com; expensive to very expensive; recommended wedding site.**

Outdoor Kissing

❦❦ **LIVERMORE VALLEY, Livermore** Escape the urban hustle of the Bay Area in the quiet Livermore Valley's wine region. Unlike the Napa and Sonoma Valleys, this area has remained relatively undeveloped, and it serves as a refuge for a number of wineries nestled among rolling hills speckled with oak trees and cattle. A mere hour's drive from nearly anywhere in the Bay Area, the Livermore Valley makes for an ideal kissing excursion. *From southbound Interstate 680, exit onto eastbound Interstate 580 and drive to the Livermore Avenue exit.*

Romantic Suggestion: If the weather makes picnicking impossible, consider eating at the casually chic **WENTE VINEYARDS RESTAURANT** (5050 Arroyo Road; 925-456-2450; www.wentevineyards.com; moderate to expensive; lunch Monday–Saturday, dinner daily, brunch Sunday), where floor-to-ceiling windows offer views of the surrounding hillsides and vineyards. The service here is affable, the wine list excellent, and the regional American cuisine notable.

"The sound of a kiss is not so loud as

that of a cannon, but its echo lasts a

great deal longer."

Oliver Wendell Holmes

South of San Francisco

The towns of Menlo Park, Saratoga, and San Jose may not conjure up as many romantic images as their northern neighbor, but that didn't stop our lips from looking! From San Francisco we ventured southward and found several inns, restaurants, and outdoor gardens perfectly suited for a weekend getaway, or anytime romance calls your name.

Woodside

The small town of Woodside is a charming place, although you'll need to drive through town to find suitable spots for kissing. As you make your way upward along breathtaking Skyline Boulevard, giant coast redwoods shelter you from the sun and a thin veil of mist creates a cozy mood for a romance-filled drive. It is along this lonely and lovely mountaintop road that you'll find three romantic spots worth visiting.

Hotel/Bed and Breakfast Kissing

❀❀❀ **THE LODGE AT SKYLONDA, Woodside** Refreshment, rejuvenation, and romance merge into one at this lodge sheltered high in a redwood forest above the Pacific. Once you enter through the unassuming gates, the hectic world as you know it suddenly disappears. The cries of ravens and the rustling of branches replace car horns and rumbling motors. A soft mist, common to these parts, envelops you as you breathe in deeply. Soon the concept of relaxation becomes a reality as you take hold of your loved one and step inside.

Hints of Japanese design, including a long sand and rock garden and a massive metal gong, blend with a traditional lodgescape of exposed log walls, massive wood-burning fireplaces in common areas, and ceilings reaching seemingly as high as the surrounding redwoods. Large windows throughout draw the glorious forest inside. There's no music, no loud noises, and no crowds. Stillness is everywhere.

Kissing comes naturally here. How could it not in such a pristine setting? However, if your lips need a break, there are plenty of other things to do. Hiking is the cornerstone of the lodge's fitness program, and you'll find everything you need to join the fun, from fanny packs to water bottles to a friendly guide who escorts guests on morning hikes, rain or shine. With thousands of acres to explore, most people venture out with the group. If you'd rather be alone, the friendly staff will provide you and your hiking partner with a trail map and directions to the best vista points. (You'll have to discover the best kissing spots for yourselves.) When you return from your morning outing, an assortment of decadent massage services are available in the lodge's peaceful, candlelit spa. Take a dip in the heated indoor pool or soak your cares away in the steaming outside hot tub set against a forested backdrop. There's also a workout studio if you still need to get your heart pumping and, in the evening, a yoga class helps you unwind.

Retreating to your room is another after-hike option, of course. While the 16 rooms are studies in simplicity designwise, each one manages to capture some romantic traits. King-size beds (or double queens) are adorned with down comforters and whimsical-patterned pillows, balconies overlook the forest below (or parking lot and forest beyond), and deep soaking tubs come complete with soothing bath salts and forest views. Plush robes, which everybody here wears in public, are provided along with handmade soaps and wonderfully scented bath amenities. What you won't find here are any electronic distractions like TVs and stereos to interrupt the blissful peace and quiet.

While the rooms may be more clean-lined than cozy, you won't be burdened by sensory overload, and the balconies are perfect places to watch the woodpeckers and giant ravens in the redwoods. After a day of rejuvenation, snuggle up on a couch in the Great Room—one space that is well deserving of its name—and enjoy evening hors d'oeuvres. Since the lodge is remotely located, all meals are provided. An emphasis on healthy gourmet cuisine rules, and tables for two are in abundance within the common dining room. **16350 Skyline Boulevard; (650) 851-6625, (800) 851-2222; www.skylondalodge.com; unbelievably expensive (breakfast, lunch, and dinner included); minimum-stay requirement.**

Romantic Note: Weekends tend to be a more popular time for couples. During the weekdays, single travelers and groups of women are the norm.

Restaurant Kissing

❀❀❀ **BELLA VISTA, Woodside** The winding scenic drive to Bella Vista is half the fun of dining here, but once you arrive, other things should keep you entertained. Time has taken its toll on this turn-of-the-century mountaintop restaurant; it leans toward the rustic side with a somewhat rundown entrance, and dark weathered wood paneling and old-fashioned lighting inside. But such a timeworn appearance adds character and is easily dismissed once you catch a glimpse of the scenery. Floor-to-ceiling windows in the dining room command endless views of a rolling procession of redwood trees. Arrive before sunset so you can have dinner as evening begins to veil the area in velvety black and the distant lights of Redwood City begin to twinkle.

Before looking at entrée choices, we urge you to order dessert first (a good philosophy in general, we might add). The light-as-a-pillow soufflés made for two take 45 minutes and are worth ordering ahead of time. Once that's done, you can move on to the main menu featuring straightforward continental fare such as filet of sole meunière, veal sautéed in Marsala wine, and broiled lamb with Dijon mustard sauce. The friendly tuxedo-clad wait staff will dazzle you by cooking and/or serving some dishes tableside. Our steak Diane lit up the entire restaurant when the wine hit the sizzling pan. Finish things off with what you've been waiting for all evening: the soufflé. One bite of the Godiva chocolate soufflé, and you'd think you were up in the clouds ... and, depending on the weather, you just might be. **13451 Skyline Boulevard; (650) 851-1229; expensive; dinner Monday–Saturday.**

Outdoor Kissing

◆◆◆◆ **FILOLI GARDENS AND ESTATE, Woodside** Filoli's 16 acres of formal gardens evoke passion in all who visit. The gardens are laid out in a sumptuous Italian-French design, with terraces, lawns, and pools that form a succession of garden rooms. More than 10,000 plants are added annually to ensure year-round splendor. The Chartres Cathedral Garden resembles a stained glass window with its roses and boxwood hedges, the Woodland Garden is Eden revisited, and the wisteria-draped mansion is similar to a European summer palace. Original furnishings and items from the Getty and de Young Museums recall an era of grand luxury. If you feel a sense of déjà vu, it may be because you have seen Filoli portraying the classy Carrington estate on the '80s television drama *Dynasty*. Or perhaps you kissed here in your most pleasant dreams. **86 Cañada Road; (650) 364-8300; www.filoli.org; $10 entrance fee per person; call for seasonal hours, special events, and guided tour reservations.** *Filoli Gardens is located about 25 miles south of San Francisco. From Interstate 280, take the Edgewood Road exit west, turn right onto Cañada Road, and then drive 1.2 miles to the entrance.*

Portola Valley

Restaurant Kissing

◆◆ **IBERIA, Portola Valley** Don't reread your directions—you're *supposed* to be in a shopping mall. We admit it's an unusual location for a romantic restaurant, but you won't have any qualms once the owner of this distinctive Spanish restaurant greets you and ushers you to the table of your choice. Everything about this restaurant is authentically Spanish, from the ambience to the menu to the wait staff. European knickknacks fill the cozy dining room, set overlooking a small grove of trees. Leaded glass partitions lend privacy to intimate tables set with lovely hand-painted dishes.

Although the menu changes periodically, you can indulge in the traditional cuisine of Iberia by savoring such peasant-style dishes as braised lamb and sweet peppers served in a clay casserole. Of course, there's the traditional shellfish paella for two as well as a bounty of seafood, poultry, game, and meat dishes on the extensive menu. Scallops flambéed with brandy and bacon, quail stuffed with raisins and pine nuts, and several *asado* (roasted meat) dishes made for two should have you singing the praises of Spanish cuisine. **190 Ladera-Alpine Road; (650) 854-1746; moderate to expensive; lunch and dinner daily.**

Menlo Park

Hotel/Bed and Breakfast Kissing

💋💋 **STANFORD PARK HOTEL, Menlo Park** A hop, skip, and jump away from beautiful Stanford University resides this pleasant and contemporary 163-room hotel, fronted by fat palm trees and a towering fountain. Despite its close proximity to a major arterial, the inn has many redeeming features for those wanting a city getaway, including nearby shopping and easy access to university sights and activities. Plus, the popular town of Saratoga is only a 20-minute drive away (see Saratoga).

The lobby, adorned with a large fireplace surrounded by overstuffed sofas and high-backed chairs, is the gateway to what we consider the hotel's centerpiece: the garden courtyard. Punctuated with modern sculptures, the inner yard is a perfect place to sit together and enjoy the California sunshine. Beyond is a small but tantalizing heated pool and modest exercise studio.

As for the rooms, those on the third floor are prime kissing spots. In addition to not having anyone above you, you'll also appreciate the high, vaulted ceilings that add a luxurious roominess. (Unfortunately, even with the extra space and large windows, the lighting isn't too bright. Luckily, that's not a requirement for romance, although it is for reading or finding things in your suitcase.) Try booking a third-floor courtyard-facing room if possible. Although the windows are soundproofed (quite well, we might add), the road-facing rooms lack view charisma. Many rooms have king-size beds fronting wood-burning fireplaces, and every room has a large granite and tiled bathroom plus the added luxury of plush robes. Evening turndown service; pleasant colors of dark green, beige, and rose; floral motif bedspreads; and plenty of elbow room put this hotel in an above-average category for service and style.

The fowl-theme **DUCK CLUB RESTAURANT** (moderate to expensive) and adjoining lounge serve breakfast, lunch, and dinner, but we can't say we were impressed with the food enough to recommend them wholeheartedly. For a romantic snack, order from the bar menu and hide yourselves in the overstuffed chairs fronting the courtyard. **100 El Camino Real; (650) 322-1234, (800) 368-2468; www.woodsidehotels.com; expensive to very expensive.**

Palo Alto

Hotel/Bed and Breakfast Kissing

❀❀❀ **GARDEN COURT HOTEL, Palo Alto** Escape the hustle and bustle of downtown Palo Alto in this Mediterranean-style villa built around an enclosed courtyard. All 62 guest rooms here have charming little balconies, many of which overlook the courtyard below. Though we were especially partial to the rooms with courtyard views, we must warn you that they directly face rooms on the opposite side of the hotel, and views of your neighbors are all too common. (For the utmost privacy, you'll have to shut the curtains.) Even the rooms that face the busy street are infused with sunlight and laden with luxurious appointments such as large, arched windows; pastel motifs; contemporary furnishings; and canopied beds draped with luscious fabrics and plush down comforters. Other amenities, such as CD players with CDs, morning newspaper delivery, and complimentary coffee and fruit help set this hotel apart from others in town. Six suites have fireplaces and Jacuzzi tubs; all offer loads of romantic potential.

Breakfast is not included in your stay, but plenty of nearby coffee shops just steps from the hotel can satisfy your morning cravings. **IL FORNAIO** (650-853-3888; www.ilfornaio.com; moderate to expensive), the restaurant on the hotel's main level, serves breakfast, lunch, and dinner. This chain Italian restaurant is too noisy and crowded to be romantic, but the garden courtyard is a lovely place to enjoy a meal. Il Fornaio also delivers to guest rooms, and those private balconies make for wonderful dinner spots. **520 Cowper Street; (650) 322-9000, (800) 824-9028; www. gardencourt.com; very expensive to unbelievably expensive; recommended wedding site.**

Romantic Warning: Unlike many hotels we've visited in northern California, the Garden Court offers smoking rooms. If you're sensitive to smoke, be sure to request a nonsmoking room. Our room smelled of stale cigarettes, which wasn't appealing at all.

Saratoga

Surrounded by forest and parkland, Saratoga is an idyllic escape from the city. Tall trees shade picturesque streets lined with charming storefronts and well-tended gardens and homes. Saratoga's main thoroughfare, BIG BASIN WAY, is surprisingly small, but teeming with award-winning restaurants that score as high on the kissing scale as they do on the culinary scale. Saratoga has more than enough romantic possibilities to fill a superlative afternoon or weekend interlude.

Romantic Warning: Due to the growing popularity of the Paul Masson concert season in the warmer months, there are times when Big Basin Way is a traffic bottleneck, the likes of which are not supposed to happen outside the city. Keep your schedule loose if you happen to be here at the end of a concert. Simply park your car and have a snack or sip cappuccino at any of the dining spots along Big Basin Way.

Hotel/Bed and Breakfast Kissing

❀❀ **THE INN AT SARATOGA, Saratoga** Nestled in the heart of picturesque Saratoga, this handsome inn strikes a perfect balance between the intimate warmth of a bed and breakfast and the comfortable practicality of a hotel. All 45 guest rooms feature private balconies and windows that overlook Saratoga Creek flowing through a small forest of sycamore, maple, and eucalyptus trees. Upscale hotel furnishings, king-size beds, double vanities, and a host of amenities provide everything seasoned travelers require and romantics yearn for, including luxurious tiled Jacuzzi tubs in seven of the rooms.

Complimentary wine and refreshments are served every afternoon in the plush lobby downstairs. In the morning, return to the lobby for a complimentary buffet-style continental breakfast; however, there aren't always enough tables to go around and, if you're a late sleeper, the pickings can be slim. Consider waking up early and taking breakfast back to the privacy of your own room. You can always go back to bed after eating. If you are *really* late sleepers and miss the A.M. offerings altogether, don't fuss. All of Saratoga's coffee shops, restaurants, and cafés are just outside your door. **20645 Fourth Street; (408) 867-5020, (800) 338-5020; www.inn atsaratoga.com; expensive to unbelievably expensive.**

Restaurant Kissing

❤❤ **LA FONDUE, Saratoga** La Fondue effortlessly lives up to its reputation as a unique restaurant. More unusual than it is romantic, the colorful dining room filled with moons, suns, and stars draws its theme from Greek mythology. Who would guess that in an atmosphere like this, the menu would offer nothing but fondues? The air is laden with delicious aromas, and the fondue selection is limitless, from classic Swiss cheese to more unusual selections like pesto and Cognac fondue and tofu fondue. Of course, you can't leave a fondue restaurant without indulging in a "dunk-your-fruit-into-chocolate" dessert. Several dipping selections should entice your taste buds, including a velvety white chocolate and old-fashioned milk chocolate. If you're wondering whether fondue can be romantic, take notice of the restaurant's "fondue rules," which state: "If a lady loses her cube in the fondue, she pays with a kiss to the man on her right." Just make sure you're not seated next to strangers. **14510 Big Basin Way; (408) 867-3332; www.lafondue.com; expensive; dinner daily.**

❤❤ **LA MÈRE MICHELLE, Saratoga** When making reservations at La Mère Michelle, you should specify whether you want to eat in the dining room or on the more casual sunporch. It's a difficult choice. Subdued, elegant, and slightly conservative, the dining room is highlighted by sparkling crystal chandeliers, fine art, and mirrored walls. Here, candles flicker at intimate tables cloaked in white linens. Though it is much more casual, the enclosed sunporch is more enticing, overlooking Saratoga's charming storefronts and encircled by a short brick wall embellished with bright flower bouquets. The traditional French menu and enchanting atmosphere of either area are sure to please. Our only complaint was the Sunday brunch, which veers away from French classical into the realm of ordinary continental fare. We were extremely disappointed with the overly sweet cheese blintzes and bland eggs Benedict. Even the croissants were burnt on top. What would the French say to this? **14467 Big Basin Way; (408) 867-5272; www.lameremichelle.com; expensive; lunch and dinner Tuesday–Sunday, brunch Sunday.**

❤❤ **LE MOUTON NOIR, Saratoga** Le Mouton Noir is anything but the black sheep of Saratoga's restaurant row. Laura Ashley prints and a combination of off-white and earth tones lend a French country charm to the very intimate and elegant dining room. French inspirations can also be found in the delectable California-style cuisine. For the ultimate in gourmet surf 'n' turf dishes, try the crispy braised sweetbreads accompanied by a Maine lobster tail. Other treats, from both land and sea, include pan-seared sea bass and medallions of venison atop creamy polenta adorned with huckleberry sauce. Elaborate desserts are served with care, so be sure to order one as you bask in the candlelight glow of this romantic treasure. **14560 Big Basin Way; (408) 867-7017; www.lemoutonnoir.com; expensive; dinner daily.**

❀❀❀ **THE PLUMED HORSE, Saratoga** Each of the intimate dining rooms at The Plumed Horse has unique detailing and character. One brims with Victorian antiques and opulent red velvet furniture; another features weathered wood walls and stained glass windows. Appropriately, horse paraphernalia and horseshoes are displayed everywhere. Best of all, the continental and seasonal menu with heavy French influences rarely disappoints. Don't by shy about trying anything, from the osso bucco to the baked Australian lobster tail. Some of the monthly specials are especially intriguing, most notably the crispy duck breast with pistachio ballotine, a polenta tower adorned with baby vegetables, and the roasted pork tenderloin covered by a Madagascar green peppercorn sauce. **14555 Big Basin Way; (408) 867-4711; www.plumedhorse.com; very expensive; dinner Monday–Saturday.**

❀❀❀ **RESTAURANT SENT SOVÍ, Saratoga** It's no surprise that Restaurant Sent Soví is the talk of the town—everything about this restaurant is just about picture-perfect. Small lights create a soft glow in the contemporary French dining room, fashioned with high ceilings and appointed with stark, modern paintings. Unique copper wainscoting adds some shine and dried flower arrangements provide texture, while stylish rugs cover the worn hardwood floors. There's only a handful of tables here, all adorned with white linens and candles. Tables set against the wall offer little elbow room, which is the only drawback about this dining room.

The innovative French menu will certainly set the right tone for a romantic evening, especially with such luscious starters as the house specialty: wild mushroom soup flecked with shaved black truffles. A noteworthy entrée is the roasted veal loin with celery root and caramelized pearl onions. The goat-cheese ravioli flavored with smoked ham and garden sage also delighted our taste buds, but our cod fillet entrée wasn't as well balanced as the other dishes. Dessert shouldn't be passed up here even if you're full—the chocolate-rum bread pudding is especially tantalizing … and small in size. **14583 Big Basin Way; (408) 867-3110; www.sentsovi.com; very expensive to unbelievably expensive; reservations recommended; dinner Tuesday–Sunday.**

Romantic Note: Popularity, combined with limited seating, makes reservations here a must. However, plan on calling twice: once to make your reservations and then again on the set date to reconfirm. How can one remember, especially with romance on the mind? All we can say is, don't forget, especially if you want to impress that special someone.

Outdoor Kissing

❀❀❀❀ **HAKONE GARDENS, Saratoga** Hidden in the hills above Saratoga is a horticultural utopia, pure and simple and sublime. Discovering this traditional Japanese garden among the sky-reaching redwoods and fragrant eucalyptus trees is a delight, especially in the early morning when the birds sing, the breeze is soft, and the crowds haven't arrived yet. At the center of the 15-acre garden is a clear pond where colorful carp, a Japanese symbol of love and longevity, languish in the still water. White water lilies float on the surface, and a cascading waterfall fills the air with mild, tranquilizing music. Sun-basking turtles, which at first resemble statues, surprise and delight when they finally slide into the water. The garden is edged with wood-fenced walkways adorned by sweet-smelling flowers. The contemplative mood of the area makes it prime territory for a walk with the one you love. Several picnic tables are situated outside the gardens, where you can enjoy a cold drink from the gift shop or your own picnic. **21000 Big Basin Way; (408) 741-4994; www.hakone.com; free admission, $5 parking fee; open weekdays 10 a.m.–5 p.m. and weekends 11 a.m.–5 p.m.; recommended wedding site.** *Take Big Basin Way west through town; about a mile up the road, you will see a turnoff sign on the left side of the street.*

❀❀❀❀ **MOUNTAIN WINERY, Saratoga** Perched above the idyllic town of Saratoga, up a long and winding country road, Mountain Winery covers some of the most august, sun-drenched earth in the entire South Bay. Everything here seems almost too picture-perfect. Graceful trees rustle in the soft breezes. Grapevines arc across the mountainside, disappearing from sight as the horizon curves to meet hill after hill. Perhaps the only flaw in this majestic setting is that the winery is not open to the public except during special events. Then again, for most of the spring, summer, and part of fall, that's not a problem. Every year, the winery presents a spectacular summer concert series featuring entertainers who appeal to just about every audience. Regardless of what you choose to hear, there is something miraculous about listening to music in the mountains with a clear sky and the sweeping countryside as your only backdrop. **14831 Pierce Road, at Highway 9; (408) 741-0763; www.chateaulacresta.com; open for con-**

certs only; recommended wedding site. *Go west on Big Basin Way, turn north onto Pierce Road, and then follow the signs to the main gate.*

Romantic Warning: On a summer day, sitting in an unshaded spot can lead to meltdown. Try to find protected seats or bring a sun visor, sunglasses, and a picnic blanket. At night, however, the mountain breezes can be cooler than you might expect. An extra sweater, combined with some cuddling, will keep shivers at a minimum.

Romantic Note: If wedding bells are in your future, facilities and services for large groups are available through a separate company adjacent to the winery. Call **CHATEAU LA CRESTA** (408-741-0763) for details. This restaurant does only banquets or catering and is not open to the public.

❦❦❦ **VILLA MONTALVO, Saratoga** Listening to beautiful music in the spectacular garden-like setting of Villa Montalvo is another way to enjoy Saratoga's bounty of cultural events. Concerts here are oriented more to the classical music listener, which seems perfectly fitting within these lush grounds punctuated by Greek statues, perfectly manicured lawns, and an aristocratic villa. Call (408) 961-5858 for summer concert ticket information. Classical tunes aren't the only music you'll hear here; wedding bells chime as well. If tying the knot beneath the trees or beside the quaint Love Temple is what you'd like, call (408) 961-5814. Even without music or weddings, the arboretum grounds and nearby hiking trails are worthy of a visit. **15400 Montalvo Road; (408) 961-5800; www.villa montalvo.org; free admission to the grounds; call for concert ticket prices; call for seasonal hours; recommended wedding site.** *From downtown Saratoga, take Saratoga–Los Gatos Road (Highway 9) south, drive a third of a mile, and turn right onto Montalvo Road. Drive one mile to the Montalvo grounds.*

San Jose

You might be wondering why anybody would go to the silicon capital of the world for anything other than computer software. We actually wondered the same thing—until we stumbled across several very romantic finds … and, thankfully, there wasn't a computer in sight.

Restaurant Kissing

❦❦ **BELLA MIA RESTAURANT, San Jose** Twenty thousand square feet of romantic possibilities await at this ever-expanding turn-of-the-century restaurant, a diamond in the rough (as they say), set among the rundown storefronts of downtown San Jose. Wood and brick lend a handsome air to the downstairs dining room, although sounds from the open kitchen can intrude on quiet conversation. If you're serious about wining and dining, head to the beautiful back dining room warmed by a fireplace and accented with candles; or, better yet, journey upstairs where tables are arranged beneath skylights and noise from the kitchen isn't a distraction. The lengthy Italian menu has something for even the pickiest palates—the freshly baked focaccia and almond prawn cocktail are both musts. More delights await from the stove (cioppino), wood grill (spit-roasted chicken), and ovens (cannelloni and eggplant parmigiana). **58 South First Street; (408) 280-1993; www.bellamia.com; moderate to expensive; lunch and dinner daily, brunch Saturday–Sunday.**

🦪🦪 **EMILE'S, San Jose** Emile's chic dining room is appointed with wall mirrors, an ornate sculpted ceiling, and tapestry-covered chairs; at its center, ultramodern track lights illuminate a massive floral arrangement. Proudly dubbed "San Jose's best," this longtime favorite restaurant offers a creative mix of contemporary European cuisines. Due to its extreme popularity and consequent crowds, the setting doesn't exactly feel intimate, but the food more than compensates. The menu changes weekly, and concentrates on what is seasonal and at its best. Whatever time of year, you're sure to find plenty of fresh seafood entrées, wild game preparations, and traditional dishes such as rack of lamb. Despite the changing dinner menu, Emile's is known for one staple on its dessert lineup: the Grand Marnier soufflé. Don't miss it. **545 South Second Street; (408) 289-1960; www.emiles.com; expensive to very expensive; dinner Tuesday–Saturday.**

🦪🦪🦪 **LA FORET, San Jose** Although you'd never guess it from its pretty interior, La Foret is just a short drive away from the high-tech world of San Jose. Located outside the city limits, the restaurant sits next to a creek in what was the first two-story adobe hotel in California. White tablecloths drape cozy tables topped with red roses in the restaurant's three dining rooms, which survey views of a wooded landscape. A sublime French menu offers a wide range of pheasant, rack of lamb, duck breast, and a few pasta entrées; service, like the food, is outstanding. Soft candlelight casts a gentle spell as you lovingly share your evening here. **21747 Bertram Road; (408) 997-3458; expensive to very expensive; dinner Tuesday–Sunday, brunch Sunday.**

"A kiss can be a comma,

a question mark or an

exclamation point.

That's basic spelling that every

woman ought to know."

Mistinguett

Lake Tahoe and Environs

Glistening in the foothills of the High Sierra peaks, Lake Tahoe is the largest alpine lake in North America, spanning 22 miles in length and 12 miles in diameter. The area's climate is also alpine in nature, which means summers are warm and dry and winters cold and snowy. Spring and fall can be a little of both. The area's breathtaking scenery, fishing, swimming, skiing, hiking—and, yes, gambling—lure tourists of all kinds. And if you're looking for some great spots for kissing, well, you've come to the right place.

Romantic Note: During the off-season, when the weather is too cold for swimming in the lake but too warm for snow skiing, many establishments are closed, especially on the north and west shores where gambling does not keep visitors coming year-round. Always call in advance to make sure your desired destination is operating at the time you wish to visit. Such efforts may even be rewarded by more-than-reasonable accommodation rates that spring up this time of year.

North Shore

Incline Village, Nevada

The affluent residential neighborhood of Incline Village sits on the Nevada side of Lake Tahoe. On this side of the state line, most of the outdated hotels have put their energy into providing captivating casinos rather than romantic accommodations, so lodging options are limited. One advantage of staying here is that the area is self-contained: skiing, shopping, swimming, and boating are all nearby.

Hotel/Bed and Breakfast Kissing

🌺🌺🌺 **HYATT REGENCY LAKE TAHOE RESORT HOTEL, Incline Village** Unlike the more developed shores of South Lake Tahoe, the North Shore has retained its natural forested setting, so you can actually stay in a big-name hotel like the Hyatt and still enjoy a moonlit stroll along the sandy beach or around the property. The Hyatt's main building typically draws in conference-going clientele, but a unit in one of the 24 lakeside cottages could inspire a lot more than a business meeting. Wood furnishings, richly colored decor, stone fireplaces, and private decks with up-close views of the sparkling lake create an alpine lodge look and an amorous mood. The cottages are arranged in the shape of a horseshoe so that each one has a water view; we recommend booking a room in the Alverson, Baldwin, Lincoln, or Knight Cottages since they are closest to the magnificent sandy beach. Each cottage has a master bedroom and an additional bedroom (both with private baths), as well as a granite-top kitchen and a living room equipped with a stereo and TV. You can book the entire cottage, the master bedroom and living area, or just the second bedroom, which has its own private entrance. Whichever way, you are assured a high degree of privacy. Breakfast isn't included with the cottage rental, so bring your own fixings or venture to the Hyatt (or an in-town café) for morning munchies.

The 458 guest rooms in the 12-story, 1970s-looking main building are standard, albeit nice, hotel rooms, but not worthy of a romantic getaway. If you must stay here, book a room on the Regency Club level (located on the top two floors of the hotel), where complimentary afternoon wine, hors d'oeuvres, and an expanded continental breakfast are served in the private common room. That way you can avoid the distracting casino downstairs. **Country Club Drive and Lakeshore Boulevard; (775) 832-1234, (800) 233-1234; www.hyatt-tahoe.com; unbelievably expensive.**

Restaurant Kissing

❧❧ **LONE EAGLE GRILLE, Incline Village** Although the Lone Eagle is owned by the Hyatt, you'd never guess from its location. The restaurant is set across the street from the high-rise hotel and nestled in the woods right on the lakeshore. From the main entrance, descend a sweeping staircase into a magnificent lodgelike setting. First to catch your eye are two river-rock fireplaces that soar 25 feet upward into the open-beam ceiling. Next you'll notice the wrought-iron chandeliers, massive wooden beams, and the vintage skis, snowshoes, and fishing baskets decorating the walls. With windows wrapping around two sides of the restaurant, diners risk becoming mesmerized by the beauty of Lake Tahoe, which shimmers in the sun like a dazzling sapphire. Most of the candle-topped, linen-draped tables provide this glorious view; however, the farther back you are seated, the closer you are to the busy exhibition kitchen. Vistas of the lake are even better on the outdoor patio where teak tables and chairs are sheltered from the breeze by glass walls. Unfortunately, the service, which is almost too laid-back, doesn't match up to the spectacular surroundings.

The extensive American menu has something for everyone, and concentrates on rotisserie and grilled meats. Some noteworthy dishes include chile-lime sea bass, ginger-roasted duck, and a selection of Black Angus steaks grilled to perfection over mesquite coals. Although it might be better prepared outside on the beach, the popular entrée called the North Lake Tahoe clambake will appeal to those who enjoy lobster, shrimp, mussels, clams, and scallops. When the dessert tray arrives, any choice should satisfy your sweet tooth. **Country Club Drive, at the Hyatt Regency Lake Tahoe Resort Hotel; (775) 832-3250; www.hyatt-tahoe.com; expensive to very expensive; lunch and dinner daily, brunch Sunday.**

Romantic Suggestion: Dinner prices here can empty your wallet in no time flat. A delightful and less expensive alternative is to sit in the equally appealing bar area, bordered on three sides by towering bookshelves, a wall of windows, and one of the massive stone fireplaces mentioned above. With glass of wine in hand, you and your honey can slip into the big leather chairs or snuggle up in front of the fireplace.

Outdoor Kissing

❤️❤️❤️ **DIAMOND PEAK CROSS COUNTRY AND SNOWSHOE CENTER, Incline Village** If a kiss gives you that top-of-the-world feeling, just wait until you kiss at Diamond Peak. High on a mountaintop, groomed cross-country ski trails lead through pristine forest to spectacular, eagle's-eye views of crystalline Lake Tahoe and its ring of snowcapped peaks. Beginners will find rentals, lessons, and one easy trail here; try the rolling intermediate trails if you can laugh together at your snow-softened falls. Along the intermediate Vista View loop, climb up the aptly named "Knock Your Socks Off Rock" and you'll know what kissing on top of the world is all about. Tables are provided at the base of the rock for chilly but heart-warming picnics. **Mount Rose Highway (Route 431); (775) 832-1177; www.diamondpeak.com; $14 for an adult day-pass.** *From Incline Village, drive five miles out of Incline Village along the Mount Rose Highway (Route 431) toward Reno. Near the crest of the mountain, park in the highway turnout. Follow signs to the center, which is located just up the path in the woods.*

Crystal Bay

Restaurant Kissing

❤️❤️❤️ **THE SOULE DOMAIN, Crystal Bay** Nestled in a Lilliputian pine grove next to a hulking 1950s-style casino, this rustic 1935 log cabin is not only one of old Tahoe's precious remnants, but also one of the lake's most romantic restaurants. (It is continually rated as the "Best Place to Take a Date" by the local newspaper.) A crackling fire in the stone hearth casts a cozy glow on the intimate dining room, illuminating its walls of rotund pine logs caulked with rope. Chef and owner Charles Edward Soule's motto is "Every dish is a specialty of the house." This sentiment is quite evident in the ever-changing, creative menu. From the fiery Thai curried scallops to the Queen of Sheba flourless chocolate cake, everything is delicious. Specials such as linguine with lobster, scallops, and shrimp; rack of lamb chops; and filet mignon topped with shiitake mushrooms, Gorgonzola, brandy, and burgundy butter are certain to please. A romantic dinner here with your favorite date will certainly earn you brownie points or, better yet, a kiss. **A half block up Stateline Drive, across from the Tahoe Biltmore; (530) 546-7529; expensive; reservations recommended; dinner daily.**

Tahoe Vista

Tahoe Vista doesn't offer much more than a busy street of wall-to-wall businesses. Most likely you'll quickly travel through here on your way to the slopes and won't feel inspired to linger, unless you stay at THE SHORE HOUSE (see Hotel/Bed and Breakfast Kissing) or dine at one of the lakefront restaurants we recommend (see Restaurant Kissing).

Hotel/Bed and Breakfast Kissing

❤❤❤❤ **THE SHORE HOUSE, Tahoe Vista** The charming Shore House certainly lives up to its name. Located smack-dab on the shores of Lake Tahoe, it is one of the only bed and breakfasts in the area that can truly be classified as waterfront. (Most bed and breakfasts describe themselves as waterfront even when a road separates them from the water.) At The Shore House, undisturbed views of the lake are part of the package. On a beautiful summer day, the fabulous lake-fronting lawn, dotted with cushioned furniture, is as inviting as a sweet kiss. When snow caps the mountains, soak in Tahoe vistas from the comfort of the bubbling outdoor hot tub. Lakefront views continue to impress from inside the cozy dining room, where several log-pole tables and a river-rock fireplace create a minilodge-like setting. Wine and hors d'oeuvres are served here nightly and, come morning, guests are treated to such scrumptious delights as Belgian waffles topped with blackberries, French toast stuffed with Neufchâtel cheese, or the innkeeper's award-winning Monte Cristo sandwiches.

All nine rooms are wonderfully inviting, with private entrances, gas-log fireplaces, and bright, beautifully tiled bathrooms. Custom-built log furnishings and beds, down comforters, and local watercolors give each room a rustic, clean finish. What's missing from this picture are TVs and phones, but with the lake right outside the door, you'll have all the entertainment you'll ever need. (Not all rooms have direct lake views, so be sure to specify your preference when making reservations.) The main building houses seven guest quarters, including the Lakeview Room, which affords wonderful lake views from the comfort of the queen-size bed. Snuggle up in the large, dark Moon Room, complete with a step-up jetted tub in the bathroom and a king-size bed.

Of all the rooms here (and perhaps in all of Lake Tahoe), the self-contained Honeymoon Cottage is *the* place to kiss and kiss and kiss some more. Set a few feet from the lapping waters, this one-room wonder comes romantically equipped with a two-person jetted tub fronting sensational water views and a queen-size bed set against the lakefront windows. Last but not least, the self-contained Studio Cottage remains another smart choice for romance-seeking couples. Although it doesn't have much of a view or a jetted tub, the Studio is just as private as the Honeymoon Cottage. Practice drawing on the provided artist's sketchboard, and perhaps the owners will place your masterpiece on the wall along with those of previous guests. **7170 North Lake Boulevard; (530) 546-7270, (800) 207-5160; www. tahoeinn.com; expensive to unbelievably expensive; minimum-stay requirement on weekends and holidays; recommended wedding site.**

Restaurant Kissing

☙❶ LE PETIT PIER, Tahoe Vista Development along the lake is so dense in Tahoe Vista that you could easily miss this gem of a French restaurant, perched literally at the water's edge. Inside, the incredible views and the savory aromas are a welcome invasion of the senses. A lantern glows at each table, and the contemporary decor is enhanced by white linens and modern artwork. Classic French dishes are exquisitely prepared. Enticing entrées include lavender-honey–glazed duck breast, peppercorn-crusted filet mignon au Roquefort, and New Zealand venison topped with a garlic rub and accompanied by a shiitake, portobello, and burgundy reduction. **7238 North Lake Boulevard; (530) 546-4464; www.lepetitpier.com; expensive to unbelievably expensive; dinner Wednesday–Monday.**

☙☙❶ SUNSETS ON THE LAKE, Tahoe Vista Here's one place where the name fits so perfectly that there's little else we can add to the description. Set beside the water, Sunsets on the Lake captures south-facing lake views and fiery sunsets like a beautiful painting. From just about any table or booth, the two of you can hold hands and gaze out the floor-to-ceiling windows at the lake and snowcapped mountains, undisturbed by commercial sights or lights. The large, spacious interior weaves the clean lines of California design with a touch of the lodge look. A two-sided fireplace warms the dining room, which is sprinkled with tables and booths nicely spaced apart. Stylish dark wood chairs, white tablecloths, and color accents reminiscent of Lake Tahoe's Mediterranean blue waters finish off the dining scene. In the summer, a beautiful terraced patio is the prime place to catch some rays while you dine.

The only thing that will take your eyes off the views and each other is the food, which comes in Lake Tahoe–size portions. For starters, don't miss the well-seasoned and refreshing pear and Gorgonzola salad. Our fresh fish of the day, pan-roasted halibut served over a zesty corn salsa, was divine, as was the wood-fired pork tenderloin on couscous served with vanilla-glazed sweet potatoes and carrots. Many entrée items come hot off the grill, including a grilled vegetable salad and spit-roasted garlic chicken. When the sun delivers its final performance, as it should at this namesake restaurant, linger over the hard-to-resist chocolate tiramisu: a perfect end to a perfect day together. **7320 North Lake Boulevard; (530) 546-3640; www.sunsetslaketahoe.com; expensive; reservations recommended; call for seasonal hours.**

Tahoe City

Like Tahoe Vista, Tahoe City is a bustling waterfront community filled with businesses. Luckily for those seeking a place to smooch, the town holds a handful of excellent restaurants and some very kissworthy bed and breakfasts, many of which are located along West Lake Boulevard outside of town proper.

Hotel/Bed and Breakfast Kissing

❧❧ **CHANEY HOUSE, Tahoe City** Driving along West Lake Boulevard, you might just cruise past this stately home sheltered from view by large native pines. Only a small sign reveals the home's location, so keep your eyes peeled. (We emphasize this because the lake views are quite mesmerizing.) Built in 1928 by Italian masons, this impressive stone structure resides across the road from Lake Tahoe and has much to offer those looking for something other than western-style lodge decor. You can't help but imagine you've entered a cozy European castle as you step through the enormous front door. A roaring fire blazes in the living room, casting a warm glow on the 18-inch-thick stone walls. Cathedral ceilings, Gothic doors, and original pine woodwork throughout lend an air of medieval appeal.

If you'd like to create your own little Camelot, head to the Honeymoon Hideaway, by far the best place for serious smooching. Located behind the main home, this two-story stone cottage features all that's necessary for kissing and cuddling: a queen-size bed tucked into an alcove, a flip-on gas fireplace for instant ambience (and heat), and an oval jetted tub complete with bubble bath. If requested, the innkeepers will even serve you breakfast on a semiprivate patio set between the Hideaway and main house. Three more guest rooms, all with private baths, await in the main house and vary in terms of heart-tugging ambience. We like the handsome Russell's Suite, entered via a unique spiral staircase. This hidden-away room is simply decorated with knotty pine walls and plaid motifs, although the stuffed deer head over the queen-size bed is an odd touch. The inn's brochure states that there is a "lake view" from this room and that's true. What it neglects to mention is that you'll need to be on the floor looking out through the knee-high windows in order to appreciate it. (See why we write this book?) The remaining two rooms—the second-floor Master Suite and the main-floor Jeanine's Room—struck us as more ordinary than extraordinary.

A formal breakfast buffet is served in the equally formal dining room or on the kitchen-side patio when weather permits. Enjoy fresh fruit, scrumptious egg dishes served with homemade sauces, and the house specialty, baked stuffed French toast topped with hot, homemade blackberry sauce. This is one morning lineup that will definitely keep your stomachs satisfied until suppertime. **4725 West Lake Boulevard; (530) 525-7333; www. chaneyhouse.com; moderate to very expensive.**

❤❤❤ **THE COTTAGE INN, Tahoe City** You'll feel like pioneers in this little village of rustic cabins set beside the lake. Far from the glitz of the casinos and the sterility of the high-rise hotels, The Cottage Inn embraces nature rather than trying to overwhelm it. Set in a half-circle, the 15 duplex cabins are designed for privacy. All units feature private entrances and some even have front porches. Each cottage is unique, but all share a rustic, western feel accentuated by hardwood floors, knotty-pine walls, charming decorations, and local artwork. For kissing purposes, we highly recommend the Romantic Hideaway, featuring a massive river-rock waterfall that descends into a deep Jacuzzi tub. The nearby Evergreen Heaven Suite is also overflowing with romantic goodies, including a thermal massage tub for two set into a cozy alcove. Each room, from the most basic studio style to the deluxe rooms, has the luxury of a gas fireplace, a modern private bathroom, a tucked-away TV/VCR, and—most unique of all—two flannel nightshirts perfect for keeping you warm on nippy nights.

If you care to emerge from your cozy little cottage, warm yourselves by the fire in the 61-year-old main cottage, where home-baked treats are laid out in the evening and a full country breakfast is served in the morning. (If you're in the mood for a secluded start to the day, request that breakfast be left on your doorstep.) After a day of hiking or skiing, indulge in an evening sauna or stroll to the nearby beach, where you can dig your toes into the cool sand and kiss to the lullaby of Lake Tahoe's quiet, lapping waters. **1690 West Lake Boulevard; (530) 581-4073, (800) 581-4073; www.thecottageinn.com; expensive to very expensive; minimum-stay requirement on weekends and holidays.**

❦❦ **MAYFIELD HOUSE, Tahoe City** Highly trafficked Tahoe City can be a bit of a hassle to drive through, which is why we recommend staying at this traditional bed and breakfast. Located on a side road away from the hustle and bustle, the 1932 all-stone Mayfield House retains many of its original features and caters to those who enjoy a sense of yesteryear mixed in with romance. While the historical element is strong (especially on the exterior), new owners have brought a breath of fresh air to the interior. All common areas and rooms exude a comfortable, mountain-country look. Baskets hang from the rafters in the sunny living room, creatively displayed pine-cones and country antiques line the bookshelves, white lights border the river-rock fireplace, and antique crates and suitcases have been turned into functional side tables in some of the bedrooms. Hardwood floors accented by vibrant throw rugs and large paned windows provide splashes of color, texture, and light.

Three of the six guest rooms have private detached bathrooms, a fact that wouldn't normally rank them high on our romance scale. However, we made an exception for one such room, simply called the Guest Room. Romantic twosomes adore its tucked-away, mezzanine-level location and, although the bathroom is down a flight of stairs (robes and slippers are provided), such a journey is easily forgiven once you see the tempting steam shower surrounded by glass and slate. For those wanting en suite bathrooms, The Study, The Mayfield Room, and The Cottage all deliver. Although tight on space, The Cottage, located behind the main house, is *numero uno* for privacy. Skylights over the queen-size bed and in the bathroom help lighten up this romantic hideaway. In the main home, the upstairs May-field Room ranks high for romance with its country-western motif, deep jetted tub in the bathroom, large king-size bed, and enough room for some (slow) country dancing. For those who love fly-fishing, the downstairs Study features plenty of "gone fishin'" gear, as well as a king-size bed that's very inviting after a day on the lake or the slopes.

After a morning walk about town, along the lake, or across the street to the golf course, return to find breakfast waiting. Waffles topped with fresh whipped cream and strawberries, apple-walnut pancakes, and chocolate-chip banana bread are just some of the treats certain to tempt you into having seconds. **236 Grove Street; (530) 583-1001, (888) 518-8898;**

www.mayfieldhouse.com; inexpensive to very expensive; minimum-stay requirement seasonally.

❀❀❦ **SUNNYSIDE LODGE, Tahoe City** A true, gabled mountain lodge built of wood and stone, Sunnyside takes full advantage of its perch on Lake Tahoe's forested northwest shore. In the warmer months, put a blush in your cheeks out on its expansive, sun-soaked wooden deck; in winter, a blazing fire crackles in the large river-rock fireplace in the lounge. Sailors and skiers will appreciate the nautical and ski memorabilia found throughout the lodge, and everyone with a healthy appetite and desire for a view will love the pleasant waterfront restaurant known as the **CHRIS CRAFT DINING ROOM** (see Restaurant Kissing).

Sunnyside continues its pleasing ways with 23 comfortable and airy guest rooms, all adorned with high ceilings, modest wall coverings, vintage chests functioning as coffee tables, and nautical, Audubon, or skiing artwork and photographs decorating the walls. Five rooms even feature fireplaces. With the exception of the four garden-view rooms, all rooms are oriented toward the sparkling lake, so stand together on your balcony, kiss, and imagine you're on the prow of your own private yacht. In the morning, enjoy a complimentary continental breakfast and, later on, savor the afternoon tea. If that's not enough to fill you up, venture to the restaurant for summertime lunches on the deck and nightly dinners inside the classy dining room. Even if the weather isn't on the "sunny side," this lodge is one place that will certainly brighten up any romantic getaway. **1850 West Lake Boulevard; (530) 583-7200, (800) 822-2SKI; www.hulapie.com; inexpensive to very expensive; minimum-stay requirement on weekends.**

Restaurant Kissing

❀❀❦ **CHRIS CRAFT DINING ROOM, Tahoe City** The nautically inspired Chris Craft Dining Room, located in the **SUNNYSIDE LODGE** (see Hotel/Bed and Breakfast Kissing), is so close to the lake that you might think it's floating. You might also think you're inside a vintage Chris Craft powerboat, thanks to the sleek mahogany paneling, nautical-style lighting, and photographs and miniature models of vintage powerboats and sailboats. Summer months tempt most diners outside to the spacious deck where colorful umbrellas and equally vibrant canvas chairs create a festive atmosphere by the lake.

Although the restaurant is situated in northern California, its menu takes a cruise southward by highlighting a fantastic selection of Southwest-inspired creations. We started with the world-famous crispy zucchini plate followed by an exceptional chile-crusted salmon served on a corn husk, and a big plate of smoked chicken pasta tossed with roasted corn, pine nuts, and tequila cream. Nightly specials bring forth grilled meats, from smoked pork chops to Black Angus prime rib. Dinners come with a choice of soup or salad, making a meal here quite reasonable and filling. Even though our stomachs registered "full," we couldn't resist the signature dessert, Kimo's Hula Pie. The menu states it's "what the sailors swam ashore for in Lahaina (Hawaii)" and we believe it. Don't miss this macadamia-nut ice cream dessert. **1850 West Lake Boulevard, at the Sunnyside Lodge; (530) 583-7200, (800) 822-2SKI; www.hulapie.com; moderate to expensive; call for seasonal hours.**

❦❦❦ **CHRISTY HILL RESTAURANT, Tahoe City** Reflections of glorious Lake Tahoe sunsets dance on the surface waters outside of Christy Hill most evenings. Make your reservations for a pre-sunset dinner and, if you time it right, you'll be just lingering over dessert when the fiery hues begin to color the lake and distant mountains. If the sun isn't putting on its final performance due to cloud cover, no worries. Christy Hill's dining room is romantic rain or shine, cloud or no cloud. Picture windows take in undisturbed views of the lake in all its glory, watercolor paintings accentuate the cushioned booths and tables, and a two-way fireplace in the restaurant's center warms up winter nights. Tall birch branches, adorned with holiday lights and placed alongside the windows, bring a little of the alpine scenery inside.

The northern California–style cuisine is certainly some of the best in Tahoe. Although the menu changes with the season, favorites include Australian lamb loin, fresh oven-baked halibut, and duck confit ravioli. Seasonal berries and fruit highlight the signature dessert cobblers. Topped with homemade ice cream, these hot-from-the-oven numbers are the best way to end an evening right. **115 Grove Street; (530) 583-8551; www.christyhill.com; expensive; reservations recommended; dinner Tuesday–Sunday.**

Romantic Suggestion: Christy Hill has one of the finest outdoor patios in town. Reservations for al fresco dining by the lake are highly recommended.

❦❦ **TRUFFULA, Tahoe City** Romantics seeking a reprieve from rustic, lodge-style decor will find Truffula's ultramodern interior a welcome alternative. Journey upstairs to this second-story dining room, where only a dozen tables await. A picture window frames the lake and, if you're lucky, you may get the table that fronts it. If not, sit side by side in windowed alcove seats or, weather permitting, on the outside deck. Celery-colored walls, slick hardwood floors, black beams, and stylish linen-topped tables set the scene with modern flair, while the 1960s-style curvaceous black chairs and funky soundboard ceiling lend a retro touch.

"Wild food from land and sea" is how Truffula's advertises its fare.

Dishes such as black horn antelope with roasted five-spice sweet potatoes, and grilled sturgeon adorned with preserved-lemon artichoke slaw are wild enough. Other entrées can be classified as more creative: artichoke-bread salad, duck breast with cumin-scented carrots, and seared scallops with fennel ratatouille. Desserts are certainly stylish presentations, although the prices (high) don't match the portion size (small). Nonetheless, our three bites of the strawberry shortcake proved excellent. **550 North Lake Boulevard; (530) 581-3362; expensive; dinner Thursday–Monday.**

💋💋 **WOLFDALE'S RESTAURANT, Tahoe City** The food at Wolfdale's is so good that it almost compensates for the lack of direct lake views. The ever-changing menu blends Asian and European flavors in a California style that the restaurant has dubbed "cuisine unique." Truly, it is. Entrées such as sea bass tempura with dashi daikon dip, Asian braised duck leg and breast, and a coconut crêpe stuffed with vegetable stir-fry aren't found on just any restaurant's menu. Be a little bit daring here since whatever you order will be delicious, albeit different.

As for the interior, the two pleasant dining rooms are punctuated by a collection of provocative modern art. We are especially partial to the first dining room, with its hardwood floors, white tablecloths, and exotic orchids at each table. Hand-thrown Japanese-style plates and bowls adorn each table, and the wall near the entryway displays them like a gallery. If you like the dishes your food arrives on, you'll be happy to know that they—along with those in the display—are for sale. **640 North Lake Boulevard; (530) 583-5700; www.wolfdales.com; expensive; dinner daily.**

Outdoor Kissing

💋💋💋💋 **MOUNTAIN HIGH BALLOONS** If you're thinking that a hot-air balloon ride sounds like a frivolous, expensive, childish sort of excursion, you're right. If you also think it sounds like an unforgettable experience, you're right again. Both the enormous mass of billowing material overhead and the loud, blistering dragon fire that heats the air filling the balloon are astonishing. Once you're aloft, the wind guides your craft high above treetops and shimmering water, and the world seems more peaceful than you ever thought possible. From this perspective, Lake Tahoe glitters like a diamond and the shore appears to have brilliant emeralds scattered along the water's edge. This is a thoroughly transcendent experience, meant to be shared with someone you love. **(530) 587-6922, (888) 462-2683; $85 per person for a half-hour balloon ride, $145 per person for an hour balloon ride.** *The main office is located in the town of Truckee, approximately 14 miles north of Tahoe City. Call for directions and reservations.*

Squaw Valley

From Tahoe City, follow Highway 28 to the junction of Highway 89 and go north. Take the Squaw Valley exit and drive two miles to the ski area. From Interstate 80, take Highway 89 south to Squaw Valley Road. Turn right on Squaw Valley Road and drive two miles to the ski area.

Nestled at the base of jagged peaks, Squaw Valley is one of the High Sierras' most picturesque settings; the soaring mountains rival the Swiss Alps in their rugged beauty. A village of hotels, condominiums, and restaurants is tucked away at the upper end of the valley, along with stables, golf courses, and other recreational facilities. Although this first-class ski resort first gained renown for hosting the 1960 Winter Olympics, sports buffs convene here year-round.

Hotel/Bed and Breakfast Kissing

❦❦❧ **PLUMPJACK SQUAW VALLEY INN, Squaw Valley** This two-story, wood-shingled lodge is strategically situated at the base of the mountain, next to Squaw Valley Resort's gondola and parking lot. In other words, this is Grand Central Station come ski season. Still, if you can ignore the crowds, Plumpjack is an amiable and very convenient place to stay. But most of all, it is unlike any other ski lodge for miles around. The 61 guest rooms and suites can best be described as medieval-meets-modern. Swirls of metallic shapes accent lamps and sconces throughout, and many furnishings are artsy conversation pieces (especially the couches shaped like fluffy clouds and the side tables resembling seashells). All regular guest rooms feature similar decor and amenities: stylish furnishings, metal lamps and wall sconces, king- or two queen-size beds topped with thick down comforters, and color schemes of metallic grays, taupes, olives, and creams. Juxtaposing such San Francisco–chic decor is a selection of beautifully framed classical paintings. Go figure.

Although slightly more pricey, the six specialty suites are worth the extra cash, especially if you have romance on your mind. Luxurious amenities abound, including Jacuzzi tubs (in four of the suites), wet bars, magnificent beds, big-screen TVs (in some), and separate sitting areas. We especially like the two third-floor penthouse suites where you can smooch in high style.

Prominent granite slabs surround the heated pool and two hot tubs on the spacious outdoor patio. The direct mountain view from this spot is definitely worthy of a kiss ... if you don't mind having lots of company.

Breakfast isn't included in your stay, but guests (and hungry skiers in general) can enjoy a morning meal at the modern-attired **PLUMPJACK CAFE** (moderate to very expensive; reservations recommended; breakfast, lunch, and dinner daily), adjacent to the pool area. Unfortunately the linen-covered tables are much too close together for quiet conversations, and the small, narrow room can get noisy, especially during dinner. Also, when compared to its popular cousin in San Francisco (see **PLUMPJACK CAFE** in San Francisco), the California-Mediterranean–style food isn't as tasty. However, the café is worth a visit, if only to see the unusual medieval/modern decor. **1920 Squaw Valley Road; (530) 583-1576, (800) 323-7666; moderate to unbelievably expensive; minimum-stay requirement on weekends and holidays; recommended wedding site.**

❦❦❦ **SQUAW VALLEY LODGE, Squaw Valley** It was the whirlpool tubs that won us over—three of them, just off the exercise room, with a fireplace in the corner and a view of the snowy peaks outside. Or maybe it was the 178 spacious, contemporary rental condominiums equipped with full kitchens that make possible a late-night cup of cocoa or a no-hassle bathrobe breakfast. Then again, the location, adjacent to some of the best skiing in the Tahoe area, is a definite plus. If your toes get cold while you're outside, you can simply ski off the mountain and straight to your room.

Unlike regular hotel rooms, each rental condo's decor is somewhat dependent upon the owner. All the rooms we saw were tastefully decorated, although some fared better than others. Styles range from plain and simple to interior-designer perfect. Although you can't pick the decor, you can choose from open studio suites (perfect for one couple); one-bedroom suites with full kitchens, living areas, and private bedrooms; two-bedroom suites with fireplaces; or studio lofts with the master bedroom upstairs. All have cooking areas, and the modern bathrooms come equipped with big oval tubs. (We prefer the communal whirlpool tubs for serious soaking.) Best of all, large windows let in plenty of sunshine, and from some condos you and your sweetheart can enjoy close-up views of the mighty mountains. **201 Squaw Peak Road; (530) 583-5500, (800) 922-9970; www. squawvalleylodge.com; moderate to unbelievably expensive; minimum-stay requirement seasonally.**

Romantic Alternative: THE RESORT AT SQUAW CREEK (400 Squaw Creek Road; 530-583-6300, 800-327-3353; www.squawcreek.com; unbelievably expensive) looks a little out of place with its black-tinted glass tower set against the mountainside. However, once you step inside you won't care. The dramatic lobby alone is worth a peek, with its wall of cathedral-high windows framing the mountain face. Outside, the resort is even more spectacular, with a waterfall cascading past the skating rink (basketball court in the summer) down to three outdoor Jacuzzi tubs, two swimming pools, and one 110-foot-long water slide. Every amenity of a modern resort is within your reach, from a shopping arcade to a spa and health center, from airport shuttle service to five restaurants. Plus, guests have ski-in/ski-out access from the lift beside the resort. Surprisingly, the 403 unbelievably expensive guest rooms are merely standard, with a comfortable but comparatively unimaginative hotel feel. What does set these rooms apart from others in Squaw Valley are the unsurpassed mountain views (especially from the Valley View Rooms) that get better the higher you go. Whether you stay here or not, start a romantic evening off at **GLISSANDI** (see Restaurant Kissing), where views of the Sierras are complemented by contemporary California cuisine.

Restaurant Kissing

❀❀❀ **GLISSANDI, Squaw Valley** The commanding presence of the windows in the lobby at **THE RESORT AT SQUAW CREEK** (see Hotel/Bed and Breakfast Kissing) is enough to seduce anyone into staying. Luckily, you can stare out the immense windows in the resort's formal restaurant even if you're not an overnight guest. Shaped like an arrowhead, the restaurant features tables that take in glorious views of the mountains and sky above. The best vantage points are, of course, from the windowside tables. The restaurant's conservatively elegant decor, featuring blond wood chairs and subdued colors of merlot and gray-violet, does not compete with the surrounding splendor.

Creative California cuisine graces the menu. We started our meal with warm asparagus and Yukon gold potatoes, sprinkled with bread crumbs and almonds, and continued on the appetizer craze with light and refreshing smoked duck, mango, and Thai-basil salad rolls. Nightly fish specials are always interesting, but we couldn't resist the breast of pheasant served with morels and surrounded by a Madeira sauce. Only the fabulous desserts may divert your attention away from the view and each other. Our coffee ice-cream cake creation topped with spun sugar was as delicious as it looked. **400 Squaw Creek, at The Resort at Squaw Creek; (530) 581-6621; www.squawcreek.com; very expensive; reservations recommended; dinner daily.**

❀❀❀❀ **GRAHAM'S, Squaw Valley** After a day of slicing up the slopes, there's nothing better than to sit with your favorite ski partner in front of a blazing fire, share a bottle of wine, and replenish yourselves with hearty, country-style food. Graham's is an excellent choice for doing all three and, luckily, you won't have to venture far from the slopes to find this cozy restaurant. Located in the upper reaches of Squaw Valley, this shingled building (one of the oldest in the area) holds a perfectly divine dining room with fewer than a dozen candlelit tables. Although it's intimate, you won't get the feeling of being scrunched together. Pine-planked vaulted ceilings, skylights, and a massive stone fireplace set directly opposite an equally enormous mirror contribute to the restaurant's spaciousness. Textured butter-colored walls and Italian-scene artwork lend a distinct Tuscan touch.

Mediterranean "country cuisine" best describes the robust, flavorful dishes that arrive at your table, all guaranteed to give you energy for whatever romantic plans you have later on. Pine-nut-crusted rack of lamb served alongside mint-mustard sauce, muscovy duck breast with blackberry port wine sauce, and plump lobster-stuffed ravioli swimming in sage-scented brown butter should more than satisfy. The fresh catch of the day is grilled and topped with fresh herbs from the garden, and sometimes Moroccan dishes (lamb shank with couscous) and Spanish specialties (paella) are showcased as nightly specials. Whatever you order, end dinner by splitting a generous slice of the tiramisu, and don't worry about all those calories … they'll quickly be used up kissing. **1650 Squaw Valley Road; (530) 581-0454; www.dinewine.com; expensive; reservations recommended; dinner Wednesday–Sunday.**

Outdoor Kissing

❦❦❦ **OLYMPIC ICE PAVILION, Squaw Valley** Having frequented Tahoe for many years, we thought we had seen the most magnificent views the area could afford—that is, until we rode the cable car to the Olympic Ice Pavilion at High Camp. Riding the aerial tramway is an adventure in itself, as you soar above the hawks, over a pinnacle, then high to the apex of the mountaintop at 8,200 feet. On the edge of the summit, almost like a gateway to heaven in the rosy light of sunset, the outdoor skating rink overlooks the vast expanse of the valley far below. In the distance, Lake Tahoe winks on the horizon. After a kiss here, you'll never be the same. **1960 Squaw Valley Road, at High Camp; (530) 583-6955, (800) 545-4350; www.squaw.com; $14 for cable car only, $19 for cable car, skate pass, and skate rental combined ($12 after 5 p.m.).** *Look for the cable car building at the base of Squaw Valley Ski Resort. Take the Cable Car aerial tramway to the top of the mountain at High Camp.*

Romantic Note: Located next to the Olympic Ice Pavilion, **THE TERRACE RESTAURANT** (530-583-1742; moderate; call for seasonal hours) shares the same extraordinary panorama. Lunch features basic American hamburgers, chili, and sandwiches served cafeteria-style at very reasonable prices. This may be the only cafeteria in the world that inspires kissing. Nearby, **ALEXANDER'S** affords views of the lake, while the **POOLSIDE CAFE AND BAR** (both: 530-583-1742; inexpensive to moderate; call for seasonal hours) looks out over a swimming pool ($19 for cable car and swim pass, $12 after 5 P.M.; call for seasonal hours) and the peaks and valleys beyond.

West Shore

Homewood

Of the three developed shores of Lake Tahoe, the West Shore remains the most pristine. You won't find big hotels, flashy casinos, or shopping centers in tiny Homewood. What you will find are a few romantic establishments set amid towering pines.

Hotel/Bed and Breakfast Kissing

❧❧ **ROCKWOOD LODGE, Homewood** You will immediately feel comfortable upon entering this stone "Old Tahoe"–style home, so take off your shoes (required) and relax a while. Honey-colored knotty pine walls, hand-hewn open-beam ceilings, and soft cream carpets (hence the no-shoes policy) provide a soothing, homelike ambience. If this atmosphere alone doesn't shake the chill off snow-kissed cheeks, then a snuggle by the roaring fire in the living room and some kisses from your beloved should do the trick.

Although the home's knotty pine interior suggests rusticity, the five guest rooms are quite stylish. Each one is decorated with Laura Ashley linens and window treatments, and filled with utilitarian-type antiques such as an 1800s workbench and an old New England cobbler's bench. Cozy down comforters cover puffed-up feather beds, and fresh flowers brighten the mood. Each room has its own private bath and warm, terry-cloth bathrobes. Both the Secret Harbor and the Rubicon Bay Rooms offer filtered views of the lake, as well as tiled tubs with dual shower heads. We especially like Secret Harbor's Russian wedding bed: a hand-painted, four-poster wood canopy. The third-floor Zephyr Cove Room surveys views of the surrounding forest and a nearby building, and provides the most seclusion for sweethearts. Although a tiny room, the Emerald Bay boasts the best bathroom: Its seven-foot-long Roman tub (equipped to hold 100 gallons of water) comes with two shower heads for double the fun. Unfortunately, you'll be doing a hallway dash to reach this wonder.

When weather permits, an ample full breakfast is served in the backyard beneath tall pines or, if the road noise doesn't bother you, on the front patio next to the outdoor stone fireplace. If the day is gray, morning treats are served at a large table in the rather plain dining room. **5295 West Lake Boulevard; (530) 525-5273, (800) 538-2463; www.rockwoodlodge. com; expensive to very expensive; minimum-stay requirement on weekends and holidays.**

Romantic Suggestion: For spectacular views of the glistening lake while rushing down the slopes, try carving some turns at HOMEWOOD MOUNTAIN RESORT (5145 West Lake Boulevard; 530-525-2900, 530-525-2992; www.skihomewood.com; call for rates). The resort, which bills itself as a friendly, family-style kind of place, is within walking distance of Rockwood Lodge.

Restaurant Kissing

❤❤ **SWISS LAKEWOOD RESTAURANT, Homewood** Old Swiss photographs, cowbells, and other memorabilia fill every nook and cranny of Swiss Lakewood's dining room, all backdropped by bright red walls. Sound a little garish? We thought so at first, but after we were greeted by a charming international staff and had a scrumptious meal, we decided this place was "tastefully cluttered." French continental cuisine graces the menu year-round, but fondue—cheese or beef—is the specialty during winter. Feeding this tasty treat to each other is a fun way to warm hungry stomachs and playful hearts. **5055 West Lake Boulevard; (530) 525-5211; expensive; reservations required; dinner Tuesday–Sunday.**

Outdoor Kissing

❤❤❤❤ **D. L. BLISS STATE PARK, Homewood** Bliss is a fitting name for this park that hugs the shore of brilliant Lake Tahoe. Inviting sand is visible through its transparent waters, and snowcapped Sierra peaks ascend in the distance. The best place to kiss in all of Tahoe is located here at RUBICON POINT, a quarter-mile hike from the last accessible parking lot. Views of the lake grow more magnificent at every turn as you traverse a well-worn path that weaves along the shore and winds higher and higher into the rocky cliffs above. Though Rubicon Point is not well marked, you'll know when you've arrived—the already gorgeous view becomes almost spellbinding. Pine trees give way to a panoramic view of the lake, mountains, and neighboring inlet. Waves lap gently at the rocky shore below, and the sound of chattering birds and wind rustling in the trees provides background music for a long kiss. **Highway 89; (530) 525-7277, (800) 444-7275; www.cal-parks.ca.gov; $5 day-use fee per vehicle.** *From Highway 89 south, follow signs to the park. It is on your right, between Emerald Bay and Meeks Bay.*

South Shore

South Lake Tahoe

If you want to elope, South Lake Tahoe is the place for you—as long as you don't mind pledging "I do" in a roadside chapel, surrounded by an endless sea of neon lights, casinos, and strip malls. Tahoe's south shore sits astride the California and Nevada state borders and is known for its economy hotels, traffic jams, gambling casinos, and wedding chapels. "No thanks," you say? Don't worry—there's something here for nature enthusiasts too. South Lake Tahoe's **HEAVENLY SKI RESORT** (775-586-7000, 800-2HEAVEN; www.skiheavenly.com; call for rates) is one of America's largest, encompassing 4,800 acres of terrain and dazzling panoramic views of Lake Tahoe.

Hotel/Bed and Breakfast Kissing

❀❀❀❀ **BLACK BEAR INN, South Lake Tahoe** Every once in a while we come across a new inn that leaves us breathless (just like a kiss). The Black Bear Inn, located on the road to Heavenly Ski Resort, is one such place. Modeled after some of the West's great lodges, this seven-room inn captures all their majesty and rustic style, but offers a more intimate experience without the crowds, fanfare, or enormous size. Put simply, it's a scaled-down lodge perfectly suited for cuddling couples.

One look at the impressive Great Room and you'll want to stay. The centerpiece—a 34-foot-high river-rock fireplace—parallels equally magnificent rough-hewn log poles that stretch up into the cathedral ceilings. Opposite the fireplace is a river-rock wall with French doors opening to the backyard patio. Museum-quality country and farm antiques accent the interior, including vintage sleighs, snowshoes, and some interesting conversation pieces, such as a pie safe (designed to keep sweet tooths from sampling the goods) and spikes from the old Truckee railroad. Guests can continue to admire the Great Room during the evening wine-and-cheese hour, when tempting treats are set out on an antique workman's bench fronting the fireplace.

Five rooms in the main lodge, also exemplifying the lodge theme, continue to impress. Our favorites? We recommend the second-floor Fallen Leaf Room, where you can share a smooch on the private balcony, and the spacious Sequoia Room, a tucked-away retreat for those wanting complete privacy. No matter where you decide to stay, all rooms are delightfully decorated and feature private entrances, TV/VCRs hidden in armoires, king-size beds with hard and soft pillows, private bathrooms done in slate and pine, and glass-enclosed showers large enough for two. Create instant romantic ambience anytime by flipping on the gas fireplace via a bedside switch.

Out in the backyard, more kissing spots await, in particular the sheltered hot tub, perfect for post-ski soaks. There's also a charming duplex cabin, which holds two equally lovely rooms decorated similarly to those in the main lodge. At the time of our visit, two additional cabins were being built that look like they will be just as romantically promising when completed.

Come breakfast time, the innkeepers take full advantage of their interesting antique collection. Fresh-baked muffins are presented on an old grocery counter, and an old-fashioned washbasin is filled with glass bottles of orange juice and milk. Sit at one of the tables together and enjoy such treats as eggs Benedict, blueberry strudel, or (our favorite) a green apple, walnut, and Brie omelet. After such a feast, you're certain to have enough energy for both skiing and kissing. **1202 Ski Run Boulevard; (530) 544-4451, (877) BEAR-INN; www.tahoeblackbear.com; expensive to very expensive; minimum-stay requirement seasonally.**

❤❤ EMBASSY SUITES RESORT, South Lake Tahoe Situated yards away from the Nevada state line, this massive hotel surveys neon casino country. If casinos aren't your thing, neither is this hotel—its flashy neighbors are hard to ignore. On the other hand, if you're in the mood to try your luck at the one-armed bandits or roulette table, the Embassy Suites is one of the best (and most tasteful) options in the nearby area.

The centerpiece of this Bavarian-motif hotel is the series of three soaring nine-story-tall atriums. In the first, water splashes over a paddle wheel and down a flume to a decorative pool surrounded by lush greenery. Umbrella-crowned café tables fill the patios of the other atriums, where complimentary breakfast and afternoon cocktails and hors d'oeuvres are served. Several glass-sided elevators transport you to the 400 hotel-style two-room suites, the kind typically associated with Embassy Suites. There's plenty of space in each suite to stretch out after a day playing on the slopes or at the slots; other than that, the suites are similar in decor and amenities to upscale hotel rooms anywhere. If possible, try booking a lakefront-view room, but be prepared to pay premium prices. **4130 Lake Tahoe Boulevard; (530) 544-5400, (800) 988-9894; www.embassytahoe.com; expensive to unbelievably expensive.**

❦❦ INN AT HEAVENLY, South Lake Tahoe

The Inn at Heavenly may look like a motel on the outside, with its two long buildings separated by a parking lot; but take a closer look and you'll be pleasantly surprised. Each of the 13 guest rooms is individually decorated in traditional alpine motifs such as black bears, canoes, or trout. Continuing to delight are hand-stenciled walls, queen- or king-size beds covered by quilts, and some of the more impressive river-rock fireplaces we've seen. Most rooms have kitchenettes and all feature private though unremarkable bathrooms. Space is at a premium in many rooms, so if you and your honey bring along all your recreational gear, expect a tight fit.

One area of the inn has been converted into a sauna, hot tub, and steam bath sanctuary. Reservations are required, which may take some fun out of a spontaneous soak. No reservations are required, however, for kissing on the two acres of park behind the inn or pedaling to your hearts' content on the complimentary bikes (available summer only). An expanded continental breakfast is served daily in the homey gathering room. **1261 Ski Run Boulevard; (530) 544-4244, (800) MY-CABIN; www.800mycabin.com; moderate to expensive; minimum-stay requirement seasonally.**

Romantic Note: The Inn at Heavenly also offers several cabins for rent (very expensive to unbelievably expensive; minimum-stay requirement). Options include renting a single bedroom in one of the cabins or taking over an entire three- or four-bedroom cabin, although we must say the latter choice is better suited for groups than for cuddling couples. Each cabin features a hot tub and full kitchen, while some offer fireplaces and porches.

❦❦❦ TAHOE SEASONS RESORT, South Lake Tahoe

For snow lovers, what could be nicer than rolling out of bed in the morning and walking just a few steps to the slopes? Well, how about returning to your room after a day on the hill and sinking into your own private whirlpool tub? All these and more can be yours at this resort, situated across the street from Heavenly Ski Resort.

Each of the 182 sumptuous mini-suites features a pleasantly appointed living room and bedroom, separated by an oversize whirlpool tub enclosed by shoji screens. A gas fire flickers in the hearth of nearly every guest room, while microwaves and refrigerators make inventive after-skiing snacks a romantic possibility. Request one of the upper mountain-facing rooms for the best views. The lake-facing views only offer peekaboo glimpses over the neighborhood rooftops.

For the absolute best views, grab your tennis racket and favorite partner and journey to the rooftop, where several courts and fabulous vistas await. Back on earth, a small pool and hot tub are unromantically located next to the bar and lounge area, so don't expect to have much privacy while you soak. The resort's restaurant, **NEEDLES** (inexpensive to moderate; breakfast, lunch, and dinner daily), is one of the nicer casual hotel restaurants we've seen. **3901 Saddle Road; (530) 541-6700, (800) 540-4874; www.tahoeseasons.com; moderate to very expensive.**

Restaurant Kissing

❤❤❤❦ CAFE FIORE, South Lake Tahoe You don't have to worry about distractions at Cafe Fiore—there are only seven tables. It doesn't get more intimate than this. Candles glow at each of the windowside tables arranged in the cozy, wood-paneled dining room. In the summer, more tables are set up outside, but the view of the parking lot isn't particularly attractive. Wherever you sit, you're certain to enjoy the northern Italian cuisine, featuring seafood and traditional pastas, numerous chicken dishes, and plenty of veal specialties. Unlike the extensive entrée menu, dessert choices are limited, but are out-of-this-world nonetheless. Dig into the homemade white chocolate ice cream or share a snowball, an ice-cream sundae creation unique to Cafe Fiore. **1169 Ski Run Boulevard, No. 5; (530) 541-2908; www.cafe fiore.com; expensive; reservations required; dinner daily.**

Romantic Alternative: Because Cafe Fiore has so few tables, reservations are hard to come by. Luckily, **NEPHELES** (1169 Ski Run Boulevard; 530-544-8130; www.nepheles.com; expensive; dinner daily) is located next door and, though not as intimate as Cafe Fiore, it has a romantic appeal of its own. A large stained glass window depicting a smiling sun sets the mood for tasty, creative California cuisine and adds a rustic touch to the otherwise standard dining rooms. Besides filling up on food, you and your sweetheart also have the option of getting soaked here as well. Behind the restaurant, sheltered within a fenced-in courtyard, are several private hot tubs available for rent. Under clear or snowy skies, listen to piped-in stereo music while enjoying full cocktail service from Nepheles. Reservations are required, and showers and towels are provided.

❤❤ THE CHRISTIANIA INN RESTAURANT, South Lake Tahoe This old alpine-style inn is so close to Heavenly's slopes that you could almost ski right over, although we recommend changing into something more comfortable than your ski outfit. Accented by lace curtains, intimate booths, and beams decorated with tiny white lights and garlic braids, the European country–style dining room is the perfect place to enjoy heartwarming dishes. After working up an appetite on the slopes, savor such specialties as breast of duck served with an Asian blackberry glaze, or grilled pork tenderloin accompanied by a sun-dried cherry port sauce. You'll have no trouble finding the right wine to go with your meal; the wine list offers more than 200 choices. For a romantic finale, share a dessert for two. We highly recommend the bananas flambé, cherries jubilee, or baked Alaska, all flamed tableside. **3819 Saddle Road, at The Christiania Inn; (530) 544-7337; www.christianiainn.com; expensive; dinner daily.**

Romantic Warning: THE CHRISTIANIA INN (moderate to expensive), situated above the restaurant, offers two rooms and four suites. Although the location is ideal and the fireplaces and other romantic amenities sound sweet, our visit was soured by the timeworn feel, mismatched decor, and dark corridors. Stay here only if you have skiing on your mind, not romance.

❧❧❧❧ EVANS AMERICAN GOURMET CAFE, South Lake Tahoe

The food at Evans was so divine, it's hard for us to remember anything but the succulent flavor of our grilled halibut topped with a citrus beurre blanc and the grand finale of tiramisu swimming in a coffee-flavored crème anglaise. Normally we're eager to share our entrées and our desserts, but not this time—we wanted to savor every last bite of this impeccably delicious meal. Not that the surroundings weren't lovely—floral window coverings, lovely watercolors, and fresh flowers at every table infuse the intimate café with color. But the food … simply unforgettable. **536 Emerald Bay Road; (530) 542-1990; www.evanstahoe.com; expensive; reservations recommended; dinner daily.**

❧❧ MONUMENT PEAK RESTAURANT, South Lake Tahoe

It's no surprise that Mark Twain called the view from here "the fairest picture the whole earth affords." Witness the splendor with your own eyes from a large tram that climbs to a soaring 2,000 feet above Lake Tahoe. Once on top, forgo the cafeteria, which caters to heavy-booted skiers, and head to the Monument Peak Restaurant, which appeals to those seeking finer cuisine and ambience. Linen tablecloths and fresh flowers add a touch of elegance to the three-tiered dining room, but the real draw is the wall of windows framing a heavenly view of crystal-blue Lake Tahoe enfolded by jagged, often snowcapped, mountain peaks. If you come for dinner in the summer, be sure to arrive before sunset.

The menu features standard American fare like shrimp scampi, steak, chicken, and seafood dishes. Although the cuisine is usually quite good, it's not nearly as impressive as the views. Entrées tend toward the expensive side, so if you're searching for a bargain, start at the bottom of the hill. At the ticket booth, purchase a tram-dinner package for $29.95 per person. That includes a round-trip tram ride, plus your choice of entrée. Drinks, dessert, and extras are left up to you. Views and kissing are, of course, free of charge. **Heavenly Valley Ski Resort, at Top of the Tram; (530) 542-5222; expensive; $12.50 per person for tram ride; call for seasonal hours.**

Outdoor Kissing

❀❀❀ **BORGES CARRIAGE & SLEIGH RIDES, South Lake Tahoe** "Dashing through the snow, in a one-horse open sleigh" are more than familiar words of a Christmas carol to the Borges family. They offer rides on a selection of sleighs, from six- to 20-passenger rigs pulled by two Belgian draft horses to two-person, one-horse cutters. It's wonderful to skim through a snowy meadow overlooking the sapphire lake. Plus, an intriguing history lesson gives you a new perspective on glitzy South Lake Tahoe. **Lake Parkway and Highway 50; (775) 588-2953, (800) 726-RIDE; www.sleigh ride.com; $15 per adult, $60 for a half-hour private ride for two, $100 for a one-hour private ride for two.** *Call ahead for reservations and directions.*

Stateline, Nevada

Restaurant Kissing

❀❀❀❀ **THE SUMMIT RESTAURANT, Stateline** A romantic restaurant in Harrah's? You would never guess this restaurant is situated on an upper floor of one of Nevada's best-known casinos. This lofty setting once served as Harrah's Star Suite, the secluded aerie reserved for visiting royalty and Hollywood VIPs. Luckily, you don't have to be a high roller or a star to enjoy such luxury.

A fire blazes in the two-way fireplace and candles flicker from a candelabra on the ebony piano, where a tuxedo-clad virtuoso plays. Each dining area is intimate and romantically lit, whether you sit by the fire or climb the stairs to the mezzanine with its smoked-glass balustrade. Windowside tables look out at the city lights and the velvet expanse of Lake Tahoe far below. The continental cuisine is as heavenly as the ambience. Feast on appetizers like pumpkin fettuccine with Gorgonzola cream or smoked-salmon cheesecake with lemon aioli, salads so beautiful they could double as centerpieces, and grilled venison medallions or macadamia-nut-crusted sea bass in a spicy Thai coconut sauce. Be sure to end such a fancy and formal dinner with a fitting dessert such as a chocolate tuxedo torte or a Grand Marnier soufflé. The Summit is a touch of heaven—possibly the only touch this side of the state border. **16th floor of Harrah's Hotel and Casino; (775) 588-6611; www.harrahstahoe.com; very expensive to unbelievably expensive; call for seasonal hours.**

Gold Country

Highway 49 travels directly through most of the Gold Country towns. From San Francisco, take Interstate 80 east toward Sacramento. From Sacramento, continue on Interstate 80 to intersect with Highway 49 in Auburn, or take Interstate 50 to Highway 49 in Placerville.

When news spread in 1848 that gold had been discovered in the Sierra Nevada foothills, people from all walks of life flocked to the promised land of California. Determined to find riches, this sudden flood of settlers made the Gold Country a ruthless, gun-toting region. Finding the mother lode was the prime objective, and the end, for many, often justified the means. Although many travelers still think of California as a desirable destination for the pursuit of fame and riches, gold fever is a thing of the past. However, the Sierras' Western heritage still reigns, and romance continues to thrive.

At the height of the gold rush, little Nevada City, at the northern tip of Gold Country, was as populous as Sacramento is today. Tucked amid rolling golden hills and valleys, towns like Auburn, Coloma, Sutter Creek, Jackson, and Jamestown bustled with activity. As the gold supply began to dwindle, settlers deserted the area just as quickly as they had come. Today, many of the original buildings remain, creating a ghost-town feeling in some of these now-quiet small towns. History buffs will want to stop and read the countless historical markers that dot the highway, and who knows? You might even strike it rich in the memories you bring home together.

Romantic Warning: Highway 49, which runs directly through most of the Gold Country towns, is a surprisingly busy two-lane road. Expect driving to be a hassle on weekends, especially during summer. Also, unless the place you stay has soundproof windows or a location far from the highway, it is hard to escape traffic noise.

Sacramento

Despite the fact that it is a four-county metropolis and one of the ten fastest-growing regions in the United States, the capital of the Golden State exudes an amiable, small-town charm. Year-round sunshine graces Sacramento's wide streets, which are lined with tall shade trees and renovated turn-of-the-century homes. Coffeehouses, antique stores, stylish restaurants, and a handful of elegant Victorian bed and breakfasts enrich Sacramento's friendly allure. But even though Sacramento may *feel* like a small town, keep in mind that it is not. Traffic noise is a near constant, although you probably won't even notice—you'll be too busy kissing.

Romantic Note: Most of the inns and bed and breakfasts in the Sacramento area cater to business clientele during the week; however, this should have no disagreeable impact on your stay, especially if you plan your romantic getaway for a weekend.

Hotel/Bed and Breakfast Kissing

❤❤❤❤ **AMBER HOUSE, Sacramento** Poets, artists, and musicians inspired the decor at Amber House, and now it's your turn to be inspired. Set on a quiet residential street in downtown Sacramento, the inn consists of three turn-of-the-century homes called the Poet's Refuge, the Artist's Retreat, and Musician's Manor. Guests are typically greeted at the Poet's Refuge, a Craftsman-style home where comfortable furnishings, a dark brick hearth, and beautiful hardwood accents in the parlor create a welcoming atmosphere. After initial introductions, guests are escorted to their quarters for an in-room check-in, quite a fancy touch for a bed and breakfast.

Eleven of the 14 guest rooms have Jacuzzi tubs in bathrooms, a fact that's bound to inspire plenty of smooching. Rooms without Jacuzzi tubs feature antique tubs, and all are wonderfully elegant and romantic. In the Poet's Refuge, we were especially taken with the Lord Byron Room, with its wrought-iron canopy bed draped with floral linens and white fabric, not to mention the circular two-person Jacuzzi tub in the sensuous marble bathroom. Surrounding windows fill the airy Emily Dickinson Room with sunlight, and the romantic mood is enhanced by a double-sided fireplace that warms the bedroom on one side and the bathroom's double Jacuzzi tub on the other.

Bright colors give the accommodations in the neighboring Artist's Retreat a cheerful disposition. A stunning, bright yellow bedroom opens to a solarium-like bathroom with a double Jacuzzi tub and a glass-enclosed shower in the lovely Van Gogh Room. Rose-patterned linens drape a king-size wrought-iron canopy bed in the Renoir Room, which also has a double whirlpool tub. All of the rooms in this building feature reproductions of masterpieces by their respective namesakes.

Slip in your favorite classical music CD for a night of romance in the Musician's Manor. This yellow and purple Colonial home boasts some of our favorite rooms. Hide away in the upstairs Vivaldi Room that features a four-poster bed, a snug little gas fireplace, and a bathroom with an oval Jacuzzi tub. There's also a private balcony, an ideal place to have breakfast. Another romantic winner is the first-floor Mozart Room, complete with all the romantic amenities of the Vivaldi Room, but with the advantage of a heart-shaped Jacuzzi tub.

A full, delicious breakfast is served anywhere you'd like, from the backyard garden of the Musician's Manor to your own room. Don't worry if you have trouble resisting temptation and overeat: Bicycles are on hand so you can burn off those extra calories as you pedal through Sacramento's lovely old-fashioned neighborhoods. **1315 22nd Street; (916) 444-8085, (800) 755-6526; www.amberhouse.com; expensive to unbelievably expensive.**

Romantic Note: Many of Sacramento's trendiest and best restaurants are within a few blocks of Amber House. Ask the innkeeper about arranging a horse-drawn carriage ride to and from dinner (approximately $35 round-trip per couple).

❤❤ **CAPITOL PARK BED AND BREAKFAST INN, Sacramento** Set in a nondescript Sacramento neighborhood just blocks from the state Capitol, this 1910 Federalist home has plenty to offer those wanting an in-town retreat. Sebastian, the four-legged greeter, is the first to wag 'n' welcome you into the parlor, a formal room that still retains its original polished woodwork, inlaid cabinets, coved ceilings, and hardwood floors. Upstairs, four various-sized guest rooms await, each painted in soothing pastel tones, lightly sprinkled with artwork, and simply decorated with American and European antiques. Neatly pressed and starched sheets hidden beneath designer bedspreads add a subtle, classy touch.

When it comes to matters of the heart, book the Huntington Room. This large corner room, done up in a European theme, comes outfitted with a king-size bed, a window sitting area, and an antique armoire. However, the jewel in the crown is its sunlit bathroom, where you can open the plantation-style shutters, soak in the two-person Jacuzzi tub, and admire the palm tree outside. Combine that with a kiss, and you're in your own little paradise. The front-facing Crocker Room, equipped with a modern en suite bathroom (shower only), can be called cozy for two people who like being close. The two remaining rooms require some compromise for the romantically inclined. They hit the bull's eye on decor and romantic ambience, especially the Hopkins Room with its wall of windows, elegant linens, and queen-size iron canopy bed facing a gas fireplace. However, both the Hopkins Room and the adjacent Stanford Room have separate, private baths across the hall. If you can deal with this inconvenience, book the Hopkins Room, since its bathroom sports an extra-long jetted tub set windowside. (By the way, both bathrooms match the decor of their accompanying room, just in case you forget which is yours.)

Breakfast is served at the time of your choosing in the formal dining room. Tables for two come appointed with fresh flowers, and the olive-colored satin linens are topped with the finest crystal, Lenox china, and silver coffeepots. Select from a breakfast menu of buttermilk pancakes, French toast, an omelet du jour, or eggs any style, while you savor the moment. **1300 T Street; (916) 414-1300, (877) 753-9982; www.capitol parkinn.iggp.com; moderate to expensive.**

❤❤ HARTLEY HOUSE INN, Sacramento A certain straightforward simplicity dominates this turn-of-the-century Colonial Revival home, situated on a corner in a busy residential neighborhood. Hartley House's dark-stained woodwork, hardwood floors, distinctive Oriental carpets, leaded and stained glass windows, and tick-tocking old clocks will appeal to many guests as a fresh alternative to the frilly accoutrements of other bed and breakfasts in the area. Although Hartley House caters to executives during the week, weekends are prime time for romantic getaways.

Five small guest rooms are handsomely outfitted with lush feather beds, antique wardrobes, claw-foot and antique tubs, and floral bed coverings. Solid-colored walls and plantation-style shutters—along with classic artwork—give this inn a slightly modern edge. Brighton is the brightest room in the inn: Daylight streams in through a dozen windows in this sunporch-turned-guest-room. The Dover Room wins over romantics as well, thanks to its king-size bed and large claw-foot tub in the sunny bathroom.

Breakfast is a made-to-order affair and guests can choose from among such offerings as apple pancakes, cheese blintzes, and other items. (Just don't order the waffles; ours were rock-hard.) Private, two-person tables in the formal dining room await your seating. Later in the day, cuddle together on the front porch swing or savor a soak in the communal hot tub enclosed by the courtyard gazebo. **700 22nd Street; (916) 447-7829, (800) 831-5806; www.hartleyhouse.com; moderate to expensive.**

❤❤❤ THE STERLING HOTEL, Sacramento This baronial Victorian mansion, set in the heart of downtown, is a multi-use property if there ever was one. During the week, business executives flock here to take advantage of its central location. On weekends, The Sterling caters primarily to couples in search of relaxation, and wedding parties who take over the stunning Victorian ballroom downstairs. No matter what day you decide to visit, the personality of this hotel is sure to please. Manicured gardens surround the landmark building; inside, understated Victorian elegance prevails.

Each of the 17 handsome guest rooms features classic artwork, a four-poster or canopy bed topped with floral linens, and a marble-tiled double Jacuzzi tub (several of these sport impressively unique designs). Two rooms have nonfunctional fireplaces, more for looks than for heating purposes, and sunlight streams through stained glass windows in most of the bathrooms. Views range from fair (the neighborhood street) to poor (a nearby rundown building). If you are going to splurge here, we suggest doing so on the spacious Bridal Suite. The bedroom, besides being enormous, isn't anything extraordinary, but the bathroom certainly is. An elevated double Jacuzzi tub flanked by tall white Grecian columns is surrounded by floor-to-ceiling Italian gray marble. If that's not enough, a glass-enclosed double-headed shower should do the trick. Even if you're not newlyweds, this is the place to pretend you're on your honeymoon.

An extended continental breakfast, consisting of cereals, fruits, home-made pastries, and breads, is served in the sparse breakfast room downstairs, or it can be taken back to your room. Guests also have the added luxury of ordering lunch and dinner via room service from **CHANTERELLE** (see Restaurant Kissing), the hotel's intimate restaurant. **1300 H Street; (916) 448-1300, (800) 365-7660; www.sleepingsacramento.com; expensive to unbelievably expensive; recommended wedding site.**

❀❀ **VIZCAYA, Sacramento** Although there are some resemblances, you might not guess that Vizcaya is the younger sibling to the noted **STERLING HOTEL** (see review above). While both are landmark Victorians and play host to hundreds of weddings each year, Vizcaya lacks some of the elegance and polish of its urbane sibling. Located in a residential city neighborhood, this property certainly shines on the outside with its manicured gardens, flowing fountain, and brick courtyard embellished by stately trees. Also breathtaking is the Romanesque-style Pavilion, where weddings, receptions, and meeting are held. What disappoints are some of the guest rooms deemed romantic. Amenities in four of the nine rooms include marble-tiled fireplaces, and five rooms feature Jacuzzi tubs. Room decor is often an eclectic, mismatched combination of modern and antique furnishings and patterns that seem out of place in such elegant surroundings. The top-floor Penthouse Suite is the prime example and didn't captivate our hearts despite its Jacuzzi tub and tucked-away setting. The three Carriage House rooms in back are the most preferable options, both in terms of decor and location (they are farthest from the adjacent busy street). We also like the second-floor Room No. 2, where a four-poster bed fronts the marble fireplace and a skylight brightens the double Jacuzzi tub and double shower in the spacious bathroom. If you stay in the Carriage House, you'll have to venture to the main home's dining room to partake in a full breakfast with such basics as waffles and cooked-to-order eggs.

Weddings are the specialty at Vizcaya, and on the weekends you're likely to see and/or hear one or two or three. (The average is about five each weekend.) Many couples do exchange vows here, and Vizcaya has perfected the art of producing wedding ceremonies with all of the frills. We just wouldn't recommend spending a honeymoon night in the room pegged for newlyweds, the drab Garden Suite. It's a spacious area in which to get ready for your wedding, but the bedroom itself doesn't inspire romantic thoughts. While the management is making efforts to upgrade bed linens and so forth throughout the inn, hopefully an interior decorator will be hired to smooth out the mismatched edges. **2019 21st Street; (916) 455-5243, (800) 456-2019; moderate to very expensive; recommended wedding site.**

Restaurant Kissing

❧❧ **CHANTERELLE, Sacramento** Set in the heart of downtown Sacramento in the popular **STERLING HOTEL** (see Hotel/Bed and Breakfast Kissing), Chanterelle is housed in a daylight basement and fronted by a brick terrace appointed with patio furniture. Sunlight sifts through its leaded glass windows into two separate dining rooms adorned with provocative modern paintings. Black metal chairs make a sharp contrast with layers of white linen on each table. The dining rooms are perfect for a dark or chilly day; however, if the sun's out and the temperature's right, choose to dine at an umbrella-covered table on the patio.

Start your meal with the unusual-looking spinach and cheese dumplings. While these little green globs don't appear particularly appealing, the rich, cheesy taste proves that first impressions are often misleading. Dishes such as Jamaican pork tenderloin served with wild mushroom risotto or the mustard-and-goat-cheese-crusted rack of lamb are sure to satisfy. Finish in style with a taste of tiramisu or a slice of chocolate decadence cake resting on a bed of raspberry sauce. **1300 H Street, at The Sterling Hotel; (916) 442-0451, (800) 365-7660; www.sleepingsacramento.com; moderate to expensive; lunch Monday–Friday, dinner daily, brunch Sunday.**

Romantic Warning: When there is a special event happening at The Sterling Hotel, which is quite often, noise from the nearby ballroom can carry over into the dining room, disrupting your peace and quiet.

❧❧ **CITY TREASURE RESTAURANT, Sacramento** We can't think of a better name for this urban jewel, located in a residential neighborhood of Sacramento. Floor-to-ceiling windows look out to a small outdoor terrace and the street beyond. Triangular lamps suspended from exposed ceiling pipes give the small dining room a modern flair, although exotic flower arrangements, miniature white lights, and watercolor paintings soften the effect. The closely arranged tables are each adorned with a single fresh flower and a flickering candle.

In typical California fashion, City Treasure features a large, enticing menu. However talk about town is that the food can be hit or miss. Hopefully, you'll hit it right by starting with the flavor-packed ginger-spiced prawns with wasabi crème fraîche and then moving on to such entrées as braised beef and pork cannelloni with porcini bechamel or zinfandel-glazed pork tenderloin. Desserts tend toward the unusual; the spiced apple-almond cheesecake with biscotti crust goes perfectly with a cup of coffee, and the chocolate ecstasy is one item that dessert lovers should share. **1730 L Street; (916) 447-7380; moderate to expensive; lunch Monday–Friday, dinner daily, brunch Sunday.**

Romantic Alternative: BIBA (2801 Capitol Avenue; 916-455-BIBA; www.biba-restaurant.com; expensive; lunch Monday–Friday, dinner Monday–Saturday) is another romantic dining possibility in downtown Sacramento. Reservations are a must at this extremely busy Italian eatery, which is highlighted by square white pillars, arched windows, surrounding mirrors, and modern artwork. Fresh flowers add a dash of color to the animated atmosphere, where cozy, linen-draped tables are much too close together for intimate conversation. Don't miss the homemade pasta specialties. Our goat-cheese ravioli surrounded by a sage-butter sauce was superb, as was the grilled pork chop served with a white bean purée and stuffed roasted peppers. Traditional Italian desserts dominate the menu; the creamy, oh-so-delicate cannoli took the cake. Service can be a bit stuffy and, due to the restaurant's popularity, it can also be a bit slow at times.

❤❤❤ **TWENTY-EIGHT, Sacramento** The section between J and N Streets on 28th Avenue is referred to as Restaurant Row, mostly by the company that owns six restaurants here. Standing apart from its five more casual siblings is the luxurious Twenty-Eight, a sophisticated neighborhood restaurant both inside and out. In fact, its taupe stuccoed facade looks too elegant for this neck of the woods, but don't let that stop you from entering. Inside, the decor sings the praises of gold and olive-green color combinations offset by creamy white tablecloths, tailored window treatments, and crystal chandeliers shaped like suns. Comfortable padded booths line the windows and dominate the dining room, making privacy a plus. A little alcoved room in back sports only two tables, so request this area for supreme privacy.

New American cuisine with Asian, Mediterranean, and classical influences marks the small but diverse menu. Be sure to start off with the succulent lobster pot stickers, swimming in a delicious curry sauce. The house specialty, sesame-crusted ahi with crispy noodles and shiitake mushrooms, is nothing outstanding, but the fish is incredibly fresh. For more robust tastes, try the grilled lamb chops with artichoke risotto or pan-seared scallops with sweet-pea mashed potatoes. A variety of creative desserts finishes off the menu. We decided to go tropical by sharing the luscious coconut rice pudding topped with mangos; the smooth tastes will wow anyone looking for a cool finale. **2730 N Street; (916) 456-2800; www. paragarys.com; expensive; reservations recommended; lunch Monday–Friday, dinner Monday–Saturday.**

Romantic Alternative: Twenty-Eight tends toward a darker, intimate decor, which may not be what you want on a sunny summer day. If you're after some rays, head across the street to **PARAGARY'S** (1401 28th Street; 916-457-5737; www.paragarys.com; moderate to expensive; lunch Monday–Friday, dinner daily) and grab a courtyard table. Be sure to go early, since this spot is popular! Three waterfalls, flowing over modern metal sculptures, not only bring beauty and coolness to the courtyard, but also enough natural noise to allow for private conversation between the two of you. A massive outdoor corner fireplace helps heat things up when the sun goes down. The atmosphere is stylish-casual and the Italian menu features wood-fired pizzas, grilled fish, pastas, and salads.

Outdoor Kissing

❧❧ **HIGHBOURNE TRANSPORTATION AND LIVERY, LTD., Sacramento** No need to be highborn to taste a little of the high life. Cruising around town in a chauffeured vintage Rolls Royce or Mercedes Benz is an option for all romantics … provided they can open their pocketbook very wide for a day. Once inside your luxurious automobile of choice, the driver will take you almost anywhere your hearts desire, from a local restaurant, to San Francisco for shopping, even to **NAPA VALLEY** or **SHENANDOAH VALLEY** to engage in some serious sipping (see Wine Kissing in Napa Valley and Shenandoah Valley for recommended wineries). Romantic picnics can also be arranged, attended to by a uniformed waiter and served at the site of your choice. **(916) 444-8500; www.highbourne. com; rental prices start at $125 per hour; reservations required.** *Call for information about pickup and drop-off locations.*

Old Sacramento

Take the Old Sacramento exit off Interstate 80 and follow signs to the area.

The restored western-style facades lining Old Sacramento's narrow streets are just authentic enough to make you feel as though you've stepped into a John Wayne movie. Unfortunately, this is as nostalgic as it gets (and if you're not a John Wayne fan, you might be less than amused). The neighboring highways, cheap tourist shops, and casts of thousands tarnish the rustic character of this little village, and the horse-drawn buggies seem sadly out of place. Nevertheless, an afternoon spent here isn't a waste of time, especially if you take a stroll along the placid Sacramento River, indulge in an ice-cream cone, or investigate the **WELLS FARGO HISTORY MUSEUM** in the B. F. Hastings Building (1000 Second Street; 916-440-4263; www.wellsfargo.com/about/museum/info; free admission; open daily).

Restaurant Kissing

❤❤ **THE DELTA KING, Old Sacramento** Take a dockside voyage into the past on a restored stern-wheel paddleboat, the kind so often associated with the Mississippi River. The *Delta King* plied the river between Sacramento and San Francisco from 1927 to 1940. It was a floating pleasure palace for flappers when Prohibition outlawed drinking in landlocked lounges. Today, it looks much the same inside as it did in its heyday. A broad staircase sweeps up to the refined saloon, aglow with lovingly polished mahogany and teak, where two-person tables are arranged beneath windows that overlook the river's swirling waters on one side and the vintage western-style facades of Old Sacramento on the other. The Pilothouse, an oak-paneled restaurant on the lower floor, is similar in appearance, brimming with small tables covered with white linens and illuminated by softly lit wall sconces. Because of the river views and vintage setting, the restaurant rates high on romantic ambience; unfortunately, the cuisine, which concentrates on steak and seafood, has sunk into mediocrity. **1000 Front Street; (916) 441-4440; www.deltaking.com; expensive; lunch and dinner daily, brunch Sunday; recommended wedding site.**

    Romantic Alternative: Next door, **RIO CITY CAFE** (1110 Front Street; 916-442-8226; moderate to expensive; lunch and dinner daily, brunch Sunday) may be more casual than its neighbor, but affords much of the same view, plus an inventive, flavor-filled menu that will please those whose palates have been dulled by boring food. The large, airy restaurant with windows facing the Sacramento River sports a light California-contemporary design: blond wood chairs, crisp white linens, cement and wood floors, and stuccoed walls highlighting a few pieces of modern art. Choice kissing tables are secluded along the floor-to-ceiling windows or on the riverfront patio. Entrées focus heavily on seafood, including mesquite-broiled salmon and the house favorite, ginger-crusted ahi tuna with soy-lime vinaigrette. We pretended we were back on the bayou and shared a big bowl of spicy

Cajun jambalaya overflowing with chicken, pork, and fish. Continuing on the Southern theme, we concluded lunch with warm pecan pie topped with Jack Daniels crème fraîche. Portions are not for dainty eaters, so bring a big appetite.

❦❦❦❦ **THE FIREHOUSE, Old Sacramento** Venture into The Firehouse, and the alluring atmosphere will help you ignite the flames of passion. This unexpected find is well hidden among the storefronts of Old Sacramento, but well worth your search. In accordance with its name, The Firehouse revels in its rich history, which dates back to 1853. Unusually high cathedral ceilings are offset by red brick walls, while a wrought-iron spiral staircase cascades down into the bar area, and a shiny brass fire pole nearby serves as the most vivid reminder that this restaurant was once Fire Station No. 3. Victorian opulence adds a finishing touch to the historical fixtures. Elaborate mirrors and life-size oil paintings trimmed with ornate gold frames are the first images to capture your attention after your eyes adjust to the dimly lit interior. Massive floral arrangements are set around the two dining rooms, and tables, adorned with lamp-like candles, fine linens, and gold-rimmed china, are spaced nicely apart.

Out in back, a European feel takes hold in the brick courtyard, where large trees provide ample shade to the wrought-iron tables and chairs. This is a thoroughly engaging lunch spot, and at night tiny white lights set the trees aglow. Whatever time you dine, a burbling fountain drowns out any street noise that might otherwise be a distraction.

The Firehouse prides itself on service, which we must say is excellent. The classical American cuisine, however, is of the hit-and-miss variety. The glazed duck breast, complemented by a blueberry and cabernet sauce, wakes up the taste buds with flavor, as does the traditional rack of lamb. Grilled asparagus topped with prosciutto and Asiago cheese also charmed our palates. However, the pork tenderloin covered by an apple brandy cream disappointed us with no flavor. Luckily, the dessert tray is a winner. Chocolate mousse swirled within a chocolate cup or the traditional tiramisu, best downed with a cup of java, should provide enough fuel to help fan the flames of love. **1112 Second Street; (916) 442-4772; www.firehouse oldsac.com; expensive to very expensive; lunch Monday–Friday, dinner Tuesday–Saturday.**

Fair Oaks

At first glance, there is nothing remotely romantic about this Sacramento suburb overflowing with the usual strip malls and cookie-cutter office complexes. But upon closer inspection, we discovered a kissable oasis called **SLOCUM HOUSE** (see Restaurant Kissing). Although the 30- to 50-minute drive (depending on traffic) from downtown Sacramento may be a detour, a trip to this restaurant is definitely worth the effort.

Restaurant Kissing

☙☙☙❧ **SLOCUM HOUSE, Fair Oaks** Sometimes you have to travel far to strike it rich with romance. Such a lengthy journey is necessary to find the Slocum House, located 30 to 50 minutes from downtown Sacramento. This 1925 historical bungalow, set on a forested knoll surrounded by lush, slightly wild gardens, is filled with romantic nooks and crannies inside and out. If the weather permits, plant yourselves in the large back courtyard, which is the top spot for those wanting to engage the lips. A selection of tables, sheltered beneath magnificent maples, are amply spaced apart for private conversations and smooching in the moonlight. Vine-covered fences and manicured hedges delight the eye with greenery, and the strutting roosters—who think they own the place—provide plenty of entertainment. The prime al fresco table is No. 94, hidden behind overlapping ivy and beneath lush trees. Let it be known that this little number was voted the most romantic table in the Sacramento area by the local press, so it's usually occupied. (You can request it, but there are no guarantees.) Other patio tables located in pods away from the central area are equally nice, but not as secluded.

Inside, several cozy rooms, especially those with only four or five tables, allow for romantic repasts any time of the day. The interior comes across as pleasant and subtle, decorated with conservative pastel wallpaper, creative twig arrangements, and antique photographs of the home and Slocum family. Don't expect excitement with the table decor; dull gray linens and matching mauve napkins add little pizzazz.

Although prices for the California-contemporary cuisine are higher than average, each entrée comes with soup or salad, fresh vegetables, and thick slices of homemade bread. We opted for the nightly fish special: seared halibut atop mashed potatoes swimming in a luscious Dijon-chive beurre blanc. Seafood lovers will also appreciate the Pacific Rim ahi tuna, served with a soy-lime vinaigrette. Other noteworthy dishes include Caribbean jerk pork; spicy Black Angus New York Steak; and a smoked butternut squash, portobello mushroom, and baby spinach risotto. Special dinners should always end on a sweet note, and that's easy to do here. If the two of you are celebrating a special occasion, have the restaurant's staff write your heartfelt thoughts on the dessert with chocolate syrup. (Be sure to call ahead if you want it to be a surprise!) We recommend writing those three little words of love on the Hawaiian Paradise, a chocolate mousse cake topped with coconut sorbet that's sure to inspire sweet thoughts. **7992 California Avenue; (916) 961-7211; www.slocum-house.com; expensive; reservations recommended; lunch Tuesday–Friday, dinner Tuesday–Sunday, brunch Sunday; recommended wedding site.**

Nevada City

You might expect a place named Nevada City to be full of flashing lights, casinos, nondescript motels, and oversize hotels; instead, it is one of the most picturesque towns in Gold Country, abounding with quality accommodations. Nevada City has been compared to a rural New England community, and on crisp fall afternoons, after the leaves have turned myriad shades of red, orange, gold, and purple (yes, purple!), you'll see why. Many of the area's earliest settlers were from New England, and some brought along their favorite trees as they journeyed west a hundred and fifty years ago.

Romantic Suggestion: Give yourselves at least a day to behold the grand display of fall colors, then visit the shops and restaurants downtown. The annual blaze of autumn glory usually begins early in October and lasts about six weeks. For more information and a walking map of the town, contact the **NEVADA CITY CHAMBER OF COMMERCE** (132 Main Street, Nevada City, CA 95959; 530-265-2692, 800-655-NJOY; www.nc gold.com).

Hotel/Bed and Breakfast Kissing

❀❀❀ **DEER CREEK INN, Nevada City** Countless establishments are named after lakes or rivers, even if they are not remotely near the picturesque site, but the Deer Creek Inn is genuine. This venerable blue Queen Anne Victorian sits at the edge of Deer Creek, just as the name implies. All that separates the house from the rushing stream is a grassy backyard dotted with fountains, flower beds, and cushioned chairs and hammocks for endless lounging.

The five guest rooms feature private marble baths, canopy or four-poster beds, down comforters, air-conditioning, and antique furnishings. Some have their own private verandas. Elaine's Room has been dubbed the Honeymoon Suite because of its private entrance, wrought-iron canopy bed, garden patio facing the grassy yard and creek, and Roman tub and shower for two. Dressed in violets, the upstairs Winifred's Room is also extremely popular with romantics who like the claw-foot tub at the foot of the bed and the excellent creek view from the patio. Each room is decorated differently, but comfortable elegance is a constant.

Wine and appetizers are served by the creek each afternoon, and the hospitable innkeeper's freshly baked cookies and brownies will keep your sweet tooth satisfied all day. Breakfast is a three-course bonanza of sweet and savory treats that may include specialty egg casseroles accompanied by sausage, fresh fruit salad, and delicious fruit-stuffed oven pancakes. The deck overlooking the creek is the ideal place to enjoy the morning offerings, as is the formal dining room on cooler days. Despite all the activities the Gold Country offers, staying at Deer Creek all day is a perfect plan. In addition to kissing by the creek, the two of you can pan for gold (pans provided), cast your fly rods into the clear waters (bring your own fishing equipment), or just dangle those tootsies over the rocky edge. Such a life. **116 Nevada Street; (530) 265-0363, (800) 655-0363; www.deer creekinn.com; moderate to expensive; minimum-stay requirement on weekends and holidays; recommended wedding site.**

❤❤ DOWNEY HOUSE BED AND BREAKFAST, Nevada City Colorful and romantic times await at the Downey House, located just a block from the town's center. At first glance you'd expect this 1869 Eastlake Victorian to be filled with the familiar frills and antiques associated with such homes. Not here. Each of the six small but comfortable rooms is vividly painted, with colors ranging from fire-engine red to sea blue to creamy mint. Such surroundings, we must say, are a breath of fresh air compared to the popular butter-colored walls seen elsewhere. In addition, each room is soundproofed and completely kiss-worthy thanks in part to down comforters, central air-conditioning, and private baths. Two rooms have double beds, but the others feature queen-size beds. Since room space is at a minimum, the inn presents guests with several common areas. The formal parlor, its ceiling adorned with Bradbury & Bradbury wallpaper, is a perfect spot for sitting when the weather is cold. Any day is fine for gazing out onto the treetops from the upstairs sunporch, which is painted a cool spearmint green and adorned with white wicker chairs. When things get too hot, cool off in the downstairs garden room or, better yet, outside in the green-trimmed garden pocketed with comfortable chairs and tables.

Of course, we highly recommend the garden as your breakfast spot, weather permitting. Otherwise enjoy such mouth-watering treats as Dutch babies or chiles rellenos in the simple, somewhat dark, dining room. Throughout the day, decadent brownies are available for snacking and, come evening, local wines are served alongside appetizers. **517 West Broad Street; (530) 265-2815, (800) 258-2815; www.downeyhouse.com; moderate; minimum-stay requirement on weekends seasonally.**

❀❀❀ **EMMA NEVADA HOUSE, Nevada City** Built in 1856, this pictur-esque beige Victorian was home to 19th-century opera singer Emma Nevada, the glamorous diva of her day. Today, impressive renovations have made her home into one that sings of romance, beauty, and love. Red roses line the white picket fence that encloses the lush yard fronting this architectural delight. While the home may look small at first glance, outward appearances are deceptive. The elongated structure reaches far back into the property and, inside, tall ceilings and generous windows give the home a wonderful spacious feeling.

Of the six guest rooms, we prefer the three on the main floor, with their high ceilings and extra space. In Nightingale's Bower, luxurious Italian bedding drapes a queen-size bed set into front yard–facing bay windows. (If you've got serious romancing in mind, we recommend drawing the drapes for privacy.) An oval Jacuzzi tub is the highlight of the small bathroom, and a charming antique stove rounds out the romantic picture.

Touted as the honeymoon suite, the light and bright Empress' Chamber features a hand-carved queen-size bed covered with pristine white linens; a Jacuzzi tub for two awaits in the lovely bathroom. The Mignon's Boudoir, also on the main floor, has a decidedly French-country feeling, with pansy-motif linens, hardwood floors, and a pretty bathroom with a claw-foot tub. A flip-on gas fireplace adds some degree of ambience. The remaining three bedrooms, tucked upstairs under the gables, are slightly smaller. Though these rooms are snug, plush down comforters and private baths with claw-foot tubs make them comfortable places to stay.

With its peaked cathedral ceiling and circular wall of windows, the airy sunroom is a delightful place for a filling breakfast of Belgian waffles, onion-caraway quiche, and fruit cobbler. If you're up early (and the sun's out), you may be lucky enough to claim the table on the adjacent veranda overlooking the backyard parking lot and the trees beyond. After breakfast, descend the veranda stairs to the creekside garden, where the owners have placed secluded benches with one purpose in mind: kissing, of course. **528 East Broad Street; (530) 265-4415, (800) 916-EMMA; www.nevada cityinns.com/emma.htm; moderate to expensive; minimum-stay requirement on weekends.**

❀❀❀ **GRANDMERE'S INN, Nevada City** Grandmere's Inn, like its sister property **EMMA NEVADA HOUSE** (see review above), is certainly a sight to behold. This grand dame stands tall at the top of a hill, showing off Colonial Revival flair with impressive white columns flanked by mature trees. A wrought-iron fence encloses this stately white 1856 home and, in back, beautifully landscaped, flower-filled grounds come dotted with stone benches. Daylight fills the comfortable parlor, which is appointed with a cozy cushioned window seat and a mixture of modern and antique furnishings.

The six commodious guest rooms have been beautifully decorated with simple but endearing country-style furnishings, including antique pine pieces, handworked patchwork quilts, and baskets. Light gray walls, white trim, and stylish plantation shutters lend a contemporary touch. The two-room Susan B. Anthony Suite boasts a private sunporch overlooking the garden; Ellen's Garden Room, secluded below the home, features a private garden entrance and an oversize tub; and the large Diplomat's Suite, handsomely decorated in gray and dark blue, comes with a lovely four-poster bed. A private front porch entrance leads to the two-room Senator's Chambers, a perfect place for those wanting to sit and watch the world go by. In the larger room of this suite you'll find hardwood floors, delightful country knickknacks, a beautiful four-poster king-size pine bed covered with white linens, and a rather odd sunporch, which offers no access but does present guests with a lovely rocking chair and teddy bear display to view. A clawfoot tub awaits in the pretty, countrified private bath.

A full country breakfast is served in the dining room, but we suggest you take your trays to a secluded spot in the terraced garden. This is a wonderful place to spend some affectionate time together planning the rest of the day. **449 Broad Street; (530) 265-4660; www.nevadacityinns.com/grand mere.htm; moderate to very expensive; minimum-stay requirement on weekends and holidays seasonally; recommended wedding site.**

❧❧ **RED CASTLE HISTORIC LODGINGS, Nevada City** Tucked into a forested hillside above Nevada City, this imposing four-story red-brick mansion with wraparound verandas and intricate white trim offers guests a chance to step back in history. Everything about this Gothic Revival home (one of only a few on the West Coast) is designed to make you feel as if you live in the Victorian era, from the stately antiques decorating every inch of space, to the afternoon teas served in the parlor, to the absence of telephones, TVs, and alarm clocks. Only the ticking of the grandfather clock echoes from the hallway. After a few minutes here, you might just start believing you are in the 1800s.

We must warn you, when visiting this inn, not to arrive before the designated check-in time. Several notes by the front door, not to mention a small clock, remind guests what time they're welcome. Once ushered inside (at the correct time, of course), you are immediately enveloped by Victorian opulence. Deep-colored walls, lace curtains fronted by heavy draperies, overlapping floral patterns, chandeliers, and magnificent ornate mirrors set the mood. Keeping in character with typical Victorian homes, many of the rooms are very dark, even during the day. Luckily, ample antique lights help brighten up the scene.

Of the seven guest rooms, the more spacious ones on the entry level are recommended despite their proximity to the front door and parlor. All three entry-level rooms feature queen-size beds, high ceilings, and private en suite bathrooms with antique or antique reproduction fixtures. Each of these rooms also has access to a semiprivate patio or porch. Vintage antiques and ornate wallpapers, chandeliers, French doors, and four-poster or canopy beds provide Victorian charm at every turn. Of all the rooms, we especially liked the Forest View Room, a private little hideaway on the ground level. A centerpiece claw-foot tub, a canopy bed with a dimming chandelier above, and your own private veranda make this place prime kissing territory. On the more unusual side, its bathroom features a unique toilet and shower combination in which both facilities share one space (a curtain separates the two, but they share the same tiled floor). Such a setup is common in Europe but seldom seen here. As for the remaining three rooms, the two middle-level ones are much too small to be considered comfortable. On the top floor, the two-bedroom Garret Suite has a detached bathroom down a short flight of stairs, which doesn't make it preferable for romantic interludes.

A five-course lavish breakfast, featuring all sorts of goodies from a savory tomato, onion, and Gruyère tart to a sweet tarte Tatin, is served buffet-style in the entry-level foyer. Guests are welcome to savor breakfast privately in their room or on the veranda, or to find a secluded spot near the garden fountain. With half an acre of lovely terraced gardens here, finding an intimate site shouldn't be difficult. **109 Prospect Street; (530) 265-5135, (800) 761-4766; www.innsofthegoldcountry.com/red.htm; moderate to expensive; minimum-stay requirement on weekends seasonally.**

Romantic Suggestion: On this hillside, you are far enough away to escape the rush of busy little Nevada City (although you might hear some freeway noise during the day). If you are in the mood to explore the area, a winding pathway leads through trees and greenery to the town below. It is only about a five-minute walk, and since the path is well lit at night you may even want to walk to dinner.

Restaurant Kissing

❦❦❦ **CITRONÉE, Nevada City** Citronée, one of the top restaurants in the area, offers diners a choice in mood-setting decors. Whether you have a taste for a casual lunch or an intimate candlelit dinner, this downtown restaurant delivers—along with some of the tastiest food this side of the Sierras. The front, street-facing dining room is best described as Tuscan chic. Textured butter-colored walls are adorned with framed posters, blond wood tables and chairs top tiled floors, and a long bar, offset by a brilliant floral display, commands the space on one side of the window-filled room. This is the perfect place to enjoy lunch, especially on a glorious sunny day. Those who want to hit the mother lode when it comes to romance should make their way to the back dining room. Rough-hewn beams, a wood-planked ceiling, and aged brick walls give the sense of descending into a gold mine. Luckily, little tea candles, modern artwork illuminated by halogen lamps, and white linen–covered tables contribute softness and elegance to the cozy, rustic space.

Citronée may reside in a small town, but its menu spans the world. The sea bass with wasabi mashed potatoes and caramelized lemongrass sauce is superb, as is the stuffed pork chop filled with mushroom duxelles served over polenta. Other interesting entrées worth ordering are braised garlic short ribs or vegetarian phyllo purses filled with wild mushrooms and baby spinach. The desserts don't rate high on originality or selection, but that didn't prevent us from quickly consuming the cream-filled profiteroles covered in chocolate sauce and accompanied by vanilla ice cream. **320 Broad Street; (530) 265-5697; expensive; lunch Monday–Friday, dinner Monday–Saturday.**

☙☙ **THE COUNTRY ROSE CAFE, Nevada City** Historic brick buildings abound in these little gold-rush towns, and one of them houses the very charming Country Rose Cafe. High ceilings, exposed-brick walls, floral table linens, and carved oak chairs create a casual, countrified setting; high-backed booths along one wall provide a small amount of privacy. On a summer day, try to secure a table on the shady deck. Lunch consists of soups, sandwiches, and salads, while dinner offers a hearty variety of French-influenced fare, from five types of raviolis to *poulet Escoffier* to roast game hen with jalapeño-tequila sauce. The menu changes daily and is plainly presented on a write-on/wipe-off board. Service is friendly but rushed at times due to the cafe's popularity. **300 Commercial Street; (530) 265-6252, (530) 265-6248; moderate to expensive; lunch and dinner daily, brunch Sunday.**

☙☙ **KIRBY'S CREEKSIDE RESTAURANT AND BAR, Nevada City** Kirby's could definitely be classified as more casual than romantic, but once you are seated on the pleasant creekside patio you will probably forgive all the informality and just enjoy the setting. Leafy oaks and lush greenery trim the deck that resides just a few feet above the clear creek. The rushing water drowns out most of the traffic noise from the nearby bridge. Indoors, stake your claim at one of the booths along the walls or, on chilly nights, by the gas fireplace. Little brass lamps embedded in rock adorn every table, and recessed lighting overhead creates just the right glow.

A variety of pasta, meat, and seafood dishes are available, but we recommend ordering one of the chef's culinary adventures. Available in three-, four-, five-, or six-course options, these dinners showcase the best the kitchen produces. Try the delicious crusted shrimp with lemongrass glaze or the seared duck breast adorned with a sun-dried cherry sauce. Portions are generous, and service is small-town friendly. **101 Broad Street; (530) 265-3445; moderate to expensive; lunch Monday–Saturday, dinner daily, brunch Sunday.**

Outdoor Kissing

❤❤❤ **INDEPENDENCE TRAIL, Nevada City** In this dry and dusty region, you may find yourselves searching for water, and not just for drinking purposes. Independence Trail leads to waterfalls and pools that will quench your desire to be near refreshing, clear blue water. This wheelchair-accessible trail is paved and extremely well maintained. Depending on your pace, the walk takes about an hour round-trip. *From Nevada City, travel north on Highway 49. The trailhead is on the right, just before a sharp bend in the road and a large bridge crossing the South Yuba River.*

Grass Valley

Grass Valley was the most heavily mined area in the northern section of Gold Country, and that working-town feel still remains today. There are some charming little shops, a few good restaurants, and some stately Victorian homes worth admiring. The folks who live here will make you feel welcome and comfortable.

Hotel/Bed and Breakfast Kissing

❤❤ **MURPHY'S INN, Grass Valley** Manicured ivy and lovely gardens trim this opulent estate, built in 1866 by one of Gold Country's most successful mine owners as a wedding present for his wife. A hammock swings lazily in the breeze between two trees on the lovely grounds near a gently trickling water fountain. Inside, brightly colored modern carpeting and visible TVs contrast sharply with the otherwise old-fashioned Victorian mood of the six guest rooms in the main house. White lace curtains, floral wallpapers, and canopy or four-poster beds are authentic, though the entire decor is somewhat mismatched. Two rooms have the added luxury of fireplaces, but if these rooms happen to be booked, you can seek out the two fireside sitting rooms on the main floor. Wherever you decide to relax, there are enough common areas to keep you from feeling crowded by other guests. The best seats in the house await on the deck or on the covered, wraparound porch in front. A full breakfast is served at two tables in the breakfast room. **318 Neal Street; (530) 273-6873, (800) 895-2488; www. murphysinn.com; moderate to expensive; minimum-stay requirement on weekends and holidays.**

Romantic Note: The Donation House, a separate Victorian home across the street, has two rooms, each with a fireplace and a private bath with a double-headed shower. One sports a queen-size bed; the other, a king. Families with children are encouraged to stay here, so unless you have to bring the kids along on your romantic getaway, ask for a room in the main house.

Restaurant Kissing

❦❦ **ARLETTA'S DINING ROOM AT THE HOLBROOKE HOTEL, Grass Valley** Step off the dusty trail and into this vintage hotel that looks and feels much as it did in the late 1850s, rowdy saloon and all. Tucked down the hall and just past the front desk, this old-fashioned restaurant is an elegant surprise. Several globe chandeliers hang from the high ceiling, green library lamps illuminate most of the wooden tables, and brick walls and archways make cozy alcoves for intimate dining. Plantation shutters and rotating displays of modern artwork contribute a modern-day touch to the scene. Seasonal menu offerings focus on American regional cuisine and might showcase classics such as "Not like mom's pot roast" or fancier fare, most noteworthy a fresh fettuccine mixed with asparagus, morel mushrooms, and roasted red peppers. Another favorite is the grilled tuna in a green curry sauce. The fine food is sure to delight, but try to save room for the dessert, as the menu quite boldly suggests. Homemade apple pie à la mode, one of the many daily dessert choices, is sure to inspire some sweet kisses later on. **212 West Main Street, at The Holbrook Hotel; (530) 273-1353, (800) 933-7077; www.holbrooke.com; moderate; lunch and dinner daily, brunch Sunday.**

Romantic Note: The historic HOLBROOKE HOTEL (inexpensive to expensive) has a variety of antiquated and timeworn rooms upstairs, but we don't recommend them for a romantic encounter. Legendary individuals such as Mark Twain and Ulysses S. Grant supposedly stayed here, but if their rooms were anywhere near the noisy saloon on the main floor, they certainly didn't sleep well.

Coloma

Ensconced in the wooded section of the American River canyon, the tiny town of Coloma is actually part of a 275-acre park formally known as **MARSHALL GOLD DISCOVERY STATE HISTORIC PARK** (310 Back Street, P.O. Box 265, Coloma, CA 95613; 530-622-3470; www.isgnet.com/coloma; $5 entrance fee per vehicle, $2 walk-in entrance fee per person). With a population of around 175, Coloma hasn't changed much since its prime in the 1850s as a gold-rush town. You can find the local tinsmith and blacksmith hard at work in their workshops, or hopeful visitors panning for gold in the south fork of the American River. While the dry, rural scenery here is spectacular and hosts an abundance of outdoor adventure opportunities, keep in mind that the town of Coloma tends to gear itself toward tour groups, which are (needless to say) *never* romantic. To avoid getting swept away by the crowds during your visit here, we recommend checking into the **COLOMA COUNTRY INN** (see Hotel/Bed and Breakfast Kissing).

Hotel/Bed and Breakfast Kissing

❀❀❀ **COLOMA COUNTRY INN, Coloma** Five acres of quiet country surround this picturesque gray and white clapboard-style farmhouse and Carriage House, hemmed in by flower gardens and a white picket fence. Domestic chickens run freely through the yard, a small wishing well awaits your most romantic wishes, and a rope swing, suspended from a high bough, swings right out over a small duck pond.

Hands-on service is a focal point here. In the afternoon, fresh lemonade and iced tea are served in the gazebo, and baskets are provided for guests who want to hand-pick local berries. In the morning a breakfast of home-baked breads, seasonal fruits, and hearty granola is served in the formal dining room or, on especially warm days, outside under the pergola overlooking the pond.

Although all seven guest rooms are comfortable places to call home for an evening or two, the Carriage House's Geranium Suite struck our hearts as being the most romantic. Set back from the main house and enveloped by gardens, the 1898 Carriage House has a storybook appearance, with window boxes, flower-covered trellises, and an antique weather vane. With its private kitchenette, white-wood queen-size bed, and French doors that open onto a charming garden patio, the Geranium Suite is designed for couples who want quiet time alone together. Couples traveling together will appreciate the Carriage House's other room, the Cottage Suite, which features two bedrooms and a sitting room. These rooms are nicely appointed with French-country antiques, floral fabrics and linens, and abundant charm. In the main farmhouse, handmade quilts, country art, and American antiques lend a homespun flavor to most of the rooms. We especially like the light and bright Lavender Room with its quilt-covered queen-size bed and claw-foot tub in the private bathroom. Some rooms in the main house share a hallway bathroom and some have tiny double beds, so be sure to specify your preferences when making reservations. **345 High Street; (530) 622-6919; www.colomacountryinn.com; inexpensive to very expensive; no credit cards; minimum-stay requirement on holidays.**

Romantic Note: Though many are drawn to the Coloma Country Inn because of its picturesque, serene setting, many more arrive looking for adventures. Hot-air balloon rides, white-water rafting trips, hikes, and, of course, gold-panning expeditions can be incorporated into your stay. Indicate which adventures interest you most when booking your reservation.

Plymouth

Plymouth is best known as the gateway to the Shenandoah Valley: wine country paradise. Acres upon acres of well-tended vineyards grace the sloping Sierra Nevada foothills, creating a wondrous setting for bed and breakfasts and award-winning wineries, not to mention kissing.

Hotel/Bed and Breakfast Kissing

❤❦ **AMADOR HARVEST INN, Plymouth** Nestled between the vineyards in the heart of the Shenandoah Valley, this picturesque East Coast–style bed and breakfast offers one of the most stunning settings in Gold Country. A massive black walnut tree, set among the sprawling manicured lawns, partially embraces the gray and white home. Just below the inn, a fully stocked lake (catch-and-release only) awaits, bordered by weeping willows, stately oaks, and hilly vineyards. Plus, for those interested in wine, **DEAVER VINEYARDS** (209-245-4099; www.deavervineyard.com; open 11 A.M.– 5 P.M. daily) has a tasting room on-site, and numerous other wineries are within a grape's throw. For those interested in sips, this is your place. As for people interested in lips, well, there are some kissing possibilities here as well.

The inn's four guest rooms, located upstairs, are of the standard variety: clean, comfortable, and simply decorated with oak furnishings, rocking chairs, and a painting here and there. The smallest room, Chardonnay, is our favorite because it has an en suite bathroom and accesses a shared deck with million-dollar views. For more space, book the Zinfandel Suite, complete with a king-size bed and private bathroom. (One guest room has a bath down the hall.) Amador Harvest Inn's rooms may not inspire gushes of romantic thoughts, but the surroundings certainly will. This is the perfect setting for romancing the day away at local wineries or beneath a tree by the lake.

A full breakfast is served in the dining room each morning. Come evening, take in spectacular views of the lake as you sit on the back porch and enjoy hors d'oeuvres. **12455 Steiner Road; (209) 245-5512, (800) 217-2304; www.amadorharvestinn.com; inexpensive to moderate; minimum-stay requirement on weekends.**

Romantic Note: Peace and quiet are guaranteed at this bucolic bed and breakfast, whose motto is "the loudest noise you're likely to hear is a frog croaking or a cork popping." However, such celestial solitude means that modern conveniences, such as restaurants and local shops, are a 25- or 35-minute drive along country roads and Highway 49.

❦❦❦❦ **INDIAN CREEK BED AND BREAKFAST, Plymouth** The romance of the Old West is alive and well in the Gold Country, especially if you stay at this charming bed and breakfast. Built in 1932 by a Hollywood producer, this refined two-story log house is sequestered on the edge of ten acres of woodland. Endowed with a wonderful bucolic elegance, the home's interior has been masterfully crafted, with pine walls and Douglas fir floors. A two-and-a-half-story fireplace constructed of quartz warms the large living room, where Hollywood's select were entertained in the 1930s and '40s. Today, green leather couches, Southwest-motif rugs and throw blankets, and Native American artwork and relics give the home an intriguing lodge-style flavor. A hallway leads to the back of the house, where swinging doors open into an authentic "cowboy bar" with tractor-seat bar stools and decorator ropes, halters, and boots. "It's never too late to become a cowboy," claim the owners. Apparently not.

A wooden staircase climbs to a manzanita-wood balcony overlooking the living room, and to four upstairs guest rooms, all of which have queen-size beds, private bathrooms, and air-conditioning. A hand-painted wood floor and a mural of birch trees decorate the Margaret Breen Room, which also features a four-poster pine bed, dimming lights, a fireplace, and French doors that open to a private wraparound deck. Horseshoes are welded to an antique-iron bed draped with a denim duvet in the Way Out West Room, while a saddle adds that definitive western touch. This corner room also sports a long bathtub for soaking, a cozy reading alcove to curl up in together, and a private balcony and patio for savoring your morning brew in peace and quiet. Though it is the smallest and least expensive, the Indian Summer Room is attractive, with sponge-painted walls and a wrought-iron demi-canopy bed. The Dances with Wolves Room features wolf pictures and horse-patterned linens. A beautiful pine ceiling offsets the textured walls, which display Native American art and artifact replicas.

Afternoon beverages are included with your stay and in the morning a full gourmet breakfast awaits in the ranch-style dining room. Fresh fruits and smoothies, egg baskets (similar to eggs Benedict, but better), salsa omelets, stuffed French toast with berries, and all sorts of baked goodies will have you off your diet in no time.

During the day, guests can lounge by the outdoor pool and Jacuzzi tub, sway in a creekside hammock, or walk along the seasonal creek that (nine months out of the year) purls through Indian Creek's ten wooded acres and is home to trout, otters, and frogs. The large, covered front porch, adorned with lounge chairs, is the perfect perch from which to watch the feathered ones, most notably wild turkeys, quail families, and dozens of hummingbirds. Last, but not least, there's a gold mine on the property, although it's barricaded for safety purposes. But that's OK, since Indian Creek Bed and Breakfast is a treasure in itself. **21950 Highway 49; (209) 245-4648; www.indiancreek.com; moderate to expensive; minimum-stay requirement.**

Shenandoah Valley

For a closer look at the beautiful Shenandoah Valley, take a day or two and tour the host of wineries here, set in the gently sloping Sierra foothills. Many of the wineries offer sublime views of the countryside in addition to tastes of the superb, award-winning local wines. Although most of the wineries are worth visiting, the list below reflects our particular favorites. For more information, contact **AMADOR VINTNERS** (P.O. Box 667, Plymouth, CA 95669; 209-267-2297; www.amadorwine.com).

Wine Kissing

❀❀ **AMADOR FOOTHILL WINERY, Plymouth** Perched high on a hillside, the Amador Foothill Winery offers exquisite views of the orchards, vineyards, and shimmering lakes in the valley below. This entire scene is offset by the distant Sierras, which are snowcapped in the winter and spring. The view and the award-winning zinfandel and fumé blanc are what draw visitors to this winery. Unfortunately, the sun-drenched picnic tables, where you can survey the pastoral scenery, are situated in front of unattractive wine-making equipment. Just face eastward and try ignoring the equipment strewn about the place. **12500 Steiner Road; (209) 245-6307, (800) 778-WINE; www.amadorfoothill.com; open noon–5 p.m. Friday–Sunday and most holidays.**

❧❧ **KARLY, Plymouth** A long, winding, and dusty drive past sprawling oaks and rows of grapevines brings you to Karly's beautifully landscaped winery. Views of the surrounding country are almost as delicious as Karly's robust zinfandels. There is only one picnic table set within a sunny courtyard, so seating choices are slim. **11076 Bell Road; (209) 245-3922, (800) 654-0880; open noon–4 p.m. daily.**

❧❧ **SHENANDOAH VINEYARDS, Plymouth** Partake of classic vintages while you browse in the contemporary art and ceramics gallery set among the wine barrels. On sunny days, admire views of the vineyards from cozy picnic tables situated beneath a grove of trees. **12300 Steiner Road; (209) 245-4455; www.sobonwine.com; open 10 a.m.–5 p.m. daily.**

❧❧❧ **STORY WINERY, Plymouth** The Story Winery is more like a fairy tale. Far off the beaten path, this family-operated winery takes pride in its vineyards, which are more than 50 years old and continue to produce extraordinary vintages. Sip wine to your hearts' content as you bask in the visual splendor of the gorgeous Cosumnes River canyon. Plenty of picnic tables nicely spaced apart under the oaks make this our favorite choice for a picnic with a view. **10525 Bell Road; (209) 245-6208, (800) 713-6390; www.zin.com; open noon–4 p.m. Monday–Friday and 11 a.m.–5 p.m. on weekends.**

❧❧❧ **YOUNG'S VINEYARDS, Plymouth** By far the most picture-perfect setting around, Young's Vineyard delights those seeking the beauty of flowers, manicured lawns, and sprawling vineyards as they sip their favorite vintage. The tasting room, housed inside a renovated barn, is surrounded by California poppies, blooming roses, and other flowering delights. Journey down the gravel pathway to the stone fence that encloses a sprawling lawn. Two picnic tables beneath the oaks let you sit in the shade and admire the nearby pond. **10120 Shenandoah Road; (209) 245-3005; open 10:30 a.m.–5 p.m. Saturday–Sunday.**

Amador City

Restaurant Kissing

❧❧❧ **IMPERIAL HOTEL RESTAURANT, Amador City** Though you can't elude the past anywhere in Gold Country, the Imperial Hotel is one of the few places that encourages you to feel at home in the present. The brick interior of this gold-rush mercantile establishment turned hotel lends warmth to the airy dining room, which is enhanced by high ceilings and elaborate local artwork that's bound to bring out the critic in you. The linen-covered tables come embellished with fresh flowers, and sunflowers adorn the hanging lamps. If you enjoy fresh-air dining, sit outside under Japanese lanterns on a charming patio made of native stone, surrounded by plants, flowers, and a murmuring fountain.

Ambience isn't the only thing the Imperial does right—the food here is heavenly. The menu changes seasonally, so everything is as fresh as possible. Portobello mushrooms stuffed with spinach and blue cheese atop garlic mashed potatoes is one succulent choice, as is filet mignon served with a porcini mushroom butter. (This is a dish visitors return for time and time again.) More on the hit-and-miss side is the thick, somewhat heavy, breadcrumb-encased pork loin surrounded by a tart cherry sauce. Entrées come with soup or salad and can be ordered in full- or half-size portions, the latter being a smart choice if you also plan on choosing a decadent slice of chocolate torte or the Grand Marnier crème brûlée. **14202 Highway 49, at the Imperial Hotel; (209) 267-9172, (800) 242-5594; www. imperialamador.com; moderate to expensive; dinner daily.**

Romantic Note: The **IMPERIAL HOTEL** (inexpensive to moderate) offers six upstairs guest rooms. However, due to the hotel's location smack dab along Highway 49, they are difficult to wholeheartedly recommend for a quiet romantic evening. The nicely restored rooms come complete with brick interiors, hardwood floors, Oriental carpets, colorful art pieces, and an eclectic mix of furnishings. All rooms here have private baths, air-conditioning, and reasonable price tags (even on weekends and holidays), so they're worth knowing about if you're traveling on a budget.

Sutter Creek

Set in the golden velvet folds of the surrounding hills, the former gold-rush town of Sutter Creek has retained its whitewashed overhanging balconies, balustrades, and western-style storefronts. Boardwalks hemmed with antique shops, gift boutiques, and casual cafés invite a relaxing stroll together.

Romantic Warning: All the inns and bed and breakfasts listed in this section face Highway 49, so traffic noise can be a disruption. Either bring earplugs or request a room as far back from the road as possible. Luckily, traffic dies down after 10 P.M., but picks up again quite early.

Hotel/Bed and Breakfast Kissing

❀❀❀ **THE FOXES BED AND BREAKFAST IN SUTTER CREEK, Sutter Creek** This beautifully restored 1857 New England–style farmhouse is one of the best finds in Gold Country. Set in the heart of Sutter Creek, the Foxes Bed and Breakfast is tucked far enough away from the road to ensure privacy, but is centrally located so guests can walk to restaurants, shops, or the theater. A shaded garden, pocketed with places to sit and smooch, surrounds the house, and a bubbling fountain keeps the ears occupied. Simple country and Victorian furnishings throughout the inn are elegant and set about with a designer's touch. In the large country kitchen, polished silver tea sets gleam in the sunlight, hinting at the lovely gourmet breakfasts delivered to your room each morning. Unlike other bed and breakfasts, meals here are cooked to order, so you will have several dishes to choose from.

Walk through a private garden entrance to the spacious Honeymoon Suite, which features an antique claw-foot tub and a half-canopy bed warmed by a wood-burning fireplace. (Wood fires also crackle in the hearths of three other rooms, including the cozy private library in the Fox Den and in the two-room Hideaway Suite.) The two upstairs suites in the main home—the Anniversary Suite and Victorian Suite—are especially appealing for lovebirds. Even if it's not your special day, we recommend inventing a celebration in order to claim the Anniversary Suite as your own. A magnificently carved nine-foot-tall headboard and equally astounding dresser and armoire take center stage in the light, window-filled room with vaulted ceilings. A claw-foot tub set windowside lets you soak as you view the gardens below. Unfortunately, this room faces the street, so traffic noise might be a problem. A quieter option is across the hall in the Victorian Suite, a handsome room done up in the soft, warm colors of fall. This suite offers cuddling couples a queen-size bed fronting a gas fireplace. The tiled, sun-filled bathroom features a step-up claw-foot tub, a walk-in shower, two comfortable robes, and dimming lights throughout. The inn's other rooms are located at the back of the house and are sheltered from direct street noise. Regardless where you stay, each of the seven rooms is spotless, spacious, and lovingly decorated. Some common touches include silk flowers, a mix of elegant antiques, light-filled modern bathrooms, leather or wicker chairs, and beautifully set tables where breakfast is served at the hour you request. An ample selection of CDs and videos is available to rooms equipped with TV/VCR and/or stereo systems. **77 Main Street (Highway 49); (209) 267-5882, (800) 987-3344; www.foxesinn.com; moderate to very expensive; minimum-stay requirement on weekends and holidays.**

❦❦❦ **GREY GABLES INN, Sutter Creek** A dash of the English country-side has been transplanted to Gold Country in the form of the Grey Gables Inn. This sprawling gray and white Victorian, encircled by flowering gardens, sits along Highway 49 just outside Sutter Creek's town center. Comforts such as private baths, air-conditioning, and gas-log fireplaces are found in the eight delightful rooms, each named after an English poet. As an extra touch, a poem composed by the room's namesake is beautifully framed above the fireplace. The very elegant Byron Room has light mauve walls, hunter green appointments, and rich mahogany furnishings. Country Victorian antiques beautify the Browning Room, with its brass bed, lace curtains, and claw-foot tub. Tucked away on the inn's top floor is the pretty Victorian Suite, with arched ceilings, soft pink walls, lace curtains, and a claw-foot tub. Windows in all of these picture-perfect rooms are quite soundproof, so road noise should not be a problem despite the inn's proximity to the main road.

In proper British tradition, afternoon tea is presented daily by the English innkeepers, and wine and hors d'oeuvres are served in the formal parlor each evening. At breakfast, fine china and complete silver service enhance a satisfying gourmet meal. Four tables are set up in the dining room, so you may be able to secure a table for two; if you want to ensure privacy, you can request that breakfast be delivered to your room. It is options like these that make an establishment truly romantic. **161 Hanford Street (Highway 49); (209) 267-1039, (800) 473-9422; www.grey gables.com; moderate to expensive; minimum-stay requirement on weekends.**

❦❦❦ **THE HANFORD HOUSE, Sutter Creek** As you drive southbound into Sutter Creek, you can't help admiring The Hanford House's beautiful brick building. Wrapped in a coat of ivy, the historical building radiates charm both inside and out. California pine furnishings; country antiques; high ceilings; and colors of peach, sage, and taupe lend an air of clean spaciousness to each simply decorated room. Of the six guest rooms and three suites, our two favorites are the most expensive (but still reasonably priced) and the most spacious: the Gallery Suite and the adjacent Gold Country Escape. A gorgeous cherrywood king-size canopy bed bedecked with white draperies and warm blue linens welcomes you in the Gallery Suite, which also has a fireplace, a comfortable seating area, and plenty of room for falling in love. Romantics will appreciate the two-person Jacuzzi tub and private sundeck in the Gold Country Escape, not to mention the beautiful pewter and brass queen-size bed surrounded by ivory drapes and covered by tapestried linens. Dimming rose-hued lights in both suites help set an amorous mood, and their tucked-away, upstairs location ensures the utmost privacy. If you stay in the suites, hot morning beverages, home-baked treats, and a newspaper are brought to your door before breakfast. Although both these rooms are close to perfect, they do front Highway 49, so light sleepers should take note.

Even if you opt for one of the other rooms, you'll find plenty of space in each for ample kissing, plus pleasantly decorated surroundings, private baths, Ralph Lauren linens, and fluffy robes. Baked goods and coffee are set out in the common hallway prior to breakfast. For outdoor kissing, head upward to the sunny redwood deck overlooking town rooftops and the oak-knobbed hills, or relax on the sun-dappled patio on the west side of the inn. A full breakfast is served in the cheerful breakfast room, where guests have left their names and appreciative comments on every inch of the walls and ceiling. (Definitely different, but guests seem to think it's a fun touch.) Savor such treats as vegetable quiche, basil crêpes with creamy eggs, or fruit-topped Belgian waffles, all of which incorporate organic and/or local products. If you get hungry later on (which is highly unlikely after such a feast), venture to the guest pantry where you'll find such goodies as low-fat biscotti, specialty iced teas and lemonades, and a carafe of wine. **61 Hanford Street (Highway 49); (209) 267-0747, (800) 871-5839; www. hanfordhouse.com; inexpensive to expensive; minimum-stay requirement on weekends for suites.**

Restaurant Kissing

❀❀ **SUSAN'S PLACE WINE BAR AND EATERY, Sutter Creek** Casual yet charming, this bistro is nestled in the back of the lively Eureka Street outdoor courtyard, which adjoins gift shops and several other restaurants. Enjoy the open air at one of the picnic tables with purple umbrellas and gingham tablecloths or, if you prefer more privacy, eat inside where wine bottles surround you and the scent of freshly baked goods wafts through the country-style dining room. Consider a create-your-own wine and cheese board, which includes samples of wine, cheese, pâtés, and meats, served with an array of vegetables. If that's not ample enough, try the interesting mix-and-match menu. You choose a main course—the catch of the day, chicken, Black Angus steak, pork tenderloin, or vegetable—and then select an accompanying sauce, such as orange-ginger teriyaki, garlic honey mustard, or Southwestern salsa. A soup or salad and your choice of side dish comes along, too. A hearty appetite and a taste for variety are prerequisites for dining here. **15 Eureka Street; (209) 267-0945; inexpensive to moderate; lunch Wednesday–Sunday, dinner Wednesday–Saturday.**

❀❀ **SUTTER CREEK PALACE RESTAURANT AND SALOON, Sutter Creek** Finding a restaurant that combines the flair of the Old West with a sprinkling of romance is a bit like looking for gold—it's difficult to find, but not impossible. Luckily, there's one restaurant that sports an authentic gold-rush atmosphere and still sparkles with romance: the Sutter Creek Palace.

This downtown establishment has been a restaurant and saloon since the days when gold miners sat at the stools and ladies weren't allowed in the bar. A real, honest-to-goodness saloon and modern piano bar are first to catch your eye. If you're more interesting in blowing kisses than blowing suds off beer, venture farther back to the cozier adjoining restaurant. Decorated in an old-fashioned country theme, the restaurant's back dining room is prime smooching territory. A handful of tables, bedecked with thick tapestried linens, fancy folded napkins, and flickering lamp-like candles, all front an old-fashioned stove, perfect for wintertime dining. In the heat of the summer, gravitate to the tiny backyard patio where five tables are spaced far enough apart to ensure privacy. On a warm evening, mist-makers refresh you, and small lights and tiki torches cast a perfect glow. There's even a bubbling mermaid fountain designed to cover up traffic noise. We highly recommend the back room of the restaurant and the backyard patio; the two front dining rooms are nicely decorated in an Old West theme, but saloon noise is very distracting. Luckily, specific tables can be reserved, so call ahead.

The straightforward steak-pasta-chicken-seafood menu is well liked by both visitors and locals, many of whom flock here on the weekend when prime rib is on special. We tried the mild-tasting red snapper Santa Fe, topped with green chiles and roasted red peppers in a cream sauce, and the pepper steak accompanied by a brandy-mushroom sauce. Both were nearly perfect. The kitchen's got its pastas down pat too, including a wild mushroom fettuccine and traditional spaghetti carbonara. Since this is wine country, end dinner with some local flavor. A slice of cheesecake topped with your choice of raspberry-chocolate pinot noir sauce or a coffee-merlot chocolate sauce is the perfect finale. If that's not enough, order a glass of the house wine, so reasonably priced you won't believe you're in California. **76 Main Street; (209) 267-1300; moderate to expensive; lunch and dinner Friday–Tuesday.**

❀❀ **ZINFANDELS AT SUTTER CREEK, Sutter Creek** Set smack-dab on the edge of Highway 49, this blue and white country farmhouse really belongs out in the country amid trees and lush foliage. Despite the misplaced surroundings, Zinfandels is worth visiting while you're in Gold Country. The house's original living areas have been transformed into intimate dining rooms, where wax-covered empty zinfandel bottles serve as candleholders and clusters of grapes and grape leaves accent the table-cloths and curtains. The adept kitchen regularly amazes diners and has won regular patrons over with the grilled polenta appetizer topped with assorted mushrooms, roasted sweet red peppers, and fresh herbs and cream. In fact, the polenta is such a popular item that it is the only fixture on the ever-changing menu. You'll also find pastas, risottos, and entrées such as the catch of the day topped with a citrus ginger sauce; filet mignon mari-nated in red wine, rosemary, and garlic; and lemon-pepper linguine with wild mushrooms and roasted garlic cloves. Certainly, any of these dishes would go well with a glass of the restaurant's namesake. **51 Hanford Street (Highway 49); (209) 267-5008; moderate to expensive; reservations recommended; dinner Thursday–Sunday.**

Ione

Outdoor Kissing

❧❧❧ **SUTTER CREEK–IONE ROAD, Ione** Those interested in exploring Ione's enchanting countryside can veer off the highway and take the road less traveled. This backcountry road winds for ten miles through velvety rolling hills and valleys speckled with venerable oaks and grazing cattle. Every season imparts a beauty of its own: Autumn leaves heighten the al-ready bronzed landscape, winter brings rain (when there isn't a drought) and turns the hillsides a delicious green, and wildflowers dab color everywhere in the spring and summer. Be sure to stop along the way and share a kiss among this natural splendor. *From Ione's Main Street, turn east onto Preston, then right onto Highway 24. Watch for signs to Sutter Creek–Ione Road.*

Wine Kissing

❧❧❧ **CLOS DU LAC CELLARS/GREENSTONE WINERY, Ione** The set-ting of this majestic winery is as beguiling as its award-winning vintages. A long drive rambles over vineyard-laden hills, past a duck pond, to a stately stone structure that looks like a French country manor. In the modern tast-ing room, sunlight pours through multipaned windows set high near the cathedral ceiling, casting a golden glow over the wood paneling. Outside, picnic tables set in natural greenstone outcroppings and shaded by old oak trees overlook Eden-like fields and Bacchus Pond. Beyond them is a stretch of Miwok Indian land. Complete this dreamy vision with a picnic lunch and a bottle of the winery's finest. **3151 Highway 88, at Jackson Valley Road; (209) 274-2238; open 10 a.m.–4 p.m. Wednesday–Sunday.**

Lodi

The trick to finding Lodi and having a nice outing along the way is to enter from the west side of town via Turner Road, so you drive past farmland and acres of vineyards before hitting the main part of town. Lodi is a rich agricultural area, not a tourist town or a romantic destination. However, one establishment here specializes in matters of the heart. If you're headed to **WINE AND ROSES COUNTRY INN** (see Hotel/Bed and Breakfast Kissing), you won't be disappointed.

Hotel/Bed and Breakfast Kissing

❧❧❧ **WINE AND ROSES COUNTRY INN, Lodi** The name of this five-acre country estate is well suited, but falls short in its description. The grounds are replete with flowers of every imaginable color and kind: azaleas, impatiens, violets, daisies, and, of course, roses. Flowers are not the only thing blossoming here. Diamond engagement rings are frequently presented over filet mignon or rosemary lamb chops in the intimate country dining room. Proposals are a specialty at Wine and Roses Country Inn, as are the garden weddings that follow.

The Victorian farmhouse, which houses both the inn and restaurant, has been beautifully renovated and radiates fresh country charm. All ten guest rooms located on the first and second floors are equally engaging. Moonlight and Roses is one of the more romantic rooms, with deep burgundy carpet, a white brass bed, a sitting area surrounded by windows, and a claw-foot tub. White Lace and Promises is a lovely two-room honeymoon attic suite exulting in garden views from its own private terrace. It's the place to stay when you want to be completely alone together. Whichever room is yours, special touches, such as wine and cookies upon arrival, rose petals in the toilet (different, but nice), room service from the restaurant, and a cooked-to-order breakfast, make this a pleasant place to stay. The TVs in each room, a necessity for the midweek business clientele, can be removed upon request so as not to distract you from more affectionate activities. **2505 West Turner Road; (209) 334-6988; www.winerose.com; moderate to expensive; call for seasonal hours; recommended wedding site.**

Romantic Warning: Heavily trafficked West Turner Road runs adjacent to the inn. Although Wine and Roses is wonderfully sheltered by tall trees that hide views of the road, the whiz of cars during rush hour invades the otherwise tranquil country setting.

Romantic Suggestion: When planning a romantic lunch, dinner, or Sunday brunch at the restaurant (moderate to expensive), we urge you to call and confirm that it will be open during your stay or visit. Often, big weddings take over and the small restaurant closes to accommodate the party's needs. It would be a shame to miss a meal here, especially since Lodi isn't loaded with intimate dining options.

Jackson

As the Amador County seat in the heart of Gold Country, Jackson is home to most of the businesses in the area. It's not exactly a prime romantic destination; rather, it is where folks from surrounding towns do their shopping. This is great for provisions, but definitely not for maximizing moments together.

Hotel/Bed and Breakfast Kissing

❤❤ **GATE HOUSE INN, Jackson** Set deep in Jackson's residential countryside, the Gate House Inn is a truly quiet escape. Guests are encouraged to explore the colorful grounds (flower identification maps are provided), wander past the trickling water fountain, and enjoy a refreshing dip in the large (unheated) outdoor pool. Rosebushes trim the walkway leading up to the turn-of-the-century beige and green Victorian. Meticulous renovations have brought back to life the home's historic elegance, securing the inn a spot on the National Register of Historic Places. Beautiful antiques and impressive architectural touches provide intrigue and keep the eyes entertained. Oriental rugs in the dining room and entry hall accent the mahogany-inlaid oak parquet floors. In the living room, you'll find a French rosewood center table with a carved urn at its base, among other imposing antiques. Breakfast is served by candlelight in the formal parlor at one large antique dining table.

You're guaranteed to sleep well here—the owners have a penchant for angels and claim the inn is protected by them. A seven-foot angel ornaments the chimney's exterior, and guests who share the owners' passion will find the living room and dining room areas thoughtfully adorned with darling cherubs. Surprising as it may sound, the angel theme is not obvious throughout the inn's four guest rooms and additional cottage. Some of the rooms are plainer than others, but all of them are comfortable, with private baths, queen-size beds, and an interesting blend of antiques. The upstairs French Room is the most impressive, with its commanding views of the north garden and its Louis XIV bedroom set trimmed in gold. The first-floor Parlor Room sports an extra-long antique tub for extra-long soaks together. Secluded in the backyard, a renovated woodshed has been converted into the charming, self-contained Summer House. Rustic and cozy, the cottage features knotty cedar walls, a wood-burning stove, and a two-person Jacuzzi tub. It's a perfect spot to spend some quality time together. **1330 Jackson Gate Road; (209) 223-3500, (800) 841-1072; www.gate houseinn.com; moderate to expensive; minimum-stay requirement on holidays; recommended wedding site.**

❦❦ **THE WEDGEWOOD INN, Jackson** "Country" is the operative word at The Wedgewood Inn, set about eight miles outside downtown Jackson. Antiques and country artifacts fill the homey parlor and common rooms in this Victorian replica built to serve as a bed and breakfast. There's also a store overflowing with Victorian collectibles as well as an art gallery featuring the works of Thomas Kinkade. Breakfast is considered "conversational" and served in several courses on elegant china at one large table topped with candles. If you'd rather not engage in conversation with anyone except your sweetie, breakfast can be delivered to the larger guest rooms upon request. At any hour, guests can help themselves to complimentary beverages and microwave popcorn in the pantry. Other nice touches at The Wedgewood include chocolate truffles at turndown, mood-setting candles in some rooms, and a warm, toe-sniffing welcome by Wags, the four-legged cutie. When the weather is warm and beautiful (which is most of the time in Gold Country), take advantage of the paths that cover the carefully landscaped grounds. Walk through a rose arbor to a Victorian gazebo, a perfect place for kissing any time, day or night.

The six comfortable and spacious guest rooms, all of which have private baths, continue in the country-Victorian theme. Interesting antiques, vintage clothing and accessories, shelves filled with old and new books, black-and-white photographs, and family heirlooms abound. No empty space is neglected. In the Wedgewood Cameo Room, a family wedding dress is on display, and a white embroidered bedspread embellishes a hand-carved queen-size bed. There's also a private balcony and a double whirlpool tub set against a greenhouse-style window. At the top of the house, Granny's Attic lives up to its name with cozy peaked ceilings, a brick hearth, a handmade patchwork quilt, and a picture of the woman herself. The self-contained two-room Carriage House Suite adjacent to the inn offers the most space and seclusion, with its private entrance, sitting room, and enclosed patio overlooking the forest. Here, cathedral ceilings enhance a sense of space, floral-patterned embroidered linens drape a wooden bed, and a pink-tiled two-person whirlpool tub is embraced by a bright window alcove. Stepping into this suite, however, is much like entering a museum. A loft area displays a staged collection of children's toys, dozens of antique kitchen items reside on a vintage stove, and an assortment of dolls rest in a wooden case. There is so much for the eye to see here, it's overwhelming. We suggest closing your eyes while kissing. **11941 Narcissus Road; (209) 296-4300, (800) 933-4393; www.wedgewoodinn.com; moderate to expensive; minimum-stay on holiday weekends.**

Restaurant Kissing

❦❦ **UPSTAIRS RESTAURANT, Jackson** Hidden above a storefront in the heart of downtown Jackson, the Upstairs Restaurant is a small but appealing place for an evening out. Walk (you guessed it!) upstairs to the elongated and narrow dining room, bordered by windows on one side that peer out onto the roof next door. White and blue tablecloths topped with fresh flowers and oil lanterns cover a handful of Scandinavian-style tables, and local-flavored artwork dresses up the white cinder-block walls. (The art can be purchased if something particularly strikes your fancy.) Try snagging a two-person table by the street-facing window; they're the best suited for quiet conversation.

A vein of creativity runs strong through the restaurant's international menu. Bring a sense of adventure with you and try such specialties as coffee bean– and Szechuan peppercorn–encrusted steak, Caribbean-spiced catfish, or boneless duck breast that's grilled and topped with a fig and port sauce. Of course, there's also the run-of-the-mill entrées, such as New York steak, coconut shrimp, and pasta puttanesca for those who don't want to tempt their taste buds too much. The menu changes weekly, and nightly five-course dinners (with or without wine) will have adventurous gourmets thinking they've hit the mother lode. **164 Main Street; (209) 223-3342; expensive to very expensive; dinner daily.**

Romantic Note: Lunch is served in the downstairs dining room, which is too casual to be classified as romantic.

Murphys

"Above the fog and below the snow," as the locals say, sits the quaint little town of Murphys, at an elevation of 2,200 feet. As you ascend, pine trees become more prevalent and the air grows a bit cooler. Walk along the main street of town on raised wooden boardwalks, past buildings with western-style facades that now house boutiques, galleries, a historic saloon, several restaurants, and an ice cream shop. You'll feel like you've stepped back in time.

Romantic Suggestion: Ascend farther up Highway 4 to reach **BIG TREES STATE PARK**, where you can picnic or hike among giant sequoias.

Romantic Warning: Events are scheduled in Murphys almost every summer weekend, overloading this tiny community. On a busy weekend you might feel more like getting out of town.

Hotel/Bed and Breakfast Kissing

❤❤❤❤ **DUNBAR HOUSE, 1880, Murphys** Touted as the crown jewel of Gold Country, this 1880 Italianate Victorian is a sight to behold. A white picket fence and lovingly tended flower gardens envelop the home's expansive grassy yard, where hummingbirds flit above a water fountain and a large hammock swings beneath the trees. From the moment you cross the threshold of this country refuge, you will be indulged with old-fashioned hospitality and romance. Chocolate chip cookies, along with coffee, tea, and cocoa, are served in the dining room every afternoon. Breakfast is an affair to remember. (Hint: Bring your camera; you'll want to take a picture of the meal.) It is served at the time and place of your choosing, be it the dining room, your own room, or on the patio. Later in the day, plan a picnic for two. Dunbar House provides the basket, blanket, cooler, and even sun hats for a day touring the countryside.

Each of the four beautiful, countrified guest suites has a wood-burning stove, so you can warm yourselves as you toast each other with the complimentary bottle of wine affectionately provided by the innkeepers. Chocolates are left on your pillows at turndown service, and a welcome plate of appetizers awaits guests in every room upon arrival. Antiques, hardwood floors graced with Oriental carpets, and queen-size beds covered with lush down comforters add to the romantic climate. The pleasant Ponderosa Room, although less impressive than the other accommodations here, offers views of the gardens and a claw-foot tub in the bathroom. In the handsome Sequoia Room, settle into a bubble bath in the claw-foot tub set next to the woodstove. The Sugar Pine Room upstairs is beautifully adorned with country pine furnishings. Views from this second-story delight can be had from two vantage points: the claw-foot tub overlooking the garden and the charming little balcony residing just above the home's entryway. In the spacious Cedar Suite, commonly reserved by couples looking for a special romantic getaway, you can cuddle on the white brass bed in front of a warm woodstove, relax on your private sunporch in the late afternoon, or pamper yourselves in the two-person whirlpool bathtub surrounded by candlelight. There's also a private patio where you can enjoy the sounds of the burbling backyard fountain. This suite is adjacent to the dining room, which may prove bothersome if everyone else in the inn decides to eat an early breakfast there. However, during our stay we didn't find the location to be noisy at all. No matter which room is yours, you'll feel rejuvenated and romantically charged after spending time at this inn of inns. **271 Jones Street; (209) 728-2897, (800) 692-6006; www.dunbarhouse.com; expensive to very expensive; minimum-stay requirement on weekends.**

❀❀❀ **REDBUD INN, Murphys** Tucked away on a side street, the Redbud Inn provides romantic refuge in the heart of Murphys. This self-enclosed cedar-shingle inn with stone chimneys houses 12 guest rooms, each decorated in slightly different fashion but all wonderfully private and attractive. Many rooms hold folk-art pieces, others have antique furnishings, and some are done in a more contemporary style. Gold Fields, one of the smallest and least expensive rooms, has an intimate French-country atmosphere with warm saffron walls, hardwood floors, a colorful bedspread, and a claw-foot tub. In the Fireside Room, a two-person claw-foot tub in front of the fireplace helps heat things up. Snug Skyview, one of the smaller rooms, offers hardwood floors, a four-poster feather bed, and a small patio that faces a neighboring building (hence the name Skyview, since the only view from here is if you look up). The top-of-the-line Anniversary Suite, done in shades of peach, is equipped with a pool-size two-person spa tub, a double-sided wood-burning fireplace, and a wet bar. Also romantically appealing is the Wisteria, located in a separate building. A deep Roman soaking tub with built-in lounging chairs, a wood-burning fireplace, a private entrance, complimentary champagne, and abundant square footage contribute to the very expensive cost of this room but, then again, it is the most private. Be sure to ask about romantic amenities when booking any of the remaining rooms; several rooms have wood-burning fireplaces or antique stoves, some have whirlpool tubs for two, while others sport claw-foot tubs. All have balconies. Wine and hors d'oeuvres are served in the early evening, and a full breakfast is also included with your stay.

Overall, the Redbud Inn is a great value. When an inn offers rooms priced in the moderate range that are decorated just as nicely as the most expensive suites, we must congratulate the management. Check out the Redbud for yourselves; it's blooming with romantic possibilities. **402 Main Street; (209) 728-8533, (800) 827-8533; www.redbudinn.com; inexpensive to very expensive; minimum-stay requirement on weekends and holidays; recommended wedding site.**

Restaurant Kissing

❀❀ **GROUNDS, Murphys** Although Grounds is an extremely casual little restaurant, we found it quite charming and the food excellent. Pale hardwood floors with Turkish rugs, bare birch tables and chairs, modern art, and mirrors framed with salvaged barn wood give this dining room an open, airy, slightly contemporary feeling. There is a walk-up counter at the front of the restaurant if you are just stopping in for espresso, or you may choose to sit in the back dining room or on the outside patio. Morning pastries are rich and delicious, lunches are fresh and healthy, and dinners are some of the best in town. Our pasta creation, a mix of spinach, grilled chicken, and portobello mushrooms in a chardonnay–black pepper sauce, was finished in no time flat. Other pasta, steak, and seafood dishes line the small but flavorful menu. For dessert, indulge in the chocolate suicide cake. As our waitress put it, "It's rich, it's creamy, it's an oh-so-dreamy chocolate cake to die for." Well said. **402 Main Street; (209) 728-8663; inexpensive to moderate; breakfast and lunch daily, dinner Wednesday–Monday.**

Calaveras County

Welcome to a wine-growing region where getting to the winery is half the fun. If you have been to the Napa or Sonoma Valley and were most impressed with wineries located off the beaten path, you will love the Calaveras wine country. Although this is one of the oldest wine-growing regions in California, wineries here are ensconced in rural seclusion. These small establishments have a down-home warmth, but the vintners take a serious approach to wine-making. The following are some of our favorite wineries, where sipping and kissing make a wonderful combination.

Approximately seven wineries operate in the Murphys vicinity. For additional information, contact the **CALAVERAS WINE ASSOCIATION** (800-225-3764, ext. 25; www.calaveraswines.org) or the **CALAVERAS VISITORS BUREAU** (P.O. Box 637, Angels Camp, CA 95222; 800-225-3764; www.visitcalaveras.org).

Wine Kissing

❧❧ **CHATOM VINEYARDS, Douglas Flat** Lovely gardens and vineyards surround the Chatom Vineyards' unusual rammed-earth building. Picnic grounds allow you to soak in the beauty while tasting the flavors of the region. **1969 Highway 4; (209) 736-6500, (800) 435-8852; open 11 a.m.–5 p.m. daily.**

❧❧❧ **KAUTZ IRONSTONE VINEYARDS, Murphys** Colorful gardens lead to massive iron doors that open to the tasting room and gift shop of this impressive family-run facility. A massive stone fireplace marks the center of the room, and a cathedral ceiling caps the grand interior. A full gourmet deli (inexpensive; open daily) off to one side offers an impressive variety of salads, sandwiches, desserts, and fresh breads. Two-person picnics that include wine are affordably priced under $20. **1894 Six Mile Road; (209) 728-1251; www.ironstonevineyards.com; open 10 a.m.–6 p.m. daily.**

❤❤❤ **STEVENOT WINERY, Murphys** Stevenot Winery is a place to discover together. In the rustic, sod-roofed tasting room, you can sample wines, specialty mustards, scrumptious chocolate sauce, and delectable kiwi jam; then choose one of each, add Brie and bread, and enjoy your repast at one of the picnic tables outside beneath the lush arbor. Except for the winery buildings themselves, all you'll see around you are acres of idyllic vineyards and forested rolling hills. **2690 San Domingo Road; (209) 728-3436; www.stevenotwinery.com; open 10 a.m.–5 p.m. daily.**

Angels Camp

Hotel/Bed and Breakfast Kissing

❤❤ **THE COTTAGES AT GREENHORN CREEK, Angels Camp** If you've ever dreamed of living in a luxurious residential neighborhood set beside a golf course, here's your chance. The ten cottages that comprise this 20-room accommodation are clustered together in a quiet cul-de-sac within sight of Greenhorn Creek's gorgeous fairways. This unusual but delightful setup is worth checking out, especially for couples who love to golf. The brand-new Craftsman-style cottages each house two bedrooms (most with double queen- or double twin-size beds), and several room options are available. Guests can rent the entire cottage and both bedrooms, the main cottage (which includes the master bedroom, private bathroom, kitchen, and living room), or one guest room with private bathroom and private entrance. Whichever option you choose, the contemporary English country–style furnishings are pleasant and the overall feel is light and bright. Private decks, fully equipped kitchens, and CD players come with the full cottage or main cottage options. If budget matters come into play, don't hesitate booking one of the guest rooms, which are inexpensive and perfect for two. Cottage Nos. 706 and 698 face a tree-lined creek while others, such as No. 697, have front-porch views of distant foothills.

Breakfast isn't included with your stay, but morning refreshment is easily obtained at **THE TURN** (209-736-8185; inexpensive; breakfast and lunch daily), Greenhorn Creek's casual golf-course grill. Guests also have use of the nearby fitness center and outdoor pool. Golf-and-stay packages, advertised mainly during the off-season, offer some unbelievable bargains, so be sure to ask for details when making reservations. When the sun starts to dip, walk over to **CAMPS RESTAURANT** (see Restaurant Kissing) for a romantic dinner and sunset viewing. Such easy living is just par for the course here. **676 McCauley Ranch Road; (209) 736-8180, (888) 736-5900; www.greenhorncreek.com; inexpensive to unbelievably expensive; minimum-stay requirement on weekends.**

Restaurant Kissing

☙☙ **CAMPS RESTAURANT, Angels Camp** Golf course restaurants aren't typically places we recommend for kissing, but if there's a romantic element to them, we're game. Luckily, Camps Restaurant at Greenhorn Creek strives to facilitate romantic agendas. While it does tend to draw a golf-oriented, country-club crowd, the dining room's serene views of the expansive golf course and rolling hills dotted with oak trees will appeal to everyone. Modern glass chandeliers hang from the dining room's cathedral ceilings, and candle lanterns illuminate every table. The lulling melodies of a player piano are an appealing romantic touch. The stylish wood tables and leather chairs are spaced far enough apart so no one can hear you reveal your golf score, and tables situated away from the exhibition kitchen are better suited for quiet conversations. Service is efficient and the gourmet menu focuses on meat and seafood. We enjoyed the daily special: fresh grilled halibut topped with a pineapple-ginger salsa. Another favorite is pork medallions with sweet-potato hash browns, a menu standard. Whether you come here to putt around or just to savor the views, a stop at Camps should be on your list. **676 McCauley Ranch Road; (209) 736-8181; moderate to expensive; lunch Tuesday–Saturday, dinner Wednesday–Sunday, brunch Sunday.**

Columbia

As you walk along Columbia's narrow streets, hemmed with Old West storefronts and overhanging balconies, you escape from the cares of today and enter the nostalgia of yesterday. **COLUMBIA STATE HISTORIC PARK**, the best-restored and most unusual of Gold Country's portals to the past, includes approximately two blocks of old-fashioned shops. Vehicles are not allowed inside the park, with the exception of the Wells Fargo stagecoach and assorted ponies. Shopkeepers and wait staffs in period costume greet visitors at the antique stores and old-fashioned restaurants. Fiddlers and banjo players enliven the street with foot-stomping tunes, and children clamber onto the stagecoach for a ride about town. If all this action isn't enough, panning for gold is also a possibility in the seeded wooden troughs. Tourist attractions might not be very intimate, but the ones here certainly are entertaining. For more information, contact the **COLUMBIA CHAMBER OF COMMERCE** (P.O. Box 1824, Columbia, CA 95310; 209-536-1672; www.sierra.parks.state.ca.us).

Hotel/Bed and Breakfast Kissing

❧ **BLUE NILE INN, Columbia** Named after a lavender-tinted rose, the Blue Nile is a Victorian replica set in a residential neighborhood just a block from **COLUMBIA STATE HISTORIC PARK**. Four guest rooms upstairs are decorated in a subtle country theme, with hardwood floors, floral throw rugs, and silk flower accents. Classic art reproductions adorn the cream-colored walls. These rooms can't quite be classified as warm and cozy, but they are free from needless frills and are large and light. We only recommend two for romance, the Angel Room and Victorian Garden, both of which have a jetted tub for two in the bathroom and a flip-on fireplace for instant ambience. As for breakfast, we can't tell you much, other than you'll get one. When we paid a visit, the innkeepers refused to divulge what guests eat in the morning. We don't understand the secrecy of such information, since this is a bed and *breakfast*. Who knows what you're in for here? **11250 Pacific Street; (209) 532-8041; www.blue-nile-inn.com; moderate; minimum-stay requirement on holiday weekends.**

Restaurant Kissing

❧❧ **CITY HOTEL RESTAURANT, Columbia** With its high-backed leather chairs, burgundy velvet draperies, brass chandeliers, classical music, and elegant cuisine, the City Hotel Restaurant is a relatively refined departure from rough-and-ready Columbia. Established in 1856, this is where the wealthy celebrated their fortunes away from the dusty trails. Today it is a training kitchen for hotel management students from nearby Columbia College. Eager beginning chefs create such entrées as rack of lamb with rosemary sauce and baked ratatouille in phyllo, or grilled beef tenderloin with smoked mushroom sauce and potato gratin. The signature dessert, a lemon soufflé with Grand Marnier sauce, takes 30 minutes to prepare, but is worth the wait. Meals aren't always perfect here, but they are always interesting. **Main Street, at the City Hotel; (209) 532-1479; www.cityhotel. com; expensive; dinner Tuesday–Sunday, brunch Sunday.**

Sonora

Sonora is a shock to the senses if you've spent time in the rest of Gold Country, because it is significantly larger and more populated than most of the other gold-rush towns. Sonora, too, flaunts its history with vintage old-fashioned storefronts and inns, but the development here is a glaring reminder of what century you're really in. In some ways, though, Sonora's size is its primary advantage: Your kissing options are increased significantly.

Hotel/Bed and Breakfast Kissing

❧❧ **RYAN HOUSE, 1855, Sonora** If you stop to smell the roses at the Ryan House, your senses will be more than satiated by the time you reach the front door. A long garden walkway lined with blooming bushes summons you into this small 1850s Victorian. Pretty in its homespun simplicity, the interior decor is clean and uncluttered, with soft lavenders and blues accented in patchwork quilts and dried-flower wreaths. The upstairs Honeymoon Suite, endowed with a spacious private parlor and a large two-person soaking tub, offers the most privacy and is really the reason to stay here. The inn's emphasis is on old-fashioned comfort, from its ultra-cozy beds in the three guest rooms to the warm aromas of baking—cookies for the afternoon sherry break or fresh scones for breakfast. In the evening you can share a favorite book on the love seat by the woodstove in the library downstairs or venture out for a kiss beneath the branches of the hawthorn tree. **153 South Shepherd Street; (209) 533-3445, (800) 831-4897; www. ryanhouse.com; inexpensive to expensive; minimum-stay requirement on holiday weekends.**

❧❧❧ **SERENITY, Sonora** You'll drive a way out of town to reach this country-Victorian home but, then again, you are trying to find Serenity, aren't you? Aptly named, the inn is sheltered on six acres of woodland and exudes quiet country elegance at every turn. Unwind with a glass of fresh lemonade on the breezy veranda or in front of the wood-burning stove in the parlor. The four guest rooms are modestly pleasant and feature private baths, lace-trimmed linens, antique furnishings, and bright color schemes (sometimes a little too bright). Gas fireplaces in the two upstairs bedrooms (Lilac Time and Violets Are Blue) can actually be turned on via remote control from bed. A queen-size sleigh bed makes the fireside Lilac Time Room especially inviting, while a garden scene complete with life-size sunflowers and foxgloves in the Host of Golden Daffodils Room is also enticing. Peruse the floor-to-ceiling bookshelves lining the walls of the library, where sunlight spills through a tall arched window. Breakfast is the clincher. As you relish carved pineapple boats or eggs Florentine, remember to save room for dessert: Strawberry shortcake and boysenberry cobbler are summertime favorites, while a slice of fresh-from-the-oven gingerbread cake makes winter mornings much warmer. **15305 Bear Cub Drive; (209) 533-1441, (800) 426-1441; www.serenity-inn.com; moderate; minimum-stay requirement on holiday weekends.**

Restaurant Kissing

❧ **GOOD HEAVENS, Sonora** This unassuming eatery is a favorite lunch spot for locals. Exposed brick comprises one wall, and windows peeking out to Sonora's small-town main street line another. In between, café tables topped with country-style floral cloths and linen napkins fanned in wine goblets invite visitors to enjoy hearty lunch specials, quiches, and sandwiches. Every entrée comes with a complimentary basket of warm mini-biscuits with which you can sample the selection of homemade jams. Both lunch and dinner bring plenty of down-home comfort foods to the table. Savor such dishes as boneless baby back ribs, pot roast, honey-baked ham, and country fried steak covered with gravy. No meal here would be complete without sampling the specialty Bundt cakes (flavors change daily) or an old-fashioned piece of pie. **49 North Washington Street (Highway 49); (209) 532-3663; inexpensive to moderate; lunch Wednesday–Monday, dinner Friday–Saturday.**

❧❧ **HEMINGWAY'S CAFE RESTAURANT, Sonora** The unusual combination of dinner and live entertainment at this contemporary, family-run bistro can be a lot of fun, but you have to be in the mood for it. The eccentric, multitalented chef plays piano and the waitresses sing Broadway tunes between taking orders. Several small dining rooms compose the restaurant, which is located a block from Sonora's main street in a residential neighborhood. Dark green tablecloths and fresh flowers adorn the handful of tables, most of which are illuminated by candlelight. While the surroundings are certainly conducive to kissing, some problems exist. The tableside performances can easily distract you from one another, and you might be left waiting for your meal if the chef decides to play the piano for ten minutes or so. Nevertheless, this is a fun place to spend an evening if you like music—all it takes is the right mind-set.

As for the menu, it changes with the chef's whim, but is typically filled with tasty creations. When we visited, the five-course set dinner (with à la carte options) focused on authentic Hawaiian fare. That's quite different for this neck of the woods but, then again, so is this restaurant. **362 South Stewart Street; (209) 532-4900; expensive to very expensive; call for seasonal hours.**

❧❧❧ **JOSEPHINE'S, Sonora** Sometimes in Gold Country you have to look hard to find little treasures. Josephine's is such a case. Hidden in the back of the historic Gunn House Hotel a few blocks south of the bustling downtown strip, this restaurant is certainly set off the beaten path. Candles and a stained glass window help create a romantic glow in this one-room restaurant, while textured rose-colored walls and hand-stenciled vines, along with classic still-life paintings and a magnificent mirror, give hints of European elegance. Framed by strands of garlic, chile peppers, and dried flowers, the open kitchen doesn't distract much from the quiet atmosphere and proves entertaining to watch. When the weather cooperates, a patio above the outdoor swimming pool makes for the most romantic seating area.

The kitchen turns out average northern Italian dishes, all with a California twist. Gorgonzola cheese seems to be a popular ingredient in many dishes, most notably the popular grilled portobello appetizer topped with creamy Gorgonzola sauce, and the popular bay shrimp Gorgonzola salad. Our pasta with grilled portobello mushrooms and filet tips was tasty, but the fatty meat disappointed. (Try ordering it without the meat.) Stick to the mesquite-grilled or wood-burning-oven-baked items, such as grilled filet mignon, sage-roasted pork tenderloin, and grilled chicken. As for sweet endings, our tiramisu proved rich and creamy enough, but was timid on the coffee flavor. Nonetheless, we enjoyed. **286 South Washington, at the Gunn House Hotel; (209) 533-4111; moderate to expensive; dinner Tuesday–Sunday.**

Romantic Warning: One of the first two-story adobe structures built in Sonora (around 1850), the **GUNN HOUSE HOTEL** (209-532-3421; very inexpensive) may be historically appealing, but the worn-out guest rooms leave much to be desired. Venture here only to visit Josephine's.

Twain Harte

The tiny hamlet of Twain Harte (named after writers Mark Twain and Bret Harte) is a bit removed from the rest of Gold Country, both in looks and location. At an elevation of approximately 4,000 feet, the setting takes on a distinctly alpine appearance as the foothills start turning into full-fledged mountains. After a quick visit in town, continue ascending until you reach **MCCAFFREY HOUSE BED AND BREAKFAST INN** (see Hotel/Bed and Breakfast Kissing), *the* place in Twain Harte for heart-tugging romance.

Hotel/Bed and Breakfast Kissing

❤❤❤ MCCAFFREY HOUSE BED AND BREAKFAST INN, Twain Harte

From the golden valley of Gold Country, climb up to 4,000 feet above sea level to reach this bed and breakfast nestled among the trees. Located off

Highway 108 and bordered by a forest of cedar, pine, and oak, this seven-room inn is well worth the ten-minute drive from Sonora. You'll first be greeted by three friendly dogs and one cat, who gladly escort you into the large, contemporary home filled with the innkeepers' family photos, treasures from world travels, and a well-chosen and varied art collection. In the common living room, sit on soft couches and sip a glass of wine. If the weather's nice, head outside to the home's most outstanding feature: a series of terraced decks adorned with shaded tables that look out into the dense woods. On one such deck is the communal hot tub, perfect for bubbling beneath the moonlight.

Two guest rooms are tucked away downstairs and the rest are located upstairs on the second floor; of course, the latter offer better forest views. Done up in a mix of floral prints and solid colors, each lovingly decorated room exudes country elegance, especially when complemented by pine queen-size beds (in four-poster or sleigh styles), matching armoires, and vibrant quilts. All rooms feature down pillows, fluffy robes, lovely bay windows or patios, and gas fireplaces that are equipped with timers so you can fall asleep together in warm comfort. Each room has a TV/VCR hidden within the armoire, and guests have a choice of hundreds of videos from the innkeepers' extensive collection. While every room is wonderful, we have a particular fancy for the Green Room. From our private, forest-facing balcony we spent an afternoon watching a Steller's jay feed its young in a nest only 30 feet away.

When the morning sun starts filtering through the trees, enjoy your coffee on the deck, or take a pre-breakfast walk through the woods. When you return, breakfast will be waiting in the dining room at a series of two- and four-person tables. (Request a table for two if you want to dine alone.) Morning entrées rotate from sweet to savory and include a fruit starter course, mini-muffins, juice, and plenty of robust coffee. We loved the apple Dutch pancake on the first morning and quickly consumed the zesty Southwest egg specialty the next. After breakfast, be sure to explore the world of recreational opportunities just minutes away. Twain Harte is the gateway to the **STANISLAUS NATIONAL FOREST** (209-532-3671; www.r5.fs.fed.us/stanislaus; free admission), home to 1,100 miles of hiking trails, 78 lakes, and, of course, millions of al fresco kissing spots. **23251 Highway 108; (209) 586-0757, (888) 586-0757; www.mccaffreyhouse.com; moderate to expensive.**

Restaurant Kissing

❧ **NATASHA'S CAFÉ, Twain Harte** Never judge a book by its cover—or, in this case, never judge a restaurant by its exterior. This small, operating-on-a-budget dining establishment is set in a roadside shack of sorts—looking like something most of us would dismiss as a biker's hangout (and, actually, the bar next door is exactly that!). But once you enter through the side door, you'll see that this little restaurant is budding with romance. The husband-and-wife owners have tried hard to make the decor appealing. Fine linens and flowers adorn the tables, flowing fabrics and white holiday lights drape the windows, and classical music plays softly in the background. Since there are only eight tables in the dining room, you're pretty much guaranteed quiet conversation. Unfortunately, the outdated metal chairs and an exposed air-conditioning unit aren't particularly attractive but, then again, this isn't a big-budget operation.

What shines more than the ambience is the creative menu, which is brimming with rabbit, lamb, salmon, and veal dishes. Included with your dinner is a big bowl of homemade soup and an equally large salad. On our visit, we savored saffron-chicken soup followed by a strawberry-and-mixed-greens salad. We then feasted on honey-glazed quail and an outstanding Chinese roast pork loin glazed with a Mandarin orange sauce. A peach bread pudding, topped with a scoop of potent brandy ice cream, ended the evening just right. If you don't let first impressions fool you, try this rustic little restaurant for a pleasantly surprising evening. **23370 Highway 108, at The Confidence Inn; (209) 586-2936; expensive; no credit cards; reservations recommended; dinner Wednesday–Sunday, Sunday brunch seasonally.**

"Where kisses are repeated

and arms hold there is no

telling where time is."

Ted Hughes

Yosemite National Park and Environs

Oakhurst

If you've ever been to Oakhurst, you might wonder why we bother to include this nondescript town as a romantic destination. Most people pass through without blinking an eye (or wanting to stop) on their way to Yosemite National Park. Well, no longer. CHATEAU DU SUREAU (see Hotel/Bed and Breakfast Kissing) and ERNA'S ELDERBERRY HOUSE (see Restaurant Kissing) have become nationally known attractions, making Oakhurst a four-lip destination.

Hotel/Bed and Breakfast Kissing

💋💋💋💋 CHATEAU DU SUREAU, Oakhurst A four-lip rating system fails us when we run across a property like Chateau du Sureau, which warrants at least ten lips (if not more). In fact, we were tempted to revise our entire rating system because nothing we've seen compares to the luxurious grandeur of this authentic French Provincial country estate. There aren't enough words (or lips) to describe what makes this place so extraordinary—you have to see it for yourselves to believe it.

Wrought-iron gates swing open to reveal a luminous white stucco castle with a stone turret and red tiled roof, ensconced on nine acres of wooded hillside. Stone walkways meander past a murmuring fountain, a stream-fed swimming pool, lovely gardens, and even a life-size chessboard.

Inside the manor walls you are greeted like royalty and ushered past common areas brimming with luxurious appointments to the palatial comfort of your room. Soon after, a plate of delicious appetizers arrives at your door, the first of many pampering touches. Chandeliers add elegance to each of the ten guest rooms, which are appointed with fine European antiques, richly colored linens, fresh flowers, and French doors that open onto private balconies or patios. CD players are tucked discreetly in antique cabinets, a fire crackles in the stone hearth in colder months, and every light switch has a dimmer to set the right romantic mood. Nearly as large as bedrooms themselves, the beautiful, spacious bathrooms feature luxurious robes, handmade French tilework, and soaking tubs. Rooms located on the second floor have more expansive views and enhanced privacy.

Extraordinary doesn't begin to describe the service here, which caters to your every desire and whim (almost to the point of being overdone).

Long-stemmed roses and decadent chocolates appear on your pillows after turndown service. You can even ask to have your bags unpacked and your pajamas laid out. For a slight fee, a picnic lunch can be prepared for you to enjoy on a day hike; upon your return, the staff will be happy to oblige you with some "magic to pamper tired feet"—a foot massage. (Fortunately, gratuities are added to your bill to save you the trouble of tipping along the way.)

In the morning, freshly squeezed orange juice, banana-bread French toast, corn cakes stuffed with smoked salmon, and melt-in-your-mouth croissants, among other delicacies, await guests in the sunny terra-cotta–tiled breakfast room. When weather permits, your morning repast may be served at wrought-iron tables on the outdoor breakfast patio.

Just as our four-lip rating fails to illustrate the grand opulence of the chateau, our price category of "unbelievably expensive" fails to accurately reflect the cost of staying at the new self-contained Villa du Sureau. Nestled among the pine trees, this Paris Manor–style home can be yours and yours alone—if you're willing to pay the $2,500-a-night price tag. Although the Villa was under construction at the time of our visit, we have no doubt this will be an incredible, albeit expensive, place to kiss. Fourteen-foot ceilings rise above an impressive collection of European antiques and exquisite paintings, while two bedrooms, two bathrooms, a mini-kitchen, a library/drawing room (with a baby grand piano), and a breakfast balcony complete the picture. Enormous bathrooms come equipped with free-standing steam showers, whirlpool tubs, bidets, and elegant marble accents. One of the bedrooms features a raised bed crowned with a stained glass window and enclosed by thick ceiling-to-floor drapery. You'll want for nothing here, but if you do, simply push a button in any of the rooms to summon your own personal butler, who lives downstairs. Once you've played king and queen here for a day, you'll find that returning to reality is almost too much to bear. **48688 Victoria Lane, at Highway 41; (559) 683-6860; www.integra.fr/relaischateaux/sureau; unbelievably expensive; minimum-stay requirement on weekends and holidays; recommended wedding site.**

❤❤❤ **THE HOMESTEAD, Oakhurst** Set on 160 wooded acres outside of Oakhurst, The Homestead's four sophisticated cottages are enfolded by ancient oak trees and surrounded by country quiet. While the setting appeals primarily to naturalists who are looking to escape the city, the cabins are beautifully appointed and offer plenty of modern comforts: gas fireplaces, TV/VCRs, comfy robes, and private full baths. Knotty pine walls, cathedral ceilings, and saltillo-tile floors lend rural style, and inviting linens drape either four-poster or canopy beds in the separate bedrooms. You'll be even more amazed to learn that these adobe, stone, and cedar cottages were designed and built by the amiable innkeepers themselves.

Although the cabins are similar in design and amenities, subtle differences in style and theme grant each one its distinct personality. Cowboy hats, lariats, and other memorabilia give the Ranch Cottage its Western look (there's even a horseshoe over the front door for good luck!), while the Garden Cottage is as fresh as spring with its lovely wall stenciling, floral fabrics, and ivy-entwined four-poster bedframe. An equestrian theme enlivens the Country Cottage, and Native American artwork distinguishes the fourth cottage. A basket of baked goods and fresh fruit awaits in the fully equipped kitchen, so once you arrive you're on your own and your privacy is ensured. A centrally located gas barbecue and accompanying picnic table are also available for use by all guests.

Set on the second floor of the owners' quarters, the Star Gazing Loft is the fifth and least expensive accommodation on the property. Though slightly smaller than the cabins, this one-room studio offers similar amenities: a private entrance, a kitchenette stocked with breakfast goodies, a TV/VCR, handcrafted pine furniture, and views of the countryside (and the stars in the evening) through a large picture window. Its wicker furnishings and eclectic decor make the loft a casual and cozy hideaway. **41110 Road 600; (559) 683-0495, (800) 483-0495; www.homesteadcottages.com; expensive to very expensive; minimum-stay requirement on weekends and holidays.**

❦❦❦ **HOUNDS TOOTH INN, Oakhurst** This sprawling, Victorian-style home, cream with dark green trim, resides 12 miles from Yosemite's South Entrance. Highway 41 borders one side of the property but, luckily, your entrance consists of a descent down a steep driveway to the inn, leaving the road mostly out of sight (although not completely out of mind). Once inside, start things off right with complimentary cookies and wine served at a lovely bar area next to a glowing fireplace.

Twelve distinctly decorated guest rooms comprise the first and second floors of the home. We liked the spaciousness of the second-floor rooms with their vaulted ceilings and large windows, although the five rooms on the ground floor offer private entrances via the wraparound cement patio. All guest rooms feature private baths, ceiling fans, feathertop mattresses, and sunny dispositions. Five have whirlpool tubs and one room comes equipped with a refrigerator, wet bar, and microwave. Unfortunately, visible air-conditioning units and TVs set out on the most convenient piece of furniture detract from the otherwise attractive rooms, but such eyesores will easily be forgiven if you book a stay in one of our top picks for romance.

Done up in a striking taupe and black color scheme, the Hounds Tooth Room made our hearts go pitter-patter. A sumptuous king-size bed is a dorned with handsome linens and faces the mantle, where a TV is discreetly tucked away above the gas fireplace. In a corner of the bedroom, you'll find a two-person whirlpool tub set next to a window affording views of the adjacent treetops. This room also features a couch perfect for snuggling, a handsome cherry-wood desk for writing those love notes, and a large bathroom. We also liked the Tower Room, otherwise known as the Honeymoon Room, for its whimsical wrought-iron bedframe encircled with sheer netting and ivy. This light and bright room features a whirlpool tub next to the queen-size bed. Those looking for a masculine touch will prefer the Firelight Room, with its cherry-wood furniture, wingback chairs, and maroon linens draping a king-size bed.

Road noise is only a problem if you venture outside to relax on the flower-filled patio or stroll around the two-and-a-half-acre property. A buffet-style breakfast of cereal, pastries, sweet breads, quiche, fresh fruit, and coffee is served in the sunny main-floor breakfast nook each morning. **42071 Highway 41; (559) 642-6600, (888) 642-6610; www.hounds toothinn.com; inexpensive to expensive.**

Restaurant Kissing

❦❦❦❦ **ERNA'S ELDERBERRY HOUSE, Oakhurst** People drive for hours just to dine at Erna's Elderberry House. You might wonder why a restaurant in such an obscure location merits so much time in a car, but once you've spent a blissful evening at this luxurious French restaurant, you too will undoubtedly be willing to drive for hours. Nestled among elderberry trees adjacent to the **CHATEAU DU SUREAU** (see Hotel/Bed and Breakfast Kissing), the restaurant showcases views of the castle, the gardens, and the sun setting behind the property's ponderosa pines. Large chandeliers with glowing candles illuminate the main dining room, which is appointed with rich red walls, cathedral ceilings, tapestries, paintings, and mirrors with gilded frames. Beautifully upholstered chairs accompany cozy tables dressed in white tablecloths and topped with flickering votive candles. A fire crackling in the hearth fans the flames of romance in the cooler months.

Erna's exquisitely presented six-course, prix-fixe dinners change daily and are served by an exceedingly formal and gracious wait staff. We savored a poached quail egg topped with caviar, followed by tuna tartare with miso-basil sauce. An interesting combination of flavors were united in the curried New England clam chowder; our Sonoma lamb noisettes were embellished with a tarragon-tomato essence sauce; and our crisp salad topped with apples and Roquefort cheese proved delicious. The finale? Chocolate terrine with fresh fruit and homemade ice cream. Utter perfection! **48688 Victoria Lane, at Chateau du Sureau; (559) 683-6800; www.integra.fr/relaischateaux/sureau; unbelievably expensive; lunch Wednesday–Saturday, dinner daily, brunch Sunday; recommended wedding site.**

Bass Lake

Located just 14 miles outside Yosemite National Park, Bass Lake is a sizable freshwater lake surrounded by evergreens and Sierra Nevada peaks. Although much of the lakeshore has become crowded by residences and lodges, one side remains free from development, adding to its romantic allure and beauty.

Hotel/Bed and Breakfast Kissing

❦❦ **DUCEY'S ON THE LAKE, Bass Lake** Reminiscent of a ski lodge, Ducey's on the Lake features 20 suites, most with lake and marina views. Though the decor is fairly standard, with pine armoires, green carpeting, pink walls, and floral bedspreads, romantic amenities such as private balconies, wet bars, sitting areas, wood-burning fireplaces, and provided bathrobes make Ducey's an extremely comfortable place to call home for a night or two. In addition, two-person spa tubs in some of the rooms are sure to assuage weary outdoor enthusiasts. Those who aren't so weary can take advantage of the resort's tennis courts, sauna and hot tubs, outdoor swimming pool, and lake recreation (boating, water-skiing, fishing, and swimming), not to mention Yosemite National Park—a mere 14 miles away.

As for evening entertainment, dinner at the on-site restaurant (see Restaurant Kissing) is one option; jazz concerts performed on the lakeside deck every Friday night in the summer are another. Guests receive a coupon for a complimentary continental breakfast or 30 percent off any menu item served at the casual Pines Restaurant on the upper part of the property. Unfortunately, the mediocre food and western-theme decor won't inspire any kisses. **39255 Marina Drive; (559) 642-3121, (800) 350-7463; www.basslake.com; very expensive to unbelievably expensive; minimum-stay requirement on weekends.**

Romantic Note: Ducey's on the Lake shares the same property and facilities with the Pines Chalets. These 84 duplex-style cabins have older, somewhat dated furnishings and are geared mostly toward families. We recommend only the Ducey's suites for romance.

Restaurant Kissing

❧ **DUCEY'S RESTAURANT, Bass Lake** Ducey's is not fine dining by any stretch of the imagination, but it is the only game in town when it comes to romance. Glowing candles at every table and knotty pine walls decorated with antique skis and snowshoes lend rustic warmth to the two-tiered dining room overlooking Pines Marina on Bass Lake. Polished wood tables and cozy booths create a casual atmosphere for enjoying steaks, seafood, or pasta. We found the prices a bit steep for the quality of food, but what you're really paying for here is a serene view of the lake and the convenient location. Hint: The kitchen is heavy-handed with the condiments—whether it's salad drowning in dressing or thick butter piled high on your baked potato—so request yours on the side. Also, steer clear of the very dry baked halibut encrusted with herbs and Parmesan cheese. Luckily, the pleasant service and lovely lake view help compensate for the kitchen's shortcomings. **39255 Marina Drive; (559) 642-3131, (800) 350-7463; www.bass lake.com; expensive; restaurant: dinner daily, brunch Sunday, bar and grill: lunch and dinner daily.**

Fish Camp

Hotel/Bed and Breakfast Kissing

❧❧ **TENAYA LODGE, Fish Camp** The fact that awe-inspiring Yosemite National Park is minutes from Tenaya Lodge might be incentive enough to stay here. Set just off the highway, Tenaya commands views of a luscious valley hemmed by trees rising in succession to the horizon. This view would be heavenly if it weren't for the sprawling parking lot that surrounds the hotel. Still, there are advantages to staying here. You might not have uninterrupted views of Yosemite's splendor, but at least you get what you pay for in terms of accommodations, service, and amenities.

Enormous iron chandeliers trimmed with candles hang from cathedral ceilings in the large, slightly dated hotel lobby, where a fire crackles in an immense stone fireplace, and canoes and hunting trophies adorn the dark wood walls. A recent renovation has given the 244 guest rooms an updated look with new furnishings, attractive bedspreads, and Native American patterns in shades of green, burgundy, and tan. All rooms feature standard baths and TVs hidden in armoires. For slightly higher prices, the Luxury and Honeymoon Suites offer hand-carved four-poster beds, private balconies, soaking tubs, and extra space. Treat yourselves to a massage and then dine at one of the hotel's restaurants. An indoor pool, fitness center, sauna, Jacuzzi tub, and rental bicycles are available for guests who still have energy after breathtaking tours of Yosemite. **1122 Highway 41; (559) 683-6555, (800) 635-5807; www.tenayalodge.com; very expensive to unbelievably expensive.**

Yosemite National Park

Yosemite National Park can be accessed via one of its four entrances. From Fresno, drive 89 miles north along Highway 41 to the park's South Entrance; from Merced, follow Highway 140 approximately 80 miles to the Arch Rock Entrance; and from San Francisco, make the four-and-a-half-hour journey along Highway 120 to the Big Oak Flat Entrance. There's also an East Entrance (closed in winter) accessed via Highway 120 from the town of Lee Vining.

To say that Yosemite National Park is paradise on earth is not an exaggeration. We could use every adjective in the thesaurus and still not begin to describe Yosemite in its full glory. No matter which entrance you take to get into the park, your first view of Yosemite will literally take your breath away. Myriad waterfalls cascade over towering rock formations that rise thousands of feet above lush valleys and meadows, surrounding you with sublime splendor.

Winter, spring, summer, or fall—there's a season for everyone at Yosemite. Snowfall brings a host of activities including downhill or cross-country skiing at Badger's Pass, ice skating at Curry Village's outdoor rink, or snowshoeing and snow camping in more untouched areas. During the warmer months, when the Valley is awash in the brilliant colors of spring and summer, outdoor enthusiasts come to camp, horseback ride, bike, rock climb, and, of course, hike. With 840 miles of trails, Yosemite is prime hiking territory. For information about trails and conditions, call (209) 372-0200.

A visit to this extraordinary park could easily change your life, giving you a newfound respect for nature. Although 89 percent of Yosemite's 1,170 square miles is designated wilderness, the millions of tourists who visit each year are taking a toll on park resources. Visitors are asked to tread lightly and disturb the land and the wildlife as little as possible.

A word about reservations: Due to Yosemite's popularity—more than 4 million people visit each year—reservations for accommodations within the park are often hard to come by, especially during the popular summer months. Planning ahead (even up to a year in advance) is your best strategy to reserve your spot among the natural splendor. Call the Yosemite reservation line at (559) 252-4848. Other options include visiting from November through March, when midweek rates may drop as much as 25 percent, or staying in any of the kiss-worthy accommodations located just outside the park. For campground information, contact the **CAMPGROUND OFFICE** at (209) 372-0200.

Romantic Note: From late fall to early spring, California state law requires park visitors to carry chains in their cars. Call (209) 372-0200 for updated information about road and weather conditions.

Hotel/Bed and Breakfast Kissing

❧❧❧ THE AHWAHNEE HOTEL, Yosemite Valley Even if you've never been to Yosemite, you're probably familiar with pictures of the legendary Ahwahnee Hotel. Built in 1927, this landmark six-story hotel, made of native granite and concrete stained to look like redwood, is an architectural masterpiece set beneath Yosemite's majestic Royal Arches. Inside, Native American mosaics, rugs, and artwork adorn the many common areas. Walk-in-size fireplaces warm a colossal lounge where wrought-iron chandeliers hang from cathedral ceilings, and floor-to-ceiling windows capture wondrous views of Yosemite's sheer rock walls. Tall windows in the sunny, relatively less-visited solarium provide the perfect place to pucker up while taking in stunning views of **GLACIER POINT** (see Outdoor Kissing).

In 1997, a two-year, $1.5 million renovation was completed, with the Ahwahnee's guest rooms and public areas benefiting from new fabrics and a general freshening up. The 99 standard guest rooms are simply nice hotel rooms with a Native American theme and your basic amenities. These rooms offer comfortable sitting areas, TVs hidden in armoires, king-size beds with standard linens, awkward walk-in closets, robes, and ordinary baths. Location, not ambience, is what you are paying for here—and, while the prices are very high, we must say that the location is incredible.

If kissing in the heart of Yosemite is foremost on your mind (and if you have a credit limit higher than Half Dome), we suggest you reserve one of the six Penthouse Suites located on the hotel's private-access top floor. These palatial wonders vary in design and decor, although they all feature separate sitting areas and elegant appointments. One has mahogany paneling, a fireplace, and leaded glass windows reminiscent of a Swiss chalet; another offers a Jacuzzi tub with shutters that open onto a sunken living room.

An option between the high-end Penthouse Suites and the standard guest rooms are the hotel's four Parlor Suites, appointed with subtle color schemes, European-style furnishings, wood-burning fireplaces, and lots of windows. These suites can be rented as either two- or three-room units. Also on the property are 24 cottages that form a series of duplexes and pentplexes in the wooded area behind the main building. Although much more rustic than the rooms in the main building, they boast surprisingly large bathrooms and innovative headboards created by a local artist. **One Ahwahnee Road; (559) 252-4848; www.yosemitepark.com; very expensive to unbelievably expensive.**

Romantic Note: The Ahwahnee attracts an overabundance of tourists year-round. Reservations are hard to get, so be sure to plan ahead or consider visiting midweek or during the off-season.

Romantic Suggestion: Ask about the Ahwahnee's romance package, which may include such extras as champagne and roses upon arrival, down comforters, satin sheets, and breakfast in bed, or a special in-room candlelight dinner for two.

No lips YOSEMITE LODGE, Yosemite Valley Located near the base of Yosemite Falls, this lodge is the only other hotel option in the valley beside **THE AHWAHNEE HOTEL** (see review above). Its 245 rooms range from standard to substandard (most with multiple beds), and the grounds are constantly inundated with people and noisy tour buses. Although your wallet may be satisfied with these accommodations, your lips will undoubtedly be disappointed. **Yosemite Valley; (559) 252-4848; www.yosemitepark. com; inexpensive to moderate.**

Restaurant Kissing

❦❦ AHWAHNEE DINING ROOM, Yosemite Valley Climbing to the top of Bridalveil Falls seems to be easier than finding good food and a romantic ambience for dining in Yosemite Valley. If a day of hiking and sightseeing has left you hungry for a decent meal, head to the **MOUNTAIN ROOM RESTAURANT** (see Romantic Alternative below) to refuel for another day of adventure. If the park's surrounding splendor has aroused your passion for romance, we suggest you wine and dine your sweetheart at the Ahwahnee Dining Room.

Grand sugar-pine trestles and granite pillars endow the enormous dining room with rustic elegance. Thirty-four-foot ceilings soar above tables draped in pink linens, while rugs and draperies in bright shades of yellow, green, and red add splashes of color. During the day, full-length windows let in ample sunshine, as well as views of Yosemite Falls and **GLACIER POINT** (see Outdoor Kissing). In the evening, chandeliers hanging from the cathedral ceiling and slim candles in wrought-iron holders provide soft light for the cozy tables.

Meals are presented on the Ahwahnee's signature china—an event that comes off as more touristy than attractive in such a large hotel. The menu features mostly meat and seafood dishes, from filet mignon and braised lamb shank to pan-seared salmon and broiled ahi. Mediocre describes both the food and the service, but at least you have that spectacular view and your special someone to keep your mind on romance. Oh, and about dessert: The lemon sorbet will help you pucker up for that goodnight kiss! **One Ahwahnee Road, at The Ahwahnee Hotel; (559) 372-1489; expensive to very expensive; dinner reservations required; breakfast, lunch, and dinner daily, brunch Sunday.**

Romantic Alternative: The MOUNTAIN ROOM RESTAURANT (Yosemite Lodge; 559-372-1281; moderate to expensive; call for seasonal hours) is the only other dining option in Yosemite Valley. Surrounded by colorful photographs depicting Yosemite scenes, the dining room is attractive but casual. The food is quite good (standouts include the Caesar salad and the salmon rubbed with Brazilian spices), the prices are more than reasonable, and the service is attentive without being intrusive.

Outdoor Kissing

❧❧❧ **GLACIER POINT, Yosemite National Park** No matter where you go, Yosemite abounds with spectacular views, but Glacier Point beats them all. The one-hour drive (accessible in summer only) winds through fertile meadows and dense forest, setting the mood for the visual ecstasy that awaits. Perched 3,214 feet above Yosemite Valley, Glacier Point commands mesmerizing panoramic views of the valley below, as well as Nevada Falls, Vernal Falls, the Merced River, and the Sierras rising in the distance. Yosemite's near-constant tourist traffic deters much of the wildlife from wandering here, but red-tailed hawks often soar effortlessly overhead, and coyotes and deer sometimes emerge from the forest. *Take Highway 41 to Chinquapin and follow Glacier Point Road to Glacier Point.*

Romantic Note: An abundance of hiking trails originate at Glacier Point. Follow signs to these trails or get more information at the VISITOR CENTER located in Yosemite Valley: (209) 372-0200.

❧❧ **MARIPOSA GROVE, Yosemite National Park** This awesome grove of giant sequoias is right out of a storybook—you almost expect the trees to talk. What better place to pucker up than under the shade of the Grizzly Giant? (It takes 27 fifth-graders to reach around the trunk of this monstrous tree.) Cars are not allowed here (except for shuttle buses), so wander on foot through the hushed forest to your hearts' content. *From the park's South Entrance, follow signs to the Mariposa Grove on your immediate right.*

❦❦❦❦ **TIOGA ROAD, Yosemite National Park** Thirty-nine miles of scenic roadway might sound like a lot of driving, but Tioga Road boasts a multitude of spectacular turnouts, vistas, and natural attractions to keep you occupied. This long and winding road climbs high into the Sierras, past forested hillsides, luxuriant meadows, and steep granite slopes. Be sure to stop at **TENAYA LAKE,** where mammoth granite mountains plummet right into a clear blue lake fringed with evergreens and rocky rubble. Farther on you'll discover **TUOLUMNE MEADOWS,** a peaceful roadside glen framed by mountains. If you continue to the eastern side of the Sierra Nevada, you'll find **MONO LAKE,** one of the oldest and most beautiful lakes in North America. Because of its high concentrations of salt and alkali, this crystal blue lake is outlined by "Tufa Towers," white calcium deposits that have been sculpted over time to resemble artistic sand castles. *From Yosemite Valley, follow Big Oak Flat Road (Highway 120 West) to Tioga Road and turn right.*

Groveland

The town of Groveland sprang to life in the heart of the 1849 California gold rush, although in those days it was known as Garrotte (after the hangman's noose) and filled with rugged individuals seeking their fortune in the foothills of the Sierra Nevada. Today, Groveland is a sleepy little community where wooden sidewalks and historic buildings are reminders of the past. While this once-bustling gold-rush town isn't exactly a destination spot on its own, its location just 23 miles west of Yosemite National Park makes it a smart stopping point for park visitors.

Hotel/Bed and Breakfast Kissing

❦❦❦ **THE GROVELAND HOTEL, Groveland** There may not be much gold left in California's Gold Country, but one precious gem remains: The Groveland Hotel. Set alongside Highway 120, the original adobe section of this historic inn was built in 1849. The other half of the inn, a Queen Anne–style building, was added around the turn of the century. Today, after being saved from demolition and undergoing a massive restoration, this pastel yellow hotel combines romance with plenty of historic charm.

Upon arrival, you'll receive a coupon for a complimentary glass of wine, served either in the authentic gold-rush saloon or in the VICTORIAN ROOM restaurant (see Restaurant Kissing). Take in some California sunshine in the peaceful courtyard, or unwind on the inn's expansive wraparound porch (which unfortunately allows easy glimpses into many of the guest rooms). Four modest guest rooms are located on the second floor of the original house; the other 13 reside in the building next door. Country-style Victorian florals and 19th-century furnishings grace every room, while couches, down comforters, and carpeting from the current era ensure comfort. Some rooms have the cozy charm of grandma's house and others feature elegant appointments. The three suites with separate sitting areas, gas fireplaces, and spa tubs are especially popular with romantic travelers. Another frequently requested unit is Lyle's Room, said to be the dwelling place of the resident ghost. (Apparently this friendly spirit has preferences regarding where items are placed in his room, and he sneaks mints from guests' pillows from time to time. Ask anyone at the hotel about Lyle: He's the talk of the inn.)

After a good night's rest (if you weren't too spooked to sleep), a European-style continental breakfast is served in the main building's dining room. You'll realize you've struck gold once you see the lovely buffet of cereals, fruit, bagels, English muffins, cinnamon rolls, coffee, teas, and juices. Afterward, you'll be ready for a day of exploring the magnificent park; the entrance is only about an hour's drive away. **18767 Main Street; (209) 962-4000, (800) 273-3314; www.groveland.com; moderate to very expensive.**

Romantic Note: Trying to keep the mystery in your relationship? Ask about the hotel's Murder Mystery Weekends, which include a cocktail party, dinner, dessert, and Sunday brunch, along with plenty of old-fashioned fun ($100 per person, lodging not included). For special occasions at The Groveland Hotel, a romance package is also available, featuring a welcome basket full of goodies, an in-room gourmet dinner, and other pampering touches along the way.

Restaurant Kissing

❧❧❧ **THE GROVELAND HOTEL VICTORIAN ROOM, Groveland** The Victorian Room is the only fine dining establishment in these parts, and it is definitely worth your romantic and gastronomical consideration. Set on the main floor of a historic gold-rush hostelry, this casually elegant country Victorian restaurant is subtly lit by brass chandeliers. Pale pink walls provide the backdrop for three whimsical angels who hover in flight above a stream of gold gauze, while mauve-colored wainscoting and window treatments add a rosy warmth. Each of the cozy tables in the dining room is topped with a white tablecloth, fresh flowers, and a glowing candle, and some tables look out onto the hotel's veranda. Visit Saturday night to enjoy live keyboard melodies while you dine.

Warm hospitality and swift service make dinner here an affable experience. The kitchen consistently turns out artistically presented gourmet cuisine prepared with local seasonal ingredients. Seafood lovers won't want to miss the incredible snow crab bisque, followed by the aptly named yum yum shrimp: giant shrimp sautéed in a cross-cultural blend of Indian ginger ghee, sake, garlic, cilantro, scallions, lime, and tomatoes. The rack of lamb is a house specialty, and other favorites include rib-eye steak and grilled salmon. Those who wouldn't mind death by chocolate will come close to heaven with the dessert known simply as "chocolate suicide." **18767 Main Street, at The Groveland Hotel; (209) 962-4000, (800) 273-3314; www.groveland.com; expensive; dinner daily.**

"Kissing power is stronger

than will power . . . "

Abigail Van Buren

South Coast

Traveling the coastline of California is the visual experience of a lifetime. For literally hundreds of miles, the power of the ocean and the majestic scenery are nothing less than scintillating. Despite this seemingly unending spectacle, there are distinct differences between the coastal areas south and north of San Francisco.

While the North Coast's seaside villages are more rural, with laid-back personalities, the communities scattered along the South Coast are chic, urbane, and densely populated. Carmel, Monterey, and Pebble Beach are far more upscale and cosmopolitan than any of the little towns found up north—or, for that matter, in most other regions of northern California. If you and your beloved like to shop in stylish boutiques, eat at choice restaurants, and relax in quality lodgings, the South Coast will more than live up to your dreams. And so will the area's numerous accessible beaches and incredible, dramatic views of the mighty Pacific.

Pacifica

Restaurant Kissing

☙☙ **MOONRAKER RESTAURANT, Pacifica** Floor-to-ceiling windows in the Moonraker's series of softly lit dining rooms showcase views of the crashing ocean surf, which practically laps at the foot of the property. These are the best views in town, at least from the vantage point of a restaurant. Actually, the Moonraker looks more like a lounge than a dining room. Deep, curved leather booths encourage intimacy and face the ocean, taking full advantage of the spectacular display. Tiny white lights strewn across the ceiling to create the effect of a star-filled sky, and red lanterns perched atop wharf posts, set an amorous mood. Unfortunately, the seafood-oriented menu, with its ample selection of grilled meats, isn't as reliable as the views. Luckily, any one of the luscious desserts is sure to inspire a kiss. **105 Rockaway Beach Avenue; (650) 359-0303; expensive; dinner daily, brunch Sunday.**

Moss Beach

Unlike its neighbors, Moss Beach has been spared from overdevelopment, and its small neighborhood setting remains intact. Tourists travel from far and wide to visit Moss Bay's **FITZGERALD MARINE RESERVE**, where they can trek along oceanfront trails and observe tide pools teeming with aquatic life. This rocky intertidal habitat is sheltered from the crashing surf by a series of offshore terraces. Visitors are encouraged to tread lightly and respectfully when exploring the 30 acres of reef exposed during low tide. After a day of discovery, seek out nearby diminutive **MOSS BEACH,** a picture-perfect spot to observe the sun's nightly dip into the ocean.

Romantic Warning: Most of the inns listed in the Moss Beach, Princeton, and Half Moon Bay areas have facilities for small business conferences, so don't be surprised if you run into cell-phone-toting types during the day. If this concerns you, call the inn to find out if any conferences are being held during your stay.

Hotel/Bed and Breakfast Kissing

❤❤❤❤ **SEAL COVE INN, Moss Beach** The owner of this distinctive property is a well-known travel writer, so it's not at all surprising that the details at Seal Cove Inn are so beautifully rendered. All the nuances for an enamored escape from city life are here, a mere 30 minutes south of San Francisco. Surrounded by herb and flower gardens, the expansive inn enjoys narrow glimpses of the ocean beyond a dense stand of lofty cypress trees. Guests can walk through the property to rugged oceanside bluffs and spend hours exploring the neighboring marine reserve and tide-pool beaches.

Many couples find the absence of frills and fuzzy teddy bears to be a welcome change of pace. Simple and pleasing country decor sets the stage in each of the ten guest rooms, accented by wonderful wood-framed beds, grandfather clocks, watercolor paintings, and comfortable seating areas. The spacious rooms feature an abundance of romantic highlights, from the luxurious linens gracing the beds to wood-burning fireplaces that enhance cozy sitting areas. TVs with VCRs are tastefully tucked away in armoires. Fresh flowers, towel warmers, an assortment of complimentary beverages, evening turndown service, and morning newspaper and coffee delivery to your door are extra touches at this sophisticated inn. Each room has a private bath and a deck or terrace that overlooks the property's resplendent gardens. Vaulted ceilings lend an added feeling of spaciousness to the upstairs rooms, and Jacuzzi tubs in the Cypress and Fitzgerald Suites are well worth the extra expense.

If privacy is your priority, a continental breakfast can be served to your room; otherwise, start your day with hot entrées like Grand Marnier French toast or blueberry pancakes in the formal, sun-filled dining room with other guests. After a day of tide-pool exploring or beachcombing, return to find wine and appetizers waiting in the comfortable living room beside a blazing fire. **221 Cypress Avenue; (650) 728-4114, (800) 995-9987; www.sealcoveinn.com; very expensive to unbelievably expensive; minimum-stay requirement on weekends.**

Princeton

Hotel/Bed and Breakfast Kissing

❤❤❣ **PILLAR POINT INN, Princeton** Escape to Cape Cod for the weekend without leaving the West Coast. How? By staying at this comfortably modern seaside inn that looks as if it were transplanted from a New England fishing village. Despite its location on a well-traveled street, the soundproof windows and sprawling architectural design make each room a haven unto itself.

Ten of the 11 rooms feature bay windows with spectacular views of the ocean. Recline in the window seat and watch the fishing boats as they enter the harbor with the day's catch. The only room that does not face the ocean overlooks a meadow and a well-kept, hedged garden. Each room has a beautifully tiled fireplace, a downy European feather bed, and the usual hotel-like amenities, such as a telephone, refrigerator, and concealed TV; all have private, standard baths. Vaulted ceilings in several of the upstairs rooms add a light, airy touch. The best views can be had from Room Nos. 6 and 10, where you and your sweetheart can cuddle up in comfy window seats encased beneath large arched windows.

The glowing fireplace in the breakfast room is sure to warm your hearts. Large windows allow you to bask in the morning sunshine as you enjoy delicious homemade granola, fresh muffins, coffee cake, Belgian waffles, chile pepper quiche, or cheese blintzes. Stroll into the parlor for a fireside glass of sherry (available at all hours), or don your jackets, walk to the wharf, and see what the fishing boats brought home. **380 Capistrano Road; (650) 728-7377, (800) 400-8281; www.pillarpointinn.com; expensive to very expensive; minimum-stay requirement on weekends.**

Romantic Suggestion: About a quarter of a mile away from Pillar Point Inn is the lively Italian restaurant, **MEZZA LUNA** (459 Prospect Way; 650-728-8108; moderate; lunch and dinner daily; live music on weekends), housed in a historic hotel. Although the acoustics aren't conducive to intimate conversation and there's no ocean view, the sunny Tuscan interior, standard but varied Italian fare, and delicious desserts are worth the walk.

Half Moon Bay

When the rest of the world is heading north of San Francisco to Stinson Beach and other points along the exquisite northern coastline, you can wind your way south to Half Moon Bay. A mere 25 miles from San Francisco, this quaint little hamlet by the water feels worlds away from big-city life.

Half Moon Bay hugs the seaside along the rocky Pacific Coast Highway. In a location such as this, with epic scenery at every turn, it's difficult to find a place that *isn't* suitable for hugging and kissing. Replete with miles of sandy beaches, the area also has an abundance of equestrian trails and bicycle paths. Adventurers can arrange fishing charters, sailing sessions, and whale-watching expeditions. Local wineries, charming little lunch spots, and plenty of parks will help round out your day. At night, visit one of the restaurants serving up an eclectic assortment of cuisines, or a club featuring classical and jazz music. Both can keep you busy well into the wee hours of morning—unless, of course, you can find something better to do.

Hotel/Bed and Breakfast Kissing

❀❀❀ BEACH HOUSE INN AT HALF MOON BAY, Half Moon Bay A

view with a kiss or a kiss with a view: Luckily, you'll get both if you book an oceanfront room at the Beach House. This Nantucket shingle-style inn, accented by flower-filled window boxes and a bubbling fountain, is one of the newer accommodations on the southern coastline and offers refreshingly modern rooms with upscale amenities.

The 54 guest accommodations are similar in design and size; it's the differing views that determine price and romantic potential. We highly recommend splurging for an ocean-view room, where a California king-size bed faces the sea and where you'll have no visual reminders of the inn's roadside location. Each comfortable guest room includes a lovely sitting area, a granite-topped kitchenette, a sparkling white bathroom, and a sandstone fireplace. From your private balcony or patio, you can hear the waves lap against the barrier rocks and the sea grass rustle in the wind. The only thing that may interrupt these sounds of nature is the low honk of a distant foghorn. If you choose to venture from your comfy quarters, you'll find a communal hot tub overlooking the ocean and a small heated pool residing at the property's edge. A continental breakfast is served in the lobby each morning. **4100 North Cabrillo Highway (Highway 1); (650) 712-3300, (800) 315-9366; www.beach-house.com; very expensive to unbelievably expensive; minimum-stay requirement on holiday weekends.**

❀❀❀❀ CYPRESS INN ON MIRAMAR BEACH, Half Moon Bay The

melodic rhythm of crashing waves, the cry of gulls, and the invigorating smell of salty air are all part of the sensory package at this picturesque inn. The two contemporary beach houses that comprise the Cypress Inn sit directly across the street from the ocean, so you won't be wanting for beach sights, sounds, and smells. Designed in celebration of nature and folk art, the inn's original building showcases a colorful collection of hand-carved Mexican sculptures and artwork. The eight smallish rooms in this building survey breathtaking ocean views and incorporate the elements with names like *La Luna* (moon), *Las Nubes* (clouds), and *El Cielo* (sky). Vividly colored stucco walls, terra-cotta–tiled floors, and natural-fiber furnishings lend the rooms a simple yet Southwest-sophisticated distinction. Luxurious white linens accent the fluffy feather beds, and a gas fireplace glows in every room. Although the spacious Penthouse Suite is the only room with a Jacuzzi tub (built for two), all of the rooms have private bathrooms and private balconies where you can sit and listen to the raging Pacific perform its eternal symphony.

Four luxury suites occupy the second beach house, set directly behind the original inn. Located a little farther from the water, these rooms compensate for the lack of direct ocean views with such sumptuous details and romantic amenities as gas fireplaces, extra-deep jetted tubs (in two rooms), elegant bathrooms, expansive decks in some rooms, and striking contemporary color schemes. Seashell-motif fabrics, rich in texture, surround the king-size canopy beds. Seals, sea otters, and strands of kelp float gracefully in a beautifully painted seascape mural that runs the length of the entry hall; the same elements reappear on the walls in several of the rooms.

In the morning, share sweet kisses during a bountiful breakfast brought directly to your room or served family-style in the inn's cheery dining room. Choices might include peaches-and-cream French toast, vegetarian eggs Benedict topped with steamed asparagus, or a light yogurt parfait. Wine and hors d'oeuvres are served in the twilight hours, and, later on in the evening, a sweet treat awaits on your pillow. **407 Mirada Road; (650) 726-6002, (800) 83-BEACH; www.cypressinn.com; expensive to unbelievably expensive; minimum-stay requirement on weekends.**

❧❧❧❧ **MILL ROSE INN, Half Moon Bay** Framed by a classic white picket fence, a lush garden bursting with brilliant colors welcomes you to the Mill Rose Inn. From the lovingly manicured rose garden in the courtyard to the luscious chocolates and liqueurs found in the guest rooms, every detail shows the full attention bestowed by the longtime owners. This English country inn is well taken care of, and, as guests, you will be too.

Antiques and photos of the owners' prized poodles fill the cozy common areas, where guests can take in the ambience of bygone days while sampling wine, cheese, and decadent desserts in the early evening. In the six intimate guest rooms, luxurious linens adorn unbelievably plush European feather beds, and extravagant bouquets of silk and fresh-cut flowers brighten every room. Ornate Bradbury & Bradbury wallpaper, ultraplush window treatments, claw-foot tubs, European antiques, and hand-painted tile fireplaces (in all but one room) re-create authentic turn-of-the-century elegance. Modern conveniences like TVs, VCRs, and stereos are hidden in armoires; mini-refrigerators are stocked with complimentary beverages; and each suite has its own private entrance. Turndown service and morning newspaper delivery round out the pretty picture.

An ample whirlpool tub (large enough for two) highlights the Bordeaux Rose Suite, but all guests have access to a flower-shielded gazebo that encloses a Jacuzzi spa enhanced by lush greenery, more flowers, and a bubbling fountain. Don't worry about finding a crowd in the spa—you can reserve time here for a private, steamy soak of your own.

After a good night's sleep, enjoy a champagne breakfast at your own private table in the dining room or, better yet, have it delivered to your room or to a table in the peaceful rose garden. An apple-cranberry crunch topped with whipped cream, a frothy banana-orange frappé, and an outstanding artichoke frittata served with spicy salsa kept us going until dinnertime. Mill Rose Inn also prides itself on offering special, affectionate services, such as the use of blankets, coolers, and a fully equipped picnic basket (you supply the food and drinks) for your beach outings. **615 Mill Street; (650) 726-8750, (800) 900-ROSE; www.millroseinn.com; very expensive to unbelievably expensive; minimum-stay requirement on weekends; recommended wedding site.**

❤❤ **OLD THYME INN, Half Moon Bay** Spicing up your love life is simple at this bed and breakfast in downtown Half Moon Bay. Handsomely renovated and well maintained by its owners, this Queen Anne Victorian is a delightful place for those seeking a traditional bed-and-breakfast experience. A blend of modern and old-fashioned touches is apparent in each of the seven rooms, both upstairs and down. Works from the owners' art collection adorn walls painted in soothing solid colors. Luxurious designer linens blanket the beds, and claw-foot tubs and authentic stained glass windows are highlights in some of the bathrooms. Other rooms are romantically equipped with fireplaces and whirlpool tubs. Extra touches like fresh flowers brighten the rooms, and a video library overflowing with "snuggling up" movies entices you to stay put. By far the most romantic and spacious room is the Garden Suite, with its own private entrance off the herb garden, a double Jacuzzi tub set beneath a large skylight, and a canopied bed fronting the fireplace. A subtle Japanese motif lends a simple yet comfortable feeling to this special retreat. Guests here have the indulgent option of having breakfast delivered at their leisure.

Breakfast offerings may include scrambled-egg tortillas, lemon cheese-cakes, eggs Florentine, harvest-grain breads, and, of course, a selection of herbal teas. Specials, such as lemon-rosemary crumb cake, showcase delights from the inn's productive herb garden, which contains dozens of aromatic varieties, all available for tasting by inquisitive guests. Breakfast is served to guests (except those in the Garden Suite) at a common table in the living room or on the garden patio when weather permits. After a stay here, it is easy to see how love (not to mention hundreds of flowers and herbs) can bloom so easily at the Old Thyme Inn. **779 Main Street; (650) 726-1616, (800) 720-4277; www.oldthymeinn.com; moderate to very expensive; minimum-stay requirement on weekends.**

Restaurant Kissing

❦❦ MIRAMAR BEACH RESTAURANT AND BAR, Half Moon Bay

Known more for its location than its ambience, the Miramar Beach Restaurant delights in glorious views of the azure Pacific. Many of the wooden tables throughout the dining room are positioned next to windows and offer unobstructed views of spectacular sunsets and crashing waves. Table lamps and wall sconces soften the effect of dark wood accents and a clubbish interior, and fresh flowers at every table dress up the otherwise uninspired mood. While oceanfront seating is preferred, there is a small table in back next to the fireplace that is highly romantic and should be reserved if privacy is paramount.

All of the seafood on the menu is delicious, especially the generous crab cakes and the "fresh catch of the day," delivered by local fishermen. Other dishes tend toward the typical, including filet mignon, pasta primavera, and Cajun fettuccine. **131 Mirada Road; (650) 726-9053; inexpensive to expensive; lunch and dinner daily, brunch Sunday.**

❦❦❦ PASTA MOON, Half Moon Bay

It seems only fitting to find a restaurant called Pasta Moon in the town of Half Moon Bay. Set among the small boutiques that line Main Street, this restaurant offers tantalizing Italian dishes in a refined café atmosphere. Glowing candles, white tablecloths, and soft Mediterranean music conspire to create an affectionate ambience worthy of a kiss or two. Most tables are spaced reasonably apart so private conversations can be just that. The best table choices are next to the large picture windows, where noise from the open kitchen is less audible.

Culinary-keen locals say Pasta Moon's food is the best in town and we couldn't agree more. We started our meal by savoring the succulent grilled prawns and then indulged in one of the noteworthy pastas, a housemade pappardelle tossed with roasted beets, goat cheese, and walnuts. The catch

331

of the day—seared halibut topped with grilled asparagus—proved exceptionally light and fresh. Overall, every dish validated the restaurant's reputation for well-flavored and generous dishes. Be sure to save room for dessert, because the tiramisu is definitely out of this world. As for the service, the friendly wait staff would gladly bring you the moon if they could. **315 Main Street; (650) 726-5125; moderate to expensive; lunch and dinner daily.**

Pescadero

The stretch of land between Half Moon Bay and Santa Cruz provides spectacular ocean scenery, but few places for a romantic rendezvous. If you happen along Highway 1, you'll eventually see signs for Pescadero, which resides off the beaten path. There's not much to see in this one-stop-sign town but, luckily, high above in the hills, there's a bed and breakfast worth the detour.

Hotel/Bed and Breakfast Kissing

❦❦ **OLD SAW MILL LODGE, Pescadero** After driving almost three miles up a winding, mountainous road you'll wonder if there is actually something up here besides the clouds. Keep going! Once you reach your destination and settle into your room at this traditional bed and breakfast, you'll know the long journey was worth it. The highlight of the large, lodge-like home is the back deck, from which you can savor views of the Santa Cruz mountain range and the distant Pacific. Such scenery will take your breath away, while the quietness and the fresh, cool air will refresh your spirits. Inside, a lodge theme is evident in the common area, replete with big-game trophies, old saws and farming antiques, a sizable river-rock fireplace, and plenty of games and books. A small pool and even smaller Jacuzzi tub are housed in the slightly weathered solarium.

The five rooms—three with decks and four with en suite bathrooms—are pleasantly decorated in a stylish contemporary fashion and are outfitted with down duvets or plush quilts, king- or queen-size beds, and robes and slippers. For those rainy, snowy, or nippy nights, curl up in bed with a bowl of popcorn and watch a movie on your TV/VCR. (Popcorn and a video selection are available.) The two large corner rooms, the Head Bullmaster's Room and the Head Faller's Room, boast the best kissing potential, in part due to private decks and king-size beds. In the Head Bullmaster's Room, the California king-size bed faces the window, making it the ideal place to have breakfast. (It's the only room where breakfast is delivered to your bed and the only room with a telescope.) The Head Faller's

Room, adorned with a beautiful four-post king-size bed, caters to early birds who love the morning sun streaming through their windows. The other rooms are small and pleasant, and while they aren't loaded with romantic perks, the prices are certainly reasonable, and you can't beat the mountaintop location.

For breakfast, guests (other than those residing in the Bullmaster's Room) sit on comfy peeled-log chairs at tables for two in the sunny dining room. On warm summer mornings, take your fixings out to the deck and watch the birds as you eat. A full country breakfast, served buffet-style, will have you in gear for the rest of the day. You can burn off those scrumptious pecan sticky buns on the various hiking trails that meander through the 60-acre wooded property. If you'd rather be a beach bum, the Pacific is only a 15-minute descent by car. **700 Ranch Road West; (650) 879-0111, (800) 596-6455; www.oldsawmill.com; moderate to expensive; minimum-stay requirement on weekends seasonally.**

Romantic Suggestion: Once you're up here, you might not want to make the effort to leave, especially at night. Many guests bring an easy-to-fix dinner and prepare it in the small community kitchen that's complete with refrigerator, microwave, and some cooking utensils. Savoring a sunset dinner on the porch swing has to be the most romantic dining for miles around.

Santa Cruz

In the spring and summer, hordes of tourists flock to Santa Cruz to stroll the commercialized (and sometimes seedy) oceanfront boardwalk, eat cotton candy and caramel corn, and ride the roller coaster. Locals spike volleyballs over nets scattered across a long stretch of sandy beach, and crowds of sunbathers bake in rows as far as the eye can see. But even though its beachfront and boardwalk are what Santa Cruz is best known for, there's much more to this crowded oceanfront town than is first apparent.

More than 30 wineries dot the nearby Santa Cruz Mountains, boasting award-winning wines and pastoral vistas. If being enveloped by nature is your idea of romantic, the options in this area are limitless. Travel north along winding, narrow Highway 9 to **HENRY COWELL REDWOOD STATE PARK**, where dense groves of towering redwoods extend for miles. Here, hiking paths meander through lush meadows and deep forests, and California sunshine spills through the canopy, illuminating the trails.

The **UNIVERSITY OF CALIFORNIA SANTA CRUZ ARBORETUM** (High Street between the east and west entrances of UC Santa Cruz; 831-427-2998; open daily 9 A.M.–5 P.M.) offers slightly tamer views of Mother Nature, and in the summer often hosts small musical festivals and concerts. After treating the ears to beautiful sounds, wander past fragrant flower and herb gardens to a vine-covered trellis set at the edge of a hillside and engage the lips.

For the adventurous at heart, yacht charters, scenic cruises, and sailing lessons are available from **O'NEILL YACHT CENTER** (2222 East Cliff Drive; 831-476-5202; www.oneillnet.com) and **PACIFIC YACHTING AND SAILING** (790 Mariner Parkway; 831-423-SAIL, 800-374-2626; www.pacificsail.com). Hop into a kayak and paddle away with each other by calling **KAYAK CONNECTION** (831-479-1121; www.cruzio.com/~kayakcon) or **ADVENTURE QUEST** (831-425-8445). The **BICYCLE RENTAL CENTER**, just two blocks from the municipal wharf on Center Street (831-426-8687; www.bikeandtour.com), provides tandem bicycles as well as mountain and cruising bikes for self-guided tours of the area. If you're after the ultimate California experience, **RICHARD SCHMIDT SCHOOL OF SURFING** (831-423-0928; www.primitive.com/schmidt) provides surfing lessons to people of all ages and athletic abilities. Contact each company listed above for prices and details.

Hotel/Bed and Breakfast Kissing

❀❀❀❀ **BABBLING BROOK INN, Santa Cruz** An acre of greenery is the backdrop for this rambling wooden inn—a true nature lover's oasis. Picturesque footbridges and meandering footpaths offer close-up views of breathtaking redwoods, pines, flowering gardens, tumbling waterfalls, and a massive waterwheel that churns in the inn's namesake: a babbling brook. Guests are welcomed in a cozy country parlor, where the aroma of freshly baked chocolate chip cookies is too tempting to resist. Wine and hors d'oeuvres are also served here in the evening, next to a glowing fire.

Eight of the property's 13 guest rooms and cottages are named after famous French painters. Beautifully framed reproductions of paintings by Cézanne, van Gogh, and Monet (among others) establish the theme in each of these rooms. Special romantic touches add character to the winsome French-country decor in all rooms. A ten-foot-tall white wrought-iron bed from the University of California at Santa Cruz's production of *Romeo and Juliet* is the highlight of the Degas Room. A private deck in the hidden Fern Grotto Room boasts close-up views of a small cascading waterfall and waterwheel, and for those painting a picture of love in the Artist's Retreat, an outdoor hot tub awaits on your own deck. Individual entrances, private decks, and wood-burning stoves in every room help to keep the fire burning (so to speak), and the double whirlpool tubs in two of the rooms are romantic bonuses.

Take advantage of the fact that the boardwalk, beach, and sparkling Pacific Ocean are a mere ten-minute stroll from the inn. In the morning, a generous country repast served buffet-style in the parlor will give you plenty of energy to battle the crowds and build sand castles at the nearby beach to your hearts' content. **1025 Laurel Street; (831) 427-2456, (800) 866-1131; www.babblingbrookinn.com; expensive to very expensive; minimum-stay requirement on weekends; recommended wedding site.**

Romantic Warning: The Babbling Brook Inn fronts a very busy street, and traffic noise is most noticeable during the day and early evening. Hopefully, you'll be so enchanted by the murmur of the babbling brook and the turning waterwheel that you'll scarcely notice. What we noticed more was the noisy child bouncing off the walls in the room below. Unromantic? Yes, but the inn claims that children don't visit often.

Restaurant Kissing

❤❤ **CASABLANCA RESTAURANT, Santa Cruz** If you're looking for a restaurant with a water view, you need look no further. Casablanca Restaurant sits directly across the street from the beach, and the dining room's tall, stately windows overlook the crowded boardwalk and crashing ocean surf. Candle lanterns at every table illuminate the small dining room, which is decorated with leafy palm trees, cushioned rattan chairs, and crisp white linens. Fried Brie with jalapeño jelly is an unusual prelude to such classic continental dishes as pan-roasted chicken breast with basil pesto, fresh halibut encrusted in macadamia nuts, and roast rack of lamb covered by an ancho chile and dried-cherry demi-glace. After an enjoyable dinner don't be surprised if the one you're with reaches for your hand, gazes into your eyes, and recites those famous lines, "This could be the beginning of a beautiful friendship." **101 Main Street; (831) 426-9063; expensive; dinner daily.**

Romantic Warning: There is nothing romantic about the **CASA BLANCA INN** (831-423-1570, 800-644-1570; www.casablancasantacruz. com; expensive to very expensive), attached to the restaurant; it's just your basic motel.

❤❤ **LINWOOD'S, Santa Cruz** Linwood's is not quite a restaurant but, then again, it doesn't exactly look like a true-blue bar either. This somewhat undefinable eating establishment does have one sure thing going for it: It boasts one of the finest panoramic views of Santa Cruz and the bay beyond, which is why it is listed in our book.

The interior is fresh and contemporary, with taupe and black striped chairs, stylish halogen lighting, a large fireplace, and some cozy tables for two. There's also a sophisticated bar and, if the weather's nice, a spacious outdoor patio for al fresco dining. Two silent televisions and a pool table are the only evidence that Linwood's is more of a bar than a restaurant; fortunately, both can be ignored if you face westward to watch the sunset. An à la carte menu featuring the average lineup of sandwiches, salads, grilled meats, and seafood won't win any awards for originality, but most are satisfying.

The only drawback about dining here is not knowing who your neighbors will be. Chaminade, where Linwood's is located, is a popular conference center and depending on your luck (and the day of the week) you may be surrounded by busy bee conventioneers, or it just may be the two of you and the sunset. We hope you experience the latter. **One Chaminade Lane, at Chaminade at Santa Cruz; (831) 475-5600, (800) 283-6569; www. chaminade.com; moderate; lunch and dinner daily.**

Romantic Note: Accommodations at CHAMINADE AT SANTA CRUZ (very expensive; minimum-stay requirement on holiday weekends) cater primarily to business travelers and conference attendees. The 152 standard, hotel-style rooms in this sprawling Mediterranean-style complex offer just enough amenities to keep you comfortable, but not enough to inspire any serious kissing.

Outdoor Kissing

❧❧ **NATURAL BRIDGES STATE PARK, Santa Cruz** Once upon a time, a beautiful orange-and-black monarch butterfly came to court its mate in a wooded canyon near the seashore. Before long, other wooing butterflies discovered this lover's lure. Today, hundreds of thousands of monarchs return to this spot each winter, creating a kaleidoscope of color among the sweet-scented eucalyptus. Stroll hand in hand into this storybook setting along a wooden walkway that leads down into the woods to a platform nested in the monarchs' winter home. Once there, you can simply lie on the platform and watch them flutter above you like colorful stars. Sixty-five acres of forest, beach, and tide pools nearby invite additional kissing as you wander toward the ocean. **West Cliff Drive; (831) 423-4609; $6 entrance fee per vehicle.** *From the Santa Cruz boardwalk, follow West Cliff Drive north along the shore to the park entrance.*

Romantic Note: The best time to visit is midday in late November to early February. Monarch migration times vary, but you can always call ahead to make sure the colorful creatures have arrived. Also, be aware that this site is popular with elementary and junior high school science classes during the school year, which can be a noisy distraction.

Capitola, Soquel, and Aptos

Capitola is a quaint seaside village with just enough handicraft stores and clothing boutiques to make it interesting for shoppers, but not so many they detract from the melodic Pacific surf. Traffic can be tough, however, and getting to the beach might prove difficult depending on the day and weather. Though it is farther north than its affluent seaside neighbor, Carmel, Capitola has a decidedly Southern California feel. When the surf's up, dry suit–clad surfers skim through the waves, and when the sun's out, college students play beach games and couples picnic on the sand. A promenade stretches along the shore, and the view stretches even farther north and south along the coastline. Benches face the ocean, so you can sit, embrace, and daydream together.

Nearby and inland, Soquel and Aptos also have a certain amount of charm. Although they don't share Capitola's ocean drama, they offer quiet seclusion and country appeal. Spectacular sunsets are a daily treat at our two favorite nearby beaches, **MANRESA STATE BEACH** (831-763-7064; $6 day-use fee) and **SUNSET STATE BEACH** (831-763-7064; $6 day-use fee), where you can wander for miles along the water's edge.

Hotel/Bed and Breakfast Kissing

❤❤ **THE BAYVIEW HOTEL, Aptos** From the road, you might miss this grand Italianate Victorian hotel. During the spring and summer, most of the three-story building is hidden by a magnificent magnolia. Such a tree is a blessing since it shelters the inn from afternoon sun and, more importantly, from the unsightly parking lot and road in front. The Bayview Hotel is the oldest operating hotel in the Monterey Bay area (it was built in 1878) and offers surprisingly good old-fashioned charm and comfort. The hotel's 11 guest rooms have high ceilings, but are otherwise on the small side. Plush feather beds covered with beautiful linens are complemented by local art and solid-color walls accented by beautiful trim or hand-painted murals. Antique beds, dressers, and armoires are intermixed with contemporary sofas and chairs, creating an authentic Victorian feel with modern comforts. Third-floor rooms have the advantage of being more spacious and having larger beds, plus they exude a much more contemporary tone. Two of the most romantically appealing rooms up here, Seacliff and Rio del Mar, have soaking tubs in their spacious tiled bathrooms, and gas-burning fireplaces. None of the rooms have air-conditioning, which might pose a problem especially for those rooms catching a lot of sunlight. In the morning, a deluxe continental breakfast is served in the pleasant but ordinary dining room. We highly recommend requesting that breakfast be brought to your room.

Guests staying here have the added convenience of eating at the **WHITE MAGNOLIA RESTAURANT** (831-662-1890; moderate to expensive; call for seasonal hours), housed in the Bayview's ground floor, but operating under different ownership. The stunning bar radiates modernism, while the dining room (most of which is housed in the sunporch) is classically styled and relatively conservative in its appointments. **8041 Soquel Drive; (831) 688-5128, (800) 422-9843; www.bayviewhotel.com; moderate to expensive.**

Romantic Warning: Noise from the restaurant and bar is most discernible in the second-floor rooms.

❀❀❀ **BLUE SPRUCE INN, Soquel** Good things often come in small packages, which is the case with the unpretentious and heartwarming Blue Spruce Inn. Enclosed by a white picket fence, the beautifully renovated Victorian farmhouse is fresh and endearing. Colorful Amish quilts drape luxurious feather beds in the six guest rooms located throughout the Main Home and adjoining Garden Area. Local artists were commissioned by the innkeepers to echo the colors and motifs of the quilts in paintings that adorn the walls.

Although the guest rooms are quite small, most offer private entrances and patios. Romantic luxuries in some of the rooms also help to compensate: Three rooms have Jacuzzi tubs, five offer gas fireplaces, and all have skylights that let in plenty of sunshine. An outdoor hot tub nestled in a garden courtyard is available for all guests to use, although it is far from private. Seascape, a first-floor room decorated in ocean blues and greens, features wicker chairs, an inviting feather bed, a gas stove, a bow-shaped double Jacuzzi tub, and a private entrance. The teeny Two Hearts room is a cozy second-story hideaway with a red heart–patterned quilt and dormer ceilings. Its private, pink-colored bathroom may be tiny, but it packs a punch with its four-jetted massage shower (dubbed "The Human Car Wash"). In the spacious Carriage House, skylights just above the headboard of the raised bed invite kissing beneath the stars, and a two-person Jacuzzi tub set in the living room offers bubbling pleasures aplenty. The tucked-away Summer Afternoon Room features a lovely seating area, plus a very unique feature: an outdoor claw-foot tub for soaking beneath the stars.

The delightful innkeepers love to cook and that shows in their morning treats: hot blueberry pudding topped with crème fraîche, sourdough Belgian waffles with an assortment of syrups, or spinach-feta strata presented with smoked chicken and apple sausage. The full breakfast, which also includes a fruit dish, freshly baked muffins or scones, and fresh-squeezed orange juice, is served to guests in the cheery dining room, which is adorned with the innkeepers' angel collection. **2815 South Main Street; (831) 464-1137, (800) 559-1137; www.bluespruce.com; inexpensive to expensive; minimum-stay requirement on weekends.**

❦❦❦❦ **INN AT DEPOT HILL, Capitola** If ever an inn deserved to enter the annals of romance, this one does. If we could extend our kiss rating we would, because the Inn at Depot Hill deserves ten lips, possibly even more. Built in 1901, this opulent establishment once served as a turn-of-the-century railroad depot. (In the dining room, a hand-painted mural depicting a train window and a pastoral landscape recalls the past.) Hop on board and select one of the lavishly decorated rooms that evoke the world's most romantic destinations. You can kiss in a Parisian pied-à-terre, in a Mediterranean retreat on the Côte d'Azur, in a simple Japanese hideaway in Kyoto, or in an Italian coastal villa in Portofino. Each guest room truly reflects the essence of these locales.

No matter which "destination" you choose, prepare yourselves for luxury and pampering along the way. The 12 spectacularly decorated rooms are magazine material, with architectural touches such as domed ceilings, handsome wallpapers and paintings, and two-sided fireplaces. Sumptuous fabrics drape unbelievably plush, canopied feather beds, and magnificent antique furnishings enhance the foreign flair in every room. A blue-and-white Dutch tiled hearth warms the Delft Room, where a cushioned window seat overlooks a private garden. Frescoed walls in the Portofino Room create the impression of a coastal Italian villa. Decorated in royal red, the Railroad Baron's Room is adorned with handcrafted furniture covered with silk. The simple Kyoto Room, fronted by a serene Japanese garden, holds a deep soaking tub and a shower with a window. The spacious marble bathroom in each room comes equipped with all the amenities you could ever need (and many more). Each room also features a wood-burning fireplace, an irresistible two-person shower, a stereo system with appropriate music to complement your room's decor, TV/VCR (concealed unobtrusively in a cabinet), and plenty of fresh flowers.

We could fill a book with each room description, and we haven't even begun to tell you about the lovely courtyard or the deliciously cozy common areas. Four guest rooms have private outdoor Jacuzzi tubs; guests in those that don't can reserve time in the communal soaking tub set outside behind a latticed fence in the garden courtyard. Full breakfasts, afternoon wine with appetizers, and evening desserts, all prepared by the inn's executive chef, ensure energy for continuous kissing. **250 Monterey Avenue; (831) 462-3376, (800) 572-2632; www.innatdepothill.com; very expensive to unbelievably expensive; minimum-stay requirement on weekends and holidays; recommended wedding site.**

☙☙ **INN AT MANRESA BEACH, Aptos** If it looks like this 1867 Victorian mansion was just plunked down in the middle of flowering fields, it's because that's exactly what happened. The owners actually moved the massive structure several miles and then proceeded to renovate both inside and out. The result is a unique inn that offers something for romantics ... and for tennis fanatics who aim to keep the score at love-love.

When you walk in the main entrance, you might think you have stepped into a pub. There's a wooden bar and stools, a corner TV tuned to a 24-hour sports channel, and an assortment of tables. The walls are decorated—if that's the word—with business certificates and tennis rackets. While this is quite unusual decor for a bed and breakfast, you may understand why when you learn that tennis is the main game here (followed closely by romance). The inn is noted for its two clay courts and one grass court, not to mention year-round tennis tournaments and private lessons.

Thankfully, the eight rooms aren't so sports oriented, but more spiritually centered. The innkeepers hired a color psychologist and feng shui expert to help create rooms that appealed to all. The result: a California-casual look with walls painted in solid, primary colors and accented by modern art. Lovely sleigh and four-post beds topped by elegant duvets, and gorgeous, but simple, window treatments round out the picture. Romantic amenities weren't neglected in the creation of the rooms either: Five rooms have two-person jetted tubs and all feature gas fireplaces. Most of the beds move, too, with adjustable massage settings, although we prefer the human touch. Our favorite rooms are the second-floor Champagne and Cabernet Rooms. Those seeking rich, dark colors and an escape from sunny rooms might like the Champagne Room, decorated in elegant eggplant, gold, and scarlet. There's a two-person Jacuzzi tub in the bathroom and a queen-size bed fronting a fireplace. The Cabernet Room's highlight is the two-person Jacuzzi tub set smack-dab in the sunny bedroom. The other rooms are all lovely, but for privacy and to avoid noise we recommend those on the second floor only. Breakfast is served in your room—a big romantic plus—or downstairs in the pub-like dining room, which might detour any romantic plans if your sweetie is a sports fan. **1258 San Andreas**

Road; (831) 728-1000, (888) 523-2244; www.indevelopment.com; expensive to very expensive.

Romantic Warning: Although this one-of-a-kind inn certainly has its attractions, both romantically and athletically, we have two concerns about its kissability. The first and foremost is that children are welcomed with open arms. In fact, some rooms offer futon beds specifically for little ones. We adore children, but having them along or around does not a romantic getaway make. Our second and more minor concern is that the largest suite available is actually the innkeeper's living quarters. On weekends they move out while some unsuspecting couple moves in.

❀❀❀ **MANGELS HOUSE, Aptos** During the Victorian heyday, the elite vacationed far from the cares of the city, in fabulous country homes equipped with every imaginable luxury. Built in 1886 by California's sugar beet king, Mangels House is one of the most secluded and best restored of these homes. Set at the edge of 10,000-acre **NISENE MARKS STATE PARK** (see Outdoor Kissing) and encompassed by four acres of lush English gardens, the whitewashed Italianate Victorian mansion is a sight to behold. Guests are ushered into a stunning ballroom-size parlor, where the grand piano seems dwarfed. Hardwood floors gleam under Oriental carpets, and comfortable overstuffed sofas are clustered around a massive stone fireplace, where a fire blazes in the cooler months.

Fresh, contemporary color schemes and a vast collection of art, sculpture, and paintings brighten the six immensely spacious guest rooms upstairs. Decorated in a variety of styles, these rooms have their own eclectic flair and delightfully romantic touches. Murmurs from the garden's fountain are audible in the gigantic Guest Room, which has its own private porch, plenty of room for a party of two, and a private en suite bathroom. A fire crackles in the hearth of the Mauve Room, next to windows that overlook the lawn and trees. Nicholas' Room is handsomely decorated with an outstanding collection of artifacts from Zaire and Kenya, along with rich brown and cream colored walls, bold geometric African prints, and a mosquito net draped over the king-size canopy bed. The smallest room of all, the Mediterranean, is perhaps the most cheerful, with a bright private bath, queen-size bed, and soothing colors of green and blue. Cuddling couples should be aware that two rooms (Timothy's Room and Maria's Room) have private but detached bathrooms. While robes are provided, the hallway dash in this large home is more like a 50-yard sprint.

A full breakfast is served to guests at one large table in the elegant, formal dining room, which is adorned by large portraits of somber aristocrats. The limitless array of freshly baked oatmeal scones, popovers, coffee cake, apple pancakes, and tea (or coffee) served in silver teapots makes breakfast an affair to remember. You don't have to feel guilty about gorging yourselves, either; remember that 10,000 acres of hikable wilderness are right outside the front door. **570 Aptos Creek Road; (831) 688-7982, (800) 320-7401; www.innaccess.com/mangels; moderate to expensive; minimum-stay requirement weekends and holidays.**

☙☙ **MARVISTA, Aptos** The Spanish-style stucco exterior of this two-story home gives no indication that a stylish bed and breakfast awaits inside. The two guest rooms here are decorated in a comfortable, contemporary fashion with down comforters, wicker chairs, beige carpeting, and Pottery Barn–style furnishings. In the Palo Alto Room, warm up next to the gas stove or recline on the four-poster king-size bed where you can watch the sea. An enormous en suite bathroom (so big you can hear an echo) has a two-headed shower and a wonderful tiled Jacuzzi tub that looks out onto the garden. Manresa, the smaller room with a detached bath across the hall, has a French-country feel, with blue and yellow linens, a skylight, and a gas stove. Amenities in both rooms include TVs, telephones, small refrigerators, fluffy robes and slippers, and little semiprivate balconies with ocean views beyond neighborhood rooftops.

If the glow from the gas stove in your room does not provide the effect you desire, there is a wood-burning fireplace in the Arts and Crafts–style living room. Full breakfasts, which might feature blueberry pancakes or egg soufflés, are served each morning in the casual dining room. **212 Martin Drive; (831) 684-9311; expensive to very expensive; minimum-stay requirement on weekends.**

☙❨ **SEASCAPE RESORT, Aptos** First impressions count for a lot, but they're not everything. This is especially true at Seascape Resort. At first glance, there is nothing remotely romantic about the resort's sprawling, apartment-like buildings. But you can't argue with the prime location, atop a series of oceanfront bluffs. Enjoy spectacular views of the lovely natural setting from a cushioned fireside window seat in the hotel's expansive, elegant lobby. Although the water is partially hidden behind a dense grove of cypress trees, a steep footpath winds through a tree-laden ravine right to the ocean and six miles of soft sandy beach.

While most of Seascape's 290 guest rooms are typical of a standard resort/hotel, they all have unexpected touches of romance, with fireplaces, private balconies, fully equipped kitchens, upscale linens, and comfortable but ordinary furniture. Most (but not all) rooms have ocean views, so be sure to ask ahead of time. (Rooms in the north wing are particularly enticing because of their wonderful views of the water beyond the trees.) Surprisingly, for a resort this large, there are only six rooms with Jacuzzi tubs.

For added enjoyment, the resort features three heated pools, three outdoor Jacuzzi tubs, tennis courts (for a fee), and complimentary use of the sports club across the street. If you'd like private outdoor activities, opt for the beach bonfire special for two ($49 per couple). A staff member will transport the two of you, via golf cart, to the beach, build a bonfire, and leave so you can smooch for as long as the fire stays lit. Scrumptious s'mores are provided, as well as an after-fire pickup. How's that for heating up the night? **One Seascape Resort Drive; (831) 688-6800, (800) 929-7727; www.seascaperesort.com; very expensive to unbelievably expensive; recommended wedding site.**

Romantic Suggestion: Distant water views are the main attraction at the property's restaurant, SANDERLINGS (831-662-7120; moderate to expensive; breakfast, lunch, and dinner daily, brunch Sunday), which is decorated with tall green plants, white linens, and cloth umbrellas suspended from the high ceilings. Casual outdoor patio seating is available during warm weather. The kitchen serves up better-than-average California cuisine, including local Monterey Bay cioppino; roasted vegetable ravioli; and a tempting tempura trio of nori-wrapped ahi, soft-shell crab, and prawns.

Romantic Note: With all the amenities and the beachfront before you, it's no wonder this is a popular place for families. If you are traveling with children, but want some time for a momentary romantic escape, the resort offers a Kid's Club program. Plenty of activities will keep the young ones entertained while you pursue more amorous adventures.

Restaurant Kissing

☙☙ **BITTERSWEET BISTRO, Aptos** If you love chocolate as much as you love your sweetheart, Bittersweet Bistro is a dream come true. Chocoholics come from miles around for these dessert creations, most of which are perfectly sized for two. Yet sweet tooths aren't the only ones who flock here. People who seek out good food buzz like bees around the flower garden that fronts the entrance to this popular place. (Hint: Make reservations so you won't have to wait.) Inside, the various dining areas are all decorated in a warm Mediterranean decor. Wrought-iron sconces and bold modern prints fill the wall space, while fresh flowers and candles adorn butcher paper-topped tables complete with crayons for writing colorful love poems. The main dining room near the entrance is too crowded to be romantic, so opt for the room in the back or hide yourselves in a bar booth as a last resort. When the weather is warm, the outdoor patio is a pleasant spot to dine.

The menu lists a variety of pasta, seafood, and meat dishes; we recommend trying the more intriguing nightly specials. If in season, the towering asparagus salad, topped with shaved Reggiano cheese, is a must. Our roasted escolar, adorned with a mushroom sauce, was less unusual than it was hearty. When our grand finale arrived—a chocolate mousse cake sided by a scoop of pistachio ice cream—all heads in the dining room turned to see. The sweet endings here are all architectural wonders, with plenty of swirling sugar creations and mile-high presentations. If you can't decide on one of the many desserts *or* dessert specials, try the trio of specialty chocolate treats, perfect for sharing. Whatever you order, your dining experience here will be more sweet than bittersweet. **787 Rio del Mar Boulevard; (831) 662-9799; moderate to expensive; reservations recommended; lunch Wednesday–Friday, dinner Tuesday–Sunday, brunch Sunday.**

❤ **CAFÉ CRUZ, Soquel** More often than not, the locals can tell you where to find the best food in town. Listen to them and you'll wind up at Café Cruz. What this place lacks in romantic charisma it makes up for in outstanding food, generous portions at moderate prices, and an easygoing atmosphere. Just be sure to enter through the back patio, or else you might get the wrong impression. The front entrance is dark and dim but, inside, large windows light up the various dining rooms that are accented by tropical plants, stucco walls, and large murals. The back dining room boasts the only indoor fireplace but also holds the sometimes busy bar area, so it's a hit-and-miss option. Sunshine brings diners to the casual back patio, although heat lamps and a cozy fireplace should keep things comfy when it's cloudy.

If you don't mind such a casual atmosphere and plenty of people, the California comfort cuisine more than compensates for any romantic shortcomings. Organic produce, fresh fish, and generous portions are the hallmarks of the kitchen. Red pepper tortellini topped with blackened chicken and a rich mustard sauce delighted our palate. The homemade lemon bars, drizzled with mango and raspberry sauces, should have you puckering up in no time. **2621 41st Avenue; (831) 476-3801; moderate; lunch and dinner daily.**

❤❤ **CAFE SPARROW, Aptos** Treat yourselves to a taste of the French countryside at Cafe Sparrow. Food this good is usually found in a more refined setting, but the casual provincial ambience is a breath of fresh air for most city folks. Blue and pink sponge-painted walls, floral tablecloths, Impressionist-motif seat cushions, and a worn wood floor give the restaurant its quaint, rustic feel. Charming hand-painted knickknacks fill each nook and cranny, while dried-flower wreaths and rows of wine bottles adorn the walls. Although similar in decor, the two dining rooms have distinct personalities. Bright and airy, the main dining room is warmed by sunlight streaming through a large window that overlooks Soquel Drive. The second dining room is slightly more dark and formal, with a ceiling of flowing fabric that draws into a centerpiece of hanging baskets. The proximity of the open kitchen, however, makes this area less desirable.

Open for both lunch and dinner, Cafe Sparrow offers a variety of savory French dishes prepared with California flair. With its delicate blend of cheddar, Gruyère, and Brie, the fromage baguette is a cheese lover's dream come true! As for the albacore cheese puff, tuna just doesn't get any better than this. Dinner entrées include filet mignon and rack of lamb. For dessert, indulge yourselves with the profiteroles, light pastries filled with your choice of ice cream or pastry cream and sprinkled with chocolate.

Our only hesitation about Cafe Sparrow is that the casual atmosphere seems to have rubbed off on the wait staff; the service may be a little too leisurely for fast-paced city dwellers. **8042 Soquel Drive; (831) 688-6238; moderate; lunch and dinner daily, brunch Sunday.**

♥♥♥ **CHEZ RENÉE, Aptos** Embedded in a small business complex, the exterior of this simple French restaurant resembles a dentist's office. Fortunately, there's nothing office-like about its cozy interior. Lengths of leaf-patterned fabric adorn the barrel ceilings in the restaurant's four intimate but unpretentious dining rooms. A blazing fire spreads warmth throughout the restaurant, and a handful of cozy tables draped in white linen and topped with flickering candles encourage quiet conversation (and a few discerning pecks). Some aspects of the decor are a bit outdated, most notably the '80s-style wicker chairs, but, then again, you don't have to look at them, just sit on them. When weather permits, you can choose to dine on an outdoor patio, although nearby freeway noise can be bothersome.

The award-winning California cuisine is spiced with French and Italian accents, among others. Standouts include duckling garnished with an apricot chutney, and pan-grilled sturgeon served with sautéed shiitake mushrooms in a red wine sauce. Desserts are equally tantalizing. **9051 Soquel Drive; (831) 688-5566; expensive; lunch Wednesday–Friday, dinner Tuesday–Saturday.**

♥ **COUNTRY COURT TEA ROOM, Capitola** Small but brimming with charm, this authentic teahouse specializes in fireside lunches and genuine English-style high teas. Set beside a busy residential street, the cozy, countrified dining room is warmed by a fireplace and holds only a handful of tables. Trailing ivy is painted on the walls, and local art, country collectibles, and antiques garnish every shelf. Since all are for sale, the decor is forever changing. No matter what time of day you dine, the homemade soups, breads, and pastries are always a treat. Loyal fans flock here weekly for an abundant Sunday afternoon high tea. Be sure to request the "Two for Tea" booth for romantic dining or, on a sunny afternoon, sit in the interior courtyard sheltered underneath a magnolia tree. **911B Capitola Avenue; (831) 462-2498; inexpensive; no credit cards; call for seasonal hours.**

Romantic Warning: Ladies who lunch and mother-daughter combos are more common at this eatery than kissing couples.

❦❦❦ **SHADOWBROOK, Capitola** Located on the banks of Soquel Creek, this unique and exceedingly popular restaurant is reached via a steep, winding footpath surrounded by greenery. (You can also hop on board a little red cable car that rolls down its tracks to drop you at the restaurant's front door.) Nearly swallowed by dense, lush foliage, the lodge-style chalet has an enchanting storybook appearance. Multilevel dining rooms scattered throughout the enormous restaurant offer a variety of views and surroundings in which to enjoy a romantic repast. The Greenhouse and Main Dining Room are atrium-like in appearance, with plenty of ivy and ferns, flowing waterfalls, and windows looking out to the creek. The Wine Cellar is a small room tucked in back and surrounded by handsome wood walls, a beautiful tapestry, and plenty of wine bottles neatly arranged in racks. A massive brick fireplace, fronted by one table, is *the* spot to sit in the cellar. Our favorite room, however, is the Garden Room, famous for the redwood tree that grows inside. Here you'll have garden and creek views along with more privacy than the other rooms. Despite the many dining areas, things can get bustling, and you are almost guaranteed to hear at least one version of "Happy Birthday" in this quintessential celebration spot.

If you can't get reservations (which isn't uncommon), opt for having dinner, a drink, or a light supper in the bar area, aka the Rock Room, which is the most handsome room of all. Cathedral ceilings constructed of redwood wine barrels, and a sprawling rock wall complete with plants and a waterfall easily entertain the eye. Copper pots above the wood-burning fireplace, reasonably comfortable teak furniture, and plenty of small tables make this the place to romance the night away. Plus, for all those on a budget, happy hour is the bargain du jour. Although the nearby entryway can be packed with people, you can tuck yourselves away by the fire and forget the world.

The traditional California-style cuisine, focusing on grilled meats and fresh seafood, is about average in taste and presentation, although you have to give the kitchen some credit for creativity. Our oh-so-ordinary teriyaki-glazed salmon sat atop a bed of seaweed and was surrounded by a spicy wasabi-ginger sauce. Other entrées will appeal to more conservative tastes. Our dessert was divine: vanilla custard wrapped inside two crêpes and surrounded by a pool of caramel sauce. **1750 Wharf Road; (831) 475-1511; moderate to expensive; reservations recommended; lunch Monday–Friday, dinner daily, brunch Sunday.**

❀❀❀ **THEO'S, Soquel** Nestled within a quiet residential area, Theo's is a bungalow-turned-restaurant with a quaint front courtyard and a terra-cotta and brick exterior. Inside, contemporary artwork and wine bottles add European flair to the modest decor in the two dining rooms, each with peaked ceilings and linen-draped tables. The main dining area is made even cozier by its large stone fireplace.

French doors open to a rock patio that wraps around to the back of the house. Guests are encouraged to retreat there, wineglass in hand, to enjoy the cool evening breeze or explore the expansive herb garden that contributes fresh flavors to the chef's inspired creations. During warm weather (or when the heat lamps are on), guests can dine on the back patio overlooking a large grassy lawn.

Fresh salmon, homemade ravioli stuffed with goat's-milk ricotta, and roasted Muscovy duck breast are just a few of the consistently well-prepared main courses. Our assortment of three Hawaiian fish bathed in a coriander and ginger broth proved exceptionally light and flavorful. Desserts are much more decadent: The deep-fried chocolate truffles served with vanilla-bean ice cream are certain to raise an eyebrow or two. More ordinary, yet equally as extraordinary, is the mascarpone cheesecake atop a pistachio crust. Everything about Theo's reflects understated elegance, from the warm decor to the beautifully presented food and the refined service. You'll leave in love with this place and, of course, each other. **3101 North Main Street; (831) 462-3657; www.theosrestaurant.net; expensive; dinner Tuesday–Saturday.**

Outdoor Kissing

❀❀❀ **THE FOREST OF NISENE MARKS STATE PARK, Aptos** The Forest of Nisene Marks State Park is a wonderful place to sample nature's splendor. Patches of sunlight stream through breaks in the leafy canopy above, dappling the dense tangle of trees and bushes below. Nature-loving romantics will discover a number of uncrowded picnic areas scattered throughout the park. More than 30 miles of hiking trails, open to the public, offer suitable challenges for both casual walkers and hard-core hikers.

Even if you're not the outdoor type, you can experience the park's natural beauty from the comfort of your car. We recommend putting in a tape of classical music, reaching for your loved one's hand (hopefully your car has an automatic transmission), and driving through the tunnel of arching trees that line the main road. Just make sure you keep your windows closed, because other touring vehicles can stir up a tremendous amount of dust.

No matter how you choose to experience this incredible refuge, an afternoon in the solitude of Nisene Marks State Park is bound to nurture your appreciation for the earth as well as for each other. **(831) 763-7063; free admission, $3 parking fee.** *From southbound Highway 1, take the Seacliff Beach exit and turn east over the freeway to the first light. Turn right onto Soquel Drive. Continue about one-half mile, turn left onto Trout Gulch Road, and follow it to the entrance of the park.*

Romantic Suggestion: If you're planning a picnic or a romantic outing of some sort, stop by **GAYLE'S BAKERY AND ROSTICCERIA** (504 Bay Avenue, Capitola; 831-462-1200; inexpensive to moderate; open daily). Before choosing your meal, you'll want to wade through the bustling crowd to peruse the pastry cases that span the entire length of the bakery. The outstanding spit-roasted chicken, gourmet salads and pastas, and sinful desserts are some of the best deals in town.

Monterey

The sound of barking seals resounds throughout this well-known seaside town that rises from the blue-green waters of Monterey Bay and an adjoining marine sanctuary. Pelicans and otters frolic in the gentle surf, and year-round sunshine bathes the rocky beaches and picturesque residential streets in golden warmth. Monterey has a rich heritage that is reflected in its venerable Spanish-style adobe homes and meticulously maintained waterfront parks bursting with flowers. In December many of these historic sites are decorated for the holidays and opened to the public for fascinating self-guided tours.

Of course, **FISHERMAN'S WHARF** and the **MONTEREY BAY AQUARIUM** (see Outdoor Kissing for reviews of both) are prime tourist attractions, and they draw year-round crowds. And speaking of popular destinations, **CANNERY ROW** is a bustling reminder that the more things change, the more they stay the same. This building complex once thrived on the business of catching and canning sardines. Now it's the site of a series of shops and restaurants in the business of catching tourists (who are often packed tight like sardines). Why would you want to kiss here? Well, you probably wouldn't. Instead, take the opportunity to explore Cannery Row's endless array of boutiques, art galleries, and gift stores. And while browsing isn't exactly romantic, it can be enjoyable, and that's a good prelude to just about anything—including kissing.

Hotel/Bed and Breakfast Kissing

💋💋💋 **HOTEL PACIFIC, Monterey** With so many bed and breakfasts and charming inns to choose from on the Monterey Peninsula, it's hard to believe anyone would want to stay at a big hotel. Hard to believe, that is, until you see some of the very chic, exceedingly lavish hotels that have been developed in this area. Hotel Pacific is one of them, and it seems more like a romantic retreat than a traditional hotel. Plus, it goes one step further than most of the big names with its noteworthy approaches to the flavors of Monterey's rich past, starting with the decor. A circular fountain fronts the entrance to the Spanish Colonial–style inn, and dense flowering vines line the pathways that meander through two fountain-filled brick courtyards. Tucked into a historical section of town, Hotel Pacific gives little indication that it is much newer than the century-old buildings surrounding it.

Terra-cotta tiles, cream-colored stucco walls, and Santa Fe–style fabrics accent the 105 guest rooms, where you'll also find gas fireplaces, cushy feather beds, separate living areas with comfortable furnishings, and private patios or balconies facing the inner courtyard or surrounding neighborhood. Top-floor rooms are particularly appealing, with high beamed ceilings and curtained, canopied beds made from sandblasted pine logs. Although the hotel is close to Monterey's interesting sights and sounds, don't be surprised if you're tempted to spend the duration of your visit in the comfortable confines of your suite.

A complimentary continental breakfast is served buffet-style in a small, plush lobby filled with overstuffed couches and chairs. Appetizers are also served here in the evening. Either way, there aren't enough seats in this room, but even if there were, it is far too cramped to accommodate so many guests. We took our pastries, fruit, and coffee out to the garden-trimmed courtyard, sat at the fountain's edge, and planned our day in peace and quiet. **300 Pacific Street; (831) 373-5700, (800) 554-5542; www. hotelpacific.com; very expensive to unbelievably expensive; minimum-stay requirement on weekends seasonally.**

💋💋 **THE JABBERWOCK, Monterey** At first glance, this 1911 Craftsman-style home looks like any other bed and breakfast, complete with hedges, brick pathways and driveway, and lovely gardens. But once you venture "through the looking glass" and into The Jabberwock, you'll find yourselves in the topsy-turvy world of *Alice in Wonderland*. Don't be surprised to discover a breakfast menu with funny names, a "burbling" room for private telephone conversations, and other delightful surprises along the way.

This bed and breakfast has heaps of character and a charming home-like ambience that feels friendly and comfortable. Although four of the seven rooms share baths, romantic touches add a sense of enchantment to the otherwise modestly furnished accommodations. You're likely to forget this home was previously a convent once you see the tempting two-person Jacuzzi tub and enormous king-size bed in the sun-filled Mome Rath Room, the Toves' eight-foot carved walnut bed and secret garden, or Borogove's fireplace and spacious sitting area. The highlight of Jabberwock, however, has to be the lovely gardens embellished by brick walkways, iron benches and chairs, and a lovely waterfall garden. If you can't enjoy such beauty due to bad weather, the enclosed wraparound sundeck is the next best thing.

Each morning, you'll wake up to sweet and savory gourmet breakfasts with such tongue-twisting names as "snarkelberry flumptuous" (crêpes) or "deleeksious tweedledumps" (quiche). After imbibing some "jabber juice" and engaging in some "jabbertalk" with others in the dining room, you can spend the day whispering sweet nothings to each other in the garden. If you want to avoid all the gibberish completely, have breakfast delivered to your room. The only thing missing in such a wonderland is the Cheshire cat, but you will see plenty of smiles nonetheless. **598 Laine Street; (831) 372-4777, (888) 428-7253; www.jabberwockinn.com; moderate to very expensive; minimum-stay requirement on weekends.**

❤❤❦ **MONTEREY PLAZA HOTEL AND SPA, Monterey** The Monterey Plaza Hotel is so large it hugs *both* sides of Cannery Row, with a skywalk connecting buildings on opposite sides of the street. Wrought-iron balconies with potted plants add a quaint touch to the white stucco exterior, while polished elegance reigns inside. The expansive lobby dazzles with Italian marble floors, Brazilian teakwood walls, candle-style sconces, and a grand piano. An expansive outdoor terrace, popular with lovers and tourists alike, juts out over the water as if it were part of the jagged coastline. It's the perfect place to admire the blue water dotted with sailboats and kayaks.

The 290 guest rooms and suites have a luxury hotel feel, and are tastefully decorated in greens, creams, and rose hues. All feature classic mahogany and walnut Biedermeier-style furnishings and leather chairs, marble bathrooms, and European duvets covering king-size beds. When making a reservation, be sure to request a room with a water view; only half of the rooms afford such vistas, but to tell the truth, the ocean panorama is the primary attraction at the Monterey Plaza Hotel. Corner rooms in Building 1 offer the best views of the bay, thanks to their extra windows and large decks. Rooms in Building 2 directly face the water but, unfortunately, many take in noise from the often-crowded terrace below. No matter which waterfront room you choose, you're guaranteed to hear the squawking of seagulls mixed with the gentle sound of lapping waves below. The balconies, with seats for two, make wonderful places to sit, snuggle, and watch the tide roll in. **400 Cannery Row; (831) 646-1700, (800) 631-1339; www.woodsidehotels.com; very expensive to unbelievably expensive; minimum-stay requirement on holiday weekends.**

Romantic Note: After a day of sea-gazing, head downstairs to dine at THE DUCK CLUB RESTAURANT (831-646-1701; moderate to expensive; breakfast and dinner daily). Well-spaced tables with handsome leather and wood chairs are surrounded by cherrywood paneling, green plants, Audubon art and statues, and enormous windows commanding waterfront views. The open kitchen serves up a standard but tasty array of homemade pastas, seafood, and wood-roasted specialties including, not surprisingly, several duck preparations. If you're lucky enough to get a seat near the windows, you can watch the shimmering moon dance across the bay as the lights of the city sparkle in the distance.

Romantic Alternative: Just up the street from the Monterey Plaza Hotel, at the entrance to Cannery Row, is the MONTEREY BAY INN (242 Cannery Row; 831-373-6242, 800-424-6242; www.montereybayinn.com; expensive to unbelievably expensive). Fronted by an emerald green park, this nondescript white stucco building enjoys splendid views of the ocean, harbor, and marine sanctuary. This is the property's only real romantic draw, however. Unless you reserve a room with full-on ocean views, the obtrusive cement decks, standard bathrooms, and hotel-style furnishings are not particularly impressive.

❤❤❤❤ **OLD MONTEREY INN, Monterey** Nestled on a quiet hillside far from the bustle of town, the Old Monterey Inn is the kind of place you fall in love with the moment you enter the garden gate. Terra-cotta pots filled with flowers hang like jewels from the gnarled branches of ancient trees in the front yard, while meandering paths lead to lovingly tended gardens and secluded niches where you can kiss to your hearts' content. Attention to affectionate details is equally evident inside the 1929 English Tudor inn, where every room offers something special for those seeking romance.

The ten rooms—nine with fireplaces and three with jetted tubs—blend masculine and feminine styles together to please all preferences. Original woodwork and cabinetry, English style antiques, and plush feather beds with down comforters make any room an enviable place to stay. In the main house we prefer the handsome Library Room, with its bed tucked into a windowed alcove. This second-floor room also has a private patio where you can sit and read from one of the many novels provided. One of the most appealing rooms for cuddling couples is the Chawton Room, hidden behind the house. Although small and darker than the other rooms, it warms the heart with whimsical cherub art, hand-stenciled walls, a fireplace, and a beautifully tiled two-person jetted tub. Soft coral hues and dimming lights make everyone glow with beauty here. The most private room of all (and the most expensive) is the Garden Cottage, which has its own entrance, a linen-and-lace crown canopy above the bed, and a tiled fireplace that warms the comfortably furnished sitting room.

Hot beverages and freshly baked cookies are available at all hours, and a lavish spread of wine and cheese is served every afternoon in the homey fireside parlor. Morning brings big decisions, namely, where to have breakfast. Choice one: Enjoy a hot breakfast served on hand-painted china in the elegant dining room overlooking the gardens. Choice two (and our favorite): Indulge in breakfast in bed. Choice three: Have breakfast served in the room, but not in bed. Choice four: In the warmer months, savor your first meal while seated on the brick patio surrounded by a profusion of pink and white impatiens, roses, wisteria, and boxwood hedges. Such choices, and such romance! There can be no question that this is a real slice of paradise. **500 Martin Street; (831) 375-8284, (800) 350-2344; www. oldmontereyinn.com; very expensive to unbelievably expensive; minimum-stay requirement on weekends.**

❤❤❤❤ **SPINDRIFT INN, Monterey** Standing at the water's edge in the middle of Cannery Row, the Spindrift Inn is ultrachic and European in its styling and architecturally impressive throughout. To get the utmost of what this boutique hotel offers, we suggest you splurge for a waterfront room. Here, the tang of salt water wafts through the air and the sound of waves right below your room enhances the mood. Binoculars and window seats in the oceanside rooms allow you to watch seals, otters, pelicans, and other marine animals at play in the kelp beds. Behind you, a wood-burning fireplace casts an amber glow on the hardwood floors, stylish carpets, and sumptuous fabrics. The 42 rooms here also feature down comforters and feather beds (some sleigh beds, some canopies), TV/VCRs hidden in armoires, and spacious marble bathrooms. If it's a warm evening, only one option could possibly tempt you away from all this newfound comfort: a short stroll along the silvery moonlit beach. In the morning, a continental breakfast arrives at your door on a silver tray. Wine and appetizers are served every afternoon in the lobby where they can be enjoyed in the company of other guests or taken up to the rooftop garden for a panoramic picnic. **652 Cannery Row; (831) 646-8900, (800) 841-1879; www.spin driftinn.com; expensive to unbelievably expensive; minimum-stay requirement on weekends.**

❧❧ **VICTORIAN INN, Monterey** Although the name may lead you to envision a charming little bed and breakfast, the Victorian Inn is more like a hotel than a traditional inn. Located on busy Foam Street near Cannery Row, the property resembles a cross between a small park and a motel, with a stone walking path leading across the grounds to the main building. The lobby is certainly Victorian in style; the antique furniture, high ceilings, banister staircase, and sunny window seat exhibit classic elegance. Once you leave the tiny lobby to find your room, however, you may be disappointed by the plain, hotel-like interiors. That is why we highly recommend the 14 rooms on the Concierge Level. These top-floor rooms come with extra-special touches, including feather beds, robes, CD players, turn-down service, and morning newspaper delivery. Four have whirlpool tubs. Room 301, a spacious corner room, holds all the amenities for a romantic getaway: a king-size bed fronting the fireplace, a window seat with over-the-rooftop views of Monterey, and—last but not least—a double-jetted tub and two-person shower. The standard rooms are just that, but each comes with a fireplace and either a private balcony or patio, and the prices are some of the more reasonable in town.

A generous continental breakfast is served in the lovely parlor just off the lobby. Here a grandfather clock stands guard among marble busts, ornate mirrors, pretty chandeliers, and classic settees. Several cozy tables provide a relaxing place to begin your day over fresh fruit, home-baked breads, and croissants. **487 Foam Street, at McClellan; (831) 373-8000, (800) 232-4141; www.victorianinn.com; expensive to unbelievably expensive; minimum-stay requirement seasonally.**

Restaurant Kissing

❧❧ **CAFE FINA, Monterey** Although Cafe Fina doesn't look very promising from the outside—its yellow facade blends in with the other seafood vendors on the pier—you'll be surprised by its handsome interior. Vintage black-and-white photos depicting hardworking fishermen and members of the owner's seafaring family adorn the walls both upstairs and downstairs, adding a homespun touch to the simple decor. Stylish halogen lights spotlight each photo as well as each table. Mauve cloth napkins bring a splash of color to the tables, which are draped in white tablecloths and accompanied by either black lacquered chairs or cushioned banquettes.

The elongated downstairs dining area isn't our first choice for romance since the tables are too close and only four come with decent views. But just journey upstairs, where fewer than a dozen tables—all with views—create an intimate dining experience. For an extra-special rendezvous, request the table for two in the upstairs corner; it has the best views in the house. If you manage to snap up the prized window seats, you'll be treated to views of the clear turquoise water below, sea lions sunning themselves on the rocks along the water's edge, and anchored sailboats bobbing in the background.

Cafe Fina uses a wood-burning oven for its meat and pizza entrées. If it's seafood you're fishing for, try the sautéed mussels or the deep-fried Monterey calamari. Fish can be blackened Cajun-style or broiled over mesquite charcoal if so desired. Cafe Fina also offers favorite Italian classics, including ricotta and spinach ravioli in marinara sauce and seafood pastas in several combinations. Order any one of the classic Italian desserts and call the evening a success. **47 Fisherman's Wharf; (831) 372-5200, (800) 843-3462; www.cafefina.com; moderate; lunch and dinner daily.**

💋💋 **CIBO, Monterey** *Cibo* may merely mean "food" in Italian, but *Cibo* in this case means elegance, romance, jazz, and wonderful Sicilian cuisine. Italian owned and operated, Cibo offers an ample variety of pizza, pasta, and grilled meat and seafood dishes, all garnished with locally grown herbs and vegetables. Creative interpretations of traditional Sicilian recipes are prepared in the open kitchen that spans the entire back wall of the restaurant. On our visit, the catch of the day was seared monkfish on a bed of roasted-corn mashed potatoes surrounded by a luscious bacon beurre blanc. While it didn't sound too Italian to us, it was delicious. The only disappointment was dessert. Our tiramisu had that "been-in-the-refrigerator-too-long" taste.

Cibo's decor handsomely blends neoclassic, urban, and rustic elements. Painted a fiery burnt sienna, the plaster walls are adorned with classical architectural drawings. Niches in the walls hold large vases, ivy vines trail from pots near the entryway, and bushels of wheat decorate the archways that separate the various rooms. The lighting is stark, and dark wood tables, some a little too close for comfort, fill the dining areas. Snuggle close in the cushioned booths while you enjoy live jazz Tuesday through Sunday evenings. **301 Alvarado Street, at Del Monte; (831) 649-8151; www.cibo. com; moderate; dinner daily.**

💋💋💋 **FRESH CREAM, Monterey** Fresh Cream has a long-standing reputation as the crème de la crème of French dining in Monterey. Spectacular views of the harbor create a romantic backdrop in the three separate dining rooms with floor-to-ceiling windows. (There is a fourth dining area, but the view is nil.) Light and dark gray tablecloths accentuate the blond wood of the chairs and walls. Well-spaced tables, fresh flower bouquets, and glass oil lamps are more than conducive to amorous conversation and loving looks. The simple architectural design gives the restaurant a sophisticated yet warm personality, and the service definitely complements it; Fresh Cream has one of the most gracious and refined wait staffs we've encountered.

Hearty portions of classic French dishes with California accents are artistically presented and so delicately scrumptious that you will savor every bite. We highly recommend the lobster ravioli appetizer, a creation akin to eating a lobster soufflé stuffed inside handmade pasta. The two salad choices included with dinner are far from your average garden variety: Our greens were tossed in a light balsamic vinaigrette and topped with goat cheese and toasted pecans. As for dinner, you certainly won't be disappointed by the grilled filet mignon surrounded by roasted portobellos and a truffle-Madeira sauce. Desserts are culinary works of art. We had a chocolate "sack" filled with a frothy mocha milkshake and topped with fresh whipped cream. Two straws are included, and you'll have to get close enough to kiss in order to share this cool sensation. **99 Pacific Street, at the corner of Scott and Pacific Streets; (831) 375-9798; www.fresh cream.com; very expensive; dinner daily.**

MONTRIO, AN AMERICAN BISTRO, Monterey Locals throng to Montrio's upbeat, tightly packed dining room, where tables are jammed almost on top of each other. Though the crowds present an obvious distraction, Montrio's unusual interior and enticing, artistically presented seafood dishes and desserts are its saving grace. Billowing white clouds hover beneath the sky blue ceiling, and twisted metal sculptures and artwork are tucked into alcoves and corners. Black track lights dangle from exposed ceiling pipes, illuminating closely spaced tables covered with white linens, brightly colored crayons, and blank paper that beckons to your creative senses. (When was the last time you composed a passionate sonnet for your beloved?) A second dining room upstairs is slightly less funky but equally noisy due to crowded tables and an adjacent open bar. Fortunately, the service is gracious and the California-style cuisine is better than average, especially the single oven-roasted portobello mushroom or the grilled gulf prawns presented with caramelized-leek risotto. **414 Calle Principal; (831) 648-8880; www.montrio.com; moderate to expensive; lunch and dinner daily.**

PARADISO TRATTORIA, Monterey The fresh, tantalizing antipasti displayed in the front window draw patrons into this Mediterranean-style trattoria, but it's the spectacular waterfront setting that convinces them to stay. An abundance of two-person tables are placed next to oversize windows that capture views of otters and pelicans diving for fish in Monterey Bay. Ceramic fruit sculptures, bright green chairs, and tropical flower arrangements give the oceanfront dining room an artsy, if not a bit outdated, flair. Delicious fresh seafood and Italian specialties, including polenta vegetable towers and Mediterranean cioppino, are available noon and night. Sunset is definitely the most romantic time to dine (at least as far as the views are concerned), although this is also when you're likely to encounter the most competition for a window table. **654 Cannery Row; (831) 375-4155; moderate to expensive; lunch and dinner daily.**

❀❀❀ **STOKES ADOBE, Monterey** Part of the charm of visiting downtown Monterey is strolling along and admiring the clusters of historic Spanish-Colonial buildings and homes. Although most in the downtown core have been taken over by business firms, there is one historical home-turned-restaurant that offers plenty of romantic potential: Stokes Adobe. This large, sunset-pink stucco home, built in 1833, is one of the prettiest buildings in town, and the simple beauty of its exterior continues inside. Softly colored textured walls, rough-hewn chairs and tables, and Mexican tile floors add a definitive Southwest touch. More contemporary accents, including unique "pear tree" chandeliers and large modern paintings, blend easily into this historic setting. The main dining room is surrounded on three sides by large paned windows with views of the neighborhood. While some tables are much too close, there are the quintessential corner tables, well suited for intimate repasts.

A California-inspired menu offers some Spanish twists, starting with the impressive tapas selection. At such reasonable prices, it is worth ordering a few of these appetizers. The crispy polenta with mushrooms and the Tuscan white bean bruschetta are both excellent, although a bit heavy on the oils. Try the cured salmon or seared ahi for lighter fare. As for the entrées, a grilled pork chop served alongside a savory bread pudding and pear chutney proves pleasurable to the palate as does the seared hanger steak with a spinach cheese tart. For dessert, we tried the classic Spanish flan, but found the addition of lemon zest more chewy than flavorful. **500 Hartnell Street; (831) 373-1110; moderate to expensive; lunch Monday–Saturday, dinner daily.**

Outdoor Kissing

❀❀❀❀ **ADVENTURES BY THE SEA, Monterey** Kayaking side by side or in a two-person kayak on the gentle waters of Monterey Bay is a special experience you'll remember long after you return home. Pelicans skim the water's surface, seals sun themselves on rocky outcroppings, and frolicking otters loop in and out of the kelp, sometimes even plopping playfully on the front of your kayak. Beneath you, dazzling colors and textures come alive in the sunlight, punctuated with bright orange and gold starfish. These stable boats are made for laid-back drifting, interspersed with unhurried paddling. Far from the crowds of Cannery Row, you can hold hands and perhaps even rock the boat with a kiss. You'll stay nice and dry during your outing, thanks to spray skirts that fit over you and the kayak. If you pack a picnic before heading out, you can pull up onto a beach or share it right on the water. Adventures by the Sea also rents bikes or in-line skates so landlubbers can admire the views from the safety of the shore. **299 Cannery Row; (831) 372-1807; www.adventuresbythesea.com; call for rental prices for kayaks, bikes, and in-line skates.** *Between Reeside and Drake on Cannery Row, across from the Monterey Plaza Hotel.*

❦ **FISHERMAN'S WHARF, Monterey** Due to its oceanfront location, Fisherman's Wharf is definitely worth visiting for an hour or two on a sunny afternoon. The wharf is home to the usual souvenir shops, stands selling mediocre seafood fast food, and many sit-down restaurants boasting views of the bay. If the smell of the sea arouses your hunger, stop by **CAFE FINA** (see Restaurant Kissing), about two-thirds of the way down the wharf, port side. As you and your loved one continue down the boardwalk, your senses will be tickled by the smell and taste of the salty ocean breezes. Stop and watch as pelicans and seagulls soar overhead, while boats rock gently in the nearby harbor. *At the intersection of Scott and Oliver Streets.*

❦❦ **JACKS PEAK COUNTY PARK, Monterey** Just outside Monterey is a delightful park known as Jacks Peak. Explore the eight and a half miles of riding and hiking trails (each trail is roughly a mile long) or simply share your midday meal at one of the many picnic areas. Nature lovers will befriend Steller's jays and gray squirrels beneath sheltering pines. Ridgetop views overlooking the Monterey Peninsula are found throughout the 525-acre park; for an extraordinary vista, however, follow the Skyline Self-Guided Nature Trail to the summit of Jacks Peak. **(831) 755-4899, (888) 588-2267; $2–$3 entrance fee per vehicle; open daily 10:30 a.m.– 5:30 p.m.** *Head north from Monterey on Highway 68 and watch for signs that direct you to the park.*

❦❦❦ **MONTEREY BAY AQUARIUM, Monterey** At the end of Cannery Row is another of the city's tourist attractions, but this one presents a not-to-be-missed opportunity to view the marine life that abounds below the water's surface. Housed in an unbelievably realistic underwater setting, the

Monterey Bay Aquarium is one of the world's largest and best. The illuminated jellyfish exhibit is especially stunning, as is the kelp forest display. Hold hands and brave the crowds for a few hours; you'll be glad you did. **886 Cannery Row; (831) 648-4888, (800) 756-3737 in California; www. mbayaq.org; $15.95 entrance fee per person; open daily.**

Romantic Note: Tickets to the aquarium are available at the front door, but you'll probably have to stand in a long line. Many participating hotels and bed and breakfasts sell tickets so you can avoid the wait. Advance tickets can also be purchased by phone and are highly recommended during holidays and summer.

❧❧❧ **RENT-A-ROADSTER, Monterey** We never knew driving could be so much fun! With a toot of the *"ah-ooga"* horn, we were off to tour the coastline in our reproduction 1929 Model A roadster. The top was down, the sun was shining, waves were crashing, and people waved to us as we trundled by. This unusual company offers Model As, a 1929 Mercedes, and a 1930 Phaeton for rent, all very easy to drive, with modern engines capable of doing 55 miles per hour—but why hurry? Be sure to allow enough time to stop by the seashore along **LOVERS POINT** near Pacific Grove, which is only a few minutes away from Rent-A-Roadster. Or plan on doing the **17-MILE DRIVE** in style (see Outdoor Kissing in Pacific Grove). If you know another romantically inclined couple, they can join the fun in the Model A's rumble seat. **229 Cannery Row; (831) 647-1929; www.rent-a-roadster.com; $30–$35 per hour per vehicle.**

Romantic Alternative: Another playful way to tool around Monterey is to rent a pedal surrey or a bicycle built for two at **BAY BIKES** (640 Wave Street; 831-646-9090). The surreys have two sets of pedals and a brightly striped, fringed roof that's perfect cover from the afternoon sun. You can pedal them only on Monterey's bike path along Cannery Row: The surreys aren't allowed on streets. Athletic romantics can pedal their tandem bicycle along the 17-Mile Drive or all the way to Carmel (about 14 miles).

Pacific Grove

Unlike neighboring Monterey and Carmel, which are often crowded to the point of overflowing, you can still find a measure of peace and solitude in the enchanting oceanfront town of Pacific Grove. Picturesque Victorian mansions line Ocean View Boulevard, where the tide laps at the endless stretch of sandy shoreline. Not only is Pacific Grove's quiet charm a welcome change of pace, the bevy of bed and breakfasts and restaurants here include some of the most impressive properties we've encountered along the South Coast.

Hotel/Bed and Breakfast Kissing

❤❤ **THE CENTRELLA INN, Pacific Grove** Harbored in a residential neighborhood, this renovated turn-of-the-century home specializes in friendly hospitality. Every afternoon, freshly baked cookies and a carafe of cream sherry sit on an old oak table in the bright parlor, where the sun beams in through a wall of beveled glass windows. Here you can relax by the fire after a long, unhurried afternoon of window shopping or strolling along the waterfront. In the morning, the scent of freshly brewed coffee and homemade breakfast goodies provides all the incentive you'll need to get out of bed.

Down comforters, old-fashioned wallpaper, and ordinary antique furniture create an authentic Victorian atmosphere in the 21 rooms found in the main house. This authentic mood is unfortunately intensified by creaky floors and rickety doors and doorknobs. Although the rooms on the first and second floors are rather small, in need of minor touch-ups, and somewhat confining (especially those with shared baths), your romantic options here are still plentiful. Two spacious attic suites tucked under skylights on the third floor offer considerably more space and privacy. Outside, a brick walkway bordered by camellias and gardenias leads to five additional cottage suites with private entrances, fireplaces, and cozy sitting areas. If you aren't up for hearing squeaky floors and closing doors, opt for these accommodations.

Last but certainly not least is the Garden Room, The Centrella's honeymoon quarters. Regardless of whether you're celebrating a honeymoon or not, this self-contained unit (attached to the main house) is the ultimate for romantic encounters. A private entrance ensures seclusion in this spacious room, replete with a wood-burning fireplace, beautiful Ralph Lauren linens, and a two-person Jacuzzi tub in the black-and-white tiled bathroom. **612 Central Avenue; (831) 372-3372, (800) 233-3372; www.centrella inn.com; expensive to very expensive; minimum-stay requirement on weekends.**

❤❤❤ **THE GATEHOUSE INN, Pacific Grove** Built as a seaside "cottage" in 1884, this cheerfully restored Victorian flaunts trappings and amenities its original builders would envy. Elaborate, custom-designed, hand-silk-screened wallpapers adorn the walls and ceilings in the homey parlor and snug, antique-filled guest rooms. You'll want to lie in bed together just to admire the intricate Middle East–inspired patterns above you. In the spacious Langford Suite, a beautifully adorned white-lace bed faces the bay and a potbellied stove warms the room. The Sun Room, which features a white wrought-iron bed and a glimpse of the nearby ocean, feels almost like an indoor garden. Wine-colored curtains cast a rosy glow over the sexy Victorian Room's sumptuous burgundy linens and claw-foot tub. For those who want additional privacy, five of the nine rooms have their own entrances and three adjoin secluded brick patios.

The owners do everything to make this feel like your home away from home. Cookies, fresh fruit, and tea and coffee are available at all hours, or you can help yourselves to the fully stocked refrigerator filled with juices, sodas, and milk (for those cookies, of course). After a short walk to the beach, we returned to find an array of afternoon wine and appetizers waiting, including delicious homemade cheeses. In the morning a full breakfast buffet of specialties, such as pumpkin-cornmeal pancakes or a cheese strata, provide the perfect start to a romantic day by the sea. **225 Central Avenue; (831) 649-8436, (800) 753-1881; www.sueandlewinns.com; moderate to expensive; minimum-stay requirement on weekends.**

❧❧ **GOSBY HOUSE INN, Pacific Grove** Since its early years as a boardinghouse, this yellow and white Victorian inn has undergone several renovations while retaining all of its charm. (The house's history is illustrated in a series of black-and-white photographs inside.) Of the 22 rooms here, 20 comprise the main house (five of which have private entrances); the other two are located in the Carriage House. The guest rooms are a mix and match of sizes, shapes, and lighting moods; some have that dark-in-the-daytime look, while others are flooded with sunshine. Floral wallpaper, antique wood furnishings, and white embroidered bedspreads are common to each. What differs a bit are a room's amenities (or lack thereof): ten rooms feature fireplaces, only six rooms have TVs, and all but two have private baths. Private balconies in the second-floor Gosby and Holman Rooms are quite enticing. Rooms in the Carriage House come equipped with whirlpool tubs and separate showers. The pretty floral parlor in the main house is a beautiful setting in which to enjoy a delicious country breakfast or afternoon tea. If you'd rather have breakfast en suite, it's an extra $5 per person.

Every effort has been made to make your stay as comfortable as possible, right down to the teddy bears placed on each of the beds. If there is any hesitation at all in our enthusiasm about the Gosby House Inn, it is that the decor may be a bit too flowery for some tastes and some of the first-floor rooms are too close to the busy kitchen and dining room. **643 Lighthouse Avenue; (831) 375-1287, (800) 527-8828; www.four sisters.com/gosby.html; moderate to expensive.**

❧❧❧❧ **GRAND VIEW INN, Pacific Grove** If you're familiar with Pacific Grove's famous SEVEN GABLES INN (see review below), you know what kind of luxury to expect from its sister property. Situated right next door, the Grand View Inn is managed by the same discriminating owners and shares Seven Gables' spectacular oceanfront setting. Not surprisingly, it also shares a well-deserved four-lip rating. If you're wondering about the differences between the two properties, we'll take the word of the inn-keeper: Seven Gables is ornate and the Grand View is more sedate. Additionally, the Grand View is an Edwardian mansion (versus its Victorian sister next door), so the interior tends toward the handsome side, highlighting natural woods, square shapes, and large, comfortable furnishings.

A small creek trickles through boulders and greenery in the beautifully landscaped yard that fronts this expansive blue and white 1910 home. Notable for their simple elegance and sleek lines, the ten guest rooms boast high ceilings, marble bathrooms, blond wood detailing, and ample space. Chandeliers cast a formal light on brass and canopied beds and other enticing period touches. A beautifully handcrafted wood staircase spirals to the top of the house, where bay windows in the Rocky Shores Room showcase the best views on the property. Non-oceanside rooms overlook the Grand View's lovely rambling gardens.

Afternoon hors d'oeuvres and an all-you-can-eat breakfast of baked egg dishes, muffins, pastries, fruit, yogurt, and much more are served at two large tables in the lovely oceanfront dining room. After filling up on a meal of this magnitude, you can easily go without lunch. Instead, take the time to explore this section of the wondrous California coast that's right outside the door. **557 Ocean View Boulevard; (831) 372-4341; www. 7gables-grandview.com; expensive to unbelievably expensive; minimum-stay requirement on weekends.**

🌸🌸🌸 **GREEN GABLES INN, Pacific Grove** From the moment you step inside this Queen Anne Victorian, you'll know you are in for an enchanting experience. The Green Gables Inn, as its name suggests, is a multigabled structure with leaded glass windows that afford dreamy views of Monterey Bay. A collection of antiques decorate the parlor, where a brightly painted carousel horse sits behind a sofa, stained glass panels frame the fireplace, and freshly cut flowers are arranged about the room. Halfway up the stairway that leads to the guest rooms, a gang of teddy bears plan mischief on a small bookshelf.

Most of the 11 rooms are decorated in paisley and country floral prints. Some rooms have sloped ceilings, while others offer bay windows, comfortable sitting areas, fireplaces, and scintillating views of the nearby ocean. One room with angled ceilings and a love-seat bench resembles a small chapel (which might or might not be romantic, depending on your religious views). The Lacey Suite is the largest room at the inn; located adjacent to the parlor, it is beautifully appointed, with hardwood floors, a four-poster canopy bed, a tiled fireplace, and an antique claw-foot tub in the private marble bathroom. The five rooms in the Carriage House are all spacious, but the ocean view isn't as grand. To make up for such a shortcoming, these rooms will entice you with their fireplaces and private baths; four sport Jacuzzi tubs for two.

Regardless of which room is yours, you can indulge in a full country-style breakfast, served beside a fireplace and expansive windows that face the shimmering sea. In the afternoon, more food comes your way when trays of housemade appetizers, cheeses, and vegetables are served alongside a selection of wine. There's also tea and hot coffee accompanied by a sweet treat. **104 Fifth Street; (831) 375-2095, (800) 722-1774; www.foursisters.com/green.html; moderate to very expensive.**

Romantic Warning: Except for the Lacey Suite and Jennifer Room, all of the rooms in the main house share bathrooms, which in our opinion is not conducive to uninterrupted kissing. Be sure to request a room with private facilities, unless your ability to partake in continual smooching here is contingent upon lower-priced accommodations.

❤❤❤ **LIGHTHOUSE LODGE SUITES, Pacific Grove** A large cypress shades the colorful manicured gardens and immense rock outcroppings that highlight this assembly of Craftsman-style cedar-shingled accommodations. A welcome change of pace from the all-too-familiar Victorian bed and breakfasts found along the South Coast, these 31 pleasantly decorated guest rooms are perfectly designed for romantic seclusion. Private entrances and decks ensure solitude, while vaulted ceilings, rich color schemes, and standard but handsome furnishings guarantee comfort. Everything you need for a romantic evening is at your fingertips, including a wet bar, gas fireplace, Jacuzzi tub set in a seductive marble bathroom, and even a bedside dimmer switch to help set an amorous mood. Although there is no reason to leave this lap of luxury, the ocean is only a short walk from your front door.

Every morning guests gather in the spacious dining room, located in the middle of the property. A complimentary, cooked-to-order breakfast is served at two-person tables while fireplaces at both ends of the room help take off that morning chill. If you'd rather not venture out, have breakfast delivered to your room. In the afternoon, a noteworthy selection of complimentary appetizers and local wines invite quiet conversation after a busy day of touring together. If that's not enough, the affiliated Lighthouse Lodge across the street features a complimentary barbecue each evening for guests staying in the suites. **1249 Lighthouse Avenue; (831) 655-2111, (800)**

858-1249; www.lhls.com; very expensive to unbelievably expensive; minimum-stay requirement on weekends.

Romantic Warning: Two separate properties comprise the Lighthouse Lodge Suites. When making your reservations, be absolutely sure that you reserve a Lighthouse Lodge *suite* rather than a unit in the separate Lighthouse Lodge hotel. Otherwise you will end up with a mediocre, motel-style room that isn't even remotely romantic.

❀❀❀ **THE OLD ST. ANGELA INN, Pacific Grove** This 1910 Cape Cod–style home, originally built as a summer residence, still retains that fresh, festive, and light feel associated with warm-weather retreats. Large windows and numerous skylights throughout let ample amounts of sunshine flood the country-inspired common rooms, sea breezes flow forth in the ocean-facing rooms, and a colorful garden affords a pleasant place to sit and watch little winged ones play in the birdbath. Although the home is located in a residential neighborhood along a somewhat busy street, the tranquillity of Monterey Bay and its long walking path are just one block west.

Recently redecorated, all nine rooms are delightful, bright, and comfortable. Common denominators include skylights and ceiling fans, large windows, lovely linens, and hardwood floors covered with decorative rugs. Our romantic favorites are the four rooms upstairs: the nautically inspired Crow's Nest, the blue and white Whale Watch with its private deck, the roomy Garden Gable, and the Bay View, which boasts the best ocean views. Most rooms are warmed by fireplaces and many have one-person jetted tubs in the bathrooms. (Thanks to the owner's foresight in putting the water faucet in the tub's center, two people can usually squeeze in ... and we mean *squeeze*.) Otter's Cove, a cozy room off the garden, may be small, but it offers a charming curtain-enclosed window seat perfect for snuggling up with a book (or each other). It's also the least expensive room and ideally suited for those wanting privacy at a reasonable price.

A small sunroom overlooking the garden is where guests gather to partake in a full breakfast of juices, homemade muffins, bagels, fruit, and a delicious main course. Potato pancakes chock-full of toasted pecans, egg casseroles filled with crab or Canadian bacon, and strawberry-stuffed French toast topped with homemade whipped cream are just some of the choices. Decadent delights don't end in the morning either. Come evening, a generous wine-and-cheese hour brings plenty of appetizers to the living room table and, later on, brownies, cookies, or a cheesecake are presented for sweet tooths to savor. Some people who stay here don't even bother going out for dinner. **321 Central Avenue; (831) 372-3246, (800) 748-6306; www.sueandlewinns.com; moderate to expensive; minimum-stay requirement on weekends.**

❧❧❧❧ **SEVEN GABLES INN, Pacific Grove** Truly a sight to behold, this immense yellow and white Victorian mansion holds court on a rocky promontory in Pacific Grove. Every plush, stately room offers satisfactory-to-outstanding views of the glistening ocean and rugged coastal mountains. Built in 1886, this celestial bed and breakfast has been painstakingly renovated, and an extensive collection of fine art and museum-quality antiques set it off to perfection. Tiffany glass windows, Persian carpets, 18th-century oil paintings, marble statues, and crystal chandeliers are just some of the collector's items crowded into the inn's opulent common areas. However, with such a formal polish, the common areas may not be the place where you will feel like making yourselves at home.

Luckily, the 14 guest rooms are inviting, cozy retreats with private, albeit standard bathrooms and varied ocean views. Broad windows trimmed with lace and balloon valances make the rooms bright and sunny by day. At night, classic lighting fixtures shed a soft, warm glow. Oriental carpets, canopy beds, and classical artwork add to the historic flavor of every room. We especially liked the eight rooms spread out between three cottages and a guest house behind the main building, which enjoy similar ocean views and enhanced privacy. On most weekends you will find at least one or two couples spending their wedding night at the Seven Gables Inn. But even if it's not your honeymoon, all that romance is sure to rub off!

Breakfast, served family-style, is a grand affair of freshly baked muffins, croissants, and special egg dishes. A generous, proper high tea, also served in the exquisite dining room, features tortes, homemade fudge, and a large assortment of pastries, not to mention a stunning view of the water. **555 Ocean View Boulevard; (831) 372-4341; www.7gables-grandview. com; expensive to unbelievably expensive; minimum-stay requirement on weekends.**

Restaurant Kissing

❧❧❧ **CYPRESS GROVE, Pacific Grove** A romantic dining experience is a simple formula, really. Blend together well-flavored food, attentive service, a candlelit room with chairs reasonably spaced apart, and presto! You have all the makings for an intimate evening out. Luckily, Cypress Grove does too. An exciting, innovative, and flavorful menu pleases the palate, while the small, French country–style dining room charms those seeking a respite from big, loud, and busy. Butter-colored walls are adorned with gilt-framed mirrors, velvety ruby-red drapes and delicate curtains hide the street from view, and fancy chandeliers and tall candles create a seductive romantic glow. Blue wooden chairs, distressed brick walls and tile floors, and plenty of wine racks in the back add that French flair. A dozen or so tables, dressed up in linens and topped with tea candles, are spaced at least an arm's length apart to ensure private conversation.

The menu brings forth some of the most creative dishes in town. Start with a white corn flan, so creamy and sweet you'll think you're eating dessert. A delightful stinging nettle soup holds a surprise treat—a poached quail's egg—and the Belgian endive salad will win the hearts of salad lovers and non-salad lovers alike. Our main course, the seared halibut, was a gift from the sea and from the kitchen rolled into one. End this culinary experience with a tapioca martini "stirred not shaken"—made with real tapioca and a hint of vodka. An array of interesting flavors comes through with each bite of the orange-scented mascarpone cheesecake in a hazelnut crust with rosemary sauce. Certainly, the recipe for romance is here at Cypress Grove; all you need to do is add the kissing. **663 Lighthouse Avenue; (831) 375-1743; moderate to expensive; dinner Tuesday–Sunday, brunch Saturday–Sunday.**

❧❧❧ **FANDANGO, Pacific Grove** Although the name of this restaurant may stir up images of the fast and furious gypsy dancing of southern Spain, you won't find any fancy footwork here. What you might hear instead is sultry Flamenco music, and you'll definitely taste the robust flavors of Spain, Italy, and France.

For an intimate dining experience, request seating in one of the three front rooms or in the cozy wine cellar with its thick rock walls, vintage wine bottles, and copper pots hanging from the rafters. Tables are appointed with bottles of olive oil on white tablecloths, bold and colorful curtains frame the windows, magnificent flower arrangements grace each table, and the worn wood floors and numerous fireplaces add a touch of warmth. Near the back of the restaurant, a more casual, informal, and noisy environment awaits in the glass-roof terrace, where the open grill is sure to entice you with the scent of seafood and poultry being cooked over mesquite and fruitwood. There's also a sunny outside patio fronting the road that is just right for a casual lunch or Sunday brunch.

Explore the entire Mediterranean as you peruse the menu. For a taste of North Africa, try the outstanding couscous Algérois, made according to a century-old family recipe. France is represented by rack of lamb à la Provençal, Spain and Italy by wonderful paellas and pastas. Swordfish, salmon, and scallops are examples of the sea's bounty. These are but a handful of Fandango's creatively prepared dishes; you'll have to discover the rest on your own. **223 17th Street; (831) 372-3456; www.fandango.com; moderate** to expensive; reservations recommended; lunch and dinner daily, brunch Sunday.

GERNOT'S VICTORIA HOUSE, Pacific Grove This stately mansion/restaurant once reigned supreme in the town of Pacific Grove. Now it tends to be overshadowed by other restaurants, but still holds romantic potential for those who like to kiss in Victorian-inspired settings. The home holds three circular dining rooms, each decorated in traditional style with ornate floral wallpaper, lace curtains, hardwood floors, and Oriental rugs. One room features a cozy fireplace tucked away near a handful of intimate tables, while the warm glow of candlelight throughout the restaurant makes this a perfect place for a heartfelt rendezvous. The continental menu won't win any creativity awards, but Austrian Wiener schnitzel and fresh salmon are standards that should please. Dinners include soup and salad, so pace yourselves if you're planning on dessert. **649 Lighthouse Avenue; (831) 646-1477; expensive; dinner Tuesday–Sunday.**

JOE ROMBI'S LA MIA CUCINA, Pacific Grove If you're seeking a sleek, stylish place to dine, Joe Rombi's fills the bill. A handful of tables with white linens and black chairs are organized around the perimeter of this small but lively restaurant. Dramatically illuminated by track lights, European advertisement posters from the late 1800s stand out as the only splashes of color against the stark white walls. Despite the restaurant's limited size, each table is adequately spaced apart so you'll have plenty of elbow room.

La Mia Cucina means "my kitchen," and it's guaranteed you won't be disappointed by what comes forth. Savory pastas, including three kinds of raviolis, grilled New York steak with basil butter, fresh fish of the day specials, and succulent entrées like chicken piccata highlight the menu. **208 17th Street; (831) 373-2416; moderate; dinner Wednesday–Sunday.**

THE OLD BATH HOUSE, Pacific Grove The Old Bath House is a time-honored establishment cherished by locals and visitors alike. Set at the edge of **LOVERS POINT PARK**, the restaurant is known for intimate oceanside dining and scrumptious desserts. Dark wood walls, dim track lighting, and gracious service create a private world where you can enjoy the view and each other's company. Cozy tables, softly illuminated by candlelight, face large picture windows. As the sun begins to set, watch as otters play in the surf and lovers stroll along the nearby park arm in arm. When the sea finally swallows up the sun, distant city lights mingle with the flickering flames of candles alight all throughout the restaurant. Little can compete with the intimacy this place sparks, except the food, which is best described as regional California cuisine with European influences. Desserts are created by the kitchen's own pastry chef and worth every sinfully rich calorie. Order the bananas Foster and watch the flames light up the room. **620 Ocean View Boulevard; (831) 375-5195; expensive; dinner daily.**

Romantic Suggestion: For those wanting a taste of the good life while still pinching pennies, The Old Bath House offers four-course, early-bird dinners at moderate prices. If you time it right, the sunset will be waiting outside after dinner at nearby **LOVERS POINT.**

❀❀ **PASTA MIA, Pacific Grove** Set in the heart of Pacific Grove, this renovated Victorian home looks more like a private residence than an Italian restaurant—at least from the outside. Inside, smooth hardwood floors and lace window treatments in the former dining and living areas are the only traces that remain of the home's historic past. Garlic braids, chiles, and culinary knickknacks adorn the walls. Freshly cut red roses accent tables draped with white linens in the casual dining rooms. For more privacy, request a table in the cozy window alcove that overlooks Pacific Grove's charming store-lined streets.

Hearty homemade soups and pastas are the kitchen's specialties; try the half-moon pasta stuffed with pesto in a zesty lemon cream sauce or the prawns sautéed in a champagne cream sauce. For dessert, Pasta Mia serves up some of the best tiramisu in town. **481 Lighthouse Avenue; (831) 375-7709; moderate; dinner daily.**

❀ **THAI BISTRO, Pacific Grove** Located on busy Central Avenue, Thai Bistro is a great place for a casual lunch, especially if you're seeking a respite from the all-too-familiar California cuisine. Thai soups, spicy salads, fried rice, and curry and noodle dishes are featured on the extensive menu. Decorated in nautical blues and whites, the restaurant has a small bar at the entryway and curvaceous adobe walls adorned with art du jour. (During our visit, charming photographs of Monterey Bay seals and otters were prominent.) Although the tables are a bit too close for comfort, the striped cushions and pillows help create a cozy atmosphere. If you don't mind plastic chairs, take advantage of the outdoor patio seating available most sunny days. **159 Central Avenue; (831) 372-8700; inexpensive to moderate; lunch and dinner daily.**

Outdoor Kissing

❀❀❀❀ **17-MILE DRIVE, Pacific Grove** Plan on taking an entire day to tour the 17-Mile Drive. It is so awesome and resplendent that you will want to take much longer to travel this unspoiled terrain than its 17-mile length suggests. Stop along the way to observe the infinite variations as ocean and land converge along the Monterey Peninsula. White, foamy waves wash up on black rocks, sending a spray of sea into the crisp, clean air. Seagulls' cries pierce the misty air as unruffled pelicans glide near the water's surface.

As you round one spiral of road, you'll spy a crescent-shaped, sandy cove that provides a calm place to pause. Here, sunlight shimmers on the vast Pacific, and in the distance a sailing vessel slowly makes its way across the horizon. Other turns in the road reveal undulating sand dunes, violently frothing sea currents, and abundant marine life sanctuaries. Watch for the stark beauty of a lone cypress clinging to the side of a cliff, and be sure to stop at **SEAL AND BIRD ROCK** to witness a multitude of marine mammals and birds basking in the sun and frolicking in the water.

As you continue on your passage up a hill, turning to the east, you enter a deeply wooded area that shelters palatial homes and estates and several world-class golf courses. Unless watching the rich and famous is your idea of an intimate interlude, continue on and in a few more turns the natural beauty of the peninsula will be yours again. If you are hungry or would like to pause, you can visit one of the restaurants at **THE INN AT SPANISH BAY** or **THE LODGE AT PEBBLE BEACH** (see Hotel/Bed and Breakfast Kissing in Pebble Beach for reviews of both). Many of these restaurants overlook the stunningly profound landscape below and, at some, the food almost equals the views. As an added bonus, show your entrance receipt after enjoying lunch or dinner and the restaurant will reimburse your entrance fee. **$7.50 entrance fee per vehicle.** *From Highway 1, take Highway 68 west to Sunset Drive, and go west again to the Pacific Grove entrance gate.*

❀❀❀❀ **PACIFIC GROVE SHORELINE, Pacific Grove** Take time to saunter hand in hand along **OCEAN VIEW BOULEVARD**, where a whisper of salt water gently caresses you as waves thunder against the rocks at water's edge. Here you can watch sea otters splashing in kelp beds and pelicans perching in sunny spots. If the time of year is right, you might even catch sight of a whale or two swimming by on their migration route. If you expect your walk to take you to **LOVERS POINT PARK**, at the southern tip of Monterey Bay, consider packing a picnic to share beneath the shade of a tree or on one of the benches bordering the park.

For more breathtaking ocean views and a look at Monterey County's past, be sure to visit the **POINT PINOS LIGHTHOUSE**, situated at the northernmost tip of the Monterey Peninsula. This National Historic Landmark was built in 1855 to guide mariners past the hazards of the rocky coast. Now the oldest operating lighthouse on the West Coast, it is fascinating to explore, and an ideal vantage point for savoring magnificent ocean vistas. If you crave isolation, be sure to traverse the glorious, windswept sands of nearby **ASILOMAR BEACH**. *Take Highway 1 to westbound Highway 68. Highway 68 becomes Forest Avenue; follow it all the way to the ocean.*

Pebble Beach

Elite Pebble Beach, securely established on **17-MILE DRIVE** (see Outdoor Kissing in Pacific Grove), is home to millionaires, deluxe accommodations, five-star restaurants, and the dramatic meeting of surf and shore. It is probably best known for its championship golf courses, which, on occasion, host the U.S. Open. Regardless of whether or not you play golf, it is the sheer beauty of Pebble Beach's coastline that makes this a kissworthy destination. Unfortunately, views of this caliber merit higher rates, so don't expect to find reasonably priced accommodations here.

Hotel/Bed and Breakfast Kissing

❤❤❤❤ **THE INN AT SPANISH BAY, Pebble Beach** Although the exclusive Inn at Spanish Bay looks like a condominium complex and feels like a country club, your affectionate inclinations will not be repressed. Not only does this world-class resort cater to your every imaginable need, it also has breathtaking ocean views beyond a rolling, emerald green golf course bordered by windswept grasslands and sand dunes. Deer graze at their leisure in this serene setting and occasionally a small fox will run by. At dusk a lone bagpiper, dressed in traditional Scottish garb, walks along the inn's perimeter, playing melodies that drift in with the sea breeze. In addition to mood-setting music and spectacular views, the resort has a full-service fitness club, a tennis pavilion complete with eight championship courts, a golf course par excellence, several choice restaurants, and an exemplary staff that will spoil you rotten.

Guest rooms with ocean vistas are preferred, but they are also considerably more expensive. Many rooms command refreshing views of cypress forests instead and are much more reasonably priced (keep in mind that "reasonable" is a relative term here). No matter what kind of view your budget allows, you are sure to appreciate the modern artwork and elegant decor. The 270 rooms are equipped with gas fireplaces, deep soaking tubs with separate glass-enclosed showers, and all the amenities you'd expect from a luxury resort.

Once you've arrived at this prime locale, you probably won't want to leave. Luckily, the inn has two excellent dining options: **ROY'S AT PEBBLE BEACH** and **THE BAY CLUB** (see Restaurant Kissing for reviews of both). There's also a spacious outdoor patio overlooking the windswept dunes and golf course, where drinks and snacks are served. When the sun begins to set, strategically placed fire pits help keep off the evening chill as you listen to the bagpiper and steal a kiss or two. **2700 17-Mile Drive; (831) 647-7500, (800) 654-9300; www.pebble-beach.com; unbelievably expensive; recommended wedding site.**

THE LODGE AT PEBBLE BEACH, Pebble Beach Upscale and refined, The Lodge at Pebble Beach is a luxury resort for romance-seekers with deep pockets and a desire for elegance. (Don't be fooled by the word "lodge"; you won't find any antlers on the walls here, just a plethora of golf-related mementos and photographs.) Built in 1919, this world-renowned piece of heaven has attracted golfers and lovers alike for decades. Although the service is a bit stuffy at times, that shouldn't distract you from enjoying the golf course, shopping square, fitness area, tennis club, and equestrian center.

The lobby is simply breathtaking. Two large marble fireplaces comprise opposite ends of the enormous sitting area. Plaster sculptures, leafy green plants, and framed paintings add splashes of color to the rich cream decor. Plush sofas and chairs are clustered around glass tables and a stately grand piano. Lining the entire far wall, immense floor-to-ceiling windows look out over a perfectly manicured golf course and beyond to the dramatic ocean surf. Step outside on the wrought-iron deck for a panoramic view of the grounds.

Although the property itself is too large to be considered intimate, the incredibly posh rooms more than compensate. Each of the 161 luxury suites and guest rooms is appointed with polished, contemporary furnishings and all the right amenities to make your stay extremely comfortable. All are decorated differently, so describing each room's deluxe decor might take up a novel. Forty-seven rooms offer fantastic ocean views with nothing standing between you and the sea. Sixty-five have what management calls garden views, which really means they overlook the expansive main lawn and the award-winning 18-hole golf course. Rooms with scenic vistas have partial views of the ocean. After a day on the green, you and your loved one can retire to your suite and relax in the wonderful Jacuzzi tub or deep soaking tub. Then cuddle up in front of a wood-burning fireplace as the murmur of the Pacific Ocean lulls you to sleep.

If all those indoor and outdoor sports have worked up an appetite, merely walk to the Lodge's main building for culinary gratification. Located on the lower level, **CLUB XIX** (expensive to very expensive; lunch and dinner daily) doubles as a casual Parisian café by day and an intimate French restaurant by night. Whether you decide on lunch or dinner, you'll enjoy the view: Club XIX's windows face Carmel Bay and the celebrated 18th green. Each table is coupled with plush chairs and adorned with white linens, gold-rimmed china, and candles. Wine bottles are stored in the light wood walls, and a small open bar stands near the entryway. The chef's specialties include fresh salmon baked to perfection in a tender corn pancake or a mouthwatering herb-crusted rack of lamb complemented by a black olive jus. Desserts are like artwork, although very small pieces of art we might add.

For fresh regional seafood, we recommend **THE STILLWATER BAR AND GRILL** (moderate to expensive), on the entrance level of the main building. Light wood furnishings, glass-top tables and counters, and colorful modern art give the space an airy cosmopolitan elegance, while large windows offer spectacular views of the bay. Specialties include applewood-smoked sea bass, and monkfish braised in a broth of fennel, Hungarian paprika, and fresh herbs. Breakfast, lunch, and dinner are served daily, and there is a lavish Sunday brunch. It's the perfect place to catch a casual meal before teeing off. **17-Mile Drive; (831) 624-3811, (800) 654-9300; www. pebble-beach.com; unbelievably expensive; recommended wedding site.**

Romantic Warning: Due to its famous reputation and Pebble Beach locale, The Lodge attracts camcorder-toting tourists by the dozen. If you'd rather not be part of this picture, we suggest staying at The Lodge's sister property, **THE INN AT SPANISH BAY** (see review above). This off-the-beaten-path inn does have people, but doesn't seem to attract as many gawkers.

Restaurant Kissing

❤❤❤ **ROY'S AT PEBBLE BEACH, Pebble Beach** During our romantic travels, we've dined at all of Roy's restaurants in Hawaii as well as the Seattle location. While each of these restaurants—all owned by star chef Roy Yamaguchi—has its redeeming features, we must say that the views from this Roy's are the most romantically inspiring. The split-level restaurant commands multimillion-dollar panoramas of The Links golf course, windswept dunes, and brilliant Pacific through floor-to-ceiling windows. The contemporary look created by blond wood floors and columns is balanced by the rich hues of the stylish rugs and upholstered chairs. Peaked copper ceilings and art deco–style chandeliers and sconces put the finishing touches on this aesthetically pleasing place. A busy and bustling open kitchen, common to all Roy's restaurants, can be a distraction, but luckily most of your attention won't be focused there. The wait staff is friendly and efficient, although we can't say the same for the hostess.

The restaurant's popularity means quiet intimacy is hard to come by, but the splendid ocean scenery and faultless Eurasian cuisine will take your mind off the crowds. What to order? Now is the time to be adventurous—you simply can't go wrong at Roy's. We recommend any of Roy's "classic" or "original" creations, including hibachi-style salmon, blackened rare ahi, and "Da Kine" wok steamed clams and mussels. If you aren't fond of seafood, the island-style honey-mustard garlic grilled short ribs is more than a mouthful; it's terrific tasting, too. For dessert, the melting-hot chocolate raspberry cake is an absolute must. However, this dessert needs to be ordered before your main course, so refrain from gazing into each others' eyes long enough to order it first! **2700 17-Mile Drive, at The Inn at Spanish Bay; (831) 647-7423; www.roys-restaurants.com; moderate to expensive; breakfast, lunch, and dinner daily.**

Romantic Alternative: Although The Inn at Spanish Bay's BAY CLUB (831-647-7490; expensive to very expensive; dinner daily) lacks a nationwide reputation, its hearty northern Italian cuisine is delicious. If your priority is quiet time together, the Bay Club's serene atmosphere is a preferable alternative to upbeat Roy's. Sleek and sophisticated, the dining room is appointed with high-backed plush chairs, track lighting, and, as a centerpiece, a life-size black and gold gondola filled with lavish flower arrangements. Soft classical music sets the mood for quiet conversation and romance. Although some of the elegantly attired tables set against the walls are too close for comfort, tables next to the bay windows have inspiring ocean views and adequate privacy.

Carmel

Artists, poets, and playwrights congregated in this seaside hamlet at the turn of the century; even today Carmel retains much of its Bohemian charm, although with a ritzy twist. Upscale boutiques, fashionable art galleries, quaint inns, and fine-dining restaurants occupy the rows of storybook cottages cloistered in Carmel's one-square-mile city limits. There are no streetlights, and in the evenings lamps in storefronts and restaurants illuminate the town's narrow boulevards. Streetlights aren't the only big city amenities missing in Carmel—you won't find address numbers, billboards, parking meters, or neon signs either. Carmel is also a very pet-friendly city, with some restaurants reserving rooms for people who wish to dine with their pooches!

Naturalists and romantics will appreciate Carmel's serene seaside location. Beautiful white sandy beaches provide a more restful setting in which to while away the hours. Without question, you will find yourselves captivated by this town's charm and its flawless natural surroundings.

Romantic Note: Part of Carmel's appeal is its small size. As we mentioned, most establishments don't even have numbers on their doors. Consequently, most of the reviews in this section use street junctions instead of formal addresses. Once you are in Carmel, this will be more than enough to help you find your destination.

Romantic Warning: Idyllic Carmel is the South Coast's most popular destination. Be forewarned that most weekends are disturbingly crowded. During the summer the town is full to the point of bursting. We recommend timing your visit on a weekday or in the off-season.

Hotel/Bed and Breakfast Kissing

❦❦ **CARMEL GARDEN COURT INN, Carmel** Hidden from the hustle of the downtown shops and restaurants but within easy walking distance of both, the Carmel Garden Court Inn is a delightful place to retreat from the world. Follow the brick pathway through a garden accented with wooden trestles, hanging pots of greenery, and bubbling fountains. Stroll among the oak trees or rest on a park bench surrounded by beautiful bougainvillea. At the end of the day, you can create your own secluded haven simply by closing the gate to your private flower-filled patio.

All nine rooms at the inn have wood-burning fireplaces, private entrances, and a few unexpected amenities, such as towel warmers, VCRs, and refrigerators, to make your stay as comfortable as possible. Although individually decorated, they share a simple country theme of knotty pine walls, wicker furnishings, floral prints, and homey, sometimes mismatched, knickknacks. The five mini-suites have large picture windows overlooking lovely secluded patios, as well as cozy eating nooks furnished with intimate tables for two. The four remaining rooms are attached to the main building and do not have private patios; however, the largest upstairs room does offer a full kitchen and a lovely antique headboard. At check-in, decide where you'd like your expanded continental breakfast to be served: in the privacy of your room, on the patio, or in the lobby. Whichever way you choose, champagne is included. **Torres and Fourth; (831) 624-6926; very expensive to unbelievably expensive; minimum-stay requirement on weekends.**

Romantic Warning: Since our last visit, the prices for the prime patio mini-suites have hit the unbelievably expensive mark. Perhaps if management invested some money in updating the mismatched, homey decor we'd be more willing to accept the increase.

❦❦❦ **CARRIAGE HOUSE INN, Carmel** Although this wood-shingled country inn is nestled in the heart of picturesque Carmel, you'll feel worlds away from the bustling village once you've settled inside your room. All 13 comfortably appointed guest rooms are spacious retreats with wood-burning fireplaces, king-size beds, and down comforters. There's all the electronic entertainment equipment you'll ever need, as well as a basket of books for those who prefer more cerebral activities. Lace curtains, old-fashioned wallpapers, and country antiques give each room an upscale turn-of-the-century character, although some rooms have been nicely redecorated with contemporary, cream colored wallpapers and more modern window treatments. Upstairs rooms have open-beam cathedral ceilings and one-person whirlpool bathtubs. Of these rooms, Nos. 8 and 11 are the most popular, thanks to their corner locations and abundant windows. Only two rooms offer Jacuzzi tubs for two. All rooms exceed normal hotel space standards, although those wanting even more square footage should book Room No. 1, a two-room suite residing over the lobby. The only potential drawback to staying at the Carriage House Inn is that most of the guest rooms front an unappealing parking lot and the echo of engines could disrupt your sleep.

An assortment of wines and cheeses is served every afternoon in the lobby. After returning from dinner, you'll find mints on the pillow and all the lights dimmed in your room. Before you get too cozy, venture to the lobby where a selection of ports, sherries, and specialty coffee drinks awaits. Come morning, a generous continental breakfast is delivered to each room on an old-fashioned platter. **Junipero, between Seventh and Eighth; (831) 625-2585, (800) 433-4732; www.webdzine.com/inns; very expensive to unbelievably expensive; minimum-stay requirement on weekends.**

❦❦❦ **COBBLESTONE INN, Carmel** The Cobblestone Inn has a reputation as one of Carmel's best-run bed-and-breakfast establishments (and that's saying a lot), so you'll be pleased to know that it also has some of the more reasonable prices in town. Teddy bears and country knickknacks accent the cheery living room, which fronts a cobblestone courtyard. In this comfortable setting, a lavish breakfast buffet and afternoon hors d'oeuvres are served next to a massive stone fireplace.

White shutters ensure privacy in the 24 countrified guest rooms, each decorated with floral wallpaper, watercolor paintings, and plaid linens. Antique brass beds and river-rock fireplaces are the romantic highlights of every room. Although the lower-priced rooms are quite small, they are still charming and comfortable. In the larger rooms, comfy couches face the fireplace in the additional sitting areas. All of the rooms, regardless of price, feature standard private baths, and the largest window in every room looks out toward the courtyard, which unfortunately also doubles as a parking lot, limiting your privacy when the shutters are open. **Junipero, between Seventh and Eighth; (831) 625-5222, (800) 833-8836; www.four sisters.com/cobblest.html; moderate to very expensive.**

CYPRESS INN, Carmel With its Moorish Mediterranean architecture, The Cypress Inn is an attractive display of white stucco walls, red tile roof, and Spanish arches. This stately, 33-room inn wraps around a lovely garden courtyard overflowing with flowers and greenery. After enjoying a continental breakfast in the courtyard, relax in one of two parlors. Part library and part lounge, the smaller sitting area features a full-service bar and dignified reading tables. Movie star Doris Day owns this inn, and posters from her stellar career adorn the walls of this common area. Elegantly decorated in shades of pale apricot, the main lobby is a great place to curl up in front of the white marble fireplace. Evenly spaced windows and a peaked wood-beamed ceiling give this room its spacious, sunny atmosphere.

The recently redecorated guest rooms match the refined elegance of the lobby, but remain relatively simple in their decor. No two rooms are alike, but all are equally lovely. Colorful ceramics, Turkish rugs, and copper bowls adorn the stucco walls and large windowsills. Wrought-iron and wicker furniture complements the earth-toned interiors, while black-and-white photographs embellish the lovely marbled bathrooms that feature glass-enclosed showers and deep soaking tubs. Some rooms have verandas with far-off glimpses of blue sea, and those in the deluxe category offer fireplaces, wet bars, jetted tubs, and plenty of space. The inn's charming design and engaging ambience can evoke the appropriate frame of mind for encounters of the heart. **Lincoln and Seventh; (831) 624-3871, (800) 443-7443; www.cypress-inn.com; moderate to very expensive; minimum-stay requirement on weekends.**

LA PLAYA HOTEL, Carmel At the grand La Playa Hotel, the Pacific Ocean is visible through pine and cypress trees, and the sound of the dramatic surf echoes in the distance. This sprawling pink Mediterranean-style villa is the place to stay if you long for a tranquil setting and all the amenities of a full-service hotel.

La Playa's lobby is warmed by an enormous fireplace and decorated with hand-loomed area rugs and lovely antiques. A sweeping staircase, accented by vivid tilework, winds upstairs to 75 basic guest rooms filled with hand-carved furnishings, including whimsical mermaid motif head-boards. Peach tones add warmth to the sunny interiors, which are complemented by wooden shutters and recessed lighting. While the standard rooms are certainly nice, we were a little disappointed by the stark white bathrooms and the absence of certain creature comforts—namely robes—which aren't included. Some accommodations in the main building are small, but just right for couples who want to be closer than usual, and some offer stunning ocean views. Our favorite rooms are situated on the lower floor, with private terraces that open onto the property's lush inner courtyard and two acres of formal gardens. Not too far away, you'll also find a heated pool encircled by orange poppies swaying on slender stems.

Five storybook cottages are nestled in a nearby garden grove. Although these retreats offer all the privacy in the world, they are also the most expensive units at La Playa. Each has a full kitchen or wet bar, a terrace or garden patio, a wood-stocked fireplace, and an assortment of eclectic antiques. Bordering on rustic, the cottages' countrified interiors are not as upscale or elegant as La Playa's other accommodations. **Camino Real and Eighth; (831) 624-6476, (800) 582-8900; moderate to unbelievably expensive; minimum-stay requirement on weekends and holidays; recommended wedding site.**

Romantic Suggestion: Although breakfast is not included with your stay, it is available at La Playa's semicasual **TERRACE GRILL RESTAURANT** (moderate to expensive), which is also open for lunch, dinner, and Sunday brunch. The California grill–style menu includes standard items like sandwiches, pastas, steak, and seafood, and the views of the lovely inner courtyard and resplendent gardens are wonderful. There's also an outdoor deck complete with heat lamps for al fresco dining.

❧ **LINCOLN GREEN COTTAGES, Carmel** Far from Carmel's bustling town center, these four quaint English country cottages reside beside lovely gardens in a quiet neighborhood, mere blocks from Carmel's legendary beachfront. A white picket fence encloses the picturesque foursome, and each is painted white with forest green trim; they're named Robin Hood, Little John, Friar Tuck, and Maid Marian. To our surprise and dismay, their interiors lack much of the setting's exterior charm. Despite beamed cathedral ceilings and stone fireplaces, the dated kitchens (for preparing your own meals) and other amenities are purely utilitarian, lacking any sense of style or élan. At these prices you definitely expect more. What makes them worth your romantic consideration are the peaceful setting and nearby beaches. From this vantage point, you may never know that the summer crowds are only a mile down the street. **Carmelo, between**

15th and 16th; reservations through Vagabond's House Inn, (831) 624-7738, (800) 262-1262; expensive; minimum-stay requirement on weekends.

❦❧ **MISSION RANCH, Carmel** A short distance from the often crowded city of Carmel lies a down-home surprise. Worth visiting for its setting alone, the Mission Ranch looks as if it were transported here straight from the ranchlands of Texas. (The six championship tennis courts, exercise room, and banquet facilities seem oddly out of place.) The renovated 1850s farmhouse and a handful of white cottages with green trim are scattered on this rambling property, surrounded by cypress trees, sheep pastures, and rolling hills that reach down to the fringes of the ocean.

Mismatched antiques, old-fashioned colors and fabrics, and exposed electrical cords give many of the ranch's 31 guest rooms a dated, motel-style look. Luckily, some aspects are romantically redeeming, most notably the queen- or king-size beds draped with floral or country-style patchwork quilts, and the picture windows surveying enticing views of lush green meadows. The Meadow View Room and the Hay Loft Bedroom feature gas fireplaces and one-person whirlpool tubs. The Bunkhouse Cottage is equipped with a full kitchen in case you want to cook a lovers' feast and dine in together. Our favorite spots for some easygoing country togetherness are the six guest rooms in the picturesque farmhouse. These rooms feature hardwood floors and lovely antiques, and share a wide wraparound veranda with trailing bougainvillea. **26270 Dolores Street; (831) 624-6436, (800) 538-8221; moderate to very expensive; minimum-stay requirement on weekends.**

Romantic Warning: The bar and grill–style RESTAURANT AT MISSION RANCH (831-625-9040; moderate; lunch Saturday, dinner daily, brunch Sunday) serves up standard steak and seafood in an informal atmosphere. Look elsewhere for romantic, intimate dining.

❦❧ **VAGABOND'S HOUSE INN, Carmel** A large, gnarled oak stands guard at the center of the Vagabond's small inner courtyard, where a waterfall spills over rocks, and potted camellias, rhododendrons, and ferns are caressed by the breeze. Many of the guest rooms in this unpretentious English Tudor home face this quiet scene. Special amenities in the 11 modestly decorated rooms include kitchenettes, wood-burning fireplaces, and a decanter of sherry beside each bed. Knotty pine walls lend rustic charm to several rooms, while marbled bathrooms add a touch of elegance. Our favorite room features a direct view of the massive oak, which is adorned with tiny white lights that could almost be mistaken for twinkling stars against the midnight sky. In the morning, an extended continental breakfast of fruit, freshly baked breads, and egg dishes can be served directly to your room. Best of all, the price is right, making the Vagabond's House a relatively inexpensive place to call home for a few days. **Fourth and Dolores; (831) 624-7738, (800) 262-1262; inexpensive to expensive; minimum-stay requirement on weekends.**

Restaurant Kissing

❀❀❀ **ANTON AND MICHEL, Carmel** Anton and Michel prides itself on having "just the right touch." True enough, almost everything about this luxurious restaurant is impressive and memorable. Oil paintings featuring fair ladies and flowers embellish the peach and cream colored walls, Corinthian columns separate the dining rooms from one another, and an entire wall of windows in one room looks out to a lovely courtyard. Candle lanterns placed on linen-draped tables cast a soft, romantic glow, inspiring intimate conversation—that is, until the food arrives. We highly recommend ordering one of the restaurant's well-known dishes such as the ostrich scaloppini crusted with pink and black peppercorns, Black Angus filet mignon, or the tableside presentations of rack of lamb or Châteaubriand. We guarantee you'll be satisfied with those; just stay away from the specials. Our nightly number tasted like leftovers the chef wanted to get rid of: linguine tossed with every root vegetable imaginable, freezer-burnt Alaskan king crab, and day-old scallops. If you stick to the standards, you'll be happy and can easily enjoy dessert. Try the cherries jubilee or bananas Foster, both flambéed right before your eyes. **Mission, between Ocean and Seventh; (831) 624-2406; www.carmelsbest.com; expensive; lunch and dinner daily.**

❀❀❀ **CASANOVA, Carmel** Tucked away on one of Carmel's quiet side streets, this charming restaurant bills itself as the town's most romantic dining establishment. (No doubt the name has something to do with it.) Such a claim may or may not be true, depending on where you sit. If the weather's nice, the small brick patio fronting the restaurant would be an ideal spot, if it weren't for its proximity to the entrance. The interior courtyard is divine on a summer's day, but the tables are so close together that you could kiss your neighbor without even stretching your neck. Inside, the romantic ambience definitely improves. Romantic repasts, accompanied by lively international music, can be had in any of the cozy dining rooms outfitted with only a few tables. The decor is subdued and country rustic. Striped curtains adorn the windows, low hanging lamps add just the right amount of light, and pastoral odds and ends decorate the earthy straw and clay walls.

Drawing on the country cuisines of France, Italy, and Spain, entrées include paella for two, seafood linguine tossed in a white wine and lemon cream sauce, and thyme-seasoned pork tenderloin au jus accompanied by onion marmalade and confit of tomato. All dinners come with three courses, including antipasto and a variety of scrumptious appetizers, which may help explain the very expensive dinner prices. **Fifth, between San Carlos and Mission; (831) 625-0501; www.casanovarestaurant.com; expensive to very expensive; lunch and dinner daily, brunch Sunday.**

❀❀ **FLYING FISH GRILL, Carmel** Imagine a redwood-planked den where flying fish soar overhead as you enjoy mouthwatering and innovative Asian-fusion creations. If this sounds inviting, make your way down the steps of Carmel Plaza to discover Kenny Fukumoto's Flying Fish Grill. Dark and intimate, the interior has that Japanese restaurant feel, but without the traditional minimalist atmosphere. In fact, there's a cozy fireplace and even cozier booths that encourage snuggling and hand holding. Blue linens make a splash on the bare wood tables, accented with a fan of chopsticks, and the warm glow of candlelight illuminates the whimsical papier-mâché fish swimming overhead.

You'll have difficulty deciding between the many tempting seafood dishes waiting to please your palate. We recommend the California rolls, tempura prawns, or yin-yan salmon bathed in a soy–lime cream sauce. Vegetables prepared to perfection accompany most meals. If you're ready for a feast, try the seafood clay pot for two, a steaming medley of seafood, vegetables, tofu, noodles, sauces, and rice. Cool off by dipping your spoons into one of three different kinds of sundaes: traditional hot fudge, basic banana, and a luscious green tea creation. **Mission, between Ocean and Seventh, in Carmel Plaza; (831) 625-1962; moderate to expensive; dinner Wednesday–Monday.**

❀❀❀ **THE FRENCH POODLE, Carmel** Naming a classic restaurant The French Poodle is a bit odd, but we'll run with it and say you won't be left in the doghouse after an evening here. Exquisite crystal chandeliers cast a soft, warm glow in the exceedingly small and intimate dining room, appointed with mauve walls and luxurious draperies. Candles flicker in oversized wineglasses placed atop every linen-draped table. As you would guess, the specialty is authentic French cuisine, from escargot to abalone. Desserts include traditional French denouements like cheese and fruit plates, in addition to not-so-traditional homemade sorbets and strawberries laced with Grand Marnier.

In spite of all this praise, we must warn you that even for a classic French restaurant, The French Poodle takes formality to an exceedingly high plane. While you'll be spoiled beyond belief, the never-ending replacement of silverware and such can be intrusive and distracting to those seeking intimate conversation. **Junipero, at Fifth; (831) 624-8643; expensive; dinner Monday–Saturday.**

☙☙ **RAFFAELLO RESTAURANT, Carmel** Raffaello claims to be the oldest singularly owned restaurant in Carmel and it just may be true. The 80-plus-year-old chef/owner, known to everyone as "Mama," still comes in every morning to make the soup and cannelloni! Sometimes Mama does the cooking, but on the night we visited, her son was in command. One bite of the delectable dinner, however, and we knew Mama had taught him well.

Traditional Italian entrées ranging from seafood to veal to free-range chicken appear on the menu, along with a selection of pasta dishes. Many entrées, most notably the pastas, can be ordered à la carte or with a soup and salad. Whatever you choose, you'll be delighted. Mama's cannelloni is an absolute must-try for pasta fans; our robust chicken cacciatore was the best we've tasted; and the homemade dessert crêpes are just right for sharing with your sweetheart. Service is formal but personable, and most dishes, from the salads onward, are brought out and prepared tableside.

The atmosphere is formal, conservative, and simple, with only 12 tables enclosed by light pink stucco walls. Heavy draperies cover the two windows, creating an environment that is dark even during daytime. An artificial fireplace does little to add to the ambience, but the soft candlelight at each table certainly makes up for it ... and makes everyone look wonderful, too. As with the lighting, the classical music is set low, so sweet nothings can easily be whispered from across the table. Unlike other restaurants in town, Raffaello caters to the locals, who frequent it often. After a dinner here, you'll join them in admiration of the quiet atmosphere and, of course, Mama's cooking. **Mission, between Ocean and Seventh; (831) 624-1541; expensive; dinner Wednesday–Monday.**

☙☙☙ **SANS SOUCI, Carmel** Locals have been finding romance at Sans Souci for more than 30 years and we understand why. Soft classical music, subdued lighting, and ultraformal service create an atmosphere where couples can talk without competing with background noise or needless hustle and bustle. Elegance and warmth are provided by the crystal chandeliers and a blazing fire in the hearth. A lush flower bouquet serves as the restaurant's centerpiece, and is surrounded by linen-covered tables adorned with candles and single red roses.

While the decor is very appealing, the classic French menu with modern nuances proved somewhat uninspiring to our taste buds. The salad vinaigrette was too oily, and the smoked tomato glaze for the sea bass reminded us of plain old barbecue sauce. Luckily, the Muscovy duck breast turned out to be fabulous, as did some of the made-to-order desserts. Half of the listed desserts cater just to twosomes. We recommend the cherries jubilee or crêpes filled with fruit and ice cream, both prepared tableside. **Lincoln, between Fifth and Sixth; (831) 624-6220; expensive to very expensive; dinner Thursday–Tuesday.**

💋💋 **SIMPSON'S RESTAURANT AND BAR, Carmel** Playful Maxfield Parrish–style murals depicting characters in popular nursery rhymes decorate the unusual dining room at Simpson's. The life-size pictures are a refreshing change from standard restaurant decor and add to the already unique character of this one-of-a-kind Carmel restaurant. Although the murals are entertaining for the eye, there is some serious romantic potential here for the heart as well. Hanging lamps cast soft light on tables, while a handful of cozy red booths set against the walls offer perfect places to snuggle up. White linens and fresh flowers give each table a fresh, formal appearance, and the soft butterscotch colored walls combine with the lighting to make everything look radiant.

Like the decor, the menu is a refreshing change of pace from the plethora of Italian and French food about town. Honest-to-goodness, home-cooked comfort food reigns supreme at this longtime family-owned establishment. Although the selection changes daily, there are some dishes you can count on. Slow-roasted prime rib, the house specialty, is served every Saturday night; Thursday night is turkey time accompanied by all the fixin's; and classical pot roast presented alongside pan-roasted vegetables is on the menu every Tuesday and Wednesday. When the fish are biting, salmon straight from Monterey Bay graces the menu, compliments of a family member who owns a fishing boat. Good, old-fashioned hospitality comes with every order, too. **San Carlos, at Fifth; (831) 624-5755; moderate to expensive; dinner Tuesday–Saturday.**

💋💋 **TUTTO MONDO TRATTORIA, Carmel** This rustic Italian trattoria looks like it belongs in the rolling hills of Tuscany instead of downtown Carmel. A fire warms the bucolic dining room, softly illuminating the brick floor and the ceiling where open beams are bedecked with wine bottles, large copper pots, and long garlic braids. If that's not enough visual stimulation, you can admire the plethora of pictures featuring the owner posing with various movie stars and sports figures. A large wrought-iron chandelier crowns a handful of dark wood tables topped with dried flower arrangements and bottles of olive oil. Although some of the tables are arranged too closely for our romantic preferences, cozy floral booths set against the wall allow for quiet moments.

The kitchen serves up delicious northern and southern Italian fare, ranging from savory bruschetta (nine varieties) to more than two dozen pasta creations, all accented with fresh Parmesan and Romano cheese. There are also several salad entrées and flat-bread pizzas, various antipasto platters, and several seafood specials. Mondo's dessert tray, loaded with creamy Italian creations, is too tempting to pass up. We couldn't resist the cool panna cotta topped with fresh strawberries. *Perfetto!* **Delores, between Ocean and Seventh; (831) 624-8977; www.mondos.com; moderate; lunch and dinner daily.**

Outdoor Kissing

❤❤ **CARMEL BEACH, Carmel** Carmel Beach is an awesome stretch of surf and white sand. Those lucky souls with houses bordering this mile-long parcel of heaven are in an enviable position. The landscape is an inspiring combination of surging waves, rolling hills, and endless ocean. A sandy stroll in the foggy morning (before the populace wakes up) or at sunset, when the sky is burnished with fire, can renew the soul. All kinds of sparks can be kindled from kissing here. Don't miss it. *From Highway 1, turn west onto Ocean Avenue and follow it until it dead-ends at the beach parking lot.*

❤❤ **POINT LOBOS STATE RESERVE, Carmel** It's been called "the greatest meeting of land and water in the world." Where better to share a lasting kiss? Almost as exhilarating as love itself, Point Lobos is one of our favorite spots in the Carmel area. At the Sea Lion Point parking lot, the first sounds you'll hear are the sharp barks of these stalwart creatures. A short trail along a hillside blanketed with ice plants leads to the promontory, where you'll see them crowded on the water-washed rocks. Nearby are tide pools you can explore together, searching out scrambling crabs and purple sea urchins. If you wish, follow one of the less traveled trails that hug the cliffs of this rugged coastline. Seclusion and spectacular scenery are yours to share. **(831) 624-4909; $7 day-use fee per vehicle; open during daylight hours; no pets allowed.** *Located on the ocean side of Highway 1, four miles south of Carmel.*

❤❤❤ **ROBINSON JEFFERS' TOR HOUSE, Carmel** Even those who have never heard of the poet Robinson Jeffers will be inspired by his ocean-view homestead. A simple stone cottage finished in 1919, Tor House is where Jeffers wrote all of his major works and most of his poetry. ("Tor" is an old Irish word for a craggy knoll.) More important, this is where he lived happily with his wife, Una, and their twin sons. Loving epigrams are carved into the timbers throughout the home. Jeffers built the Hawk Tower by hand, making "stone love stone," as a treasured retreat for Una and a magical playground for the children. In Una's room, at the very top of the tower, an epigram carved in the wooden mantel of the fireplace reads, "THEY MAKE THEIR DREAMS FOR THEMSELVES," truly reflecting Jeffers' lifestyle, and perhaps expressing the affections of others who come here. **26304 Ocean View Avenue; (831) 624-1813; www.torhouse.org; $7 entrance fee; reservations recommended; open by guided tour only on Friday and Saturday, from 10 a.m.–3 p.m.** *From Highway 1, turn onto Ocean Avenue and head through downtown Carmel. Turn left onto Scenic Drive, left onto Stewart Street, and then left again onto Ocean View Avenue. Look for Tor House and its stone Hawk Tower on the left.*

Carmel Valley

Hotel/Bed and Breakfast Kissing

Unrated BERNARDUS LODGE, Carmel Valley Bernardus Lodge was on the brink of opening at the time of our visit, so in all fairness to our readers, we can't give it an accurate kiss rating. However, by the looks of things, we are sure this new boutique resort nestled in the lush and sunny Carmel Valley will inspire many kisses once it is up and running. (Even before the cement had dried, the high-and-mighty travel magazines were declaring it a fabulous getaway.) Besides boasting a pastoral setting, the 57 accommodations provide supreme privacy, and the variety of on-site amenities, including a full spa, outdoor pool, croquet lawn, and restaurant, ensure that you won't have to leave this lap of luxury before you're ready.

The spacious guest rooms, located in nine single- and two-story adobe-style buildings, come complete with all the romantic accoutrements common in first-class resorts: vaulted ceilings, wood-burning fireplaces, balconies or patios, marbled bathrooms with deep soaking tubs and separate glass showers, king-size beds adorned with featherbeds and down comforters, and more. Add to such luxury fresh flower bouquets, a private check-in with wine, and nightly turndown service with complimentary wine and cheese, and you'll want for nothing. It's not surprising that wine is a focal point here, considering the lodge's proprietor also owns the acclaimed **BERNARDUS WINERY**, located not too far from the lodge.

Bernardus wine and other culinary delights can be found in the lodge's full-service restaurant, **MARINUS AT BERNARDUS LODGE** (expensive; breakfast, lunch, and dinner daily, brunch Sunday), where the tastes of the central coast are brought to the table. Seared Monterey Bay prawns and pancetta-wrapped venison with chanterelle mushrooms are just two of the many specialties prepared by the noted chef. What wowed us, however, was the unbelievably romantic dessert offering. After the two of you finish your entrées, order a plate of chocolate-covered strawberries, champagne, and a bubble bath. Yes, that's right. As you linger over an after-dinner coffee, a staff member will deliver the succulent strawberries to your room, put the champagne on ice, and draw the bath. When you arrive, the rest of dessert is up to the two of you. **415 Carmel Valley Road, at Laurles Grade; (831) 659-3131, (888) 648-9463; unbelievably expensive; minimum-stay requirement on weekends and holidays; recommended wedding site.**

❀❀❀❀ **CARMEL VALLEY RANCH RESORT, Carmel Valley** Even if you're not a celebrity, you'll feel like one as you pass through the gated entrance of this exclusive estate. Upon arrival, you are greeted by name and chauffeured via golf cart to your secluded, luxurious suite (this is especially handy if you haven't mastered the art of packing light). Nestled in the rolling hills of the Carmel Valley, 1,200 acres of this 1,700-acre wooded property remain pristine and undeveloped. Deer and wild turkeys are frequently seen beneath the aged, sculpted oaks that shade the sprawling grounds.

A scattering of contemporary ranch-style guest buildings fits right into this sensational natural setting. Privacy is guaranteed in each of the 144 upscale guest suites, and seven room styles are available. Each room features a private entrance, deck, and all the comforts of home. Cathedral ceilings soar above modern appointments, soft floral watercolors set a relaxing mood, and white shutters open to reveal stunning views of the valley. A gas fireplace radiates warmth in the stylish living room, and a second fireplace in the bedroom promises late-night romance. Sparkling white tiled bathrooms hold separate showers and extra-long soaking tubs, many fronted by a window. If you have the good fortune of reserving a spa suite (our top romantic pick), you can indulge in a romantic soak beneath the stars: Your own hot tub awaits on a wraparound deck set high in the trees—a true nest for lovebirds. Couples seeking a more remote place to rendezvous should book one of the 44 new suites located away from the main cluster of accommodations. While the decor is similar, these suites are perfect for people particular about bathrooms; here they are larger and come equipped with double vanities and jetted tubs.

Exclusive usually translates into expensive, and Carmel Valley Ranch is no exception. Fortunately, you get what you pay for here, and there are a variety of specialty golf, tennis, spa, and romance packages worth looking into. Your comfort is the ranch's top priority, and the gracious staff is a phone call (and golf cart) away. Nightly turndown service delivers freshly baked cookies to your room. Other amenities cater to the athletically inclined. Choices include golfing on an 18-hole championship course, playing tennis, horseback riding, hiking, and swimming. You'll want for nothing during your stay here, except more time to relish the breathtaking scenery and quiet surroundings. **One Old Ranch Road; (831) 625-9500, (888) GRAN-BAY; www.grandbay.com; unbelievably expensive; minimum-stay requirement on weekends.**

Romantic Note: Although Carmel is a relatively short drive (15 minutes) from the ranch, you won't have to go that far for good food. Adjacent to the lobby, **THE OAKS** (831-626-2533; moderate to very expensive) is open daily for breakfast, lunch, and dinner, as well as brunch on Sunday. Well-spaced tables covered with all the finery of a first-class restaurant look out to views of the oak-dotted valley. Relish a zesty Spanish omelet for breakfast. For dinner try the rack of Colorado spring lamb or the grilled rosemary-thyme chicken. Special "light" options, including golden red lentils and pan-seared sea bass, help those watching their waistline. Artfully presented and flawlessly served, the kitchen's masterpieces are complemented by an award-winning wine list, a fire crackling in an immense stone hearth, and the clear tones of a grand piano that seems like it is being played just for you.

❦❦❦ QUAIL LODGE RESORT AND GOLF CLUB, Carmel Valley As
you would expect, the Quail Lodge Resort and Golf Club is a resort built around an 18-hole golf course. If the two of you don't fare well on a fairway, you can dine at **THE COVEY RESTAURANT** (see Restaurant Kissing) and head for home—unless you are tempted to utilize the resort's tennis facilities, swimming pools, or jogging and hiking trails. For golf lovers, however, this 600-acre resort makes a convenient place to stay while visiting Carmel Valley.

With 100 guest accommodations, Quail Lodge is far from small. Yet, once you pass through a private gate into your own secluded patio, you'll feel worlds away from everything and everybody. The entryway patio, adorned with native plants and a Japanese rock pool filled with clear water and floating flowers, is a peaceful place designed to draw nature into your immediate surroundings. Inside, blond wood accents, contemporary and Asian-style furnishings, and beds perfectly swaddled in stylish linens lighten up these spacious retreats. Bathrooms are big, bright, and beautiful with garden-facing windows and shutters opening into the bedrooms. After a day on the green, put your shoes in the two-way butler's pantry for cleaning (one of the many distinctive touches here) and then ease into the extra-long tub for a soak. More relaxation can be had on the cozy couch fronting the fireplace or on your private backyard patio with views of the lakes, gardens, or golf course. Eight room categories are available, ranging from superior to fireplace king to two-bedroom suites, and none come cheap. With such glorious surroundings, new room renovations, and an exceptionally fine restaurant, Quail Lodge is the perfect place to make your own little love nest. **8205 Valley Greens Drive; (831) 624-2888, (888) 828-8787; www.quail-lodge-resort.com; very expensive to unbelievably expensive; minimum-stay requirement on holidays.**

Romantic Note: When we visited, room renovations were just starting to take place, so this review is based on the mock-up rooms we saw.

❦❦❦❦ STONEPINE, AN ESTATE RESORT, Carmel Valley Lined with

gnarled oaks, a mile-long access road crosses a wooden bridge over a swiftly running creek and passes corrals full of energetic horses on the way to Stonepine. As the wrought-iron reception gate swings open, a formidable French country manor covered with ivy comes into view. If you opt for an airport pick-up (from Monterey Airport), you'll see all this splendor from the backseat of Stonepine's own Phantom V Rolls Royce. Such first-class service is merely commonplace at this aristocratic estate that caters to the rich and famous of the world.

Morning light floods through a gallery of windows in the spacious foyer and living room of the main house (dubbed Chateau Noel), enhancing the subtle elegance of the damask-covered sofas and love seats. A handwoven Chinese rug, threaded with rose tones, stretches across the hardwood floor, and golden flames flicker warmly in an oversized limestone hearth. In the evening, this room is often graced by the sounds of a string ensemble.

Eight of Stonepine's fashionable accommodations are located in the main house. Lavish draperies, carpets, and other appointments surround guests with old-world style and modern luxury. A sexy, Roman marble bath with a Jacuzzi tub and his-and-her bathrooms are enticing features of the Taittinger Suite. Revive your spirits in the Don Quixote Room, which has a king-size bed, two bathrooms, and French doors that lead to a private garden and patio. Even the petite Dong Kingman Suite is captivating, with its peaches and cream color scheme and full marble bath overlooking the rose garden. Fireplaces and canopy beds in many of the rooms are romantic grace notes. About a mile away, the four suites in the ranch-style Paddock House have Jacuzzi tubs and the use of a fully equipped country kitchen. The most secluded unit of all is the self-contained, two-bedroom Briar Rose Cottage, with a rustic stone fireplace and its own porch overlooking a fragrant rose garden. Also on the property you'll find a 5,000-square-foot villa known as the Hermes House, sporting a fresh French-country architecture, and a mini-estate called Gate House, which will appeal more to families than to romance-seeking couples.

Stonepine prides itself on a gracious European-trained staff that caters to your every need and desire. No matter which room you choose, you and your beloved can count on being thoroughly indulged. Afternoon tea and a complimentary gourmet breakfast are served in the lovely formal dining room, which boasts burnished oak paneling, cathedral ceilings, and an immense fireplace. A superb, five-course dinner is also served here, but is not included with your stay (unbelievably expensive; reservations required). **150 East Carmel Valley Road; (831) 659-2245; www.stonepinecalifornia. com; unbelievably expensive; minimum-stay requirement on weekends and holidays; recommended wedding site.**

Romantic Suggestion: Stonepine also runs an equestrian center, where you can saddle up two horses and explore some 300 prodigious acres of forest, meadow, and bridle trails. Do keep in mind, however, that the center is not exclusively for guest use.

Restaurant Kissing

❧❧❧ **THE COVEY RESTAURANT, Carmel Valley** We can't think of a name more appropriate for this restaurant than The Covey. Its blond wood paneling displays flocks of partridges, ducks, and other game birds painted in deep colors. A peaked ceiling overhead features heavy, exposed beams and track lighting. Wine cabinets hold select vintages, and exotic plant arrangements add visual punctuation. Along the far wall, large windows reveal a charming pond with an illuminated fountain and arched footbridge.

The Covey's main dining room is split into two levels. Booths with colorful contemporary designs complement the larger tables of the upper level. For better views and a more intimate setting, however, request a table on the lower level, closer to the windows. Several smaller, more secluded dining areas branch off from the main room, and one even has a fireplace. Although somewhat close together, the tables are beautifully appointed with white linens, fresh flowers, and silver place settings set aglow by soft candlelight. If warm weather comes your way, don't pass up an opportunity to dine on the deck overlooking the pond. Glass banisters shelter you from the wind, heat lamps take off any evening chill, and the casual wood chairs and tables are spaced well apart.

The excellent Euro-California cuisine here is often garnished with flavorful artichokes that are grown locally. Angus New York steak, Australian lobster tail, and grilled beef tenderloin are but a few of the scrumptious entrées from which to choose. Before or after your meal, stop by the small adjacent lounge for a drink. A tall brick hearth decorated with stoneware overshadows a handful of tiny tables, while the grand piano in the corner soothes with its romantic melodies. You can enjoy the same wonderful views from here, although you may be too busy gazing into your sweetheart's eyes to notice. **8205 Valley Greens Drive, at Quail Lodge Resort and Golf Club; (831) 624-2888; www.quail-lodge-resort.com; expensive to very expensive; reservations recommended; breakfast and dinner daily.**

Carmel Highlands

Located four miles south of the town of Carmel, the Highlands are the gateway to celebrated Big Sur. This region's unparalleled views of the churning Pacific Ocean thundering against craggy bluffs justify the exorbitant price tags on the posh, elite properties found here. If you're tempted to splurge, you couldn't pick a better place to spend your hard-earned money. The Highlands' ocean views provide a visual feast to last a lifetime. And you won't have any regrets—even after the bill arrives.

Hotel/Bed and Breakfast Kissing

❦❦❦❦ **HIGHLANDS INN, Carmel Highlands** Some places you have to see to believe and this exclusive inn is one such must-see. Views of the coastline from the Highlands Inn will literally take your breath away. The unparalleled panorama takes in windswept trees, white surf breaking over sharp rock outcroppings, and an occasional pod of spouting whales on the distant horizon.

Most of the 142 sleek rooms, clustered in small groups and terraced into the hillside, share the same incredible view. You can even glimpse the ocean from the beautifully tiled, jetted tubs in the spa-equipped suites, enclosed behind sliding doors that open to the bedroom and the views beyond. Wood-burning fireplaces and dimming lights give every room a romantic glow, and modern furnishings create a comfortable, relaxing atmosphere. Most guest rooms have the added convenience of a full kitchen, TV/VCR, CD player, and binoculars. If you do stay here, we highly recommend requesting a room without anyone above you. Suffice it to say the soundproofing could be improved.

Outside, a sloping staircase winds past cypress trees and gardens to an outdoor heated pool surrounded by patio furniture and umbrella-shaded tables. You won't have to wander far for superb meals. The inn's exceptional **PACIFIC'S EDGE** (see Restaurant Kissing) serves outstanding views along with lunch and dinner, while the more relaxed **CALIFORNIA MARKET** (inexpensive to expensive) draws those seeking casual breakfasts, lunches, and dinners. The staff at the California Market also packs picnic baskets in case you're heading off to Big Sur. From start to finish, everything here is very first-class, very California, and very romantic. **4 miles south of Carmel on Highway 1; (831) 624-3801, (800) 682-4811; www. highlands-inn.com; very expensive to unbelievably expensive; recommended wedding site.**

❀❀❀❀ **TICKLE PINK INN, Carmel Highlands** With a name like Tickle Pink Inn, it's hard to envision that this could be anything more than a tacky pink eyesore. Forget the name—there is nothing tacky or pink in sight. (The inn is actually a light beige color and named after former State Senator Tickle.) Perched atop rugged shoreline cliffs, Tickle Pink Inn overlooks endless miles of the Pacific coast, and all but one of the 35 rooms share this colossal view. Although some of the lower-priced rooms have average-looking linens and appointments, you won't be disappointed with any of the mini-suites. River-rock fireplaces and wrought-iron king-size beds draped with twists of fabric are lovely romantic elements. Blond wood furnishings, black-tiled bathrooms, pretty floral bedspreads, and semi-private and private decks are equally inspiring. Four suites even have two-person Jacuzzi tubs; we prefer the three suites where the tub resides in the living room. If your room doesn't come with one of these tubs, the communal outdoor Jacuzzi tub should suffice. A separate stone cottage ensconced lower on the hillside offers the most seclusion, along with two bedrooms, a fireplace, an outdoor deck, and a jetted tub in the bathroom.

Check-in brings fresh cookies, and later in the evening complimentary fruit, wines, breads, and cheeses are served on the glass-enclosed wood patio overlooking the crashing waves. When the winds are blowing, guests can congregate in the plush fireside lobby furnished with comfy, overstuffed sofas. Continental breakfast is also served here, unless you ask to have it delivered to your room, which is something that definitely tickles our fancy. **155 Highland Drive; (831) 624-1244, (800) 635-4774; www.tickle pink.com; very expensive to unbelievably expensive; minimum-stay requirement on weekends.**

Restaurant Kissing

❀❀❀❀ **PACIFIC'S EDGE, Carmel Highlands** Views of the untamed ocean from this formal dining room are alone worth the price of dinner at Pacific's

Edge. Every table offers a glimpse or more of the ocean through expansive floor-to-ceiling windows that front two sides of the restaurant. Even if you opt for drinks only, the contemporary fireside lobby is just as wonderful a place to watch the sunset, especially when the sky explodes in an array of intoxicating, evocative colors.

Blond wood and stone accents lend natural elegance to the airy, spacious dining room. Colorful plates resembling the smooth, seaworn glass you'd find on the beach adorn each table, along with tall, slender oil lamps. The ever-changing California cuisine is as irresistibly sensuous as the views and is sure to inspire some passionate kisses. We enjoyed sharing a roasted beet salad with fresh asparagus, followed by entrées of grilled rack of lamb alongside creamy polenta and seared yellowfin tuna topped with a wasabi-mustard sauce. It's doubtful you'll have much room for dessert, but can you really resist a molten chocolate cake erupting with oozing chocolate sauce? Luckily this temptation takes about ten minutes to create, so sit back, relax, and enjoy sharing the sunset together before this dessert comes your way. **4 miles south of Carmel on Highway 1, at Highlands Inn; (831) 624-3801; expensive to very expensive; lunch and dinner daily, brunch Sunday.**

Big Sur

Big Sur is only about 30 miles from the packed streets of Carmel, but it seems worlds apart. This coastal town spreads out over a portion of Highway 1 and has become well known for its New Age attitude, laid-back atmosphere, and the highly acclaimed, upscale establishments along its coastline. The dramatic cliffs, aquamarine waters, and breathtaking vistas of this area inspire couples to slow down and get in touch with the natural beauty around them. Just be forewarned that such a setting demands a premium price.

Hotel/Bed and Breakfast Kissing

❦❦❦❦ **POST RANCH INN, Big Sur** Environment-conscious design meets exclusive luxury at Post Ranch Inn, set high atop the coastal cliffs of Big Sur. The unusual glass-and-wood units discreetly blend into their spectacular surroundings of California redwoods and oaks, dramatic sea cliffs, crashing waves, and rolling mountains. Given this prime location, the upscale atmosphere, and the amenities of a full-service resort, it is not surprising that this spectacular inn has become a choice destination. (Many rooms book up a year in advance.)

The inn's 30 accommodations are spread across the cliffside acreage, with some hidden in the trees while others perch on the cliff. Setting and layout vary, but, like the exterior, the interiors are stylish yet subtle, incorporating natural wood and stone elements. Huge picture windows allow the encompassing natural beauty to pour in from every angle, and each room has its own terrace, king-size bed with a denim duvet, cushioned wicker chairs, wood-burning fireplace, slate-tiled bathroom with a Japanese-style spa tub, and a pull-out massage table for in-room treatments. There are no TVs, but a state-of-the-art CD stereo system provides 30 channels of musical programming via satellite. A small refrigerator is stocked with complimentary snacks and nonalcoholic beverages, and a lavish continental breakfast is presented in **SIERRA MAR**, the inn's breathtaking restaurant (see Restaurant Kissing).

The single-standing Ocean House units are built into the side of the ocean bluff and have curved-beam sod roofs where grass and wildflowers grow. Prices for these rooms go far beyond the unbelievably expensive category, but the ocean views from the bed, bath, window seat, and terrace are perhaps some of the best in northern California. Another place to savor the view is the heated cliffside pool, where you can soak your cares away amid breathtaking scenery. If you'd like to complement your romantic experience with outdoor activities, then join in the guided morning nature walks (available on select mornings) or head to the yoga yurt to stretch those muscles.

It will cost you to stay here, as the management makes very clear. A sign at the bottom of the long driveway posts the unbelievably expensive rates and states that the restaurant is "by reservation only." While a bit unwelcoming, it does detour the general public, making Post Ranch Inn all the more private, quiet, and delightful. **28 miles south of Carmel on Highway 1; (831) 667-2200, (800) 527-2200; www.postranchinn.com; unbelievably expensive; minimum-stay requirement on weekends.**

❤❤❤ **VENTANA, Big Sur** The rocky slopes and jagged outcroppings of the Santa Lucia Mountains abut Big Sur's astonishing coastline, creating the illusion that these unspoiled mountains are tumbling directly into the sea. Ventana, set on 243 acres of forested mountainside, has a ringside view of all this, and its amenities will satisfy every other need you might have for a special weekend away. Soothe your senses in two Japanese hot baths, two heated pools, a sauna, and a Jacuzzi tub; then don a fluffy robe and retreat to your room. Rustic elegance is the name of the game here. All 62 accommodations, spread out between a dozen or so buildings, feature roaring wood-burning fireplaces, all-wood interiors, cedar furnishings with pastel accents, and private patios facing either the forest and towering mountains or the endless ocean in the distance. Some accommodations even have hot tubs on the deck, making these prime kissing spots.

In the afternoon, a wine and cheese buffet is offered in the lobby. In the morning, a continental breakfast buffet is presented here or in the library adjacent to the outdoor patio. Breakfast can be delivered to your room for no additional charge. For lunch and dinner, follow the wooded path to CIELO (see Restaurant Kissing), a restaurant noted for wonderful views and excellent food. For extra diversion, consider treating yourselves to an in-room massage or venturing to the new spa for one of the two-and-a-half-hour couple's massage treatments, aptly named "intimate ocean experience," "intimate earth experience," or "intimate aromatherapy experience." Regardless of an intimate duo massage or not, the feelings of intimacy that will fill your hearts during your stay will surpass every expectation. **Highway 1; (831) 667-2331, (831) 624-4812, (800) 628-6500; www.ventanainn.com; unbelievably expensive; minimum-stay requirement on weekends.**

Restaurant Kissing

❀❀❀❀ **CIELO, Big Sur** Overnight guests at VENTANA (see Hotel/Bed and Breakfast Kissing) can stroll along a wilderness path that leads to the inn's elegantly rustic restaurant. Accompanied by the sounds of singing birds and rustling leaves, your walk will lead you through rolling meadows and massive oak groves. It takes only about ten minutes, so slow down and savor the quiet: Ventana inspires a sense of tranquillity that truly can "nourish your spirit," as the brochure claims.

The natural materials found in the inn are echoed in the restaurant. An abundance of rustic cedar is evident from the high, open-beamed ceiling down to the polished floor. A cozy bar area sits off to one side of the restaurant, and expansive windows face an outdoor terrace and the beauty of nature all around. White linens, single flowers, and little candle lanterns at each table add romantic flair, but when the restaurant is full (a regular event on summer weekends), the tables are a little too close to one another for comfort. If the weather allows, less-crowded seating and spectacular ocean views can be found on the fireside terrace fronting the restaurant. It is here that you can truly find *cielo* (heaven).

Fresh regional ingredients are featured on the seasonally changing menu. Grilled New Zealand lamb chops, black pepper–crusted ahi, and succulent grilled quail are just a few of the interesting entrées. There's also a chef's tasting menu featuring a choice of three or four courses. Desserts, such as apple tarte Tatin topped with honey crème fraîche sorbet, are as delectable and beautifully presented as one can imagine. Exemplary service enhances the flawless meal, and if you are a guest at the inn, the quiet walk back to your room on the well-lit path is an affectionate finale to the day. **Highway 1, at Ventana; (831) 667-4242, (800) 628-6500; www.ventana inn.com; expensive to very expensive; lunch and dinner daily.**

Romantic Suggestion: If you aren't staying at the inn and would like to make a day visit here (with dinner), spend the afternoon pampering yourselves at Ventana's new spa (831-667-2331, 800-628-6500) which was being constructed when we visited.

GLEN OAKS RESTAURANT, Big Sur Glen Oaks Restaurant may not have Cielo's perfect patio, Nepenthe's star-studded past, or Sierra Mar's view, but what it lacks in glamour it makes up for in charisma, friendly service, and tables spaced very far apart. In fact, reservations are highly recommended due to the fact that there are less than a dozen tables spread out between the two dining rooms. Asian-Mediterranean cuisine, a charming cabin-style exterior, and an intimate candlelit interior resplendent with peach walls, local artwork, and a corner fireplace, make Glen Oaks a location ripe for kissing. Gauze curtains shield any distractions from Highway 1, and the husband and wife team running the restaurant do everything to ensure your meal is enjoyable. As for the food, it's hearty and delicious. Vietnamese-style spring rolls served with a refreshingly tangy dipping sauce make an appetizing starter. Move on to the sea scallops in black bean and garlic sauce or the five-spice grilled game hen. Those seeking more Mediterranean tastes may want to indulge in the homemade linguine or the prawns sautéed in garlic, shallots, and olive oil and finished with brandy and sweet butter. Desserts draw from all regions, including the central coast. Try the luscious custard infused with Big Sur wildflower honey for a sweet finale. **Highway 1; (831) 667-2264; moderate to expensive; reservations recommended; dinner Wednesday–Monday; closed January.**

NEPENTHE, Big Sur Nepenthe is hardly a secret—you may even call it a landmark or tourist attraction of sorts. Interesting metal sculptures cover the expansive landscaped grounds, a gift shop sells an array of earth-friendly mementos, and wind chimes play a soft melody in the breeze. At the top of an outdoor staircase, a massive redwood carving of a phoenix marks the entry to the well-known restaurant. A student of Frank Lloyd Wright designed the building, and the fact that this was the honeymoon cottage of Rita Hayworth and Orson Welles adds to the mystique. Inside, the atmosphere is very relaxed and earthy, the menu typical American cuisine, the food average and plentiful, and service just standard. What makes it a suitable kissing location? How about its perch on a cliff 800 feet above the Big Sur shoreline? This feature alone is enough to make an otherwise ordinary meal here a rapturous adventure.

Nepenthe is a word derived from Greek meaning "no sorrow." You won't be feeling any sorrow here, especially if you come with your loved one around sunset. As the fiery orb begins to sink into the ocean, its light penetrates the drifting clouds with a pale lavender-blue haze. Suddenly these dusky colors shift to an intense golden amber, culminating in a deep red that sets the sky ablaze. Window seats are perfectly arranged to take advantage of the sun's exit, and outdoor seating is equally good. Weather permitting, this show is performed nightly along the coastline. **Highway 1; (831) 667-2345; www.nepenthebigsur.com; moderate to expensive; lunch and dinner daily.**

Romantic Note: If outside dining appeals to you, **CAFE KEVAH** (inexpensive to moderate; closed January–February), set one level lower than Nepenthe, is another option. Breakfast and brunch dishes are ordered at a walk-up order counter, and canvas umbrella–shaded tables are set on a spacious patio overlooking the Big Sur coast. It's more casual than romantic, but the views are divine.

❀❀❀❀ **SIERRA MAR, Big Sur** Simply put, Sierra Mar boasts the best vantage point on the entire south coast. The exclusive restaurant of the **POST RANCH INN** (see Hotel/Bed and Breakfast Kissing) perches on a cliff 1,100 feet above the luminescent ocean. From almost any seat, floor-to-ceiling windows allow you to look straight down onto the rocky shoreline and kelp beds; southern views take in much of the rugged coastline beyond. From the outdoor deck, pinpoint the telescope on migrating whales, lounging seals, and the magnificent hawks flying *below* you. The views are heart-stopping, but a kiss or two ought to resuscitate you in no time.

Even if the weather turns gray, this avant-garde restaurant is a breathtaking place to dine, with its ultrastylish decor and fantastic food. Slate floors, peeled log beams, and simple blond-wood chairs add to a sophisticated, modern atmosphere. Candles set in stones and exotic little floral arrangements are placed at every table, while suspended track lighting imparts a warm glow.

Elegantly prepared regional California cuisine is typically served in a four-course, prix fixe format, but any appetizer or entrée can be ordered à la carte. While the menu changes nightly, you might start by ordering grilled quail adorned with fig compote, followed by seafood chowder tinted with saffron. Entrée choices range from seared halibut accompanied by a red pepper sauce to roast duck breast served alongside potstickers and an orange-sesame vinaigrette. Beautifully presented desserts span the taste horizons from tart lemon mousse to a heavenly crème brûlée. If the sun is still above the horizon when you finish, linger over a cappuccino or after-dinner drink—you don't want to miss watching the day come to a close at one of the coast's most spectacular settings. **28 miles south of Carmel on Highway 1, at Post Ranch Inn; (831) 667-2800, (800) 527-2200; www.postranchinn.com; very expensive to unbelievably expensive; reservations required; lunch and dinner daily.**

Outdoor Kissing

❀❀❀❀ **BIG SUR COASTLINE, Big Sur** The drive from Carmel to Big Sur provides unsurpassed scenery in which to lose yourselves in an afternoon together. The road along this rugged, arduous coastline offers some of the most glorious, breathtaking views you may ever see. We guarantee that once you've passed through Big Sur, its potent impact will be felt in your lives for years to come. Take it slow through here: An experience of this magnitude should be approached with patient appreciation and reverent awe. Besides, there is no real destination to head for, because there isn't an actual town of Big Sur. According to the signs, though, Big Sur stretches for about six miles along Highway 1 and then continues south for more of the same impeccable scenery.

What makes all this such a heartthrob? The road penetrates a precariously severe landscape, literally snaking its way along the unblemished shoreline. Beneath you, the relentless surf pounds the jagged outcroppings along the water's edge as nature continues to refine her sculpted masterpiece. Isolated beaches and secluded spots in the wilderness nearby provide momentary respite from the road for those who want to stop for private showcase views. Hard as it is to believe, each mile seems more remarkable and intoxicating than the one before. Every moment you share here will be as seductive and as passionate as the first. *Along Highway 1, about 150 miles south of San Francisco and approximately 30 miles south of Carmel.*

Romantic Suggestion: Do not confuse **JULIA PFEIFFER BURNS STATE PARK** with Pfeiffer Big Sur State Park; Julia is 11 miles south of the other, but it offers what feels like 100 miles more privacy and landscape. Pfeiffer Big Sur State Park is exceedingly popular and disappointingly developed. Julia Pfeiffer Burns State Park, on the other hand, is 2,000 acres of prime hiking territory in nature's virgin wonderland. Enchanting waterfalls, sequestered beaches, and spellbinding views are scattered along the way.

Also in the Big Sur area, **PFEIFFER BEACH** (just off Highway 1 on Sycamore Canyon Road) is an exhilarating seascape crowded with massive, eroded outcroppings and haystack rocks that are approachable during low tide. Watching the sunset from this vantage point could be a life-altering proposition (or could inspire one).

Index

A

A. Rafanelli Winery, 144
Abigail Hotel, 183
Above the West Hot-Air
   Ballooning, 90
Acquerello, 169
Adventure Quest, 334
Adventures by the Sea, 356
Agate Cove Inn, 49
Ahwahnee Dining
   Room, 319
Ahwahnee Hotel, The,
   318, 319
Alamere Falls, 18
Alamo Square, 150, 191
Albion, 42
Albion River Inn, 42, 43
Albion River Inn
   Restaurant, 43
Alexander's, 256
All Seasons Café and Wine
   Shop, 113
Amador City, 288
Amador Foothill
   Winery, 287
Amador Harvest Inn, 285
Amador Vintners, 287
Amber House, 266
Angel Island, 191
Angel Island Company, 191
Angels Camp, 302
Antique Tours Limousine
   Service, 70
Anton and Michel, 378
Applewood Inn, 143
Aptos, 337
Archbishop's Mansion,
   The, 149
Arletta's Dining Room at the
   Holbrooke Hotel, 283
Asilomar Beach, 369
Atlas Peak, 84
Auberge du Soleil, 83, 92
Auberge du Soleil Restaurant
   and Lounge, 93
Augustin Bernal Park, 226
Augustino's, 78
Ayala Cove, 191

B

Babbling Brook Inn, 334
Bale Grist Mill State Historic
   Park, 104
Bar and Grill, The, 371
Bass Lake, 315
Bauer's Transportation, 70
Bay Bikes, 358
Bay Club, The, 370, 372
Bay Hill Mansion, 21
Bayview Hotel, The, 337
Beach House Inn at Half
   Moon Bay, 328
Bed and Breakfast Inn,
   The, 151
Bella Mia Restaurant, 238
Bella Vista, 230
Belle de Jour Inn, 136
Beltane Ranch, 125
Benbow Inn, 62
Benbow Inn Restaurant, 63
Benziger Family Winery, 129
Berkeley, 218
Berkeley Municipal Rose
   Garden, 221
Bernardus Lodge, 383
Bernardus Winery, 383
Biba, 271
Bicycle Rental Center, 334
Big Basin Way, 234
Big 4, The, 159
Big Sur, 390
Big Sur Coastline, 395
Big Trees State Park, 298
Bistro Don Giovanni, 78
Bistro Jeanty, 87
Bittersweet Bistro, 343
Bix, 169
Black Bear Inn, 258
Blackthorne Inn, 9
Blue and Gold Fleet,
   193, 204
Blue Heron Inn, The, 60
Blue Nile Inn, 304
Blue Spruce Inn, 338

Blue Violet Mansion, 71
Blue Waters Kayaking, 16
Bodega, 20
Bodega Bay, 21
Bodega Bay and Beyond
   Vacation Rentals, 22
Bodega Bay Lodge, 23
Borges Carriage & Sleigh
   Rides, 263
Brannan's Grill, 113
Breakers Inn, 29
Bridges Restaurant, 224
Buena Vista Winery, 123
Burgess Cellars, 105

C

C. O. Packard House, 49
Cafe Beaujolais, 58
Café Cruz, 344
Cafe Fina, 353, 357
Cafe Fiore, 261
Cafe Jacqueline, 170
Cafe Kevah, 394
Cafe Majestic, 156, 170
Café Mozart, 170
Cafe Sparrow, 344
Calaveras County, 301
Calaveras Visitors Bureau, 301
Calaveras Wine
   Association, 301
Calderwood Inn, 137
California Canoe and
   Kayak, 217
California Market, 389
Calistoga, 106
Calistoga Chamber of
   Commerce, 106
Calistoga Inn, 114
Calistoga Inn Restaurant
   & Brewery, 113
Camellia Inn, 137
Campground Office, 317
Camps Restaurant, 303
Campton Place Hotel,
   151, 172
Campton Place
   Restaurant, 171

Cannery Row, 348
Cantinetta Delicatessen, 104
Capitol Park Bed and
  Breakfast Inn, 267
Capitola, 337
Caprice Restaurant, 203
Carmel, 372
Carmel Beach, 382
Carmel Garden Court
  Inn, 373
Carmel Highlands, 388
Carmel Valley, 383
Carmel Valley Ranch
  Resort, 384
Carnelian Room, The, 172
Carriage House Inn, 374
Carter House, 66
Casa Blanca Inn, 335
Casa del Mar, 6
Casa Madrona Hotel,
  197, 200
Casablanca Restaurant, 335
Casanova, 378
Catch a Canoe and Bicycles,
  Too, 56
Cazadero, 25
Cedar Gables Inn, 72
Centrella Inn, The, 359
Chaminade at Santa
  Cruz, 336
Chaney House, 246
Chanterelle, 269, 270
Chart House, The, 201
Chateau du Sureau, 311, 314
Chateau la Cresta, 238
Chateau Souverain Café at
  the Winery, 147
Chateau St. Jean, 130
Chatom Vineyards, 301
Chestelson House, 95
Chez Panisse, 219
Chez Renée, 345
Chicken Ranch, 13
Chris Craft Dining Room, 249
Christiania Inn, The, 262
Christiania Inn Restaurant,
  The, 261
Christopher's Inn, 107
Christy Hill Restaurant, 250
Churchill Manor, 73
Cibo, 354

Cielo, 392
Citronée, 280
City Hotel Restaurant, 304
City Treasure Restaurant, 270
Claremont Resort and Spa,
  The, 213
Clementine, 172
Cliff House, The, 173
Clift Hotel, 152
Clos du Lac Cellars/
  Greenstone Winery, 294
Clos Pegase, 114
Club XIX, 371
Coast Guard House Historic
  Inn, 35
Coast Retreats, 50
Cobblestone Inn, 375
Coit Tower, 194
Coloma, 284
Coloma Country Inn, 284
Columbia, 303
Columbia Chamber of
  Commerce, 304
Columbia State Historic
  Park, 303, 304
Compass Rose, The, 173
Cottage Grove Inn, 107
Cottage Inn, The, 247
Cottages at Greenhorn
  Creek, The, 302
Cottages on the Beach, 10
Country Court Tea Room, 345
Country Rose Cafe, The, 281
Covey Restaurant, The,
  385, 387
Cross Roads Inn, 83
Crystal Bay, 243
Curley's Grill, 64
Cypress Cove, 51, 52
Cypress Grove, 364
Cypress Inn, 375
Cypress Inn on Miramar
  Beach, 328

D

D. L. Bliss State Park, 257
Dancing Coyote Beach Guest
  Cottages, 11
Danville, 224
Deer Creek Inn, 276
Della Santina's, 122

Delta King, The, 273
Diamond Peak Cross
  Country and Snowshoe
  Center, 243
Dining Room at The Ritz-
  Carlton, The, 165, 174
Dockside Boat and Bed,
  194, 214
Domaine Carneros, 79
Domaine Chandon, 88
Domaine Chandon Winery, 89
Doran Beach Regional
  Park, 23
Downey House Bed and
  Breakfast, 277
Dry Creek Vineyard, 145
Ducey's on the Lake, 315
Ducey's Restaurant, 316
Duck Club Restaurant
  (Bodega Bay), 24
Duck Club Restaurant
  (Lafayette), 223
Duck Club Restaurant
  (Menlo Park), 233
Duck Club Restaurant
  (Monterey), The, 351
Dunbar House 1880, 299

E

EAST BAY, 213
East Brother Light
  Station, 221
Edward II Bed and
  Breakfast, 153
El Dorado Hotel, 116
El Drisco Hotel, 153
El Paseo, 206
El Quijote, 209
Élan Vital, 174
Elk, 38
Elk Cove Inn, 38
Elms, The, 108
Embassy Suites Resort, 259
Emile's, 239
Emma Nevada House, 278
Erna's Elderberry House,
  311, 314
Eureka, 65
Evans American Gourmet
  Cafe, 262
Everett Ridge Vineyards &
  Winery, 145
Evergreen, 225

Index

F

Fair Oaks, 274
Fairmont Hotel, 154
Fandango, 365
Ferndale, 63
Ferrari-Carano Winery, 144
Filoli Gardens and Estate, 231
Firehouse, The, 274
Fish Camp, 316
Fisherman's Wharf, 348, 357
Fitzgerald Marine
    Reserve, 325
Five Brooks Stables, 19
Fleur de Lys, 175
Flora Springs Winery, 105
Flying Fish Grill, 379
Fontina Caffé Italiano, 220
Food Company, The, 35
Foothill House, 109
Forest of Nisene Marks State
    Park, The, 341, 347
Fort Ross, 26
Fort Ross Lodge, 26
Fournou's Ovens, 176
Foxes Bed and Breakfast in
    Sutter Creek, The, 290
French Laundry, 89
French Poodle, The, 379
Fresh Cream, 354

G

Gables, The, 131
Gables Inn, The, 198
Gaige House Inn, 125
Garberville, 62
Garden Cafe and Bar, 60
Garden Court, 176
Garden Court Hotel, 233
Garden's Grill, 61
Gate House Inn, 296
Gatehouse Inn, The, 359
Gayle's Bakery and
    Rosticceria, 348
Gaylord India Restaurant, 177
General's Daughter, The, 122
Genova Delicatessen, 83
Gernot's Victoria House, 366
Gerstle Park, 212
Gerstle Park Inn, 211
Geyserville, 146

Gingerbread Mansion Inn, 63
Glacier Point, 318, 319, 320
Glen Ellen, 125
Glen Ellen Inn Restaurant, 127
Glen Oaks Restaurant, 393
Glendeven Inn, 44
Glenelly Inn, 126
Glissandi, 254
Gloria Ferrer Champagne
    Caves, 124
Goat Rock State Park, 24
GOLD COUNTRY, 265
Golden Gate Bridge, 192
Golden Gate Ferry, 197
Golden Gate National
    Recreation Area, 6, 202
Golden Gate Park, 149, 192
Golden Gate Promenade, 193
Good Heavens, 306
Gosby House Inn, 360
Graham's, 254
Grand Cafe, The, 157
Grand View Inn, 360
Grandmere's Inn, 278
Grandviews Restaurant and
    Lounge, 177
Grape Leaf Inn, 138
Grass Valley, 282
Gray's Retreat, 11
Green Gables Inn, 361
Greenbrae, 210
Greenwood Pier Cafe, 40, 42
Greenwood Pier Inn, 40
Grey Gables Inn, 291
Grey Whale Bar and Cafe, 59
Greystone Restaurant, 100
Griffin House at Greenwood
    Cove, 41
Grille, The, 119, 123
Grounds, 300
Groveland, 321
Groveland Hotel, The, 321
Groveland Hotel Victorian
    Room, The, 322
Gualala, 29
Guaymas, 203
Gunn House Hotel, 307

H

Hakone Gardens, 237
Half Moon Bay, 327

Hanford House, The, 291
Harbor House Inn, The, 41
Hartley House Inn, 268
Harvest Inn, 96
Haydon Street Inn, 138
Hayloft, The, 52
Headlands Inn, The, 52
Healdsburg, 135
Healdsburg Chamber of
    Commerce, 136
Healdsburg Inn on the
    Plaza, 139
Health Spa Napa Valley, 97
Heart's Desire Beach, 19
Heavenly Ski Resort, 258
Hemingway's Cafe
    Restaurant, 306
Hennessey House, The, 74
Henry Cowell Redwood
    State Park, 333
Heritage House, 45
Heritage House
    Restaurant, 47
Hess Collection Winery,
    The, 80
Highbourne Transportation
    and Livery, Ltd., 272
Highlands Inn, 388
Highway 1, 5
Holbrooke Hotel, The, 283
Homestead, The, 312
Homewood, 256
Homewood Mountain
    Resort, 257
Honor Mansion, The, 140
Hop Kiln Winery, 145
Hope-Bosworth House, 146
Hope-Merrill House, 146
Hotel Carter, 65
Hotel Inverness, 12
Hotel la Rose, 133
Hotel Majestic, The, 155
Hotel Monaco, 156
Hotel Pacific, 349
Hotel Sausalito, 198
Hotel Triton, 157
Hotel Vintage Court, 158
Hounds Tooth Inn, 313
Huntington Hotel, The, 158
Hyatt Regency Lake Tahoe
    Resort Hotel, 241

I

Iberia, 231
Il Fornaio, 233
Il Mulino, 128
Il Pescatore, 215
Imperial Hotel
    Restaurant, 288
Incline Village, Nevada, 241
Independence Trail, 282
Indian Creek Bed and
    Breakfast, 286
Ink House, 96
Inn Above Tide, The, 199
Inn at Depot Hill, 339
Inn at Heavenly, 260
Inn at Manresa Beach, 340
Inn at Occidental, The, 134
Inn at Saratoga, The, 234
Inn at Schoolhouse Creek, 45
Inn at Southbridge, The, 97
Inn at Spanish Bay, The, 368,
    369, 371
Inn at the Opera, The, 184
Inn at Union Square,The, 159
Inverness, 9
Ione, 294

J

Jabberwock, The, 349
Jack London Square,
    215, 216
Jack London State Historic
    Park, 128
Jack London Village, 128
Jacks Peak County Park, 357
Jackson, 296
Jackson Court, 159
Japanese Tea Garden, 192
Jardinière, 178
Jarvis, 80
Jasmine Cottage, 12
Jenner, 24
Joe Lococo's, 210
Joe Rombi's la Mia
    Cucina, 366
John Ash & Co., 132
Johnson's Oyster
    Company, 19
Jordan's, 214
Josef's Restaurant and
    Bar, 132

Joseph Phelps Vineyard, 105
Josephine's, 306
Joshua Grindle Inn, The, 53
Julia Pfeiffer Burns State
    Park, 395
Julius' Castle, 178, 194

K

Karly, 288
Kautz Ironstone
    Vineyards, 301
Kayak Connection, 334
Kayaking, 34
Kenwood, 129
Kenwood Inn & Spa,
    The, 129
Kenwood Restaurant and
    Bar, 130
Kirby's Creekside Restaurant
    and Bar, 281
Korbel Champagne
    Cellars, 145
Kruse Rhododendron
    Reserve, 25

L

La Belle Epoque, 74
La Boucane, 79
La Chaumière, 110
La Folie, 179
La Fondue, 235
La Foret, 239
La Mère Michelle, 235
La Playa Hotel, 376
La Residence, 75
La Scene Cafe, 168, 179
La Toque, 94
Lafayette, 222
Lafayette Park, 156
Lafayette Park Hotel, 222
Lake Merritt, 217
**LAKE TAHOE AND
    ENVIRONS, 241**
Lambert Bridge Winery, 145
Lark Creek Inn, 209
Larkspur, 209
Lavender Hill Spa, 115
Le Mouton Noir, 235
Le Petit Pier, 245
Ledford House Restaurant,
    The, 43
Lighthouse Lodge Suites, 362

Lincoln Avenue Spa, 116
Lincoln Green Cottages, 376
Linwood's, 335
Lisa Hemenway's Bistro, 133
Little River, 44
Little River Inn, 46
Livermore, 226
Livermore Valley, 227
Lobby Lounge, The, 164
Lodge at Pebble Beach, The,
    368, 370
Lodge at Skylonda, The, 229
Lodi, 295
Lone Eagle Grille, 242
Lovers Point, 358, 367
Lovers Point Park, 366, 368

M

MacArthur Place, 117
MacCallum House Inn,
    The, 59
MacCallum House
    Restaurant, 58
MacKerricher State Park, 62
Madrona Manor, 141, 142
Madrona Manor
    Restaurant, 142
Magic Flute, The, 180
Maison Fleurie, 84
Manchester, 37
Mandarin, The, 180
Mandarin Oriental, 160, 188
Mangels House, 341
Manka's Inverness Lodge, 13
Manka's Inverness Lodge
    Restaurant, 17
Manresa State Beach, 337
MARIN COUNTY, 197
Marin Headlands, 201
Marine Park, 193
Marinus at Bernardus
    Lodge, 384
Mariposa Grove, 320
Marsh Cottage Bed and
    Breakfast, 14
Marshall, 20
Marshall Gold Discovery
    State Historic Park, 284
Marvista, 342
Masa's, 158, 181
Mason's, 181

Mason's Restaurant, 155
Matanzas Creek Winery, 134
Mayfield House, 248
McCaffrey House Bed and
  Breakfast Inn, 307
McCormick & Kuleto's, 182
Meadowood, 97, 98
Mendocino, 48
Mendocino Bakery, The, 61
Mendocino Coast Botanical
  Gardens, 61
Mendocino Headlands State
  Park, 53, 62
Mendocino Hotel Victorian
  Dining Room, 59
Mendocino Seaside
  Cottage, 53
Menlo Park, 232
Merryvale Vineyards, 106
Mezza Luna, 327
Mikayla, 198, 200
Mill Rose Inn, 329
Mill Valley, 204
Mill Valley Inn, 204
Millennium, 182
Miramar Beach Restaurant
  and Bar, 331
Mission Ranch, 377
Mono Lake, 321
Monterey, 348
Monterey Bay Aquarium,
  348, 357
Monterey Bay Inn, 351
Monterey Plaza Hotel and
  Spa, 350
Monticello Vineyards, 81
Montrio, an American
  Bistro, 355
Monument Peak
  Restaurant, 262
Moonraker Restaurant, 325
Moosse Café, The, 60
Moss Beach, 325
Moss Beach, 326
Mount Tamalpais, 204,
  205, 207
Mount Tamalpais State
  Park, 204, 208
Mountain High Balloons, 251
Mountain Home Inn,
  205, 207

Mountain Home Inn
  Restaurant, 206, 207
Mountain Room Restaurant,
  319, 320
Mountain Winery, 237
Mudd's, 224
Muir Beach, 202
Muir Woods National
  Monument, 204, 208
Mumm Napa Valley, 92
Murphys, 298
Murphy's Inn, 282
Mustards Grill, 90

N

Napa, 71
Napa Valley, 70, 272
Napa Valley Balloons, Inc., 90
Napa Valley Conference and
  Visitors Bureau, 70
Napa Valley Model A
  Rentals, 91
Napa Valley Wine Train, 81
Natasha's Café, 308
Natural Bridges State
  Park, 336
Needles, 261
Neiman Marcus Rotunda
  Restaurant, 183
Neon Rose, The, 14
Nepenthe, 393
Nepheles, 261
Nevada City, 276
Nevada City Chamber of
  Commerce, 276
955 Ukiah Street
  Restaurant, 57
Nisene Marks State Park,
  341, 347
Nob Hill Inn, 161
Nob Hill Lambourne, 161
NORTH COAST, 5
North Coast Country Inn, 30
North Shore of Lake
  Tahoe, 241

O

Oak Knoll Inn, 76
Oakhurst, 311
Oakland, 213
Oaks, The, 385
Oakville, 92
Oakville Grocery, 71
Occidental, 134

Ocean View Boulevard, 368
Old Bath House, The, 366
Old Milano Hotel, The, 33
Old Milano Hotel
  Restaurant, The, 33
Old Monterey Inn, 351
Old Sacramento, 272
Old Saw Mill Lodge, 332
Old St. Angela Inn, The, 363
Old Thyme Inn, 330
Old World Inn, 77
Oleander House, 85
Olema, 7
Olema Inn, 9
Olema Inn Restaurant, 8
Olympic Ice Pavilion, 255
O'Neill Yacht Center, 334
Ovation at the Opera, 184

P

Pacific Grove, 358
Pacific Grove Shoreline, 368
Pacific Yachting and
  Sailing, 334
Pacifica, 325
Pacific's Edge, 389
Pairs Parkside Cafe, 101
Palace of Fine Arts, 149, 193
Palo Alto, 233
Pane e Vino Trattoria, 184
Pangaea, 36
Paradise Beach Park, 203
Paradiso Trattoria, 355
Paragary's, 272
Park Hyatt, 162
Pasta Mia, 367
Pasta Moon, 331
Pebble Beach, 369
Pescadero, 332
Petit Logis, 85
Petite and Grand Cafes,
  The, 157
Petite Auberge, 163
Petite Cafe, The, 157
Pfeiffer Beach, 396
Piatti Restaurant, 117
Piazza d'Angelo, 207
Pillar Point Inn, 327
Pink Mansion, The, 111
Pinot Blanc, 101
Pleasanton, 225
Plumed Horse, The, 236

Plumpjack Cafe (San Francisco), 184, 253

Plumpjack Cafe (Squaw Valley), 253

Plush Room, The, 185

Plymouth, 285

Poet's Loft, 20

Point Arena, 35

Point Lobos State Reserve, 382

Point Pinos Lighthouse, 368

Point Reyes Lighthouse, 18, 19

Point Reyes National Seashore, 7, 9, 14, 18

Point Reyes Seashore Lodge, 7

Point Reyes Station, 9

Point Richmond, 221

Poolside Cafe and Bar, 256

Portola Valley, 231

Post Ranch Inn, 390, 394

Postino, 223

Postrio, 164, 186

Prescott Hotel, The, 163

Presidio, The, 194

Princeton, 327

Purple Orchid Inn, The, 226

Q

Quail Lodge Resort and Golf Club, 385

R

Raffaello Restaurant, 380

Ramekins, 118

Ravenous, 142

Ravens, The, 56

Red Castle Historic Lodgings, 279

Redbud Inn, 300

Redwood Room, 153, 186

Reed Manor, 54

Rent-A-Roadster, 358

Resort at Squaw Creek, The, 253, 254

Restaurant at Meadowood, The, 98, 102

Restaurant at Mission Ranch, 377

Restaurant Sent Soví, 236

Restaurant 301 at the Hotel Carter, 66

Richard Schmidt School of Surfing, 334

Richardson Bay Audubon Center and Sanctuary, 202

Rio City Cafe, 273

Ristorante Bacco, 187

Ritz Bar, The, 165, 187

Ritz-Carlton, The, 154, 164

River's End, 24

RMS Distillery, 82

Robinson Jeffers' Tor House, 382

Rochioli Vineyard and Winery, 145

Rockwood Lodge, 256

Rodeo Beach at the Marin Headlands, 202

Rose Garden Inn, 218

Roundstone Farm, 8

Roy's at Pebble Beach, 370, 371

Rubicon Point, 257

Russian River Area, 143

Russian River Area Wineries Tour, 144

Russian River Region Visitors Bureau, 144

Russian River Wine Road, 144

Russian River Wine Road Information Line, 144

Rutherford, 92

Rutherford Hill Winery, 94

Ryan House 1855, 305

S

S. Anderson Vineyard, 91

Sacramento, 265

Saddles, 118

Salt Point State Park, 25

SAN FRANCISCO, 149

San Jose, 238

San Rafael, 211

San Ramon, 224

Sanderlings, 343

Sandy Cove Inn, 15

Sans Souci, 380

Santa Cruz, 333

Santa Rosa, 130

Saratoga, 234

Sausalito, 197

Schramsberg Vineyards, 115

Scoma's, 200

Scott Courtyard, 111

Scott's Seafood Grill and Bar, 216

Sea Ranch, 27

Sea Ranch Escape, 27

Sea Ranch Lodge, 28

Sea Ranch Restaurant, 28

Sea Rock Bed and Breakfast Inn, 55

Sea Star Cottage, 16

Seacliff, 31

Seal and Bird Rock, 368

Seal Cove Inn, 326

Seascape Resort, 342

Serenity, 305

Seven Gables Inn, 360, 364

17-Mile Drive, 358, 367, 369

Shadowbrook, 346

Shell Beach, 25

Shenandoah Valley, 287, 272

Shenandoah Vineyards, 288

Sherman House, The, 165

Shore House, The, 244

Showley's at Miramonte, 103

Sierra Mar, 391, 394

Silks, 161, 188

Silver Rose Inn & Spa, 112

Silverado Trail, 70

Simpson's Restaurant and Bar, 381

Skates on the Bay, 220

Slocum House, 275

Sonoma, 116

Sonoma Cheese Factory, 124

Sonoma Coast Villa, 20

Sonoma Mission Inn & Spa, 119, 123

Sonoma Valley, 116

Sonoma Valley Visitors Bureau, 116

Sonora, 304

Soquel, 337

Soule Domain, The, 243

SOUTH COAST, 325

South Lake Tahoe, 258

SOUTH OF SAN FRANCISCO, 229

South Shore of Lake Tahoe, 258

Spa, The, 118

Index

Spencer House, The, 167
Spindrift Inn, 352
Spinnaker, The, 201
Squaw Valley, 252
Squaw Valley Lodge, 253
St. Clement Vineyard, 106
St. Helena, 95
St. Orres Inn, 32
St. Orres Restaurant, 32, 33
Stanford Inn by the Sea, 56
Stanford Park Hotel, 232
Stanislaus National
  Forest, 308
Stateline, Nevada, 263
Steep Ravine Trail, 208
Sterling Hotel, The, 268,
  269, 270
Stevenot Winery, 302
Stevenswood Lodge, 47, 48
Stevenswood Restaurant,
  47, 48
Stinson Beach, 6
Stinson Beach State Park, 6
Stokes Adobe, 356
Stonepine, an Estate
  Resort, 386
Story Winery, 288
Strybing Arboretum, 192
Style 'n Comfort
  Limousine, 70
Summit Restaurant,
  The, 263
Sunnyside Lodge, 249
Sunset State Beach, 337
Sunsets on the Lake, 245
Susan's Place Wine Bar and
  Eatery, 292
Sutter Creek, 289
Sutter Creek–Ione Road, 294
Sutter Creek Palace
  Restaurant and
  Saloon, 293
Swiss Lakewood
  Restaurant, 257

T

Tahoe City, 246
Tahoe Seasons Resort, 260
Tahoe Vista, 244
Telegraph Hill, 194
Ten Inverness Way, 13
Tenaya Lake, 321

Tenaya Lodge, 316
Terra Restaurant, 103
Terrace, The
  (San Francisco), 165
Terrace Grill Restaurant
  (Carmel), 376
Terrace Restaurant, The
  (Squaw Valley), 255
Thai Bistro, 367
Theo's, 347
Thistle Dew Inn, 120
Tiburon, 202
Tickle Pink Inn, 389
Tilden Regional Park, 221
Timberhill Ranch, 25
Tioga Road, 321
Tomales Bay Foods, 18
Tomales Bay Oyster
  Company, 19
Tomales Point, 18
Tommy Toy's, 188
Top of the Cliff, 34
Tra Vigne, 104
Trojan Horse Inn, 121
Truffula, 250
Tuba Garden, 189
Tuolumne Meadows, 321
Turn, The, 302
Tutto Mondo Trattoria, 381
Twain Harte, 307
Twenty-Eight, 271
Twin Peaks, 187, 195

U

University of California
  Santa Cruz Arboretum, 333
Upstairs Restaurant, 298

V

Vagabond's House Inn, 377
Ventana, 391, 392
Viansa Winery, 124
Victorian Garden Inn, 121
Victorian Gardens, 37
Victorian Inn, 353
Villa Montalvo, 238
Villagio Inn and Spa, 86
Vineyard Country Inn, 99
Vintage Inn, 86
Vintners Inn, 131, 132
Violette's at the Mansion, 72

Vision Cottage, 16
Visitor Center (Yosemite
  National Park), 320
Vivande Ristorante, 189
Vizcaya, 269

W

Wappo Bar & Bistro, 114
Warwick Regis Hotel,
  The, 167, 179
Waterfront Plaza Hotel, 215
Waterfront Restaurant and
  Cafe, The, 190
Wedgewood Inn, The, 297
Wells Fargo History
  Museum, 273
Wente Vineyards
  Restaurant, 227
**West Shore of Lake
  Tahoe, 256**
Whale Watch Inn, 32
Whale Watching, 19
Wharf Master's Inn, 36
White Magnolia
  Restaurant, 338
White Swan Inn, 168
Whitegate Inn, 56
Wildcat Beach, 19
William Hill Winery, 82
Willowside Cafe, 133
Wine and Roses Country
  Inn, 295
WINE COUNTRY, 69
Wine Country Inn, 99
Wolfdale's Restaurant, 251
Woodside, 229

Y

York Hotel, 185
Yosemite Lodge, 319
Yosemite National Park, 317
**YOSEMITE NATIONAL
  PARK AND
  ENVIRONS, 311**
Young's Vineyards, 288
Yountville, 83
Yountville Inn, 87
YoYo Bistro, 190

Z

Zinfandel Inn, 99
Zinfandels at Sutter
  Creek, 293